P9-DGJ-453

ENCYCLOPEDIA OF
GENOCIDE

Volume I
A–H

A classic photograph of the Holocaust, showing the moment when the Jews photographed here were taken out of their hiding place in a bunker in Warsaw, Poland. (Yad Vashem, Jerusalem)

ENCYCLOPEDIA OF GENOCIDE

Volume I
A–H

Israel W. Charny
editor in chief

Forewords by
Archbishop Desmond M. Tutu
and Simon Wiesenthal

ABC-CLIO
Santa Barbara, California
Denver, Colorado
Oxford, England

Library of Congress Cataloging-in-Publication Data
Encyclopedia of genocide / Israel W. Charny, editor in chief.
p. cm.
Includes bibliographical references and index.
Summary: Alphabetical entries define names, places, and events associated with genocide, and major sections deal with the Armenian genocide, the Holocaust, and the process, detection, denial, and prevention of genocide.
ISBN 0-87436-928-2 (alk. paper)
1. Genocide—Encyclopedias. [1. Genocide—Encyclopedias.] I. Charny, Israel W.

HV6322.7 .E53 1999
364.15'1'03—dc21

99-052695
CIP

05 04 03 02 01 00 10 9 8 7 6 5 4 3

ABC-CLIO, Inc.
130 Cremona Drive, P.O. Box 1911
Santa Barbara, California 93116-1911

This book is printed on acid-free paper ♾.
Manufactured in the United States of America.

I REMEMBER

I remember: it happened yesterday or eternities ago. A young Jewish boy discovered the kingdom of night. I remember his bewilderment, I remember his anguish. It all happened so fast. The ghetto. The deportation. The sealed cattle car. The fiery altar upon which the history of our people and the future of mankind were meant to be sacrificed . . . and now the boy is turning to me: "What have you done with my future? What have you done with my life?" and I tell him that I have tried. That I have tried to keep memory alive, and I have tried to fight those who would forget. Because if we forget, we are guilty, we are accomplices.

—Elie Wiesel, in accepting the Nobel Peace Prize in Oslo, 1986

ON BECOMING HUMAN

To be human is to recognize the cultural perspectives that bind us to a tribe, sect, religion, or nation, and to rise above them. It is to feel the pain of the dispossessed, the downtrodden, the refugee, the slave, the starving child.

To be human is to break the ties of cultural conformity and group-think, and to use one's own mind. It is to recognize good and evil, and to choose good. It is to consider with the heart. It is to act with conscience.

To be human is to be courageous. It is to choose the path of compassion, rather than the path of complacency. It is to break the silence, and be an unrelenting advocate of human decency and dignity. It is to sacrifice for what is just.

To be human is to breathe with the rhythm of life, and to recognize our kinship with all forms of life. It is to appreciate every drop of water. It is to feel the warmth of the sun, and to marvel at the beauty and expanse of the night sky. It is to stand in awe of who we are and where we live. It is to see the Earth with the eyes of an astronaut.

To be human is to be aware of our dependence upon the whole of the universe, and of the miracle that we are. It is to open our eyes to the simple and extraordinary beauty that is all about us. It is to live with deep respect for the sacred gift of life. It is to love.

To be human is to seek to find ourselves behind our names. It is to explore the depths and boundaries of our existence. It is to learn from those who have preceded us, and to act with due concern for those who will follow us.

To be human is to plant the seeds of peace, and to nurture them. It is to find peace and make peace. It is to help mend the web of life. It is to be a healer of the planet.

To be human is to say an unconditional No! to warfare, and particularly to the use of weapons of mass destruction. It is to take a firm stand against all who profit from warfare and its preparation.

To be human is not always to succeed, but it is always to learn. It is to move forward despite the obstacles.

We are all born with the potential to become human. How we choose to live will be the measure of our humanness. Civilization does not assure our civility. Nor does being born into the human species assure our humanity. We must each find our own path to becoming human.

—David Krieger

Produced by the Institute on the Holocaust and Genocide, Jerusalem

The *ENCYCLOPEDIA OF GENOCIDE* is a basic and comprehensive reference work with major sections on the events of THE ARMENIAN GENOCIDE and THE HOLOCAUST and on DENIAL OF GENOCIDE and, throughout the work, emphasis on the COMPARATIVE STUDY OF THE GENOCIDES OF ALL PEOPLES (in the past, present, and tragically the future as well), the PROCESS OF GENOCIDE, EARLY WARNING SYSTEMS FOR GENOCIDE, legal deterrents and punishment in LAW AND GENOCIDE, and other means of PREVENTION OF GENOCIDE.

The basic value position of the Encyclopedia is that ALL HUMAN LIFE IS SACRED, and that the study of genocide is devoted to the preservation of all human life.

What Editorial Reviewers Said about the Encyclopedia

- Every person who picks up this volume will find a way to personally relate to its contents. Its scope is so wide and varied that any reader will be captivated from cover to cover by the material presented here. Although this encyclopedia will be consulted for specific information, it can easily be read in its entirety, and can quickly become an intellectual addiction as the reader plows through its contents.
- Staggering! A remarkable manuscript. This is a milestone in the field of Genocide Studies.
- Truly a tour de force. I was not prepared for the power of this manuscript. As I read it, I find myself exclaiming in agreement, appreciation, and even joy as I encounter brilliant, creative, provocative statements by authoritative, dedicated scholars. This is truly a magnificent work of scholarship. This Encyclopedia will be in thousands of libraries all over the world.
- I read the Encyclopedia end to end with relish and in awe of its vision for the prevention of genocide. The Encyclopedia will stand as an enduring testament. It is a comprehensive reference work for Genocide Studies, unique and original, a searching light across our knowledge of genocide.

How to Use the Encyclopedia

The Encyclopedia is designed in an innovative structure that combines four types of entries:

- ***Traditional Entries,*** or basic encyclopedic summaries of the knowledge in a typical area or field of study;
- ***Feature Entries,*** which include innovative analyses, reinterpretations, and human-interest essays that probe basic conceptual issues in the study and prevention of genocide.
- ***Features,*** which are similar to feature stories and reports of background information in newspapers, through which the reader will be exposed to more affective writing and information to accompany the basic traditional encyclopedic entry;
- ***Source Documents,*** which provide the verbatim texts of important and informative documents in the genesis of a genocide event—such as the verdict of the Turkish Military Court that at one point convicted the perpetrators of the Armenian Genocide; the Protocol of the infamous Wannsee Conference in which the Nazis took their final formal decision to implement the Final Solution of the Holocaust; and the text of the United Nations Convention on the Prevention and Punishment of the Crime of Genocide.

The Encyclopedia also features throughout pertinent and meaningful photographs, works of art, maps, and tabular representations to enhance the reader's knowledge and facilitate the intellectual and emotional comprehension of the academic entries.

The purpose is to create for the reader an unfolding invitation to a broad intellectual, emotional, and even spiritual experience.

This basic reference work marks a further stage in the development of the field of genocide studies which is a subject of study which cuts across traditional disciplines and is being studied in many different college and university departments, so that the Encyclopedia will provide an easily recognizable access for students and researchers from many different fields of inquiry.

TO LOCATE SPECIFIC INFORMATION

1. Search the alphabetical Table of Contents for the topic you wish to investigate.
2. Pay close attention to listings of *groups of entries* which include a sequence of entries under an inclusive grouping topic.
3. Note also the branching lists of *cross-references* that are provided after the names of many entries. These lists are printed in *italics.*

The Table of Contents is designed to continuously invite the reader to see the movement from one topic to related topics: from one event of genocide to another; from the narratives of various genocides to comparative analyses of the processes of different events; from the historical sequences of events to understanding triggers, causes, and structural dynamics; from events of genocide to means of intervention and prevention; all together creating a picture of genocide as a universal problem for mankind, past, present, and future.

4. Look up the topic, any other key words and associated topics, and names of people and places associated with this topic, in the detailed INDEX at the end of the Encyclopedia.

The topical structure of the Index has been planned to be coordinated with the Indices that have appeared in each of the four volumes of the series, *Genocide: A Critical Bibliographic Review,* thus facilitating additional reference work for scholars.

List of Entries

The following is an alphabetical listing of entries, with titles of feature entries (all capital letters), features (capitals and lowercase), and source documents indented after the titles of the entries they accompany. For a more detailed listing, including contributors' names and cross-references, see the table of contents.

Volume I

THE ARMENIAN GENOCIDE

DENIALS OF GENOCIDE

Volume II

Contents

Volume I

Part I: Definitions of Genocide and the Study of Genocide

Part II: Genocidal Events, Intervention, and Prevention

A

THE ARMENIAN GENOCIDE

D

DENIALS OF GENOCIDE

FILMS OF THE HOLOCAUST, GENOCIDE, AND FUTURISTIC DESTRUCTION

G

THE HOLOCAUST

THE HOLOCAUST: CONCENTRATION CAMPS AND DEATH CAMPS IN THE HOLOCAUST

THE HOLOCAUST: UNDERSTANDING THE HOLOCAUST AND ITS IMPLICATIONS

Volume II

I

K

YUGOSLAVIA, GENOCIDE IN

Foreword: Why Is It Important to Learn about the Holocaust and the Genocides of *All* Peoples?

The Most Reverend Archbishop Emeritus Desmond M. Tutu

In December 1995, fifty years after the end of World War II, I sat in the very courtroom where the Nuremberg trial was held. I was part of a BBC TV panel discussion on the legacy of Nuremberg. Afterward I visited the site of the former Nazi concentration camp at Dachau. The Germans seemed determined to ensure that their nation would never forget the atrocities that had been committed for the sake of Hitler's obsession with Aryanism. In Dachau there was a museum above whose entrance the haunting words by George Santayana were inscribed: "Those who forget the past are doomed to repeat it."

The compelling reason why we should learn about the Holocaust, and the genocides committed against other peoples as well, is so that we might be filled with a revulsion at what took place and thus be inspired, indeed galvanized, to commit ourselves to ensure that such atrocities should never happen again. It is sadly true what a cynic has said, that we learn from history that we do *not* learn from history. And yet it is possible that if the world had been conscious of the genocide that was committed by the Ottoman Turks against the Armenians, the first genocide of the twentieth century, then perhaps humanity might have been more alert to the warning signs that were being given before Hitler's madness was unleashed on an unbelieving world. For there are telltale signs, which those with eyes to see can discern, that should make us more vigilant. When tyrants feel insecure and under threat and personal liberties are eroded, then our antennae should be particularly sensitive. In times of rapid change and flux or when there is turmoil and social and economic upheaval and political unrest, then those in power will usually be on the lookout for scapegoats to take the blame for why things are going awry. The world might have been a little more vigilant when such symptoms began appearing in the Germany of the 1930s.

We want to learn about the Holocaust and other instances of genocide because we have so frequently been dazzled by the remarkable technological strides that humankind has made—space travel, landing on the moon, lightning-quick communication—that these achievements have made us not just properly proud but overweaning in a presumptuous arrogance that has believed in automatic progress. The sobering fact is that our technological achievements have not been matched by an equal moral advance. We are wonderfully intelligent but dwarfish in moral stature. We spend obscene amounts on budgets of death and destruction when a minute fraction of these huge defense budgets would ensure that God's children everywhere would have enough to eat, access to clean water, adequate health care, and a good education in a safe environment.

We have the capacity to feed the entire world population many times over, but children die of starvation and easily preventable deficiency diseases whilst we dump excess food to maintain food prices. The instances of genocide and the occurrence of the Holocaust are stark reminders that we have an extraordinary capacity for evil. Particularly devastating is the realization that some of the most awful instances were committed not by illiterate, barbaric savages but by some of the most sophisticated, the most learned, those who claimed to be Christian. It would give us reason to pause as we thought to preen ourselves—that these things were done by what appeared to be normal, ordinary human beings, the ultimate proof of the banality of evil.

But we have had wonderful accounts too in nearly all these instances of evil of the capacity of people for good—extraordinary examples of bravery, magnanimity, goodness. We learn too that we do have remarkable capacity for good, which we should harness to make this a better world.

It should all awaken in us the desire to value human life as precious, all human life, so that we would refuse to demonize even adversaries. What makes genocide possible is that the victims are seen as less than human. In Africa we have something called *ubuntu,* the essence of being human, when we recognize that our humanity is bound up in that of others. We say a person is a person through other persons. We are created for interdependence, togetherness, and complementarity. Genocide happens because people are intolerant of difference. *Ubuntu* celebrates diversity. Our differences should make us realize our need of one another. The completely self-sufficient person is subhuman. *Ubuntu* speaks about hospitality, generosity, caring, and compassion.

It is important to note a very important lesson—that ultimately those who are responsible for such atrocities come a cropper. This is, in fact, a moral universe; right and wrong matter; and evil, however rampant and apparently unstoppable, does not have the last word. In the end, good does prevail. Where are Hitler, Amin, Bokassa, Pinochet, Pol Pot, et al.? The world deprecates them. Those whom the world honors are in the end good people. Good matters; right matters. They have the last word.

We learn about the Holocaust and other genocides so that we can be more human, more gentle, more caring, more compassionate, valuing every person as being of infinite worth, so precious that we know that such atrocities will never happen again, and that the world will be a more humane place that is hostile to such horrendous occurrences.

We will remember them so that we are not doomed to repeat them.

This *Encyclopedia of Genocide* is an invaluable tool toward that end.

Foreword: Why Is It Important to Learn about the Holocaust and the Genocides of *All* Peoples?

Simon Wiesenthal

For many, many years it has been my opinion that in a humane, in a political, and in an educational sense, we Jews failed to stress the point that we were persecuted and suffered in concentration camps, together with people from 18 other nations, during the Nazi reign.

Right after the war, I dreamed about the formation of a brotherhood of victims that could also be a fighting body against any new—or old—forms of National Socialism. After all, this was the first time in our common 2,000-year-old history of living together that we had had the same enemy. But we were not able to make use of the opportunity, just as there are whole nations that have chapters in their history called "missed chances."

In the 1950s I appealed to all to not always talk just about the six million Jews who had been murdered and ignore the others; this reduced National Socialism to an exclusively Jewish problem. No one was prepared to listen to me. When I agreed to give my name to a center that was about to be built in Los Angeles in 1977, my one condition was that it would be dedicated to the six million Jews and the millions of others who had suffered with us. You can imagine how all at once a chorus of hateful people accused me of wanting to reduce the meaning of the Holocaust. My explanation that this expanded emphasis only increased the Nazis' guilt was not accepted. I proved to these critics that there are more non-Jewish survivors of concentration camps living in the United States than those of Jewish descent, and in order to fight anti-semitism and Nazi and racist tendencies in the United States, we need the help of the others.

It is also important for the State of Israel to have friends in this world. And our most reliable friends have always been those who suffered together with us, as well as their children. Be it in Europe or elsewhere, I tried to point out our similarities. There are countries where the victims' organizations are not solely Jewish, such as Holland, Denmark, Norway, and Italy. These organizations definitely do not belittle the uniqueness of our Holocaust because it is undisputed. It simply does not suffice to stress just the uniqueness of our Holocaust and not to think about the future, about those who have been and will remain our friends. It is true that when a dictatorship is installed in a specific country, the Jews are often the first victims, but then, the others get their share of abuse too.

I am very happy about the publication of the first *Encyclopedia of Genocide* that treats at great length the Holocaust, along with the genocides of a great many other peoples.

Editor's Introduction: The Dawning of a New Age of Opposition to Genocide

Israel W. Charny

The *Encyclopedia of Genocide* is a rededication to human life. It is an encyclopedia of humankind's *beginning* struggle to control and prevent the mass slaughters of unarmed human beings that, tragically, take place very often on our planet.

Already before World War II, in the 1930s, Raphael Lemkin, a Polish jurist who was Jewish, proposed to the League of Nations international legislation against the extermination of a race or people. A few years later, Lemkin lost his entire large family in the Holocaust while he escaped to the United States. For a brief period he taught at Duke University and at Yale University Law Schools, but he stopped working in order to devote himself selflessly to a single-handed campaign to have legislation passed by the United Nations against genocide. Thanks to his efforts, the UN Convention on Genocide, which is the world's major legal statement to date on genocide, was passed on January 12, 1951.

It is Lemkin who coined the new word *genocide:*

> *geno* = species;
> *cide* = murder of:
> *the murder of a people!*

Notwithstanding the law of the UN, even today Planet Earth is a world of mass murders: Past genocides in the twentieth century include:

- the Armenian Genocide at the hands of the Turks
- the Holocaust—of course of the Jews, who were defined by the Nazis as the ultimate nonhumans "deserving" of extermination, but also of Gypsies, homosexuals, and others including Jehovah's Witnesses, political opponents, and "plain" civilians in occupied countries in addition to prisoners of war
- many different nationalities and peoples in the Soviet Union by Stalin (recent scholarship by University of Hawaii political scientist R. J. Rummel estimates no fewer than *54 million people* were murdered by Stalin)
- the Chinese in Manchuria by the Japanese in the 1930s (at this writing the Japanese government has finally begun a halting measure of acknowledgment of its genocide of the Chinese)
- various indigenous tribes in a variety of countries, for example, Australia, Brazil and the United States
- Cambodia's killing fields by Pol Pot and the Khmer Rouge
- Burundi and Rwanda in a seesawing series of genocides by two peoples—the Hutu and Tutsi—of one another over many years
- the gassing of Kurds and other destruction of village populations of the Kurds in Iraq by Saddam Hussein
- genocidal murders along with forced migration for dreaded "eth-

nic cleansing" in the Former Yugoslavia
- and so, so many other cases that caring human beings must grieve and be outraged at this record of our species and planet.

There are also many who question whether nuclear destruction, as well as other mass annihilations by megabombing, are to be considered allowable acts of *war* even when committed against objectively totalitarian warmaking governments, or are to be looked at critically as possible acts of genocide against civilian populations.

Can the Need to Kill Masses of People Ever Be Overcome by Our Species?

Can it be that our species cannot be otherwise, by our very "nature," in our genetic reality? Is it possible that "nature" requires humans to reduce overpopulation through genocide (as well as other means of wars and killer illnesses)?

How can genocide be stopped?

By legal means? By political and social evolution? Through moral and spiritual development? With the aid of better educational programs, or with the creative contribution of mass media that, at long last, perhaps in response to public pressures or new legislation against the pornography of violence, would adopt a policy of promoting human life and opposing violence against all unprotected people?

The *Encyclopedia of Genocide* is dedicated by its editors to *HUMAN LIFE.*

It is a text with a definite *bias* toward respect for the sanctity of all human life, and the responsibility of all human systems—governments in particular but also all the professions such as medicine and education, and also all human organizations such as business and communications—to contribute to a maximum life opportunity for *all* people.

Needless to say, this is also a text with a bias against any and all forms of prejudice, bigotry, discrimination. domination, superiority, dehumanization, or devaluing of any people—on any basis of religion, ethnicity, physical makeup, political identity, social class, health status, sexual identity, sexual preference—*whatever* the basis will be the next times.

It is intended as a text pertaining not only to the past and present but to the future of our human life on Planet Earth.

The *Encyclopedia of Genocide* is an encyclopedia of scholarship *to support the efforts of all those who seek to protect and enhance the lives of all people and peoples, now and in the future.*

Is the Twenty-first Century to Be a New Age of International Indictment and Action against Genocide?

This first *Encyclopedia of Genocide* goes to press at a time when, remarkably, barriers of "unknowing" and ignorance, indifference, and denial of genocide are rapidly falling off in Western civilization; and time-honored escapes behind the screens of "sovereign rights" and the right of governments to deal with "internal affairs" are being rejected in new and daring political and legal developments. The NATO military campaign against Serbia in Kosovo as of March 1999 represents the first clear-cut large-scale international intervention for humanitarian purposes [see YUGOSLAVIA, GENOCIDE IN: ETHNIC CLEANSING AND GENOCIDE IN KOSOVO AND A CONTROVERSIAL MAJOR INTERNATIONAL RESPONSE BY NATO, 1999]. Thus, Vaclav Havel, president of the Czech Republic, said, "This is probably the first war that has not been waged in the name of natural interest but rather in the name of principles and values. If one can say of any war that it is ethical or that it is being waged for ethical reasons, then it is true of this war." Of course, one must also hasten to note that there are many peace-loving people who criticize the NATO action as unduly destructive to civilians; many critics of the NATO action decry it as a co-optation of the UN by a constellation of powers led by a superpower United States as well as a basic failure to use negotiation instead of force. There are also serious criticisms of the failure of NATO to plan correctly to stop the Serbs' ethnic cleansing, which in fact actually intensified first in response to the withdrawal of NATO observers who had been present in Kosovo and left in preparation for NATO military actions, and then in response to the NATO bombings. Nonetheless, even most of the critics concede that the purposes of the NATO attack were not self-aggrandizing but a genuine humanitarian effort to stop genocidal ethnic cleansing.

The years 1998 and 1999 have also seen renewed interest in creating various levels of early warning systems for genocide [see GENOCIDE EARLY WARNING SYSTEMS], in the public-educational context of proposals to the city fathers of Berlin to include a "Genocide Situation Room" or "Genocide Watch" display in their planning of a museum devoted to the Holocaust, and on the level of a formal government function per an announcement by President Clinton that the United States would create a "Genocide Warning Center." Again, the critics are not lacking. At this writing, it appears that the proposal in Berlin may have fallen by the wayside insofar as the Genocide Situation Room was part of an overall architectural proposal for the museum that did not win out; and President Clinton's proposal promptly earned a scathing rebuttal by a columnist in the *Wall Street Journal* who called it "peculiar" on the basis of an assertion that "genocide is extremely rare" and a tortuous argument that only Hitler's killings were truly or mainly genocidal, whereas the "ultimate purpose" of Stalin, Mao, the Khmer Rouge, and others was for "totalitarian rule, not genocide"; hence their millions of dead were not the victims of genocide, thus illustrating the significance of our definitions of genocide [see Part I of the Encyclopedia]. Again notwithstanding the setbacks and criticisms of programs for awareness of the dangers of genocide, it seems that the subject of community, government, and international warnings and action against genocide is, at long last, increasingly *on the agendas* of more and more leaders and institutions.

On the legal side, there are no less dramatic and perhaps even less controversial developments toward opposing genocide. The process of creating international jurisdiction for perpetrators of genocide began largely with the Nuremberg Tribunal and other post–World War II trials of war criminals under international jurisdiction and continued with the adoption of the *United Nations Universal Declaration of Human Rights* and the *United Nations Convention on the Prevention and Punishment of the Crime of Genocide* in 1948 [see entries on all these subjects]. In the years that followed, it seemed for the most part that these lofty expressions of principle would remain just that, and that a cynical world would not really move to counteract the tyrants who forever emerge in human politics to turn to mass murder. In 1998 and 1999, however, as the new millennium was being ushered in by Planet Earth, a rapid succession of transformational events has given notice that a major shift toward developing international machinery for prosecuting perpetrators of genocide may at long last be taking place.

In 1998 an International Criminal Court [see entry] was created. During the same year, trials by the International Criminal Tribunal for Rwanda brought in convictions of perpetrators of genocide in Rwanda, including, in September 1998, the indictment of the former prime minister of Rwanda for genocide and crimes against humanity [see TRIALS FOR GENOCIDE AND WAR

CRIMES: TRIALS FOR GENOCIDE IN RWANDA]. In March 1999, *England's* high court ruled that London could respond to a request by *Spain* for extradition of *Chile's* former dictator Augusto Pinochet, who was visiting England, to be tried in Spain for crimes against humanity—thus transferring jurisdiction to two countries entirely removed geographically from the scenes of the reported crimes [see PINOCHET, AUGUSTO, AND A NEW LEGAL PRECEDENT TOWARD EXTRADITION ON CHARGES OF GENOCIDE], which is the kind of universal jurisdiction that the UN Whitaker Commission on the UN Convention on Genocide recommended to a seemingly indifferent world in 1985. In May 1999, the International Criminal Tribunal for the Former Yugoslavia announced a warrant for the arrest of Slobodan Milosevic, the first indictment of a reigning head of state, along with four of his associates for crimes against humanity and genocide [see again the entry on Kosovo cited above]. The indictments were hailed by the *Washington Post* as neither "revenge" nor "just a sidelight of the wars in Bosnia and Kosovo, but a search for justice and accountability that is at the very center [of the events]." Kingsley Chiedu Moghalu, a legal adviser to the International Criminal Tribunal for Rwanda, called the indictment of Milosevic, a standing head of state, "part of a revolutionary trend in international law." He noted that it builds on the previous conviction by the Hague's Rwanda Tribunal in September 1998 of Jean Kumbanda, former prime minister of Rwanda, to life imprisonment for genocide and crimes against humanity (noted above). The indictment of Milosevic, he said, "is an important signal that international justice for crimes in which humanity is the victim is a reality of our time."

So, altogether, something at long last is happening at multiple levels of the international system in response to the evils of genocide. It is also possible that the publication of this Encyclopedia, which no scholar or publisher would have dreamed of not that many years ago, is very much part of a process announcing a welcome change that *the world is beginning to care about putting an end to genocide.*

Differences of Opinion and the Passions of Differences of Opinion and Controversies in Holocaust and Genocide Studies

As in any field of study, there are considerable and even major differences of opinion among scholars about a wide range of subjects. The single most frequent focus of controversy in the subject of Holocaust and genocide studies is the process of defining events as genocidal. Thus, were the murders of homosexuals by the Nazis during the Holocaust *genocide* or not? Were the murders of huge numbers of black slaves taken forcibly from Africa to the United States, and the killing conditions of life for many slaves thereafter, *genocide* or not? There are many scholars who want to have "pure definitions" of genocide. For example, one scholar writes that "torching villages, killing men, and even wiping out communities are often done without the intent to eliminate an entire people," and therefore for this scholar these events may be called "mass murder," "massacre" or "slaughter," "human rights abuses," "annihilation," "pogroms"—or anything but *genocide.* Thus, another scholar has written, "There were no non-Jewish victims in the Holocaust, since the Holocaust is the name only for the murders of the Jews," a point of view that definitely has not been accepted in this Encyclopedia [see entries such as "HOLOCAUST": THE WORD AND ITS USAGE and THE HOLOCAUST, NON-JEWISH VICTIMS IN]. In another instance, a scholar has written of the Nazis' "euthanasia" of the mentally retarded and ill, which was in fact the first program of mass extermination by the Nazis: "Euthanasia *per se* is not, nor pretends to be genocide; literally it is a kind of 'pruning,' the removal of excess or unwanted *individuals* in order to *preserve* race of which they—the mentally retarded, the emotionally disturbed, the dependent aged, the physically crippled, and the otherwise handicapped—are nevertheless, biologically an integral though imperfect part . . . their killing was *not* on account of their race." This is, in fact, the kind of writing that has characterized the genocidal ideas advanced in eugenics [see EUGENICS AND GENOCIDE: EUGENICS AND THE HOLOCAUST; EUGENICS AND THE DANGERS OF ACADEMIC RACISM; and "LIFE UNWORTHY OF LIVING"]. It is unacceptable in this Encyclopedia—although, let it be added, the author *may* be right that the "euthanasia" killings and the murders of the Jews were intrinsically parallel processes (the "euthanasia" preceded the mass murders of the Jews, and there are many scholars who believe that the initial program of mass killing paved the way for the larger Holocaust) and that ghettos and extermination camps for Jews *may* have developed even if there had been no previous program of "euthanasia."

The argumentation gets more complicated insofar as historical analyses are marshaled to justify the claims that only a given people, say the Jews, were the objects of "total" annihilation. In fact many of these arguments are at least partially incorrect, for example, the argument that the Armenians in Turkey were safe if they lived in Smyrna or Constantinople, when in fact the initial roundup of Armenian intelligentsia was in Constantinople and Vahakn Dadrian has shown that thousands more were deported from Constantinople and killed; also the Armenians in Smyrna were slaughtered in a later genocidal attack in 1922. Perhaps in retaliation against such thinking, at least one Armenian scholar has emphasized that some 40,000 Jewish residents of Germany survived the Holocaust, which means the Jews weren't "totally" annihilated. Indeed, we know of various exceptions to the inferno of the Holocaust, such as in the earlier years when certain prominent Jews were allowed to escape Germany, or cases when those who held US passports or received visas to the United States were actually released from German concentration camps. Even in the later years, some Jews were traded for trucks. But in all these illustrations it is logically wrong, and inherently childish and disrespectful, to test a definition against *totalities.* Not *all* people need to be killed to prove that there was clear-cut intentional *genocide,* the most terrible crime humankind can commit.

The reader is advised that throughout this Encyclopedia, there is a tension of degrees of differences among numerous writers and editors as to the purity or totality of the concept of genocide, and even times when a given writer will move back and forth between opposing positions. Thus, there will be instances in this Encyclopedia where one writer will refer alternately to the mass murder of homosexuals by the Nazis as "genocide" or "the gay genocide" and then render an opinion that the killings of the homosexuals were *not* genocidal, let alone that another writer will insist that the murders of the homosexuals should be characterized as "mass murder" or some other designation of persecution and massacre. As the editor, I have chosen *not* to squelch this dissent but at the same time to advance steadily throughout this work the point of view that all mass murders of unarmed people (or barely armed and in effect incapable of meaningful self-defense) constitute genocide, and that we dare not create situations where any mass of dead human beings will be relegated to a "lesser" category than genocide. At the same time, I strongly espouse careful, scientific scholarship to delineate the specific characteristics of each genocide and to group events in categories that spell out the similarities among certain groups of events as well as their differences from other groups of events. Such subclassifications of genocide are the necessary basis for social science research as well as for the development of proper legal tools for differential punishment of different kinds of genocidal events. For example, there is a difference between the "murder-one" or premeditated murder that characterizes intentional genocides that define a specific target people said to be deserving of total or even large-scale extermination and the more "manslaughterlike" meaning of genocidal events that are the result of negligent, indifferent policies, such as could be the case in careless, indifferent construction of a nuclear facility with little regard for the safety and welfare of civilians in the area, or unintended hunger and starvation as a result of negligent and abusive government administration.

It is my observation that there is perhaps no other field of study that evokes such strong passions in scholars in their differences of opinion and disputations. I have puzzled over this phenomenon for many years, and I am inclined to believe that what is happening actually touches on some of the very basic dynamics that are at work in creating genocidal processes to begin with! For the ways in which we define our positions about the deaths of human beings partake of no few of the fervors of our own identifications with our own ethnicity, religion, nationality, "race," or political identity, and it is the passion of such identification with *our* identities versus the *others* that is, after all, at the heart of enabling the dehumanization and demonization of other people that are basic to genocide. I fear that in the matter of genocide studies, there are no few scholars who become disrespectful, insulting, incensed, and tyrannical. *I therefore appeal to all scholars, students, and other readers of this Encyclopedia to undertake their study of the subject matter presented here in a reverent and respectful manner,* to record differences of opinion and all manner of disagreements and disputes with the writers and editors of the Encyclopedia for further discussion and rejoinders but with a prior commitment to maintaining a respectful discourse even when one feels passionate about a subject. One might hope that our mature use of the Encyclopedia can in turn contribute to far greater tolerance for diversity of opinions, and also to greater multicultural tolerance and acceptance of differences between peoples. Some day dehumanization and demonization of others need to be infinitely less acceptable in the prevailing mind-patterns in our civilization.

Indeed, there were considerable differences of opinion among the editors of this work as well, and sometimes the results were even humorous. Thus, one entry in this Encyclopedia was evaluated by one editor as totally unacceptable because, he claimed, its scholarship base was poor and in his judgment the entry was also written very unclearly, but another editor took pains to write a special note of gratitude and appreciation for the publication of that very same article, which he characterized as outstandingly creative and excellently written. In another instance, when experts on nuclear policy proposed that the pounding of the planet with nuclear explosions may be responsible for an increase in earthquakes and volcanic activities, one of our editors objected that the correlation is highly speculative and constitutes the construction of a doomsday scenario from unrelated facts that seem to coincide, but the decision was made to present the opinion of the scholars of nuclear policy. In any case, our readers should know that our board of editors did take under advisement the danger of overly passionate expression of differences of opinion, and that we succeeded in creating and maintaining a mutually respectful atmosphere in sharing our opinions with one another and agreeing to disagree.

The reader should also note that while there was considerable editing for consistency in the Encyclopedia, there is also respectful allowance for the expression of other differences in information and certainly in interpretation (in a number of cases, the reader's attention is directed explicitly to such different points of view). Thus, there are differences in reports of statistics of the number of dead in any given genocide, for example, the number killed in the genocide in Indonesia is reported variously as 100,000 to 500,000. R. J. Rummel, the political scientist who has distinguished himself in his brilliant summaries of the multiple sources of information about many genocidal events, and whose work is reported extensively in the Encyclopedia, points out that one can actually create three levels of estimates for many cases of genocide: a low level, a mid level, and a high level. In continuation of our policy of respecting the scholarship of the very remarkable group of contributors that has been assembled to write this Encyclopedia, we have left discrepancies in numbers as given by the different writers. The reader is invited in any instance to check the index for multiple references to a given case of genocide and to track the differences in the numbers cited, and it is recommended that such information be noted without anyone becoming overly upset about the "inaccuracy" of the information given. Counting mass bodies is not exactly an ordinary task, let alone that humankind's awareness of genocide is in a way just beginning at this time in the history of civilization. As previously noted, several differences between contributors as to what did and did not constitute *genocide* were also left intact. The only issue that we intended never to waver on throughout the Encyclopedia was the sacredness of human life, and that the very purpose of this Encyclopedia is rooted in commitment to that sacredness.

Structure and Emphases of the Encyclopedia

The Encyclopedia is designed in an innovative structure that combines four types of entries:

- *Traditional Entries* are basic encyclopedic summaries of the knowledge in a typical area or field of study.
- *Feature Entries* include innovative analyses, reinterpretations, and human-interest essays that probe basic conceptual issues in the study and prevention of genocide.
- *Features* are similar to feature stories, sidebars, and reports of background information in newspapers through which the reader will be exposed to more affective writing and information to accompany the basic traditional encyclopedic entry.
- *Source Documents* provide the verbatim texts of important and informative documents in the genesis of a genocide event—such as the verdict of the Turkish Military Court, which at one point convicted the perpetrators of the Armenian Genocide, the Protocol of the infamous Wannsee Conference in which the Nazis took their final formal decision to implement the Final Solution of the Holocaust, and the text of the *United Nations Convention on the Prevention and Punishment of the Crime of Genocide,* which constitutes the world's first basic law against genocide.

The *Encyclopedia of Genocide* is a basic and comprehensive reference work with major treatments of the events of the Armenian Genocide and the Holocaust and of denials of the Holocaust and other genocides; throughout the work there is emphasis on the comparative study of the genocides of all peoples (in the past, present, and tragically the future as well), the process of genocide, early warning systems for genocide, legal deterrents and punishment in law and genocide, and other means of prevention of genocide.

The Encyclopedia also features throughout pertinent and meaningful photographs, works of art, maps, and tabular representations to enhance the reader's knowledge and facilitate the intellectual and emotional comprehension of the academic entries. The purpose is to create for the reader an unfolding invitation to a broad intellectual, emotional, and even spiritual experience.

This basic reference work marks a further stage in the development of the field of genocide studies, which is a subject of study that cuts across traditional disciplines and is being studied in many different college and university departments, so that the Encyclopedia will provide an easily recognizable access for students and researchers from many different fields of inquiry.

Emphases on the Holocaust and the Armenian Genocide

Back around 1979, I had a meeting with the late Gideon Hausner, who had been Israel's attorney general and was the prosecuting attorney at the Eichmann trial and who subsequently served as chairman of the international board of Yad Vashem in Jerusalem. He was irate that we had dared to found the Institute on the Holocaust and Genocide in Jerusalem, which combined the concepts of Holocaust *and* genocide studies and would be organizing an international conference on "Holocaust and genocide" in 1982. To him the Holocaust could not be discussed in any comparative context (subsequently, Mr. Hausner became an ardent supporter of the publication of our Institute, *Internet on the Holocaust and Genocide*). That same year, I met with a distinguished social scientist in Europe whose reaction was that it was commendable that we were initiating an institute devoted to genocide studies, but why, he asked, did we have to include the name "Holocaust" in the title of our institute?

The considerable emphasis on the Holocaust in this Encyclopedia will please many readers and irritate others ("There is a little too much focus on the Holocaust"), but it is my opinion that the Holocaust has been and is an archetypal transformative event in the history of Western civilization that has brought home, as no genocidal event before it ever did, the enormity of the crime of mass destruction of human life owing to the uniqueness of the policy of murders by an extraordinarily advanced people and civilization that committed the finest of its resources and technology to nothing more foul than the systematic mass extermination of human beings, and also to the fact that the victims were the original "People of the Bible."

Similarly, there will be many who celebrate the considerable emphasis given in this Encyclopedia to the Armenian Genocide earlier in the century, but many others who will decry the seemingly disproportionate emphasis ("There are so many pages on the Armenian Genocide and too few on other cases such as the Ukraine Famine or the Cambodian Genocide"). In this case, it is the editor's judgment that the Armenian Genocide represents the first major genocide of the murderous twentieth century in which the awesome power of the state machinery was applied for systematic killing (one Israeli scholar has since characterized the Armenian Genocide as "a dress rehearsal for the Holocaust"); moreover, the Armenian Genocide has succeeded in recent years in generating a considerable body of scholarship second only to scholarship on the Holocaust.

Nonetheless, one must hasten to admit that there is more information available on other cases of genocide than will be reported in this Encyclopedia, and that the relative emphases on the two cases of the Holocaust and the Armenian Genocide must also be admitted to represent a relative emphasis on the mass murders of two Western white peoples who stand at the heart of our familiar Judeo-Christian civilization and with whom the majority of scholars and perhaps also readers of this Encyclopedia most naturally identify. Such positive emphatic identifications are in no way to be regretted, of course, but what is regrettable and indeed deserving of self-criticism are the considerable difficulties we Judeo-Christian whites have in being sensitive, caring, and involved in the genocides of a good number of other peoples who are more distant from us. As I have emphasized repeatedly in lectures on the Holocaust and genocide around the world, it is *natural* for any human being to feel and care more about those to whom he or she is closest, for example, a death in one's own family as compared to the death of a neighbor, but it is also our spiritual responsibility to cultivate and develop increased capacity for caring and memorial of the genocides of all other peoples, and certainly a capacity for appropriate actions to intervene when such genocides erupt. In sum, I believe the relative emphases on the two major genocidal events of the Holocaust and the Armenian Genocide are appropriate for the reasons stated. They also make sense pedagogically in terms of the considerable number of courses now given in universities that emphasize these two events, but at the same time there is reason for respectful criticism of the Encyclopedia that so much more needs to be done to develop information, caring, and involvement about the genocides of many other peoples.

What does need to be made entirely unambiguously clear is that at no point should an emphasis given to a case of genocide in terms of extent of its coverage in the Encyclopedia be translated in any way into implying that the deaths of any people are in any way more significant, noteworthy, disturbing, tragic, or evil than the deaths of any other people.

A Major Criticism of This Encyclopedia

Clearly, this Encyclopedia is not complete. Beyond the inevitable incompleteness of any work, there is one major criticism of this work that I would like to acknowledge at the outset, and that is that *there are a considerable number of genocidal events that have not received attention in this work, let alone that one would desire far more information about any number of the events that are reported.* In no way does this Encyclopedia cover the entire history and range of genocides and genocidal massacres, even as it does provide major coverage of several pivotal cases of genocide along with coverage of a not insignificant number of other cases. No less importantly, it treats the process of genocide and its prevention as a topic of major importance, along with presenting the historical facts of genocides.

Certainly there are dozens more genocidal events in the centuries preceding the twentieth century [see GENOCIDE IN ANTIQUITY; GENOCIDES DURING THE MIDDLE AGES; AND GENOCIDES OF THE EARLY MODERN PERIOD]. Two sources that will be very helpful to readers in this connection are Chalk, Frank, and Jonassohn, Kurt (1990). *The History and Sociology of Genocide: Analysis and Case Studies.*

New Haven: Yale University Press; and more recently Jonassohn, Kurt, with Björnson, Karin Solveig (1998). *Genocide and Gross Human Rights Violations in Comparative Perspective.* New Brunswick, NJ: Transaction Publishers.] There are also other genocides in the twentieth century that have not been covered, or have been given too brief coverage. Moreover, coverage of the "non-European" continents is without doubt far weaker than deserves to be the case. There is so much that has not been told here from the subcontinent of India; so much more to be told from the emerging giant of China; and endless cases of genocide in the emerging history of Africa that have not been treated in this Encyclopedia. Indeed, I would like to acknowledge that it was our intention to provide at least introductory coverage of a number of other events, and for a variety of reasons we did not succeed in doing so in time for this first edition. When it became clear that we would not have as full coverage of genocidal events as we had hoped, we nonetheless considered that the considerable breakthrough coverage that we were achieving in this first *Encyclopedia of Genocide* justified our going to press at this time. It is very much our hope that subsequent editions of the Encyclopedia will be expanded to provide fuller coverage. Indeed, readers are encouraged to send in comments and suggestions as to such additional informations for future editions.

Styles of Biographies Used in the Encyclopedia

Living Scholars of Holocaust and Genocide

With the exception of biographies of Elie Wiesel and Simon Wiesenthal, the decision was made to not include biographies of living scholars of the Holocaust and genocide in this volume. The stories of the professional lives of pioneering scholars in this area are not uninteresting and may indeed be edifying, but it was felt that for the present edition of the Encyclopedia it was far more important to develop the basic structure of information about genocide rather than to provide biographies of scholars. In fact, the roster of contributors to the Encyclopedia, for each of whom there is at least an introductory professional biographical note, in itself is an excellent starting point for developing an acquaintance with a good number of the outstanding scholars in this new field. [Two of the associate editors of the Encyclopedia are currently preparing a book on the first generation of genocide scholars: Totten, Samuel, and Jacobs, Steven (Eds.) (forthcoming). *Pioneers of Genocide Studies.* Westport, CT: Greenwood Publishers.] The decision to provide more full biographical materials on Elie Wiesel and Simon Wiesenthal not only reflects the considerable respect each of these great men deserves as survivors of the Holocaust who went on to dedicate their lives not only to profoundly meaningful memorials of the Holocaust but also to translations of the Holocaust into a statement of a universal event; Wiesel and Wiesenthal are also honored as representing humankind's finest capacity for transforming experiences of being victimized into doing battle against genocide to all peoples.

Deceased Scholars of Holocaust and Genocide

In the same vein of minimizing the amount of material devoted to biography in this first edition of the Encyclopedia, the decision was made to provide relatively brief biographies of Raphael Lemkin and Leo Kuper and a few other very short biographical notes such as those on Martin Ennals and Luis Kutner. With regard to Lemkin, there are also repeated references to him in many entries in the Encyclopedia as the person who created the word *genocide* and who fought tirelessly and selflessly for adoption of the first anti-genocide law in world history. In the case of Leo Kuper, who was probably the most important single scholar to advance the development of genocide studies, the brief biography is also accompanied by excerpts from a number of his writings and a selection of annotated references to most of his works.

Genocidal Killers

Paradoxically, a great deal more space is devoted to biographies of some of the genocidal killers. This is done because the story of the genocides committed by these people cannot be separated from some information about the histories of the leaders of the devastating genocidal processes, and it has to be clear that hopes for prevention of genocide in the future must also address issues of knowing how to identify emerging leaders who dedicate their skills and charisma to heinous deeds of murder. The truth is that we wanted to convey that the biographical entries for these murderers are in no way intended to express respect for them as historical heroes by entering all their names in a single section as "Perpetrators of Genocide" (hardly one of humankind's proudest occupations), but the basic structural requirement of an encyclopedia to provide easy access to alphabetically organized information won out. In Pinochet's case, we were fortunate enought to link his story to an important emergent precedent toward international extradition of those indicted for crimes against humanity and genocide, and there is, of course, much other information in the Encyclopedia about trials and prosecution of perpetrators of genocide.

Deniers of the Holocaust, Armenian Genocide, and Other Cases of Genocide

Paradoxically too, there are a fair number of biographical sketches and descriptive notes about deniers, especially of the Holocaust and the Armenian Genocide. We need to know who these deniers are—in many cases their shabby credentials, in all cases their shabby ethics, and worse their disregard not only for the historical record and human memory but also their basic contempt for human life. And we need to know how they package and disseminate their lies, half-truths, deconstructions of historical reality, and relativization of the meanings of losses of life so that we can be better equipped to combat them.

About the References Cited in the Encyclopedia

The limited number of references appended to many entries were chosen in large part as *Recommended Reading* for the user of the Encyclopedia who wishes to continue further study of a given subject in genocide studies. Regrettably, in its present scope, the Encyclopedia was not seen as an appropriate place for fuller reference lists, and the references given are not necessarily the most central or important scholarly works on a subject, but they were selected in large part as recommended additional reading on a subject.

It should also be noted that, unlike scholarly journals and research volumes, encyclopedic entries do not necessarily provide references and citations to back up all statements made by the author of the encyclopedic entry. In a few instances, where a background reference is especially esoteric or hard to find, or where there is some other reason for needing to make it very clear what is the source of information, some additional references were included inside the text of an encyclopedic entry.

Cross-References

It is very much a goal of this Encyclopedia to lead readers from one case of genocide to others, from cases of genocide to analyses of the dynamics of genocide as a process, from understanding genocide as a process to consideration of means of response to genocide, including intervention in ongoing cases of genocide, preventive measures in the face of early warning signals of incipient genocide, punishment of perpetrators in an expanded legal system that will allow for universal jurisdiction and not be restricted to criminal charges against perpetrators in the countries of their origin, and other emergent visions of a future world. For example, there may be an International Peace Army with machinery for military intervention to stop genocide and protect victims, medical and relief forces to move quickly to aid victims and refugees, and community reorganization forces that will aid in rebuilding community systems and even more so in correcting (sometimes age-old) intolerance and prejudice that surface again and again in dehumanization and demonization. The reader is urged to review the Table of Contents of the Encyclopedia as a kind of map that invites the study of interrelationships between entries. In addition, the detailed Index, ably prepared by the publisher and Marc I. Sherman, should be consulted repeatedly for multiple references to given names, places, events, and processes. In addition, a judicious selection of cross-references has been provided in the course of some entries where it was felt that an additional emphasis would be helpful to the reader.

Appreciations

A pioneering project of this magnitude involves the participation of a wide range of people to each of whom we are seriously indebted.

I am particularly grateful to the devoted group of Associate Editors, each of whom not only contributed considerable scholarly writing to the Encyclopedia but accompanied the huge task of preparing the entire work tirelessly and devotedly in many consultations, reviews of entries, and critiques of the entire manuscript.

Rouben Paul Adalian is Director of the Armenian National Institute (ANI) in Washington, DC. He specializes in the documentation of the Armenian Genocide and has created a comprehensive collection of evidence from the US Government Archives. He serves as the Encyclopedia's Resource Editor on the Armenian Genocide, and in addition, along with all the Associate Editors, as a wise reviewer of the entire manuscript.

Steven Jacobs is a practicing pulpit rabbi, a college instructor who teaches courses on genocide, and the scholar who has undertaken to reconstruct the profoundly valuable unpublished manuscripts of the great Raphael Lemkin. Among other things, he has brought to the manuscript perspectives of an American-Jewish community leader and one who is close to grassroots America.

Eric Markusen, who is a professor of both sociology and social work and who has previously published (with Robert Jay Lifton) a pathbreaking analysis of *the genocidal mentality* and (with David Kopf) a disturbing analysis of the *over*use of strategic bombing by the Allied forces in World War II as possibly genocidal, is also a heroic field researcher of ongoing genocides who has traveled dozens of times to sites of contemporary mass murder in our troubled world. His efforts at meticulous accuracy of information and a balanced perspective have been very valuable.

Samuel Totten is a professor of education who has published extensively on education about the Holocaust and genocide, has authored a major work on first-person or eyewitness reports and oral histories of genocide, and was the leader of the project, with William Parsons and me, that produced an excellent anthology of the histories of twentieth-century genocide along with oral reports of the genocides that is widely used as a college text. He brought to the editorial board a wide range of information and sensitivities on many important aspects of culture and, regarding the unfolding field of genocide studies, was an anchor person for recruiting many other contributors. In addition, he brought in his writing and editorial work a deep-felt passion of a decent man who cries out against the stupidity and evil of genocidal carnage.

Joining the above Associate Editors as Bibliographic Editor has been Marc I. Sherman, a specialist in library sciences and information services and a dedicated human rights scholar who has been our tireless "reference librarian," endlessly researching details and verifying obscure pieces of information. Along with his responsibilities for reviewing the entire manuscript, he also supervised the development of the Index of the Encyclopedia, which in itself is one of the major tools that this work generates. Insofar as this Encyclopedia may subsequently be transformed into a basis for an electronic interactive information service, there is no question that Marc Sherman will play a central role in this development.

Finally, special thanks are due to the Managing Editor of the Encyclopedia, Pauline Cooper, long-time Office Manager of the Institute on the Holocaust and Genocide and formerly Managing Editor of the *Internet on the Holocaust and Genocide.* She has brought to the Encyclopedia her characteristic charm and decency in working with people and her daunting skills for organizing and managing complex projects.

Needless to say, warm appreciations are also due the many Contributing Editors to the Encyclopedia. We also thank all other contributors as well as those who provided permission for reprinting existing materials from other sources who are acknowledged in the Credits section. Special note needs to be made of the contributions of Stephen Feinstein, Acting Director of the Center for Holocaust and Genocide Studies at the University of Minnesota, for his generous contributions of art works about the Holocaust and genocide and permissions to reproduce them.

Many thanks are also due a large number of scholars who responded to our requests to serve as reviewers of entries—a good number of which underwent arduous multiple reviews. The responses were almost uniformly gracious and timely as well as enthusiastic and encouraging of the importance of the Encyclopedia.

It is gratifying to note that there was a considerable sense of community generated among our many participants who joined together in devotion to the purpose of this Encyclopedia, which is to sound a clarion call of concern and hope that humankind can limit and put an end to genocidal killing. In addition, I would like to take special note of the fact that in agreeing to participate in this Encyclopedia, many scholars knowingly stepped out of certain traditions of being rooted largely in their own ethnic or other identities to join explicitly in creating a work that is truly multiethnic and ecumenical in respect of religion, nationality, and political orientation and also with respect to value positions held in regard to genocide in our civilization; so that appreciation is due many writers not only for the work that they did in contributing their materials but for their implicit and explicit readiness to participate in a concert that transcends personal collective identities to stand for all humanity.

To our publisher, ABC-CLIO, which is repeatedly cited by the American Library Association as an Outstanding Reference Book Publisher, our sincere thanks for their characteristic high degree of professionalism; additional appreciations are in order for a number of reasons. The idea of the Encyclopedia was born at ABC-CLIO, and not in the minds at our Institute. In this respect, the recognition of an outstanding reference book publisher that the time had come to treat the enormous yet profoundly neglected subject of genocide was a very important confirmation to us of the emerging status of the field of genocide studies, and that there was developing a new level of worldwide awareness of genocide.

In addition, there is a personal story here in that the founder of ABC-CLIO following World War II was an extraordinarily talented German-Jewish young man who survived the Holocaust, worked with the US occupation forces, and then came to make his home in the United States. Eric Boehm not only created a touching work on the stories of a number of survivors of the Holocaust (*We Survived: Fourteen Histories of the Hidden and Hunted of Nazi Germany,* originally published by Yale University Press), but in this work he gave voice to his understanding of the *universality* of the issues of prejudice, intolerance, cruelty, and readiness to do murderous harm to fellow human beings; the gift of such a universal perspective was given only to a few of those who survived the inferno of the Holocaust. It was at the Boehms' gracious home that I met one of the senior editors of ABC-CLIO, and thus a more personal groundwork was laid for the invitation that was to come some years later for me and our Institute to develop this Encyclopedia, although Boehm himself had by then retired as the chief executive of ABC-CLIO. It is our special pleasure to include in the Encyclopedia an entry as well as several thoughtful feature comments by Eric Boehm, who, it might be added, is seriously contemplating creating a major conference following the turn into the new century that will be devoted to the theme "END GENOCIDE!"

A special appreciation is also due Irving Louis Horowitz, who is in his own right one of the early major scholars of genocide (and will be found as a Contributing Editor to this Encyclopedia) and who as President of Transaction Publishers (Rutgers State University) is the publisher of the series *Genocide: A Critical Bibliographic Review* produced by our Institute on the Holocaust and Genocide in Jerusalem. These volumes are considered the standard references to a wide gamut of the literature on genocide [see BIBLIOGRAPHIES ON THE HOLOCAUST AND GENOCIDE]. They include critical essays evaluating the basic knowledge and needs in a given area of scholarship of genocide and are accompanied by extensive critical annotated bibliographies. As our publisher of the above reference series, Irving Horowitz might have taken a position that the Encyclopedia competed with the series published by Transaction, or that our affiliation with ABC-CLIO was competitive. On the contrary, from the outset Irving Horowitz has applauded the Encyclopedia and has celebrated the excellence of ABC-CLIO as a great publisher of encyclopedias—and indeed honored us greatly by joining ABC-CLIO editorial executives and ourselves in a festive dinner in London to celebrate the completion of the Encyclopedia.

In conclusion, then, I wish to thank all those who have made this first *Encyclopedia of Genocide* come to fruition.

Together, let us pray and commit ourselves to do battle for Peace and Life against the darkest forces in human existence.

Contributors

Editor in Chief

ISRAEL W. CHARNY is Executive Director of the Institute on the Holocaust and Genocide in Jerusalem, which he founded with the late Shamai Davidson, M.D., and Elie Wiesel in 1979. He is also Professor of Psychology and Family Therapy at the Hebrew University of Jerusalem.

He is widely respected and credited as a prime mover in the development of the field of Genocide Studies, in which he has persevered in his leadership for 35 years. Among his major contributions stand the historic first International Conference on the Holocaust and Genocide in Tel Aviv in 1982—which, as reported in numerous stories in the *New York Times* and other world press, he saw through to a successful conclusion, standing up against major governmental efforts to close the conference down; publication of *How Can We Commit the Unthinkable?: Genocide, the Human Cancer* (Westview Press, 1982), which was reissued in an updated Portuguese translation (Editora Rosa dos Tempos, 1998); his major proposal for a GENOCIDE EARLY WARNING SYSTEM, which has been commended by, among others, the United Nations (Whitaker Commission Report) and the *New York Times;* founding and editing the resource series *Genocide: A Critical Bibliographic Review,* in which three of the four volumes that have appeared to date were edited by him (Mansell Publishing and Facts on File, 1988 and 1991, and Transaction Publishers, 1994), and the fourth volume was under his direction as Series Editor (Transaction Publishers, 1997); founding and editing *Internet on the Holocaust and Genocide* from 1985 to 1995, the first interdisciplinary network for researchers of genocide from many different fields and the first ecumenical forum for activists from different ethnic groups (in 1995, continuation of *Internet* was transferred to the Centre for Comparative Genocide Studies at Macquarie University, Sydney, Australia); studies of denials of genocide and leadership in combatting denials, especially of the Armenian Genocide, as they have occurred in Israel and also in the United States and France; and studies of the psychology of evil, including the readiness of students in the health professions to commit themselves to doing harm and even to killing people when instructed or commanded to do so under the guise of kindness to the chronically ill or handicapped.

Since 1996, he has devoted himself to the pathbreaking work of creating the first-ever encyclopedia in the field of Genocide Studies, the *Encyclopedia of Genocide.*

Charny has been devoted to the study of the Holocaust and genocide since the mid-1960s. He is committed to the ideal that understanding the processes that brought about the unbearable evil of the

Holocaust be joined with the age-old Jewish tradition of contributing to the greater ethical development of all human civilization, and that a unique memorial to the Holocaust be forged in the development of new concepts of prevention of genocide to *all* peoples. His first publication on the subject, which appeared in *Jewish Education* in 1968, was "Teaching the Violence of the Holocaust: A Challenge to Educating Potential Future Oppressors and Victims for Nonviolence."

Associate Editors

ROUBEN PAUL ADALIAN is the Director of the Armenian National Institute (ANI) in Washington, DC. ANI (website: www.armenian-genocide.org) is dedicated to the study, research, and affirmation of the Armenian Genocide. At ANI, Adalian coordinates international efforts to document the Armenian Genocide. In 1993 he completed a project to document the Armenian Genocide in the US National Archives. As a result Chadwyck-Healey Inc. published 37,000 pages of American evidence on microfiche. The accompanying 476-page *Guide to the Armenian Genocide in the U.S. Archives, 1915–1918* was issued in 1994. Adalian has written chapters in various genocide-related publications and has contributed articles to journals, including "The Ramifications in the United States of the 1995 French Court Decision on the Denial of the Armenian Genocide and Princeton University" (*Revue du monde arménien modèrne et contemporain,* 1997, 3). He is a specialist on the Caucasus and the Middle East. He has taught at the School of Foreign Service, Georgetown University, and currently teaches at the School for Advanced International Studies, Johns Hopkins University. He is also the author of *From Humanism to Rationalism: Armenian Scholarship in the Nineteenth Century* (Scholars Press, 1992), as well as many articles on Armenia and the Armenian diaspora.

STEVEN L. JACOBS serves as the Rabbi of Temple Shalom, Huntsville, AL, and teaches courses in both Biblical Studies and Holocaust/Genocide Studies at Calhoun Community College, Huntsville, AL, and at the Martin Methodist College, Pulaski, TN, where he serves as the Zimmerman Judaic Scholar-in-Residence. He is the author of numerous reviews, essays, and books in these fields, including being international editor of the papers of Raphael Lemkin, of which he has published one volume to date, *Raphael Lemkin's Thoughts on Nazi Genocide: Not Guilty?* (Edwin Mellen Press, 1992), and an overview, "The Papers of Raphael Lemkin: A First Look" (*Journal of Genocide Research,* March, 1999). He is currently Secretary-Treasurer of the Association of Genocide Scholars.

ERIC MARKUSEN is Professor of Sociology and Social Work at Southwest State University in Minnesota. For the past twenty years he has taught and written on the nuclear threat, the Holocaust, modern warfare, genocide, and the value of education on these subjects. He is coauthor with Robert Jay Lifton of *The Genocidal Mentality* (Basic Books, 1990), and with David Kopf of *The Holocaust and Strategic Bombing: Genocide and Total War in the Twentieth Century* (Westview Press, 1995). Among his articles and book chapters are "Professions, Professionals, and Genocide," in *Genocide: A Critical Bibliographic Review, Volume 2,* edited by Israel W. Charny (Mansell Publishing and Facts on File, 1991), and with Roger Smith and Robert Jay Lifton "Professional Ethics and the Denial of the Armenian Genocide" (*Holocaust and Genocide Studies,* Spring 1995). Markusen is presently engaged in research on the genocidal killing in the Former Yugoslavia between 1991 and

1995 and in Kosovo in 1999, and on the potential contributions of the International Criminal Tribunal for the Former Yugoslavia.

SAMUEL TOTTEN is professor in the Department of Curriculum and Instruction at the University of Arkansas, Fayetteville. He is the editor of *First Person Accounts of Genocidal Acts in the Twentieth Century: An Annotated Bibliography* (Greenwood Publishers, 1995). He served as an Associate Editor of *The Widening Circle of Genocide, Volume 3 in the Series, Genocide: A Critical Bibliographic Review* (Transaction Publishers, 1994), and beginning with Volume 5 of the series, whose focus will be genocide early warning systems, Totten will begin his tenure as the new editor of the series. He has recently assumed the duties of Book Review Editor of the new *Journal of Genocide Research.*

Bibliographic Editor

MARC I. SHERMAN is Director of the Academic Research Information System (ARIS) at the Research Authority of Tel Aviv University, and Director of the *Holocaust and Genocide Bibliographic Database* at the Institute on the Holocaust and Genocide in Jerusalem. He is co-editor with Robert Krell of *Medical and Psychological Effects of Concentration Camps on Holocaust Survivors* (Transaction Publishers, 1997). He is also Associate Editor of the series *Genocide: A Critical Bibliographic Review,* and has coedited *Human Rights: An International and Comparative Law Bibliography* (Greenwood Press, 1985).

Managing Editor

PAULINE COOPER was the Managing Editor of *Internet on the Holocaust and Genocide,* 1985–1995, and is the longtime Office Manager of the Institute on the Holocaust and Genocide in Jerusalem.

Contributing Editors

YAIR AURON is Senior Lecturer at the Open University of Israel and the Kibbutzim College of Education. He specializes in Holocaust and genocide education, has developed a curriculum at the high school level in Hebrew, *Sensitivity to Suffering in the World: Genocide in the Twentieth Century* (Kibbutzim College of Education, 1995), and is currently preparing a curriculum on genocide studies for the Open University of Israel. He is the author of *The Banality of Indifference: Zionism and the Armenian Genocide* (Transaction Publishers, 1999).

PETER BALAKIAN is Professor of English and Director of the Center for Ethics and World Societies at Colgate University. He is a poet, memoirist, and literary critic devoted to the study of the literature and art of genocide, and is the author of the memoir *Black Dog of Fate* (Basic Books, 1997), and "Arshile Gorky and the Armenian Genocide" (*Art in America,* February 1996).

JENNIFER BALINT is a doctoral scholar in the Research School of Social Sciences at the Australian National University. Her doctoral dissertation, titled *Law, State Crime and Genocide: Shifting Boundaries,* places genocide within the spectrum of state crime and examines the role of law in perpetration and the limits and potentials of legal process in addressing genocide and other forms of state crime.

ALBERT BANDURA is the David Starr Jordan Professor of Social Science in Psychology at Stanford University and has done extensive research on aggressive behaviors. He is the author of many books, including *Aggression: A Social Learning Analysis* (Prentice-Hall, 1973), *Social Foundations of Thought and Action: A Social Cognitive Theory* (Prentice-

Hall, 1986), and *Self-Efficacy: The Exercise of Control* (W. H. Freeman, 1997).

DAN BAR-ON is the David Lopatie Chair of Post-Holocaust Psychological Studies at Ben Gurion University of the Negev and Codirector of PRIME (Peace Research Institute in the Middle East). He is committed to study of the psychosocial aftereffects of the Holocaust on the second and third generations of Jews and Germans, and the impact of the Holocaust on Israeli-Palestinian relations. He is the author of *Legacy of Silence: Encounters with Children of the Third Reich* (Harvard University Press, 1989).

M. CHERIF BASSIOUNI is Professor of Law and President of the International Human Rights Law Institute of DePaul University in Chicago. He is the former Chair of the United Nations Diplomatic Conference on the Establishment of an International Criminal Court in 1998; former Chair of the United Nations Commission of Experts to Investigate Violations of International Humanitarian Law in the Former Yugoslavia in 1992–1994; and the author of *Crime against Humanity* (Transnational Publishers, 2nd rev. ed., 1999).

YEHUDA BAUER is Professor Emeritus of Holocaust Studies at Hebrew University of Jerusalem and Director of the International Institute for Holocaust Research at Yad Vashem, Jerusalem. He specializes in Holocaust studies, and his most recent book is *Jews for Sale?* (Yale University Press, 1994).

MICHAEL BAZYLER is Professor of Law at Whittier Law School in Costa Mesa, CA, and is also an Associate at the Davis Center for Russian Studies at Harvard University. A second-generation Holocaust survivor, he is a Vice-President of "The 1939 Club," one of the oldest and most active Holocaust survivor groups in the United States. He is the author of numerous human rights articles, including "Litigating the Holocaust" (*University of Richmond Law Review,* May, 1999) which includes discussions of claims against European banks and insurance companies and "slave-labor actions" against manufacturing companies.

MICHAEL BERENBAUM is Professor of Theology at the University of Judaism and a Consultant to the Survivors of the Shoah Visual History Foundation. He is the former President of the Shoah Foundation, and former Director of the Research Institute of the United States Holocaust Memorial Museum and Project Director of its creation. He is the author and editor of twelve books on the history of the Holocaust and contemporary Jewish theology.

ALAN BERGER is the Raddock Eminent Scholar Chair of Holocaust Studies at Florida Atlantic University. Among his recent books is *Children of Job: American Second Generation Witnesses to the Holocaust* (SUNY Press, 1997), and he is the coeditor of *Second Generation Voices* (Syracuse University Press, 2000 [in press]).

ERIC H. BOEHM is Chairman of the International Academy at Santa Barbara, and Chairman Emeritus of ABC-CLIO and the International School of Information Management (ISIM). *We Survived: Fourteen Histories of the Hidden and Hunted in Germany* (Yale University Press, 1949), his first book, was among the early books that dealt with issues of the Holocaust.

DANIEL BROM is a clinical psychologist and psychotherapist and acts as Director of Research of AMCHA, the National Israeli Center for Psychosocial Support of Survivors of the Holocaust and the Second Generation. He specializes in trauma and has written extensively about different forms of traumatization, intervention, and therapy.

WARD CHURCHILL (enrolled Keetoowah Cherokee) is Professor of American Indian Studies and Co-Chair of the Department of Ethnic Studies at the University of Colorado at Boulder. Among his many books are *A Little Matter of Genocide: Holocaust and Denial in the Americas, 1492 to the Present* (City Lights Books, 1997), and *Struggle for the Land: Native North American Resistance to Genocide, Ecocide and Colonization* (Arbiter Ring, 1999, 2nd ed.).

ABRAHAM COOPER is a Rabbi who has been Associate Dean of the Simon Wiesenthal Center in Los Angeles since its inception in 1977, and of the Museum of Tolerance since 1993.

ROBERT CRIBB is Reader in Southeast Asian History at the University of Queensland in Brisbane, Australia. He writes widely on Indonesian political history, especially the role of violence in political change, and is editor of *The Indonesian Killings of 1965–1966* (Monash University Press, 1990).

VAHAKN DADRIAN, Professor Emeritus of Sociology at the State University of New York in Geneseo, is Director of the Genocide Study Project sponsored by the H. F. Guggenheim Foundation, and Director of Genocide Research at Zoryan Institute in Boston. He is involved in a comprehensive study of the Armenian Genocide and is the author of, among other books, *The History of the Armenian Genocide* (Berghahn, 1997), and *The Key Elements in the Turkish Denial of the Armenian Genocide* (Zoryan Institute, 1999).

SEYMOUR DRESCHER is University Professor of History and Professor of Sociology at the University of Pittsburgh. He studies Atlantic slavery in comparative context and is the author of *From Slavery to Freedom: Comparative Studies in the Rise and Fall of Atlantic Slavery* (Macmillan and Oxford University Press, 1999), and co-editor of *A Historical Guide to World Slavery* (Oxford University Press, 1998).

SIDRA DEKOVEN EZRAHI is Associate Professor of Comparative Jewish Literature at the Hebrew University of Jerusalem, and has been Visiting Professor at Duke, Princeton, Dartmouth, Susquehanna, and Yale Universities. She has written widely on critical and theoretical questions relating to the representation of the Holocaust in literature and the postwar reconstruction of Jewish culture in Israel, America, and Europe and is the author of *By Words Alone: The Holocaust in Literature* (University of Chicago Press, 1980), and *Booking Passage: Exile and Homecoming in the Modern Jewish Imagination* (University of Berkeley Press, 2000 [in press]).

HELEN FEIN is Executive Director of the Institute for the Study of Genocide in New York and a Research Associate at the Kennedy School of Government of Harvard University, and was Founding President of the Association of Genocide Scholars. She has studied both cases and comparative theory of genocide and has written two prize-winning books: *Accounting for Genocide: National Responses and Jewish Victimization During the Holocaust* (Free Press, 1979), and *Genocide: A Sociological Perspective* (Sage, 1993).

STEPHEN C. FEINSTEIN is Professor Emeritus of Russian History at the University of Wisconsin–River Falls and Director of the Center for Holocaust and Genocide Studies at the University of Minnesota. In addition to many publications, he has curated two major exhibits of art related to the Holocaust and genocide: *Witness and Legacy* and *Absence/Presence.*

BILL FRELICK is Senior Policy Analyst at the US Committee for Refugees, a nongovernmental organization based in Washington, DC. He is the editor of *Refugee Reports* and associate editor of the *World Refugee Survey,* an annual report on refugee conditions worldwide.

WILLIAM C. GAY is Professor and Chair of the Department of Philosophy at the University of North Carolina at Charlotte. He is devoted to the philosophical analysis of the many forms of violence and nonviolence, and is co-author with Michael Pearson of *The Nuclear Arms Race* (American Library Association, 1987) and with T. A. Alekseeva of *Capitalism with a Human Face: The Quest for a Middle Road in Russian Politics* (Rowman and Littlefield, 1996).

LEONARD B. GLICK is Professor of Anthropology at Hampshire College, Amherst, MA. He is author of "Religion and Genocide," in *The Widening Circle of Genocide, Volume 3 in the Series, Genocide: A Critical Bibliographic Review,* edited by Israel W. Charny (Transaction Publishers, 1994), and *Abraham's Heirs: Jews and Christians in Medieval Europe* (Syracuse University Press, 1999).

TED ROBERT GURR is Distinguished University Professor at the University of Maryland, College Park, and directs the Minorities at Risk Project, which tracks the political status and activities of more than 300 communal groups worldwide. This study provides data for his analyses of the causes and management of ethnopolitical protest and rebellion, most recently in *Peoples versus States: Ethnopolitical Conflict and Accommodation at the End of the 20th Century* (United States Institute of Peace Press, 2000 [in press]).

IAN F. HANCOCK is Professor of English, Linguistics, and Asian Studies at the University of Texas at Austin. He is the Roma representative to the United Nations and to UNICEF, is Presidium Head of the International Romani Union, and was appointed to the United States Holocaust Memorial Council by President Clinton in 1997. He was 1997 winner of the Rafto International Human Rights Prize (Norway) and 1998 Recipient of the Gamaliel Chair in Peace and Justice. He is the author of nearly 300 articles and books, most recently *The Pariah Syndrome: An Account of Gypsy Slavery and Persecution* (Karoma, 1987), and *A Handbook of Viax Romani* (Slavica, 1995), and was co-editor with Siobhan Dowd and Rajko Duric of *The Roads of the Roma: A PEN Anthology of Gypsy Writers* (University of Hertfordshire Press, 1998).

BARBARA HARFF is Professor of Political Science at the US Naval Academy in Annapolis, Maryland, and Senior Consultant to the US government's State Failure Task Force. She has published more than 40 chapters, articles, and monographs on causes, early warning, and prevention of genocides and politicides, including being coeditor with Ted Robert Gurr of *Early Warning of Communal Conflicts and Genocide: Linking Empirical Research to International Responses* (United Nations University Press, 1996).

HERBERT HIRSCH is Professor of Political Science at Virginia Commonwealth University in Richmond. His area of research and teaching is the politics of war violence and genocide, and he is author of *Genocide and the Politics of Memory* (University of North Carolina Press, 1995).

ROBERT HITCHOCK is Associate Professor of Anthropology and Coordinator of African Studies at the University of Nebraska–Lincoln. His work concentrates on indigenous peoples' human rights, and he is the co-author of "Genocide and Indigenous Peoples in Africa: A Comparative Perspective," in *The Anthropology of Genocide,* edited by Alexander Laban Hinton (University of California Press, forthcoming).

STIG HORNSHØJ-MØLLER (deceased) was a free-lance historian who was instrumental in the passage of a law to establish a Danish Center for Holocaust Studies beginning in 1999. He passed away shortly afterward.

IRVING LOUIS HOROWITZ is University Professor and Hannah Arendt Distinguished Professor Emeritus of Sociology and Political Science at Rutgers, the State University of New Jersey in New Brunswick, and Chairman of the Board and Editorial Director of Transaction Publishers. His work is focused on measuring the impact of State power on genocidal practices, and he is the author of *Taking Lives* (Transaction Publishers, 1997), and *Jewish Agonies/Israeli Ecstasies* (Oxford University Press, 1973).

MARJORIE HOUSEPIAN (DOBKIN) is a writer who was for many years Professor of English at Barnard College, Columbia University. She is the author of *Smyrna 1922: The Destruction of a City* (Newmark Press, 1998), the definitive study of the final act in the Armenian Genocide after Ataturk led his victorious army into Smyrna—thereafter known as Izmir.

FUMIKATSU INOUE is an architect living in Jerusalem who has created a plan for a major Holocaust Memorial Center Project, "Bud of the Earth." He is currently Chairman of the Japan Korczak Memorial Committee and has written a stage drama, *Dr. Korczak—The Last Journey,* published in Japan by Bungei-Yujinsha in 1995.

KURT JONASSOHN is Professor of Sociology and Codirector of the Montreal Institute for Genocide and Human Rights Studies at Concordia University in Montreal. His area is the comparative analysis of genocides throughout history, and his most recent book, with Karin Solveig Björnson, is *Genocide and Gross Human Rights Violations in Comparative Perspective* (Transaction Publishers, 1998).

GEORGE KENT is Professor and Chair of the Department of Political Science at the University of Hawaii. His professional work is centered on finding ways to strengthen the weak in the face of the strong. His most recent book is *Children in the International Political Economy* (Macmillan, 1995), and he is currently working on a computer-based tutorial titled The Human Right to Food and Nutrition.

BEN KIERNAN is the A. Whitney Griswold Professor of History and Director of the Genocide Studies Program at Yale University. He is the author of *The Pol Pot Regime: Race, Power and Genocide in Cambodia under the Khmer Rouge, 1975–1979* (Yale University Press, 1996) and is currently working on a comparative study of twentieth-century genocide.

ROSANNE KLASS is a writer, independent scholar, and policy analyst who established and headed the Afghanistan Information Center at Freedom House in New York, was co-founder of the Afghanistan Relief Committee, and was a leading independent American source of information on the Soviet-Afghan war. She is the editor and coauthor of *Afghanistan—The Great Game Revisited*

(University Press of America, rev. ed. 1990), the standard comprehensive study of that war, and has written other books and numerous articles about Afghanistan and the region.

DENNIS KLEIN is Editor of *Dimensions: Journal of Holocaust Studies,* Braun Center for Holocaust Studies, Anti-Defamation League, B'nai B'rith, New York, and is on the Faculty of Kean College of New Jersey.

DAVID KOPF is Professor of History at the University of Minnesota. His area of specialization has been India and other parts of South Asia, where he has spent some seven years and about which he has written over 60 articles and several books, one of which, *British Orientalism and the Bengal Renaissance: The Dynamics of Indian Modernization 1773–1835* (University of California Press, 1969) won the Watumull Prize awarded by the American Historical Association in 1969. He has also co-authored with Eric Markusen a work on genocide, *The Holocaust and Strategic Bombing: Genocide and Total War in the Twentieth Century* (Westview Press, 1995).

ROBERT KRELL is Professor Emeritus of Psychiatry at the University of British Columbia, Vancouver, Canada. He is a child survivor, devoted to understanding the problems of Holocaust survivor-families and their wellbeing, and is co-editor with Marc I. Sherman of *Medical and Psychological Effects of Concentration Camps on Holocaust Survivors* (Transaction Publishers, 1997).

GEORGE M. KREN is Professor of History at Kansas State University. He is co-author with Leon Rappoport of *The Holocaust and the Crisis of Human Behavior* (Holmes and Meier, 1980; 2nd ed. 1994).

DAVID KRIEGER is President of the Nuclear Age Peace Foundation. He is a leader in the global effort to abolish nuclear weapons and prevent nuclear genocide, and is the author of *Nuclear Weapons and the World Court* (Transnational, 1998).

BILL LEADBETTER is a Lecturer in History at Edith Cowan University in western Australia. He works on genocides in the pre-modern period and has published a number of articles in that field.

LYMAN H. LEGTERS is Professor Emeritus in the School of International Studies, University of Washington. A historian, he has devoted particular attention to the Soviet record with respect to genocide.

RENÉ LEMARCHAND is Professor Emeritus of Political Science at the University of Florida, Gainesville. He has written extensively on genocide, with particular reference to Rwanda and Burundi, and is the author of *Rwanda and Burundi* (Paul Mall Publishers, 1970) and *Burundi: Ethnic Conflict and Genocide* (Cambridge University Press, 1995).

ROBERT JAY LIFTON is Distinguished Professor of Psychiatry and Psychology at CUNY Graduate Center and the John Jay College of Criminal Justice in New York. He has written many works on genocide, including *The Nazi Doctors: Medical Killing and the Psychology of Genocide* (Basic Books, 1986), and is co-author with Eric Markusen of *The Genocidal Mentality: Nazi Holocaust and Nuclear Threat* (Basic Books, 1990).

FRANKLIN H. LITTELL is Professor Emeritus of Religion at Temple University and Distinguished Professor of Holocaust and Genocide Studies at the Richard Stockton College of New Jersey.

His major publications have been in the areas of religious liberty and religious persecution, and the latter concern has led him to concentrate intensely on the persecution and genocide of Jews in "Christendom." His books include *The German Church Struggle and the Holocaust* (Wayne State University Press, 1974), and *The Crucifixion of the Jews* (Harper and Row, 1975).

BARRY MEHLER is Professor of Humanities at Ferris State University in Big Rapids, MI. He is Executive Director of the Institute for the Study of Academic Racism (ISAR), which monitors academic racism and serves as a resource center for scholars, legislators, civil rights organizations, and journalists.

ROBERT MELSON is Professor of Political Science at Purdue University in West Lafayette, IN. He is the author of *Revolution and Genocide: On the Origins of the Armenian Genocide and the Holocaust* (University of Chicago Press, 1992).

SYBIL MILTON is an independent historian, formerly senior historian at the US Holocaust Memorial Museum from 1986 to 1997. She is currently serving as Vice-President of the Independent Commission of Experts: Switzerland–World War II. Her most recent publications include *In Fitting Memory* (Wayne State University Press, 1991), and the 26-volume documentation series *Archives of the Holocaust* (Garland Publishers, 1989–1995). She is Guest Co-Editor and contributor to *Photography and the Holocaust,* a special issue of *History of Photography* (December, 1999).

PEARL M. OLINER is Professor Emeritus of Education at Humboldt State University in Arcata, CA, and Research Director of the Altruistic Personality and Prosocial Behavior Institute. She is co-author with Samuel P. Oliner of the following books on altruism and caring: *Toward a Caring Society: Ideas into Action* (Praeger, 1995), and *The Altruistic Personality: Rescuers of Jews in Nazi Europe* (Free Press, 1988).

SAMUEL P. OLINER is Professor of Sociology at Humboldt State University. He teaches a variety of courses on topics such as genocide, altruism, and international race relations. He is co-author with Pearl Oliner of *Toward a Caring Society: Ideas into Action* (Praeger, 1995) and *The Altruistic Personality: Rescuers of Jews in Nazi Europe* (Free Press, 1988), and co-editor with Kathleen Lee of *Race, Ethnicity, and Gender: A Global Perspective* (Kendall/Hunt Publishing, 1997).

JACK NUSAN PORTER is Adjunct Professor of Sociology at the University of Massachusetts, Lowell. His latest interest is in post-modern controversies in Holocaust and genocide studies. His latest works are *Sexual Politics in Nazi Germany* (The Spencer Press, 1998) and *The Sociology of the Holocaust and Genocide: A Teaching and Learning Guide* (American Sociological Association, 1999).

LEON RAPPOPORT is Professor of Psychology at Kansas State University in Manhattan, KS. He is primarily concerned with the psychosocial and philosophical aspects of the Holocaust and is co-author with George Kren of *The Holocaust and the Crisis of Human Behavior* (Holmes and Meier, 1980; 2nd ed. 1994).

ALAN S. ROSENBAUM is Professor of Philosophy at Cleveland State University. He is the author of *Prosecuting Nazi War Criminals* (Westview Press, 1993), and editor of *Is the Holocaust Unique?* (Westview Press, 1996; 2nd ed. 2000 [in press]).

JOANNE WEINER RUDOF is the Archivist at the Fortunoff Video Archive for Holocaust Testimonies at Yale University. She has published papers and articles on the topic of Holocaust witness testimonies, has edited video programs, is Associate Producer of a PBS documentary, *Witness: Voices from the Holocaust,* and is co-editor of a book of the same title to be published by the Free Press.

R. J. RUMMEL is Professor Emeritus of Political Science at the University of Hawaii at Manoa. He devoted his career to the study of war, genocide, and mass murder. His latest works are *Power Kills* (Transaction Publishers, 1997) and *Statistics of Democide: Genocide and Mass Murder since 1900* (Transaction Publishers, 1999). His data, articles, and books are on his website at www2.hawaii.edu/~Rummel/.

KUMAR RUPESINGHE is Director of the Coexistence Initiative of the State of the World Forum in London. He was formerly Secretary-General of International Alert, where he succeeded the late Martin Ennals and where he served as Chair of the Forum for Early Warning and Early Action (FEWER) and Chair of the Human Rights Documentation and Exchange, International (HURIDOCS). He is co-author with Michiko Kuroda of *Early Warning and Conflict Resolution* (Macmillan-London, 1992), and author of *Civil War, Civil Peace* (Pluto Press, 1998).

RONALD E. SANTONI holds the Maria Theresa Barney Chair of Philosophy at Denison University, Granville, OH, and is a Life Member of Clare Hall, Cambridge University. He has been President of International Philosophers for the Prevention of Nuclear Omnicide, Vice-President of the American and Japanese Professionals Against Nuclear Omnicide (American Division), President of Concerned Philosophers for Peace, and is a member of the national Executive Board of Promoting Enduring Peace.

ALEX P. SCHMID holds the Synthesis Chair on Conflict Resolution at Erasmus University in Rotterdam, The Netherlands. He publishes in the fields of early warning, political conflict, human rights, and terrorism, and is currently officer-in-charge of the Terrorism Prevention Branch of the United Nations office in Vienna, Austria.

WILLIAM E. SEIDELMAN is a Professor in the Department of Family and Community Medicine at the University of Toronto. His focus is on the continuing legacy of medicine in the Third Reich, with particular emphasis on the role of the universities and research institutes as exemplified by the use of anatomical specimens derived from victims of Nazi terror.

JEFFREY SHANDLER is currently a Dorot Teaching Fellow in the Skirball Department of Hebrew and Judaic Studies at New York University. As a scholar of modern Jewish culture, he studies Holocaust remembrance in media, museums, and tourism, and his publications include *While America Watches: Televising the Holocaust* (Oxford University Press, 1999).

ROBERT SKLOOT is Professor of Theatre and Drama and Jewish Studies at the University of Wisconsin–Madison, where he serves as an Associate Vice Chancellor for Academic Affairs. He is the author of *The Darkness We Carry: The Drama of the Holocaust* (University of Wisconsin Press, 1988) and editor of *The Theatre of the Holocaust* (University of Wisconsin Press, Volume 1, 1982, and Volume 2, 1999).

ROGER W. SMITH is Professor of Government at the College of William and Mary in Williamsburg, VA. He has written extensively about genocide denial and is editor of *Genocide: Essays toward Understanding, Early-Warning, and Prevention* (Association of Genocide Scholars, 1999).

ERVIN STAUB is Professor of Psychology at the University of Massachusetts at Amherst. He has been studying individual and group psychology, social conditions, culture, and other influences leading to genocide and mass killing, with increasing focus on their prevention, and is the author of *The Roots of Evil: The Origins of Genocide and Other Group Violence* (Cambridge University Press, 1989) and of "The Origins and Prevention of Genocide, Mass Killing and Other Collective Violence" (*Peace and Conflict: Journal of Peace Psychology,* December, 1999).

MARGOT STERN STROM is Cofounder, Board President, and Executive Director of Facing History and Ourselves, a nonprofit national and international educational organization whose mission is to engage students of diverse backgrounds in civic education that encourages critical thinking skills, promotes values, and fosters the ideals needed to sustain a democratic society. She is the author and co-author of numerous books and education materials, including coauthoring with William Parsons Facing History's primary resource book, *Facing History and Ourselves: Holocaust and Human Behavior* (Facing History and Ourselves National Foundation, 1989; original edition 1982).

COLIN TATZ is Professor of Politics and Director of the Centre for Comparative Genocide Studies at Macquarie University in Sydney, Australia. He is the Supervising Editor of the *International Network on Holocaust and Genocide,* and Editor in Chief of *Genocide Perspectives.*

YVES TERNON is a physician and surgeon in Paris, and Doctor of History at Paris IV, Sorbonne. Thirty years ago he began to study the crimes of Nazi doctors and the Armenian Genocide, and more recently genocides in the twentieth century; he is the author of *L'État Criminel: Les Génocides au XXème Siècle* (Seuil, 1995).

JOHN P. THORP is Head of the Social Sciences Department at Ferris State University, Big Rapids, MI. For an analysis of the events leading up to the genocide in Bangladesh, see his article "Sheikh Mujibur Rahman, a Cyclone, and the Emergence of Bangladesh" (*South Asia Research,* 1987, 7).

MARTIN VAN BRUINESSEN is Professor of Islamic Studies at Utrecht University, The Netherlands, and one of his main research interests is religious and ethnic identities and identity politics in Turkey and its neighbors. An anthropologist, he has done extensive fieldwork among the Kurds and in Indonesia and is the author of *Agha, Shaikh and State: The Social and Political Structures of Kurdistan* (Zed Books, 1992).

ELIE WIESEL, a survivor of the Holocaust, is a Nobel laureate, University Professor, and Andrew W. Mellon Professor in the Humanities at Boston University. He is also a prolific author. See his full biography entry in the Encyclopedia.

SIMON WIESENTHAL, a survivor of the Holocaust, is Head of the Jewish Documentation Center in Vienna, Austria. Since he was liberated from the Mauthausen Concentration Camp in May 1945, he has devoted himself to tracing Nazi criminals and bringing them to trial. He is the author of a number of widely translated books, including the autobiographical *Justice Not Vengeance* (Weidenfeld and Nicolson,

1989). See his full biography entry in the Encyclopedia.

DAVID YOUNG is Research Associate at the Centre for Comparative Genocide Studies at Macquarie University in Sydney, Australia. He is the Editor of *International Network on Holocaust and Genocide.*

Other Contributors to the Encyclopedia

ROBERT H. ABZUG is Professor of History and American Studies at the University of Texas at Austin. He has written several books on a variety of topics in American cultural history, and is the author most recently of *America Views the Holocaust, 1933–1945* (Bedford/St. Martins, 1999)

KARIN SOLVEIG BJÖRNSON is a Research Associate at the Montreal Institute for Genocide and Human Rights. She is the second author with Kurt Jonassohn of *Genocide and Gross Human Rights Violations in Comparative Perspective* (Transaction Publishers, 1998).

WILLIAM R. FERNEKES is Supervisor of Social Studies at Hunterdon Central Regional High School in Flemington, NJ. He has contributed articles on Holocaust and genocide studies to *Social Education, The Social Studies,* and the *Social Science Record,* and is co-author with Beverly Edmonds of *Children's Rights: A Reference Handbook* (ABC-CLIO, 1996).

CECILE RAUSCH HERSCOVICI is a psychologist who is Co-Director of the Institute of Systems Therapies in Buenos Aires, Argentina. She is the author of *Anorexia Nervosa and Bulimia: Threats of Autonomy* (Paidos, 1990) and *The Slavery of Dieting* (Paidos, 1996).

PEDRO HERSCOVICI is a psychiatrist and Professor of Social Psychology at the Universidad del Salvador in Buenos Aires. He and Cecile Herscovici are both active in the leadership of the International Family Therapy Association, and they have firsthand knowledge of the disappearances in Argentina in 1976–1983.

ANDERS B. HANSEN is a research student at the Department of History at the University of Copenhagen who has specialized in the study of the 1947 partition of Punjab, looking into the process leading to ethnic cleansing and genocide.

ALEC ISRAEL was born in Rhodesia and immigrated to Israel in 1972. He is the Literary Editor of the *Jerusalem Post.*

TORBEN JØRGENSEN is a graduate student at the Institute for History at the University of Copenhagen. He specializes in the study of the Holocaust, and has worked especially on the recruitment and motivation of low-level perpetrators.

EDY KAUFMAN is Executive Director of the Harry S. Truman Institute for the Advancement of Peace at the Hebrew University of Jerusalem, and Senior Research Associate at the Center for International Development and Conflict Management at the University of Maryland in College Park. He has been a member of the International Executive Committee of Amnesty International, is a Board Member of Human Rights Watch/Middle East, and is currently the Chair of B'tzelem—the Israel Information Center for Human Rights in the Occupied Territories. He is the author of many works, including the forthcoming book *Human Rights in World Politics* (Tel Aviv: Ministry of Defense Publishing House).

EDWARD KISSI is Andrew W. Mellon Postdoctoral Fellow in Comparative Genocide Studies at Yale University. He is currently writing a book comparing the Ethiopian and Cambodian revolutions of the 1970s.

LEO KUPER (deceased) was Professor Emeritus of Sociology at the University of California, Los Angeles (UCLA), and was widely considered the outstanding scholar of genocide in the world. He was the author of *Genocide: Its Political Use in the Twentieth Century* (Penguin, 1981, and Yale University Press, 1982), and *The Prevention of Genocide* (Yale University Press, 1985). See his biography entry, with selections from his works, in the Encyclopedia.

DAMIR MIRKOVIC is Professor of Sociology at Brandon University in Brandon, Manitoba, Canada. His main interest is in the sociology of genocide and particularly in the historical process of destruction of Krajina Serbs in Croatia; his article on genocide in Yugoslavia during World War II appeared in *Holocaust and Genocide Studies* (1993, *2*).

The following are contributors whose materials in the Encyclopedia were taken from issues of ***Internet on the Holocaust and Genocide*** *(in several cases the affiliation given is as of the time of the original publication).*

ANNAGRET EHMANN is Director of the Education Department at Wannsee House in Berlin.

CLINTON FINK is an Affiliated Scholar at the Department of Sociology and Anthropology at Purdue University.

DAN FLEMING is Professor Emeritus in Social Studies Education at Virginia Polytechnic Institute and State University, Blacksburg, VA.

DAPHNA FROMER is on the faculty of the Bob Shapell School of Social Work at Tel Aviv University.

LILLI KOPECKY, a survivor of Auschwitz, was formerly the editor of the newsletter, *The Voice of the Auschwitz Survivor,* and contributed a regular column, "The Voice of Auschwitz Survivor 8482" to *Internet on the Holocaust and Genocide.*

DEBORAH E. LIPSTADT is Dorot Professor of Modern Jewish and Holocaust Studies and Chair, Graduate Program in Jewish Studies at Emory University, Atlanta, GA. She is the author of *Denying the Holocaust: The Growing Assault on Truth and Memory* (Free Press, 1990).

JAMES MACE, the Former Director of the United States Commission on the Ukrainian Famine, is Supervising Research Fellow in the Institute of Ethnic and Political Studies of the National Academy of Sciences of Ukraine in Kiev, and Director of the Ukrainian People's Institute of Genocide Studies in Kiev. He was responsible for the *Report to Congress* of the US Commission (US Government Printing Office, 1988), and is the author of "Soviet Man-Made Famine in Ukraine" in *Century of Genocide,* edited by Samuel Totten, William S. Parsons, and Israel W. Charny (Garland, 1997).

NAOMI PAISS is Director of Communications at the United States Holocaust Memorial Museum, Washington, DC.

JOHN SYNOTT is with the Oodgeroo Unit for Indigenous Studies and Education at Queensland University of Technology in Brisbane, Australia.

LOONG WONG is in the Faculty of Arts, Deakin University, Warrnambool, Victoria, Australia.

The following contributor's material in the Encyclopedia was excerpted from ***The***

Widening Circle of Genocide, Volume 3 in the Series, Genocide: A Critical Bibliographic Review.

JAMES DUNN is a foreign affairs and human rights specialist. One-time consul in East Timor, he was sent to Timor on an official fact-finding mission and was again there leading an aid mission when Indonesia's invasion began; he later testified before the US Congress and UN Committees.

ENCYCLOPEDIA OF
GENOCIDE

Volume I
A–H

PART I

Definitions of Genocide and the Study of Genocide

CLASSIFICATION OF GENOCIDE IN MULTIPLE CATEGORIES

"Inspired" by the uniquely systematic cruelty and evil of the Holocaust, the newly founded United Nations adopted the *Convention on the Punishment and Prevention of the Crime of Genocide* on December 9, 1948 (and it came into force after a sufficient number of ratifications by member states on January 12, 1951). However, the definition of genocide adopted in the United Nations Convention on Genocide was a political compromise that excluded mass killings of the nationals of one's own country by a government. The prevailing opinion of scholars, including the United Nations' own Whitaker Commission, is to work toward revision of this definition to include political genocide. For a period of time, an interesting but contrived scholarly solution to the problem of political genocide was to prove in some major events of mass killing, such as in Stalinist Russia or in Cambodia, that *some* of the victims were identified peoples who, although they were nationals of the country killing them, were being treated as if they were an alien group that was specifically earmarked for total extermination, thus certain nationalities in Stalin's mad world, and the Buddhist priesthood as well as a Moslem people, the Cham, in Cambodia's killing hell. But while this solution helped for a while to provide an intellectual-legal basis for identifying known killer-regimes such as the Soviet Union and Cambodia as *genocidal,* it falls far short

Martin Luther King Jr.: "I Tremble for Our World"

I tremble for our world. I do so not only from dire recall of the nightmares wreaked in the wars of yesterday, but also from dreadful realization of today's possible nuclear destructiveness, and tomorrow's even more damnable prospects.

—*Martin Luther King Jr.*

Leo Kuper: "Their Land Was Desired . . . So It Was Not Genocide"

I have listened to debates among lawyers that they get so involved in details that it is difficult to come to conclusions. The Brazilian ambassador agreed that the Indians were being killed off, but he said that it was because their land was desired and not because they were Indians, so it was not genocide.

—*Leo Kuper [at the First Raphael Lemkin Symposium at Yale University Law School]*

of reaching a point of defining all mass killings of a country's own nationals as the genocidal acts they obviously are.

In the entry DEFINITIONS OF GENOCIDE, it is noted that there is a wide range of definitions of genocide by various scholars. The extreme is an insistence on the uniqueness of one or more genocides, generally the Holocaust and perhaps the Armenian Genocide, so that only further replications of the characteristics of those particular genocides can qualify other events of mass death for the vaunted definition of "genocide"; with the result that any number of other events of mass killing are relegated to some less-valued category of "mass murder" or "mass killing," but not genocide.

It is also pointed out that among the criteria often imposed on the definition of genocide is *intentionality*—in the hands of more extreme scholars this requires a demonstration of a basic intention to exterminate *all* of the given victim people, while in other scholars' hands the proof of intention to destroy even part of a victim people is accepted as satisfying this criterion. The most liberal position presented on the continuum of definitions is that *all* mass killings, when the victims are unarmed and not engaged in a military struggle with the perpetrator, are to be defined as genocide, be they the unfit, aged, or ill, be they an ethnic group, civilians who suffer mass murder such as by gassing of villages, saturation bombings of civilian areas, nuclear bombs—all these even in the course of a bona fide war against a known aggressive government, for example, Germany or Japan in World War II. A definition extending "to all groups of human beings" was promoted by Pieter Drost as long ago as 1959, and has been advanced and extended since 1982 by Israel Charny to cover any mass of human beings, even if they do not share logically definable characteristics of a single group.

Needless to say, various scholars argue vehemently for any given position and against the definitions offered by others. In an overview of the field, Clive Foss [Introduction. In Freedman-Apsel, Joyce and Fein, Helen (1998) (Eds.), *Teaching about Genocide.* New York: Institute for the Study of Genocide] identifies in effect four main ways of defining genocide, ranging from the "all-inclusive" of Israel Charny; through a "broad approach within a careful definition" such as by Helen Fein or by Frank Chalk and Kurt Jonassohn; on to an emphasis on a given event of genocide such as the Holocaust but which emphasizes the importance of comparative studies of other genocides at the same time—as exemplified in the writings of Michael Berenbaum or in the approach of Facing History and Ourselves; and finally onto "a narrow or very restrictive approach" which insists on the uniqueness or exclusivity of a given case of genocide such as the Holocaust. Foss also makes the surprising observation that "in a practical sense, though, it hardly matters how genocide is defined, as long as students are given information to study, from which they can work out a definition." At the same time, Foss is critical of the all-inclusive definition and says that he agrees with Fein: "It is important that genocide should have a clear meaning, that it should not be trivialized and lose its force, so that some of the most monstrous examples of human behavior seem no different from events that happen all around us."

Another way to look at the definition of genocide is to assemble the various and many types of mass murder that have been included by major scholars, rather than to concentrate on how definitions are used to exclude events. Israel Charny has proposed that all events of mass murder should be treated as *genocide,* but then that each type or grouping of characteristics should be further subclassified in order to allow necessary and legitimate legal and scholarly distinctions between different subtypes of genocide. (See also the entry DEMOCIDE: A NEW INCLUSIVE CONCEPT PROPOSED for the proposal of R. J. Rummel of a new term, *democide,* for all forms of mass killing where *genocide* is a form or one subset of *democide,* although in both cases Rummel restricts his definitions to killing by governments.)

Genocide refers first of all to purposeful physical extinction of a defined collective group. In addition, if we go back to the definition offered by the originator of the concept of *genocide,* Raphael Lemkin, we have not only the purposeful effort to destroy physically a victim people by murder, but Lemkin's observations about efforts to destroy "essential foundations of the life of national groups" whose objectives "would be the disintegration of the political and social institutions of culture, language, national feelings, religion, and the economic existence of national groups, and the destruction of the personal security, liberty, health, dignity, and even the lives of the individuals belonging to such groups," genocidal actions that have been defined as "cultural genocide." This contribution too should not be discounted, even as it is clearly important to differentiate between any final termination of human lives in mass killings and processes that distress the continuity of the identity of any ethnic group but without outright mass murder.

As already noted, many major scholars of genocide have called for a broadening of the definition. Leo Kuper (1985) noted that "political affiliation can be as permanent and as immutable as racial origin" (p. 10), and further emphasized that in many cases "it is impossible to disentangle the political component from the ethnic, racial or religious" (p. 100). Helen Fein has distinguished between four overall categories of genocide: *developmental genocide,* where the perpetrators clear the way for their colonization of an area inhabited by an indigenous people; *despotic genocide,* where the perpetrators clear away the opposition to their power as for example in a political revolution; *retributive genocide,* where peoples are locked into ethnic and other stratifications of order and dominance-submission struggles; and *ideological genocide,* where a target people is defined as undeserving of life. (Fein [1984] created an outstanding teaching as well as research tool by projecting these types of genocide in a series of "fictional" scenarios where she removed the actual identifying names and places of actual events of genocide in the past, and thus created a series of templates for possible situations in which genocides can be expected in the future.) Chalk and Jonassohn proposed a typology of genocide that differentiates between "genocidal killings that are committed in the building and maintaining of empires" and "genocidal killings that are committed in the building and maintaining of nation states." Leo Kuper, definitely viewed the nuclear destruction of Hiroshima and Nagasaki as genocidal, and Eric Markusen and David Kopf have argued that saturation bombing of civilians in World War II was genocidal.

So that although many scholars have continued to argue for *exclusion* of whichever cases of mass murder from being considered genocide, inexorably the flow of human events of so many mass killings leads more and more scholars to call for the *inclusion* of a variety of real life events. Thus, British historian, Mark Levene, has struggled with instances where "*in principle,* genocide has not occurred" because the state's apparatus "has been fragmented between more than one competing group" whose warring with one another "have exhibited extreme genocidal characteristics including ethnic cleansing, selective and indiscriminate massacres, that is, of communal groups and populations regardless of age and gender." Levene concludes, albeit reluctantly, that genocide must be understood to represent "a very broad, extremely fluid continuum of mass killings with noticeably gray areas between different forms" [Levene, Mark (1994). Is the Holocaust simply another example of genocide? *Patterns of Prejudice, 28* (2), p. 5]. Similarly, even while arguing against trivialization or undue extension of the term *genocide,* Helen Fein has pressed for a broad definition of the perpetrators in her definition of genocide as "the calculated murder . . . by a government, elite staff or crowd . . ."

Charny's Typology of Many Types of Genocide

As stated, Israel Charny has proposed a solution to arguments about excluding any cases of mass murder, that *genocide* be used as a *generic definition* to cover *all* events of mass murder accompanied by a typology that subdivides, as often and in as much detail as possible, the different configurations or classes of conditions under which genocidal events take place, so that each subset can be differentiated for study of legal meanings, and ultimately disposition of appropriate punishment, and for purposes of comparative social science study of the differences and similarities between different events of genocide. Each event of genocide is to be classified into *one or more* subcategories for which it qualifies; over the course of time, there will certainly emerge new categories as the complexity of life and reality unfolds. Thus, Charny suggests it is already time to define a category of *Accomplices to Genocide* to identify the people who supply deadly weapons of mass destruction to those who commit genocide, and also a category of *Genocide as a Result of Ecological Destruction and Abuse;* and some day in the future it is possible that we will require a category, for the destruction of planets (which may be called *Planeticide, Partial Planeticide,* and *Attempted Planeticide*). Charny argues that the definition of genocide adopted in law and by social scientists must match the realities of life, so that there should be no situation in which thousands and even millions of defenseless victims of mass murder do not "qualify" as victims of genocide. Insofar as there is ever a major discrepancy between the reality of masses of dead people and our legal-scholarly definitions, it is the latter that must yield and change. The definition of genocide must also be consistent with the everyday usage of the word by reasonable people when they stand and face a mass of murdered people and naturally apply to such an event the only word there is to date in human language for such occurrences. A *generic definition of genocide does not exclude or commit to indifference any case of mass murder of any human beings,* of whatever racial, national, ethnic, biological, sexual, cultural, religious, or political definition, or any other definitions, or totally mixed groupings of any and all of the above, or random victims who share no collective identity other than having been at the same place at the same time that mass murder was committed, for example, releasing poison gas in a hub of a major city's transportation system.

Finally, Charny suggests that the definitional system will also gain if different weights or gradations are assigned to various crimes of genocide. One system for doing so that is immediately familiar for purposes of legal definition is to utilize known gradations of murder; thus, genocide in the first degree, second degree, and third degree, which are evaluated on the basis of degree of premeditation, totality or single-mindedness of purpose, resoluteness to execute policy, efforts to overcome resistance, devotion to bar escape of victims, or persecutory cruelty.

The section "A Proposed Definitional Matrix for Crimes of Genocide" following this entry presents a matrix for an encompassing *generic definition of genocide.*

Once the competition to decide which tragic events will and will not be accepted into the vaunted "genocide club" is ended, one can study the different types of genocide more honestly and come to understand their individual characteristics and differences from one another. It would be a moral absurdity and an insult to the value of human life to exclude from full historical recognition any instance of mass killing as if it were undeserving of inclusion in the record.

—*Israel W. Charny*

References and Reccomended Reading

Chalk, Frank, and Jonassohn, Kurt (1990). *The History and Sociology of Genocide: Analyses and Case Studies.* New Haven, CT: Yale University Press.

Charny, Israel W. (1994). Toward a generic definition of genocide. In Andreopolous, George (Ed.), *Genocide: Conceptual and Historical Dimensions.* Philadelphia, PA: University of Pennsylvania Press, pp. 64–94.

Drost, Pieter N. (1959). *The Crime of State: Penal Protection for Fundamental Freedoms of Persons and Peoples, Book I: International Governmental Crimes Against Individual Human Rights; Book II: Genocide. United Nations Legislation on International Criminal Law.* The Netherlands: A. W. Sythoff-Leyden.

Fein, Helen (1984). Scenarios of genocide: Models of genocide and critical responses. In Charny, Israel W. (Ed.), *Toward the Understanding and Prevention of Genocide* [Selected Presentations at the International Conference on the Holocaust and Genocide]. Boulder, CO: Westview Press; London: Bowker Publishing, pp. 3–31.

Fein, Helen (1993). *Genocide: A Sociological Perspective.* London: Sage. Originally published in *Current Sociology, 1990,* 38(1), 1–126 (whole issue).

Horowitz, Irving Louis (1997). *Taking Lives: Genocide and State Power.* Fourth Edition Expanded and Revised. New Brunswick, NJ: Transaction Publishers.

Kuper, Leo (1981). *Genocide: Its Political Use in the Twentieth Century.* London: Penguin Books, and New Haven, CT: Yale University Press (1982).

Kuper, Leo (1985). *The Prevention of Genocide.* New Haven, CT: Yale University Press.

Lemkin, Raphael (1944). *Axis Rule in Occupied Europe: Laws of Occupation, Analysis of Government, Proposals for Redress.* Washington, D.C.: Carnegie Endowment for International Peace.

Markusen, Eric, and Kopf, David (1995). *The Holocaust and Strategic Bombing: Genocide and Total War in the Twentieth Century.* Boulder, CO: Westview Press.

United Nations (1985). *Revised and Updated Report on the Question of the Prevention and Punishment of the Crime of Genocide,* prepared by Mr. B. Whitaker, Sub-Commission on Prevention of Discrimination and Protection of Minorities, 38th Sess., Item 4 (2 July 1985) E/CN.4/Sub.2/1985/6.

A PROPOSED DEFINITIONAL MATRIX FOR CRIMES OF GENOCIDE

This is a revised draft of a typology first presented at the Raphael Lemkin Symposium on Genocide at Yale University Law School in 1991 (Charny, 1994). Over time the matrix is intended to accommodate many additional classifications, and to allow for revision of definitions based on scientific observations of different events of genocidal killing.

Generic Definition of Genocide

GENOCIDE IN THE GENERIC SENSE IS THE MASS KILLING OF SUBSTANTIAL NUMBERS OF HUMAN BEINGS, WHEN NOT IN THE COURSE OF MILITARY ACTION AGAINST THE MILITARY FORCES OF AN AVOWED ENEMY, UNDER CONDITIONS OF THE ESSENTIAL DEFENSELESSNESS AND HELPLESSNESS OF THE VICTIMS.

To establish first, second or third degree, evaluate extent of:

- *Premeditation*
- *Totality or single-mindedness of purpose*
- *Resoluteness to execute policy*
- *Efforts to overcome resistance*
- *Devotion to bar escape of victims*
- *Persecutory cruelty*

[Note: An earlier proposal to define degrees of guilt for different genocides was made by Churchill, Ward (1986) (Genocide: Toward a functional definition. Alternatives, *11(3), 403–430.)]*

A. ACTUAL MASS MURDER

1. Genocidal Massacre

Mass killing as defined above in the generic definition of genocide but in which the mass murder is on a smaller scale, that is, a smaller number of human beings killed.

2. Intentional Genocide

Genocide on the basis of an explicit intention to destroy a specific targeted victim group (ethnic/religous/racial/national/political/biological/sexual or other), in whole or in any substantial part, including "ethnic cleansing" or attempt to rid an area of undesired people(s).

a. *Specific Intentional Genocide* refers to intentional genocide against a specific victim group.
b. *Multiple Intentional Genocide* refers to intentional genocide against more than one specific victim group at the same time or in closely related or contiguous actions.
c. *Omnicide* refers to simultaneous intentional genocide against numerous races, nations, religions, etc.
d. *Politicide* refers to intentional mass murder of people defined as political enemies or threats to the regime in power or seeking power.
e. *Random Genocide* refers to indiscriminate, random mass killing of accessible victims, e.g., people congregating in a transportation hub, museum, office building, hotel, etc.

3. Genocide in the Course of Colonization or Consolidation of Power

Genocide that is undertaken or allowed in the course of or incidental to the purposes of achieving a goal of colonization or development of a territory belonging to an indigenous people, or any other consolidation of political or economic power through mass killing of those perceived to be standing in the way.

4. Genocide in the Course of Aggressive ("Unjust") War

Genocide that is undertaken or allowed in the course of military action by a known aggressive power, for example, Germany and Japan in World War II, for the purpose of or incidental to a goal of aggressive war, such as massive destruction of civilian centers in order to vanquish an enemy in war.

5. War Crimes against Humanity

Crimes committed even in the course of "just wars" of self-defense against a known aggressor in the course of military actions against military targets, or in treatment of war prisoners, or in occupation policies against civilian populations which involve overuse of force or cruel and inhuman treatment and which result in unnecessary mass suffering or death.

6. Genocide as a Result of Ecological Destruction and Abuse

Genocide that takes place as a result of criminal destruction or abuse of the environment or negligent failure to protect against known ecological and environmental hazards, such as nuclear explosion and accidents involving radiation and waste from nuclear installations, pollution of the environment by chemical or biological weapons, uncontrolled poisonous air owing to industrial pollution, pollution of water resources, etc.

7. Genocide as a Result of Purposeful or Negligent Famine

Genocide that takes place as a result of willful starvation of a population group, or also as a result of cynical or indifferent negligence in providing a sustaining diet.

B. ATTEMPTED GENOCIDE

Attempts to commit any of the above types of genocide, also planning, organization and preparations to execute any of the aforesaid types of genocide.

C. ACCOMPLICES TO GENOCIDE

Persons, institutions, companies, or governments who knowingly or negligently assist individuals, organizations, or governments who are known murderers or potential murderers to gain access to mega-weapons of destruction, or otherwise to organize and execute a plan of mass murders.

D. "CULTURAL GENOCIDE" OR ETHNOCIDE

Intentional destruction of the culture of ethnic, national, religious or other people, not necessarily including destruction of actual lives.

1. Biological and Physical Ethnocide

a. Adopting measures that decrease the birthrate of an ethnic, national, religious or other group, for example, forced separation of men and women under captivity; disenfranchising children of their legal rights.
b. Harming, depleting or endangering the health of an ethnic, national, religious or other population.
c. Mass slavery, deportation, torture, rape and sexual slavery.

2. Economic Ethnocide

Destroying the foundations of the economic existence of an ethnic, national, religious or other group, for example, barring the continuity of a hunting, fishing, or farming economy.

3. Linguicide

Forbidding the use of or other intentional destruction of the language of another people.

4. Religious and Spiritual Ethnocide

Forbidding or severely disrupting the traditional practice of a religion (provided the religious practice in itself represents no danger to human life and health).

5. Social Ethnocide

a. Forbidding, censoring, or otherwise barring celebration of traditions and continuity of historical memory of an ethnic, national, religious or other group.
b. Fostering a cultural milieu in which degradation and abasement of an ethnic, national, religious or other group prevail, for example, "apartheid" or discriminatory separation and degradation of a group, encouraging or maintaining a high level of alcoholism or drugs, illiteracy, poverty, criminality or violence.

COMPARATIVE STUDY OF GENOCIDE

The comparative study of genocide entails diligent and respectful scholarship of individual cases of genocide in human history, analysis of the known causes, sequences, and outcomes of these events, and then comparison of each event with other events. In the traditions of scholarship and science, the purpose is to build up a body of knowledge of common patterns as well as differences between events, thus laying a groundwork for systematic thinking about the root causes of genocide, thinking about how to intervene when genocide looms as a threatening possibility, and also thinking about how to intervene as early as possible once an event of genocide has begun to form in order to save as many human lives as possible.

Although human thought and speech is oriented, not entirely without reason, to concepts of *more* and *less, strong* and *weak,* and so on of polarized comparatives and dichotomies, it is proving of the utmost importance to guard against such coins of speech leading to implications, even if unintentional, that the suffering, tragedy or degree of evil inflicted on any one people was somehow *more* than or *less* than that suffered by another people. Although it is natural for every human being first to experience more vividly and passionately hurt and outrage over one's own loved ones and compatriots, at the core, the value of all human life must be accorded equal status.

Historically, scholarship on genocide has grown largely out of legitimate needs for memorial of the losses suffered by each victim people; much of the scholarly process has been intended to contribute additional information for remembrance and honor to the fallen. The memorial activity of any given people has naturally been an aspect of each specific people's folklore and historical memory rather than a concern with the fates of other peoples. Since genocide has been a fact of human history from time immemorial, it has also taken on a certain quality of being expected as natural and inevitable, so that the memorial activity perhaps expressed a hope that there would be no recurrence of genocide for a given victim people, but there has been little thought about broad prevention of genocide.

Slowly but surely, however, there emerges in Earth-civilization's development, including Judaeo-Christian motifs, an anthem enjoining the killing of any other human beings and calling upon all God's children to view one another as equally deserving of life. Against the background of this emerging theme, the Holocaust exploded on the consciousness of modern civilization the horrendous knowledge that an advanced society such as Germany could turn a deaf ear to the emergent evolutionary theme of respect for human life, notwithstanding a rich culture of literature, art and music, religious institutions, educational institutions, medical institutions and legal institutions, and could even employ many of the tools associated with the development of engineering and science to "improve" the mass production of deaths of masses of people. Moreover, with their strong traditions of emphasis on learning, moral and religious thought, as well as nonviolence, the Jews as victims underscored all the more the clash between demonic destruction of life and the possible emergence of an imperative for civilization of the sacredness of human life. The calculated systematic and prolonged cruelty of the German pursuit and oppression of the Jews and the overwhelming efficiency of their systematic methods of murder and disposal of bodies shocked the world into a new cultural transition to awareness of the scourge of genocide as being a major cause of unnatural deaths of human beings. After a period of stunned shock, the result was an outpouring of enormous attention to the rich fabric of the story of the Holocaust, but not only with respect to the fates of the Jews. The intense interest in the Holocaust has created a new level of awareness of all other events of genocide, and has also brought out in many people around the world a need to understand in a new way the genocidal potential in human nature and human society.

In the academic world, the result has been seen in the emergence of a new field of genocide studies that seeks to understand the similarities and differences of the genocides of all peoples who have suffered mass destruction, and to develop tools toward the understanding of possible means of prevention and intervention for the future.

Necessarily, there exists a certain tension between those members of any given ethnic group, such as Jews concerned with memorial of the Holocaust, whose understandable caring is focused on their own memorial activity, and the students of the genocides of all peoples. Regrettably, in the scholarly literature of the Holocaust and genocide there exists a gulf between much of the literature of specific genocides and the literature of the comparative study of all genocides. The intellectual tension has also been accompanied by undue degrees of political intrigues—such as in the battles over the agendas of museums or university positions, and has given rise to degrees of acrimony and disconnection between scholars whose work should be supplementing and complementing one another rather than being competitive and adversarial. Nonetheless, the larger trend today seems to be moving in the direction of the field of comparative study of all genocides. Each new case of genocidal murder that unfolds in our world—such as in recent years in the Former Yugoslavia and in Rwanda—now seems inexorably to force on everyone but the most hard-headed zealots the necessity of our understanding genocide as a process whose threat in the future is to any and all peoples, including those who have suffered before.

Probably the biggest single step in the direction of the comparative study of genocide was constituted by the development for the first time of the basic concept of *genocide* by the late Polish-Jewish attorney, Raphael Lemkin. The fact that to this day there remain battles around the "correct definition" of this word, and whether it applies only to *some* mass murders and not to *all,* is a reflection of the tension described earlier, but again the prevailing point of view of most scholars is that all types of mass murder of unarmed civilians are coming under scrutiny and are being entered into some kind of definitional frame of reference as crimes against helpless human beings.

This Encyclopedia is dedicated to the core proposition that all human life is sacred, and that the task of our species is to expand our capacity to protect all human lives from unnatural destruction.

—*Israel W. Charny*

See References following earlier entry
CLASSIFICATION OF GENOCIDE IN MULTIPLE CATEGORIES

DEFINITIONS OF GENOCIDE

The definition of the act of genocide is both a legal and a political question, in addition to its significance for social science classification and research. Genocide was first defined by the Polish lawyer Raphael Lemkin in 1944. Lemkin wrote that "This new word, coined by the author to denote an old practice in its modern development, is made from the ancient Greek word *genos* (race, tribe) and the Latin *cide* (killing)." The term genocide was subsequently codified legally in the aftermath of the horrors and destruction of the Holocaust. In 1948 the United Nations enacted the *Convention on the Prevention and Punishment of the Crime of Genocide* (which entered into force in 1951), defining genocide not only as a crime during times of war but also a crime in times of peace.

The Convention defines genocide as follows: "In the present Convention, genocide means any of the following acts committed with intent to destroy, in whole or in part, a national, ethnical, racial or religious group, as such: (a) Killing members of the group; (b) Causing serious bodily or mental harm to members of the group; (c) Deliberately inflicting on the group conditions of life calculated to bring about its physical destruction in whole or in part; (d) Imposing measures intended to prevent births within the group; (e) Forcibly transferring children of the group."

The Convention, however, has not been accepted as the last word on the definition of genocide. The definition of the crime of genocide has provoked much scholarly and legal argument. Alternative definitions extend to the trivial and the overtly political (where not only every mass killing but every incident of mass harm is termed "genocide"). Discussion has been focused on a number of main themes: the types of victim groups to be included (possibly the most discussed issue); what it means to "destroy" and the meanings of "in whole" and "in part"; the level of "intent" required; whether genocide is committed only by governments; whether there are different types or levels of genocide; whether genocide must be systematic and sustained action or can be sporadic; whether the time period is an issue; what does "as such" mean? This entry will briefly explore the following issues: definition of the victim group, the role of intent and the agent of genocide, and the systematic nature of destruction.

Definition of the Victim Group

The definition of the group is a key issue. Athough the Convention expanded the definition of the group from Lemkin's notion of the nation or the ethnic group to the national, ethnical, racial or religious group, it does contain three notable omissions: the social group, the gendered group and the political group, all of which it has been argued have been subjects of genocide post–World War II. To ignore such groups is not to include, among other victims of genocide, 100,000 to 500,000 (estimates vary widely) Indonesians killed as members of the Communist party in 1965–1966, and to ignore the Khmer Rouge killings of an estimated 1.8 million Khmer in 1975–1979. Sociologist Helen Fein has argued that a restrictive definition of the group fails to conform with the underlying basis of the concept of genocide, being *the destruction of a group, a societal unit or basic kind.* Fein has thus defined the group as a *collectivity.* Preeminent genocide scholar, sociologist Leo Kuper also argued for the inclusion of political groups in the definition of genocide. In the contemporary world, Kuper noted, political differences are at the very least as significant a basis for massacre and annihilation as racial, national, ethnic or religious differences. In addition, as Kuper wrote, genocides against racial, national, ethnic or religious groups are generally a consequence of, or intimately related to, political conflict. In response to the omission of political groups from the Convention definition of

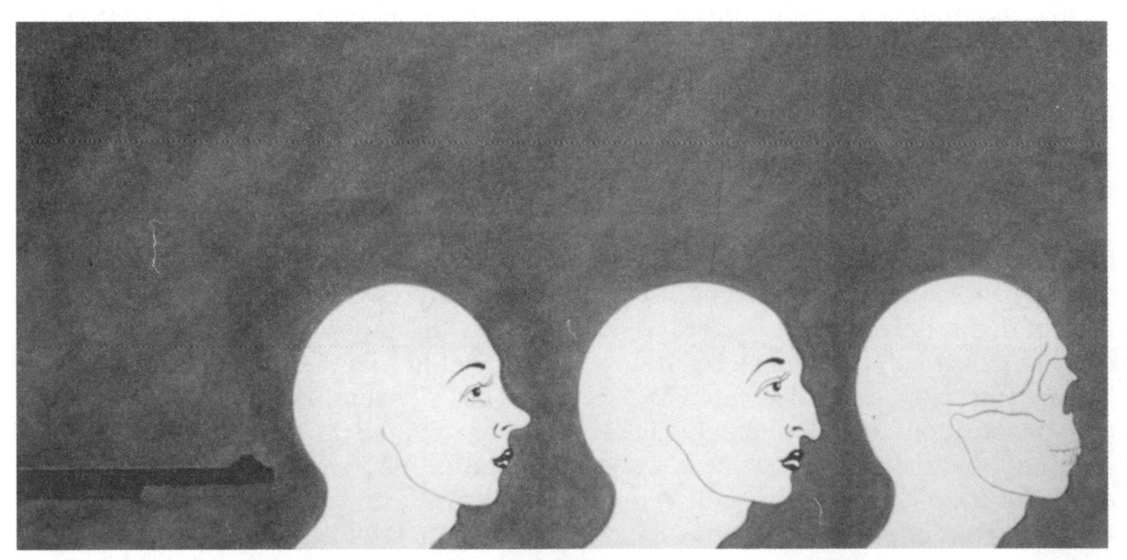

Babi Yar/Bosnia, *oil on canvas, painted by American artist Marcia Annenberg, 1992. (Courtesy of Marcia Annenberg, with the kind assistance of Stephen C. Feinstein)*

President Clinton: World Reacted Too Slowly to Rwandan Genocide

When Rwanda erupted in bloodshed, Clinton administration officials resisted appeals for intervention and spent weeks debating whether the mass killings carried out by Hutu extremists should properly be called a "genocide." In March 1998, President Bill Clinton traveled to Rwanda and acknowledged that the answer should have been simple. In 90 days, as many as a million people died in what the President called the most rapid "slaughter in this blood-filled century we are about to leave." It was a tragedy, he added, for which the United States and other members of the international community must take blame. "We did not act quickly enough after the killing began," Mr. Clinton said. "We did not immediately call these crimes by their rightful name: genocide."

—*Press Reports*

genocide, Ted Gurr and Barbara Harff have coined the term *politicide.*

Already in 1959, Pieter Drost, a legal scholar, defined genocide as *the deliberate destruction of physical life of individual human beings by reason of their membership of any human collectivity as such.* With respect to the Genocide Convention, Drost wrote that: "A Convention on genocide cannot effectively contribute to the protection of certain described minorities when it is limited to particular defined groups. On the contrary, in order to achieve its purpose such a convention must extend its protection to all groups of human beings."

Historian Frank Chalk and sociologist Kurt Jonassohn, also seeking to lay a foundation for the reinclusion of groups excluded in the U.N. Convention, have defined the group as *that group and membership as are defined by the perpetrator,* arguing that ultimately the group to be destroyed is defined by those targeting the group. Nazi Germany defined who was Jewish and who was a non-Jew. The Khmer Rouge defined who was Khmer (Cambodian) and who was non-Khmer (non-Cambodian). It is to be noted that in 1985 the United Nations Commission on Human Rights submitted a Special Rapporteur's Report written by Ben Whitaker, which recommended expanding the definition to protect political, economic and social groups. "In an era of ideology," Whitaker observed, "people are killed for ideological reasons."

Conceptual Constraints on Thinking about Genocide

Although Holocaust curricula serve important purposes, they may instill or reinforce Holocaust-based conceptions of genocide. American students, for example, may fail to recognize the annihilation of indigenous cultures of the Americas as genocidal if their central image of genocide is Auschwitz or Treblinka. Curricula that address multiple genocides and that encourage students to articulate and apply formal definitions of genocide are critical if we want students to understand history more objectively. Only through such curricula, moreover, can we help students develop the sorts of conceptual structures that will enable them to perceive and analyze the human rights catastrophes of the future.

—*David Moshman*

Intentionality of Genocide and the Agent of Genocide

The role that intent should play is another key issue. Must it be shown that the group was *intended* to be destroyed by the perpetrator group, or must it only be shown that signs of destruction (as defined in the Convention) actually exist? Can a perpetrator legitimately argue (as the Paraguayan government did with regards to the destruction of the Aché Indians), that since destruction of the group was not their main aim (the aim being the construction of roads and the clearing of land for settlers), there was no genocide? Or is it enough that *implicit* intent be demonstrated? Israel Charny has argued not only for the latter, but for any situation of mass killing, even by neglect or inadvertence, for example, careless handling of a nuclear facility. He emphasizes the danger that many events of mass murder will be disqualified from being labeled genocide if there is an obligation to establish clear-cut specific intent. Thus, some scholars so restrict the term genocide to one or another scenario, such as the Holocaust, that they exclude many other cases of mass murder. Charny argues for a "generic" definition, defining genocide as follows: "*Genocide in the generic sense is the mass killing of substantial numbers of human beings, when not in the course of military action against the military forces of an avowed enemy, under conditions of the essential defenselessness and helplessness of the victims*" [see CLASSIFICATION OF GENOCIDE IN MULTIPLE CATEGORIES].

In response, Jennifer Balint has argued for a definitional difference between genocide and mass murder, that although we must be wary of the dangers of what Charny has termed "obsessive definitionalism," we must also differentiate between the organized and intended destruction of a group, whether implicitly or explicitly intended, and the indiscriminate killings of persons. The first is defined as genocide and the second as mass murder. Genocide, she argues, is *defined through the intent and the will, whether implicit or explicit, to systematically destroy (a group of people)*.

Charny in turn argues that the distinction between intentional genocides and others, and the degree of intentionality, *are* important and should be preserved in a subclassification of different categories of genocide, but that all events of mass or collective murder be subsumed first of all as *genocide.* R. J. Rummel, a political scientist, has responded to the importance of differentiating between intentional genocide and the vast extent of mass murders by proposing a new overarching word, *democide* (*demo* for people, and *cide,* of course, for killing). Charny in turn has no conceptual objection, since this is precisely the kind of inclusive definition that will not ignore cases of mass murder that he seeks. However, unlike Rummel, he does not limit the mass murders to those done by governments and also considers mass murder as genocide or democide when the perpetrator is a competing revolutionary group, a terrorist organization, a church or cult, or whoever. Thus, Vahakn Dadrian has proposed that "the focus of attention be shifted from [only] states [also] to political parties capable of displacing state power." Charny leaves it to the "play" of scholarship in coming years whether Rummel's new word will gain usage. But until it does, Charny argues that *genocide,* which has finally been accepted by the media as the everyday word for mass murders, be used as the generic or overarching word, and that intentional genocide be an important subclassification.

The Systematic Nature of Destruction

Must the destruction be systematic and sustained, or can it be sporadic? Sociologist Irving Louis Horowitz has argued that genocide is not simply a sporadic or random event, that it must be systematic and conducted with the approval of, if not direct intervention by, the state apparatus. It is to be noted that Leo Kuper introduced the term *genocidal massacre* to cover those events that produce mass killing even in single-case episodes: for example, the French reprisal killings in the town of Setif in Algeria in 1945. Kuper argued that it is important to retain the basic concept of genocidal murder, that it is not helpful to create entirely new definitions when there exists an internationally recognized definition and a Genocide Convention that might provide the basis for some effective action, however limited the underlying conception. He argued that basically all mass killing is genocide, but at the same time the word *massacre* can be added to convey a more limited range of mass killing.

Overall, genocide can be simply defined as the destruction of a group, yet it is also clear that more sophisticated definition is essential in law and social science research. In defining and in identifying the elements that constitute genocide, we are better able to analyze how it is that genocide is perpetrated and therefore better able to possibly prevent its occurrence.

—Jennifer Balint and Israel W. Charny

See References following earlier entry
CLASSIFICATION OF GENOCIDE IN MULTIPLE CATEGORIES

DEMOCIDE: A NEW INCLUSIVE CONCEPT PROPOSED

EDITOR'S INTRODUCTION TO THE WORKS OF R. J. RUMMEL

Political scientist R. J. Rummel, of the University of Hawaii, has proposed a new inclusive word, *democide,* for all forms of mass killing. *Demo* stands for people, as in the word democracy, and *cide* for killing, as in homocide or genocide.

Rummel's concern is that when we differentiate between different forms of mass killing—for example, when we distinguish between *genocide, politicide* and *mass murder*—the definition of any one category, however correct or useful it may be, may lead us to be unaware or forget that millions more of innocent human beings have been murdered by governments, and that a true picture must include *all* killings of masses of unarmed peoples by governments. In addition, Rummel is concerned to preserve the original definition of genocide as the killing of persons *because* of group membership. In order to provide an inclusive word for all mass killings by governments, Rummel has given us the concept of *democide.* This concept may provide a partial solution when scholars argue that only such and such event was truly *genocide,* for example, the many scholars who have argued for the super-uniqueness of the Holocaust and have questioned the comparability of other events to the Holocaust and even the identification of these other events as genocide. Rummel's overarching concept transcends the controversy. What Rummel argues is, let the scholars argue whether to put a given event under the category of *genocide, politicide* or *mass murder,* but let it be clear that one is speaking about an event of mass killing by a government—or *democide.*

As was explained in the previous entries, my own solution to the problem has been to propose that the word *genocide,* which has finally gained a natural usage by people and the media for describing events of mass murder, should be retained as the generic or overarching word; but that subsumed under this overarching concept would be a classificatory system for defining the various kinds of genocide, including the three categories with which Rummel is working as well as others, for it is important, for work in the social sciences and for legal purposes, to make differentiations between different subcategories of events. Were I sure that the word-concept of *democide* would catch hold and give us an all-inclusive term that will achieve easy usage by people around the world, then I would have no objection whatsoever to Rummel's word. However, I am concerned that it has taken so many years for the word *genocide* to enter into common usage, and given the natural momentum for it to continue being the word that people turn to for describing a situation of mass murder, it seems to me advantageous for *genocide* to remain the inclusive term.

I also pointed out in the entry on DEFINITIONS OF GENOCIDE that I have a disagreement with Rummel in that I am concerned that the all-inclusive definition—whether *democide* or *genocide*—also refer to mass murders by *non*governmental agents. Rummel does include *some* quasi-governmental nongovernmental groups so long as they have their *own* governing system and control certain territory, for example, the Khmer Rouge in Cambodia and the Communists in China in the 1930s, but many other scenarios of mass murder are not covered, such as a revolutionary terrorist group that is attempting to take over a government or simply spread anarchy, other types of terrorist groups, a religious movement, or any version of megalomaniac such as a cult leader or a madman who plans the mass destruction of whatever thousands, tens of thousands or millions with the horrible weapons that are now available to humankind.

More important, along with the concept of democide, R. J. Rummel has given us a series of statistical researches of mass killings that is undoubtedly the most comprehensive series of scientific studies of genocide ever done. At the conclusion of this entry, the reader will find references to Rummel's works. He has also contributed several other entries to this encyclopedia about several major events of genocide (CAMBODIA, GENOCIDE IN: KHMER ROUGE AND CAMBODIA; CHINA, GENOCIDE IN: *THE COMMUNIST CHINESE ANTHILL;* THE NAZI GENOCIDE STATE; THE SOVIET GULAG STATE). But first of all, the reader will find in the present entry on democide an overall perspective that an incredible number of near 170,000,000 innocent human beings—as a conservative estimate!—were murdered by governments—*not as war combatants*—during the twentieth century; and since the statistics are essentially up until 1987, the final count of the century will be much higher! Note also that although Rummel does make an effort to account for a variety of countries all around the world in addition to the major cases of genocide he has studied in depth, it is very likely that he has not gathered full data for any number of events especially in respect of regions more removed from our Western eyes such as in Africa, and the implication is that the number of dead from democide is again greater than the stupefying number Rummel already has given us.

But this introduction to Rummel's amazing trail-setting work is still not complete; for in addition to the concept of *democide* and in addition to his startling accumulation of statistics, Rummel has also come up with a definitive scientific conclusion that *democide—mass killing—is far more characteristic of totalitarian or nondemocratic regimes than it is of democratic regimes.* In my opinion, R. J. Rummel's statement, *POWER KILLS, ABSOLUTE POWER KILLS ABSOLUTELY* (see later entry in this section)—is one of the most important intellectual statements ever made. It is, of course, consistent with many other sources of human wisdom about power, but it is especially noteworthy because it is rooted in a comprehensive empirical analysis of the data of the events in which millions of innocent people found their deaths at the hands of other people.

Based on empirical findings, Rummel tells us that Power is the most dangerous force poised against human life, and that only the restraints of democratic checks and balances can contain it. Without democratic checks and balances, power runs rampant. Where democracy is alive, power "can still lurk in the isolated and secret corners of government," but it is far more contained.

There are a number of critics of Rummel's work who have suggested that he has not sufficiently accounted for the extent of genocidal massacres that are nonetheless the work of democracies (although note that he does include democracies in his count to an extent, such as in the case of the US, the killing of native Indians and deaths by atomic bombs; in the case of the UK, the Boer War and area-bombing of Germany; and in the case of Israel, democide in Lebanon). He is also criticized that he has not tackled the genocidal qualities of certain unjust wars that democracies have foolishly and immorally undertaken—terribly important issues to all human beings who care about justice and about preserving human life; also that he does not address the process of historical crisis and change in which a society might pass from being democratic to totalitarian (a criticism also rendered of Horowitz' classification of genocidal and nongenocidal societies—*see* GOVERNMENT AND GENOCIDE). But the main point is that Rummel does bring convincing scientific proof that the broad sweep of the demonic genocidal capacity to exterminate identified target populations is essentially the work of totalitarian power.

Of Rummel's work, Irving Louis Horowitz, a pioneer scholar of genocide (see various entries in this Encyclopedia) and as President of Transaction Publishers of Rutgers University a distinguished leader in publishing about genocide, has commented as follows: "In the specialized world in which the grim side of the twentieth century is explored in depth and with a special poignancy that often defies words . . . none stand taller than R. J. Rummel, political scientist at the University of Hawaii. In his work, he has brought to the study of genocide the quantitative—a range of figures that is truly staggering by any scale—and the qualitative, the meaning of all these numbers in the study of the 'comparative worth' of civilizations. We can no longer work in this area without reference to this massive, yet singular effort. What Rummel has done above all others is provide a conceptual map to make future studies easier. He has made the sort of hard distinctions that are data-driven between legal and outlaw states; between genocide and democide, between democratic and authoritarian systems—all anchored firmly in numbers. The numbers are so grotesque that we must actually revise our sense and sensibilities about the comparative study of totalitarianisms to appreciate that of the two supreme systemic horrors of the century, the Communist regimes measurably surpass the fascist regimes in their life taking propensities. For buried in the data on totalitarian death mills as a whole, is the terrible sense that communism is not 'Left' and fascism is not 'Right'—both are horrors—and the former, by virtue of its capacities for destroying more of its own nationals, holds a unenviable 'lead' over the latter in life taking. We all walk taller by climbing on the shoulders of Rummel's work. He has helped us to redeem the highest aspirations of the founders of social science and yet remain perfectly true to techniques of formal analysis" (Horowitz, 1997, pp. 276–279).

—*Israel W. Charny*

THE NEW CONCEPT OF DEMOCIDE

Democide: demo for people,
cide for killing

- *Democide:* The murder of any person or people by a government, including genocide, politicide, and mass murder.
- *Genocide:* Among other things, the killing of people by a government because of their indelible group membership (race, ethnicity, religion, language).
- *Politicide:* The murder of any person or people by a government because of their politics or for political purposes.
- *Mass Murder:* The indiscriminate killing of any person or people by a government.

Genocide is horrible, an abomination of our species, and totally unacceptable. It is an obscenity—the evil of our time that all good people must work to eradicate.

Most people recognize this evil for what it is. There is no doubt that the Nazi program to kill all Jews was genocide. Nor is there any doubt that the Bosnian Serb massacre of Bosnian Moslems was genocide. But was it also genocide for government forces fighting a rebellion to massacre helpless villagers in the Sudan? How about the Indonesian army's purge of communists, the assassination of political opponents by the nationalist government on Formosa, the "land-reform" executions of landlords in the Soviet Union, or the rapid death of inmates in Vietnamese reeducation camps? What about the absorption of one culture by another, the disease spread to natives by contact with colonists, the forced deportation of a people, or African slavery?

In international conventions and the professional literature, genocide was initially defined as the intentional destruction of people because of their race, religion, ethnicity, or other permanent group membership. The origin of the concept is the 1944 work by Raphael Lemkin on *Axis Rule in Occupied Europe:* "New conceptions require new terms. By *genocide* we mean the destruction of a nation or of an ethnic group . . . Genocide is directed against the national group as an entity, the actions involved are directed against the individuals, not in their individual capacity, but as members of the national group" (p. 79).

This was written at the height of the Jewish Holocaust—a clear case of a regime trying to exterminate a whole group, its intellectual contributions, its culture, and the very lives of all its people. There was an immediate need for some way to conceptualize this horror, and "genocide" did it. During the Nuremberg trials of Nazi war criminals, and in the postwar discussion and debate over how to prevent such killing in the future, "genocide" became a commonly used term. In incredibly little time, it passed from Lemkin's pages into international law. In 1946, the United Nations General Assembly recognized that "genocide is a crime under international law which the civilized world condemns, and for the commission of which principles and accomplices are punishable." Two years later the General Assembly made this resolution concrete by passing the *Convention on the Prevention and Punishment of the Crime of Genocide.*

The Convention is consistent with Lemkin's definition and elaboration. Relevant here, however, is the fact that both define genocide as the intent to destroy in whole or part a group either by killing members of the group or *by other means,* such as by preventing births in the group or by causing serious mental harm. That is, according to both Lemkin and the Convention, genocide does *not* necessarily have to include killing. This has been the source of much confusion.

In the early years of its use, "genocide" was applied almost exclusively to the Jewish Holocaust and then, especially through the work of Armenian scholars, to the mass murder of Armenians by the Young Turk regime during World War I. However, scholars increasingly have come to realize that restricting the killing aspect of the concept to those murdered by virtue of their indelible group membership does not completely account for the millions wiped out by the Nazis.

How then do we conceptualize the purposeful government killing of protesters and dissidents, the reprisal shooting of innocent villagers, the beating to death of peasants for hiding rice, or the indiscriminate bombing of civilians? How do we conceptualize torturing people to death in prison, working them to death in concentration camps, or letting them starve to death, when such killing is done out of revenge, for an ideology, or for reasons of state having nothing to do with the social groups to which these people belong?

Because of such questions scholars have generalized the meaning of "genocide." In some cases it has been extended to include the intentional killing of people because of their politics or for political reasons, even though this aspect was explicitly excluded from the Genocide Convention. Some scholars have extended the definition of genocide to cover any mass murder by government. Some have stretched the concept much further, for example by characterizing the unintentional spread of disease to indigenous populations during European colonization, including that in the American West. To most scholars, the critical aspect of "genocide" is intentional government killing of masses of human beings.

Both of these issues are confusing. Both the nonkilling aspect of "genocide" and the need to have a concept that covers other kinds of government murder have led to the following being called genocide: the denial of ethnic Hawaiian culture by the US-run public school system in Hawaii; government policies that let one race adopt the children of another race; African slavery by Whites; South African apartheid; the murder of women by men; or death squad murders in Guatemala. The linking of such diverse acts or deaths under one label created an acute conceptual problem that begged for the invention of a new concept that covers and is *limited to* intentional government murder. Thus did both Barbara Harff and I independently develop the concept of *politicide* for a government's premeditated killing of people because of their politics or for political reasons. But this new concept was still not sufficient, since it did not apply to many mass murders by government, such as the working of POWs to death by the Japanese army in World War II or the killing of Black Africans that resisted enslavement.

Already in general use is the concept of "mass murder" or "massacre." Although usage varies, both usually mean the intentional and indiscriminate murder of a large number of people by government agents, such as the shooting down of unarmed demonstrators by police, or the lobbing of grenades into prison cells by soldiers before retreating under pressure from enemy troops. The terms can also include the random execution of civilians (as in the German reprisals against partisan sabotage in Yugoslavia), working prisoners to death (as in the Soviet Kolyma mining camps), the blanket firebombing of cities (as in the 1937–38 Japanese rape and pillage of Nanking during which Japanese soldiers probably killed some 200,000 people).

We also have the concept of "terror" as applied to government killing. This term usually means the extrajudicial execution, slaying, assassination, abduction or disappearance forever of targeted individuals. That is, the killing is discriminative. Its purpose may be to exterminate actual or potential opponents or for social prophylaxis—as Aleksandr Solzhenitsyn characterized Stalin's countrywide elimination of undesirables. Such killing also may be for the purpose of promoting fear among a people and thus ensuring their obedience and subservience.

Then there is killing that does not easily fit under any of these labels. There is, for example, murder by quota carried out by the Soviets, Chinese communists, and North Vietnamese. For the Soviet and Vietnamese communists, government (or party) agencies would order units to produce certain numbers of dead. Moreover, millions of people wasted away in labor or concentration camps not because of their social identity, their political beliefs, or who they were, but simply because they got in the way, violated some Draconian rule, did not express sufficient exuberance for the regime, innocently insulted the leader (as by sitting on a newspaper with the picture of Stalin showing), or simply because they were a body that was needed for labor (as the Nazis would grab women innocently walking along a road in Ukraine and deport them to Germany for forced labor). And there are the hundreds of thousands of peasants that slowly died of disease, malnutrition, overwork, and hunger in Cambodia as the Khmer Rouge forced them under penalty of death to labor in the collectivized fields, expropriating virtually their whole harvest and refusing them adequate medical care.

Even when applicable, the concepts of *genocide, politicide, mass murder* or *massacre,* and *terror* overlap and are sometimes used interchangeably. Clearly, a concept was needed that includes all intentional government killing in cold blood and that is comparable to the concept of murder for *private* killing.

The killing of one person by another is murder whether done because the victim was of a particular color, refused to repay a loan, or hurled an insult. It is murder whether the killing was a premeditated act or the result of reckless and wanton disregard for life. It doesn't matter whether the killing is done for high moral ends, altruistic reasons, or any other purpose. Killing is murder under Western and most other legal codes (unless officially authorized by government, as for judicial executions or military combat). However, as a crime, murder is limited by definition to taking of another's life in some way. Although we use murder metaphorically, as in someone "murdering" the language, it is not considered murder in a criminal sense to hurt someone psychologically, to steal their child, or to rob them of their culture.

I thus offer, as a concept analogous to public murder, the concept of *democide,* or *murder by government agents acting authoritatively.* Its one root is the Greek *demos,* or people; the other is the same as for genocide, which is from the Latin *caedere,* to kill. Democide's necessary and sufficient meaning is the intentional government killing of unarmed persons or people. Unlike the concept of genocide, it is restricted to intentional killing of people and does not extend to attempts to eliminate cultures, races, or peoples by other means. Moreover, democide is not limited to the killing of genocide, nor to politicide, mass murder, massacre, or terror. It includes them all, as long as the killing is a purposive act, policy, process by an institution of government.

In detail, *democide* is any action by government:

1. designed to kill or cause the death of people
   - 1.1 because of their religion, race, language, ethnicity, national origin, class, politics, speech, actions construed as opposing the government or wrecking social policy, or by virtue of their relationship to such people;
   - 1.2 in order to fulfill a quota or requisition system;
   - 1.3 in furtherance of a system of forced labor or enslavement;
   - 1.4 by massacre;
   - 1.5 through imposition of lethal living conditions; or
   - 1.6 by directly targeting noncombatants during a war or violent conflict; or
2. that causes death by virtue of an intentionally or knowingly reckless and depraved disregard for life (which constitutes *practical* intentionality); as in
   - 2.1 deadly prison, concentration camp, forced labor, prisoner of war, or recruit camp conditions;
   - 2.2 murderous medical or scientific experiments on humans;
   - 2.3 torture or beatings;
   - 2.4 encouraged or condoned murder, or rape, looting, and pillage during which people are killed;
   - 2.5 a famine or epidemic during which government authorities withhold aid, or knowingly act in a way to make it more deadly; or
   - 2.6 forced deportations and expulsions causing deaths.

This definition has the following qualifications and clarifications.

a. "Government" includes de facto governance—as by the Communist Party of the People's Republic of China—or by a rebel or warlord army over a region and population it has conquered—as by the brief rule of Moslem Turks (East Turkistan Republic) over part of Sinkiang province (1944–46).

b. "Action by governments" comprises official or authoritative action by government officials, including the police, military, or secret service; or nongovernmental action (e.g., by brigands, press-gangs, or secret societies) that has or is receiving government approval, aid, or acceptance.

c. Clause 1.1 includes, for example, directly targeting noncombatants during a war or violent conflict out of hatred or revenge, or to depopulate an enemy region, or to terrorize civilians into urging surrender. Concrete examples of such instances could include indiscriminate urban bombing or shelling, or blockades that cause mass starvation.

d. "Relationship to such people" (clause 1.1) includes relatives, colleagues, coworkers, teachers, and students.

e. "Massacre" (clause 1.4) includes the mass killing of prisoners of war and of captured rebels.

f. "Quota" system (clause 1.2) includes randomly selecting people for execution in order to meet a quota; or arresting people according to a quota, some of whom are then executed.

g. "Requisition" system (clause 1.2) includes taking from peasants or farmers all their food and produce, leaving them to starve to death.

h. Excluded from the definition are:

h.1 execution for what are internationally considered capital crimes, such as murder, rape, spying, treason, and the like, so long as evidence does not exist that such allegations were invented by the government in order to execute the accused;

h.2 actions taken against armed civilians during mob action or riot (e.g., killing people with weapons in their hands is not democide); and

h.3 the death of noncombatants killed during attacks on military target, so long as the primary target is military (e.g., during bombing of enemy logistics).

TABLE 1
Sources of Mass Death

Sources of Mass Death
Intentional
War
international/domestic
Democide
genocide
Nazi killing of Jews or Gypsies
Khmer Rouge killing of Vietnamese
Soviet killing of Volga Germans
politicide
Hitler's 1934 purge of the SA
Viet Minh murder of nationalists
Libya bombing of a civilian airliner
mass murder/massacre
Nazi reprisals in Yugoslavia
Vietnamese murder by quota
Japanese rape of Nanking
terror
Guatemala death squads
Stalin's 1936–1938 purge of communists
Argentina's disappearances
Unintentional
Famine
by nature
China's 1936 famine
government-created[a]
China's 1959–1962 Great Famine
Disease
by nature
1918 influenza pandemic
government-created[a]
Soviet 1918–1923 typhus epidemic
Disaster
storm
earthquake
fire
etc.

[a]Intentionally man-made famine or disease is included under democide and may constitute genocide, politicide, or mass murder.

Table 1 gives an overview of the concept of democide in relation to the other concepts mentioned previously and placing them within the context of democidal sources of mass death.

Democide is meant to define the killing by government, just as the concept of murder defines individual killing in domestic society. Here, intentionality (premeditation) is critical, including *practical* intentionality. If a government causes deaths through a reckless and depraved indifference to human life, the deaths are as though intended.

A death constitutes democide if it is the intentional killing of an unarmed or disarmed person by government agents acting in their authoritative capacity and pursuant to government policy or high command (as in the Nazi gassing of the Jews). It is also democide if the death was the result of such authoritative government actions carried out with reckless and wanton disregard for the lives of those affected (as putting people in concentration camps in which the forced labor and starvation rations were such as to cause the death of inmates). It is democide if government promoted or turned a blind eye to the death even though it was murder carried out "unofficially" or by private groups (as by death squads in Guatemala or El Salvador). And the death also may be democide if high government officials purposely allowed conditions to continue that were causing mass deaths and issued no public warning (as in the Ethiopian famines of the 1970s). All extrajudicial or summary executions comprise democide. Even judicial executions may be democide, as in the Soviet show trials of the late 1930s. Judicial executions for "crimes" internationally considered trivial or noncapital—as of peasants picking up grain at the edge of a collective's fields, or a worker telling an antigovernment joke, or of an engineer making a miscalculation—are also democide.

I have found that in the vast majority of events and episodes, democide is unambiguous. When under the command of higher authorities soldiers force villagers into a field and then machine-gun them, there should be no question about definition. When a group armed by the government for this purpose turns the teachers and students out of school, lines up those of a particular tribe, and shoots them, it is surely democide. When all foodstuffs are systematically removed from a region by government authorities and a food blockade put in place, the resulting deaths must be considered democide. Sad to say, *most cases of government killing in this century are that clear.* The number of deaths will be hazy for many of these cases; the perpetrators and intent will not.

—*R. J. Rummel*

POWER KILLS, ABSOLUTE POWER KILLS ABSOLUTELY

Power gradually extirpates for the mind every humane and gentle virtue.
—*Edmund Burke, A Vindication of Natural Society*

Power, like a desolating pestilence, Pollutes whate'er it touches.
—*Percy Bysshe Shelley, "Queen Mab III"*

Power tends to corrupt; absolute power corrupts absolutely.
—*Lord Acton, Letter to Bishop Creighton*

The conclusion that "power corrupts" is the message emerging from work on the causes of war and comparative study of genocide, politicide, and mass murder—what I call *democide,* or the killing of masses of people—in this century.

The more power a government has, the more it can act arbitrarily according to the whims and desires of the elite, the more it will make war on others and murder its foreign and domestic subjects. The more constrained the power of governments, the more it is diffused, checked and balanced, the less it will aggress on others and commit democide. At the extremes of Power, totalitarian communist governments slaughter their people by the tens of millions, while many democracies can barely bring themselves to execute even serial murderers.

These assertions are extreme and categorical, but so is the evidence so far accumulated. Consider first war. Table 2 shows the occurrence of war between nations since 1816. In no case has there been a war involving violent military action between stable democracies, although they have fought, as everyone knows, nondemocracies. Most wars are between nondemocracies. Indeed, we have here a general principle that is gaining acceptance among students of international relations and war, namely that *democracies rarely make war on each other.* To this I would add that the less democratic two states, the more likely that they will fight each other.

TABLE 2
Wars between Democracies and Nondemocracies, 1816–1991

Dyads[a]	*Wars*[b]
Democracies vs. democracies	0
Democracies vs. nondemocracies	155
Nondemocracies vs. nondemocracies	198
Total	353

[a]Stable democracies. This only excludes the war between an ephemeral republican France and republican Rome in 1849.
[b]Defined as any military action in which at least 1,000 persons are killed. [From Small, M., and Singer, J. (1976). The war proneness of democratic regimes, 1816–1965. *Jerusalem Journal International Relations,* 1 (summer), 50–69; Small, M., and Singer, J. (1982). *Resort to Arms: International and Civil Wars, 1816–1980.* Beverly Hills, CA: Sage; more recent estimates from the author.]

Moreover, this is historically true of democracies as well. If one relaxes the definition of democracy to mean simply the restraint on Power by the participation of middle and lower classes in the determination of power holders and policymaking, then there have been many democracies throughout history. And whether considering the classical Greek democracies, the forest democracies of medieval Switzerland, or modern democracies, they did or do not fight each other (depending on how war and democracy are defined, some might prefer to say that they *rarely* fought or fight each other). Moreover, once those states that had been mortal enemies, that had frequently gone to war (as have France and Germany in recent centuries), became democratic, war ceased between them. Paradigmatic of this is Western Europe since 1945. The cauldron of our most disastrous wars for many centuries, in 1945 one would not find an expert so foolhardy as to predict not only forty-five years of peace, but that at the end of that time there would be a European community with central government institutions, moves toward a joint European military force by France and Germany, and zero expectation of violence between any of these formerly hostile states. Yet such has happened. All because they are all democracies.

Even if all to be said about absolute and arbitrary Power was that it causes war and the attendant slaughter of the young and most capable of our species, this would be enough. But the reality is much worse, as case studies attest, even without the excuse of combat. Power also massacres in cold blood those helpless people it controls—in fact *several times more of them* than it kills in wars. Consider Table 2 and Figure 1: the list and its graph of this century's *megamurderers*—those states killing in cold blood, aside from warfare, 1 million or more men, women, and children. These fifteen megamurderers have wiped out over 151 million people, almost four times the almost 36,500,000 battle dead from all this century's international and civil wars up to 1987. *The most absolute Powers—namely, communist USSR, China, and preceding-Mao guerrillas; Khmer Rouge Cambodia, Vietnam, and Yugoslavia, and*

TABLE 3
Twentieth-Century Democide

Regimes	*Years*	*Democide (000)*[a]			*Annual Rate (%)*[b]
		Total	*Domestic*	*Genocide*	
Megamurderers	1900–87	151,491	116,380	33,476	.92[d]
Deka-megamurderers	1900–87	128,168	100,842	26,690	.18[d]
USSR	1917–87	61,911	54,769	10,000	.42
China (PRC)	1949–87	35,236	35,236	375	.12
Germany	1933–45	20,946	762	16,315	.09
China (KMT)	1928–49	10,075	10,075	nil	.07[e]
Lesser Megamurderers	1900–87	19,178	12,237	6,184	1.63[d]
Japan	1936–45	5,964	nil	nil	nil
China (Mao Soviets)[c]	1923–49	3,466	3,466	nil	.05[e]
Cambodia	1975–79	2,035	2,000	541	8.16
Turkey	1909–18	1,883	1,752	1,883	.96
Vietnam	1945–87	1,678	944	nil	.10
Poland	1945–48	1,585	1,585	1,585	1.99
Pakistan	1958–87	1,503	1,503	1,500	.06
Yugoslavia (Tito)	1944–87	1,072	987	675	.12
Suspected Megamurderers	1900–87	4,145	3,301	602	.24[d]
North Korea	1948–87	1,663	1,293	nil	.25
Mexico	1900–20	1,417	1,417	100	.45
Russia	1900–17	1,066	591	502	.02
Centi-Kilomurderers	1900–87	14,918	10,812	4,071	.26[d]
Top 5	1900 87	4,074	2,192	1,078	.89[d]
China (warlords)	1917–49	910	910	nil	.02
Turkey (Ataturk)	1919–23	878	703	878	2.64
United Kingdom	1900–87	816	nil	nil	nil
Portugal (dictatorship)	1926–82	741	nil	nil	nil
Indonesia	1965–87	729	579	200	.02
Lesser Murderers	1900–87	2,792	2,355	1,019	.13[d]
World Total	1900–87	169,202	129,547	38,566	.09[f]

[a]Includes genocide, politicide, and mass murder; excludes war dead. These are most probable mid-estimates in low to high ranges. Figures may not sum due to rounding.
[b]The percent of a population killed in democide per year of the regime.
[c]Guerrilla period.
[d]Average.
[e]The rate is the average of that for three successive periods.
[f]The world annual rate is calculated for the 1944 global population.

fascist Nazi Germany—account for nearly 128 million of them, or 84 percent.

Table 3 also shows the annual percentage democide rate (the percent of its population that a regime murders per year) for each megamurderer; Figure 1 graphically overlays the plot of this on the total murdered. Massive megamurderers such as the Soviet Union and communist China had huge populations with a resulting small annual democide rate. Lesser megamurderers were far more lethal to their own populations.

Table 4 lists the fifteen most lethal regimes, and Figure 2 bar graphs them. As can be seen, no other megamurderer comes even close to the lethality of the communist Khmer Rouge in Cambodia

FIGURE 1
Megamurderers and Their Annual Rates of Democide (From Table 3)

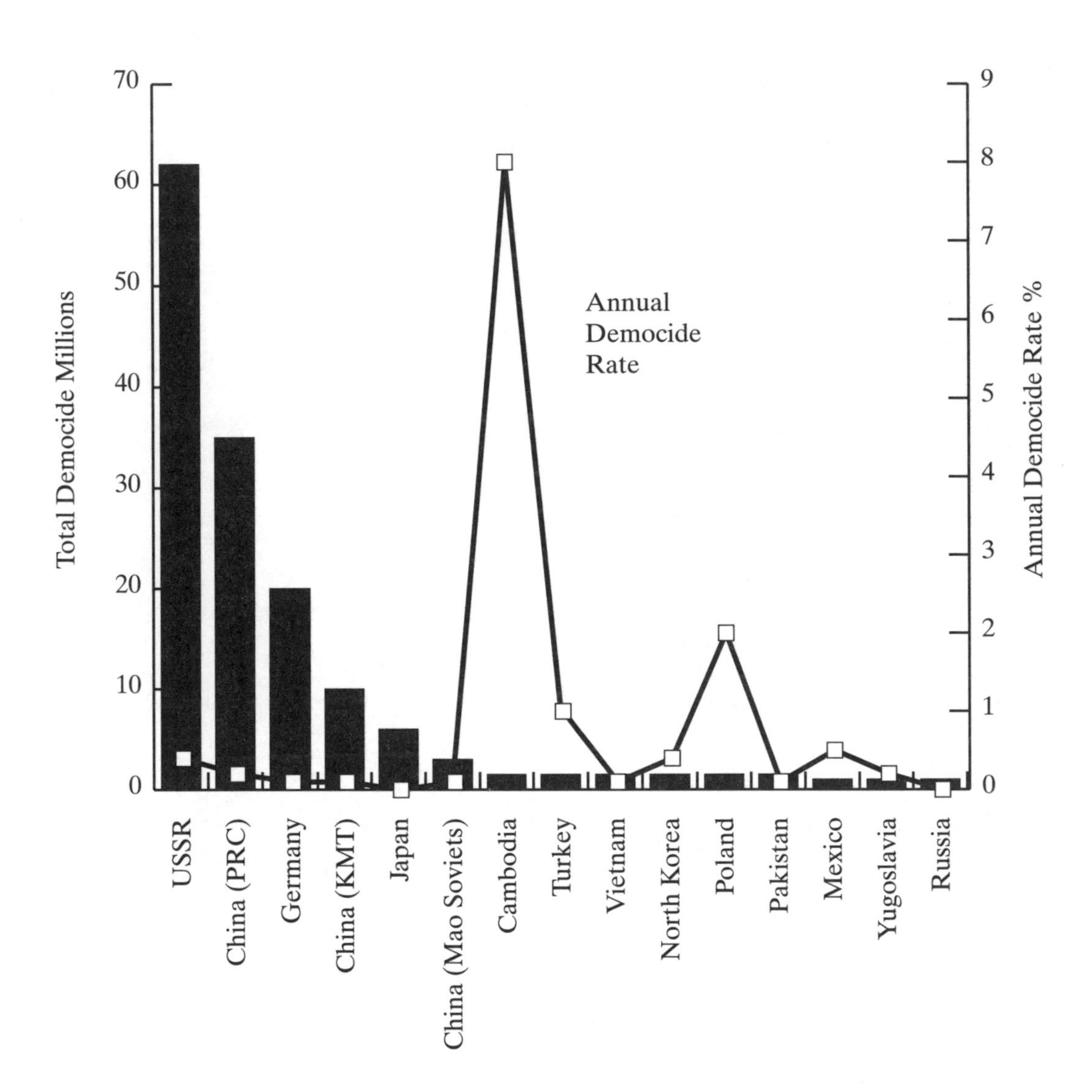

during their 1975 through 1978 rule. In less than four years of governing they exterminated over 31 percent of their men, women, and children; the odds of any Cambodian surviving these four long years was only about 2.2 to 1.

Then there are the kilomurderers, or those states that have killed innocents by the tens or hundreds of thousands, such as the top five listed in Table 3: China's Warlords (1917–1949), Ataturk's Turkey (1919–1923), the United Kingdom (primarily due to the 1914–1919 food blockade of the Central Powers in and after World War I, and the 1940–1945 indiscriminate bombing of German cities), Portugal (1926–1982), and Indonesia (1965–1987). Some lesser kilomurderers were communist Afghanistan, Angola, Albania, Romania, and Ethiopia, as well as authoritarian Hungary, Burundi, Croatia (1941–1944), Czechoslovakia (1945–1946), Indonesia, Iraq, Russia, and Uganda. For its indiscriminate bombing of German and Japanese civilians, the United States must also be added to this list. These and other kilo-

TABLE 4
Fifteen Most Lethal Regimes

Regime[a]	*Regime*			*Annual*	*Domestic*	*Midperiod*
	Years	*Duration (years)*	*Type*	*Rate (%)*[b]	*Democide (000)*	*Population (000)*
Cambodia (Khmer Rouge)	1975–79	3.83	C	8.16	2,000	6,399
Turkey (Ataturk)	1919–23	4.08	A	2.64	703	6,500
Yugoslavia (Croatia)	1941–45	4.17	A	2.51	655	6,250
Poland (Post–World War II)	1945–48	3.33	A	1.99	1,585	23,930
Turkey (Young Turks)	1909–18	9.17	A	.96	1,752	20,000
Czechoslovakia (Post–World War II)	1945–48	2.83	A	.54	197	12,916
Mexico	1900–20	21.00	A	.45	1,417	15,000
USSR	1917–87	71.00	C	.42	54,769	184,750
Cambodia (Samrin)	1979–87	8.92	C	.40	230	6,478
Uganda (Amin)	1971–79	8.33	A	.31	300	11,550
Angola	1975–87	12.17	C	.30	125	3,400
Romania (Carol/Michael)	1938–48	10.08	A	.29	484	16,271
North Korea	1948–87	39.33	C	.25	1,293	13,140
Uganda (Post-Amin)	1979–87	8.75	A	.20	255	14,300
Mongolia	1926–87	61.17	C	.19	100	873
World	1900–87	17.46[c]		.24[c]	129,909[d]	2,325,000[e]

Key: A = authoritarian; C = communist
[a]State regimes older than one year and having a population greater than 750,000.
[b]Percent of citizens killed through democide per year of the regime.
[c]Average.
[d]Total.
[e]For 1944.

murders add about 15 million people killed to the democide for this century, as shown in Table 3.

Of course, saying that a state or regime is a murderer is a convenient personification of an abstraction. Regimes are in reality people with the power to command a whole society. It is these people that have committed the kilo- and megamurders of our century, and we must not hide their identity under the abstraction of "state," "regime," "government," or "communist." Table 5 lists the men most notoriously and singularly responsible for the megamurders of this century.

Stalin, by far, leads the list. He ordered the death of millions, knowingly set in motion events leading to the death of millions of others, and as the ultimate dictator, was responsible for the death of still millions more killed by his henchman. It may come as a surprise to find Mao Tse-tung next in line as this century's greatest murderer, but this would only be because the full extent of communist killing in China under his leadership has not been widely known in the West. Hitler and Pol Pot are of course among these bloody tyrants, and there are others whose names may appear strange but whose megamurders have been documented. The monstrous bloodletting of these nine men should be entered into a Hall of Infamy. Their names should forever warn us of the deadly potential of Power.

The major and better-known episodes and institutions for which these and other murderers were responsible are listed in

FIGURE 2
Democide Lethality

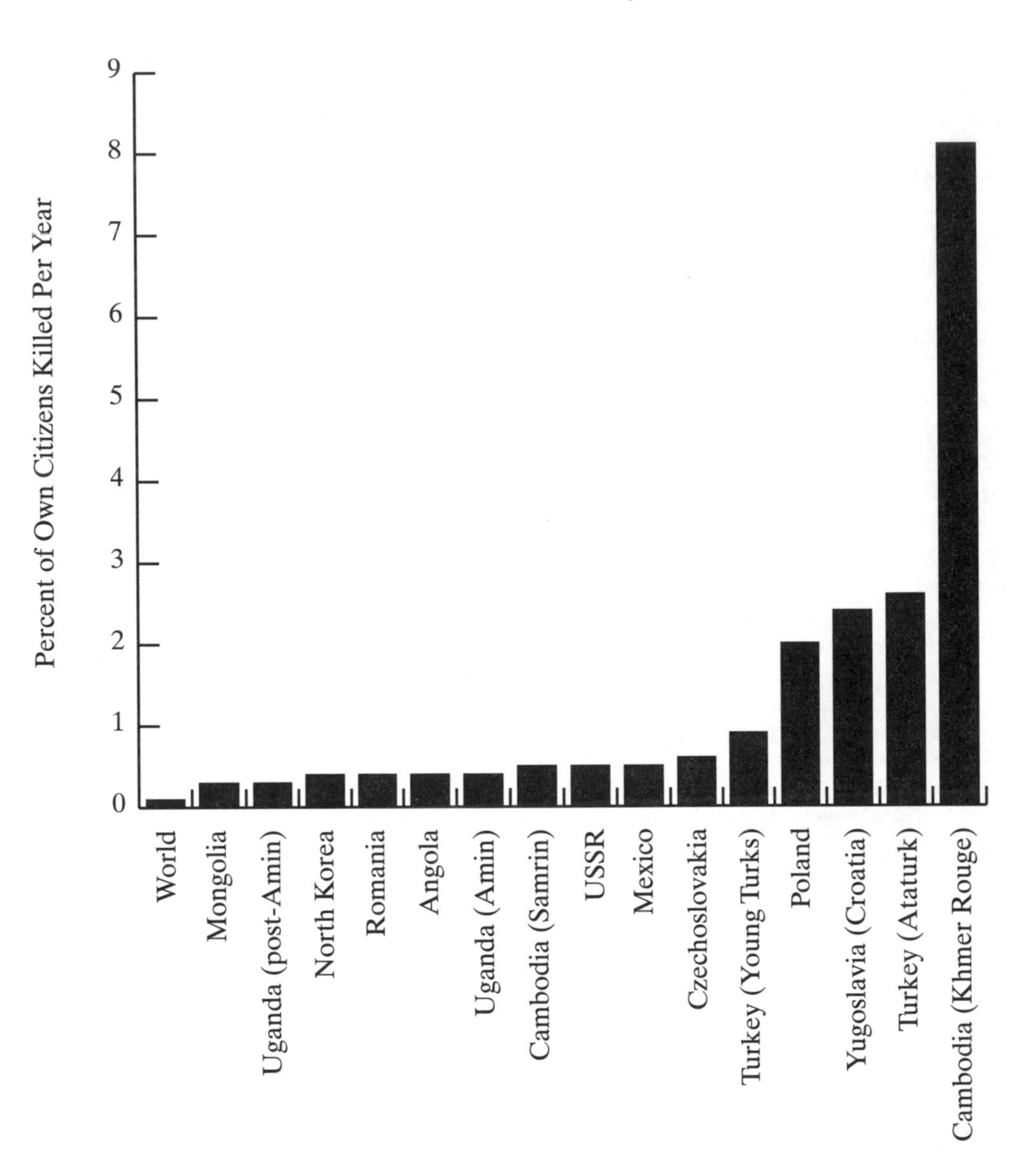

Table 6. Far above all is gulag—the Soviet slave-labor system created by Lenin and built up under Stalin. In some 70 years it likely chewed up almost 40 million lives, well over *twice* as many as probably died in some 400 years of the African slave trade, from capture to sale in an Arab, Oriental, or New World market.

In total, during the first eighty-eight years of this century, almost 170 million men, women, and children were shot, beaten, tortured, knifed, burned, starved, frozen, crushed, or worked to death; buried alive, drowned, hanged, bombed, or killed in any other of the myriad ways governments have inflicted death on unarmed, helpless citizens and foreigners. Depending on whether one uses high or more conservative estimates, the dead could conceivably be nearly 360 million people. It is as though our species has been devastated by a modern Black Plague. And indeed it has, but a plague of Power, not germs.

TABLE 5
The Twentieth Century's Bloodiest Megamurderers

Dictator	*Ideology*	*Country*	*Years*	*Murdered (000)*[a]
Joseph Stalin	C	USSR	1929–53	42,672[b]
Mao Tse-tung	C	China	1923–76	37,828[c]
Adolf Hitler	F	Germany	1933–45	20,946
Chiang Kai-shek	M/F	China	1921–48	10,214[d]
Vladimir Lenin	C	USSR	1917–24	4,017[e]
Tojo Hidcki	M/F	Japan	1941–45	3,990[f]
Pol Pot	C	Cambodia	1968–87	2,397[c]
Yahya Khan	M	Pakistan	1971	1,500
Josip Broz Tito	C	Yugoslavia	1941–87	1,172[c]

Key: C = communist; F = fascist; M/F = militarist/facist; M = militarist
[a]These are the most probable estimates from a low to high range. Estimates are from or based on Rummel 1990, 1991, 1992 and *Statistics of Democide.*
[b]Citizens only.
[c]Includes his guerrilla period.
[d]Includes his warlord period.
[e]Includes one-third the democide for the NEP period 1923–28.
[f]Estimated as one-half the 1937–45 democide in China plus the World War II democide.

The souls of this monstrous pile of dead have created a new land, a new nation, among us. In Shakespeare's words, "This Land be calle'd The field of Golgotha, and dead men's Skulls." As is clear from the megamurderers listed in Table 3 alone, this land is multicultural and multiethnic. Its inhabitants followed all the world's religions and spoke all its languages. Its demography has yet to be precisely measured.

Table 7 summarizes the most prudent estimate of democide and contrasts them to this century's battle dead. Figure 3 gives a bar chart of these totals. Note immediately in the figure that the human cost of democide is far greater than that of war for authoritarian and totalitarian regimes. Democracies show a reverse pattern, however, they suffer far fewer deaths than do other regimes. In evaluating the battle dead for democracies, also keep in mind that most of these dead were the result of wars that democracies fought against authoritarian or totalitarian aggression, particularly World War I and II and the Korean and Vietnam Wars.

Putting the human cost of war and democide together, a midrange estimate is that Power has killed over 203 million people in this century. If one were to sit at a table and have this many people come in one door, walk at three miles per hour across the room with three feet between then (assume generously that each person is also one foot thick, navel to spine), and exit an opposite door, it would take over five years and nine months for them all to pass, twenty-four hours a day, 365 days a year. If all these dead were laid out head to toe assuming each to be an average of 5 feet tall, they would reach from Honolulu, Hawaii, across the vast Pacific and then the huge continental United States to Washington, DC, on the East Coast, and then back again almost twenty times.

Now, as shown in Table 7 and Figure 3, democracies themselves are responsible for some of the democide. Almost of this, however, is foreign democide during war, and consists mainly of those enemy civilians killed in indiscriminate urban bombing, as of Germany and Japan in World

TABLE 6
Some Major Democide Episodes and Cases

Episodes/Cases	*Democide (000)*[a]	*Years*	*Victims*	*Regime(s)*
Concentration/labor camps	39,464	1917–87	anyone	USSR
Jewish Holocaust	5,291	1942–45	European Jews	Hitler
Intentional famine in Ukraine	5,000	1932–33	peasants	Stalin
China land reform	4,500	1949–53	rich/landlords	Mao Tse-tung
Collectivization	3,133	1928–35	peasants/landlords	Stalin
Cambodian Hell	2,000	1975–79	Cambodian people	Pol Pot
Cultural Revolution	1,613	1964–75	Communists/officials/ intellectuals	Mao Tse-tung
German expulsion	1,583	1945–48	German ethnics	Poland
Bengal/Hindu genocide	1,500	1971	Hindus/Bengali leaders/ intellectuals	Pakistan
Armenian genocide	1,404	1915–18	Turkey's Armenians	Young Turks
Great Terror	1,000	1936–38	Communists	Stalin
Serbian genocide	655	1941–45	Serbs/Jews/Gypsies	Croatian Ustashi
Indonesian massacre	509	1965–66	Communists/ sympathizers	Indonesian army
Ugandan massacres	300	1971–79	Critics/opponents/ tribesmen	Idi Amin
Boat people	250	1975–87	Vietnamese/Chinese	Vietnam
Spanish Civil War	200	1936–39	Republicans/Nationalists	Spanish Republican Government/ Nationalist Army
Rape of Nanking	200	1937–38	Chinese	Japanese Army
"La Violencia" massacres	180	1948–58	Liberals/conservatives	Colombia Liberal/ Conservative Governments
Tribal massacres	150	1971–72	Hutu educated/leaders	Burundi Tutsi
East Timor massacres	150	1975–87	Timorese	Indonesian army
Colonial massacres	132	1900–18	Hereros/Hottentots/ others	German Kaiser

[a]Most probable estimates from a low to high range. Estimates are from or based on Rummel 1990, 1991, 1992, and various tables of sources and estimates published in *Statistics of Democide*.

Note: These statistics do not include recent cases of democide, even when reported elsewhere in the Encyclopedia, such as genocide in the Former Yugoslavia (1991–1995) or Rwanda (1994). —Ed.

War II. Democide by democracies also includes the large-scale massacres of Filipinos during the bloody US colonization of the Philippines at the beginning of this century, deaths in British concentration camps in South Africa during the Boer War, civilian death due to starvation during the British blockade of Germany in and after World War I, the rape and murder of helpless Chinese in and around Peking in 1900, the atrocities committed by Americans in Vietnam, the murder of

TABLE 7
Democide and Power

Regime[a]	*Regime Power*	*Killed (000)*[b]			*Rate (%)*[c]	
		Total	*Domestic*	*Foreign*	*Overall*	*Annual*
Democide						
Democratic	least	2,028	159	1,858	0.04	0.01
Authoritarian	mid	28,676	26,092	2,584	1.06	0.21
Totalitarian	high	137,977	103,194	34,783	4.15	0.40
Communist	highest	110,286	101,929	8,357	5.35	0.52
Others[d]		518	464	54		
World		169,198	129,908	39,278	7.28[e]	0.083[e]

War	*Regime Power*	*Total*	*Domestic*	*International*	*Per War*[f]	*% Population*[g]
Democratic	least	4,370	5	4,365	62	0.24
Authoritarian	mid	15,298	4,774	10,523	86	0.33
Totalitarian	high	14,354	68	14,286	399	0.64
Communist	highest	9,784	68	9,715	326	0.53
World		34,021	4,848	29,174	120	1.46[h]
World Total		203,219	134,756	68,452		8.74[i]

[a]These are regimes in states, quasi-states, and nonstate groups. Classification of regimes is based on Small and Singer 1976 and Ted Robert Gurr's Polity I and II data.
[b]Figures for democide are the sums of the most probable mid-values in a low-high range over the period 1900–1987. Figures for war are a regime's battle dead in excess of 1,000 for 1900–1980 based on Small and Singer 1982, modified by additional data. Figures may not add up due to rounding.
[c]"Overall" is the average of each regime's percent of mid-period population killed through democide during the period 1900–1987. "Annual" is this average per year.
[d]These are groups for which a regime could not be specified, such as international terrorists and domestic guerrillas.
[e]The world rate is calculated for the 1944 global population.
[f]Average regime's battle dead per foreign war.
[g]Average percent of a regime's population killed in international wars.
[h]Percent of the world's 1944 population killed in all wars, 1900–1980. The annual percentage is .018.
[i]Percent of the world's 1944 population killed in democide, 1900–1987, and wars, 1900–1980.

helpless Algerians during the Algerian War by the French, and the unnatural deaths of German prisoners of war in French and US POW camps after World War II.

All this killing of foreigners by democracies may seem to violate the Power Principle, but really it underlines it. For, in each case the killing was carried out in a highly undemocratic fashion: in secret, behind a conscious cover of lies and deceit, and by agencies and power holders that had the wartime authority to operate autonomously. All were shielded by tight censorship of the press and control of journalists. Even the indiscriminate bombing of German cities by the British was disguised before the House of Commons and in press releases as attacks on German military targets. That the general strategic bombing policy was to attack working men's homes was kept secret still long after the war.

So Power kills, and absolute Power kills absolutely. What then can be said of those alleged causes or factors in war, genocide,

FIGURE 3
Deaths from Democide Compared to Deaths from International War (from Table 7)

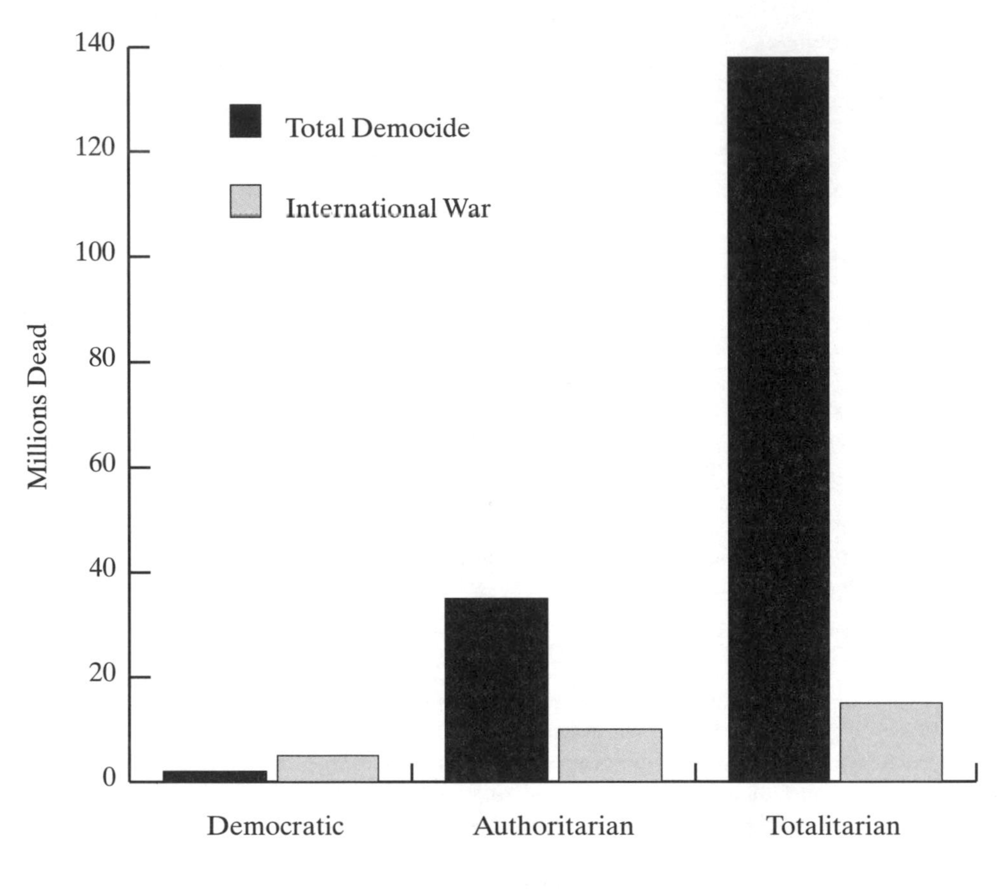

and mass murder favored by students of genocide? What about cultural-ethnic differences, ingroup-outgroup conflict, misperception, frustration-aggression, relative deprivation, ideological imperatives, dehumanization, resource competition, etc.? At one time or another, for one regime or another, one or more of these factors plays an important role in democide. They are essential for understanding some genocides, as of the Jews or Armenians; some politicides, as of "enemies of the people," bourgeoisie, and clergy; some massacres, as of competing religious-ethnic groups; or some atrocities, as of those committed against poor and helpless villagers by victorious soldiers. But they do not explain all the killing. They only accelerate the likelihood of war or democide once some trigger event occurs and absolute or nearly absolute Power is present. That is, *Power is a necessary cause for war or democide.* When the elite have absolute power, war or democide follows a common process.

However, relative power never remains constant. It shifts as the interests, capabilities, and wills of the parties change. The death of a charismatic leader, the outrage of significant groups, the loss of foreign support by outgroups, the entry into war and the resulting freedom of the elite to use force under the guise of wartime necessity, and so on, can significantly alter the balance of power between groups. Where such a shift in power is in favor of the governing elite, Power can now achieve its potential. Where also the elite has built-up frustrations regarding those who have lost power or feels threatened by them; where it sees them as outside the moral universe, or where it has dehumanized them; where the outgroup is culturally or ethnically distinct and perceived by the elite as inferior; or where any other such factors are present, Power will achieve its murderous potential. It simply waits for an excuse, an event of some sort, an assassination, a massacre in a neighboring country, an attempted coup, a famine, or a natural disaster, to justify the beginning of murder en masse. Most democides occur under the cover of war, revolution or guerrilla war, or in their aftermath.

The result of such violence will be a new balance of power and attendant social contract. In some cases this may end the democide, for example by eliminating the "inferior" group (as the Turks did to the Armenians). In many cases this will subdue the survivors (as happened with the Ukrainians who lived through Stalin's collectivization campaign and intentional famine). In some cases, this establishes a new balance of power so skewed toward the elite that they may throughout their reign continue to murder at will: Murder as public policy becomes part of the new social order. Consider the social orders of Hitler, Stalin, Mao, Pol Pot, and their henchmen.

It is not apparent, however, why, among states where Power is limited and accountable, war and significant democide are much less likely to take place. Two concepts explain this: (1) *cross-pressures* and (2) the associated political *culture*. Where Power is diffused, checked, and accountable, society is driven by myriad independent groups, disparate institutions, and multiple interests. These overlap and contend; they section loyalties and divide desires and wants. Churches, unions, corporations, government bureaucracies, political parties, the media, special interest groups, and such, fight for and protect their interests. Individuals and the elite are pushed and pulled by their membership in several such groups and institutions. It is difficult for any one driving interest to form. Interests are divided, weak, ambivalent; they are cross-pressured. For the elite to sufficiently coalesce so as to commit itself to murdering its own citizens, there must be a nearly fanatical, driving interest. But even were such to be present among a few, the diversity of interests across the political elite and associated bureaucracies, the freedom of the media to dig out what is being planned or done, and the ever-present potential for leaks and fear of such leaks from disaffected elite to the media brake such tendencies.

As to the possibility of war between democracies, diversity and resulting cross-pressures operate as well. Not only is it very difficult for the elite to unify public interests and opinion sufficiently to make war, but there are usually diverse economic, social, and political bonds between democracies that tie them together and oppose violence.

But there is more to these restraints on Power in a democracy. Cross-pressure is a *social force* that operates wherever individual and group freedom predominates. It is natural to a spontaneous social field. But human behavior is not only a matter of social forces—it also depends on the meanings, values, and norms that are present. That is, democratic *culture* is also essential. When Power is checked and accountable, when cross-pressures limit the operation of Power, a particular democratic culture develops. This culture involves debate, demonstrations, and protests as well as negotiation, compromise, and tolerance. It involves the art of conflict resolution and the acceptance of democratic procedures at all levels of society. The ballot replaces the bullet, and people and groups come to accept a loss on this or that interest as only an unfortunate outcome of the way the legitimate game is played. "Lose today, win tomorrow."

This picture of Power and its human costs is new. Few are aware of the sheer democide that has been inflicted on our fellow human beings.

Even more, our appreciation of the incredible scale of this century's genocide, politicide, and mass murder has been stultified by lack of concepts. Democide is committed by absolute Power; its agency is government. The discipline for studying and analyzing power and government and associated genocide and mass murder is political science. But except for a few specific cases, such as the Holocaust and Armenian Genocide, and a precious few more general works, one is hard put to find political science research specifically on this topic.

What is needed is a reconceptualization of government and politics consistent with what we now know about democide and related misery. New concepts have to be invented, old ones realigned to correct—dare I write "modernize"—our perception of Power. We need to invent concepts for governments that turn their states into a border-to-border concentration camp, that purposely starve to death millions—millions!—of their citizens, and that set up quotas of those that should be killed from one village or town to another (although murder by quota was carried out by the Soviets, Chinese communists, and Vietnamese, I could not find in any introductory or general political science literature even a recognition that governments can be so incredibly inhumane). We have no concept for murder as an aim of public policy, determined by discussion among the governing elite in the highest councils, and imposed through government.

In any case, the empirical and theoretical conclusion is this: The way to end war and virtually eliminate democide appears to be through restricting and checking Power, that is, through *fostering democratic freedom.*

Epilogue

One university course I teach is Introduction to Political Science. Each semester I review several possible introductory texts (the best measure of the discipline) for the course. I often just shake my head at what I find. At this stage of my research on democide, the concepts and views promoted in these texts appear grossly unrealistic. They just do not fit or explain, or are even contradictory to the existence of a Hell-State like Pol Pot's Cambodia, a Gulag-State like Stalin's Soviet Union, or a Genocide-State like Hitler's Germany.

—R. J. Rummel

References and Recommended Reading

Works of R. J. Rummel

Rummel, R. J. (1990). *Lethal Politics: Soviet Genocide and Mass Murder Since 1917.* New Brunswick, NJ: Transaction Publishers.

Rummel, R. J. (1991). *China's Bloody Century: Genocide and Mass Murder since 1900.* New Brunswick, NJ: Transaction Publishers.

Rummel, R. J. (1991). *Democide: Nazi Genocide and Mass Murder.* New Brunswick, NJ: Transaction Publishers.

Rummel, R. J. (1992). Power kills. Absolute power kills absolutely. *Internet on the Holocaust and Genocide, Special Issue 38.* Jerusalem: Institute on the Holocaust and Genocide.

Rummel, R. J. (1994). *Death by Government.* New Brunswick, NJ: Transaction Publishers.

Rummel, R. J. (1999). *Statistics of Democide: Genocide and Mass Murder since 1900.* New Brunswick, NJ: Transaction Publishers.

Rummel, R. J. (1997). *Power Kills: Democracy as a Method of Nonviolence.* New Brunswick, NJ: Transaction Publishers.

Other References

Eliot, Gil (1972). *Twentieth Century Book of the Dead.* London: Penguin.

Harff, Barbara, and Gurr, Ted Robert (1988). Toward empirical theory of genocide and politicides: Identification and measurement of cases since 1945. *International Studies Quarterly,* 32(4), 359–371.

Horowitz, Irving Louis (1997). *Taking Lives: Genocide and State Power.* Fourth Edition Expanded and Revised. New Brunswick, NJ: Transaction Publishers.

Lemkin, Raphael (1944). *Axis Rule in Occupied Europe: Laws of Occupation, Analysis of Government Proposals for Redress.* Washington, DC: Carnegie Endowment for International Peace.

"GENOCIDE," FRIVOLOUS USE OF THE TERM

Frivolous use of the term "genocide" is rampant in today's world. Well-intentioned but ill-informed individuals and groups use the term to describe a wide array of social ills, "oppression of one form or another," and/or any situation they either feel passionate about or believe merits the use of a "dramatic" term. At a minimum, many of those who misuse or abuse the term seem well aware of the term's ability to capture the ear of even the most blasé public; many also use the term to simply "hype" their issue or cause.

Examples of such misuse and abuse over the past thirty years are rife. Indeed, as early as 1982 Jack Nusan Porter noted that, "Since 'genocide' has become such a powerful catch-word, it is often used in political and cultural rhetoric." In his introduction to *Genocide and Human Rights,* Porter delineated numerous examples as to how the term was misused: "Genocide has been applied to all of the following: 'race-mixing' (integration of blacks and nonblacks); the practice of birth control and abortions among Third World people; sterilization and 'Mississippi appendectomies' (tubal ligations and hysterectomies); medical treatment of Catholics; and the closing of synagogues in the Soviet Union." *[One should note that systematic programs to reduce the birthrate of a people, or to suppress a people's culture can qualify as "cultural genocide," but even then the designation should be made clearly and not by the term "genocide" alone.—Ed.]*

More recent examples also abound. In the 1980s, AIDs activists asserted that President Ronald Reagan's lack of support for research on AIDs constituted genocide against homosexuals. Certain Palestinians and their supporters have claimed that the Israelis' actions against the Palestinians during the intifada was genocide. Throughout the 1990s, various African-American groups and certain others decried the US government policy of allowing whites to adopt black children as being genocidal. In the mid-1990s, certain activists asserted that the US government purposely implemented an ineffective drug policy that led to rampant drug availability, sales and use in the inner cities of the United States, and that such a situation was genocidal. Throughout the 1990s the most fervid antiabortion activists have claimed that the rate of abortions in the United States was genocidal.

There are, of course, also propaganda uses of charges of "genocide," even by some actual perpetrators of genocide who attempt to reverse the truth of the actual situation and accuse the victims of being perpetrators. Frivolous misuse of the term also includes political accusations such as when, during NATO air attacks against Bosnia Serb military targets in 1995, Russia charged the Serbs were facing "genocide" from the West.

Frivolous use of the term is bound to lead many members of the public to become lazy and indiscriminate in making key distinctions between what is and is not truly genocide or genocidal. When genocide is used in a loose and irresponsible manner, not only does it distort the true meaning of the term, but it diminishes the significance of and minimizes those actions that are truly genocidal in nature. Misuse and overuse of the term many also contribute to inuring some people to the horror of the reality of genocide—one of the most egregious human rights violations known to humanity.

—*Samuel Totten*

References and Recommended Reading

Porter, Jack Nusan (1982). Introduction. In Porter, Jack Nusan (Ed.), *Genocide and Human Rights: A Global Anthology.* Washington, DC: University Press of America, pp. 2–32.

Totten, Samuel (1998). Defining genocide: Words do matter. In Danks, Carol, and Rabinsky, Leatrice

(Eds.), *Teaching for a Tolerant World: Essays and Resources.* Urbana, IL: National Council of Teachers of English, pp. 141–151.

GENOCIDE, STUDY OF

Like many catastrophic natural events and incurable terminal illnesses, genocide for many years has simply been an event that happened, often with little to no warning, and for reasons unknown. Even many of the peoples who themselves suffered genocide did not seek much beyond a "Bad Man" or prejudice-discrimination explanation of how and why an enemy did them in. Today, however, one can look with some satisfaction on the increasing emergence of scholarship and the scientific study of genocide as a process whose origins and lawful development can be tracked with some measure of understanding and even predictability, and therefore one may also dare begin to think some day of possibilities for preventing genocide.

When Does Genocide Take Place?

One of the first questions addressed in genocide scholarship was the conditions under which genocide is most likely to take place. One of the earliest scholars of genocide, sociologist Irving Louis Horowitz, argued that genocide is not a random or sporadic event, but a special sort of mass destruction that requires the approval of the State, which uses genocide as a technique for national solidarity. He proposed a framework for categorizing societies at large that included genocidal societies, deportation or incarceration societies, torture societies, and harassment societies.

Leo Kuper created a classification of genocide that specifies some of the conditions under which genocide is more frequent: "1. Genocide against indigenous peoples (e.g., the murder of Indians in South American countries such as Paraguay); 2. Genocide following decolonization of a two-tier structure of domination (e.g., the Hutu in genocidal massacres by the Tutsi in Rwanda and Burundi); 3. Genocide in the process of struggles for power by ethnic or racial or religious groups, or struggles for greater autonomy or for secession (e.g., Bangladesh in 1971); 4. Genocide against hostage or scapegoat groups (e.g., the Armenians by the Turks in 1915, and the persecution of the Jews by the Nazis in the Holocaust)." Kuper further noted that "domestic genocides," that is, genocides that arise on the basis of cleavages within a society, are a phenomenon of plural societies in which there are sharp cleavages between ethnic, racial or religious groups. They arise under a variety of circumstances: struggles for power, consolidations of despotic regimes, annihilation of hostage groups in situations of crisis for host societies, economic expansion into areas inhabited by hunting and gathering groups, and under the facilitating conditions of international civil wars.

Jack Porter undertook to formulate the clustering of characteristics that predict the occurrence of genocide and also the contrasting convergence of characteristics that predict the reduced likelihood of genocide (see Table 1). He noted that genocide is most prevalent in times of war, colonization, and tribal conflict.

The most stunning empirical researches on the actual extent of genocides have been compiled by University of Hawaii political scientist, R. J. Rummel. He has shown that a *conservative* estimate of the number of victims of mass murder of unarmed civilians by states—which he called *democide*—in the twentieth century is around 170 million! Deriving from his research, Rummel has also demonstrated empirically an overwhelming relationship between totalitarian governments and genocide, and that *the best single prophylaxis for genocide at this time is democratic government* [see DEMOCIDE].

TABLE 1
Genocide Prediction

Predict Genocide	*Predict Genocide Unlikely*
• Minority group is considered an outsider	• Pervasive tolerance for minorities
• Racist ideology	• Strong minority with ready access to legal and human rights
• Strong dependence on military	• Temperate attitude to military
• Power exclusion of political parties	• Democratic political structure
• Leadership has strong territorial ambitions	• Weak territorial and imperial ambitions
• Power of the state has been reduced by defeat and war or internal strife	• No such precipitant events
• Possibility of retaliation for genocide from some source is at minimum	• Possibility of retaliation or interference by outside nations is considerable

Source: Porter, Jack (1982). *Genocide and Human Rights: A Global Anthology.* Washington, DC: University Press of America.

Definition of Genocide

From the outset of genocide research and continuing to this day, a great deal of scholarly energy has been devoted to efforts to define *genocide.* Since this subject is treated separately in the earlier entries in Part I of the Encyclopedia [see CLASSIFICATION OF GENOCIDE IN MULTIPLE CATEGORIES and DEFINITIONS OF GENOCIDE], it will not be discussed here other than to comment that the center position in scholarly debates is well represented by Helen Fein who has emphasized the objective helplessness of the victims, and has fought both for an inclusive definition of genocide that encompasses all situations where a victim group is defined by the perpetrator as deserving of mass murder, but also for rigorous distinctions between genocide and other forms of mass murder.

The Process of Genocide

Charny with Rapaport proposed that we look at how societies are organized both around *forces that promote human life* and *forces that move toward the destruction of life* long before an actual genocidal event emerges as a basis for prediction of genocidal dangers. Their analytic schema is an effort to relate the principles of psychology of the *normal* life experience processes of individuals and their behaviors in the family, groups and society to macrosocietal processes that lead to genocide, and culminates in a series of *genocide early warning processes,* which are systematic exaggerations and distortions of what are originally normal life experience processes [see GENOCIDE EARLY WARNING SYSTEMS].

There have been many other important contributions to our understanding of the process of how genocide unfolds including Kelman on crimes of obedience; Lifton—in a brilliant series of studies including survivors of Hiroshima, Vietnam veterans, the Nazi physicians in the concentration camps, and with Eric Markusen of "the genocidal mentality"—has given us the concept of how extremely the human mind can split off from knowing what it is doing ("doubling"), and has taught us a great deal about the psychology of seeking immortality; and Staub and Charny have described the stages of a society as it moves to genocide [see GENOCIDE AS A PROCESS]. Gurr and Harff have pioneered the study of *politicide*—or genocidal murders targeting a political enemy, and the development of empirical measures of politicide as well as the larger vital area of minorities at risk [see section on GENOCIDE EARLY WARNING SYSTEMS; MINORITIES AND GENOCIDE: EARLY WARNING AND MINORITIES AT RISK AROUND THE WORLD]. Harff has also been a leading scholar of the concept of humanitarian intervention.

Denial of Genocide

It has become clear that the last stage of the genocidal process is the denial that the genocide took place. Fein notes that once genocide has taken place, the most common way for the perpetrator to deny that it ever happened is to declare that the actions were justified as defensive responses to attacks by the victims on the perpetrator [see the various entries on DENIAL].

Who Commits Genocide?

Genocide is generally fomented—including planned, inspired and led—by leaders and their followers who are committed to the mass murder of the targeted people. And yet, at the same time, the conclusion that has reluctantly emerged over the years is that the "normal" and "ordinary" people are the bulk of those who commit genocide. These *perpetrators* perform the killing along with major constituencies of people who are *accomplices* or *bystanders* while the genocidal process takes place; while the latter do not play the active roles of perpetrators, they represent—as individuals, groups, societies and governments—the huge majority of people who also are responsible for the events of mass murder [see "ORDINARY PEOPLE" AS PERPETRATORS OF GENOCIDE].

Culture and Genocide

Needless to say, the possibilities of genocide are deeply affected by the prevailing culture. At this point in civilization, it is doubtful that *any* culture is "genocide-proof," although as Rummel has shown democratic societies are far less likely to engage in genocide, and it is likely that cultures, including religions, which genuinely promote a reverence for human life as sacred, will produce greater resistance to processes of genocide as well as more people who will make efforts to be rescuers of potential victims.

Professional and Organizational Initiatives

A few professional and organizational initiatives stand out in recent years concerned with the study of genocide as a process and an accompanying conception of the possibilities of prevention of some events of genocide in the future.

The International Conference on the Holocaust and Genocide in Tel Aviv in 1982 represented a pioneering effort to bring together many different peoples, such as Jews and Armenians, who normally are involved each in the memorial of their own history of genocide, and also to bring together many different professions in the interdisciplinary study of genocide as a process. The conference ran into considerable political pressures to close it down, beginning with Turkish threats against certain Jews if the Armenians were allowed to participate, followed by Israeli government pressures to close the conference down because of its interpretation of its responsibility to protect Jewish lives. It has been suggested that many if not all efforts to create public events on the subject of genocide will inevitably evoke various forms of resistance from the very people who otherwise legitimize genocide. *A certain measure of courage and political will to withstand hate group and political forces would seem to be a requirement of scholarly and professional activities aiming at the study and prevention of genocide.*

The 1982 conference was followed by the establishment of the Institute on the

Holocaust and Genocide in Jerusalem by Israel Charny, Shamai Davidson and Elie Wiesel. Since then a small but growing number of institutes and organizations devoted to the study and/or prevention of genocide have developed including the Institute for the Study of Genocide, New York, and the Centre for Comparative Genocide Studies, Macquarie University, Sydney, Australia. In 1985, a new worldwide organization was launched, International Alert, whose purpose was to respond on a political level to news of and indications of probable genocide, mass murder and massacres. In 1994, a professional organization, Association of Genocide Scholars [see entry], was formed with Helen Fein as its first President. In 1985 the Institute on the Holocaust and Genocide in Jerusalem launched an international newsletter, *Internet on the Holocaust and Genocide;* and in 1986 a new scholarly journal entitled *Holocaust and Genocide Studies* made its appearance edited by the Israeli Holocaust scholar, Yehuda Bauer. Steadily, museums are also developing as major institutions for the study of the Holocaust and to some extent also the study of intolerance and the genocides of other peoples. In schools, colleges and universities, there is an increasing number of study units and courses on the Holocaust in particular; in a growing number of programs there is also study of the Armenian Genocide; and there is also a meaningful tendency toward completing such courses by some degree of comparative study of other genocides and consideration of genocide as a recurring process. In addition, there are courses that from the outset undertake to study man's various and all too numerous cases of genocide, and which undertake to study in greater depth genocide as a process, political and legal responses to genocide, early warning systems and other means for reponse to genocide and its prevention.

Finally, interestingly and hopefully, on the community level, especially in smaller communities, there is evidence of grassroots cooperation among different ethnicities, especially Jews and Armenians but also others, in creating ecumenical events of joint memorials and/or joint support of human rights events. The common sense that we must all join together, and that there can be no hierarchy of importance of genocides, takes over in the practicalities of living together in communities, even if some scholars and some powerful politicians of ethnic communities continue to push aside affirmations of the commonality of all human beings in the battle against genocide of any and all peoples.

Intervention and Prevention of Genocide

The Prevention of Genocide by Leo Kuper published in 1985 by Yale University Press addressed the hope for possibilities of growth in the United Nations system for preventing genocide, but concluded reluctantly that the UN record had been dismal: "The performance of the United Nations in response to genocide is as negative as its performance on charges of political mass murder. There are the same evasions of responsibility and protection of offending government and the same overriding concern for state interests and preoccupation with ideological and regional alliances" (p. 160).

The Whitaker Report, an official UN Commission, also in 1985 established the principle that there is an inherent justification of intervention by all governments "to prevent and punish violations of the crime by others." The report recommended including in the definition of genocide political genocide, mass murder of a sexual group, genocide of one's own people, and also recommended the possible consideration of apartheid as well as cultural genocide or ethnocide, as well as the consideration of ecocide—adverse impacts on the ecological environment. Since expansion of the definition of genocide under the United Nations Convention in itself implies an increased pressure on peoples and governments who might otherwise undertake any of the various types of mass killing, the Commission's recommendations can also be considered tools for prevention.

The Whitaker Report also sought to place responsibility on individuals for their actions in mass killings even if they are following orders given by their superiors. "The Special Rapporteur recommends that explicit wording should be added to the Convention . . . that 'in judging culpability, a plea of superior orders is not an excusing defence,'" and called on national codes for "armed forces, prison staffs, police officers, doctors and others, to advise and warn them that it is not only their right to disobey orders violating human rights, such as to carry out genocide and torture, but their legal duty so to disobey."

Indeed, in recent years albeit in a stumbling and highly irregular process, society has seen new levels of intervention by the international system—sometimes under the identity of NATO, yet also under the UN—such as in the Former Yugoslavia and Rwanda. Overall, there is a beginning sense that the UN is becoming more responsible for causing the cessation of genocides, and invoking sanctions and punishments of the crime. Accompanying these political developments there are new developments in international law of genocide, such as the establishment of an International Court of Criminal Justice, and trials of perpetrators by the international system such as in Yugoslavia and Rwanda. These developments in law—along with beginning if also sporadic and flawed efforts at actual implementation—seem to be laying down for the first time in human history the principle that genocide is to be outlawed by the civilized community [see LAW RESPONDS TO THE HOLOCAUST AND GENOCIDE: REDRESS AND PERPETRATION, and other entries on law and genocide cross-referenced there].

Conclusion

Today, we are somewhat beyond the unknowingness and impotence that characterized responses to genocide barely twenty years ago. On the other hand, the study of genocide as a process has only recently begun, and there are many years ahead of us before we can expect to see real fruits of such work. There are many who fear that today our world is moving resolutely toward the destruction of greater numbers of people than ever before, the desolation of life over vast geographical areas, conceivably even the destruction of most or all human life on planet Earth, and possibly the destruction of the planet itself. The new weapons of the atomic era portend future instances of "nuclear genocide," "multiple genocide" (where several different peoples can be annihilated at one and the same time), "omnicide" (the broad destruction of many people and sections of the earth) [see entries under each of these terms] and "ecocide" (adverse alterations of the environment, often irremediable, perhaps through nuclear explosions, chemical weapons, and so forth). The ultimate irony is that there may no longer be a civilization on planet Earth at the time when we might have been ready to prevent genocidal murders.

—*Israel W. Charny*

Reference Note: This essay can be read as introducing a good many contributions to the Encyclopedia. Contributions by the scholars referred to in this entry and references to their major works, along with other entries mentioned here, can also be found easily through the Index.

"HOLOCAUST": THE WORD AND ITS USAGE

There are a variety of questions as to the "correct" usage of the word *holocaust.*

Holocaust is from the Greek "holokaustos," a compound word consisting of the root "holos," meaning "whole," and "kaustos" meaning "burnt," hence meaning either "burning whole" or "total consummation by fire." Its original meaning is that of an offering the whole of which is burnt, and it also has a second meaning of great or total destruction of life especially by fire. The word appears originally in the Greek translation of the biblical sacrifice known as "olah," which was a wholly burnt offering given entirely to the Lord—there were other sacrifices that were partial or shared as food. The word then also is used as a translation of "shoah" in the biblical Hebrew (where it appears in several places, for example, *Isaiah* 47:11, *Psalms* 35:8, and *Proverbs* 3:25), as a word that describes "total destruction," "utter destruction," and "overwhelming catastrophe."

The resulting *possible* aspect of meaning of "holocaust" in contemporary language as a sacrifice that is offered to God in positive intention, which is prayerfully expected to be received by God in appeasement and forgiveness of the suffering of human beings, presents quite serious religious-theological problems. Putting aside the connotative religious implication of which most people are not aware, and staying with the meaning of the word as such as total consumption, *the word "holocaust" can be understood as total destruction or devastation.* As such, it is entirely appropriate to the Nazi German intention and actual undertaking to destroy the Jewish people.

In the wake of World War II, the usage of the word was so widely and clearly devoted to the Nazi destruction of the Jewish people that for a while it seemed as if there should be no question about this being its language meaning. Indeed, many writers, including the editor of this Encyclopedia, have chosen to capitalize "Holocaust" to define the destruction of the Jewish people as a major historic, specific and archetypal event.

Slowly but surely, however, questions have arisen as to the proper language meaning of the word, including the realization that the "Holocaust" itself certainly included the destruction of a variety of non-Jewish peoples, such as the Sinti-Romani (Gypsies) by the Nazis in the same total program of destruction; also that "holocaust" had been used as World War II unfolded to describe all of Hitler's destruction of numerous victims; and continuing with the revelations that the word "holocaust" actually had been in usage far before the World War II event for great catastrophes as well as for earlier instances of mass murder.

One early example from 1833 cited by the *Oxford English Dictionary* quotes L. Richie that "Louis VII . . . once made a holocaust of thirteen hundred persons in a church." So too, well before World War II, the word "holocaust" had been used to describe prior events of destruction of Jews, such as of hundreds of years earlier in the Crusades, or in Cossack pogroms in the seventeenth century.

Approaching World War II, an editorial in the *London Times Literary Supplement* on August 26, 1939 observed that "the inflammatory fever which has been consuming Germany in recent years threatens a holocaust, a wholesale incineration." An article in *Life Magazine* in September 1939 said Hitler "has proved that he could summon the holocaust." Jonathan Petrie [*The Genocide Forum,* September 1997, 4 (1), p. 8] has pointed out that, "By the end of 1942 'holocaust' in the sense of 'a mass killing' was being used to refer to German mass murder of civilians—both Jews and non-Jews. The British Ministry of Information in 1942 referred to a 'holocaust of Catholics' (Laqueur, Walter, Hitler's Holocaust. *Encounter,* July 1980, Vol. LV, No.1, p. 20)."

Perhaps most important for students of genocide are a variety of instances in which the word "holocaust" was used long before World War II to describe the Armenian Genocide. As a matter of record, the word "holocaust" was used to describe each of the large-scale massacres (1895, 1909, 1915) that visited the Armenian people in the Ottoman Empire, and the usage of the word was invoked for the very reason that the killings were invariably associated, especially in 1895 and 1909, with the burning of the Armenian neighborhoods. One very specific event had much to do in creating the association of the word "holocaust" with the destruction of the Armenian population; the burning of the cathedral of Urfa (Edessa) in 1895 with 3,000 congregants who had taken refuge in it. Reporting on atrocities, a September 10, 1895, *New York Times* headline read: "Another Armenian Holocaust: Five Villages Burned, Five Thousand Persons Made Homeless . . ." Armenians themselves used the word "holocaust" to describe the 1909 torching of a vast swath of the city of Adana and other Armenian-inhabited towns. Dr. N. Daghavarian and Khosrov (pen-name for Armen Ardontz) authored in English in April 1911, *The Young Turks: The Truth about the Holocaust at Adana, Asia Minor, During April 1909.* US Ambassador Henry Morgenthau is reported to have used the word "holocaust" in private communication to his son in 1915. More publicly, wartime British Prime Minister David Lloyd George, in his *Memoirs of a Peace Conference* (1939), wrote: "The action of the British Government led inevitably to the terrible massacres of 1895–97, 1909 and worst of all to the holocausts of 1915. By these atrocities, almost unparalleled in the black record of Turkish misrule, the Armenian population was reduced in numbers by well over a million" (p. 811). Winston Churchill, in his book, *The World Crisis, Vol. 5: Aftermath* [1929, p. 158] wrote: "As for Turkish marching till they dropped dead the greater part of the garrison at Kut; massacring uncounted thousands of helpless Armenians, men, women and children together, whole districts blotted out at one administrative holocaust—these were beyond human redress." Similarly in 1915, in *The Murder of a Nation,* Arnold Toynbee used the words "Armenian Holocaust" to describe the unfolding genocide. It is evident from the regular use of the word "holocaust" in describing the many outrages committed against the Armenians that, before Raphael Lemkin's coining of the word *genocide,* the term "holocaust" was used in the English language to indicate wholesale and organized destruction of a civilian population.

Nonetheless, it is clear that in the immediate aftermath of World War II, as the world was shocked by the realization of the unheard-of inhumanity of the Nazi "assembly line" for destruction of the Jews, the word "holocaust" became identified in particular with the genocide of the Jews. (Some scholars credit Elie Wiesel with establishing the term for the destruction of European Jewry as his writings touched the world deeply.) At the same time, there is no question that the apparent and often intended exclusivity of the the word "holocaust" only for the murder of the Jews is not accurate. As noted, the word has an extensive history of use for prior genocidal massacres of Jews as well as for genocidal massacres of other peoples, let alone that one cannot exclude from the record of the Nazi destruction the killings of other peoples at the same time the Jews were being slaughtered. Ian Hancock points out that Roma were included "with no regard to the degree of their racial impurity" in the transport order issued by Himmler, acting upon a direct order from Hitler, following the Wannsee Conference in 1942.

Nonetheless, since symbolic meanings are also of importance alongside the hard facts of history and language, there is justification for preserving the sense of shock that our civilized world suffered at learning of the fate of the Jews at the hands of Germany. The word "Holocaust," with a capital H, has taken on a connotative meaning as the mass destruction by the Nazis especially but not only of the Jews. See, for example, in the *Merriam-Webster's Collegiate Dictionary* the additional definitions of holocaust as follows: "often cap: the mass slaughter of European civilians and esp. Jews by the Nazis during World War II . . . ; a mass slaughter of people; esp: GENOCIDE."

This Encyclopedia continues the established usage of the capitalized word "Holocaust" to refer to the destruction of the Jews; at the same time also to the murder of all other victim peoples selected at the same time for extermination by the Nazis; and also accepts usage of the word "holocaust" with regard to other major genocides such as the Armenian Genocide, while exercising care not to allow "hijacking" of the term for human rights injustices and abuses other than genocidal mass murders.

One might note that the Sinti-Romani people also have a word in their Romani language for the tragedy of their destruction in the Holocaust by the Nazis and that is *Porrajmos* [paw-rye-mos], which means, quite similarly to holocaust, "The Devouring."

A further note about the original word for "holocaust" in biblical Hebrew, "shoah." Some scholars in both the Jewish and Christian communities have opted to take the Hebrew word and attribute to it somehow an even more particular meaning as the ultimate word for the destruction of the Jewish people in World War II by the Nazis, perhaps now with an additional aura that the word being used in itself is a Hebrew word describing the plight of the victim Hebrew people. While there is no objection to this kind of symbolic emphasis, again from a historical point of view, insofar as the translation of the word into "holocaust" is concerned, all that was previously stated remains true—whatever the biblical origin of the word, at least in its translation, it does not belong exclusively to the Hebrew people. Moreover, it might be noted that even in Hebrew, there have been any number of references in contemporary writing in the Israeli press and books to the "Armenian shoah."

To conclude, "Holocaust" (with a capital letter) and "shoah" are both primarily descriptions of the *Jewish* aspects of the destruction by the Nazis, the latter more because it is an originally Hebrew word in the Bible; but even "Holocaust" cannot be divorced from the genocidal killings of other peoples such as the Sinti-Romani during the same period; and the generic word "holocaust," while still reverberating with the meaning it took on after World War II as the genocide of the Jews belongs historically to *all* peoples who suffer cataclysmic extermination and annihilation.

Whatever the usage adopted, it is always important to maintain a sensitivity that the affirmation of any one or more people's suffering not become a basis for excluding the suffering of any other people.

—Israel W. Charny, with contributions by Rouben Paul Adalian and Steven L. Jacobs

PART II

Genocidal Events, Intervention, and Prevention

ADANA MASSACRE

The Adana Massacre was the second series of large-scale massacres of Armenians to break out in the Ottoman Empire. The atrocities committed in the province of Adana in April 1909 coincided with the counter-revolution staged by supporters of Sultan Abdul Hamid (Abdulhamit) II (1876–1909) who had been forced to restore the Ottoman Constitution as a result of the 1908 Young Turk Revolution led by the Committee of Union and Progress (CUP). A prosperous region on the Mediterranean coast encompassing the old principality of Cilicia, once an independent Armenian state between the eleventh and fourteenth centuries, the province of Adana had been spared the 1890s massacres. The disturbances were most severe in the city of Adana where a reported 4,437 Armenian dwellings were torched, resulting in the razing of nearly half the town and prompting some to describe the resulting inferno as a "holocaust." The outbreaks spread throughout the district and an estimated 30,000 Armenians were reported killed. While attempts at resistance in Adana proved futile, and Armenians in smaller outlying villages were brutally slaughtered, two towns inhabited mostly by Armenians organized a successful defense. Hadjin (Hajen in Armenian) in the Cilician Mountains withstood a siege, while the 10,000 Armenians of Dortyol (Chorkmarzban in Armenian) held off 7,000 Turks who had surrounded their town and cut off its water supply.

The intensity of the carnage prompted the government to open an investigation, but the failure to prosecute dashed Armenian expectations of liberal reforms by the new regime. The reactionary elements of the Ottoman Empire were suspected of instigating the massacres to discredit the CUP, but the Young Turks were also implicated. The Adana Massacre exposed the twin composition of the Young Turk Movement, which consisted of both liberal and radical nationalist elements. It also demonstrated the convergent interests of the nationalists with the reactionary and conservative elements of Ottoman state in their policies toward a progressive-minded minority. For the Young Turks, the Adana Massacre proved a rehearsal for gauging the depth of Turkish animosity in the Ottoman Empire toward Christian minorities and for testing their skills in marshaling those forces for political ends. Despite the restoration of a constitutional government, the specter of mass violence was reintroduced as a mechanism of state power.

—Rouben Paul Adalian

References and Recommended Reading

Dadrian, Vahakn N. (1988). The circumstances surrounding the 1909 Adana holocaust. *Armenian Review,* 41(4), 1–16.

AFGHANISTAN, GENOCIDE IN

Afghanistan has experienced genocide twice. In 1219–1221, Genghis Khan transformed it from a major hub of trade and culture into a depopulated backwater. Between 1978 and 1992, a second genocide was perpetrated, initially by the Afghan Communist puppet regime that seized power in April 1978 with Russian assistance and then more systematically by Soviet forces that invaded in December 1979.

In 1978, the new Afghan communist leaders announced, "We only need one million people to make a revolution. What happens to the rest doesn't matter." They immediately moved to implement that policy. Pul-i-Charkhi prison in Kabul, built to house 6,000 common criminals, was turned into a political prison crammed with 20,000 men, women and children; as the regime moved to eliminate the entire noncommunist educated class, an estimated 32,000 prisoners were executed there in the first 18 months of the regime. Torture became, and remained, routine. Thousands simply disappeared; their fates are still unknown. An estimated 50,000–100,000 educated Afghans fled to Europe, the United States, the Middle East and Australia.

Until the Russians took over, atrocities in the provinces were primarily punitive and exemplary, aimed at villagers who resisted Marxist policies. In northern Samagan, 1,500 villagers were bound and thrown into the Oxus River to drown. In Kunar province, hundreds of men and boys were called to a town meeting and machine-gunned. In Laghman province, 650 villagers were buried alive. The rural exodus from affected areas began: some 250,000 refugees were huddled in improvised camps in Pakistan even before the Soviet invasion.

From January 1980 on, however, the Soviets made genocide a coherent, systematic policy.

Multi-ethnic Afghanistan has never had a census. The pre-1978 population, over 95 percent rural and scattered across a country the size of France, was officially estimated at 15 to 17 million, but extrapolations from a confidential sample census conducted in Kabul in the mid-1970s suggested that in fact it was only 12.5 to 15 million. About 40–45 percent (5.6 to 7.6 million) were Pushtuns (also known as Pukhtuns or Pathans), the fractious, fiercely independent ethnolinguistic group who has given Afghanistan its special character for three thousand years and ruled the modern country from its founding in 1747 until 1992.

Soviet and local communist forces targeted the rural civilian population, not the armed resistance. After the Russians invaded and took direct control in December 1979, operational patterns (particularly air attacks) indicated a systematic effort to depopulate selected areas on an ethnic basis. Although all parts of Afghanistan were brutalized to some degree, the treatment of civilian populations in Pushtun and non-Pushtun areas differed significantly. Overall Soviet strategy focused on emptying out the predominantly Pushtun areas, thereby altering the ethnic makeup of Afghanistan. This emptying of the Pushtun areas would facilitate the eventual integration of its strategically important and mineral-rich northern provinces into Soviet Central Asia, where Afghan Tajiks, Uzbeks, and Turkomans have ethnic kinsmen. Thousands of very young children were (often forcibly) sent to the USSR and Eastern Europe for ten years for preparatory indoctrination; few if any have returned.

Air attacks throughout the southern and eastern provinces—the Pushtun heartland—methodically killed hundreds of thousands and resulted in the mass exodus of millions, creating a depopulated no-man's-land in large areas along the

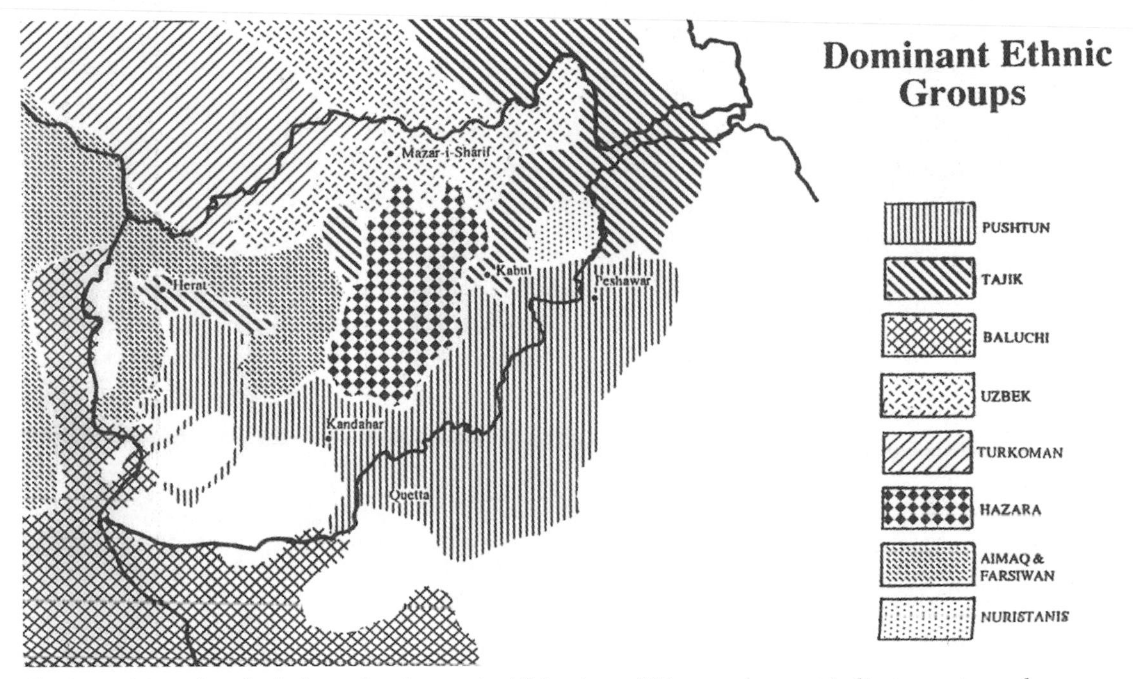

Comparative regional ethnic predominance in Afghanistan. This map does not indicate greater or lesser population density, relative numbers of a particular ethnic group, or a particular group's share of total population. (Map drawn by Steven Ginsberg)

Afghanistan-Pakistan border. In addition to the bombings, which reached their peak in 1986, the Soviets used terror—chemical weapons, weapons targeting children, gruesome localized atrocities, and the destruction of crops, orchards, animals, food supplies and water sources—to empty out whole districts. Since it was intended that those who fled should not return, the irrigation systems on which Afghan agriculture depends were destroyed, turning the land into desert.

Moscow openly imposed stringent controls to prevent information from reaching the world's attention. Independent journalists were barred; those who entered clandestinely were threatened with death. The International Red Cross was ordered out of the country. Strenuous efforts were made to interdict clandestine medical and humanitarian aid efforts mounted by Western nongovernmental organizations (NGOs). Journalists and medical personnel were hunted and attacked; several were captured, imprisoned and even killed. In addition, there was an intensive world-wide Soviet disinformation campaign to control and discredit those reports that did come out, especially those that (accurately) reported the use of chemical weapons.

By 1985, Afghans made up half of all the world's refugees, and the exodus still continued. According to official Pakistani and Iranian figures for registered refugees, at least six million Afghans—35 percent to 48 percent of the total prewar population, and 80 percent to 85 percent of them Pushtuns—were driven into exile in those neighboring countries. Death could not be recorded systematically, but the United Nations has used estimates of 1.5 to 2 million people killed between 1978 and 1992, which would be 10 percent to 16 percent of the total prewar population. Combined with 6 million exiles, that adds up to a loss of 47 percent to well over 50 percent of Afghanistan's total prewar population (all ethnic groups). In addition, several hundred thousands have been maimed, blinded and incapacitated.

The percentages are even higher for Pushtuns, singled out for "ethnic cleansing." Two-thirds to three-quarters or more of the victims in all categories were probably Pushtuns, which would suggest that 25 percent or more of the Pushtun population may have been killed; and more than five million Pushtuns became refugees. When mortality estimates are combined with refugee figures, they add up to a loss of 80 percent or more of the Pushtun population, leaving the Tajiks and other Persian-speakers, formerly about 22 percent of the population, as the dominant group.

The ostensible Russian withdrawal in 1989 masked continuing Soviet control and massive support for its puppet regime, which would still be in power if the USSR had not unexpectedly collapsed. In that case, few of the refugees would have returned and Moscow's genocidal policies would have succeeded in erasing the Pushtun presence and transforming the character of the region. Indeed, they may have done so: theoretically the refugees can return—but given the devastation and the turmoil resulting from the war and the civil war that has followed (as regional powers struggle to dominate Afghanistan through local proxies), it is not clear how many of them will do so. As of 1997 most still remain in exile, even though a Pakistan-supported Pushtun force, the Taliban, seized control of most of the country in 1995–1996.

And, as was true 700 years earlier, much of the cultural and social disintegration may prove to be irremediable. The traditional social structure has been shattered, and abandoned to chaos and ethnic conflict encouraged by foreign interests. Most of Afghanistan's artistic and cultural treasures have vanished—some destroyed, some stolen and dispersed to the clandestine international art market, some to a fate thus far unknown.

Reports of the genocide in Afghanistan met with widespread denial and disbelief while it was happening; since the withdrawal of Soviet troops and the collapse of the USSR, the Afghan genocide and its aftermath have been ignored by the rest of the world.

—Rosanne Klass

References and Recommended Reading

Klass, Rosanne (1994). Genocide in Afghanistan 1978–1992. In Charny, Israel W. (Ed.), *The Widening Circle of Genocide. Volume 3 in the Series, Genocide: A Critical Bibliographic Review.* New Brunswick, NJ: Transaction Publishers, pp. 129–164.

Klass, Rosanne (Ed.). (1990). *Afghanistan: The Great Game Revisited.* Enlarged 2nd edition. New York: Freedom House.

Laber, Jeri, and Rubin, Barnett R. (1988). *"A Nation Is Dying": Afghanistan under the Soviets, 1979–1987.* Evanston, IL: Northwestern University Press.

ANTISEMITISM

Antisemitism, an obsessive hatred of Jews and Judaism, is among the longest lasting social pathologies in history. Although the term itself originated only in the late nineteenth century, the phenomenon is rooted in antiquity even as its manifestations have assumed different forms. The one constant associated with Judaeophobia is a negative assessment on the part of the dominant culture of "otherness." Jews have historically been viewed as the pre-eminent "other." It is as if the biblical admonition, "Lo, it is a people that shall dwell alone, and shall not be reckoned among the nations" (*Numbers* 23:9) were prophetic. For a negative obsession with the Jews is found in the writings and teachings of pagan cultures, in Christianity, among anti-Christians, in the medieval period, in modernity, and in contemporary culture. Certainly the Holocaust, which is far from being mono-causal, would have been inconceivable without a millennial tradition of antisemitism.

There are both continuities and discontinuities between the various forms of antisemtism such as cultural, religious,

A Christian Memory Hole: Christian-Jews during the Holocaust

Christians who have joined Jews in memorializing the Holocaust and its Jewish victims focus on the Final Solution as an act of genocide affecting Jews and their descendants for which, they feel, they share a measure of guilt. They acknowledge that Christian antisemitism and Christian collaboration were an integral part of the Third Reich's racist assault on European Jewry. As contrite Christians, they feel compelled to express in prayer and public confession the sins of the established churches and their coreligionists during the Nazi era. But that is a slightly myopic view, however laudable its intention.

There is a far more direct connecting thread linking Christians to the annihilation of Jews by Nazi Germany. In most middle-sized and large German Christian parishes, both Catholic and Protestant, there was at least one parishioner who was a convert from Judaism. In many cases, there were several such parishioners, even second and third generation descendants of Jewish converts in the nineteenth century. By 1933, most of these Christians had all but forgotten their Jewish origins. For the most part, their fellow congregants also gave little thought to their fellow Christians of Jewish origin.

September 1935 changed all that abruptly; the issuance of the Nuremberg Racial Laws identified every person genealogically as "Aryan" or "Jewish," regardless of contemporary religious affiliation. Overnight, several thousand people fully integrated into Christian communities became officially Jews, and, by extension, *Jewish* Christrians, or Christians of non-Aryan standing, that is, Jews in the eyes of the state, and therefore to be treated as Jews throughout German society including the parishes.

What were the responses of the Catholic and Protestant clergy and hierarchies to these racial classifications of congregants? Were there loud protests? Did the millions of Catholics and Lutherans in Germany rally in Christian fellowship and solidarity around their fellow Christians, regardless of "race?" Did they offer these outcasts the warmth of spiritual comfort? Did priests and pastors encourage their flocks to walk in the compassionate footsteps of the Master who empathized with all outcasts, from lepers to prostitutes? Where are the sermons that embodied the essence of Christian teaching to defy Caesar, to turn against the unchristian values of the godless German City of Man? How many volunteered to protect, to hide, to protest, to help, etc.? How many survivors owed their lives to the congregation? Did the majority Aryan Christian spouses married to a "Jewish" Christian refuse to heed the Nazi state's admonition to divorce or separate? And in the end, how many Christians volunteered to be deported along with their "Jewish" loved ones? The questions are, of course, primarily rhetorical.

Parishes today should ask if, knowing the failures of past Christian congregations, can one expect a heightened sense of loyalty to each other in the face of similar governmental pressure in the future. Thus in recent years, what happened in Rwanda is less than inspiring: there, Christians quickly degenerated into bloodthirsty Hutus, including priests.

—Henry R. Huttenbach

antireligious, secular, political, economic, and racial Jew-hatred. Furthermore, there are historical differences as well. For example, medieval expressions of antisemitism, which focused on the association of Jews with the Devil differ from modern secular Judaephobia, which asserts that Jews are racially inferior. And a new post-Auschwitz form of antisemitism emerges in the form of Holocaust denial and in certain expressions of anti-Zionism.

Etiology of Antisemitism: Pagan Forms

It is instructive to note pagan objections to Jews and Judaism. The religious beliefs and rituals of Judaism set its tradition apart from the pagan world. Consequently, monotheism and dietary laws were viewed with suspicion by the Greeks. Cumulatively, Greek writers charged the Jews with aloofness, not respecting pagan deities, and being abnormal. Greeks believed that *brit milah* [circumcision, a visible and eternal sign of the Abrahamic covenant] was a barbaric practice because it tampered with the human form.

Philosophers and intellectuals gave voice and rationale to anti-Jewish feelings. Heraclitus of Abdera (fourth century B.C.E.) termed Judaism "an inhospitable and anti-human form of living." Josephus quotes Manetho, a Greek-speaking Egyptian priest, as interpreting the Exodus from Egypt as the expulsion of a leper colony. The Egyptian Pharaoh, Ramses II, for his part admonished his countrymen to "deal wisely [with the Israelites], lest they multiply, and [if there be a war] they join themselves unto our enemies, and fight against us." Further, Ramses ordered the murder of all Jewish male infants. This attempted genocide, of course, was overcome through the Exodus as reported in the Bible.

The *Scroll of Esther* in the Hebrew Bible reports another genocidal plot against the Jewish people because of their perceived otherness. Haman, the evil prime minister of the kingdom of Shushan, informs his dull-witted king that: "There is a certain people scattered abroad and dispersed among the people in all the provinces of the kingdom, and their laws are diverse from all people, neither keep they the king's law, therefore it is not in the king's benefit to suffer them." The evil plot is thwarted by Esther and her uncle Mordechai, and the would-be genocider himself is executed. While the tale itself may or may not be historically accurate, the charges reported leveled against the Jews of Shushan again reveal that in the eyes of

French Catholic Church Apologizes for Participation in Holocaust

In October 1997, the Roman Catholic Church in France apologized to the Jews for its failure, silence and acquiescence in French collaboration with the Holocaust. Archbishop Olivier de Berranger declared that the bishops of France acquiesced through their silence to a "murderous process" that should have been met immediately by protest and protection of the Jews. "We confess this error," he said. "We beg for the pardon of God and we ask the Jewish people to hear this word of repentance." The statement came just before the fifty-seventh anniversary of the promulgation on October 3, 1940, of the first of more than 160 antisemitic laws and decrees passed by the Vichy regime that progressively excluded Jews from French public life and opened the way for the dispatch of about 76,000 of them to their deaths.

—*Press Reports*

pagans Jews and Judaism were viewed as unassimilable.

Christian Anti-Judaism: The Religious Factor

The issue of Christian anti-Judaism profoundly influenced the spread of anti-Judaic sentiment. Scholars have noted the theological and psychological tensions between the two traditions. For example, Richard Rubenstein comments that the relationship between Judaism and Christianity was one of disconfirming otherness; for one to be true the other was to be false. Theologically, as one progresses from the writings of Paul (ca. 50 C.E.), arguably the founder of Christianity and certainly the tradition's first systematic theologian, through the synoptic gospels and, finally, to the Gospel of John (ca. 100 C.E.), one sees a growing estrangement between Judaism and the gentile majority.

Yet even the Pauline distinction between law (Judaism), which is defined as deadening, and spirit (Christianity), which is seen as giving life, set the stage for the emergence of a Christian Theology of Supercession and the Teaching of Contempt. Jews are portrayed as children of the Devil who do not love God (Jesus). Even granting the fact that the term "the Jews" was quite probably applied to all those the writer viewed as opponents, it soon was applied specifically to actual Jews. But the Gospel of Matthew is equally devastating in asserting that Jews bear collective and eternal guilt for the death of Jesus: "His blood be on us and on our children!" (*Matthew* 27:24). Furthermore, the Jews were accused of being unable to properly read their own scriptures, and killing their own prophets.

Events in the political sphere were, moreover, viewed through a theological lens. This led to the increasing isolation and marginalizing of the Jews. For instance, the destruction of the Jerusalem Temple (70 C.E.) was seen by both Jews and Christians as bearing religious significance, a divine judgment on the House of Israel. But the reason for this judgment differed radically. Judaism viewed it as punishment for straying from the covenantal path. The early Christian movement contended that it was a punishment for deicide. When, in the fourth century Christianity became the official religion of the Roman Empire, the church's negative teaching about Jews and Judaism became civil policy.

Adversus Judaeos

The teaching of contempt is embodied in the *adversus judaeos* (refutation of Judaism) tradition. Based on the writings of the Church Fathers (St. Justin, St. John Chrysostom, and St. Augustine, *inter alia*) this tradition stresses several themes: the guilt of the Jewish people for deicide; the assertion that the Hebrew Bible, which in condescending fashion is designated the *Old Testament,* is a preparation for what Christians termed the *New Testament* and, therefore, contains references to the coming of Jesus; and that Jewish teachers are blind guides. Neither this tradition nor Christianity, however, officially called for the extermination of the Jews. But the reason for this restraint is deplorable. For example, St. Augustine observed that the Jews should be spared in order that all could see what happens to those who reject the messiahship of Jesus. The Jews are condemned to eternal reprobation, a visible sign of God's displeasure.

The Medieval Period

The anti-Judaism of medieval Christianity associated Jews with those figures whom society most feared and despised: witches, sorcerers, murderers, well-poisoners, and the Devil. This period also ushered in the Crusades, a series of campaigns whose purpose was ostensibly to free the Holy city of Jerusalem from the

Pope Concedes that Christians Advanced Antisemitism

In March 1998 the Vatican issued a long-awaited document, "We Remember: A Reflection on the Shoah [Holocaust]" in which it expressed remorse for the cowardice of some Christians during the Holocaust. The 12-page document went beyond the Holocaust and condemned other mass killings in this century, mentioning Armenians, Gypsies, Cambodians and Chinese as victims, among others.

The statement on the Roman Catholic Church's role during World War II came a decade after it was promised by Pope John Paul II. The document praised Pope Pius XII as a wise diplomat, though he has long been criticized for failing to speak out forcefully against Nazi persecution.

Jewish leaders criticized the defense of the actions of wartime Pope Pius XII and the weak tone of the condemnation of the Holocaust. "It is too little, too late," Meir Lau, Israel's Chief Rabbi and a Holocaust survivor, said in Tel Aviv. "I have no doubt that the church did not do everything it could have to save people. His [Pope Pius XII's] silence cost millions of human lives."

Earlier the same year, speaking at a theological symposium in Rome on the origins of anti-Judaism, Pope John Paul II said that certain Christian teachings, based on "wrong and unjust" interpretations of the New Testament, had helped contribute to the Holocaust and the persecution of Jews in Europe over the centuries. As he had done several times before, the Pope condemned antisemitism as "totally unjustifiable and absolutely condemnable," and called it a "pagan" notion contrary to Christian doctrine. But the Pope stopped short of the kind of direct apology that many Jews wait to hear from the Vatican, both for its muted protests during the Holocaust and for its centuries-old tolerance of antisemitism in its ranks and in its liturgy, which until 30 years ago contained references to "perfidious Jews." The Pope's statement joined other Roman Catholic theologians in acknowledging that by blaming the Jews for the death of Jesus, certain Christian teachings had helped fuel antisemitism. "In the Christian world—I do not say on the part of the church as such—the wrong and unjust interpretations of the *New Testament* relating to the Jewish people and their presumed guilt circulated for too long, contributing to feeling of hostility toward these people. These contributed to soothing consciences, to the point that when a wave of persecution swept Europe fueled by a pagan antisemitism—which in its essence was equal to anti-Christianism—next to those Christians who did everything to save the persecuted at the risk of their own lives, the spiritual resistance of many was not that which humanity expected from the disciples of Christ."

In another statement, the Vatican said that Christians who are anti-Jewish offend God, and told Roman Catholics to admit past errors toward Jews and not repeat them.

—Press Reports

hold of the infidels, for example, Muslims. En route, the crusaders murdered thousands of Jews. Leon Poliakov observes that the consequences of the Crusades played a major role in shaping the "singular and unique" destiny of European Jewry. Pope Urban II preached the first Crusade on 27 November 1095; the marchers began their murderous activity in May of the following year. Before they were done, ten thousand Jews—approximately one-third of the Jewish population of Germany and Northern France—had been martyred; electing to die for the sanctification of God's Name *(al kiddush HaShem)* rather than be forcibly baptized. Robert Wistrich notes that the crusades marked a "decisive turning point for the worse" in Jewish-Christian relations. Jews were viewed as powerless, Christians as ruthless murderers. Closely associated with subsequent crusades, the second of which was preached by Pope Eugenius III in 1146, was the charge of ritual murder.

According to the canard, which was first asserted in England in 1144, Jews murdered a Christian boy "in mockery of the Passion of the Savior." Further, as Poliakov notes, there was a closely associated notion that the event had been planned far in advance by a meeting of rabbis. Over time, the accusation assumed various forms. For example, Jews were alleged to use the blood of Christians both to bake their *matza* (unleavened bread) and to add to the Passover wine. In theological terms, this practice was viewed as a profanation of the Christian eucharist. The association with the Devil also received expression in the arts, for example, Michelangelo's statue of Moses in the Sistine Chapel. Mistranslating the biblical expression "rays" of light as "horns" of light emanating from Moses's head, the artist captured the sentiment of popular culture in imagining the Jews as devils.

The response of Martin Luther to Judaism and the Jews reveals the structural tension between Judaism and Christianity. At first Luther was sympathetic to the Jews. However, after it became clear that the Jews were not going to convert, the founder of the Reformation wrote *On the Jews and Their Lies.* This vicious diatribe called for, among other things, the burning of Jewish synagogues, prohibition of their religion, and their expulsion from the Christian polity.

Moreover, the association of Jews with economic affairs led to unfortunate events. For example, Jews were forbidden to own land, but could and did dwell in cities where they dealt with money matters. The emergence of Jews as tax farmers, that is, those who collected taxes from peasants who worked on land owned by nobility, earned them the opprobrium of both groups.

Modernity

Modernity witnessed several important, and terrible, developments in the phenomenon of antisemitism. First of all, the term itself was employed by Wilhelm Marr in 1879. An antiseptic and scientific-sounding phrase, it was meant to disguise the vulgar sounding "Jew-hatred" which would have been unacceptable according to Enlightenment standards. Yet, everyone knew that antisemitism designated only Jews. Further, even as the religious teachings of Christianity became discredited by the eighteenth century's stress on reason, Christianity's negative teachings about Jews and Judaism remained in force. Many of the leading French philosophers like Voltaire despised Judaism both for giving rise to Christianity and for what he perceived as its retrograde superstitious ways.

Modernity also gave birth to political antisemtism. Politicians such as Bismarck ran on antisemitic platforms. In addition, race-theory began to emerge as a prominent way of looking at the difference between peoples. Racist writers such as the Frenchman Arthur de Gobineau and the Englishman Houston Stewart Chamberlain advanced the position that race determines destiny. Moreover, the Enlightenment goal of achieving what Jacob Katz terms the religiously "neutral" society was never achieved. In its place there emerged the "semi-neutral" society; one in which a person's religion—and race—counted heavily in assessing whether one belonged in a particular country or place.

The Enlightenment was a failure as far as Judaism is concerned. In France, three powerful groups, the aristocracy, the military, and the Catholic Church never accepted equality for the Jews. The Dreyfus Affair in which Captain Alfred Dreyfus was falsely accused of betraying France revealed the extent to which the trial was actually a referendum on Judaism. Further, Napoleon's challenge to the Sanhedrin (council composed of rabbinic and religious leaders) in which he asked Jewish communal representatives to declare themselves Frenchman first and Jews second, led to the emergence of the "hyphenated Jew": French-Jew, German-Jew, American-Jew, thereby reinforcing the xenophobic and racist notions that Jews were aliens in their various "host" countries.

By the advent of the twentieth century, Jews were viewed as embodying the antinomies of power and powerlessness. They were despised and envied. Conspiracy theories centered on Jews. For example, the infamous czarist forgery, *The Protocols of the Elders of Zion,* which described the alleged plotting of the Jews to take over everywhere, was translated into German and enjoyed a wide readership. While not all Germans or other Europeans were rabid antisemites, there existed a diffuse cultural antisemitism upon which demagogues, racists and annihilationists could readily draw.

The Holocaust

The Holocaust was engendered by a variety of factors including modernity itself, acceptance of mass death as evidenced in World War I, advanced technology, a highly systematized bureaucracy, "scientific" theories of racial hygiene, a complacent populace, and an indifferent world. All of these factors were necessary but not sufficient enablers of the *Shoah.* Antisemitism was the poisonous glue cementing all these deadly factors. After centuries of the teaching of contempt, Jews were viewed as residing outside the Christian universe of moral obligation. Joseph Goebbels was undoubtedly correct in observing that, in his view, Nazi Germany was doing the world a favor in exterminating the Jewish people.

But Nazism added a metaphysical dimension to antisemitism. Hitler was attempting to create nothing less than a new world, one that would be free of Jews *(Judenrein).* Scholars such as Steven Katz and Saul Friedlander convincingly argue the position for "metaphysical antisemitism." For example, Katz contends that Nazis singled out Jews for "metaphysical, i.e., racial and manichaean reasons." Friedlander, in a similar manner, discusses Hitler's "redemptive antisemitism" as opposed to "merely" racial manifestations of Jew hatred. Thus, antisemitism during the Holocaust had nothing to do with the possibility of converting the Jews or murdering them to "save" their souls. Rather, Hitler and his followers viewed the very existence of Jews as a barrier to achieving the new world order—the thousand-year *Reich.*

Contemporary Manifestations

Holocaust denial and some expressions of anti-Zionism are the two main types of contemporary antisemitism. Frequently, the two phenomena are inextricably related. For example, Jew-haters such as Robert Faurisson, Bradley Smith, and Arthur Butz all deny the Holocaust and claim that it is a "Zionist plot" to extort money for supporting Israel. Concerning denial of the Holocaust, it is important to note that those who today deny or minimize the Shoah are precisely the same people who would have been the first to applaud its successful completion. After Auschwitz, those who deny the Holocaust in effect claim that they are for gas chambers and crematoria.

—Alan L. Berger

Antisemitism campaign against Jews in France portraying a Jew dominating the French economy. (Yad Vashem, Jerusalem)

References and Recommended Reading

Friedlander, Saul (1997). *Nazi Germany and the Jews. Volume 1. The Years of Persecution, 1933–1939.* New York: HarperCollins.

Johnson, Paul (1987). *A History of the Jews.* New York: Harper and Row.

Katz, Steven T. (1994). *The Holocaust in Historical Context. Volume 1. The Holocaust and Mass Death Before the Modern Age.* New York: Oxford University Press.

Rubenstein, Richard L. (1992). The dean and the chosen people. Chapter in *After Auschwitz: History, Theology, and Contemporary Judaism.* Second Edition. Baltimore, MD: Johns Hopkins University Press, pp. 3–13.

ARENDT, HANNAH

[This entry is restricted to a consideration of Hannah Arendt's general approach to issues of genocide. See EICHMANN IN JERUSALEM: A REPORT ON THE BANALITY OF EVIL *for her specific evaluation of the Holocaust.—ILH]*

Hannah Arendt was born in Hanover, Germany, of German-Jewish parentage, in 1906. She was educated in Konigsberg and later Heidelberg. After fleeing to France from Germany in the late 1930s, she emigrated to the United States in 1941. She was naturalized as an American citizen in 1950. Most of her life was spent in the academy. She was a Guggenheim fellow in 1952–1953; visiting professor at the University of California at Berkeley in 1955; the first woman appointed to a full professorship at Princeton in 1959; and visiting professor of government at Columbia University in 1960. From 1963 to 1967 she was university professor at the University of Chicago. And in 1967 until her death in 1975 she served as university professor at the New School for Social Research. It is fair to say that Arendt was an intensely urban person, and that being proximate to San Francisco, Chicago and New York meant at least as much to her as the university affiliations as such.

The publication of *The Origins of Totalitarianism* in 1951 established her as a major figure in postwar political theory. In that work she attempted to provide a unitary approach to totalitarianism as such, seeing differences between National Socialism and Communism as of lesser significance than the organizational and cultural linkages that such systems have with each other. Such systems have a common base in the leadership principle, in single party politics based on mass mobilization rather than individual voluntary participation, and not the least in a near insatiable desire to expand from nation to empire—whether directly through military adventure or indirectly through political infiltration.

Antisemitism functioned differently in Germany under Hitler and Russia under Stalin, but had the same common roots: the existence of disparities between social classes and *the need for objectifying an enemy responsible for all shortcomings and defeats suffered by nations and systems—a scapegoat.* Arendt's powerful critique of antisemitism was directly linked to her participation in Jewish affairs once she came to the United States. She served as Research Director of the Conference on Jewish Relations between 1944 and 1946; and then as executive director of Jewish Cultural Reconstruction in New York between 1949 and 1952; or just prior to her famc and assumption of the round of university posts spoken of earlier.

Arendt's views on genocide extended far beyond her *Eichmann in Jerusalem* volume. Indeed, unconstrained by journalistic narrative, she developed a general theory of totalitarianism, in which the subject of genocide was thoroughly explored. In defining nazism she argued against the idea that it is simply a distorted extension of Western culture as such. "Nazism owes nothing to any part of the Western tradition, be it German or not, Catholic or Protestant, Christian,

Greek or Roman. . . . On the contrary, Nazism is actually the breakdown of all German and European traditions, the good as well as the bad."

Arendt, rather than view genocide as a special property of Germans or Austrians (or any other people), considered it as nihilism in action, "basing itself on the intoxication of destruction as an actual experience, dreaming the stupid dream of producing the void." Not a few of Arendt's critics consider this formulation as apologetics, a way in which she was able to reconcile personal relationships with politically conservative mentors and lovers like Martin Heidegger with a larger series of politically liberal, and sometimes radical, claims. But whatever the truth of such strongly biographical claims, her views on national types is well within the mainstream of twentieth century social theory.

The single most important element in *The Origins of Totalitarianism* as it pertains to genocide is that the prospect for mass murder and selective mayhem is embodied in the structure of totalitarianism as a system rather than the special national characteristics of any particular people. *The forms of totalitarianism may vary—Nazi, Fascist, Communist—but the content allows for genocidal acts whatever the ideological proclivities of the extremist regime may proclaim.*

The ground for such genocidal actions is prepared by the denial of citizenship, of political and legal rights of the victim class. In a brilliant examination and support of Edmund Burke's critique of abstract arguments of human rights that are divested of concrete sentiments of those natural rights that spring from being part of a nation, Arendt notes that "The survivors of the extermination camps, the inmates of concentration and internment camps and even the comparatively contented people could see without Burke's arguments that the abstract nakedness of being nothing but human was their greatest danger. Because of it they were regarded as savages and, afraid that they might end by being considered beasts, they insisted on their nationality, the sign of their former citizenship, as their only remaining and recognized tie with humanity." And in a stunning conclusion to the segment on imperialism, Arendt points out "that a man who is nothing but a man has lost the very qualities which make it possible for other people to treat him as a fellow man." And this stripping the Jews of legal rights through deprivation of the rights of citizens per se is the essential necessary (if not sufficient) condition for genocide to take place.

There is an ambiguity in her formulation, in that at times it is the size and power of government as such that provides the seeds for totalitarian rule, while at other times, it is the cultural and psychological conditions that define prospects for totalitarian domination. So it turns out that totalitarianism depends on the assumption of power by the extremists at a point in time when state machinery is "frozen," that it is calcified and unable to remain a process. But it also turns out totalitarianism is made possible by the widespread installation of fear and what she calls "total terror." And the totalitarian system is one in which victims and executioners alike are selected without regard to personal conviction or sympathies, but only in terms of rigid "objective" standards: that is, who is a Jew, and who is an Aryan.

The Origins of Totalitarianism ends on a creative ambiguity, one hardly restricted to Arendt. A great deal of argument within political theory after World War II focused on just such examination of the causes of extremism and the breakdown of law and democratic order. We need to know whether it is politics or culture that defines the limits of power. For otherwise, not only are we limited in understanding or responding to such ultimate horrors as the Holocaust, but the nature of democratic options as such remain in precarious limbo.

Arendt attends to this ambiguity in a work that appeared a decade later. After *The Human Condition,* which might well be seen as an interlude, she returns squarely to the problem of totalitarian systems and political change in what may well be her most underrated effort: *On Revolution.* Indeed, this work too is dedicated to her mentor, Karl Jaspers, when she noted that he uniquely in *The Future of Mankind* "dared to face both the horrors of nuclear weapons and the threat of totalitarianism." *On Revolution* addressed the world one step further. With nuclear power at a stalemate, revolutions have become the principal political factor of our time. To understand revolution for her became the key to unlock the future.

While *On Revolution* does not directly address issues of genocide, in coming to a psychological profile of political absolutism, a sense of how the "passion" and the "taste" for power leads to the genocidal state emerges, Arendt does illumine new directions. She takes Robespierre's theory of revolutionary dictatorship as the quintessential model of the European encounter with politics, an encounter that ends in antipolitique. "The thirst and will to power as such, regardless of any passion for distinction, although characteristics of the tyrannical man, is no longer a typically political vice, but rather that quality which tends to destroy all political life, its vices no less than virtues." With the appeal to the political as a framework for rational discourse, the sort of unique qualities that endeared American and British civilization to Arendt, there can be no democratic society. So that even in Revolutionary France from 1789 to 1794, the shouts of the day were "Long Live the Republic," and not "Up with Democracy."

Arendt remained in all her works the jurist, the legal analyst. Her concerns were to plumb the depths of legitimacy, not as an abstract discourse on nationalism, but as an effort to review the grounds that permit a people to survive even harsh and tyrannical conditions. In this, she was neither a conservative nor liberal, at least not in any conventional modes of those concepts. To be sure, Arendt's resistance to easy characterization may be the quality that has proven most irritating as well as elusive to critics. For example, Arendt saw in modern conservatism (in contrast to the writings of ancient Greek philosophers) a profound two-hundred-year response to the French Revolution, seeing it as a polemic in the hands of Edmund Burke, Alexis de Toqueville, Eric Voegelin, and their modern followers; while liberals, for their part, were doomed to provide an uneasy rationalization for a totalitarian Revolution they could neither quite understand, accept in full, nor reject. But the ambiguity of such formulations notwithstanding, in this way she compelled a fresh reading of historical events of enormous magnitude.

As someone steeped in classical German legal philosophy, the juridical order of things was critical to Arendt through her career. The legal system is that logical artifact that both makes possible and calls forth the loftiest aims of human beings, and at the other extreme prevents or at least curbs the implementation of their most venal desires. These strongly ancient Jewish and classical Greek appeals to the legal as the logical were invoked by Arendt both to illustrate the survival of the human race, and their function *to limit and ultimately thwart the totalitarian temptation behind the genocidal invocation.*

—Irving Louis Horowitz

References and Recommended Reading

Arendt, Hannah (1989). *The Human Condition.* Chicago, IL: University of Chicago Press (original edition, 1950).

Arendt, Hannah (1963). *On Revolution.* New York: Viking Press.

Arendt, Hannah (1966). *The Origins of Totalitarianism.* New York: Harcourt, Brace and World (original edition, 1951).
Arendt, Hannah (1977). *Between Past and Future: Eight Exercises in Political Thought.* Enlarged Edition. New York: Penguin Books.
Arendt, Hannah (1982). *Lectures on Kant's Political Philosophy* (edited by Ronald Beiner). Chicago, IL: University of Chicago Press.
Arendt, Hannah (1987). *Eichmann in Jerusalem: A Report on the Banality of Evil.* Revised and Enlarged Edition. New York: Penguin Books (original edition, 1963).
Arendt, Hannah (1996). *Love and Saint Augustine* (edited by Joanna Vecchiarelli-Scott and Judith Chelius Stark). Chicago, IL: University of Chicago Press.

THE ARMENIAN GENOCIDE

ARMENIAN GENOCIDE

In April 1915 the Ottoman government embarked upon the systematic decimation of its civilian Armenian population. The persecutions continued with varying intensity until 1923 when the Ottoman Empire ceased to exist and was replaced by the Republic of Turkey. The Armenian population of the Ottoman state was reported at about two million in 1915. An estimated one million had perished by 1918, while hundreds of thousands had become homeless and stateless refugees. By 1923 virtually the entire Armenian population of Anatolian Turkey had disappeared.

The Ottoman Empire was ruled by the Turks who had conquered lands extending across West Asia, North Africa and Southeast Europe. The Ottoman government was centered in Istanbul (Constantinople) and was headed by a sultan who was vested with absolute power. The Turks practiced Islam and were a martial people. The Armenians, a Christian minority, lived as second class citizens subject to legal restrictions that denied them normal safeguards. Neither their lives nor their properties were guaranteed security. As non-Muslims they were also obligated to pay discriminatory taxes and denied participation in government. Scattered across the empire, the status of the Armenians was further complicated by the fact that the territory of historic Armenia was divided between the Ottomans and the Russians.

In its heyday in the sixteenth century, the Ottoman Empire was a powerful state. Its minority populations prospered with the growth of its economy. By the nineteenth century, the empire was in serious decline. It had been reduced in size and by 1914 had lost virtually all its lands in Europe and Africa. This decline created enormous internal political and economic pressures that contributed to the intensification of ethnic tensions. Armenian aspirations for representation and participation in government aroused suspicions among the Muslim Turks who had never shared power in their country with any minority, and who also saw nationalist movements in the Balkans result in the secession of former Ottoman territories. Demands by Armenian political organizations for administrative reforms in the Armenian-inhabited provinces and better police protection from predatory tribes among the Kurds only invited further repression. The government was determined to avoid resolving the so-called Armenian Question in any way that altered the traditional system of administration. During the reign of Sultan Abdul Hamid (Abdulhamit) II (1876–1909), a series of massacres throughout the empire meant to frighten Armenians and so dampen their expectations, cost up to three hundred thousand lives by some estimates and inflicted enormous material losses on a majority of Armenians.

In response to the crisis in the Ottoman Empire, a new political group

The 1915 Armenian Genocide in the Turkish Empire

This map illustrates three prevailing aspects of the 1915 Armenian Genocide: the deportations, the massacres, and the concentration camps. The deportations affected the majority of Armenians in the Turkish Empire. From as far north as the Black Sea and as far west as European Turkey, Armenians were forcibly removed to the Syrian desert. From the onset the deportations were marked by atrocities. At select sites, large-scale massacres were carried out. The survivors were dispersed across Syria, Iraq, and as far south as Palestine (see inset), where they were left in inhospitable places. Starvation, thirst, and epidemic diseases destroyed vast numbers of those confined to these places of concentration. The deportees in many concentration camps were eventually killed through further massacres. As this map demonstrates, the total effect of the policies of the Turkish government was the mass destruction of the Armenian people.

ANI
ARMENIAN NATIONAL INSTITUTE
122 C Street, NW
Suite 360
Washington, DC 20001
Phone: 202-383-9009
Fax: 202-383-9012
e-mail: ani@aaainc.org
www.armenian-genocide.org

"THE UNREMEMBERED GENOCIDE"

In 1915, the Young Turk regime of the Ottoman Empire set out to exterminate its Armenian population, an Indo-European people with an ancient civilization based in Asia Minor for over 2,000 years and the first nation to adopt Christianity in 301 C.E. An order signed by Talaat Pasha, Minister of the Interior and mastermind of the genocide, reads in part: "The government [has decided] to destroy all the Armenians living in the Empire. An end must be put to their existence, however criminal the measures taken may be, and no regard must be paid to age, or sex, or conscientious scruple [first published in the *London Daily Telegraph,* reporting on the *Memoirs of Naim Bey;* authenticated in Dadrian, 1986].

The procedure for annihilation followed a pattern set by the central government. Turkish gendarmes and militia in all parts of Turkey except Constantinople and Smyrna (where, because of large numbers of foreign eyewitnesses, orders were "to apply gentle measures" for the time), first sent to their deaths writers, poets and community leaders. Next, able-bodied men who appeared to be between 14 and 60 were drafted into special "labor battalions," taken aside, set to digging ditches, then shot. And lastly, unarmed women, children and the aged, on pretext of "relocation," where many presumed they would meet their men, were set on foot toward the Syrian desert. US Ambassador Henry Morgenthau stalwartly protested the measures visited on these helpless people, reporting that "they could be seen winding in and out of every valley and climbing up the sides of every mountain." American missionaries, German newsmen and military officials reported that in the first six months alone, over 1.2 million of a population of 2.1 million people joined this "unearthly procession."

Gendarmes flogged them when they paused to rest, forbade them drink when they passed wells and streams, stole their bread and their clothes, tortured, raped and mutilated them, joined by prisoners loosed from the jails and the villagers and tribesmen called out to join in the work of killing "by hand." Favorite military sports were to line up children for target practice and throw infants into the air and catch them on bayonets. Young women were forced to dance, whipped and taunted the while, then doused with kerosene and burned alive while the mobs cheered.

To date, successive Turkish governments continue to mount increasingly virulent campaigns of denial, despite abundantly documented accounts of foreign diplomatic and missionary eyewitnesses including the national archives of Germany, Turkey's wartime ally. Turkey's use of its geopolitical position as blackmail has encouraged its present allies, notably the United States, to refrain from referring to the World War I treatment of the Anatolian Armenians as "genocide."

Turkish spokesmen and their academic mercenaries (e.g., the writings of revisionists Justin McCarthy and Stanford Shaw) insist that the Armenians during the first World War were conniving with the Russians and fighting a "civil war in the northeast." The Turkish position on the Armenian Genocide deliberately confuses the Turkish and Russian sides of Turkey's northeastern frontier during World War I. When Russia—with a significant Armenian population of its own—was fighting

continues

continued

against Turkey, at various times its armies advanced into the Ottoman territories and retreated. Thus, when Armenians barricaded themselves in the ancient city of Van, and were saved by the Russian army, the Armenians fled to Russia when that army retreated. These events are further and quite deliberately confused with the postwar (1919–1920) fighting in the Russian Caucasus when, after recognizing a fledgling Armenian republic in 1918, Turkey proceeded to attack it, and the Armenians in this case fought fiercely for their lives. The Turkish view also ignores the fact that during the genocide, Armenians as far west as Bursa and Izmit, not to mention Adapazar, only 20 kilometers from Constantinople, were sent by trains in cattle cars to Konya, there held in "concentration camps," and sent on a death march in small groups.

In justifying his genocidal intentions on the eve of his invasion of Poland, Hitler, some of whose highest ranking generals had served in Turkey during the First World War, could truthfully declare a scant 24 years after the Armenian Genocide: "Who, after all, speaks today of the annihilation of the Armenians!" [first published by Louis Lochner, Associated Press correspondent in Berlin to 1942, in "What About Germany?"; authenticated by Bardakjian, 1985].

[This entry is a continuation of a classic article in Commentary *in 1966 that played a major role in bringing the forgotten Armenian Genocide to the attention of Western scholars.—Ed.]*

—Marjorie Housepian

References and Recommended Reading

Bardakjian, Kevork B. (1985). *Hitler and the Armenian Genocide.* Cambridge, MA: Zoryan Institute.

Dadrian, Vahakn N. (1986). The Naim-Andonian documents on the World War I destruction of the Ottoman Armenians: The anatomy of a genocide. *International Journal of Middle East Studies,* 18(3) 311–360.

Housepian, Marjorie (1966). The unremembered genocide. *Commentary,* 42(3), 55–60.

Lochner, Louis (1942). *What about Germany?* New York: Dodd, Mead.

called the Young Turks seized power by revolution in 1908. From the Young Turks, the Committee of Union and Progress (CUP), *Ittihad ve Terakki Jemiyeti,* emerged at the head of the government in a coup staged in 1913. It was led by a triumvirate: Enver, Minister of War; Talaat, Minister of the Interior (Grand Vizier in 1917); and Jemal, Minister of the Marine. The CUP espoused an ultranationalistic ideology that advocated the formation of an exclusively Turkish state. It also subscribed to an ideology of aggrandizement through conquest directed eastward toward other regions inhabited by Turkic peoples, at that time subject to the Russian Empire. The CUP also steered Istanbul toward closer diplomatic and military relations with Imperial Germany. When World War I broke out in August 1914, the Ottoman Empire formed part of the Triple Alliance with the other Central Powers, Germany and Austria-Hungary, and it declared war on Russia and its Western allies, Great Britain and France.

The Ottoman armies initially suffered a string of defeats, which they made up with a series of easy military victories in the Caucasus in 1918 before the Central Powers capitulated later that same year. Whether retreating or advancing, the Ottoman army used the occasion of war to wage a collateral campaign of massacre

Photograph by Armin T. Wegner of Armenians on the path of forced deportation. (Courtesy of Deutsches Literaturarchiv, Marbach, and United States Holocaust Memorial Museum)

against the civilian Armenian population in the regions in which warfare was being conducted. These measures were part of the genocidal program secretly adopted by the CUP and implemented under the cover of war. They coincided with the CUP's larger program to eradicate the Armenians from Turkey and neighboring countries for the purpose of creating a new Pan-Turanian empire. Through the spring and summer of 1915, in all areas outside the war zones, the Armenian population was ordered deported from their homes. Convoys consisting of tens of thousands including men, women, and children were driven hundreds of miles toward the Syrian Desert.

The deportations were disguised as a resettlement program. The brutal treatment of the deportees, most of whom were made to walk to their destinations, made it apparent that the deportations were mainly intended as death marches. Moreover, the policy of deportation surgically removed the Armenians from the rest of society and disposed of great masses of people with little or no destruction of property. The displacement process, therefore, also served as a major opportunity orchestrated by the CUP for the plundering of the material wealth of the Armenians and proved an effortless method of expropriating all of their immovable properties.

The genocidal intent of the CUP measures was also evidenced by the mass killings that accompanied the deportations. Earlier, Armenian soldiers in the Ottoman forces had been disarmed and either worked to death in labor battalions or executed outright in small batches. With the elimination of the

The Cream of the Armenian Leadership Is Murdered

Istanbul—On April 24, 1915, the cream of Western Armenian intelligentsia in Istanbul included 195 writers, 165 painters, 55 composers—including Gomidas Vartabed, 340 physicians, pharmacists and dentists, 175 teachers and professors, 170 lawyers and architects.

Among the murdered were world-class Armenian Ottoman poets like Krikor Zohrab, Daniel Varoujan, Yeroukhan (Yervat Sirmakesian), Siamanto (Adom Yerjanian), Roupen Zartarian, Melkon Gurjian, Roupen Sevag, Ardashes Harutiunian, and Dikran Chugurian.

All were arrested arbitrarily, without any reason or warrants, and sent into exile to Anatolia where they were subsequently executed by Turkish gendarmes. Only Gomidas was spared, and later spent his broken life in Paris for unsuccessful treatment of mental anguish.

—Press Reports

Harput—On the night of June 23, 1915, several hundred of the most prominent Armenians were sent away in ox carts from the local prison to an unknown destination. Among them were the bishop of the Gregorian Church, most of the professors and instructors in Euphrates College, and many of the leading merchants and professional men in Harput and Mamouret-ul-Aziz. Not one of these men escaped and for a long time nothing definite was known about their fate. I wrote the Embassy in cipher about the matter immediately, as the arrests had reached such proportions that they could not be looked upon with indifference and as American institutions were being seriously affected by them. It was afterwards learned that nearly all of these men were massacred somewhere near Arghana Maden, about halfway between Harput and Diarbekir.

—From Official Reports of Leslie A. Davis, American Consul in Harput, Turkey

able-bodied men from the Armenian population, the deportations proceeded with little resistance. The convoys were frequently attacked by bands of killers specifically organized for the purpose of slaughtering the Armenians. As its instrument of extermination, the government had authorized the formation of gangs of butchers—mostly convicts released from prison expressly enlisted in the units of the so-called Special Organization, *Teskilâti Mahsusa.* This secret outfit was headed by the most ferocious partisans of the CUP who took it upon themselves to carry out the orders of the central government with the covert instructions of their party leaders. A sizable portion of the deportees, including women and children, were indiscriminately killed in massacres along the deportation routes. The cruelty characterizing the killing process was heightened by the fact that it was frequently carried out by the sword in terrifying episodes of bloodshed. Furthermore, for the survivors, witnessing the murder of friends and relatives in the mass of innocent persons was the source of serious trauma. Many younger women and some orphaned children were also abducted and placed in bondage in Turkish and Muslim homes resulting in another type of trauma characterized by the shock of losing both family and one's sense of

Eyewitness Account of Armenian Genocide by a US Diplomat

The Slaughterhouse Province: An American Diplomat's Report on the Armenian Genocide, 1915–1917 (edited by Susan K. Blair. New Rochelle, NY: Aristide D. Caratzas, 1989) is based on a long forgotten report under the same title by Leslie A. Davis, an American diplomat and eyewitness to the massacres of the Armenians in Turkey.

When Davis, US Consul at Harput from 1915–1917, ventured out of the city, he found that the Ottoman policy of deportation of Armenians went much further than forcible relocation (the document ordering the deportations is reproduced together with the official US State Department translation). In his repeated hikes through the countryside, he saw the bodies of thousands of Armenians. He realized the need for a detailed record of the atrocities and brought along a doctor who determined and described the causes of death. Davis also photographed victims, and his pictures are published with the report.

Davis summarized his findings in a report submitted to the US State Department in 1918. At the time little attention was paid to it, and it was filed away in an archive. Susan K. Blair, a scholar doing research in US government archives on Turkey and the Near East, came upon the report. Although Blair first found a clue in 1980 that the American consul had "actually seen" massacre sites, it took five years of searching to locate the account which was misfiled among a box of documents in the National Archives in Washington. Earlier, Blair's investigations had turned up the diplomat's long-lost photographs in the custody of two 95-year-old residents of Ithaca, NY.

It was the historian Barbara Tuchman who first confirmed that this find was "of great importance," said Blair. Then she notified the publisher Caratzas, after another publisher, fearing controversy, turned her down.

Blair says harassment attempts began soon after the first announcement about discovery of the long-lost documents and the forthcoming book were made. A bomb threat brought law enforcement and security experts into the picture, and Blair and her family left their home and went into hiding.

Diplomat Davis describes as "certain death" the original Turkish intention to relocate the Armenian population from the province under his jurisdiction to an area miles across the desert. "A massacre, however horrible the word may sound, would be humane in comparison," Mr. Davis wrote to the US Ambassador, Henry Morgenthau Sr. He later reported that the massacre was the intention. "The country is to be purely Moslem and nothing else," Davis wrote in a follow-up letter, which outlined the Young Turks' regime's goal of uniting the nations on the basis of religious unity, excluding Christian Armenians.

Horrified by the brutality, and the tens of thousands of corpses he observed on three separate investigations, Davis found little to indicate mass death from famine or epidemic.

The Slaughterhouse Province consists of Davis' reports, his consular dispatches sent from Harput to the US embassy in Constantinople, his photographs of victims, and introduction by Susan Blair, the deportation proclamation, and other documents relating to the genocide. The endpapers of the book reproduce a later Turkish Army contour map of the area, permitting the reader to follow the author's description.

—*Internet on the Holocaust and Genocide*

Photograph by Armin T. Wegner of Armenians slaughtered on the path of the Armenian Genocide. (Courtesy of Deutsches Literaturarchiv, Marbach, and United States Holocaust Memorial Museum)

identity. These women and children were frequently forbidden to grieve, were employed as unpaid laborers, and were required to assimilate the language and religion of their captors.

The government had made no provisions for the feeding of the deported population. Starvation took an enormous toll much as exhaustion felled the elderly, the weaker and the infirm. Deportees were denied food and water in a deliberate effort to hasten death. The survivors who reached northern Syria were collected at a number of concentration camps whence they were sent further south to die under the scorching sun of the desert. Through methodically organized deportation, systematic massacre, deliberate starvation and dehydration, and continuous brutalization, the Ottoman government reduced its Armenian population to a frightened mass of famished individuals whose families and communities had been destroyed in a single stroke.

Resistance to the deportations was infrequent. Only in one instance did the entire population of an Armenian settlement manage to evade death. The mountaineers of Musa Dagh defended themselves in the heights above their villages until French naval vessels in the eastern Mediterranean detected them and transported them to safety. The inhabitants of the city of Van in eastern Armenia defended themselves until relieved by advancing Russian forces. They abandoned the city in May 1915, a month after the siege was lifted, when the Russian Army withdrew. The fleeing population was hunted down mercilessly by Turkish irregular forces. Inland towns that resisted, such as Urfa (Edessa), were reduced to rubble by artillery. The survival of the Armenians in large part is credited not

THE ARMENIAN GENOCIDE AND THE HOLOCAUST COMPARED

The Armenian Genocide and the Holocaust were the quintessential instances of total genocide in the modern era. Four reasons may be cited for this claim. First, both mass-murders were the products of state-initiated policies whose intentions were the elimination of the Armenian community from the Ottoman Empire and of the Jews from Germany and Europe and even beyond Europe. These were unmistakable instances of what the United Nations has called "genocide-in-whole," or "total genocide," to distinguish such instances from "genocide-in-part" or "partial genocide." Examples of partial genocide from which both differ are the destruction of Overseas Chinese in Indonesia in 1965, Ibos in Northern Nigeria in 1967, and Muslims in Bosnia in 1992–1996.

Second, both victimized groups were ethnoreligious communities that had been partially integrated and assimilated into the larger society, the Ottoman Empire and European society respectively. Their destruction was not only a war against foreign strangers. It was a mass-murder that commenced with an attack on an internal domestic segment of the state's own society. Thus the Armenian Genocide and the Holocaust were instances not only of "total genocide" but of "total domestic genocide"—to differentiate these two cases from the genocide of foreign groups, that is, foreign with regards to the borders of the state. For example, the Armenian Genocide and the Holocaust differ from the destruction of foreign peoples such as the men of Melos by the Athenians, Carthage by Rome, and a host of native communities by the Europeans in the New World and Africa.

Third, Armenians and Jews were unmistakably communal or ethnic groups, not political groups or classes whose noninclusion under the original UN definition of genocide has generated much criticism. Although Armenians and Jews may have occupied certain strata in the social structures of the Ottoman Empire, Germany and Europe, they were not social classes like, for example, the Kulaks of the Soviet Union and the urban Cambodians that were destroyed by the Stalinists and the Khmer Rouge, respectively.

Fourth, both the Armenian Genocide and the Holocaust were the products of modern ideologies and the circumstances of revolution and war. The Armenian Genocide occurred under the circumstances of the Turkish revolution and the First World War, while the Holocaust was a product of the Nazi revolution and the Second World War.

For centuries Armenians had been tolerated as a minority *(dhimmi)* millet in the Ottoman Empire. They welcomed the Young Turk revolution of 1908, hoping that it would improve their situation, which had become increasingly desperate under the regime of Sultan Abdul Hamid II. However, following the Ottoman military disasters of 1908–1912, the Young Turks abandoned Ottoman tolerance for the ideology of Pan-Turkism, a variant of contemporary organic or integral nationalism, and by 1915, under the circumstances of the First World War, they deported and destroyed the Armenian community.

The Jews of Imperial Germany had been emancipated by 1871, and, despite the rise of the antisemitic movement, they hoped to be assimilated and accepted in the wider German and Euro-

continues

continued

pean society. Following the disasters of the First World War, the inflation of the 1920s, and the Great Depression, the democratic Weimar Republic collapsed and the Nazis rose to power. They were motivated by a world view that fused radical antisemitism with racism and under the circumstances of the Second World War they committed total genocide against the Jews and Gypsies and partial genocide against other groups like the Poles.

Although there are striking similarities between the Armenian Genocide and the Holocaust, there are differences as well. Three may be briefly listed: First, the Armenian millct in the Ottoman Empire, like the Jews of Europe, occupied a distinctively inferior status; however, unlike the Jews, Armenians were never stigmatized as deicides, killers of God. The Jews being viewed as deicides, on the one hand, and their demands for inclusion on the other, may explain why the Jews were met by a racialist antisemitic movement that demonized and excluded them in a manner quite distinct from the Armenians in the Ottoman Empire.

Second, Armenians were largely a peasant society living on its own lands in Cilicia and the eastern provinces of Anatolia, while the Jews were largely an urban community scattered throughout Germany and Europe and not concentrated on its ancestral lands. The result was that in the period of nationalism, there existed Armenian nationalist political parties demanding territorial autonomy and self-administration; while, with the exception of the Zionist movement, the Jews of Europe were hoping for assimilation and inclusion in their countries of domicile. The Armenian Genocide, in contrast to the Holocaust, therefore, included not only a destruction of the Armenian community, but also the loss of ancestral Armenian lands dating back to the pre-Christian era.

Third, in contrast to the Young Turks who had nationalist and imperial aspirations, the Nazis were a totalitarian movement whose racialist antisemitic ideology had global scope. The result was that the Holocaust, in contrast to the Armenian and other genocides, was global in its intentions and scope as well. For example, the Nazis demanded of their Japanese allies that they hand over their Jews for destruction. Although the Japanese refused, this example illustrates the difference in ideological intentions between the Nazis and the Young Turks. The former saw themselves in a global war against the Jews, while the latter wished to eliminate the Armenians from Anatolia and the rest of their Pan-Turkic realm. Unlike the Nazis, the Young Turks did not aspire to exterminate their victims the world over.

—Robert Melson

References and Recommended Reading

Dadrian, Vahakn N. (1995). *The History of the Armenian Genocide: Ethnic Conflict from the Balkans to Anatolia to the Caucasus.* Providence, RI: Berghahn Books.

Fein, Helen (1978). A formula for genocide: A comparison of the Turkish genocide (1915) and the German Holocaust (1939–1945). In Tomasson, Richard F. (Ed.), *Comparative Studies in Sociology. Volume 1.* Greenwich, CO: JAI Press, pp. 271–293.

Melson, Robert (1992). *Revolution and Genocide: On the Origins of the Armenian Genocide and the Holocaust.* Chicago, IL: University of Chicago Press.

Ternon, Yves (1995). *L' État Criminel: Les Génocides au XXème Siècle* [*The Criminal State: The Genocides of the 20th Century*]. Paris: Éditions du Seuil.

TREATMENT OF THE ARMENIAN GENOCIDE IN REPRESENTATIVE ENCYCLOPEDIAS

As standard references created by specialists for the use of the wider public, encyclopedias play a special role in disseminating tested and established knowledge. In the selection of topics, in their representation, and in the choice of descriptive language, encyclopedias send a message to society about the accepted truth and the reliable fact. Because of this responsibility, they tend to be conservative publications, prone to weigh the range of information available and to opt for safer views on controversial subjects, which can also institutionally predispose them to accommodate rationalizations, and perhaps even make them especially vulnerable to a coordinated program of revisionism.

Regrettably, the representation of the Armenian Genocide across a host of commonly referred to encyclopedias distinctly reflects the near complete absorption of the revisionist interpretation of the Armenian Genocide. The emergence of this problematic rewriting can be traced through various editions of the same encyclopedia from the 1960s to the 1990s. The trend is an increasing dilution of the consequences of the atrocities, this in complete contrast to the growing body of scholarship about the Armenian Genocide emerging from new research that reveals the secret and extensive planning involved in the execution of the deportations and massacres.

The complications arising from a tolerance of revisionist historiography as reflected in the encyclopedias are considerable. To begin with, none of the encyclopedias reviewed carry an entry on the Armenian Genocide, not even a subsection. With the exception of the *Encyclopedia Britannica,* none other even refers to the atrocities as "genocidal." The *Encyclopedia Americana* speaks of an attempt at "physically annihilating" the Armenians, but attributes the casualties to deportation. *Collier's Encyclopedia* refers only to deportations during World War I.

Beyond the question of proper labeling, the greatest effect of revisionism is detectable in the causative explanation given for the Armenian Genocide. While earlier editions placed the events of 1915 in the context of the increasingly brutal treatment of the Armenian population of the Ottoman Empire as evidenced by a string of massacres from the 1890s onward, all newer editions reproduce the basic accusation of Armenian collaboration with Russian forces as the rationalization for the policy of deportation. With this trend, the incorporation of euphemisms is also evidenced, because the resulting deaths are depicted as having been consequential to the policy of relocation as opposed to any premeditated plan of extermination. Lastly, the dilution process is most apparent in the reduction in the number of victims, in effect representing the Armenian Genocide as a comprehensible reaction to wartime exigency, and in so doing essentially registering success for the campaign to eliminate the subject from the standard inventory of historical information.

The problematics are not restricted to the subject at the source of its most common citation, that is, the entries on Armenia and the Armenians. Entries on Turkey or the Ottoman Empire are virtually devoid of reference to the annihilation of their Armenian population.

continues

continued

Even more disturbing is the complete exculpation of Young Turk leaders whose biographical entries are purged of any mention of their role as the principal organizers of the Armenian Genocide. This aspect of the revisionist effort is most apparent in the *Encyclopedia of Islam.* Perhaps some reference works on the Middle East can be understood to often assume a measure of responsibility for seemingly rectifying Eurocentric, Islamophobic, and minority-sympathetic views, but this moderating role can be abused. Thus, too, in the *Encyclopedia of the Modern Middle East,* the 1909 massacre of the Armenians of Adana is described as "an Armenian riot," this in an entry on Jemal Pasha, one of the Young Turk triumvirs during the Armenian Genocide.

Recent encyclopedia literature on the Armenians reflects an altered reality deriving from revisionism and registers the entry of denialist authorship into the domain of standardized encyclopedic historiography.

—Rouben Paul Adalian

References and Recommended Reading

Collier's Encyclopedia (1994). *Volume 1.* New York: P. F. Collier.

Encyclopedia Americana (1993). *Volume 2.* Danbury, CT: Grolier.

Encyclopedia of Islam New Edition (1960–1993). Leiden: E.J. Brill.

Encyclopedia of the Modern Middle East (1996). New York: Macmillan Reference USA.

The New Encyclopaedia Britannica (1982). *Volumes 1 and 18.* Chicago, IL: Encyclopedia Britannica.

to acts of resistance, but to the humanitarian intervention led by American Ambassador Henry Morgenthau. Although the Allied Powers expressly warned the Ottoman government about its policy of genocide, ultimately it was through Morgenthau's efforts that the plight of the Armenians was publicized in the United States. The US Congress authorized the formation of a relief committee that raised funds to feed "the starving Armenians." Near East Relief, as the committee was eventually known, saved tens of thousands of lives. After the war, it headed a large-scale effort to rehabilitate the survivors who were mostly left to their own devices in their places of deportation. By setting up refugee camps, orphanages, medical clinics and educational facilities, Near East Relief rescued the surviving Armenian population.

In the postwar period, nearly four hundred of the key CUP officials implicated in the atrocities committed against the Armenians were arrested. A number of domestic military tribunals were convened that brought charges ranging from the unconstitutional seizure of power and subversion of the legal government, the conduct of a war of aggression, and conspiring the liquidation of the Armenian population, to more explicit capital crimes including massacre. Some of the accused were found guilty of the charges. Most significantly, the ruling triumvirate was condemned to death. They, however, eluded justice by fleeing abroad. Their escape left the matter of avenging the countless victims to a clandestine group of survivors that tracked down the CUP arch conspirators. Talaat, the principal architect of the Armenian Genocide, was killed in 1921 in Berlin where he had gone into hiding. His assassin was arrested and tried in a German court, which acquitted him.

Most of those implicated in war crimes evaded justice and many joined the new Nationalist Turkish movement led by Mustafa Kemal. In a series of military campaigns in Russian Armenia in 1920 against the refugee Armenians who had returned to Cilicia in southern Turkey in 1921, and against the Greek army that had occupied Izmir (Smyrna) where the last intact Armenian community in Anatolia still existed in 1922, the Nationalist forces completed the process of eradicating the Armenians through further expulsions and massacres. When Turkey was declared a republic in 1923 and received international recognition, the Armenian Question and all related matters of resettlement and restitution were swept aside and soon forgotten.

In all, it is estimated that up to a million and a half Armenians perished at the hands of Ottoman and Turkish military and paramilitary forces and through atrocities intentionally inflicted to eliminate the Armenian demographic presence in Turkey. In the process, the population of historic Armenia at the eastern extremity of Anatolia was wiped off the map. With their disappearance, an ancient people that had inhabited the Armenian highlands for three thousand years lost its historic homeland and was forced into exile and a new diaspora. The surviving refugees spread around the world and eventually settled in some two dozen countries on all continents of the globe. Triumphant in its total annihilation of the Armenians and relieved of any obligations to the victims and survivors, the Turkish Republic adopted a policy of dismissing the charge of genocide and denying that the deportations and atrocities had constituted part of a deliberate plan to exterminate the Armenians. When the Red Army Sovietized what remained of Russian Armenia in 1920, the Armenians had been compressed into an area amounting to no more than ten percent of the territories of their historic homeland. Armenians annually commemorate the Genocide on April 24 at the site of memorials raised by the survivors in all their communities around the world.

—Rouben Paul Adalian

References and Recommended Reading

Adalian, Rouben Paul (Ed.) (1994). *Guide to the Armenian Genocide in the U.S. Archives, 1915–1918.* Alexandria, VA: Chadwyck-Healey.

Dadrian, Vahakn N. (1995). *The History of the Armenian Genocide: Ethnic Conflict from the Balkans to Anatolia to the Caucasus.* Providence, RI: Berghahn Books.

Hovannisian, Richard G. (Ed.) (1992). *The Armenian Genocide: History, Politics, Ethics.* New York: St. Martin's Press.

Melson, Robert (1992). *Revolution and Genocide: On the Origins of the Armenian Genocide and the Holocaust.* Chicago, IL: University of Chicago Press.

Toynbee, Arnold (Ed.) (1916). Preface by Viscount Bryce. *The Treatment of Armenians in the Ottoman Empire 1915–1916: Documents Presented to Viscount Grey of Fallodon, Secretary of State for Foreign Affairs, by Viscount Bryce.* London: Sir Joseph Causton and Sons.

See also the materials provided by the Armenian National Institute (ANI) on the World Wide Web: www.armenian-genocide.org.

Source Document

NEW YORK TIMES REPORTS OF THE ARMENIAN GENOCIDE

As it took place, the Armenian Genocide in 1915 was fully reported and documented in newspapers. Over 194 articles appeared in the *New York Times* alone. The following are samples of some of the headlines in the *New York Times* at the time.

Appeal to Turkey to Stop Massacres, April 28, 1915
Morgenthau Intercedes, April 29, 1915
6,000 Armenians Killed, May 17, 1915
Allies to Punish Turks who Murder, May 24, 1915
Wholesale Massacres of Armenians by Turks, July 29, 1915
Report Turks Shot Women and Children, August 4, 1915
Armenians are Sent to Perish in Desert, August 18, 1915
Burn 1,000 Armenians, August 20, 1915
Turks Depopulate Towns of Armenia, August 27, 1915
1,500,000 Armenians Starve, September 5, 1915
Answer Morgenthau by Hanging Armenians, September 16, 1915
Mission Board Told of Turkish Horrors, September 17, 1915
500,000 Armenians Said to Have Perished, September 24, 1915
Armenian Women Put up at Auction, September 29, 1915
Armenian Officials Murdered by Turks, September 30, 1915
Government Sends Plea for Armenia, October 5, 1915
800,000 Armenians Counted Destroyed, October 7, 1915
Sends $100,000 to Aid Armenians Refugees, October 9, 1915
Spare Armenians, Pope Asks Sultan, October 11, 1915
Turkish Official Denies Atrocities, October 15, 1915
Turkey Bars Red Cross, October 19, 1915
Only 200,000 Armenians Now Left in Turkey, October 22, 1915
Germany Says She Cannot Stop Turks, October 23, 1915
Aid for Armenians Blocked by Turkey, November 1, 1915
Pope May Make New Plea to Kaiser, December 9, 1915
Million Armenians Killed or in Exile, December 15, 1915
500 Armenians Slain Under Turkish Order, January 15, 1916
Saw Armenians Go Starving to Exile, February 6, 1916
Sultan Searching Out Authors of Killings, December 7, 1918
Saw Armenians Drowned in Groups, February 2, 1919
'Ravished Armenia' in Film, February 15, 1919
Turkey Condemns its War Leaders, July 13, 1919

A sample of news stories follows, as cited in the book-length compilation of news accounts by Richard Kloian (1988), *The Armenian Genocide, News Accounts from the American Press: 1915–1922,* 3rd ed. (Richmond, CA: Armenian Genocide Resource Center, 5400 McBryde Ave, Richmond, CA 94805, fax: 510-215-0444).

The New York Times

AUGUST 4, 1915

REPORT TURKS SHOT WOMEN AND CHILDREN

Nine Thousand Armenians Massacred and Thrown Into Tigris, Socialist Committee Hears.

PARIS, Aug. 3. — B. Varazdate, a member of the Executive Committee of the Armenian Social Democratic Party, writing to L'Humanite, the Socialist daily, says that the committee has received word to the effect that Turks, after massacring all the males of the population in the region of Bitlis, Turkish Armenia, assembled 9,000 women and children and drove them to the banks of the Tigris, where they shot them and threw the bodies into the river.

These advices have not been substantiated from any other source.

The Armenian population of Cilicia, in the Turkish Vilayet of Adana, also has been subjected to persecutions, according to the reports of the committee. More than 40,000 persons already are dead and it is feared that the Armenians at Moucks and Diarbekr, in Kurdestan, also have been massacred.

Twenty members of the Armenian Social Democratic Party, M. Varzadate says, have been publicly hanged in Constantinople after being charged with wishing to found an independent Armenia.

AUGUST 20, 1915

BURN 1,000 ARMENIANS.

Turks Lock Them in a Wooden Building and Then Apply the Torch.

LONDON, Friday, Aug. 20.—A Reuter dispatch from Petrograd says:

"Almost unbelievable details of Turkish massacres of Armenians in Bitlis have reached Petrograd.

"In one village, 1,000 men, women and children are reported to have been locked in a wooden building and burned to death.

"In another large village only thirty-six persons, it is said, escaped massacre.

"In still another instance, it is asserted, several scores of men and women were tied together by chains and thrown into Lake Van."

AUGUST 25, 1915

TURKS' SOP TO ARMENIANS.

Sublime Porte Promises Not to Deport 10 Per Cent. of Them.

Special to The New York Times.

WASHINGTON, Aug. 24. — Ambassador Morgenthau has notified the State Department from Constantinople that the Turkish Government has informed him that orders have been telegraphed throughout Turkey exempting from deportation all Armenians who are members of Protestant or Catholic churches. The Ambassador said that about 90 per cent. of the Armenians belonged to the Gregorian or Armenian Church, and 10 per cent. to the Protestant or Catholic.

The Turkish Government has also granted exemption for Armenians in the employ of American Consulates.

The New York Times

August 27, 1915

TURKS DEPOPULATE TOWNS OF ARMENIA

Traveler Reports Christians of Great Territory Have Been Driven from Homes.

600,000 STARVING ON ROAD

Adds That More Than 100,000 Greeks Have Been Deported from the Mediterranean Coast.

A traveler who has just arrived in New York from Turkey, where he was long a resident, told THE TIMES yesterday of conditions as he found them in Constantinople, and of the wholesale deportations of Armenians from the interior districts of Asiatic Turkey. For reasons that are valid, the narrator does not wish to have his name published, but THE TIMES can vouch for his qualifications as an observer, especially of conditions in the Armenian district.

Leaving Sivas, where he spent some time, he proceeded to Constantinople and thence to Athens, from which port he sailed for New York. When in Constantinople about four weeks ago, he said, the tension was pretty high. In official circles it was maintained that everything was proceeding smoothly for the Turks, but there were many individuals, he said, who expressed discouragement. These put little faith in Germany's motives in aiding Turkey, and some even charged Enver Pasha with having sold out to Germany for money.

"The Armenians of the interior," he said, "have been deported in the direction of Mosul. At the time I left Sivas, two-thirds of them had gone from the city, including all Protestants, teachers, and pupils. According to my best knowledge and opinion, with the exception of Armenian soldiers and prisoners, and a very few exceptions, who for various reasons were necessary to the Government, all Armenians are gone from Sivas. According to what I consider good authority, I believe it to be true that the entire Armenian population from Erzerum to and including Gemereh, near Cesarea, and from Samsoun to and including Harpoot, has been deported."

More than 100,000 Greeks from the Marmora and Mediterranean coast have been deported.

September 16, 1915

ANSWER MORGENTHAU BY HANGING ARMENIANS

He Protests Against the War of Extermination Now in Progress.

Special Cable to THE NEW YORK TIMES.

LONDON, Thursday, Sept. 16. — A Times correspondent, lately in Salonika, says that all the reports from Turkey are agreed as to the terrible character of the Turkish atrocities against Armenians. It is believed that it is the official intention that this shall be a campaign of extermination, involving the murdering of 800,000 to 1,000,000 persons. Christians can escape murder by embracing Mohammedanism, in which case all the female members of the convert's family of marriageable age — wife, sisters, or children — are distributed around to other Turks, making the reversion to Christianity in the future practically impossible.

The American Minister at Constantinople is said to have protested recently against the massacre, in view of the danger to which they exposed the American missionaries. The only response to his protest was the hanging of twenty leading Armenians the next day in the streets of Constantinople.

The New York Times

SEPTEMBER 24, 1915

500,000 ARMENIANS SAID TO HAVE PERISHED

Washington Asked to Stop Slaughter of Christians by Turks and Kurds.

Special to The New York Times.

WASHINGTON, Sept.23.—Charles R. Crane of Chicago, a Director of Roberts College, Constantinople, and James L. Burton of Boston, Foreign Secretary of the American Board of Commissioners for Foreign Missions, visited the State Department today and conferred with Acting Secretary of State Polk and other officials regarding the slaughter of Armenians by Turks and Kurds in Asia Minor. They will attend a meeting of a general committee, to be held in New York within a few days, to devise a plan for appealing to the American people for funds and aid for as many of the unfortunate Armenians as can be helped.

It was learned, in connection with the conferences held here today, that general representations have from time to time been made to the Ottoman Government by Ambassador Morgenthau for humane treatment of Armenians. Despite these representations, the slaughter of Armenians has continued.

The records of the State Department are replete with detailed reports from American Consular officers in Asia Minor, which give harrowing tales of the treatment of the Armenian Christians by the Turks and the Kurds. These reports have not been made public. They indicate that the Turk has undertaken a war of extermination on Armenians, especially those of the Gregorian Church, to which about 90 percent of the Armenians belong. The Turkish Government originally ordered the deportation of all Armenians, but some time ago, after representations had been made by Morgenthau, the Ottoman Government gave assurances that the order would be modified so as not to embrace Catholic and Protestant Armenians. Reports reaching Washington indicate that about 500,000 Armenians have been slaughtered or lost their lives as a result of the Turkish deportation order and the resulting war of extinction. Turkish authorities drove the Gregorian Armenians out of their homes, ordered them to proceed to distant towns in the direction of Bagdad, which could only be reached by crossing long stretches of desert. During the exodus of Armenians across the deserts they have been fallen upon by Kurds and slaughtered, but some of the Armenian women and girls, in considerable numbers, have been carried off into captivity by the Kurds. The reports that have been sent to the State Department by its agents in Asia Minor fully confirm these statements made in the appeal sent to this country by Viscount Bryce, formerly the British Ambassador to the United States, to try to stop the slaughter of the Armenians. Viscount Bryce stated that the horrors through which the Armenians have passed have been unparalleled in modern times.

Special Cable to THE NEW YORK TIMES

ALEXANDRIA, Sept. 23, (Dispatch to The London Morning Post.) — British refugees from Urfa, who arrived in Alexandria yesterday, brought terrible tales of sufferings of interned allied subjects. They were not supplied with food, furniture, or servants, and were housed in an Armenian monastery the monks in which had been massacred.

They witnessed the Armenian massacres of Aug. 19. Urfa was the centre of ghastly scenes. The Turks systematically murdered men and turned women and children out into the desert, where thousands perished of starvation.

The last batch of women and children left Urfa on Aug. 24. They were delayed a fortnight at Alexandretta, awaiting a ship in filthy quarters and half starved. They finally embarked for Alexandria in an American warship

The New York Times

NOVEMBER 1, 1915

AID FOR ARMENIANS BLOCKED BY TURKEY

Attempts to Send Food to Refugees Frustrated, Says the American Committee.

PUTS VICTIMS AT 1,000,000

Careful Survey Shows 55,000 Persons Killed in the Vilayet of Van Alone.

The American Committee on Armenian Atrocities, among the members of which are Cardinal Gibbons, Cleveland H. Dodge, Bishop David H. Greer, Oscar S. Straus, Professor Samuel T. Dutton, Charles R. Crane, and many other prominent citizens, issued a statement yesterday in which it was said that authentic reports from Turkey proved that the war of extermination being waged against the Armenians was so terrible that when all the facts were known the world would realize that what had been done was "the greatest, most pathetic, and most arbitrary tragedy in history."

Attempts to furnish food to the Armenians ordered deported to distant parts of the empire were blocked by the Turkish authorities, the committee said, the Turkish officials stating that "they wished nothing to be done that would prolong their lives."

In the statement the committee makes public a report received a few days ago from an official representative of the neutral powers, who, reporting on conditions in one of the Armenian camps, says:

"I have visited their encampment and a more pitiable sight cannot be imagined. They are, almost without exception, ragged, hungry and sick. This is not surprising in view of the fact that they have been on the road for nearly two months, with no change of clothing, no chance to bathe, no shelter, and little to eat. I watched them one time when their food was brought. Wild animals could not be worse. They rushed upon the guards who carried the food and the guards beat them back with clubs, hitting hard enough to kill sometimes. To watch them one could hardly believe these people to be human beings. As one walks through the camp, mothers offer their children and beg you to take them. In fact, the Turks have been taking their choice of these children and girls for slaves or worse. There are very few men among them as most of the men were killed on the road. Women and children were also killed. The entire movement seems to be the most thoroughly organized and effective massacre this country has ever seen."

"They all agree," adds the committee, referring to the reports," as to the method of procedure, the thoroughness and cruelty of the destructive work, and the confessed purpose of the plan to wipe out the Armenian nation. The fact that the central government at Constantinople refuses to permit Armenians to leave their country is further evidence of their purpose of extermination.

"The Turks do not deny the atrocities, but claim they are a military measure to protect them against a possible attack of a race that is disloyal.

"It is impossible to estimate how many have already perished. A careful survey in the Van Vilayet gathered the names of 55,000 persons who had been killed. Others were able to escape by flight to Persia and Russia. An eyewitness who has recently made an extended journey across Asia Minor saw over 50,000 poor, dazed, helpless, starving refugees camped by the roadside in a region almost desert, with no provision for their food supply. Probably it is not an overestimate to say that 1,000,000 of the possible 2.000,000 Armenians in Turkey at the beginning of the war are either dead or in Moslem harems, or forced to profess Mohammedanism, or are on their sad journey to the desert and death."

The committee says it has cabled $106,000 to Ambassador Morgenthau at Constantinople, of which $100,000 was for relief of Armenians in Turkey, and the remainder for Armenians who had escaped into Egypt. The office of the committee, of which Mr. Crane is Treasurer, is at 70 Fifth Avenue, New York.

Source Document

RAPHAEL LEMKIN ON THE ARMENIAN GENOCIDE

From a letter to Mrs. Thelma Stevens, Methodist Women's Council, July 26, 1950

This Convention is a matter of conscience and is a test of our personal relationship to evil. I know it is very hot in July and August for work and planning, but without becoming sentimental or trying to use colorful speech, let us not forget that the heat of this month is less unbearable to us than the heat of the ovens of Auschwitz and Dachau and more lenient than the murderous heat in the desert of Aleppo which burned to death the bodies of hundreds of thousands of Christian Armenian victims of genocide in 1915.

From *Totally Unofficial,* Autobiography

In 1915 the Germans occupied the city of W. and the entire area. I used this time to read more history, to study and to watch whether national, religious, or racial groups are being destroyed. The truth came out only after the war. In Turkey, more than 1,200,000 Armenians were put to death for no other reason than they were Christians . . . After the end of the war, some 150 Turkish war criminals were arrested and interned by the British Government on the island of Malta. The Armenians sent a delegation to the peace conference in Versailles. They were demanding justice. Then one day, the delegation read in the newspapers that all Turkish war criminals were released. I was shocked. A nation was killed and the guilty persons were set free. Why is a man punished when he kills another man? Why is the killing of a million a lesser crime than the killing of a single individual?

•

I identified myself more and more with the sufferings of the victims, whose numbers grew, as I continued my study of history. I understood that the function of memory is not only to register past events, but to stimulate human conscience. Soon contemporary examples of genocide followed, such as the slaughter of the Armenians in 1915. It became clear to me that the diversity of nations, religious groups and races is essential to civilization because every one of those groups has a mission to fulfill and a contribution to make in terms of culture. . . . I decided to become a lawyer and work for the outlawing of Genocide and for its prevention through the cooperation of nations.

•

A bold plan was formulated in my mind. This consisted [of] obtaining the ratification by Turkey [of the proposed *UN Convention on Genocide*—Ed.] among the first twenty founding nations. This would be an atonement for [the] genocide of the Armenians. But how could this be achieved? . . . The Turks are proud of their republican form of government and of progressive concepts, which helped them in replacing the rule of the Ottoman Empire. The genocide convention must be put within the framework of social and international progress. I know however that in this conversation both sides will have to avoid speaking about one thing, although it would be constantly in their minds: the Armenians.

[*Source:* With permission of the Rare Books and Manuscripts Division, the New York Public Library, Astor, Lenox, and Tilden Foundations.]

Source Document

THE EUROPEAN PARLIAMENT'S RESOLUTION "ON A POLITICAL SOLUTION TO THE ARMENIAN QUESTION"

June 18, 1987

The European Parliament

Convinced that recognition of the identity of the Armenian people in Turkey as an ethnic, cultural, linguistic and religious minority follows on from recognition of its own history,

Whereas the Armenian side regards these events as planned Genocide within the meaning of the 1948 UN Charter,

Whereas the Turkish State rejects the charge of Genocide as unfounded,

Whereas, to date, the Turkish Government, by refusing to recognize the Genocide of 1915, continues to deprive the Armenian people of the right to their own history,

Whereas the historically proven Armenian Genocide has so far neither been the object of political condemnation nor received due compensation,

Whereas the recognition of the Armenian Genocide by Turkey must therefore be viewed as a profoundly humane act of moral rehabilitation towards the Armenians, which can only bring honor to the Turkish Government;

Profoundly regretting and condemning the mindless terrorism by groups of Armenians who were responsible between 1973 and 1986 for several attacks causing death or injury to innocent victims and deplored by an overwhelming majority of the Armenian people,

Whereas the obdurate stance of every Turkish Government towards the Armenian Question has in no way helped to reduce the tension,

1. Believes that the Armenian Question and the question of minorities in Turkey must be resituated within the framework of relations between Turkey and the Community; points out that democracy cannot be solidly implanted in a country unless the latter recognizes and enriches its history with its ethnic and cultural diversity;
2. Believes that the tragic events in 1915–1917 involving the Armenians living in the territory of the Ottoman Empire constitute Genocide within the meaning of the convention on the prevention and the punishment of the crime of Genocide adopted by the UN General Assembly on December 9, 1948; Recognizes however, that present Turkey cannot be held responsible for the tragedy experienced by the Armenians of the Ottoman Empire and stresses that neither political nor legal or material claims against present-day Turkey can be derived from the recognition of this historical event as an act of Genocide;
3. Calls on the Council to obtain from the present Turkish Government an acknowledgement of the Genocide perpetrated against the Armenians in 1915–1917 and promote the establishment of a political dialogue between Turkey and the representatives of the Armenians;
4. Believes that the refusal by the present Turkish Government to acknowledge the Genocide against the Armenian people committed by the Young Turk government, its reluctance to apply the principles of international law to its differences of opinion with Greece, the maintenance of Turkish occupation forces in Cyprus and the denial of the existence of the Kurdish question, together with

continues

continued

the lack of true parliamentary democracy and the failure to respect individual and collective freedoms, in particular freedom of religion, in that country are insurmountable obstacles to consideration of the possibility of Turkey's accession to the Community;

5. Conscious of those past misfortunes, supports its desire for the development of a specific identity, the securing of its minority rights and the unrestricted exercise of its people's human and civil rights as defined in the European Convention on Human Rights and its five protocols;
6. Calls for fair treatment of the Armenian minority in Turkey as regards their identity, language, religion, culture and school system, and makes an emphatic plea for improvements in the care of monuments and for the maintenance and conservation of the Armenian religious architectural heritage in Turkey and invites the Community to examine how it could make an appropriate contribution;
7. Calls on Turkey in this connection to abide faithfully by the provisions for the protection of the non-Muslim minorities as stipulated in Articles 37 to 45 of the 1923 Treaty of Lausanne which, moreover, was signed by most Member States of the Community;
8. Considers that the protection of monuments and the maintenance and conservation of the Armenian religious architectural heritage in Turkey must be regarded as part of a wider policy designed to preserve the cultural heritage of all civilizations which have developed over the centuries on present-day Turkish territory and, in particular, that of the Christian minorities that formed part of the Ottoman Empire;
9. Calls therefore on the Community to extend the Association Agreement with Turkey to the cultural field so that the remains of Christian or other civilizations such as the ancient classical, Hittite, Ottoman, etc., in that country are preserved and made generally accessible;
10. Expresses its concern at the difficulties currently being experienced by the Armenian community in Iran with respect to the Armenian language and their own education in accordance with the rules of their own religion;
11. Condemns the violations of individual freedoms committed in the Soviet Union against the Armenian population;
12. Condemns strongly any violence and any form of terrorism carried out by isolated groupings unrepresentative of the Armenian people, and calls for reconciliation between Armenians and Turks;
13. Calls on the Community Member States to dedicate a day to the memory of the genocide and crimes against humanity perpetrated in the twentieth century, specifically against the Armenians and Jews;
14. Commits itself to making substantial contribution to initiatives to encourage negotiations between the Armenian and Turkish peoples;
15. Instructs its President to forward this resolution to the Commission, the European Council, the Foreign Ministers meeting in political cooperation, the EEC in Turkey Association Council and the Turkish, Iranian and Soviet Governments and the UN Secretary General.

Source Document

JOINT DECLARATION BY FRANCE, GREAT BRITAIN, AND RUSSIA, MAY 24, 1915

Telegram
Department of State, Washington
May 29, 1915
Amembassy [American Embassy], Constantinople
French Foreign Office requests following notice be given Turkish Government. Quote. May 24th

For about a month the Kurd and Turkish population of Armenia has been massacring Armenians with the connivance and often assistance of Ottoman authorities. Such massacres took place in middle April at Erzerum, Dertchun, Eguine, Akn, Bitlis, Mush, Sassun, Zeitun, and throughout Cilicia. Inhabitants of about one hundred villages near Van were all murdered. In that city Armenian quarter is besieged by Kurds. At the same time in Constantinople Ottoman Government ill-treats inoffensive Armenian population. In view of those new crimes of Turkey against humanity and civilization, the Allied governments announce publicly to the Sublime-Porte that they will hold personally responsible [for] these crimes all members of the Ottoman government and those of their agents who are implicated in such massacres.

Unquote.
R.G. 59,867.4016/67

Source Document

PERMANENT PEOPLE'S TRIBUNAL ON THE ARMENIAN GENOCIDE

April 13–16, 1984
Paris, France
On April 6, 1984 in Paris, France, after three days of testimony and deliberation, the Permanent Peoples' Tribunal found Turkey guilty of committing the crime of genocide and called upon the United Nations and its member states to recognize the Armenian Genocide.

The 13 Representatives of the Tribunal, comprising a jury of distinguished international scholars and Nobel Prize laureates, heard reports from various historians, legal experts, and genocide survivors, and examined archival documentation to arrive at their verdict.

The independent panel of jurists concluded that "the extermination of the Armenian populations through deportation and massacre constitutes a crime of genocide . . . (and) the Young Turk government is guilty of this genocide . . ."

THE PERMANENT PEOPLES' TRIBUNAL was called upon the request of the following organizations to devote a session to the case of the genocide of the Armenians:

- Minority Rights Group (London, England)
- Cultural Survival (Cambridge, Massachusetts, U.S.A.)

continues

continued

- Gesellschaft für Bedrohte Völker (Göttingen, West Germany)

The following questions were raised:

1. Is it established that the Armenian people was the victim of deportations, massacres, etc., in the Ottoman Empire?
2. Do these facts constitute a "genocide" in the sense of the International Convention on the Prevention and Punishment of the Crime of Genocide (1948) and, consequently, do they fall under the 1968 Convention on the Non-Applicability of Statutory Limitations to War Crimes and Crimes against Humanity?
3. What are the consequences of this both for the international community and for the concerned parties?

The President of the Tribunal declared this request to be admissible in accordance with Article 11 of the statutes, and the Turkish government was informed, in application of the provision of Articles 14 and 15. The Turkish government was invited to send representatives or written documents to make its position known.

Since the Turkish government did not reply to this invitation, the Tribunal decided to insert into the record the two documents cited below, which contain the arguments of the Turkish party in support of its denial of the genocide of the Armenians.

The Tribunal held public hearings 13–14 April 1984 at the Sorbonne in Paris and the jury deliberated the matter on 15 April 1984.

At the conclusion of this discussion, the Tribunal pronounced the following verdict:

Considering the Universal Declaration of Human Rights of 10 December 1948,

Considering the Convention on the Prevention and Punishment of the Crime of Genocide of 9 December 1948,

Considering the Nuremberg principles formulated by the International Law Commission and adopted by the United Nations General Assembly in 1951,

Considering the Convention on the Non-Applicability of Statutory Limitations to War Crimes and Crimes against Humanity of 26 November 1968,

Considering the Universal Declaration on the Rights of Peoples (Algiers, 4 July 1976),

Considering the Statutes of the Permanent Peoples' Tribunal (Bologna, 24 June 1979);

Having heard reports from:

- Richard G. Hovannisian, Professor at the University of California at Los Angeles (U.S.A.), on the Armenian question from 1878 to 1923;
- Gerard J. Libaridian, historian and Director of the Zoryan Institute for Contemporary Armenian Research and Documentation (Cambridge, Massachusetts, U.S.A.), on the intent to commit genocide and the ideology of the "Young Turk" movement;
- Christopher Walker, historian and author, on British sources concerning the Armenian Genocide;
- Tessa Hoffman, Freie Universitat, West Berlin, on the Austrian and German sources concerning the Armenian Genocide;
- Yves Ternon, historian and author, on the Armenian Genocide in the Ottoman Empire in 1915–1916;
- Joe Verhoeven, Professor at the Catholic University in Louvain, on the Armenian people and international law;

continues

continued

- Dikran Kouymjian, Professor at California State University, Fresno, on the destruction of Armenian historical monuments;

Having heard testimony from:

Mr. Papgen Indjirabian (France)
Mrs. Haigouhi Boyajian (United States)
Mr. Aram Gureghian (France)
Mr. Paul Nahabedian (United States)
Survivors of the massacres;

Having heard:

- a report written by and read for Professor Leo Kuper of the University of California at Los Angeles on the concept of genocide as it applies to the massacre of the Armenians;
- a memorandum written by and read for Professor Theo Van Boven, former Director of the U.N. Human Rights Division, on the deletion of the reference to the massacre of the Armenians when the issue was under study by the United Nations Human Rights Commission;

Having taken note of:

- the many documents presented by the rapporteurs of their reports, including the documents coming from British and, in particular, from German sources;
- the important and abundant body of documentation from American sources;
- the documentation on the Unionists' trial in 1919 and the trial of Soghomon Tehlirian held in Charlottenburg, Berlin, in 1921;
- the document entitled "The Armenian Problem: Nine Questions, Nine Answers" (Foreign Policy Institute, Ankara), stating the viewpoint of the current Turkish government;
- the testimony given by Professor Ataov of the University of Ankara to the Criminal Court in Paris in January 1984, which repeats the arguments of the Turkish government.

THE VERDICT

In answer to the questions which were put to it, the Tribunal hereby finds that:

- The Armenian population did and do constitute a people whose fundamental rights, both individual and collective, should have been and shall be respected in accordance with international law;
- the extermination of the Armenian population groups through deportation and massacre constitutes a crime of genocide not subject to statutory limitations within the definition of the Convention on the Prevention and Punishment of the Crime of Genocide of December 9, 1948. With respect to the condemnation of this crime, the aforesaid Convention is declaratory of existing law in that it takes note of rules which were already in force at the time of the incriminated acts;
- the Young Turk government is guilty of this genocide, with regard to the acts perpetrated between 1915 and 1917;

continues

continued

- the Armenian Genocide is also an "international crime" for which the Turkish state must assume responsibility, without using the pretext of any discontinuity in the existence of the state to elude that responsibility;
- this responsibility implies first and foremost to obligation to recognize officially the reality of this genocide and the consequent damages suffered by the Armenian people;
- the United Nations Organization and each of its members have the right to demand this recognition and to assist the Armenian people to that end,

Members of this Permanent People's Tribunal comprising the jury for the session on the Armenian Genocide:

Madjid Bellchikh (Algeria), Professor of International Law at the University of Algiers
Georges Casalis (France), theologian, Honorary Professor of the Institut Protesant de Theologie, Paris
Harald Edelstam (Sweden), former Ambassador to Chile and Algeria
Richard Falk (USA), Professor of International Law, Princeton University
Ken Fry (Australia), member of Parliament
Andrea Giardina (Italy), Professor of International Law at the University of Rome
Sean McBride (Ireland), jurist, President of the International Peace Office, Nobel Peace Prize laureate and Lenin Peace Prize winner, American Medal for Justice
Leo Matarasso (France), lawyer at the Paris Bar
Adolfo Perez Esquivel (Argentina), Nobel Peace Prize laureate, general coordinator of "Servicio Paz y Justicia en America Latina" (Service for Peace and Justice in Latin America)
James Petras (USA), Professor of Sociology, State University of New York at Binghamton
E'ranrois Rigaux (Belgium), Professor at the Faculty of Law of the Catholic University in Louvain
Ajit Roy (India), economist and journalist
George Wald (USA), Professor Emeritus of Biology, Harvard University, Nobel Prize for Physiology and Medicine, 1967

Source Document

TREATY OF SÈVRES

The Treaty of Sèvres was signed by the British Empire, Italy, France, Japan, Belgium, Greece, Poland, Portugal, Romania, Czechoslovakia, Yugoslavia, Hijaz, Armenia, and Turkey on August 10, 1920.

Article 226

The Turkish Government recognizes the right of the Allied Powers to bring before military tribunals persons accused of having committed acts in violation of the laws and customs of war. Such persons shall, if found guilty, be sentenced to punishments laid down by law. This provision will apply notwithstanding any proceedings or prosecution before a tribunal in Turkey or in the territory of her allies.

The Turkish Government shall hand over to the Allied Powers or to such one of them as shall so request all persons accused of having committed an act in violation of the laws and customs of war, who are specified either by name or by the rank, office or employment which they held under the Turkish authorities.

Article 227

Persons guilty of criminal acts against the nationals of one of the Allied Powers shall be brought before the military tribunals of that Power.

Persons guilty of criminal acts against nationals of more than one of the Allied Powers shall be brought before military tribunals composed of members of the military tribunals of the Powers concerned.

In every case the accused shall be entitled to name his own counsel.

Article 228

The Turkish Government undertakes to furnish all documents and information of every kind, the production of which may be considered necessary to ensure the full knowledge of the incriminating acts, the prosecution of offenders and the just appreciation of responsibility.

Article 229

The provisions of Articles 226 to 228 apply similarly to the Governments of the States to which territory belonging to the former Turkish Empire has been or may be assigned, insofar as concerns persons accused of having committed acts contrary to the laws and customs of war who are in the territory or at the disposal of such States.

If the persons in question have acquired the nationality of one of the said States, the Government of such State undertakes to take, at the request of all the Allied Powers, all the measures necessary to ensure the prosecution and punishment of such persons.

Article 230

The Turkish Government undertakes to hand over to the Allied Powers the persons whose surrender may be required by the latter as being responsible for the massacres committed during the continuance of the state of war on territory which formed part of the Turkish Empire on August 1, 1914.

The Allied Powers reserve to themselves the right to designate the tribunal which shall try the persons so accused, and the Turkish Government undertakes to recognize such tribunal.

continues

continued

In the event of the League of Nations having created in sufficient time a tribunal competent to deal with the said massacres, the Allied Powers reserve to themselves the right to bring the accused persons mentioned above before such tribunal, and the Turkish Government undertakes equally to recognize such tribunal.

The provisions of Article 228 apply to the cases dealt with in this Article.

ARMENIAN GENOCIDE, COURT-MARTIAL OF PERPETRATORS

The courts-martial set up by a succession of post–World War I Ottoman governments to try the authors of the Armenian Genocide constitute an important milestone in Turkish history and specifically in Turkish legal history. This is true even though the trials were incomplete and the atmosphere surrounding them was turbulent. Despite a legacy of impunity associated with decades of persecution and intermittent massacres of one of its principal minorities, the Armenians, a succession of postwar Ottoman governments felt constrained, if not compelled to institute criminal proceedings against a plethora of high-ranking officials and Young Turk Ittihadist party chieftains suspected of complicity in the wartime, empire-wide massacre of the Armenians.

This rather bold initiative was not unrelated to the near-complete defeat of the Ottoman Turkish armed forces at the end of World War I and the prospect of stiff terms being imposed upon the vanquished empire. Three types of Inquiry Commissions went to work to collect and evaluate incriminating material on the basis of which it was determined that there was enough evidence to warrant the institution of criminal proceedings against the prima facie suspects: 1) The Executive branch's Inquiry Commission, 2) The Legislative's Inquiry Commission, and 3) The Court Martial's own Inquiry Commission. In addition to collecting documents, each one of which was authenticated by competent ministerial officials with the notation, "it conforms to the original," the Administration's Inquiry Commission compiled a mass of pretrial interrogatory evidence through interrogatories administered to the suspects orally and in writing.

The formation of the court-martial was authorized through an imperial *irade* (written decree) on 16 December 1918. Another *irade* (on 25 December 1918) involving officials suspected of complicity in the atrocities declared that trial competence of areas not under siege by martial law will devolve upon existing criminal courts so as not to vitiate the terms of Article 88 of the Constitution setting forth the conditions of jurisdiction and venue. A third *irade* (on 8 January 1919) rendered the special court-martial operational for the trial of the perpetrators of "deportations and massacres" *(tehcir ve taktil)*. The military panel of judges included a presiding judge (or chief justice) with the rank of divisional general (in the present case, Mahmud Hayret Paşa, who in March 1919 was replaced by Mustafa Nazim Paşa) and two associate judges with the rank of general, brigadier general, or colonel. These were supplied by the Defense Ministry. The attorney-general and his deputies were provided by the Ministry of Justice.

Using location *(ratione loci)* as a major criterion for its organization, the court clustered the trials around those cities that served as principal sites for the mass murder, for example, Yozgat, Trabzon, Bayburt, Erzincan, Mosul. In addition there were certain series of trials through which were prosecuted, for example, Ittihad party responsible secretaries and delegates, and the ministers of the two wartime cabinets. All these trials took place in the edifice housing the Ottoman Parliament in Istanbul. The first, the Yozgat series, began on 5 February 1919; the rest stretched over eighteen months to July 1920. Several of the series overlapped. The start of the Trabzon series, for example, coincided with the fourteenth sitting of the Yozgat series (26 March 1919), with the latter ending at the eighteenth (7 April 1919). Between the fourteenth and the fifteenth sittings of the Trabzon trials (26 and 30 April 1919), the major cabinet trial series was started (28 April). The Trabzon series ended at the twentieth sitting (17 May 1919), and that of the cabinet ministers on 5 July 1919, after several interruptions, mainly caused by the transfer to Malta of most of the Ittihadist ministers. The rising tide of defiant nationalism in defeated Turkey caused the Sultan's government and the British authorities cooperating with it to fear a Bastille style storming of the prison where these ministers were being held. Hence the British, in a surprise move, enacted the transfer at the end of May 1919—with the tacit approval of the Sultan's government.

The Key Indictment, whose particulars, or the bill of charges, can also be found in the subsidiary indictments drawn up for the series of trials of less prominent Ittihadists, warrants attention because it is the only available prosecutorial statement that refers to evidence with proof of certification, indicating the nature of the array of documents lodged with the indictment. Many of these documents are top secret orders and coded telegrams. Others are admissions of guilt and related confessions from the accused who were subjected to pretrial interrogatories administered by examining magistrates. Still others are written statements and depositions from a number of civilian and military officials supplying testimony on the complicity of the defendants.

On 3 May 1919, the attorney-general's office formally notified the court that new offenses had been discovered in the course of the investigation conducted by the examining magistrates. The amended version of the indictment, [published in the supplements *ilâve,* of the official organ of the Ottoman government, *Takvimi Vekâyi,* no. 3571, pp. 128–132], also charges that these crimes were committed "in a particularly organized way" *(teşkilâti mürettebe ile),* when the deportee convoys were set upon and destroyed. They were perpetrated "in the capital and in the provinces." The preamble to the new indictment also speaks of "the extermination of an entire people constituting a distinct community," and of the existence in the evidentiary material secured by the court of "the admission and confession" of the defendants *(kabul ve itiraf)* [*ibid.*]. The original indictment maintained that these measures were neither due to specific incidents, nor were they limited to certain localities only [*Takvimi Vekâyi,* no. 3540, p. 5]. The court also asserted that the deportations were dictated neither by military necessity, nor did they constitute a disciplinary measure [*ibid.*]. The amended text of the indictment is even more explicit on this point. These deportations "were conceived and decided upon by Ittihad's Central Committee"; "[their] tragic consequences . . . were felt in almost every corner of the Ottoman Empire" *(Memaliki Osmaniyenin hemen her tarafnda)* [*Takvimi Vekâyi,* no. 3571, p. 130]. As in Nuremberg, so in Istanbul, the tribunal relied largely on authenticated documents in its possession rather than on courtroom testimony.

In the cabinet trials verdict [*Takvimi Vekâyi,* no. 3604, pp. 217–220], Enver,

Cemal, Talât, and Dr. Nazim were convicted and condemned to death; in the Harput trials, Dr. Sakir was likewise found guilty and condemned to death [*Takvimi Vekâyi,* no. 3771, pp. 1–2]; all these sentences were imposed in absentia. Several lesser functionaries were also condemned to death in absentia. From among those who were present at their trials, only three were convicted and hanged in Istanbul. In all its subsequent verdicts, the tribunal sustained the charges relating to the destruction of the Armenians, pointing to evidence on "the organization and implementation of the crime of murder *(taktil cinayeti)* by the leaders of Ittihad. This fact has been proven and verified *(tahakkuk).*" Neither the indictment nor the court-martial proceedings are generally accessible to scholars, and no Turkish author of date has produced any work examining the trials. There are rare and scattered references to some individual issues of *Takvimi Vekâyi* in the works of some contemporary Turkish authors, but no comprehensive index of this gazette that cover the proceedings.

After Grand Vizier, Damad Ferit's third cabinet fell on 2 October 1919, and the last Ottoman Sultan's position weakened substantially, the prosecutorial zeal of the court slackened considerably. About a year later, when Ferit's fifth and final cabinet was virtually forced out by the sweeping tide of Kemalism (21 October 1920), the courts-martial ceased functioning.

—*Vahakn N. Dadrian*

References and Recommended Reading

Akçam, Taner (1996). *Armenien und der Völkermord. Die Istanbuler Prozesse und die türkische Nationalbewegung.* Hamburg: Hamburger Edition, pp. 77–364. (German)

Dadrian, Vahakn N. (1986). The Naim-Andonian documents on the World War I destruction of Ottoman Armenians: The anatomy of a genocide. *International Journal of Middle East Studies,* 18 (3), 311–360.

Dadrian, Vahakn N. (1989). Genocide as a problem of national and international law: The World War I Armenian case and its contemporary legal ramifications. *Yale Journal of International Law,* 14 (2), 291–315.

Dadrian, Vahakn N. (1991). The documentation of the World War I Armenian massacres in the Proceedings of the Turkish Military Tribunal. *International Journal of Middle East Studies,* 23 (4), 549–576.

Dadrian, Vahakn N. (1997). The Turkish Military Tribunal's prosecution of the authors of the Armenian Genocide: Four major court-martial series. *Holocaust and Genocide Studies,* 11 (1), 28–59.

Source Document

TURKISH MILITARY TRIBUNAL'S VERDICT

Excerpts from the Official Transcript of the Sentence

July 5, 1919

During the course of this trial, having heard the petitions and statements of both the defense and the prosecution; having studied and examined in detail documents relating to this case; and after holding many consultations in the interest of the proper disposition of the matters under dispute, the following verdict is handed down . . . :

The Court Martial has confirmed the following . . . points which are irrefutable, substantiating the Attorney General's demand that a verdict of guilty be arrived at . . . :

(1) On the evidence of the trial which has taken place before this Military Court, it is obvious that the massacres which took place in the Kaza of Boghazliyan (Ankara), the San-

continues

continued

jak of Yozgat, and the Vilayet of Trebizond, were organized and perpetrated by the leaders of the Ittihad and Terakki Party. *[Crimes committed against the Armenians in other districts of the Ottoman Empire were covered by other Turkish trials.]*

(2) The Defense argued that news of these crimes were communicated (to the Party) only after they had been committed. But even if this hypothesis were true, it is plain that even after news was received of the atrocities, no steps were taken to prevent their repetition; nor were arrangements made for the punishment of the original criminals. . . .

The authors of the above-mentioned crimes, representing the moral person of the Ittihad and Terakki Party, are the members of its General Assembly, the fugitives—Prime Minister Talaat Pasha and Minister of War Enver Effendi, now expelled from his military career; Djemal Effendi, Minister of the Navy, likewise expelled from the service; Dr. Nazim, Minister of Education—these were the principal criminals *(fayili asli)* and their guilt has been determined by a unanimous vote. . . .

As to the sentences: punishment is to be meted to the abovementioned persons: Talaat, Enver, Djemal and Dr. Nazim, whose crimes were the greatest according to the first paragraph of the 45th Article of the Imperial Civil Penal C; also to be punished are Djavid, Mustafa Sheref and Musa Kiazim, by virtue of the second paragraph of the same Article and in accordance with the last paragraph of the 55th Article of the same Lawbook. . . .

In accordance therefore with the abovementioned paragraphs in the law code, Talaat, Enver, Djemal and Dr. Nazim are sentenced to death, and Djavid, Mustafa Sheref and Musa Kiazim are sentenced to fifteen years at hard labor . . .

These verdicts have been rendered unanimously, *in absentia* in the cases of Talaat, Enver, Djemal, Dr. Nazim; Djavid, as well as Mustafa Sheref, Osgan and Suleyman-el Boustani *Effendis;* and in the presence of Rifaat, Hashim, and Musa Kiazim *Beys.*

July 5, 1919, (signatures): Staff Lieutenant-General (Ahmed) Mustafa Nazim Bey, President of the Extraordinary Courts-Martial; Staff Major-General Ali Nazim, Member of the Extraordinary Courts-Martial; Infantry Colonel (Mehmed Ali) Rejeb Ferdi Bey, Member of the Extraordinary Courts-Martial."

Source: Published in the Official Gazette of Turkey *(Takvimi Vekâyi)*, no. 3604 (supplement), July 22, 1919. The transcript was translated into English by Haigazn K. Kazarian and published in the *Armenian Review,* 1971, 24.

ARMENIAN GENOCIDE, DOCUMENTATION OF

DOCUMENTATION OF ARMENIAN GENOCIDE IN GERMAN SOURCES

In terms of reliability and verifiability, no other single source may compare to the critical importance of official German records on the Armenian Genocide in documenting the capital crime of the genocide.

The exigencies, commitments and friendship ties associated with the Turko-German political and military alliance were compelling enough to constrain the German civilian and military officials stationed in wartime Turkey to protect the latter's reputation under any and all circumstances. For about six weeks after the start of the organized mass murder, many of these officials did just that; without any hesitation they embraced practically all charges the Turkish propaganda machine spread indiscriminately against the Armenians. However, the initially persuasive flair of the litany of Turkish claims and anti-Armenian charges attenuated itself in short order in the face of cumulative and incontrovertible evidence. The invented stories of widespread Armenian rebellion, crippling blows by Armenian insurgents to the Turkish war effort and consequently enormous Turkish losses, and many cases of Armenian espionage and sabotage acts eventually lost their original hold on believability as well as feasibility. The story that most irked the ambassadors was the one that was deemed to be the ultimate affront, namely, the claim that the Turkish government in all its solicitousness, was providing protective care to the deportees, feeding them and transporting them to new quarters for purposes of temporary "relocation." Another instance of affront was the companion claim that the government was limiting its operations of deportation only to the zones of war, sparing the rest of the Armenian population. These falsehoods and misrepresentations lasted only until the middle of June 1915, as far as the German ambassadors were concerned. In the second half of June 1915, the avalanche of reports from the consuls finally managed to jolt the ambassadors, jarring them loose from the grip of deceptive Turkish pronouncements.

From then on the dispatch of data to Berlin is a long ritual of accurate accounting and recounting which respect the truth of the macabre saga of the Armenian Genocide; it is a pathetic recitation of the reality that bears the imprimatur of the government of Imperial Germany, the ally of Imperial Ottoman Turkey. Many of the German officials, in particular Ambassadors Wangenheim, Metternich, Kühlmann and their deputies Hohenlohe and Neurath as well as German Consuls Büge (Adana), Holstein (Mosul), Rössler (Aleppo) reacted rather sharply to what they considered to be the duplicity of the Turkish authorities and in no uncertain terms specifically denounced Talât for disseminating "blatant lies" *(krasse Lügen).*

Count Wolff-Metternich: "The Turkish Government Has Refused to Be Deterred"

In its attempt to carry out its purpose to resolve the Armenian Question by the destruction of the Armenian race, the Turkish government has refused to be deterred neither by our representations, nor by those of the American embassy, nor by the delegate of the Pope, nor by the threats of the Allied Powers, nor in deference to the public opinion of the West representing one-half of the world.

—Count Wolff-Metternich, German Ambassador to the Ottoman Empire, July 10, 1916, Cable to the German Chancellor

The significance of the emergence of an attitude of decrial of an ally in wartime cannot be overestimated for it represents a dramatic confirmation of the facts of the Armenian Genocide the denial of which by the Turkish authorities provoked these decrials in the first place. The reliability of the respective German documents is further enhanced by the fact that they were prepared strictly for internal or in-house flow of communication purposes only; as such they precluded the possibility of containing propaganda or deliberate falsehood.

The German documentation is predicated upon three types of sources. First and foremost were the consuls, vice consuls and gerents who reported from the epicenters of the mass murder that fell within the jurisdiction of their districts, especially those of Trabzon, Adana,

Mosul, Aleppo and Erzurum. The second were those German military officers who operated within the ranks of the Turkish army, in particular, the Special Organization, and in the Ottoman Ministry of War. The third source is a succession of German ambassadors and their deputies. Their close contacts with high ranking Turkish government officials, their access to the Turkish agents conducting intelligence work within the circles of the Ittihadist leadership and the Turkish military, enabled them to collect valuable information about the secret aspects of the scheme of the genocide.

The documents generated may be subsumed under the following categories:

Premeditation

German Colonel Stange, a commander of a Special Organization Detachment, 8th Regiment, in his "secret" report to the German Military Mission to Turkey clearly states that the Armenians were being destroyed "pursuant to a plan conceived a long time ago" *(einen lang gehegten Plan).* Captain Scheubner-Richter, a co-commander of Special Organization Expeditionary Force, reported the same.

The Use of Convicts

Colonel Stange, Ambassador Wangenheim, Consuls Bergfeld (Trabzon), Rössler (Aleppo) have underscored the role of the "released felons" *(entlassene Sträflinge)* in the execution of the massacres.

The Pivotal Role of Ittihad's Operatives

Ambassadors Metternich and Kühlmann, Consuls Bergfeld, Rössler, Scheubner-Richter, repeatedly pointed out the systematic control the provincial commissars and chieftains of the Ittihad party exercised in the organization of the massacres in the provinces. In doing so, all of them directed attention to the massive scale of pillage and plunder attending the killing operations.

Genocidal Intent

The most decisive feature of the ensemble of these official documents is the recurrent theme that the objective of the central authorities was the eradication of the Armenian population and the termination of the Armenian presence in Turkey. In exposing the fraudulent aspect of the Turkish claims of "deportation for the purpose of relocation," nearly all these officials consistently and uniformly use the German terms of *Ausrottung, Vernichtung, Exterminierung* to convey their firm judgment that the intent of the perpetrators was nothing less than the wholesale destruction of the Armenian population of Turkey and that the survival of pockets of the victim population was mainly due to the inability of the authorities to complete the job.

Even though German documentation is compelling and as such it renders the historical reality of the Armenian Genocide both incontestable and verifiable, there is an ironic twist to this German contribution to irrefutable historical knowledge. Circumstantial as well as some direct evidence in German and Turkish sources, official and unofficial, are such as to implicate certain German authorities, military in particular, in the decision-making to eliminate the bulk of the Armenian population of the Ottoman Empire. The complicity at issue here primarily involves the acts of "suggesting" *(Anregung)* or "approving" *(Zusage)* the massive Armenian deportation that entailed the ultimate destruction of the victim population. German responsibility in the Armenian Genocide, therefore, attaches to the facts of German connivance and German support in various forms and at various levels of the lethal anti-Armenian measures instituted by the Ottoman-Turkish authorities during World War I.

—*Vahakn N. Dadrian*

References and Recommended Reading

Dadrian, Vahakn N. (1994). Documentation of the Armenian Genocide in German and Austrian

sources. In Charny, Israel W. (Ed.), *The Widening Circle of Genocide. Volume 3 in the Series, Genocide: A Critical Bibliographic Review.* New Brunswick, NJ: Transaction Publishers, pp. 77–125.
Dadrian, Vahakn N. (1996). *German Responsibility in the Armenian Genocide: A Review of the Historical Evidence of Complicity.* Cambridge, MA: Blue Crane Books.
Lepsius, Johannes (1919). *Deutschland und Armenien 1914–1918.* Berlin-Potsdam: Tempelverlag. (German)

DOCUMENTATION OF ARMENIAN GENOCIDE IN TURKISH SOURCES

The detailed examination of the 1915–1916 Armenian Genocide, whose perpetration was considerably facilitated through the opportunities of a global war, is encumbered by a host of factors. These include the persistence of the denial of the crime; the disappearance of the bulk of the records of the Central Committee of the Young Turks' Ittihad party; before their sudden and surreptitious escape to Germany at the end of the war, destruction by Talât, Enver and Cemal, the three arch leaders of Ittihad, of most of their personal documents; the burning, by virtue of official orders, of all telegraphic material dealing with Armenian deportations and massacres; and the burning of all the evidence on the activities of the Special Organization *(Teşkilâti Mahsusa)* by one of its chiefs, Eşref Kuşcubaşi. The problem is further compounded by the use of special telegraphic apparatuses that Talât and Enver had installed in their homes to relay highly secret orders informally rather than formally. These orders often were intended for the purpose of countermanding previously relayed formal orders.

Through a number of randomly surviving Turkish official documents, it has been possible nevertheless to verify the facts of the Armenian Genocide. These documents may be subsumed under the following categories:

The Archives of the Turkish Military Tribunal

In order to be able to successfully prosecute the authors of the genocide, the Tribunal assembled as many sets of documents as it could [see ARMENIAN GENOCIDE: COURT-MARTIAL OF PERPETRATORS].

The Inquiry Commission of the Fifth Committee of the Ottoman Chamber of Deputies (Beşinci Şube Tahkikat Komisyonu)

This Commission interrogated, orally and in writing, the Ministers of the two wartime Cabinets, including the two Seyhulislams (the chief religious official in the Ottoman Empire) involved, who had not yet fled. Among the many revelations made in the course of these interrogations was the admission of ex-Grand Vizier Said Halim that the Special Organization was created without the approval of the Cabinet and that it functioned outside the purview of the government. He also admitted that the order for deportation was used to "kill" the deportees. Ex-Justice Minister Ibrahim in his testimony revealed that "a significant number *(mühim bir yekün)* of convicts" were released from the prisons and enrolled in the ranks of the Special Organization.

Parliamentary Debates

Similar admissions and voluntary confessions were made during these debates in the October-December 1918 Armistice period. Mehmed Hafiz, Deputy from Trabzon, for example, a lawyer by profession, admitted on 11 December 1918 in the Chamber of Deputies seeing personally how the Armenians were being loaded into a barge, taken to the high seas and drowned. He added that this practice reportedly was followed by the governor-general of Trabzon throughout that province located on the Black Sea coastal region. In the Senate, the President, Ahmed Riza, on 19 October 1918 in his inaugural speech, decried "the savagery" with which the Ottoman Armenians were murdered *(vahşiyane ödürülen Ermeniler)*. Senator Reşid Akif, a distinguished Ottoman statesman, on 21 November 1918, delivered a speech in the Senate in which he admitted seeing in the office of the President of the State Council a secret Ittihad party document, a circular, ordering provincial party functionaries to commence with the massacres *(mukatelei zalime)* through the brigands *(çetes)*, as soon as deportations started.

Additionally, there is a plethora of personal memoirs, foremost among which is that of former General Ali Fuad Erden, the Chief of Staff of IVth Army Commander Cemal Paşa. In it the general categorically declares that the claim of relocation of the deportees was unfounded since "there was neither preparation, nor organization to shelter the hundreds of thousands of deportees." Another author, the distinguished Turkish popular historian, Ahmed Refik (Altinay), who served in Department II, Intelligence, of the Ottoman General Staff, concluded in his memoirs that "the aim of Ittihad was to destroy the Armenians" *(Ermenileri imha etmek)*, and that "the greatest crimes against the Armenians were committed by the brigands of the Special Organization" *(en büyük cinayetleri bu çeteler ika ettiler)*.

By way of reconstructing all this evidentiary material, one gets the following general picture about the essential features of the organization of the Armenian Genocide. As a first step the targeted population was critically debilitated through the conscription of all able-bodied men in connection with the General Mobilization that then neutral Turkey instituted in the wake of signing on 2 August 1914 a secret military and political alliance with Kaiser's Germany. The next step coincides with the actual initiation of the genocide when in the spring of 1915 thousands of leading Armenian intellectuals, educators, clergymen, lawyers, merchants and other Armenian notables in all corners of the Ottoman Empire were, by synchronized surprise nightly raids, arrested and deported; very few of them escaped the ensuing operations of liquidation. Through these draconian measures the entire Armenian community was not only decapitated but was also terrorized. Istanbul Police Chief Bedri boasted to American Ambassador Henry Morgenthau that the gruesome details of the torture, to which the arrested community leaders were being subjected, "were matters of nightly discussions at the headquarters" of Ittihad, and that the perpetrators "were constantly ransacking their brains in the effort to devise some new torment." An ancillary method of terror was the creation of spectacles of public hangings in large cities of the empire.

The next and in fact most lethal step was the massive deportation of the bulk of the Armenian population consisting almost entirely of women, children and old men. Ostensibly they were being deported for the purpose of "relocation" in settlements supposedly prepared for them by the government in the deserts of Mesopotamia. In fact, however, many of the deportee convoys, those from eastern Turkey in particular, were set upon by specially engaged gangs of convicts and brigands, led by carefully selected regular army officers and were mercilessly massacred while en route. In the provinces of Bitlis, Harput, Erzurum, and parts of Van, the majority of the victims were dispatched *in loco* or within the provincial boundaries. In Muş Plain, comprising some 90 Armenian villages of various sizes, about 80,000 Armenians were burned to death in stables and haylofts. In Trabzon province, on the Black Sea littoral, some 50,000 Armenians, and in the Euphrates and its tributaries countless others were destroyed through drowning operations. Those who managed to escape or survive these and other lethal deportation mechanisms and arrived in Mesopotamia in wretched condition, especially those from western and southwestern Anatolia, were subjected in the summer of 1916 to new rounds of ferocious massacres improvised by the government in the areas of Deir Zor, Rakka, Ras ül Ain and Chabur to get rid of them as fast as possible. It is estimated that some 150,000 Armenians were thus annihilated in a "secondary" stage of the genocide. According to official Turkish statistics, 800,000 were killed in the course of deportations, exclusive of the soldiers and officers who were murdered by fellow military, and the multitudes of orphans, young girls and women who were forcibly converted to Islam, were pressed into concubinage or driven into harems. Countless other women, both young and old, were raped before being murdered; those who resisted were mutilated and then killed.

The evidence is conclusive that the Armenian Genocide was premeditated, and centrally planned, and that its conception, organization, supervision and implementation were primarily, if not exclusively, the work of Ittihad party's Central Committee functioning as a shadowy but omnipotent governing body in control of the regular organs of the state. This very same conclusion is succinctly articulated by Ottoman 3rd Army Commander General Vehib in whose command zone most of the massacres were enacted prior to his assuming command, and which massacres he personally investigated through a court-martial he personally instituted in the summer of 1916. Here is his statement: "The massacre and destruction of the Armenians and the plunder of pillage of their goods were the results of decision reached by Ittihad's Central Committee. . . . The atrocities were carried out under a program that was determined upon and involved a definite case of premeditation *(mukarrer bir program ve mutlak bir kasd tahtinda)*. . . . The executioners consisted of gallows birds and of gendarmes with blood on their hands and blood in their eyes *(eli gözü kanli jandarmalar)*. . . . One can find no such examples of atrocity and savagery in the annals of Islam *(tarihi Islamda misli görülmemiş bir zulum)*. . . . Divine justice may be delayed but it is not to be forfeited *(Adaleti Allahiyede imhal var ihmal yoktur)*."

—*Vahakn N. Dadrian*

References and Recommended Reading

Dadrian, Vahakn N. (1994). The complicity of the party, the government, and the military: Selected parliamentary and judicial documents on the Armenian Genocide in official Turkish records. *Journal of Political and Military Sociology*, Special Issue, 22(1), 29–96.

Dadrian, Vahakn N. (1994). Documentation of the Armenian Genocide in Turkish sources. In Charny, Israel W. (Ed.), *Genocide: A Critical Bibliographic Review. Volume 2.* London: Mansell Publishing; and New York: Facts on File, pp. 86–138.

Dadrian, Vahakn N. (1995). *The History of the Armenian Genocide: Ethnic Conflicts from the Balkans to Anatolia to the Caucasus.* 3rd revised edition. Providence, RI: Berghahn Books.

Dadrian, Vahakn N. (1999). *The Key Elements in the Turkish Denial of the Armenian Genocide: A Case Study of Destruction and Falsification.* Cambridge, MA: Zoryan Institute.

Source Document

TELEGRAMS BY TURKISH LEADERS ORDERING THE ARMENIAN GENOCIDE

September 3, 1915

We recommend that the operations which we have ordered you to make shall first be carried out on the men of the said people, and that you shall subject the women and children to them also. Appoint reliable officials for this.

(signed) Minister of the Interior
Talaat

September 16, 1915

It was first communicated to you that the Government, by order of the Jemiyet, had decided to destroy completely all Armenians living in Turkey. Those who oppose this order and decision cannot remain on the official staff of the Empire. An end must be put to their existence, however criminal the measures taken may be, and no regard must be paid to age, or sex, or to conscientious scruple.

(signed) Minister of the Interior
Talaat

November 15, 1915

From interventions which have recently been made by the American Ambassador at Constantinople on behalf of his government, it appears that the American consuls are obtaining information by secret means. In spite of our assurances that the Armenian deportations will be accomplished in safety and comfort, they remain unconvinced. Be careful that events attracting attention shall not take place in connection with those who are near the cities or other centers. From the point of view of the present policy it is important that foreigners who are in those parts shall be persuaded that the expulsion of the Armenians is in truth only deportation. For this reason it is important that, to save appearances, for a time a show of gentle dealing shall be made, and the usual measures be taken in suitable places. It is recommended as very important that the people who give information shall be arrested and handed over to the military authorities for trial by court-martial.

(signed) Minister of the Interior
Talaat

January 10, 1916

Inquiries having been made, it is understood that hardly ten per cent of the Armenians subjected to the general transportation have reached their destinations; the rest have died from natural causes, such as hunger and sickness. We inform you that we are working to bring about the same result with regard to those who are still alive, by using severe measures.

(signed) Abdulahad Nuri

Credit: Cited in Housepian, Marjorie (1966). "The Unremembered Genocide." *Commentary,* 42(3), 55–60. Authenticated by Dadrian, Vahakn N. (1986). The Naim-Adonian documents of the World War I destruction of the Ottoman Armenians: The anatomy of genocide, *International Journal of Middle East Studies,* 18(3), 311–360.

DOCUMENTATION OF ARMENIAN GENOCIDE IN US ARCHIVES

The United States National Archives and Library of Congress contain a microfiche set of 37,000 pages of documentation on the Armenian Genocide. It is accompanied by a 476-page *Guide*. The project was completed and edited by historian Rouben Paul Adalian, who is Director of the Armenian National Institute in Washington, DC.

The collection includes some 4,500 documents found in official US archives, thousands of which are previously unexamined and unpublished. All of the records in the publication are copies of the original documents written contemporaneously to the events described in them. The materials cover every aspect of the genocide process.

The United States National Archives holds the most comprehensive documentation in the world on the Armenian Genocide. After war broke out between the Ottoman Empire and the Allies in November 1914, the United States was left as the sole major neutral Western state with official representation at the court of the sultan. A US presence continued throughout most of the war, and Americans were on site for relief efforts afterward. A complete picture can thus be found in these documents from the Department of State and other government agencies [which] relate in chilling detail the entire process by which the Armenian population of the Ottoman Empire was made the subject of a racial policy aimed at destroying all vestiges of its existence in Armenia and Anatolia.

The *Guide* contains a complete list of documents, a Names Index and a Subject Index. Among the many key subjects covered by the documents are: methods of deportation; deportation policy; mistreatment of women and children; use of slave labor; malnutrition; forced conversions; confiscation of property; cases of resistance; and, of course, massacres. Major players are identified within the categories: Young Turk government; Young Turk officials; German officials; and others. The aftermath of the genocide is also recorded under topics such as: orphanages; refugee camps; resettlement of survivors; and humanitarian intervention.

These documents also preserve a piece of American history. They tell of valiant diplomats, like Ambassador Morgenthau, who did everything within their personal and professional means to end the carnage. Up to 1914, Great Britain, France, and Russia had been the states most involved with the question of the Armenian people in the Ottoman Empire. After war broke out between the Ottomans and the Allies in November 1914, the United States, which remained neutral until 1917, was left as the sole major Western state with official representation in the Ottoman capital of Constantinople still interested in the fate of the Armenians. In 1915, the Ottoman government, under the control of the Young Turk Committee, began implementing a policy to annihilate the Armenians of the empire through deportations and massacres. The United States Embassy in Constantinople immediately became the focal point for those reporting on the escalating violence directed against the Armenian population of the Ottoman state.

Apart from the Embassy in the capital, the United States maintained consular posts in a number of cities in Turkey, including Smyrna (present-day Izmir), Trebizond, Mersin, Harput (or Kharpert), Aleppo, Beirut, and Jerusalem. The presence of American consuls at two of these sites proved crucial for closely monitoring developments in the spring and summer of 1915 when the Ottoman government proceeded to expel the Armenians from their homes and to deport them toward the Syrian Desert. Masses of Armenians were moved through the Harput region on the Euphrates as the point of exit for the population of Armenia proper and their exodus to the south. But as was the case at Harput, where the vast majority of the deportees were destroyed within the confines of the province itself, large-scale massacres at isolated spots en route to the desert often decimated the victim population considerably. Many convoys of deportees from Armenia and Anatolia were sent on to Aleppo. From there and other collection centers further east, they were marched into the desert and left to die of thirst and exposure. Others were sent to specific killing sites, such as Ras-ul-Ain and Deir-el-Zor. On a regular basis, the American consuls at Harput and Aleppo kept the United States Embassy in Constantinople informed of the arrival of the exhausted refugees from the interior and the departure of the condemned toward the desert.

The interest of Americans in the condition of the Armenian people in Turkey grew largely out of a near century-long association between American missionaries and Armenians of the Middle East. The missionaries had established a vast network of institutions (schools, hospitals, churches) throughout the Ottoman Empire, which serviced mainly the Armenian population. American missions were located in some of the major cities of Anatolia—Sivas, Kayseri, Marash, Hadjin, Adana, Aintab, Urfa—and further east in historic Armenia—Harput, Bitlis, Erzerum, and Van. Thousands of Armenian survivors of earlier massacres had become wards of the American mission orphanages. The missionaries witnessed the daily tribulations of Armenians living under Turkish rule and, when the deportations began, became an additional source of direct information on the fate of the Armenians in the Ottoman Empire.

Independent of the consuls and the missionaries, the United States Embassy also received reports from citizens of other neutral countries, such as Sweden, Denmark, and Switzerland, and heard directly from Armenians who had survived their own particular ordeals. Alarmed at the increasing frequency of the reports of mistreatment, deportation and massacres, Henry Morgenthau, United States Ambassador to Turkey, reached the conclusion that a systematic effort was under way to liquidate the Armenian population. In a series of reports, Ambassador Morgenthau relayed his findings to the Secretary of State in Washington. His cables included the consular reports substantiating the rumors in circulation that the Armenians in Turkey were in the throes of a state-organized campaign aimed at their wholesale annihilation under the guise of a resettlement policy. In addition, the Department of State received correspondence from diplomatic sources outside the Ottoman Empire who had obtained evidence further substantiating the charge that a policy of genocide was in progress in the Ottoman Empire.

Persuaded of the gravity of the danger faced by the Armenian population, the Department of State authorized Ambassador Morgenthau to submit formal protests to the appropriate Ottoman officials. It instructed him also to warn the representatives of Germany, Turkey's ally in World War I, that, under the circumstances, their government too would be held accountable for failing to intervene in order to stop the indiscriminate killings. At the same time, Congress gave its approval for setting up a private agency, the American Committee for Armenian and Syrian Relief (better known as Near East Relief) to raise funds in the

United States for aid to the Armenian deportees. The ambassadors, consuls, and missionaries, in addition to the relief workers who arrived mainly after the end of the war, played key roles in disbursing aid to the Armenians in spite of regular interference from Ottoman officials, and, for some, at risk to their own lives.

Formal relations between the United States and the Ottoman Empire were severed in April 1917 after Congress declared war on Germany. However, the United States never declared war on Germany's ally, the Ottoman Empire, nor did it engage in hostilities against the Ottoman Empire. United States personnel returned to Constantinople upon the signing of the Mudros Armistice, which brought an end to the war in the Middle East in October 1918. After the war, Near East Relief was instrumental in providing shelter for thousands of orphans, rescuing hundreds of women from their abductors, and feeding and clothing tens of thousands of survivors. President Woodrow Wilson's Fourteen Points, with its pronounced commitment to the principle of self-determination for the oppressed peoples of the Ottoman Empire, kept the United States all the more involved in Middle Eastern affairs after the end of the Great War. Hence, throughout most of the critical years from 1915, when the extermination of the Armenians began, to 1923 when the Republic of Turkey was established and the era of deportations and massacres ended, Americans were on site in the region. They reported in detail from direct observation and through eyewitness accounts the entire course of events that enveloped the Armenian people.

Because of the multiplicity of places from which these reports originated, and their wide geographic distribution, a fairly complete picture of the Armenian Genocide can be formed with the documentation in the United States Archives.

At the local level, Consul Leslie Davis in Harput and, most exceptionally, Consul Jesse Jackson in Aleppo proved to be men of extraordinary fortitude and industry; other consuls who were equally steadfast in their duties, G. Bie Ravndal in Constantinople and W. Stanley Hollis in Jerusalem might be mentioned. The names of the ambassadors are better known, and Abram Elkus, who succeeded Henry Morgenthau, appears to have altered none of the procedures introduced during Morgenthau's tenure in transmitting all the evidence that found its way to the United States Embassy in Constantinople. For Henry Morgenthau, saving the Armenian population became a cause that he championed in and out of office. His sense of alarm as he grew aware of the scale of the campaign to eradicate the Armenians was conveyed to Secretary of State William Jennings Bryan, and his successor, Robert Lansing, in no uncertain words. They resonate to this day as the most riveting pronouncements on the fate of the Armenians in the Ottoman Empire. The unfolding tragedy made no less an impression on President Woodrow Wilson. Wilson's policies, during and after the war, were in part formed by his sympathies for populations particularly victimized by German and Turkish militarism.

What makes these reports, cables, communiques, and even simple receipts exceptional is the fact they were handled as routine business in uncommon circumstances. Only in retrospect does the full evidence begin to shed light on the magnitude of the Armenian catastrophe.

—*Rouben Paul Adalian*

References and Recommended Reading

Adalian, Rouben Paul, compiler and editor (1994). *Guide to Armenian Genocide in the U.S. Archives 1915–1918*. Alexandria, VA: Chadwyck Healey.

ARMENIAN GENOCIDE, INTERNATIONAL RECOGNITION OF

During and immediately after World War I, the atrocities committed against the Armenians of the Ottoman Empire were public knowledge. In their May 24, 1915 joint declaration, the Allied Powers, namely Great Britain, France, and Russia had accused the Young Turk regime of crimes against humanity and civilization. In 1919 the postwar Ottoman government prosecuted a number of Young Turk conspirators of the crimes of massacre and plunder. By signing the Treaty of Sèvres on August 10, 1920, Turkey obligated itself to the apprehension of those "responsible for the massacres." The international community did not question at the time the veracity of the reports on the extermination of the Armenians.

Developments intervening between the first quarter and the last quarter of the twentieth century, however, altered public perception and created the conditions for the denial of the Armenian Genocide. This regressive transformation in historical memory became the basis of the search by later generations of Armenians, descendants of the survivors, to seek international reaffirmation of the Armenian Genocide as a gesture of public acknowledgment of the terrible sufferings endured and of the crime committed against their forebears.

In 1923 the international community abandoned the Armenians when the European Powers agreed to the Treaty of Lausanne in which Turkey was absolved of further responsibility for the consequences of the policies of the expired Ottoman state. Turkey took license from this posture to embark upon a policy of denial, suppression of public discussion, and prevention of any official mention of the criminal treatment of the Armenians. The mood in Europe of escape from the horrors of WW I, isolationism in the US, and revolutionary utopianism in Russia, further stigmatized the Armenian survivors as witnesses of a catastrophe policy-makers and the public wanted to forget or bury. World War II, however, brought the problem of mass extermination into sharp relief as the revelation of the Holocaust revived the sense of international obligation toward victimized peoples. As this sense of duty to a moral order respectful of human life and of the dignity of the individual became embodied in a number of international covenants forged under the auspices of the United Nations, Armenians began to find renewed hope that their case would receive attention again. The 1948 *Convention on the Prevention and Punishment of the Crime of Genocide* attached a label to mass slaughter and a new word entered the postwar political vocabulary: *genocide.* With it came the realization among Armenians that they had been victims of a crime that at the time still lacked a name.

To retrieve the memory of their forgotten genocide, Armenians worldwide in their diaspora domiciles initiated efforts for national and international recognition. These began with the introduction of commemorative resolutions in the United States Congress in 1975 and with efforts to enter the subject on the record at the UN, which occurred with the 1985 adoption of a report on genocide by the UN Commission on Human Rights. In 1987 broader recognition was achieved with the adoption of a resolution by the European Parliament, which stated that "the tragic events of 1915–1917 . . . constitute genocide." In the following years, the legislatures of countries such as Belgium, Canada, Cyprus, France, Greece, and Russia adopted resolutions affirming the historical record on the Armenian Genocide. Acknowledgment also came through declarations by heads of states and pronouncements by legislators. Among these have been the statements issued by presidents of the United States and many members of Congress on or about April 24 extending official condolences to the Armenian people on their day of mourning, although, bowing to Turkish goverment pressure, US presidents to date have avoided the word *genocide.* These efforts have contributed to greater media attention and the education of the broader public about the legacy of genocide in the twentieth century. The continued denial by the Republic of Turkey, however, has created conditions, which in the view of many Armenians, necessitates the continuation of the search for international reaffirmation until such time as acknowledgment is made universal and irreversible.

—*Rouben Paul Adalian*

References and Recommended Reading

Sassounian, Harut (1995). *The Armenian Genocide: Documents and Declarations 1915–1995.* Glendale, CA: 80th Anniversary of the Armenian Genocide Commemorative Committee. (Pamphlet)

ARMENIAN GENOCIDE, MISSIONARIES AND

Missionaries were the first foreign eyewitnesses of the Armenian Genocide. With their successful evangelizing among Armenians of the Ottoman Empire, Protestant missionaries, mostly associated with the American Board of Commissioners for Foreign Missions (ABCFM), had created an extensive network of school, orphanages, hospitals, and colleges across Anatolia and Armenia. On account of US neutrality during the first three years of World War I, the missionaries were allowed to stay in the Ottoman Empire. Their institutions, however, were devastated by the destruction of the Armenian population. The missionaries made heroic attempts to provide for the care and feeding of the destitute, especially orphans, only to face hardships of their own at the hands of Turkish officials. Attempts to provide refuge proved futile and only provoked the ire of the government, which came to look upon them with increasing suspicion. Next to the US consuls, the American missionaries collectively became the second most important group of witnesses to the Armenian Genocide. Virtually every mission sent reports, which together with the official consular communiques, came to constitute the body of English-language eyewitness and documentary evidence about the Ottoman policy of extermination filed with the American Embassy in Constantinople and forwarded to the US Department of State in Washington. Many of these reports were compiled by Arnold Toynbee, then a young historian, and were published in Lord (James) Bryce's, *The Treatment of Armenians in the Ottoman Empire,* presented to the British Parliament in 1916 as proof of "the gigantic crime that devastated the Near East in 1915." While the Department of State classified the cables from the Embassy in Constantinople as confidential, the ABCFM was able to release the contents of the reports it received and alerted the US media and the American public. Formal US reaction to the deportations and massacres did not go beyond verbal protests to the Ottoman government. Strong public sympathy generated by the atrocity reports, however, helped in subsequent relief efforts. Swiss, Danish, and German missionaries also witnessed the Armenian Genocide. Johannes Lepsius of the Deutsche-Orient Mission, whose wartime report was suppressed by Germany upon the protest of the Turkish government, with the authorization of the postwar German government published *Deutschland und Armenien 1914–1918: Samlung diplomatischer Ak-*

American Missionaries Are Witnesses to the Armenian Genocide

American missionaries who went to Turkey as "witnesses to Christ" became, during the Armenian deportations of World War I, "witnesses to genocide." Research by Suzanne Elizabeth Moranian at the University of Wisconsin is based on the papers of the American Board of Commissioners for Foreign Missions housed at Harvard University. Scattered in stations from Istanbul throughout the interior of Turkey, the American missionaries were well acquainted with Ottoman society, spoke the native languages, and were well positioned to know the true fate of the Armenians during World War I. "The missionary accounts undercut the central Turkish claim that the Armenians were seditious," Moranian said. The validity of the missionary accounts can be seen in the fact that they corroborate each other even in cases where the authors had no contact and served in different stations. There was no motive for the missionaries to falsify in these reports. While it is true that the missionaries were sympathetic to the Armenians, they were in no sense against the Turks; on the contrary, they never deserted their initial aim which was to convert Muslims.

—*Internet on the Holocaust and Genocide*

tenstucke (1919), the second important volume of documentary evidence released during the time of the Genocide.

—*Rouben Paul Adalian*

References and Recommended Reading

Moranian, Suzanne E. (1994). *The American Missionaries and the Armenian Question: 1915–1927.* Ann Arbor, MI: UMI Ph.D. Dissertation at the University of Wisconsin, Madison.

ARMENIAN GENOCIDE MEMORIAL IN YEREVAN, ARMENIA

The Armenian Genocide Memorial in Yerevan was built in response to unauthorized and spontaneous mass demonstrations held in 1965 in the capital city of then Soviet Armenia to mark the fiftieth anniversary of the Armenian Genocide. Designed by the architects Arthur Tarkhanian, Sashur Kalashian, and the sculptor Hovhannes Khachaturian, the memorial, which was completed in 1967, overlooks Yerevan from the hilltop called Tsitesrnakaberd (Swallow's Fort).

The monument consists of two parts, a round Memorial Sanctuary and the Obelisk of Rebirth. Devoid of any decorative detail, the monument is a statement in subdued artistry. The Memorial Hall is composed of twelve basalt stelae arranged in a circle around an eternal flame at the center of the rotunda. Stairs between the stelae lead visitors inside the Memorial Hall, wherein a sense of enclosure is created by the massive walls leaning inward over the open platform around the eternal flame.

The nearby obelisk in a narrow pyramidal shape stretching forty meters into the sky symbolizes the revival of Armenia. The obelisk consists of two portions, a smaller pyramid representing the Diaspora encased by the larger representing Armenia. From a distance, the obelisk and the leaning stelae appear as contrasting silhouettes, one hugging the earth, with the other reaching for the sky. The rotunda of stelae also echoes the conical roof over Armenian church domes thereby subliminally reenforcing the memorial's connection with spirituality evoked through an archetypal structure.

The Armenian Genocide Memorial in Yerevan, Armenia, June 1998. (Photographed by Rouben Paul Adalian)

The entire complex is composed of three other understated architectural elements. A high wall runs at a distance parallel to a long walkway leading to the plaza upon which the memorial stands. By imposing a separation with the space beyond, the barrier directs the attention of the visitor toward the monument. The walkway obligates the visitor to traverse a ceremonial distance from its starting point at the remote end of the hilltop. It is also designed to create a reverential atmosphere as the visitor approaches the Memorial Sanctuary from the outside and finally descends into the rotunda enclosed by the stelae whose massive proportions are only felt from the depth of the memorial space.

During the Communist era, the monument remained without any inscriptions as a compromise to Soviet foreign policy on the memorial's potential implications to relations with neighboring Turkey. In 1998 the basalt wall lining the walk was inscribed with the names of all the major sites of the Armenian Genocide with Deir-el-Zor, the final destination of the deportations, as the last name at the end of the wall nearest the monument.

The first monument to the Armenian Genocide was raised in the 1950s in the compound of the Armenian Catholicosate in Antelias, Lebanon. Built in the form of a memorial chapel, it housed a collection of bones recovered from mass graves in the Syrian Desert. In 1965 a monument in the form of multiple cross-stones in the traditional style of Armenian medieval stone carving was erected on the grounds of the Armenian Catholicosate at Echmiadsin, in then Soviet Armenia. Beginning in the 1960s, Armenian diaspora groups began raising monuments in their respective communities.

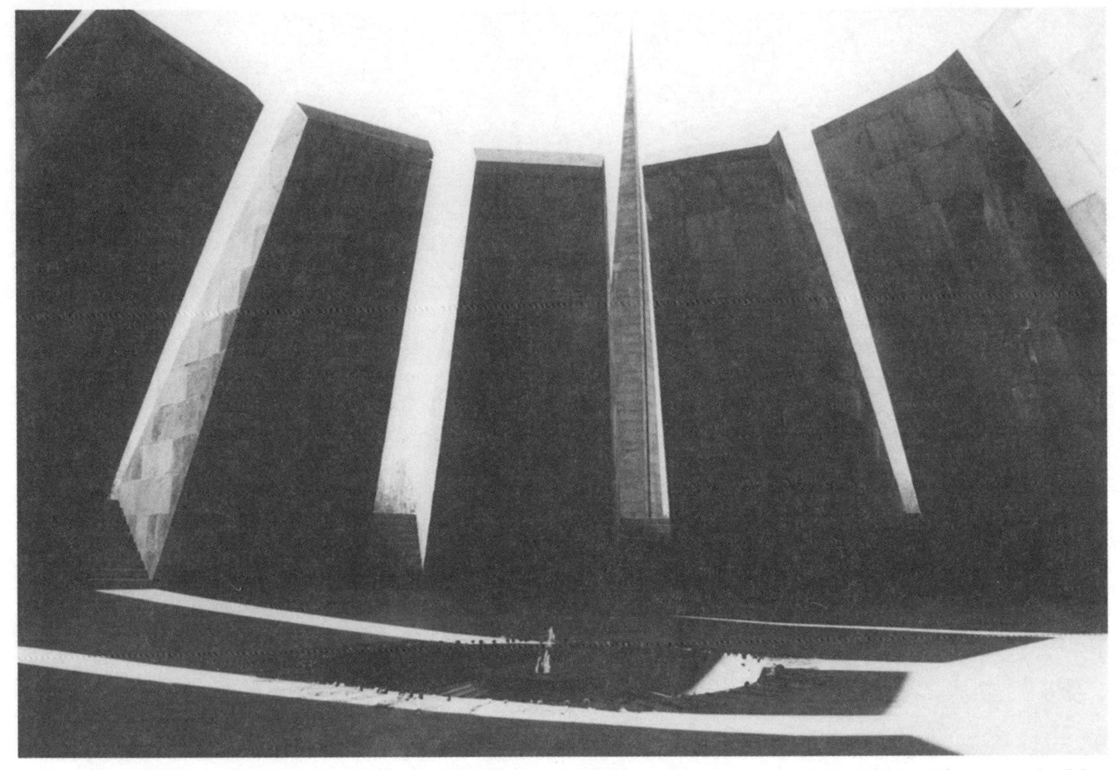

The eternal flame at the Armenian Genocide Memorial in Yerevan, Armenia, June 1998. (Photographed by Rouben Paul Adalian)

Some were placed in civic localities and their construction did not go without protest from the Turkish government. Large monuments stand in Montebello, California; Sydney, Australia; Sao Paolo, Brazil; and Buenos Aires, Argentina. Smaller monuments may be found in virtually all Armenian communities around the world including such places as Marseilles, Vienna, Stuttgart, Toronto, Montreal, Detroit, Philadelphia, and Montevideo. In 1990 a memorial chapel was constructed at Deir-el-Zor, Syria, the only monument to stand at a site associated with the Armenian Genocide. In the 1970s and 1980s many monuments were raised in the towns and cities of Soviet Armenia that had been settled by refugees and survivors. The introduction of physical monuments in Armenia, however, was proceeded in earlier decades by another phenomenon, the naming of new towns in memory of the lost communities of West Armenia, Cilicia, and Asia Minor.

Because of its central location and its grand and somber design, the Tsitesernakaberd memorial is now deeply seated in the popular imagination as the universal monument to the Armenian Genocide. It has become a place of pilgrimage for the entire Armenian nation. Throngs of up to a million persons make a silent journey from the city of Yerevan and its environs to the hilltop monument every April 24, each person bearing a single flower. By day's end a circular wall of flowers up to six feet high is constructed around the eternal flame in memory of the victims of the Armenian Genocide.

—*Rouben Paul Adalian*

References and Recommended Reading

Manukian, S. (1996). The Influence of the Armenian Genocide on the Arts: Monumental Art. In *Encyclopedia of the Armenian Question* (Edited by Kostandin Khudaverdian). Yerevan: Armenian Encyclopedic Publisher. (Armenian)

Philadelphia Armenian Monument

A public monument in Philadelphia about the Armenian Genocide is Young Meher by the sculptor Khoren Der Harootian (1909–1991). This 22 foot high monument is located next to the Philadelphia Museum of Art and is under the custody of the Fairmount Park Commission. Executed in 1975 in bronze and dedicated on April 24, 1976, the sculpture Meher symbolizes the "invincible faith of the Armenian people," its long history and "Day of Infamy, April 24, 1915." The bas-relief on the East side of the sculpture depicts a vulture peering over a field of skeletons. Meher, the subject of the title, is a legendary figure from the Middle Ages symbolizing the spirit of the Armenians. Born in Armenia, Der Harootian received his art education at the Worcester (Massachusetts) Museum School. For many years he lived in Jamaica before moving to New York.

—*Stephen C. Feinstein*

Philadelphia Armenian Monument (© Fairmont Park Commission)

ART OF THE HOLOCAUST, GENOCIDE, AND FUTURISTIC DESTRUCTION

ART OF THE HOLOCAUST

Holocaust survivors have suggested that art, in any form, can never conceptualize the Shoah. The artist R.B. Kitaj, whose paintings are dense with Holocaust imagery, agrees and has noted that the role of the artist who deals with the subject must be troublesome and elusive: "The fact is that no one can touch anything but its shadow . . . ."

Art Created in the Camps and in Hiding

At Terezin, in other camps, and in hiding, Jewish artists and even children without training created an array of a visual response that stands as a "visual memoir" to the camp experience, especially the tragedies of everyday life that are not documented by photography.

Through the art of the camps, the entire story of the Holocaust can be told. Artists like Bedrich Fritta, Otto Ungar, and Freidl Brandeis-Dicker exposed the movie-set world of Terezin. Leo Haas's drawings dramatize daily survival in Nisko while Roman Kramztyk, Halina Olomucki and Maurcy Bromberg documented the travail of life in the Warsaw Ghetto. [For more information of these and other artists of the camps, see Blatter, Janet, and Milton, Sybil (1981). *Art of the Holocaust.* New York: Routledge; and Constanza, Mary (1982). *The Living Witness.* New York: Free Press.] Felix Nussbaum, deported on the last train from Belgium to Auschwitz, left a fantastic visual record of his own persecution. These works are now preserved in a new museum dedicated to Nussbaum in Osnabruck. One of the most prolific artists of the Holocaust was Charlotte Salomon, a twenty-five-year-old woman who painted 765 paintings during 1941–1942 when she was in hiding. The series entitled *Life or Theater?* suggests the drama of optimism against a sea of pessimistic reality. [The most complete edition of the gouaches of Charlotte Salomon are found in Salomon, Charlotte (1981). *Life or Theatre?* New York: Viking Press. See also the biography of Salomon by Felstiner, Mary (1994).]

Art Produced by Those Viewing the Crime

Many artists witnessed the Holocaust as it unfolded and tried to document it as well as evoke a public response. Marc Chagall's *White Crucifixion,* a response to Kristallnacht in 1938, remains the icon among many paintings that described Jewish suffering before 1939. Chagall used the theme of a crucified "Jewish" Jesus set against vignettes of Jewish persecution that unfolded in the Nazi era. During World War II, as more information about Jewish persecution leaked out of central Europe, Chagall continued to paint crucifixion scenes where the vision of Jesus, the Jewish Messiah, became that of a tormented contemporary Jew.

Other artists during this period were also noted for their visual statements about the Holocaust: Lazar Segall produced a monumental statement on the prewar refugee crisis and results in *Emigrant Ship* (1931–1941) and *Concentration Camp* 1945. Yankel Adler painted figurative works and landscape showing the mutilation of Jewish life. Ben Shahn produced strong responses such as the famous colored poster that tersely detailed the destruction of Lidice (*This is Nazi Brutality,* 1942), and later more subtle paintings such as *Boy* (1944), *Hunger* (1946), *Cherubs and Children* (1944), *Italian Landscape II* (1944) and *Martyrology* (1962).

Rico LeBrun, an important postwar abstractionist, and non-Jew, insisted that "the Holocaust was a subject that no serious artist could neglect . . ." The contemporary American painter Leonard Baskin, LeBrun's colleague and friend, described his approach to the subject as confronting "the mind-curdling reality of the least human of human endeavors, and in paintings and drawings of dissolution, dismemberment and incineration he is saying, all is not vanity, all is horror." Baskin himself has produced a significant body of work dealing in very indirect but not obscure ways with the Holocaust.

Art by Survivors after the Holocaust

Many survivors became known artists or chose to use the visual rather than the written work to express their memory of the Holocaust. Zoran Music, Samuel Bak, Hannelore Baron, Marek Oberlander, Janusz Stern, Isaac Celnikier, Alice Cahana, and Walter Spitzer are all known for their Holocaust-inspired paintings. In some respect, the only "authentic" Holocaust art may be said to be the art of survivors. Jozef Szajna, a Polish survivor of Auschwitz and Buchenwald and a major postwar artist and theatre director in Poland, insists that only those who experienced the camps can attempt to make art about the Holocaust. These artists experienced the terror of being hidden, the ghettos and death camps. Questions of aesthetics certainly exist with their art, creating a tension between memory and witnessing versus a purely artistic approach to the subject.

Art Created by Children of Holocaust Survivors

For the second generation, art provided an appropriate entry for questions of memory, absence, presence and identity. The memory of the event that affected their parents also produced different media responses: painting, photography, video, installation art and the comic strip. Joyce Lyon, Pier Marton, Art Speigelman, Deborah Teicholz, Haim Maor, Wendy Joy Kuppermann and Mindy Weisel are just a few names from hundreds of artists in this group.

Contemporary Artists of Different Dimensions

Artists who were not directly involved with the Holocaust have also attempted to enter the subject. The art of this group cannot be "memory," for they did not experience the event itself. It may be an interpretation (derived from their own sense of vulnerability as Jews or artists), a historical narrative, reflections on place, absence and presence, or simply a confrontation with the impenetrability of the subject.

Leon Golub, Mauricio Lasansky, Larry Rivers, Audrey Flack, Jerome Witkin, Arnold Trachtman, Judy Chicago, Robert Morris, Pearl Hirshfield, Jeffrey Wollin, Susan Erony, Robert Barancik, Marlene Miller and Shirley Samberg are among hundreds of American artists who have tried to deal with the Holocaust, with varying degrees of success. Among contemporary European artists whose works integrate Holocaust and memory themes are Anselm Kiefer, Sigmar Polke, Hundertwasser, Theo Tobiasse, Christian Boltanski, and Magdalena Abakanowicz.

In Israel, artistic response to the Holocaust has been slow in developing, except among survivors and the second generation. Often, art about the Holocaust that was exhibited was not found in the major art museums, but rather in places like the art galleries at Yad Vashem and the Lochamei Hagetaot Museum of the Holocaust whose contexts reduce the concern with the aesthetic in favor of the subject matter.

Since 1993, there have been several comprehensive shows dealing with the art of the Holocaust. *Burnt Whole* (1994) at the Washington Project for the Arts; *After Auschwitz* (1994–95) at Royal Festival Hall and the Imperial War Museum; *Witness and Legacy: Contemporary Art About the Holocaust* (1995), at the Minnesota Museum of American Art; and *Where is Abel, Thy Brother?* (1996) displayed by Zacheta Gallery of Contemporary Art in Warsaw.

—*Stephen C. Feinstein*

References and Recommended Reading

Amishai-Maisels, Ziva (1993). *Depiction and Interpretation: The Influence of the Holocaust on the Visual Arts.* London: Pergamon Press.

Feinstein, Stephen C. (Ed.) (1994). *Witness and Legacy: Contemporary Art about the Holocaust.* Minneapolis, MN: Lerner Publications.

Felstiner, Mary (1994). *To Paint Her Life: Charlotte Salomon in the Nazi Era.* New York: HarperCollins.
Lasansky, Mauricio (1976). *The Nazi Drawings.* Iowa City, IA: University of Iowa Press, 30 leaves of plates.
Young, James E. (1993). *The Texture of Memory: Holocaust Memorials and Meaning.* New Haven, CT: Yale University Press.

ART OF OTHER GENOCIDES

While artistic representation of the destruction of European Jews has had a long and ongoing response in art, less is visible with other genocides. Arshile Gorky (1904–1948), the Armenian-born painter whose career flourished in the United States from the 1920s through the 1940s, infused his paintings with images inspired by his own memories of Turkish massacres of Armenians in Van. In a letter to his sister, Gorky wrote that "our beautiful Armenia which we lost and which I shall repossess in my art . . . I shall resurrect Armenia with my brush for all the world to see" [Arshile Gorky as quoted in Balakian, Peter (February 1996). Arshile Gorky and the Armenian Genocide. *Art in America,* 84(2), 59]. Karl Stojka, a member of the Roma community in Austria is the only known painter who depicted the destruction of Gypsies. Absence of visual representation has to do in part with the Roma and Sinti tradition of not talking about the dead.

In 1992, as a response to genocide in Bosnia, a major exhibit was arranged by Sarajevo's bombed out Obala Gallery and was shown in 1994 under the title of "Witnesses of Existence," at the New York Kunsthalle, Centre PasquaART in Biel, Switzerland, and the Edinburgh Festival in Scotland. Bosnian filmmaker Srdan Vuletic made a movie of the original exhibit, where viewers came to the gallery under dangerous conditions. Included in the exhibit were paintings, sculpture and installations that recalled the recent atrocities committed within eyesight of the gallery: Zoran Bogdanovíc's *Memory of People,* Edo Nuankadíc's *War Trails,* Nusret Pasíc's *Witnesses of Existence and Martyrs,* and Mustafa Skoplijak's *Sarajevo '91, '92, '93, '94.* In 1995, The Imperial War Museum in London displayed the provocative paintings of artist Peter Howson, who represented, in the tradition of World War II documentary painting, the atrocities in the former Yugoslavia and particularly mass rape of Bosnian women.

In the realm of photography, more has been accomplished, with both political agendas and aesthetic conceptions behind the works. Candan Melioglu, a Turkish photographer, produced a series of photographs that became a book about the destruction of Islamic architecture in the town of Foca-on-the-Drina in Eastern Bosnia. The photographs also documented dispossession and expulsion of the Muslim population, as well as a rape camp set up in Foca's Partisan sport's arena. A traveling photo exhibition in the United States, organized through the United States Holocaust Memorial Museum, *Faces of Sorrow: Agony of the Former Yugoslavia,* dramatically depicted via color photography, genocidal activity and concentration camps. Other photographers who have dealt with Bosnia are Gilles Peress (*Farewell to Bosnia*), M. Sugarman (*God Be With You: War in Bosnia and Croatia*), and Bellwinkel (*Bosnia: War in Europe.*). Photography of the genocide in Rwanda by Pierre-Laurent Sanner has been exhibited in Europe and reproduced in other places [Malagardes, Maria (1995). *Rwanda, le jour d'après: Récits et témoignages au lendemain de génocide.* Paris: Editions d'art Somogy]. In September 1996, the Festival of Photojournalism in Perpignan, France featured a multi-photographer exhibition, *The Lost Children of Rwanda,* which showed faces of children and their personal possessions and clothes.

Jozef Szajna, a Polish Catholic survivor of Auschwitz has created both paintings and room installations that attempt to relate the dehumanization of the Nazi genocide and the reoccurrence of genocide in Europe during the 1990s.

A distinctive characteristic of art about genocide is that it is never exhibited in the country where genocide is being committed actively. It is thus designed for the outsider, as a means of conveyance of brutality, and in a search for humane solutions, and implicitly requests the intervention of the onlooker.

—Stephen C. Feinstein

References and Recommended Reading

Howson, Peter (1994). *Bosnia.* London: Imperial War Museum.

Totten, Samuel (1988). The literature, art and film of genocide. In Charny, Israel W. (Ed.). *Genocide: A Critical Bibliographic Review.* London: Mansell Publishing; and New York: Facts on File, pp. 232–240.

ART OF FUTURISTIC DESTRUCTION

Artists have frequently had unique insights into the potential for human destruction. This has been particularly a more frequent vision since World War I. Among the artists who are distinguished for this cryptic and terrifying imagry are Salvador Dali (*Soft Construction with Boiled Beans,* and *The Premonition of Civil War,* 1936, *Ruin with Head of Medusa,* 1941); and Max Ernst (*The Horde,* 1927, *Vision,* 1931 and *Europe after the Rain II,* 1940–1942). Zoran Music, a Croatian survivor of Dachau and painter produced a series, *We Are Not the Last* (1971), which suggested, through images of mass graves, that humanity had an ongoing capacity to engage in genocide. Zdislaw Beksinski, a contemporary Polish painter has created horrific images of crucifixions, decimated humanity and landscapes that suggest the effects of genocide and nuclear catastrophe.

—Stephen C. Feinstein

References and Recommended Reading

Totten, Samuel (1988). The literature, art and film of nuclear and other futuristic destruction. In Charny, Israel W. (Ed.), *Genocide: A Critical Bibliographic Review.* London: Mansell Publishing; and New York: Facts on File, pp. 241–256.

ASSOCIATION OF GENOCIDE SCHOLARS

The Association of Genocide Scholars is an international, interdisciplinary, nonpartisan organization that seeks to further research and teaching about the nature, causes, and consequences of genocide, and advance policy studies on prevention of genocide. The Association, founded in 1994 by Israel Charny, Helen Fein, Robert Melson, and Roger Smith, meets biennially to consider comparative research, important new works, case studies, the links between genocide and gross human rights violations, and prevention and punishment of genocide. The aim of the Association is not to replace any existing professional organization, but to focus more intensively on questions of genocide than is possible in the existing two-hour format of most conferences and to draw colleagues from different disciplines into an interdisciplinary conversation. Membership is open to scholars, graduate students, and other interested persons worldwide. The Association is an autonomous affiliate of the Institute for the Study of Genocide (see entry).

For membership and conference information, contact the Association of Genocide Scholars, Department of Government, College of William and Mary, Williamsburg, Virginia 23187-8795 USA

—Roger Smith

ATATURK, MUSTAFA KEMAL

Mustafa Kemal Ataturk (1881–1938) was the founder of the Republic of Turkey and the consummator of the Armenian Genocide. He was an officer in the Turkish army whose defense of Gallipoli in 1915–1916 defeated the Allied campaign to breach the Dardanelles and quickly eliminate the Ottoman Empire from World War I. A supporter of the Committee of Union and Progress (CUP), he stayed out of politics until 1919 when he organized the Turkish Nationalist Movement in the drive to oust the Allies who had placed strategic portions of the country under occupation after its defeat. Kemal established headquarters in Ankara, amnestied CUP members who joined his movement, and regrouped the remaining Ottoman army and other irregular units under his general command.

Kemal first directed his forces against the French in Cilicia with fatal consequences for the Armenians. With Allied encouragement and promises of protection, most surviving Armenians had repatriated to their hometowns in Cilicia in 1919. The attack by Kemalist units against the city of Marash in January 1920, which was accompanied by large-scale slaughtering of the Armenians, spelled the beginning of the end for the remnant Armenian population. The Armenians of Hajen (Hadjin) put up a last desperate fight for seven months only to be reduced by October 1920 to less than five hundred survivors who fled from a city completely torched by the besieging Turks. When the French formally agreed to evacuate Cilicia in October 1921, the debacle signified a second deportation for the Armenians of the region. In the meantime, the Turkish Nationalist forces had gone to war against the Republic of Armenia. With secret instructions from the Ankara government to proceed with the physical elimination of Armenia, General Kiazim Karabekir seized half the territories of Armenia in November 1920 as Red Army units Sovietized the remaining areas. Once again the Armenian population was driven out at the point of the sword with heavy casualties as the city of Kars and its surrounding region were annexed by Turkey.

The final chapter of the Armenians in Anatolia was written in Smyrna (Izmir) as Kemalist forces routed the Greek army and entered the city in September 1922. Soon after, a fire begun in the Armenian neighborhood consumed the entire Christian sector of the city and drove the civilian population to the shore whence they sailed into exile bereft of all belongings. With this exodus from the mainland, Mustafa Kemal completed what Talaat and Enver had started in 1915, the eradication of the Armenian population of Anatolia and the termination of Armenian political aspirations in the Caucasus. With the expulsion of the Greeks, the Turkification and Islamification of Asia Minor was nearly complete.

With the restoration of Turkish sovereignty over Anatolia, Kemal turned his attention to the modernization of the country. Designated President of the newly proclaimed Republic of Turkey in

1923, he embarked upon a thoroughgoing process of westernization while promoting a secular Turkish national identity. This effort was epitomized in the adoption of the Latin alphabet for the modern Turkish language. In 1934 the Turkish Grand National Assembly hailed Kemal with the surname of Ataturk, meaning the father of the Turks, in tribute to his singular contribution in forging modern Turkey. With an eye toward securing his legacy, in 1931 Kemal founded the Turkish Historical Society, which was charged with the guardianship of the state's official history. In 1936 Kemal began to pressure France to yield the Sanjak of Alexandretta, or Iskenderun, a district on the Mediterranean under French administrative rule whose inhabitants included 23,000 Armenians. Preoccupied with the deteriorating situation in Europe, France yielded when Turkey send in its troops in 1938. Kemal died that year having prepared the annexation of the district. His action precipitated the final exodus of Armenians from Turkey in 1939 as most opted for the French offer of evacuation to Syria and Lebanon rather than risk mistreatment yet again.

—*Rouben Paul Adalian*

References and Recommended Reading

Kinross, Patrick B. (1964). *Ataturk: The Rebirth of a Nation.* London: Weidenfeld and Nicolson.

AUSTRALIAN ABORIGINES, GENOCIDE OF

Prior to white settlement in 1788, probably 500,000 indigenous people lived scattered across this huge continent in small, tribal groups. These hunter-gatherers began life here in periods varying from 20,000 to 60,000 years ago. Diseases introduced by convicts and settlers—mainly chickenpox, smallpox and measles—decimated them. Discrimination by white society, in every sphere, has been their historic lot.

But was Australia simply another case of colonialism, of indigenous people dying (regrettably) for "economic reasons" as a result of "progress" toward a cattle, timber, gold or uranium industry? Is Australia a case of "ethnocide," the extinction of a culture during colonization? Do any—or all—of the acts listed in Article II of the Genocide Convention apply to Aborigines?

Aborigines have suffered it *all:*

- intentional physical killing because they were aborigines, people considered as "other," not simply because they blocked the colonial path to what the land held (Article IIa);
- forced removal to completely isolated government and/or Christian-run missions, to be 'civilized' by the gun and the whip, or the threat thereof, in the name of the (then) protection-segregation philosophy (Article IIb and e);
- forcible removal from parents, siblings and spouses if considered "half-caste" in the name of the (then) forced assimilation policy (Article IIe);
- forcible fostered, adopted, or institutionalized in the name of "salvaging" those with a percentage of white ("civilized") blood (Article IIe);
- shackled, chained, indentured by force as laborers or sexual chattels on cattle ranches (Article IIb);
- systematically deprived of language, custom, and tradition on the grounds that such were repugnant to public policy (Article Ilb);
- subjected, at, times, to unilaterally imposed birth control injections (Article IId).

The physical genocide is well documented. For example, three years after the first white arrivals in Tasmania, the serious killings began: children were abducted for forced labor, women raped,

Genocide of Aborigines

There appear to be a number of features of the genocide of the Australian Aborigines that have been repeated in other occurrences of genocide:

1. a systematic, "scientific" and institutional dehumanization of the victim
2. a "play" or "sport" element created as an avenue for indulging in mass murder
3. an appropriation of the victim's property accompanied by claims that the victim had no right to such property
4. a propaganda campaign to ensure support from the rest of the general population for the genocide practices. This is conducted within an ideology of blaming the victim and the promotion of the belief that the victim "deserves" to be exterminated
5. an appeal to "higher authority" such as God or evolution to sanction genocide actions (in the case of Cambodia, the Khmer Rouge conducted their mass murder in the name of "Higher Organization")
6. application of superior technology to carry out the genocide
7. a subsequent processing of history in such a way as to obscure the genocide, legitimate the eradiction of the victim population, and reproduce an ideology of justified dominance on the part of the perpetrator of the genocide.

—*John P. Synott, Internet on the Holocaust and Genocide*

tortured and given poisoned flour, and the men shot—allegedly in 'retaliation' for spearing of cattle. Disposal was in one's and two's, sometimes dozens, rather than in systematic massacre. By 1935, between 3,000 and 4,000 were dead, by intent. Considered "wild animals," "vermin," "scarcely human," "hideous to humanity" and a "nuisance," white settlers killed 10,000 Aborigines in Queensland between 1824 and 1908. Such was the slaughter that a Royal Commission, appointed in 1896, recommended what became the Aboriginal Protection and Restriction of the Sale of Opium Act a year later. This is *the world's first statute to protect not an animal species but an endangered human race—from genocide.*

In 1997, *Bringing Them Home: Report of the National Inquiry into the Separation of Aboriginal and Torres Straits Islander Children from their Families* found that child removal, perhaps of the order of 50,000 over a century, was a gross violation of human rights, a denial of legal rights and, significantly, an act of genocide. The Australian Federal Government, which refuses to make an appropriate apology, contends that the standards of yesteryear cannot be applied to the mores of today, and that such removals were always intended "for their own good." Australia ratified the Genocide Convention in 1949, yet persisted in removing children until the last "assimilation home," at Bomaderry in New South Wales, was closed in 1988! The Report rightly dismisses the "assimilation-was-in-their-best-interests" motive as irrelevant to a finding of genocide: the object of late nineteenth and much of twentieth century policy was that these

Aboriginal children would disappear as Aborigines.

—*Colin Tatz*

References and Recommended Reading

Australian Government (1997). *Bringing Them Home: Report of the National Inquiry into the Separation of Aboriginal and Torres Strait Islander Children from their Families.* Sydney: Human Rights and Equal Opportunity Commission [Commissioner: Ronald Wilson; edited by Meredith Wilkie].

Manne, Robert (1998). The stolen generation. *Quadrant,* January–February, 53–63.

B

BANGLADESH, GENOCIDE IN

Bangladesh's emergence as a nation in 1971 came at the cost of three million people dead, a quarter of a million women and girls raped, ten million people fled to India, and thirty million people forced to flee their homes.

Pakistan was made up of a province on the west side of India (former Punjab et al.) and on the east side of India (former East Bengal). The army was manned and commanded by people from West Pakistan. Elections for a Constitutional Assembly were held in Pakistan in December 1970. The East Pakistan based Awami League won an outright majority of seats in this Assembly, and planned to write a constitution that would give the majority population of East Pakistan political control of the country. On the evening of March 25, 1971, the military and political elite of West Pakistan with malice aforethought loosed the Army of Pakistan (manned and commanded by West Pakistanis) on the Bengali population of East Pakistan to emasculate the Awami League as a political opponent, to rid the province of East Pakistan of its Hindu population of 10 million persons, and to terrorize the civilian population into complete and permanent submission. This plan of intimidation, brutalization, and extermination of any Bengali who would not accept West Pakistani superiority continued until the West Pakistan military capitulated to the Indian Army on December 16, 1971.

Particularly at risk were known Awami League politicians and their supporters, most of whom, however, went into hiding in the countryside or escaped to India. The armed security and police forces manned by Bengalis were an early target, but many of these also escaped with their weapons to return as guerrillas. Bengali students, professors, and intellectuals were summarily executed. The West Pakistan Army was particularly intent on killing every single Hindu they could find. Slum and squatter areas of the major cities and towns were also obliterated with all their occupants.

All able-bodied young Bengali men were considered freedom fighters. Early on, they were routinely rounded up, tortured, and killed. Very quickly, however, they fled the cities and towns for the guerrilla camps in the countryside and in India. The Army of West Pakistan turned its fury on the women and girls left behind. Girls and women were publicly raped in front of their family members. They were routinely abducted to special camps near army barracks to be gang-raped, brutalized, and killed, or to live with the eternal shame of their violation. Many committed suicide.

As the Bengali guerrilla campaign became more effective against the West Pakistan Army, the Army undertook daily retaliatory missions to destroy as many villages as possible. In December, when the Army of West Pakistan was finally forced to retreat back into its cantonments, they systematically set about killing all the influential intellectuals and professionals in each city and town where they were besieged. The genocidal campaign of the West Pakistani military elite against the Bengali population of East Pakistan stopped only when the Indian Army disarmed the Army of Pakistan to prevent the guerrilla movement from spreading to separatist elements in the Indian State of West Bengal.

Genocide as government policy failed to prevent the birth of Bangladesh. The West Pakistani military elite never recognized that Sheikh Mujibur Rahman and the Awami League had crafted a compelling vision of an independent Bangladesh arising from the blood of millions of martyrs (*shaheed*) who supported the vast guerrilla movement. The military authorities were able to recruit collaborators from Muslims who had emigrated to East Pakistan from other parts of India after Partition, and from among the East Pakistani political parties opposed to the Awami League, but to no avail in preventing the independence of Bangladesh. Retribution against the poorer of these collaborators was swift and brutal immediately after the surrender of the West Pakistani Army. Armed violence had become and remains an accepted part of ordinary Bangladeshi life. Better situated collaborators survived and by 1975 were openly participating in Bangladeshi public life. To this day, an elemental enmity between freedom fighters and collaborators continues to cause political and social turmoil.

—*John P. Thorp*

References and Recommended Reading

Jahan, Rounaq (1997). Genocide in Bangladesh. In Totten, Samuel; Parsons, William S.; and Charny, Israel W. (Eds.), *Century of Genocide: Eyewitness Accounts and Critical Views.* New York: Garland Publishing, pp. 291–316.

BARBIE, KLAUS

Klaus Barbie (1913–1991) was a brutal Nazi Gestapo officer stationed in Lyon, France, where he terrorized Jews and French Resistance members from 1942–1944. Barbie oversaw the detention and deportation of hundreds of French Jews to Nazi death camps. He was also responsible for multiple rapes, assassinations, torture and killings of French resistance leaders. In April 1944, he sent 44 Jewish children from an orphanage to Auschwitz, where they were cremated on arrival. For his brutal acts, he was known as "The Butcher of Lyon."

After World War II, Barbie was hired as an anti-communist expert by the United States, and eventually ended up in South America. For years, he was protected by Bolivia's military regime, where he lived openly under the name Klaus Altmann. He helped the regime's illicit arms dealings and cocaine trade until democracy was restored in 1982. Barbie was then deprived of Bolivian citizenship and expelled to French Guyana. Once back in France, Barbie was the first person since World War II to be charged and convicted, in 1987, of crimes against humanity. He was sentenced by France to life in prison, where he died four years later.

—*Michael J. Bazyler*

References and Recommended Reading

Finkielkraut, Alain (1992). *Remembering in Vain: The Klaus Barbie Trial and Crimes against Humanity.* Translated by Roxanne Lapidus with Sima Godfrey; Introduction by Alice Y. Kaplan. New York: Columbia University Press.

Hoyos, Ladislas de (1985). *Klaus Barbie.* Translated from the French by Nicholas Courtin. London: W. H. Allen.

BEIT HASHOAH/MUSEUM OF TOLERANCE OF THE SIMON WIESENTHAL CENTER

Beit Hashoah/Museum of Tolerance is the educational arm of the Simon Wiesenthal Center. It first opened its doors to the public on February 9, 1993,

The Museum of Tolerance

Please allow me to tell you about an institution in Los Angeles that was named after me. The Simon Wiesenthal Center has built a large museum called the Museum of Tolerance. If you have an opportunity to visit this Museum, you will be vividly informed about human rights violations and genocide—not only about the Holocaust against the Jews, but also about the ongoing challenges to the human dignity of minorities in different countries.

The Museum's impressive audio-visual presentations implore the visitor to ask: How can we prevent a repetition of such crimes in the future? At the entrance to the Museum are two doors, one marked "PREJUDICED," the other "WITHOUT PREJUDICE." The second door is permanently locked—thus challenging each visitor to deal with his and her own prejudices and biases. Tolerance is the prerequisite for the peaceful coexistence of all people on this earth and the only alternative to the hatred that led to the horrible crimes against humanity. Hatred is the evil opposite of tolerance. Hatred instills in the young the concept of an enemy even in early years; it leads to radical words that are then followed by radical action. I invite each of you and your children to visit my living legacy.

—*Simon Wiesenthal*

and in the first six years of operation has welcomed over 2 million visitors. The interactive human rights facility currently consists of four major components.

The Tolerance Center

The Tolerance Center deals with fundamental issues of personal and group prejudice and intolerance against the backdrop of American social history and current threats to human rights and dignity by hate groups and extremists worldwide. Special emphasis is placed on critical thinking and personal responsibility via exhibits like the *POV (Point of View) Diner, The Los Angeles Riots,* and *Millennium 2000.* Future displays in the permanent exhibit will also highlight the unique challenges posed by digital hate on the Internet.

The Shoah

The second section, The Shoah, is a sequenced, narrated exploration of the history of Nazi Germany and the genocide perpetrated against the Jewish people. The Shoah is presented as the definitive paradigm of intolerance and genocide in contemporary history. More than 35 distinct exhibits present history through direct engagement with pivotal events and people.

Throughout these two distinct museum experiences, the goal is to maximize the visitor's experience and to involve simultaneously both cognitive and affective educational processes. The strategies of presentation vary from interactive environments, projection theaters and dioramas recreating historic events. The presentations seek to motivate each visitor to actively reflect on and delve into controversial and often painful issues.

Multimedia Learning Center

Each visitor receives a passport-size photograph of a young Jew trapped in the Nazi Holocaust upon entering the Holocaust section of the Museum. Now the visitor learns of the ultimate fate of the child and can utilize this story as a point of entry to the Multimedia Learning Center, located on the second floor. This 30-station facility invites the visitor to access over 50,000 photographs and thousands of entries on every aspect of the Holocaust, World War II and related issues (this resource is also available via

View of the entrance to the Museum of Tolerance of the Simon Wiesenthal Center. (Copyright © Jim Mendenhall, 1993. With the kind courtesy of Rabbi Abraham Cooper, Associate Dean, Simon Wiesenthal Center)

Resource Materials at the Simon Wiesenthal Center

Genocide (VHS/BETA, Color/83 mins., 1982). Academy Award-winning Documentary tells the definitive story of the Holocaust beginning with pre-war Europe. Narrated by Orson Welles and Elizabeth Taylor.

Genocide: Critical Issues of the Holocaust. (Eds. Grobman/Landes, Rossel Books) paperback. A companion textbook to the film *Genocide.* In compelling original articles, experts in the field write on the issues surrounding the Holocaust.

"The Courage to Remember: The Holocaust 1933–1945": 40 full-color posters. Internationally acclaimed exhibit with over 200 photographs, maps, timelines and narrative. Compelling display for classroom or exhibition purposes.

The Last 7 Months of Anne Frank (VHS/BETA). Winner of a 1988 International Emmy, interviews with eight women who were with Anne Frank and her family during the final months of her life.

Hatred, Prejudice, and Genocide

In August 1995, Simon Wiesenthal represented Austria at a special meeting of the UN General Assembly to mark the United Nations Year for Tolerance, and on November 20, 1995 he gave the following speech at the Special Commemorative Meeting of the General Assembly:

> It is a great honor for me to be allowed to speak to this audience, as the representative of Austria, at the end of the Year for Tolerance. In four years we will be standing at the end of this century, which has been rightly termed "a century of crime." Thus there is a need to speak about tolerance and also to act on this principle. In this century I have myself seen Communism become a form of government under Stalin and—thankfully—I have seen its downfall. I have seen the rise of National Socialism under Hitler—and I have lived to see its downfall as well. Both of these regimes adopted measures that cost millions of lives. In the Soviet Union the victims were mainly Soviet citizens. The Nazi regime was responsible for the deaths of millions of foreign nationals. Altogether, about 50 million people, including 6 million Jewish victims, were killed as a result of the war and the innumerable crimes committed in the countries occupied by Nazi Germany. Together, these two dictatorships extinguished about 100 million human lives during this century. *[See DEMOCIDE for higher figures.—Ed.]*
>
> Underlying both Stalinism and National Socialism were two fundamentals: hate and technology.
>
> Even after the First World War, with its millions of victims, many nations had already pledged to never again wage war. On 27 August, 1928, Germany, Great Britain, Belgium, Iceland, Italy, Japan, Poland, Czechoslovakia and the United States of America signed the so-called Kellogg Agreement, with the aim of ensuring peace. This was followed by a series of disarmament conferences to reduce arms of all kinds. All of these efforts were cut short, however, when National Socialism came to power in Germany. Another terrible world war began and, with it, the loss of human rights for the suffering civilian populations. There were again millions of victims, and the Holocaust especially, the systematic extermination of 6 million Jews, has gone down in history as an unprecedented example of crime. The Holocaust has come to serve as a warning for the future of mankind and must continue to serve as a reminder to future generations. At the Nuremberg Trials, when it came to judging those responsible for the Second World War after National Socialism had collapsed, the charges also included explicit reference to the violations of the Kellogg Plan.
>
> What about the fundamental that fanned the flames of aggression at the onset of all these immense crimes—the element of hate? Can one ban hatred from people's hearts—or at least reduce it? If we succeed in reducing hatred in individuals, then politicians—who are paying increased attention to people's feelings and also incorporating this in their policies—will see to it that more emphasis is placed on the importance of tolerance in our societies. The younger generation must be warned against prejudices, especially against the prejudice of racial hatred, which has always led only to immeasurable human suffering.
>
> I would therefore like to make the following proposal: Let us try to organize a worldwide conference aimed at reducing hate. Technology without hate can be so very beneficial for mankind, but in conjunction with hatred it leads to disaster. The most important participants in such a conference—which should of course be held under the patronage of the United Nations—would be representatives of the monotheistic and other religions. Through religious networks the greater part of mankind could be

continues

continued

reached. The representatives of the various religions, in keeping with their moral duties, would work for mutual respect and support among men and against hatred. By spreading positive messages in churches, temples, mosques and synagogues, they can reach more people than all political parties put together. If religious representatives can agree to make the gradual elimination of hatred a major common concern, they will also find ways of informing and influencing their believers throughout the world.

As a survivor of the Nazi period—my wife and I lost 89 family members in the Holocaust—I have dedicated my life to the struggle for justice. The title of my last book is "Justice Not Vengeance" because my work was never motivated by hate or revenge. I would therefore feel very honored if many people of good will and with the firm intention to conquer the hate in this world were to take part in a conference having this aim.

I thank the Assembly kindly for its attention and convey to it warm greetings from the people and the Government of Austria. And I promise that we will continue to work for tolerance and human rights.

—*Simon Wiesenthal*

the Internet at motlc.wiesenthal.com). In late 1999, the Learning Center will begin to present video testimonies of Holocaust survivors compiled and presented by Steven Spielberg's Shoah Foundation.

Temporary Exhibitions

From its inception, the Museum has presented a wide range of highly acclaimed temporary exhibits, ranging from photo exhibitions on the unfolding tragedies in the Former Yugoslavia and Rwanda, to Holocaust heroes Chinue Sugihara and Simon Wiesenthal, to a special exhibition in honor of Jackie Robinson's breaking of baseball's color barrier.

Children's Museum

Current plans call for the opening of a new permanent tolerance museum facility designed for children to open in the early twenty-first century.

The uniqueness of the Beit Hashoah / Museum of Tolerance is that it mandates *tolerance education within the framework of the Holocaust.* It is an issues-oriented museum that invests heavily in empathetic communications and a moral sphere of humanistic values based on concepts of justice. In this context, the Museum has launched its *Tools for Tolerance* workshops, which annually service over 8,000 law enforcement personnel from some 70 different policies agencies. A similar program for teachers and other professionals services thousands of other adults. In each case, the museum experience is incorporated directly into the formal training of the professionals.

This museum challenges everyone entering its doors to discover moral purpose and commitment through questions we are all too often unprepared to ask. What is a just and tolerant society? What allows for the fostering of human dignity? How do we guarantee the rights of the individual and the group within the context of the needs of the many? It is a museum with an unwavering core statement that is also committed to maintaining a connection and relevance to contemporary human rights challenges.

Further Information: Simon Wiesenthal Center Museum of Tolerance, 9760 W. Pico Blvd., Los Angeles, CA 90035, USA; tel: 1-310-553-9036; Fax: 1-310-553-8007; www.wiesenthal.com; motlc.wiesenthal.com.

—*Abraham Cooper*

The Mound of Ears in Kyoto, Japan

In Kyoto, Japan, on a 30-foot-high hill, stands one of the world's more macabre war memorials. The site marks the burial place of noses and ears when, 400 years ago, Japanese Samurai warriors hacked off the noses and ears from the corpses of tens of thousands of Koreans and brought them back to Japan. Few Japanese outside Kyoto know of the Ear Mound, but almost all Koreans do. To many Koreans, it is a symbol of Japanese aggression that still lurks waiting to explode. In 1592 Japan assembled some 200,000 troops and launched an invasion of Korea that set off a war that lasted six years and by some accounts killed more than one million Koreans—close to one-third of the country's population at that time. The Ear Mound is not mentioned in most guidebooks, and it attracts few Japanese or foreign tourists. But children in the Hiroshima public schools are regularly bused to Kyoto to see the mound.

—*Press Report*

BIBLIOGRAPHIES ON THE HOLOCAUST AND GENOCIDE

As ever-increasing attention has been focused on the study of the Holocaust and genocide, numerous bibliographies have been developed and published on a wide variety of issues germane to these subjects. These have ranged from single bibliographies on particular acts of genocide and/or specialized subjects such as literature of the Holocaust or first person accounts of genocidal acts to an entire bibliographical series on various facets of genocide. They have also ranged from those in pamphlet form to those in book form to those on CD ROMs.

There are numerous annotated bibliographies by scholars on various topics germane to the Holocaust. A mere sampling of some of the more valuable and useful bibliographies provides a sense of the breadth of topics addressed in such works: Randolph Braham (19[illegible]), *The Hungarian Jewish Catastrophe: A Selected and Annotated Bibliography;* Fortunoff Video Archive for Holocaust Testimonies (1990), *Guide to Yale University Library Holocaust Video Testimonies;* Philip Friedman (1952), *The Bibliography of the Warsaw Ghetto;* Helen Kehr (1978), *Persecution and Resistance Under the Nazis;* Jacob Robinson and Mrs. Philip Friedman (1973), *The Holocaust and After; Sources and Literature in English;* Sheba Skirball (1990), *Films of the Holocaust: An Annotated Bibliography of Collections in Israel;* and the series entitled *Guide to Unpublished Material on the Holocaust Period;* each of which was edited by different individuals (among whom were Yehuda Bauer, Jacob Robinson, Shmuel Krakowski, and Aharon Weiss).

Numerous bibliographies on Holocaust literature have been published over the past twenty years, and among the most noted are: Abraham and Hershel Edelheit (1986), *Bibliography on Holocaust Literature;* Abraham and Hershel Edelheit (1990), *Bibliography on Holocaust Literature: Supplement;* Vera Laska (1985), *Nazism, Resistance and Holocaust in World War II: A Bibliography* (which includes a major section devoted to literature); David Szonyi (1985), *The Holocaust: An Annotated Bibliography and Resource Guide.* The US Holocaust Memorial Museum (1994) has also published *Annotated Bibliography,* which lists works (general history, specialized history, fiction, poetry, biographies) for use by educators. In this way, educators are guided to those works that are known to be historically accurate, developmentally appropriate for various ages, and of generally a high quality of writing.

The first bibliography on the fate of the Gypsies, *Gypsies and the Holocaust: A Bibliography and Introductory Essay,* was complied and edited by Gabrielle Trynauer in 1989. It includes citations in English, French, and German on various facets of the Gypsies' subjugation, persecution and murder at the hands of the Nazis.

Among the first bibliographies on a genocide other than the Holocaust was *The Armenian Holocaust: A Bibliography Relating to the Deportations, Massacres, and Dispersion of the Armenian People, 1915–1923* by Richard G. Hovannisian. Published in 1980, the bibliography includes more than 400 citations on memoirs, accounts, collections of documents and studies on the subject of the Armenian Genocide.

A particularly noteworthy project in the field of genocide is the bibliographical series entitled *Genocide: A Critical Bibliographic Review.* The series was initiated in 1986 by Israel Charny, Director of the Institute on the Holocaust and Genocide in Jerusalem. The purpose of this pioneer project was to bring scholars from different disciplines together to summarize the work that had been conducted in the field of genocide in their subject areas and to critically evaluate the most important print and non-print research materials. Each chapter combines a critical review and an annotated bibliography, thus providing invaluable tools for scholars. As of 1998, four volumes have been completed and published in the series: *Genocide: A Critical Bibliographic Review* was published in 1988; *Genocide: A Critical Bibliographic Review, Volume 2,* was published in 1991; *The Widening Circle of Genocide, Volume 3* was published in 1994; and *Medical and Psychological Effects of Concentration Camps on Holocaust Survivors, Volume 4,* appeared in 1997. Other volumes are in planning stages, including one on the issues of intervention and prevention of genocide.

The initial volume in the series, published in 1988, was the first bibliography to extend beyond individual occurrences of genocide, to encompass both the totality of genocide as a process and the efforts that were being made to understand and combat it. It included contributions by historians, sociologists, a psychologist, political scientist, philosopher and an educator. Among the topics addressed in the volume were the study of genocide, the history and sociology of genocidal killings, the Holocaust, the Armenian Genocide, the genocide in the USSR, the genocide in Cambodia, other selected cases of genocide and genocidal massacres, understanding the psychology of genocidal destructiveness and the literature, art and film of genocide.

The second volume, published in 1991, includes contributions by sociologists, historians, political scientists, educators, and a psychologist, and is comprised of essays and collections of annotations on such topics as the psychology of denial of known genocides, denial of the Holocaust, denial of the Armenian Genocide, documentation of the Armenian Genocide in Turkish sources, the status of basic genocide law, humanitarian intervention in genocidal situations, educating about the Holocaust and genocide, total war and nuclear omnicide, the professions and genocide, the memorialization of the Holocaust, first-person accounts of genocidal acts, righteous people in the Holocaust, and the language of extermination in genocide.

The Widening Circle of Genocide, which is the third volume and was published in 1994, includes contributions by political scientists, anthropologists, a computer specialist, an educator, a foreign affairs adviser, political scientist, psychiatrist, and sociologist. It is comprised of essays and collections of annotations on such issues as democracy and the prevention of genocide, religion and genocide, documentation of the Armenian Genocide in German and Austrian sources, genocide in Afghanistan, genocide of the Kurds in Iraq, genocide in East Timor, the fate of the Gypsies in the Holocaust, the psychiatric treatment of survivors, the mortality of children during genocidal acts, horizontal nuclear proliferation and its genocidal implications, and non-governmental organizations working on the issue of genocide.

The fourth volume, co-edited by Robert Krell and Marc I. Sherman, which was published in 1997, is a special volume fifty years after the Holocaust that assembles the literature on survivors of the Holocaust, and in addition contains chapters summarizing the history of psychiatry's relationship to the survivors and a summary of the knowledge available about Holocaust survivors.

In 1992, Michael Dobkowski and Isidor Wallimann contributed a one-volume annotated bibliography with analytical introductions that covered several topics, including ethnocide, the Holocaust, the Armenian Genocide and its denial, the Ukrainian Famine, genocide and modern war, and early warning, intervention and prevention of genocide.

In the early 1990s, Marc I. Sherman and Israel W. Charny, under the auspices of the Institute on the Holocaust and Genocide in Jerusalem, also produced the computerized *Holocaust and Genocide Bibliographic Database.* The fields covered in the interdisciplinary database include religion, psychology, sociology, law, medicine, history, economics, political science, anthropology, education, and philosophy. The database contains over 9,750 bibliographic citations of books, chapters of book, book reviews, journal articles, and dissertations. Over half of the citations contain abstracts.

First-Person Accounts of Genocidal Acts Committed in the Twentieth Century: Annotated Bibliography, compiled and edited by Samuel Totten, was the first bibliography to focus exclusively on first person accounts of a wide range of genocidal acts committed in the twentieth century. Comprised of 1275 annotations, this bibliography addresses the following genocidal acts: the German extermination of the Hereros in Southwest Africa, the Armenian Genocide, the Soviet manmade famine in the Ukraine, the Soviet deportation of whole nations, the Holocaust, the fate of the Gypsies during the Holocaust years, the Indonesian genocide of Communists and suspected Communists, genocide in Uganda, genocide in Bangladesh, genocide of the Hutus in Burundi, Indonesian genocide in East Timor, the Cambodian genocide, the threatened genocide of the Baha'is, and the genocide of various indigenous peoples.

As the field of Holocaust and genocide studies continues to evolve, more bibliographies are bound to be developed, and undoubtedly many will be made available in databases. Through the development of such works will scholars be able to keep abreast of the burgeoning literature.

—Samuel Totten

References and Recommended Reading

Bauer, Yehuda (Ed.) (1975). *Guide to Unpublished Material of the Holocaust Period—Moreshet Archives in Giv'at Haviva. Volume III.* Jerusalem: The Hebrew University of Jerusalem and Yad Vashem. 413 pp.

Bauer, Yehuda (Ed.) (1981). *Guide to Unpublished Material of the Holocaust Period—Moreshet Archives in Giv'at Haviva. Volume VI.* Jerusalem: The Hebrew University of Jerusalem and Yad Vashem. 259 pp.

Bauer, Yehuda; Krakowski, Shmuel; and Weiss, Aharon (Eds.) (1977). *Guide to Unpublished Material on the Holocaust Period. Volume IV.* Jerusalem: The

Hebrew University of Jerusalem and Yad Vashem. 389 pp.
Bauer, Yehuda; Krakowski, Shmuel; and Weiss, Aharon (Eds.) (1979). *Guide to Unpublished Material on the Holocaust Period. Volume V.* Jerusalem: The Hebrew University of Jerusalem and Yad Vashem. 436 pp.
Braham, Randolph (Ed.) (1984). *The Hungarian Jewish Catastrophe: A Selected and Annotated Bibliography.* New York: Columbia University Press. 501 pp.
Charny, Israel W. (Ed.) (1988). *Genocide: A Critical Bibliographic Review.* London: Mansell Publishing; and New York: Facts on File. 273 pp.
Charny, Israel W. (Ed.) (1991). *Genocide: A Critical Bibliographic Review. Volume 2.* London: Mansell Publishing; and New York: Facts on File. 432 pp.
Charny, Israel W. (Ed.) (1994). *The Widening Circle of Genocide. Volume 3 in the Series, Genocide: A Critical Bibliographic Review.* New Brunswick, NJ: Transaction Publishers. 375 pp.
Dobkowski, Michael N., and Wallimann, Isidor (Eds.) (1992). *Genocide in Our Time: An Annotated Bibliography with Analytical Introductions.* Ann Arbor, MI: Pierian Press. 183 pp.
Edelheit, Abraham, and Edelheit, Hershel (Eds.) (1986). *Bibliography on Holocaust Literature.* Boulder, CO: Westview Press. 842 pp.
Edelheit, Abraham, and Edelheit, Hershel (Eds.) (1990). *Bibliography on Holocaust Literature: Supplement.* Boulder, CO: Westview Press. 564 pp.
Fortunoff Video Archive for Holocaust Testimonies (Ed.) (1990). *Guide to Yale University Library Holocaust Video Testimonies.* New York: Garland Publishing, 116 pp.
Friedman, Philip (1952). The bibliography of the Warsaw Ghetto. *Jewish Book Annual,* 11, pp. 121–128. New York: Jewish Book Council of America.
Hovannisian, Richard G. (Ed.) (1980). *The Armenian Holocaust: A Bibliography Relating to the Deportations, Massacres, and Dispersion of the Armenian People, 1915–1923.* Cambridge, MA: Armenian Heritage Press. 43 pp.
Kehr, Helen (Ed.) (1978), *Persecution and Resistance Under the Nazis.* London: The Institute of Contemporary History and Wiener Library. 500 pp.
Krell, Robert, and Sherman, Marc I. (1997). *Medical and Psychological Effects of Concentration Camps on Holocaust Survivors. Volume 4 in the Series, Genocide: A Critical Bibliographic Review.* Series Editor: Israel W. Charny. New Brunswick, NJ.: Transaction Publishers. 290 pp.
Laska, Vera (Ed.) (1985). *Nazism, Resistance and Holocaust in World War II: A Bibliography.* Metuchen, NJ: Scarecrow Press. 183 pp.
Robinson, Jacob, and Bauer, Yehuda (Eds.) (1970). *Guide to Published Materials of the Holocaust Period, Volume I.* Jerusalem: Hebrew University, Institute of Contemporary Jewry, Division of Holocaust Studies. 245 pp.
Robinson, Jacob, and Bauer, Yehuda (Eds.) (1970). *Guide to Published Materials of the Holocaust Period, Volume II.* Jerusalem: Hebrew University, Institute of Contemporary Jewry, Division of Holocaust Studies. 334 pp.
Robinson, Jacob, and Friedman, Mrs. Philip (1973). *The Holocaust and After: Sources and Literature in English.* Jerusalem: Yad Vashem Martyrs' and Heroes' Memorial Authority, and YIVO Institute for Jewish Research. 353 pp.
Sherman, Marc I., and Charny, Israel W. (Eds.) (1994). *Holocaust and Genocide Computerized Bibliographic Database* [Version 2.2]. Published on computer diskettes and distributed by the Institute on the Holocaust and Genocide, Jerusalem.
Skirball, Sheba (Ed.) (1990). *Films of the Holocaust: An Annotated Bibliography of Collections in Israel.* New York and London: Garland Publishing. 273 pp.
Szonyi, David (Ed.) (1985). *The Holocaust: An Annotated Bibliography and Resource Guide.* New York: KTAV Press. 396 pp.
Totten, Samuel (Ed.) (1991). *First-Person Accounts of Genocidal Acts Committed in the Twentieth Century: Annotated Bibliography.* Westport, CT: Greenwood Publishers. 351 pp.
Tyrnauer, Gabrielle (Ed.) (1989). *Gypsies and the Holocaust: A Bibliography and Introductory Essay.* Montreal: Interuniversity Centre for European Studies and Montreal Institute for Genocide Studies. 51 pp.
The US Holocaust Memorial Museum (1994). *Annotated Bibliography.* Washington, DC: US Holocaust Memorial Museum. 32 pp.

BOKASSA

Eddine Ahmed Bokassa, born Jean Bedel Bokassa and later known to the world as Emperor Bokassa, was born the son of the village chief of Bobangui in the Central African Republic on February 22, 1921. At age eighteen, he joined the Free French Forces, served in Indochina, and had a distinguished and decorated military career of more than four decades. (Ironically, his love of all things French, including his French citizenship and his passport given him for his military service, led him to a convenient lapse of memory of his father beaten to death by French soldiers when he was a small child.)

In 1963, after the Central African Republic was given its independence by France, the French pressured its newly-elected leader, Bokassa's cousin, David Dacko, to appoint him Commander-in-Chief of the Army. Two years later, in 1965, Bokassa overthrew Dacko, making himself President-for-Life, and later crowning himself Emperor Bokassa I in 1977. Increasingly corrupt and dictatorial, his coronation consumed one-third of his country's annual budget and left it even more destitute than before. His tyrannical desire to unify the different elements and factions within the Central African Republic, without the requisite political and economic experience, led him to give the Army an increasingly greater role with himself at the helm. Thousands of dissidents were brutally killed or fled the country, though fully accurate figures are impossible to attain. Economic chaos was the order of the day. Perversely, it was his desire for all schoolchildren to wear school uniforms purchased from his own factories and thereby increasing his own personal coffers, including those who could ill afford them, that ultimately led to his undoing. In April 1979, Emperor Bokassa had hundreds of children arrested; over one hundred of them died of suffocation, bayonetting, beatings, and other brutalities. It was reported by eyewitnesses that he himself participated in this slaughter, poking out the eyes of any number of children with his royal ebony and ivory cane. In September 1979, led by French troops, whose government led by Valerie Giscard D'Estang had already distanced itself from Bokassa, he was overthrown and his cousin, David Dacko, restored to power. France refused him entry though he still held valid citizenship, and he was ultimately allowed to settle on the French Ivory Coast. A tribunal of the Central African Republic sentenced him to death in absentia.

In 1987, still believing himself indispensable to his country's future and largely innocent of those atrocities for which he was condemned, he voluntarily returned to the Central African Republic where he was again condemned to death after first arguing the stresses and difficulties of leadership. By the time of his return, the Army had returned to power. He was put on trial for genocidal massacres against his own people. However, his sentence was later commuted to life imprisonment at hard labor and in solitary confinement; but in 1993 he was released in a general amnesty.

—*Steven L. Jacobs*

References and Recommended Reading

Chirot, Daniel (1994). *Modern Tyrants: The Power and Prevalence of Evil in Our Age.* Princeton, NJ: Princeton University Press.

Bosnia and Rwanda: The Holocaust and More Recent Cases of Genocide

In Bosnia, Serbs waged war against Muslims, in the name of "ethnic cleansing," systematically raping and murdering civilians and throwing Muslims into concentration camps. In Rwanda, Hutu squads murdered hundreds of thousands of Tutsi—almost 20 per cent of the country's Tutsi population were destroyed in less than two months. Newspapers, magazines, and television illustrated the carnage with a depressing array of photographs and videotapes: starved, maimed, and hopeless survivors; corpses piled high, strewn on roads, jamming rivers. For many people in the West, these nightmarish images instantly recalled the pictures taken at Dachau, Buchenwald, and Bergen Belsen in 1945.

Those who sought intervention by other countries and the UN to stop the killing in Bosnia and Rwanda often explicitly compared these recent events to the Nazis' murder of millions of Europe's Jews and Gypsies. Correctly labeling the Hutu and Serbian actions as "genocide," they challenge the West and the world to act.

continues

continued

How useful is the analogy between these recent tragedies and the Holocaust? Clearly, the wanton destruction of lives and cultures in Bosnia and Rwanda merits the kind of moral outrage most people feel about the Holocaust.

One reason for failure to achieve peace in Bosnia and Rwanda was that both Serbian and Hutu forces pursued genocidal policies as part of long-brewing civil wars, a complication for which the Holocaust analogy does not prepare us. The Nazis attempted to isolate and murder two stateless, landless, unarmed and friendless peoples—the Jews and the Gypsies—in the cause of Aryan racial superiority, which transcended politics and borders. Unlike the Jews and Gypsies, today's victims were neither stateless nor without armed forces.

Coming between warring parties in a civil war is difficult enough, but in both Bosnia and Rwanda long-standing alliances with other countries complicate peace negotiations. Russia champions the Serbs; France retains links to the Hutu and Belgium to the Tutsi. Indeed, France's intervention in Rwanda on behalf of civilians was rejected by Tutsi rebels, who feared that it would inevitably favor the Hutu. Such facts in no way diminish the magnitude of the tragedies in Bosnia and Rwanda; they do, however, point to circumstances far different from those of the Holocaust. The absence of outside supporters was a fact of life and death for European Jews and Gypsies.

More useful analogies can be found. For instance, the Bosnian tragedy brings to mind the Spanish Civil War. Between 1936 and 1939, Spanish Loyalists and Fascists engaged in a blood-bath in which 200,000 soldiers and more than 130,000 civilians perished. The vast majority of civilians died in massacres or other acts of terrorism committed by both sides—acts quite comparable to those in Bosnia. The Fascists killed an additional 100,000 Loyalists in the years immediately following their victory. Ideology and religion figured as more prominent issues than ethnicity (although ethnic tensions surfaced as well), but the results were just as bloody as those in Bosnia and Rwanda.

Italy and Germany lent military support to the Spanish Fascists, and Stalin's Russia aided the Loyalists. The Western democracies remained neutral and even declared an arms embargo, in part because they feared a world war and in part because each side in Spain had strong lobbies in the West.

In thinking about Rwanda, the fate of break-away Biafra in the Nigerian civil war of 1967–1970 provides useful parallels. In just over two years, nearly one million Biafrans starved to death while Nigeria wore down the rebels. The outside world provided famine relief and help to refugees, but could not broker a settlement because Nigeria did not want anything less than total victory. In another African case relevant to Rwanda, it took an invasion by Tanzania to bring Idi Amin's murderous rule in Uganda to an end. But even then mass killings and civil war continued.

Sadly, such comparisons offer little hope for an end to the bloodshed in such conflicts short of victory by one side, mutual exhaustion, or decisive military intervention by outside forces. If we are to prevent future outbreaks of genocide and make cease-fires last, we must face the economic, political, and social problems of

continues

continued

potential Rwandas and Bosnias before they disintegrate into civil wars and worse. We must spend more time and money encouraging nations at risk to achieve social stability.

Both the Bosnian and Rwandan tragedies have histories that belie their sudden appearance in the headlines. Calling up the memory of Auschwitz may shock us into awareness, but each of those histories had moments when timely aid, pressure, or threats might have dampened the bloodlust that then became so hard to tame.

—*Robert H. Abzug*

BYSTANDERS TO GENOCIDE

The passivity of bystanders significantly increases the likelihood of genocide. Frequently, genocide evolves as a process that starts with discrimination and limited acts of violence against members of a victim group, which change individual perpetrators, institutions and social norms, and over time greater violence becomes possible and probable.

Bystanders are individuals and groups, including nations, that are witnesses to events and choose to ignore them. They are in a position to know, even if sometimes through psychological maneuvers or other ways they avoid knowing. I have distinguished between internal bystanders, who are members of the perpetrator group or society but not themselves perpetrators, and external bystanders, who are outside individuals and groups. Both types of bystanders usually remain passive or in various ways support perpetrators.

Preceding the Holocaust, very few Germans protested the increasing, intense persecution of Jews. Most Germans cooperated with Nazi authorities and boycotted Jewish stores, stopped relationships with Jewish friends and lovers, took over Jewish businesses and jobs. Over time, many initially passive bystanders joined the perpetrators. In other instances as well, like the genocide of the Armenians in Turkey, the population remained passive or in various ways supported the perpetrators.

External bystanders also remain passive or, by continuing with business as usual, even support perpetrators. Thus, in 1936 the nations of the world participated in the Berlin Olympics, thereby affirming Germany. US corporations were busy conducting business in Germany in the 1930s. As the genocide of the Armenians progressed, Germany, Turkey's ally in the war, remained passive. When Iraq used chemical weapons to destroy Kurdish villages, many countries continued to provide Iraq with arms and economic aid.

The bystanders' passivity and complicity affirms and encourages perpetrators. Hitler and the Nazis were surprised by the cooperation of the German people

Neutrality Is a Sin

In extreme situations when human lives and dignity are at stake, neutrality is a sin. It helps the killers, not the victims.

The opposite of love, I have learned, is not hate, but indifference. Jews were killed by the enemy but betrayed by their so-called allies, who found political reasons to justify their indifference or passivity.

—*Elie Wiesel, after Receiving the Congressional Gold Medal of Achievement at the White House in 1985* with their early anti-Jewish acts. When the community of nations at the Evian Conference refused to take in Jewish refugees from Germany, Goebbels, the Nazi propaganda minister, wrote in his diary that the whole world wants to do to the Jews what the Germans were doing but does not have the courage.

There are several likely reasons why internal bystanders remain passive. There is fear of authorities. However, Germans did act against the euthanasia killings of other Germans. Frequently, genocide begins or a genocidal system comes to power in difficult times, when the need for connection to the group is strong and risking ostracism by going against it is especially threatening. Usually the victim group is an historically devalued group, which further reduces the motivation to act. Finally, as bystanders remain passive, they reduce their guilt and empathic distress by further devaluing victims and thereby further distancing themselves from them, which then makes action by the bystanders even less likely.

Passivity and complicity by nations comes in part from their pursuit of national interest defined as power, wealth and influence. In addition, most nations have not historically regarded themselves as moral agents who are responsible for the welfare of those outside their borders. Diffusion of responsibility contributes to the passivity of all bystanders.

The potential power and therefore responsibility of bystanders is great. As violence against a victim group evolves, many of the perpetrators become intensely committed to their guiding ideology and the specific goal of destroying the victims, whom they see as the enemy of their group and of the fulfillment of the ideology. As a result, only bystanders can halt the evolution.

Although bystanders rarely act, individual bystanders and nations have great potential power. What one person says or does in an emergency when someone is in great need due to an accident or illness, greatly affects how other bystanders behave. In Le Chambon, the Huguenot village in France, the heroic actions of the villagers in helping Jewish refugees influenced some perpetrators, who then helped the villagers. The unusual instance of coordinated boycotts and sanctions against South Africa helped bring its apartheid system to an end. The limited military intervention by NATO in Bosnia stopped the ongoing violence.

Actions by bystanders can reaffirm the humanity of victims. They can make perpetrators afraid of, or actually experience, the negative consequences of their actions to themselves. Early actions, before strong commitment develops to an ideology or the destruction of a group, has the potential of bringing violence to a halt without the use of violence.

Preventive actions can aim at overcoming devaluation of victims and reconciliation between historically antagonistic groups. Helping previously victimized groups heal makes it less likely that they respond to threat with violence. Helping to create or strengthen democracy also makes genocide less likely, partly by bringing about culture change.

In order for "bystander nations" and the international community to act, it is essential to develop international standards for when action should be taken, by whom, and what kinds of action. It is also essential to develop effective institutions for early warning, activation, response and prevention.

—Ervin Staub

References and Recommended Reading

Latane, Bibb, and Darley, John M. (1970). *The Unresponsive Bystander: Why Doesn't He Help?* New York: Appleton-Crofts.

Staub, Ervin (1989). *The Roots of Evil: The Origins of Genocide and Other Group Violence.* Cambridge: Cambridge University Press.

Staub, Ervin (1996). Preventing Genocide: Activating Bystanders, Helping Victims and the Creation of Caring. *Peace and Conflict: Journal of Peace Psychology* 2(3), 189–201.

CAMBODIA, GENOCIDE IN

THE CAMBODIAN GENOCIDE AND ITS LEADERS

Pol Pot, with other Khmer Rouge leaders like Son Sen, Ieng Sary, Nuon Chea, Chhit Chocun and Khieu Samhan, conceived and directed the genocide in Cambodia from 1975 to 1979.

Pol Pot was born Saloth Sar in 1928. His family had royal connections. His brother Suong was an official in the royal palace. Pol Pot joined him in 1934, at age six. A year in a royal monastery was followed by six in a Catholic school. The palace compound was closeted, the old king a French puppet. Outside, Phnom Penh's inhabitants were mostly Chinese shopkeepers and Vietnamese workers. Few Cambodian childhoods were so removed from their vernacular culture.

In 1945, demanding independence from France, Buddhist monks led Khmer nationalists in common cause with Vietnamese communists. Three years later, Pol Pot went to study radioelectricity in Paris. Traveling through Saigon, he felt ill at ease in bustling Vietnam, like a "dark monkey from the mountains."

In France, Pol Pot joined the French Communist Party in its Stalinist heyday. Self-effacing, he kept company with Khieu Ponnary, the first Khmer woman to get the Baccalauréat. Their Paris student friends included Ieng Sary, Son Sen, and Khieu Samphan. Pol Pot had disagreements with Hou Yuon, later a popular Marxist intellectual, and one of their first victims on winning power. But Pot stood out in his choice of a *nom de plume:* the "Original Cambodia." Others preferred less racialist, modernist code-names like "Free Khmer" or "Khmer Worker."

Pol Pot failed his course three times, arriving home in 1953. King Sihanouk had declared martial law. Cambodia's independence movement was becoming radicalized by French colonial force. Pol Pot's brother, Chhay, joined the Cambodian and Vietnamese communists, and took him along. Vietnamese began teaching Pot to "work with the masses." To him, this was a patronizing slight, like his failure to quickly rise to leadership despite overseas experience. He decided that "Khmers should do everything on their own." Cambodia did not need to learn or import anything from its neighbors. Rather, it would recover its pre-Buddhist glory by rebuilding the powerful economy of the medieval Angkor kingdom, and regain ancient "lost territory" from Vietnam and Thailand. Pol Pot treasured his "race," not its individual members. National impurities included the foreign-educated (with the exception of his Paris group) and "hered-

Pol Pot, leader of the Khmer Rouge, walking in the Cambodian jungle. In July 1997 Pol Pot became the centerpiece in a show trial in western Cambodia by the Khmer Rouge leadership. Found guilty, he was sentenced to life in prison. He was reputed to have died in April 1998. (UPI/Corbis-Bettmann)

itary enemies"—especially Vietnamese, but also other ethnic minorities. To return Cambodians to their imagined "origins," Pol Pot needed war, and secrecy—"the basis" of the revolution. He never admitted that his real name was Saloth Sar, and that he was from an elite background.

After French and Vietnamese forces left Cambodia, Pol Pot rose in the Cambodian communist ranks. In 1962, he became Party leader. He consolidated his control during eight years of guerrilla warfare (1967–75), using the code-name "Pol." In 1969, embroiled in Vietnam, the US began a secret B-52 bombardment of Cambodia. A year later, Sihanouk was overthrown by the US-backed Lon Nol. The Vietnam War spilled across, and a new war tore Cambodia apart. American planes dropped 540,000 tons of bombs, killing 100,000 Khmer peasants. In 1973 the CIA reported that communist recruiters were effectively "using damage caused by B-52 strikes as the main theme of their propaganda."

The Khmer Rouge defeated the Lon Nol regime on April 17, 1975. Forced evacuation of the two million inhabitants of Phnom Penh began. Hou Yuon, who opposed the evacuation, was shot. Son Sen became Deputy Prime Minister under Pol Pot and took charge of the General Staff and Security for the Communist Party of Kampuchea, which operated in secrecy. In a 1975 victory speech, Pol Pot claimed "clean victory . . . without any foreign connection." Cambodia cut itself off from the world. Foreign and minority languages were banned, and all neighboring countries attacked. Rice and endangered wildlife were exported to China for weapons. Cambodia's Buddhist religion and culture were banned. Peasants were forced into unpaid collective labor. Spouses were separated, family meals prohibited. A Khmer Rouge document noted: "There is a little friction with the people. But we can abandon the people, there is no problem."

In this prison camp state of eight million inmates, 1.7 million were worked, starved or beaten to death. *[The author notes that this figure, at which he arrived in his studies of the genocide in Cambodia, has been accepted by the United Nations.—Ed.]* Minority and urban groups suffered disproportionately, but half the victims came from the peasant majority. Pol Pot said: "Don't be afraid to lose one or two people of bad background." He claimed to be "years ahead" of other Asian communist states. "We have no model." This disguised the influence of Stalinism, of Maoism in the call for a "Super Great Leap Forward," and even of the French Revolution, which the Khmer Rouge copied when they redesigned Cambodia's month into ten-day weeks. Dissident communists who favored "a system of plenty" were consid-

Cambodia Chronology

1954 Cambodia gains independence from France; new government, a constitutional monarchy, is led by King Norodom Sihanouk.
1960 Saloth Sar, known as Pol Pot, helps set up Khmer Rouge, a Communist party.
1961 Uprising against Sihanouk begun by Khmer Rouge.
1970 Right-wing coup, supported by United States and led by Prime Minister Lon Nol, topples Sihanouk, who joins with Khmer Rouge against government. Khmer Rouge gets Chinese and Vietnamese help.
1975 Khmer Rouge topples Lon Nol. Khmer Rouge executes ruthless instant evacuation of capital, Phnom Penh. Thousands die of exhaustion and starvation. Purges begin among Khmer Rouge leadership and ethnic minorities, then extend to population and process of genocide and "autogenocide" *[term given by UN Human Rights Commission to genocide of a people against itself rather than a definable outgroup—Ed.]* builds.
1978 Vietnam invades Cambodia to stop Khmer Rouge border attacks.
1979 Phnom Penh falls to Vietnamese, who install client regime made up mostly of Khmer Rouge defectors. Khmer Rouge retreat to Thai border, set up guerrilla bases. Khmer Rouge continue to be recognized as legal representative of Cambodia to UN for fourteen years, and receive millions of dollars of US support.

—*Press Reports*

ered corrupted by "a little prosperity," "taken to pieces" by material things.

Pol Pot did not conceive of Cambodia at peace. He shared the traditional Khmer elite's racism against Vietnamese and other minorities, and their designs on "lost territories." With the help of large scale Chinese aid, Pol Pot and Son Sen built up the Khmer Rouge army for war against Vietnam. "We could lose tremendously if we apply international law," Sen conceded in 1976. Raids on Vietnam, Thailand, and Laos began the next year. Pol Pot ordered his army to "kill the enemy at will, and the contemptible Vietnamese will surely shriek like monkeys screeching all over the forest." His troops were to "tie up the enemy by the throat, shoulders and ribs on both sides, his waist, his thighs, his knees, his calves, his ankles . . . smashing and breaking his head." Son Sen took charge of the "Highway 1 Front." On September 24, 1977, his troops crossed the Vietnamese border and massacred three hundred civilians. Three months later, Sen presided at a meeting in which Pol Pot proclaimed: "Each Cambodian is to kill thirty Vietnamese, in order to take southern Vietnam back."

Son Sen's secret police chief, Deuch, and chief interrogator and former student, Mam Nay, ran the notorious Tuol Sleng prison, known as "S-21," nerve center of the genocide. Of 16,000 prisoners held there, seven survived. Son Sen also supervised the regime's bloodiest purges, in the Eastern Zone along Highway 1. On September 24, 1977, the same day as his attack on Vietnam, he sent Pol Pot a list of 21 people in Region 22 "who have been named by enemies" under interrogation. Sen added: "Some of these people we have arrested and brought to S-21, some have been arrested in the Region. But we have not yet taken measures against most of them . . . We request that the Region follow-up those whom we suspect, and take measures according to the concrete situation." In December, Sen was promoted to the CPK Standing Committee.

Meanwhile, his wife Yun Yat was wiping out Buddhism, a "reactionary" religion, "incompatible with the revolution," whose "cultural base must be uprooted." Only 2,000 of Cambodia's 70,000 monks are known to have survived in 1979. Yat boasted in 1978 that Cambodians had "stopped believing" and that the monks had "left the temples." She added: "The problem gradually becomes extinguished. Hence there is no problem."

When Cambodian communists rebelled in the eastern zone in May 1978, Pol Pot's armies were unable to crush them quickly. The regime broadcast a call not only to "exterminate the 50 million Vietnamese" but also to "purify the masses of the people" of Cambodia. Of 1.5 million easterners, branded as "Khmer bodies with Vietnamese minds," at least 100,000 were exterminated. In 1979, surviving rebels succeeded Pol Pot, after Hanoi drove his army into Thailand.

Pol Pot had predicted that only "piles of the enemy's bones" would remain. Mass graves mark every district with the bodies of his victims. Yale University's Cambodian Genocide Program has so far located over two hundred "killing field" sites with a total of 9,500 mass grave pits. We suspect there may be another 10,000 such pits. In a briefing to his guerrilla commanders in 1988, Pol Pot blamed most of the killings on "Vietnamese agents." But he defended having massacred defeated officers, soldiers and officials. "This strata of the imperialists had to be totally destroyed," he insisted.

In 1996 Ieng Sary defected from Khmer Rouge, and was given amnesty by the Royal Cambodian Government. Further splintering followed. In June 1997, Pol Pot's last loyalists, fleeing his jungle stronghold in northern Cambodia, massacred Son Sen, Yun Yat, and eight relatives, driving trucks over the bodies as they retreated. Pol Pot was soon captured by other Khmer Rouge, led by Khieu Samphan, Nuon Chea, and Chhit Choeun, who staged a perfunctory show trial. A fair trial, and justice for the victims, never took place, but a report in January, 1998 stated that Pol Pot was under house arrest, that he was suffering from some undisclosed medical difficulty, and was no longer at the helm of the Khmer Rouge, and in April, 1998 he was reported to have died and that his body was burned reportedly in the presence of Thai officials.

—Ben Kiernan

References and Recommended Reading

Kiernan, Ben (1996). *The Pol Pot Regime: Race, Power and Genocide in Cambodia Under the Khmer Rouge, 1975–1979.* New Haven, CT: Yale University Press.

KHMER ROUGE AND CAMBODIA

In proportion to its population, Cambodia underwent a human catastrophe unparalleled in this century. Out of a 1970 population of probably nearly 7,100,000, Cambodia probably lost almost 4 million people to war, rebellion, man-made famine, genocide, politicide, and mass murder. From democide [see DEMOCIDE] alone, almost all concentrated in the years 1970 to 1980, successive governments and guerrilla groups murdered almost 3,300,000 men, women, and children (including 35,000 foreigners). Most of these, probably close to 2,400,000, were murdered by the communist Khmer Rouge.

In other areas of the world, democide has not significantly affected population

A pile of human skulls and bones sits near a memorial pagoda at the Tuol Sleng Museum of Genocidal [illegible] Khmer Rouge torture prison in Phnom Penh. (Corbis/Chris Rainier)

totals, for they are too large. The margin of error alone exceeds the magnitude of the democide. But for Cambodia the relatively small population clearly shows the demographic cataclysm.

The greatest democide during these years was committed by the Khmer Rouge. Most deadly was their general treatment of urbanites and peasants living in their controlled areas, particularly beginning in 1973. As they would do when they assumed full power, the Khmer Rouge rapidly emptied cities, dispersing the people into the countryside and forcing them to assume the lives of peasants. In occupied areas, religious practice, including the Buddhism so central to the Cambodian way of life, was forbidden. So was any religion—among those executed for exercising their religion were the priests. Money was eliminated, as were free speech and free travel, even between villages; old songs were forbidden. Farming was completely collectivized; eating was communal; peasants worked according to schedules and rules set up by the Khmer Rouge cadre, each of whom had absolute command over the life or death of each peasant. In some places one worked virtually every day from morning to well after dark; and death in the field, village, or town could come from violation of the smallest rule. In short, the Khmer Rouge instituted a system of terror.

In April of 1975, the Khmer Rouge captured the capital city of Phnom Penh and ordered everyone out of the city at gunpoint. In this and all newly occupied cities and towns, the order to evacuate was implacable. Everyone. All 2 million to almost 3 million in the capital, and in the days following perhaps 200,000 in Batambang, 130,000 in Svay Rieng, 60,000 in Kompong Chhnang, 60,000 in Kompong Speu, 50,000 in Siem Reap, and so on. Four million to nearly 4,240,000 overall; whether sick, infirm, or aged; whether being operated on or in labor with child. The order was implacable: "Go! Go! You must leave!"

And they did. Families left in any way they could: the wealthy or middle class in cars; some on heavily loaded motor scooters or bicycles; the poor on their feet. Some ill or infirm hobbled along; some thrown from hospitals crawled along on hands and knees. Failure to evacuate meant death. Failure of any in the mass of humanity that clogged the roads out of a city and in the neighboring countryside to obey Khmer Rouge orders meant death. Failure to give the Khmer Rouge what they wanted, whether car, motor scooter, bicycle, watch, whatever, meant death.

Which direction the people exited the city depended on which side of it they were on when they received the evacuation order. Those that were refugees were often told to return to their home village; but for the mass, and particularly the urbanites, where they went after evacuation and what village they were eventually settled in depended on the whim of the Khmer Rouge troops along the way. Some food was provided, and here and there shelter was occasionally available, but even for those to whom "aid" was given, the trip was hell. People were jumbled together, trudging along for days or weeks, usually with whatever clothes or covering they could grab and provisions taken at the last moment. Many had minimal supplies, since they had believed the Khmer Rouge, who had said that the evacuation would only be for a few days. The very young and old, those already sick or injured or infirm, that is, those most susceptible to the elements, sickness, and hunger, soon died on the roads or trails. One of these trudging millions, a medical doctor named Vann Hay, said that every 200 meters he saw a dead child.

Including those killed outright, the toll from this utterly outrageous and unbelievable policy is in dispute. Whether 40,000 to 80,000 evacuees died, as one scholar not unsympathetic to the Khmer Rouge at that time claims, or 280,000 to 400,000 as the CIA estimates, the sheer horror of this urban expulsion is undeniable. As word about it reached the outside world via the few foreigners remaining in the capital at the time, many were incredulous while others were shocked. *(One prestigious pacifist magazine in the*

"Comrade Ox Did Not Object When His Family Was Killed"

People were instructed to be like oxen: "Comrade Ox never refused to work. Comrade Ox was obedient. Comrade Ox did not complain. Comrade Ox did not object when his family was killed." A soldier told one "new" person that it was better that her mother had died "than a cow . . . [cows] help us a lot and do not eat rice. They are much better than you pigs." Part of this extreme devaluation stemmed from the fact that "new" people were often regarded as "war slaves." "Many times we heard soldiers shout, 'Prisoners of war, you are pigs. We have suffered much. Now you are our prisoners and you must suffer.'" While sometimes tolerated, such "enemies" were expected to work hard and be obedient. If they committed offenses, their execution would be no loss. When explaining why his commune leader both killed and ordered the execution of so many people, a prisoner notes: "We weren't quite people. We were lower forms of life, because we were enemies. Killing us was like swatting flies, a way to get rid of undesirables." Such Khmer Rouge were indoctrinated into an ideology that instructed them to have no feeling for the enemy. As one cadre told me: "We were brainwashed to cut off our heart from the enemy, to be willing to kill those who had betrayed the revolution, even if the person was a parent, sibling, friend, or relative. Everything we did was supposed to be for the party."

—*Alexander Laban Hinton*

West called for understanding of the different values of an oriental civilization in the service of a revolution to create a new democratic people's govenment. -Ed.) It should be noted, however, that the Khmer Rouge had similarly ejected people from urban areas under their control during the war. They were only faithful to their own doctrine.

As the evacuees reached their home villages or were assigned one, there was usually no relief from the horrors already suffered; they were just different in kind. Under the Khmer Rouge, no Cambodian was free. There were no political, civil, or human rights. Cambodians could not freely travel, not even from village to village. There was no freedom of speech. Religion, traditionally Buddhism, was not allowed. Freedom of organization did not exist. While freedom to pick one's husband or wife and cohabit varied from place to place, sexual freedom was severely controlled. There were no appeals, no courts, no judges, no law. No one has ever reported a trial during this period.

There were no practicing lawyers, doctors, teachers, engineers, scientists, or the like. These professions were deemed unnecessary or presumed to contain simple truths any peasant could pick up through experience. Those who had been such professionals under the old regime were either killed or had to work in the field like everyone else, depending on the local cadre and region. In other words, *the Cambodia of the Khmer Rouge was a nation-sized concentration camp in which all suffered the torments of hell.* It was divided into compounds with keepers, each applying the heat, brimstone, and pitchforks to his inmates largely as he saw fit. There were no rights, but everywhere in this hell inmates had two duties: instant and unquestioning obedience to every command of the Khmer Rouge cadre, and work. The result was terror, fatigue, hunger, disease, and death.

Some 90 percent of Cambodians believed in some form of Buddhism, and many had received a rudimentary education from the monks. So central and locally powerful an institution could not be allowed to be independent, so the Khmer Rouge set out with vigor to destroy it. Monks were defrocked; many were simply executed. All the top hierarchy and most of the others were killed—one estimate is that out of 40,000 to 60,000 monks only 800 to 1,000 survived to carry on their religion. As for the Buddhist temples that populated the landscape of Cambodia, virtually all, 95 percent, were destroyed; the few remaining were turned into warehouses or used for some other demeaning purpose. Incredibly, in the very short span of a year or so, the Cambodian people had the center of their culture, its spiritual incarnation, and its institutions wiped out. In most if not all of the country at one time or another, simply being of Chinese, Vietnamese, Thai, or Lao ancestry was sufficient for execution. Even Cambodian minorities, such as the Moslem Cham, were sought out and killed as part of a "centrally organized genocidal campaign."

This was genocide, and it was pervasive. The basic reason for most of this democide was ideological. The Khmer Rouge were fanatical communists and they wanted to establish "the most advanced and purest form of communism in the world."

The Khmer Rouge were willing to kill millions of Cambodians, even until no more than a million remained, to reconstruct a completely collectivized Cambodia with no class enemies left; no imperialists or anything foreign; no feudalists or those holding power in the past, such as the monks; no capitalists. All others would work and eat communally; all would have all their needs fulfilled by the "Organization." The family structure would be unneeded, children would be taken away from their parents at a very young age and brought up by the Organization. All would be equal; all would be happy.

Secondly, they wanted to create immediately an independent and self-sufficient Cambodia. For the Khmer Rouge, the key concept was "independence-sovereignty." Any dependence on other nations for anything—whether food, newsprint or machinery—was to be eliminated forthwith. They also wanted to recover the ancient glory and lands of the Khmer Kingdom. Part of this glory, they felt, lay in the pure soul of the Khmer that existed then, a soul that had been corrupted by modern life and Western influence. Emptying the cities, forcing the millions of urbanites to work like oxen in the fields, to learn the simple peasant life, would help achieve this purification.

Our English vocabulary, as rich as it is, simply has no word for the kind of state that was created by the Khmer Rouge in 1975. Nor do we political scientists have a concept or theory for it. These communists turned Cambodia into a gulag of nearly 7 million people, a "hell state."

—R. J. Rummel

References and Recommended Reading

Rummel, R. J. (1994). *Death by Government.* New Brunswick, NJ: Transaction Publishers.

Rummel, R. J. (1999). *Statistics of Democide: Genocide and Mass Murder since 1900.* New Brunswick, NJ: Transaction Publishers.

CEAUSESCU, NICOLAE

Born January 26, 1918, in Scornicesti, Romania, Nicolae Ceausescu was executed on December 25, 1989, together with his wife, Elena, after being overthrown in a coup that ended his decades-long dictatoral rule over his impoverished country.

Joining the Communist Party at age fifteen, he was imprisoned for his political activism at age eighteen, and again at age twenty-two. In 1967, at age forty-nine, he became President of the State Council and Prime Minister of Romania, succeeding Gheorghe Gheorghiu-Dej upon his death; in 1969, General Secretary of the Communist Party, and in 1974, first President of Romania. Originally popular as a "man of the people," and supported by the intellectual elite of Romania, his regime turned increasingly dictatorial and repressive as his repeated attempts at modernization met with recurring failures. His economic and industrial failures led to increasing impoverishment that may yet take generations to recover, if at all.

It was Ceausescu's policies of increasing suppression of dissent that merit his inclusion in the *Encyclopedia of Genocide,* and mark him, especially toward the end of his life, as one of Eastern Europe's most brutal tyrants. In 1971, upon his return from North Korea and deeply impressed with that country's leadership under Kim Il Sung, he attempted his own version of China's "cultural revolution," whereby increasing modernization became the order of the day and any criticism of either economic policy or government bureaucracy was brutally suppressed. Population relocation was also instituted. In addition, ethnic minorities within Romania were also suppressed genocidally. Though the actual numbers of victims may be somewhat smaller than other regimes, and actual figures are difficult if not impossible to obtain, Ceausescu, together with his wife, followed the classic pattern of brutal suppression of the people and the deaths of countless innocent men, women, and children. Following Stalin, despite a deteriorating situation, Ceausescu practiced a "cult of personality" with all of the appropriate accoutrements such as large photo billboards and the bestowing of additional titles of adulation on himself.

In 1989 he attempted to suppress a demonstration for human rights in the city of Timisoara, which in turn ignited a flame of rebellion and ultimately turned even the Army against him. Attempting unsuccessfully to flee Bucharest, he and his wife were captured, a hasty show trial was held, and they were both executed. After his death, in the 1990s the West learned of rampant AIDS among the children of Romania due to unsterilized syringes and infected blood, and a network of orphanages where children were underfed and grossly neglected, and regressive medical practices throughout the country.

—Steven L. Jacobs

References and Recommended Reading

Chirot, Daniel (1994). *Modern Tyrants: The Power and Prevalence of Evil in Our Age.* Princeton, NJ: Princeton University Press.

CENTRE FOR COMPARATIVE GENOCIDE STUDIES

The Centre for Comparative Genocide Studies was established in December 1993 within the School of History, Philosophy and Politics at Macquarie University, Australia, and is the only Centre of its kind in the southern hemisphere. Its main objective is to educate people about genocide and the consequences of prejudice and racism, and ideally to work toward the prevention of genocide.

Under the direction of Professor Colin Tatz, the Centre conducts a third year politics course entitled "The Politics of Genocide," organizes community education courses on genocide, Holocaust and antisemitism, and holds conferences for members of relevant professions, schools and government institutions. It regularly receives international scholars and disseminates information through its publications, both nationally and internationally.

Ongoing research projects focus on aspects of genocide in Rwanda, Australia, Bosnia, Cambodia, and Timor; on legal definitions of genocide; the nature of extremist ideologies and their relationship to genocide; the relationship between modernity and genocide; the relationship between racism and genocide; the value of the concept of "ethnocide"; and Gypsies and women in the Holocaust. Postgraduate research is being conducted on legal aspects of genocide, denialism *[denials of genocides—Ed.],* genocide and medicine, bioethics and psychiatry, the media, ancient antisemitism and blood libel, and the role of indigenous police battalions in the Holocaust. Collation and cataloguing of documents gathered by the recently disbanded Australian Special Investigations Unit, entrusted to the Centre, has begun.

The Centre publishes an international journal, *International Network on the Holocaust and Genocide,* its own annual collection of articles, *Genocide Perspectives,* a quarterly newsletter, and a monograph series consisting of distinguished postgraduate theses is scheduled. The Centre provides a reading room facility for members and students, computer facilities including the *Holocaust and Genocide Bibliographical Database* and a selection of rare books relating to genocide and racial theory not available in the main Macquarie Library.

Funding for the Centre is obtained from private donations, bequests, grants, membership subscriptions and sponsorships. The management committee is drawn from several Schools. The advisory board consists of six Macquarie University academics, representatives from other tertiary and secondary educational institutions and relevant community groups. Over fifty associates of the Centre, all national and international scholars, have registered their support for the Centre, wishing to share their expertise, to advise and cooperate on research, supervision, and teaching and to assist in the Centre's objectives. The Centre's director is Professor Colin Tatz; and the Centre's deputy director is Professor Konrad Kwiet.

For further information, contact the Centre for Comparative Genocide Studies, School of History, Philosophy and Politics, Macquarie University NSW 2109, Australia, tel: 61–2–9850–8822; fax: 61–2–9850–8892, e-mail: ctatz@laurel.ocs.mq.edu.au; website: http://genocide.sunnet.com.

—David Young

CHILDREN AND GENOCIDE

CHILDREN'S MORTALITY AND GENOCIDE

Nothing conveys the plight of children worldwide as clearly as their massive mortality rates. Estimates of the number of under-five deaths for selected years are shown in Table 1.

The number of children dying each year has been declining, but the numbers are still enormous, with around a million dying every month. Children's deaths account for about one-third of all deaths worldwide. In northern Europe or the United States children account for only two to three percent of all deaths. In many less developed countries more than half the deaths are deaths of children, which means there are more deaths

TABLE 1
Annual Children's Deaths

Year	*Child Deaths*
1960	18,900,000
1970	17,400,000
1980	14,700,000
1990	12,700,000
1991	12,821,000
1992	13,191,000
1993	13,272,000
1994	12,588,000
1995	12,465,000
1996	11,694,000

Source: United Nations Children's Fund, *The State of the World's Children* (New York: UNICEF/Oxford University Press, annual).

of young people than of old people. The median age at death in 1990 was five or lower in Angola, Burkina Faso, Ethiopia, Guinea, Malawi, Mali, Mozambique, Niger, Rwanda, Sierra Leone, Somalia, Tanzania, and Uganda. This means that in these thirteen countries at least half the deaths were of children under five. In the United States the median age at death in 1990 was 76, and in the best cases, Japan, Norway, Sweden, and Switzerland, it was 78.

The number of children who die each year can be made more meaningful by comparing it with the mortality due to warfare. There have been about 100 million fatalities in wars between the years 1700 and 1987. That yields a long-term average of about 350,000 fatalities per year. The yearly average between 1986 and 1991 has been estimated at about 427,800. These figures can be compared to the more than 12 million children's deaths in each of these years.

The most lethal war in all of human history was World War II, during which there were about 15 million battle deaths. If civilian deaths are added in, including genocide and other forms of mass murder, the number of deaths in and around World War II totaled around 51,358,000. Annualized for the six year period, the rate comes to about 8.6 million deaths a year—when children's deaths were running at well over 20 million per year. This most intense war in history resulted in a lower death rate, over a very limited period, than results from children's mortality year in and year out. Counting late additions, at the end of 1987 there were 58,156 names on the Vietnam War Memorial in Washington, DC. That is less than the number of children under five who die every two days throughout the world. A memorial for those children who die worldwide would be more than 200 times as long as the Vietnam Memorial, and a new one would be needed every year.

Children die for many different reasons. The immediate cause of death for most children is not murder, direct physical abuse, or incurable diseases such as AIDS, but, as shown in Table 2, a combination of malnutrition and quite ordinary, manageable diseases such as diarrhea, malaria, and measles. Given adequate resources, these diseases are readily managed. If enough resources and attention are given to small children, most would thrive. Many do not do well because their families are desperately poor. But focusing on the children and their families alone blinds us to the ways in which their conditions reflect the policies and actions of their societies.

The failures of governments in relation to children are partly due to bad policies and programs, but more often to absent and inadequate programs resulting from the treatment of children's programs as low priority items in national budgets. Children could be fed adequately in almost every country in the world, even the poorest among them, *if* that were regarded as high priority in government circles. Even if it can be claimed that some countries truly are too poor to care for their children, it cannot

TABLE 2
Estimated Annual Deaths of Children under 5 by Cause, 1986

Cause	*Number (millions)*	*Proportion (percentage)*
Diarrhea	5.0	35.4
Malaria	3.0	21.3
Measles	2.1	14.9
Neonatal Tetanus	0.8	5.7
Pertussis (Whooping Cough)	0.6	4.3
Other Acute Respiratory Infections	1.3	9.2
Other	1.3	9.2
Estimated Total	14.1	100.0

Source: United Nations Children's Fund, *The State of the World's Children 1987* (New York: UNICEF/Oxford University Press, 1987).

be claimed that they have been born into a world that is too poor to care for them. Massive children's mortality is not necessary and inevitable.

Most children's deaths cannot be described as murders. But that does not mean that they are accidental or natural or inevitable. They result from a form of negligent homicide. Negligent homicide is still homicide in that the deaths are avoidable and unnecessary. The deaths of children are dispersed all over the globe, and are sustained over time. There is no central command structure causing these deaths to happen. There is nothing like the Wannsee Conference of January 1942

The roundup and expulsion of Jewish children of the Lotz ghetto in Poland. (Yad Vashem, Jerusalem)

at which the Nazis systematically set out their plans for the extermination of the Jews of Europe. The widespread deliberate and sustained neglect of children is not the calculated program of a few madmen assembled at a particular moment in history. Arguably, the massive mortality of children is more frightening precisely because it occurs worldwide with no central coordination mechanism. *The culpability is not individual but systemic.*

Some argue that genocide should be defined narrowly, as deliberate extermination, to prevent the debasement and trivialization of the concept. However, a narrow definition may suggest that other kinds of large-scale mortality that are permitted to take place are less important. The alternative is to acknowledge that there are *different kinds of genocide* associated with different categories of victims and different forms of intentionality.

The massive mortality of children is not the deliberate action of readily identified actors, in a specific place and time. It differs in many ways from the Holocaust and other atrocities commonly described as genocides. The differences, however, are not sufficient to dismiss the issue. The conclusion is inescapable: *children's mortality is so massive, so persistent, and so unnecessary, it should be recognized as a kind of genocide.*

Where children's mortality rates are much higher than they need to be, the governments' policies amount to a form of genocide. When not just one child but children as a class are not adequately nourished and cared for, that constitutes an ongoing crime by society. And as a crime there should be mechanisms in law for correcting that manifest injustice, including means for calling not only parents and local communities but also governments to account.

—George Kent

References and Recommended Reading

Kent, George (1995). *Children in the International Political Economy.* London/New York: Macmillan/St. Martin's.

United Nations Children's Fund (1980– ; annual). *The State of the World's Children.* New York: UNICEF/Oxford University Press.

CHILDREN OF SURVIVORS OF GENOCIDE

The knowledge of the effects of genocide on children of survivors, who themselves have not been directly exposed to the violent impact, derives almost exclusively from the offspring of Holocaust survivors. This last group has received the attention of both clinicians and researchers since the 1960s. In the nineties, the initially divided opinions seem to become integrated in a unified view as to the effects that genocide can have on the offspring of survivors.

Concepts and Terminology

Diverse concepts have been used to indicate the effects of the Holocaust on the offspring of survivors. Each concept stems from a distinct perspective and some concepts seem to obscure more than they clarify. Examples of such concepts are: *transgenerational traumatization*—implying that the offspring is actually traumatized; *intergenerational* or *transgenerational transmission*—implying similarity between the effects on survivors and the effects on their offspring; and *second generation effects*—implying that most children of survivors are affected. Most authors using these terms clearly do not support these implications, but this has not prevented the field from being flooded by a vague terminology.

History

The deleterious effects of the Holocaust on the children of the survivors were first

CHILDREN OF VICTIMS AND PERPETRATORS OF THE HOLOCAUST IN DIALOGUE

Fifty years after the Holocaust the descendants of both sides have been able to encounter each other. A group setting was formed in which descendants of Nazi perpetrators and Jewish descendants of Holocaust survivors could face each other and initiate an open dialogue. Five encounters took place over a period of four years between a group of eight descendants of Holocaust perpetrators and a group of five American and four Israeli descendants of Holocaust survivors. The questions addressed were as follows:

1. Could they face each other genuinely?
2. Could such meetings help each party work through aspects that could not be worked through in their own 'tribal ego' setting?
3. Through such an encounter, would a common agenda emerge over and beyond the separate agendas of each side?

The first encounter was devoted to getting acquainted mainly by listening to each other's personal accounts and stories. In the remaining sessions, the scheduling of the encounters was planned by the group itself. The following are the major issues that were discussed in these encounters:

1. *The impact the Holocaust still has on my life.* Members of both groups shared their own experiences—how, when and in what ways they could trace the after-effects of the Holocaust within their own lives. For some this was a daily struggle, with sleeplessness, fears, and uncontrollable reactions—many times associated with the silence, repression or other difficult reactions of their parents.
2. *Self and social estrangement.* Acknowledgment of a personal relationship to the Holocaust was accompanied by a feeling of estrangement, both internal (from oneself) as well as external (from one's social surroundings).
3. *Feelings of uprootedness.* The Jewish members of the group suffered first of all from physical uprootedness, as their parents had immigrated to the USA or to Israel after the Holocaust. This physical uprootedness was usually accompanied by psychological uprootedness associated with the fact that their parents could not overcome the loss of so many family members and had difficulty in integrating themselves into the new society. The German members of the group shared this feeling of psychological uprootedness but for other reasons: They felt that due to the atrocities committed by their parents, their roots have been poisoned and they could no longer draw support from their origins. They had to develop new roots as did the descendants of the survivors.
4. *Difficulty in becoming socially and psychologically independent of one's parents.* "Can I

continues

continued

allow myself to live my own life, neither dependent nor counterdependent to that of my parents?" This was a major issue for members of both groups. While for the Jewish descendants separation from their parents was more difficult because their parents leaned on them emotionally, descendants of Nazi perpetrators tended to counterreact, thereby creating other problems for emotional independence. This problem becomes more severe over time, especially when the parents age and the objective need to care for them becomes a real necessity.

5. *How to live with so much death within and around oneself?* In many ways members of both groups struggle daily with dreams of death, bearing names of dead people (especially Jewish descendants of survivors), having fantasies of sacrificing themselves for a constructive human cause (especially descendants of perpetrators). One descendant of the survivors said: "We talk about our feelings, emotions and ideas, but they all concern the dead people who are in the back of our minds." Perhaps not by coincidence many members of the group belong to the helping professions.
6. *Dialogue with the victim and victimizer inside oneself.* Members of the two groups could quite easily establish an open dialogue with the *victim* in themselves. But it was much more difficult for both groups to identify and enter into an open dialogue with the *victimizer* within oneself and to let the two 'figures' talk with each other. It became clear that we all have this potential role within ourselves, and only by openly acknowledging and entering into a dialogue with the potential victimizer within us all could its uncontrolled potential be reduced for future unexpected situations.
7. *Scaling of power, suffering and heroism.* We all tend to create a scale of suffering—who suffered more, who less? It is much more difficult to relate to the experiences of the other as just being different, not more or less. As we cannot grasp the experiences our parents had during the Holocaust, the scaling helps us live with it. Something similar happened around the subject of heroism or power—who was more a hero? How to maintain the legitimacy of differences without using scaling is a problem, since scaling in itself creates unnecessary pain and humiliation.
8. *Asymmetry among the parents—symmetry among the descendants.* It was difficult but important to bear in mind that while we develop a common feeling of mutual trust and respect suggesting a new symmetry between parties in the dialogue, this by no means erased the asymmetry that still exists in our minds between our parents during the Holocaust where there were victimizers and victims. These two types of

continues

continued

relationships are difficult to maintain simultaneously.

9. *The capacity to live with the past on different levels.* Through the group experience it became clear that the outcome of this process is not to forget or to be done with the past once and for all, but to find new ways to live with it, perhaps in ways that are more conscious but also less threatening and self-destructive. By working through such massive trauma one does not end it or let it go, but one can find new ways to live with it. The Holocaust will always be a presence, but its negative impact on our lives and the lives of others can be reduced through conscious working through processes.
10. *Doing for ourselves—helping others.* From the outset of the group work there was a dilemma: How much time should we devote to ourselves and how much should we devote to working and helping other people in a similar process? At first, this group chose to use most of the time for itself; during the later meetings, attention was slowly shifted to activities of members of the group outside the group context.

—Dan Bar-On

References and Recommended Reading

Bar-On, Dan (1989). *Legacy of Silence: Encounters with Children of the Third Reich.* Cambridge, MA: Harvard University Press. Paperback edition, 1991. Also Paris: Eshel, 1991 (French); Frankfurt/Main: Campus Verlag, 1993 (German); Tokyo: Jili Tsushin Sha, 1993 (Japanese); Hamburg: Rohwolt Verlag, 1996 (Paperback) (German); Beer Sheva, Israel: Ben Gurion University of the Negev Press, 1997 (Hebrew).

Bar-On, Dan (1990). Children of perpetrators of the Holocaust: Working through one's moral self. *Psychiatry,* 53, 229–245.

Bar-On, Dan (1995). Encounters between descendants of Nazi perpetrators and descendants of Holocaust survivors. *Psychiatry,* 58(3), 225–245.

Bar-On, Dan (1995). *Fear and Hope: Life-Stories of Five Israeli Families of Holocaust Survivors, Three Generations in a Family.* Cambridge, MA: Harvard University Press. Also Tel Aviv: Lochamei Hagetaot-Hakibbutz Hameuchad, 1991 (Hebrew); Hamburg: Rottbuch (in press) (German); Taiwan: Jinni (in press) (Chinese).

noticed by clinicians who treated these children in the 1960s. They were impressed by the presence of the effects of the Holocaust in the clinical picture they observed. Further observation and analysis led them to the conclusion that children of survivors were vulnerable to specific forms of pathology. When researchers tried to confirm these observations in systematic and later on also in controlled studies, they appeared unable to do so. A gap between clinicians and researchers developed, researchers blaming the bias of clinicians and clinicians blaming the insensitive way research has tried to grasp complex clinical phenomena.

Questions

In order to map the consequences of the Holocaust on the offspring of its survivors, we can distinguish between three fields and their related questions:

1. Mental health—Do children of survivors show more signs of psychopathology than others?
2. Intrapersonal and interpersonal well-being—Has the background of the Holocaust affected the well-being and the pattern of interpersonal relations of the offspring of survivors?
3. Contents of consciousness—In what way has the Holocaust in-

fluenced the way children of survivors perceive themselves and their surrounding world?

Findings

On the question of psychopathology, it has been proven unequivocally in studies of groups of the offspring of Holocaust survivors that they do *not* show more psychopathology than control groups, and also that there is no specific diagnostic category related to the status of being offspring of survivors. There are indications in clinical practice, however, that when children of survivors do suffer from mental disorders, the disorders are more severe or more persistent. Moreover, relative to comparison groups, while the offspring of survivors appear a well-functioning group, they do show at the same time somewhat more signs of distress and these signs tend to appear in the realm of feelings of depression, guilt and anxiety, and in the regulation of aggression. The best documented differences between the offspring of survivors and control groups lie in the field of interpersonal characteristics. Although conceptualized in different ways, evidence was found that adult children of survivors feel more responsibility in the relationships with their parents, have more difficulties in maintaining boundaries in relationships with others, and more difficulties in attaining intimate and satisfying relationships. These phenomena have been conceptualized as problems in the separation and individuation of the offspring.

The gap between clinical knowledge and knowledge derived from empirical research has remained. One should realize that most statements about the effects on the offspring of survivors are based on quantitative research comparing this group with other groups, and that the conclusions in no way mean that *all* of the offspring are affected in similar ways. The mean scores on a variety of measures show statistically significant differences, but this does not say much about the strength or the prevalence of these effects in this population. It is clear that the effects mentioned are not present in the whole group and that no inferences can be made on the individual level. Research has found the offspring to be hardly different and maybe somewhat more optimistic in their world views. On

Rwandan Children Perpetrators and Victims

Most of the killings in Rwanda was done in public and by the public—including children. For many youths, the choice was to kill or be killed. Some youngsters followed their parents in frenzied machete attacks on former friends and neighbors. Others led some of the savagery, hunting Tutsis in deadly packs in an all-too-real version of the novel *Lord of the Flies.*

In a UNICEF study based on interviews with 3,030 children, nearly 80 percent of those interviewed had lost immediate family members, many witnessed the slayings, many saw their parents tortured, their mothers raped, their fathers hacked to death, their sisters nailed to trees, more than one-third saw other children take part in killings, 16 percent hid under dead bodies to escape being killed, nearly all heard family or friends plead for their lives or scream in pain, and saw corpses and hacked body parts. Many clearly are haunted by the horrors they experienced. "There's no baseline in history to compare with what we're seeing in Rwanda," said a UNICEF expert, "not even with Holocaust survivors."

—*Press Reports*

Rwanda: Post-Genocidal Post-Traumatic Stress Disorders

Rwandans are suffering from post-traumatic stress disorders (PTSD) that are off the scales most Westerners use. Survivors suffer from confusion, anxiety, depression, flashbacks, difficulty concentrating, sleep disturbances, anti-social behavior and acting out.

Criminals' impunity from justice poses a psychological hurdle for victims as well. Most killers escaped to refugee camps outside the country. The criminal justice system is only slowly becoming operational because many intellectuals, including judges and lawyers, were among the first to die in the massacres. "In environments where perpetrators are not held accountable, there is an inability of victims to heal," a psychologist said, citing studies in Argentina and Guatemala, where organized killings have occurred. "There is retraumatization and failure to reintegrate fully into the community. It's as if the government doesn't recognize what's been done to you."

For child victims, the problems are immense, said a psychologist serving as a senior adviser to the United Nations High Commissioner for Refugees in Central Africa. Many survived by hiding under dead bodies of their family and neighbors. Others just ran away. "Some kids have seen hundreds of people killed." Later, some of these children have complained of "insects crawling" in their heads, while others refused to eat meat even though they were hungry. The children have seen too much exposed flesh. Much of the killing was done with machetes. In some of the care centers, children showed profound clinging behavior.

A harrowing future lies in wait for the adolescents who were soldiers. "Their moral development is fundamentally stunted and altered," a psychologist said. "This has very powerful and long-term implications for the society." In work done in Mozambique after civil war there, it was found that adolescents who had been captured by guerrillas and told to "kill or be killed" were best healed later in the family setting if they still had one. Youths put into shelters with other children found themselves outcasts. As it stands, Hutu youth who were killers have lost their childhood, their play opportunities and their homes, and if they return to Rwanda, they would likely lose their lives.

A psychologist observed, "We don't take off the shelf what we learned in the West. It may have limited applicability in an African context." Instead, psychologists need to think about song, dance and storytelling—African modalities that are powerful and integral to local cultures. They could contribute to healing, he said. Some women's prayer groups have allowed women to talk about experiences that would be too stressful to address in direct conversation. There have been some attempts to use drawing therapy, which seems to help. The children sketched pictures of machetes, of empty houses and other disjointed scenes. But there are few programs using such therapies.

In general, foreign aid workers must be alert to unlikely sources of distress. For example, after years of civil war in Angola, when refugees were asked to name their biggest worry, the answer was that they weren't able to perform proper burial ceremonies for their dead relatives because bodies often couldn't be found or

continues

continued

identified. This was profoundly upsetting. It troubled many Angolans for years; and similar problems are cropping up in Rwanda.

Many refugee families have become dysfunctional. Mothers have grown listless and depressed and don't give their small children needed attention. Of women who are starting to have babies in the camps, there are reports that infants are being killed at birth and thrown into latrines.

—*Excerpted from the* American Psychological Association Monitor, *August 1996*

POST-GENOCIDE RECONCILIATION BETWEEN PERPETRATORS AND VICTIMS AS SEEN BY A HOLOCAUST RESEARCHER

[Reviewers of this feature pointed out correctly that the author does not present examples of actual reconciliation in a post-genocidal society, but were impressed with the clarity and potential usefulness of the preliminary conceptualization.—Ed.]

Several projects and researches of dialogue between children of perpetrators and survivors of the Holocaust have led to the following preliminary thoughts on the process of post-genocide reconciliation which may be useful in analyzing and working on the sequels of other events of genocide.

Reconciliation can have different meanings in different cultures or religions. Conflicts may change on the manifest level, but this does not necessarily mean a weakening of motives or prevention of a new outburst in the future. The best example of this is the ethnic conflict in Bosnia. If one assumed that earlier ethnic tensions were resolved under the communist regime of Yugoslavia (with an intermarriage rate of 46%), the disintegration of that regime caused the old tensions to surface and escalate into extreme bloodshed and atrocities, even between well-known neighbors and long-term acquaintances. This example demonstrates that conflicts can be suppressed on the manifest level but have not been worked through psychosocially, and may still be present in some hidden form. It is this hidden aspect which psychosocial reconciliatory acts have to address before one can expect a successful reconciliation.

In some conflicts there was no earlier phase of understanding or trust. Under such circumstances, one must expect enemies to enter into a new positive dialogue which will help water down the previous stages of hostility, violence and suffering. The one-hundred year old Israeli-Palestinian conflict is an example of a social context in which there was no initial stage of harmony, unless one wants to relate to Biblical times or to Medieval Spain when there were periods Jews and Arabs lived together peacefully. This situation may require creative procedures in which this deficiency will be taken into account rather than ignored and suppressed.

continues

continued

Rarely do violent conflicts ignite or persist between equals. Either they ignite between parties which have never been equal, for example between a majority and a minority within one nation, or they occur between a suppressed majority and an oppressing minority as in the case of South Africa. In such cases, reconciliation may mean first of all the political and socio-economic development of the 'weaker' side, while a new social context of mutual respect is being established.

Reconciliatory activity may be interpreted very differently within different cultural or religious belief-systems. For example, asking for forgiveness after the atrocities of the Holocaust is perceived differently by Jews and by Christians. While within the Christian tradition this is a necessary and sufficient act for reconciliation which every representative of the community can initiate, within the Jewish tradition no one but the victims themselves are entitled to receive forgiveness for acts done to them. In many cases, this discrepancy creates additional sources of tension because one sides assumes it did what it had to do, while the other side feels humiliated in addition to their primary feelings of pain and suffering.

Psychosocial reconciliation between parties in conflict may be more possible after at least some of the following conditions have been fulfilled:

1. A political solution has been established;
2. Legal measures have been undertaken against the perpetrators of inhuman atrocities committed within the conflict itself;
3. Financial compensation has been provided for the victims of those atrocities;
4. The parties involved have reached a new stage in which the motives for maintaining their conflict have weakened considerably or become irrelevant;
5. There was an earlier stage of trust between the parties which they may now reestablish;
6. A symmetry exists between the parties involved in the conflict, enabling them to become equal partners in the reconciliatory effort.

When many of these conditions are not met, the chances for a deeper process of reconciliation are probably low.

—Dan Bar-On

References and Recommended Reading

Bar-On, Dan (1996). Encounters between descendants of survivors and descendants of perpetrators of the Holocaust: A way to struggle with the past for the future. In Simon, Bennet, and Apfel, Roberta (Eds.), *Minefields in Their Hearts: The Mental Health of Children in War and Communal Violence.* New Haven, CT: Yale University Press, pp. 165–188.

Bar-On, Dan; Ostrovsky, Tal; and Fromer, Daphna (1998). "Who am I in relation to my past, in relation to the other?": German and Israeli students confront the Holocaust and each other. In Danieli, Yael (Ed.), *International Handbook of Multigenerational Legacies of Trauma.* New York: Plenum, pp. 97–116. Also in Bar-On, Dan; Hare, Paul A.; and Brendler, Konrad (Eds.) (1996). *"Something in the Roots Went Wrong . . .": German and Israeli Students Confront the Holocaust and Each Other.* Frankfurt: Campus Verlag, pp. 225–261 (German).

the other hand, in clinical reports there is ample evidence for the identification of the offspring with their parents' Holocaust experience, including self-perceptions as victim and survivor and including the development of symptoms that symbolically express unprocessed grief. Again this gap shows the importance of the difference between the general and the clinical populations. As a whole the offspring of survivors are a well-functioning group, but if they develop disorders, the imprint of the Holocaust background is not only visible but clinically relevant.

The current knowledge about multigenerational effects of trauma is rather limited and has been led by the work on the Holocaust. What few reports there are of work on the effects of other forms of traumatization on children of survivors have produced indications in similar directions. The interpersonal difficulties that stand out as the most prevalent and discerning characteristics of children of survivors are also a reminder of the pervasive effects of genocide on the interpersonal functioning of the survivors themselves.

—Daniel Brom

References and Recommended Reading

Danieli, Yael (Ed.) (1998). *International Handbook of Multigenerational Legacies of Trauma.* New York: Plenum.

CHINA, GENOCIDE IN: *THE CHINESE COMMUNIST ANTHILL*

Those who were shocked by the June 1989 Beijing massacre and repression of prodemocracy demonstrators should not have been. Such cruelty and mass killing are a way of life in China. Indeed, no other people in this century except Soviet citizens have suffered so much mass killing in cold blood as have the Chinese. They have been murdered by rebels conniving with their own Empress, and then with the defeat in war of the dynasty by soldiers and citizens of many other lands. They have been killed by minidespots—warlords—who ruled one part of China or another. They have been slaughtered because they happened to live where nationalists, warlords, communists, or foreign troops fought each other. They have been executed because they had the wrong beliefs or attitudes in the wrong place at the wrong time. They have been shot because they criticized or opposed their rulers. They have been butchered because they resisted rape, were raped, or tried to prevent rape. They have been wiped out because they had food or wealth that soldiers or officials wanted. They have been assassinated because they were leaders, a threat, or potential antagonists. They have been blotted out in the process of building a new society. And they have died simply because they were in the way.

After the dynasty fell in 1911, China was governed by an ineffective and disunited republican government. When General Yuan Shih-k'ai, the one unifying leader of this government, died in 1916, China was largely divided by warlords who governed their separate regions as though they were sovereign and independent countries. Many were absolute dictators, fighting hundreds of wars to gain more power or to protect their territory.

Putting available information together and making some conservative guesses, I estimate that some 910,000 people likely were murdered by the warlords or their soldiers, perhaps even a third more than this. The warlord toll alone ranks these Chinese dead among the major victims of democide [see DEMOCIDE] in this century.

The nationalists were no different than the warlords. They murdered opponents, assassinated critics, and employed terror as a device of rule. Moreover, nationalist soldiers, like many warlord soldiers, were considered scum, lower than vermin. They were beaten, mistreated, often poorly fed and ill paid; and if wounded or sick they were left to fend for themselves, often to die slow and miserable deaths. In turn, soldiers often treated civilians no better. Looting, rape and arbitrary murder were risks that helpless civilians faced from passing soldiers or from those occupying or reoccupying their villages and towns. As we will also see, from the earliest years to their final defeat on the mainland, the nationalists likely killed between almost 6,000,000 and nearly 18,500,000 helpless people, probably around 10 million of them. This incredible number is over a million greater than all the aforementioned some 9 million war dead in all the hundreds of wars and rebellions in China from the beginning of the century to the nationalist final defeat. *It ranks the nationalists as the fourth greatest megamurderers of this century, behind the Soviets, Chinese communists, and German Nazis.* This democide is even more impressive when it is realized that the nationalists never controlled all of China—perhaps no more than 50 to 60 percent of the population at its greatest.

Before passing on to the communists, we should not ignore Japanese democide in China. Japanese indiscriminate killing of Chinese became widely known and almost universally condemned as criminal in the late 1930s. World opinion was especially horrified over what became known as "The Rape of Nanking," but this was not an isolated case. From one village, town, or city to another, the Japanese often killed the inhabitants, executed suspected former nationalist soldiers, beat to death or buried alive those disobeying their orders or showing insufficient respect, and mistreating many others. Much of this killing was done in cold blood and thoughtlessly—as one would swat a fly. An example of this that most sticks in my mind is of one Japanese officer's use of Chinese prisoners for "kill practice" by his inexperienced soldiers.

Moreover, the Japanese terror-bombed Chinese cities and towns, killing civilians at random (that this was done by the Anglo-American Allies during World War II hardly excuses it—official US protests to Japan at the time condemned such "barbarism"). And they widely employed germ warfare. Over some major cities, for example, the Japanese released flies infected with deadly plague germs, causing epidemics.

Overall and quite aside from those killed in battle, the Japanese probably murdered close to 4 million Chinese during the war; even possibly as many as almost 6,300,000. Some readers who were prisoners of the Japanese during the war or who remember the Tokyo War Crimes Tribunal revelations after the war will hardly be surprised by these numbers. What is shocking is that the nationalists likely murdered some 2 million more during the war, and that this toll, or something like it, is virtually unknown. Apparently, the nationalists got away with megamurder; responsible Japanese were tried as war criminals.

As for the communists, from their very formation as a Party on the Soviet model (with the help of Soviet advisors), the Chinese communists used the same kind of repression and terror employed by the Chinese nationalists. They executed so-called counterrevolutionaries, nationalist sympathizers, and other political opponents. Up to 1 October 1949, when Mao Tse-tung officially proclaimed the People's Republic of China (PRC), the communists, acting as the de facto government of the regions they controlled, killed from almost 1,800,000 to almost 11,700,000 people, most likely close to 3,500,000.

Once control over all of China had been won and consolidated, and the proper party machinery and instruments of control put generally in place, the communists launched numerous movements to systematically destroy the traditional Chinese social and political system and replace it with a totally socialist, top-to-bottom "dictatorship of the proletariat." Their principles derived from the Marxism-Leninism, as interpreted by Mao Tse-tung. Their goals were to thoroughly transform China into a communist society. Witness what Mao himself had to say in a speech to party cadre in 1958: "What's so unusual about Emperor Shih Huang of the Chin Dynasty? He had buried alive 460 scholars only, but we have buried alive 46,000 scholars. In the course of our repression of counterrevolutionary elements, haven't we put to death a number of the counterrevolutionary scholars? I had an argument with the democratic personages. They say we are behaving worse than Emperor Shih Huang of the Chin Dynasty. That's definitely not correct. We are 100 times ahead of Emperor Shah of the Chin Dynasty in repression of counterrevolutionary scholars."

Only when these movements, and especially the final, total collectivization of the peasants and "Great Leap Forward," destroyed the agricultural system, causing the world's greatest recorded famine—27 million starved to death—did the communists begin to draw back from or slacken their drive. Shortly after this famine, in the mid-1960s, an intraparty civil war erupted between Mao Tse-tung and his followers who wanted to continue the mass-based revolution, and the more moderate, pragmatically oriented faction. The resulting "cultural revolution" probably cost over 1,600,000 lives. Mao won, but only temporarily. With his death soon after the pragmatists and the "capitalist roaders" regained power and launched China into a more open, economically experimental direction, even on a more liberal path—until the Tiananmen Square demonstrations and subsequent massacres of 1989.

Indeed, from October 1949 to 1987, the Chinese Communist Party (CCP) probably killed more than 35,200,000 of its own subjects. These were "landlords" and "rich" peasants, counterrevolutionaries" and "bandits," "leftists," "rightists," and "capitalist roaders," "bourgeoisie," scientists, intellectuals, and scholars, Kuomintang "agents" and Western "spies," "wrong" and "bad" elements, and often loved ones, relatives, and friends. Even babies. If this seems exaggerated, consider the report of the Minister of Public Security, Hsieh Fu-chih, in which he cites the case of production brigade leaders in one rural county who murdered in one day, in ten brigades, all those with "bad" personal or family backgrounds, including "landlords, rich peasants, counterrevolutionaries, bad elements, and rightists and their children, including babies."

—*R. J. Rummel*

References and Recommended Reading

Rummel, R. J. (1991). *China's Bloody Century: Genocide and Mass Murder Since 1900.* New Brunswick, NJ: Transaction Publishers.

Rummel, R. J. (1994). *Death by Government.* New Brunswick, NJ: Transaction Publishers.

Rummel, R. J. (1999). *Statistics of Democide: Genocide and Mass Murder since 1900.* New Brunswick, NJ: Transaction Publishers.

CHMIELNICKI POGROMS

The Chmielnicki Pogroms are named for the *Hetman* or leader of the Ukranian Zaporozhian Cossacks, Bogdan Chmielnicki (1595–1657). These massacres of 1648–1649 saw the estimated destruction of more than 300 Jewish communities throughout the Ukraine with an estimated loss of life approaching 100,000. Avowedly antisemitic, Chmielnicki sought to erase the very presence of Jewish life in the region while at the same time overthrowing Polish rule and aligning himself with Moscovite Russia.

Chmielnicki's revolt against the Poles began in early 1648, the catalyst for which was a Polish raiding party that kidnapped his wife and murdered his son. In

May of that same year, his troops slaughtered Jews in every community they encountered. These attacks upon Jews lasted until November with a second wave of pogroms beginning in 1649. Chmielnicki's war with the Poles, however, continued unabated until his own death in 1654. Thirteen years later (1667), the eastern part of the Ukraine was finally annexed to Russia.

Prior to World War II, Ukranian nationalists regarded Chmielnicki as igniting the desire for independence among his people, and Russian nationalists saw in him the great unifier of Russia and the Ukraine. During the Second World War, a military medal was named after him, and after that war two towns were named in his honor.

—*Steven L. Jacobs*

CONCENTRATION CAMPS AND DEATH CAMPS

Concentration camps are prison camps in which members of minority groups, political dissidents or others termed "asocial" are held, usually in indeterminate incarceration, and without equitable judicial processes and/or trials. Concentration camps have a long and dishonorable history prior to the Holocaust such as British incarceration of noncombatants in South Africa at the close of the nineteenth century. Concentration camps may be and often are scenes of brutality, torture, starvation, as well as murder. They are to be distinguished from *prisons* that are intended to be *legitimate* incarceration centers for those convicted of violations of civil or criminal statues; *prisoner-of-war camps* for captured enemy military; and *relocation, detention, refugee* or *internment camps* for postwar civilian populations. There are also instances of concentration camps that involve involuntary internment without due process of law but which are not characterized by brutality, for example, the Nisei or camps for Japanese in the United States during World War II, or even certain instances of concentration camps for Jews during World War II where for the most part serious brutality was *not* present, such as camps set up at the behest of the Nazis by the Italian fascists but who refused to carry out the extermination programs demanded by the SS, or the labor camp overseen by Oskar Schindler.

Concentration camps are also to be distinguished from *death camps, extermination camps* or *annihilation camps,* which are usually identified with the Nazis during World War II, but not only with them. *Death camps* refer to concentration camps that are designed for or develop into centers for organized mass killing of the inmates. The term is usually associated with the killing centers constructed under Nazi hegemony primarily in Poland, the purpose of which was to insure the extermination of large numbers of Jews and Sinti-Romani, first and foremost, and others labeled undesirable. The German term for these camps is *Vernichtungslager,* which is best translated as "extermination camp." For those who were not killed immediately or soon after arrival, daily brutalization was the norm, as were starvation, beatings and various manners of torture, prolonged exposure to bitter cold, intense physical labor without benefit of adequate food and caloric intake, sexual predatoriness, and selection of specific subpopulations of inmates for involuntary medical experiments without benefit of surgical anesthesia and/or exposure to gas burns and various diseases without recourse to antidotes. Random and systematic selected executions were also common, but the 'culmination' of the death camps' achievements was in the systematic mass murder of thousands of inmates a day, with the most notorious method of killing being the administration of the gas zyklon-B and then removal of the

The execution pit at the Sachsenhausen Concentration Camp, a camp which was not a death center yet in which many thousands were regularly executed. (Photographed by Israel W. Charny)

bodies to incinerators specially designed and built to enable the disposal of huge numbers of murdered people.

Any listing of concentration camps must also include, among others, the *gulags* or labor camps of the Soviet Union under Stalin, which were certainly concentration camps as described above, including such high rates of deaths as well as outright killings that they are only somewhat distinguishable from death camps; the camps employed by the Cambodians under Pol Pot, which have come to be known as *killing fields* and do in fact qualify as death camps; and in more recent times, the camps established in Bosnia-Herzegovina in what was formerly Yugoslavia.

The creation of institutions of death camps, "gulags," "killing fields," and murder-filled concentration camps in the twentieth century, whose primary agenda and *raison d'etre* is the wanton and willful taking of human life, has marked a new pathological step in genocidal activity by human beings.

—*Steven L. Jacobs*

CRIMES AGAINST HUMANITY

The term "crimes against humanity" was first utilized in international law in the 1915 joint declaration of Great Britain, France and Russia in response to the massacres of the Armenian population in Ottoman Turkey. The term was formally defined by the Nuremberg Charter, during the prosecution of the Nazi war criminals. Article 6(c) of the Charter defines crimes against humanity as "murder, extermination, enslavement, deportation, and other inhumane acts committed against any civilian population, before or during the war, or persecutions on political, racial or religious grounds in execution of or in connection with any crime within the jurisdiction of the Tribunal, whether or not in violation of the domestic law of the country where perpetrated."

The Nuremberg Charter established, therefore, "crimes against humanity" as a crime under international law. Under Article 6(c), acts constituting crimes against humanity are wide-ranging, and there is substantial overlap in the Charter's definition of "crimes against humanity" with "war crimes." Consequently, the accused Nazis were found guilty of both. Because of the considerable overlap, some scholars have proposed a combined category of "war crimes against humanity."

"Crimes against humanity" has retained its vitality as a crime under both international and municipal law throughout the post–World War II period. France has prosecuted and convicted a number of individuals (i.e., German Nazi, Klaus Barbie, in 1987 and French Nazi collaborator, Paul Touvier, in 1994) of committing the crime, and Canada and the United States likewise cited former Nazis living within their borders of committing "crimes against humanity" in their citizenship revocation proceedings. Since under both customary international law and express treaties, such as the *European Convention on the Non-Application of Statutory Limitations to Crimes against Humanity and War Crimes* (1974), no limitations period exists for prosecuting perpetrators of crimes against humanity, the existence of the crime on the "international law books" has been useful to prosecutors seeking to obtain justice against newly found or indicted individuals who have committed gross human rights violations dating back fifty years, during World War II.

The UN War Crimes Tribunal for the Former Yugoslavia has indicted both officers and low-ranking soldiers of committing crimes against humanity, for ordering or participating in the killings, rape and other cruelties of civilians during the conflict, and especially as part of the "ethnic cleansing" campaign engaged in by the Bosnian Serbs. Article 5 of the Yugoslav Tribunal's Charter defines "crimes against humanity" on the same terms as Article 6(c) of the Nuremberg Charter.

Proposals have been made for the adoption of a specialized Convention on Crimes Against Humanity and also for a permanent International Tribunal for Crimes Against Humanity.

—Michael J. Bazyler

References and Recommended Reading

Aroneanu, Eugene (1961). *Le crime contre l'humanité.* Paris: Dalloz.

Clark, Roger S. (1990). Crimes against humanity at Nuremberg. In Ginsburgs, George, and Kudriatvtsen, V. N. (Eds.), *The Nuremberg Trial and International Law.* Dordrecht, The Netherlands: Martinus Nijhoff, pp. 177–199.

D

DEHUMANIZATION—"KILLING" THE HUMANITY OF ANOTHER

Dehumanization is a psychological-symbolic removal of others from the province or group classification of *human,* and thus removes from the others any entitlement to protection or privilege as human beings. Thus, if one is enjoined from killing other human beings, the redefinition of others as *not-human* will constitute the removal of any symbolic barriers to killing them. Once a human being is regarded as so inferior as to be subhuman or not human, he or she becomes prey to being reduced to nonexistence.

The dehumanizing process divides human beings from one another. Dehumanization spawns and perpetuates classes of lower and undesirable peoples, with all the grief and pain that such distinctions bring to the less fortunate people, as well as the denuding of dignity and aliveness in those people who fall unknowingly into the trap of pretending to be better than others.

The underlying ideology or "justification" for delivering another person to death is dehumanization. Dehumanization is at the heart of the destructive process; it provides the necessary rationalization for the destruction. The mechanism of dehumanization operates every time one person takes away a quality of deserving to live from another. It is generally done in order to spare oneself from one's own dread of not feeling alive.

Dehumanization is based on the psychological mechanism of projection. It can be seen as the main dynamic through which people who are overwhelmed with fears of their own possible death seize on other people and consign them to the fate they fear for themselves.

The dehumanization process extends along a continuum to the ultimate of removing the other person's opportunity to live. The "little" everyday dehumanizations we practice on one another are stations on the way toward the ultimate act of one person taking away another's life. It is not simply the insult that we do to another that is at stake in everyday dehumanizations. It is the fact that we are learning a devastating process, rehearsing it, deriving gratification from it, and perhaps preparing ourselves to one day participate in the removal of other people's lives.

Dehumanization aims at a redefinition of the other person as not deserving the protection due members of our species. Hence, anything and everything that is destructive of the other person, even killing, does not violate nature's design. "Because I am afraid that I will be nothing, I see you as nothing. I say that you are not human because deep within myself I fear that I am not. Once I see you as not human, I can attack and kill you

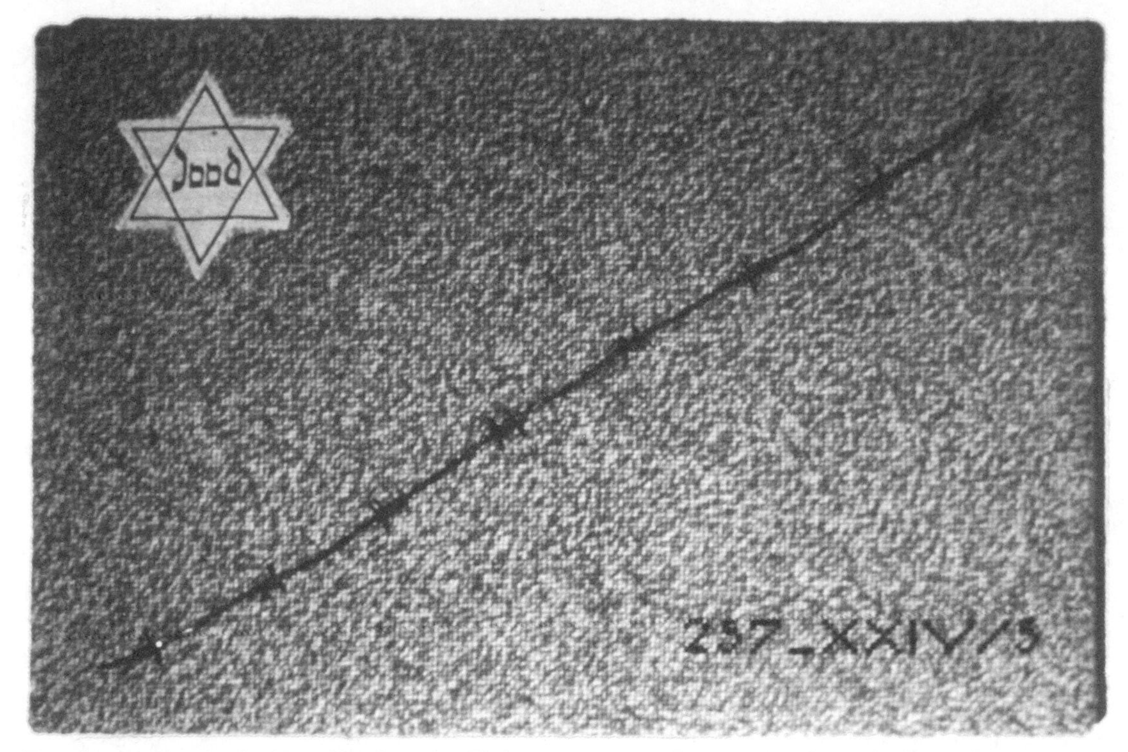

Terezin, *needlepoint by Natty Vanderpol, a Holocaust survivor from Amsterdam who is now living in the United States, 1986. (Courtesy of Natty Vanderpol, with the kind assistance of Stephen C. Feinstein)*

without fearing that I have done harm to my own kind."

The process that makes genocide possible generally does not stop at dehumanization. Dehumanizing a particular target isn't really enough to justify doing further damage to the hapless undesirables. If we are to prepare a justification for hurting those people, we need also to "prove" that they are out to hurt us. Granted that we have already projected onto them that they are less than us and not the same as us, not even as deserving of life as we are, but there is nothing yet in this bill of particulars to justify the extreme of killing them. By any test of the simple logic of man's also natural wishes to be decent, what needs to be added to justify taking away people's lives is proof that the others are also a terrible threat to our lives and that *it is their intent to take our lives away from us unless we stop them first.*

In this process too the mechanism of projection plays a key part. In addition to genuine fears we may have of the others, perhaps very realistically, we also project onto the others the hateful wishes to destroy that we cannot bear in ourselves, and thus justify our own hatred and destructiveness on the grounds that that is what the others harbor toward us.

In order to counter dehumanization, responsible people need to guard against projecting onto others responsibility for their own feelings of vulnerability and their own destructive wishes. Even when we have real reasons to fear aggression from others, and correctly need to mount our defenses against possible destruction of us, we need to guard against dehumanizing other people as if they were not of our collective mankind, hence nonhuman and therefore not deserving of life and protection. We also need to guard against being drawn into escalating conflicts based on a misperception of one another's efforts at self-defense. Especially under circumstances of conflict or incipient police or military measures, we need to be wary of a mutual escalation toward more serious destructiveness resulting from each party's viewing the other's efforts at self-defense as a confirmation of destructive intentions. People need to learn to cut these cycles without rendering themselves impotent in the face of real threats.

The underlying machinery for the dehumanization of a potential victim group is housed in the attitudes of a culture toward differences between people. Even cultures that do seek to emphasize some sense of humans' equality or godliness—that all people are God's creatures still have to deal with the powerful realities of differences between people and the natural processes those differences set off in human beings. Some of the provocative realities surrounding humankind's differences include:

1. People are remarkably different from one another—in color, build, and appearance, let alone in tradition and culture.
2. Human beings naturally tend to react very strongly to differences—with fear, distaste, and repugnance.
3. People who are different become likely objects of projection.

No matter how humanistically oriented a particular culture is toward the brotherhood of all human beings, each culture must also provide ways for dealing with the natural experiences caused by differences. Only in a relatively few instances are people educated toward accepting and enjoying differences. A positive approach to experiencing people who differ from us is that differences are the other side of the sameness and universality of human beings—both should be taught simultaneously. The prevailing situation in most cultures is to make people feel that the differences are disturbing and problematic, so people who are different are assigned one degree or another of not-being-the-same-as-us-ness and, progressively, less-than-us-ness.

—Israel W. Charny

References and Recommended Reading

Charny, Israel W. (1982). Sacrificing others to the death we fear ourselves: The ultimate illusion of self-defense. In *How Can We Commit the Unthinkable?: Genocide, The Human Cancer.* Boulder, CO: Westview Press, pp. 185–211. Republished in Portuguese with a new Introduction and Bibliography as *Anatomia do Genocídio: Uma Psicologia da Agressão Humana.* Rio de Janeiro: Editora Rosa dos Tempos, 1998.

DEMOCRACY AND GENOCIDE

R. J. Rummel, University of Hawaii political scientist, has demonstrated in his sterling researches of the statistics of many genocides that the single most correlated and therefore predictive factor as to whether or not a nation or state will engage in genocide lies in the nature of the governing system of that state, and that democracies are overwhelmingly less inclined to be genocidal than totalitarian states. This also means that in making efforts to think about means of prevention of genocide, one must not only address the creation of structures that relate directly to the emergence of genocide, for example, legal measures against incitement of genocide and the development of international means for intervening as any given nation moves toward embarking on a genocidal course, but that the single best preventative is the sponsorship, encouragement and reinforcement of democracy as a way of governance.

Rummel's interpretation of his empirical findings is that the process of power in totalitarian societies is, as power is generally understood to be in human life, corrupting. Power expands and creates momentums justifying the pursuit of greater power and the exercise of forms of power that are violent against those who would stand in the way of that power system. In democracies, there are checks and balances against the expansion of power; in totalitarian states, there are few checks and balances, and the full measure of the corruptive process of power is let loose.

While Rummel's empirical findings are largely indisputable, there have been criticisms of his writing for failing to provide sufficient information about events of genocide committed by democracies, and there have been criticisms that his conclusion creates a misleading *either-or* distinction between the goodness of democracy and the badness of totalitarian governance. Some scholars in particular warn that the very concepts of justice and freedom that are the pride marks of democratic societies are, in fact, turned blindly and self-righteously into justifications of massive genocidal policies, and are all the more disguised because the collective consciousness cannot discern the evil that is being done in the name of such lofty ideals. The same has been true of the many millions of genocidal murders committed in the names of religions who felt compelled to destroy their respective nonbelievers. A trappist Monk, Father Thomas Merton, warned that it would be the quiet, nondemented sane ones who would push the buttons of the modern technologies of nuclear destruction in the name of whatever ideals of protecting the institutions of their society. Scholars of the fates of indigenous peoples note that many Euro-American peoples—including the Spanish, Portuguese, English and American—justified their ruthless destruction of indigenous peoples in the names of their rights to develop their ostensibly more *progressive* societies and the 'manifest destiny' of their cultures, and so on of conceptions and a rhetoric that were not, as in the case of the Nazis or the Stalinists, persecutory, discriminatory or openly committed to destroying the victims. But the truth is that, at the core, the same concepts of dehumanization of the victim peoples and the legitimization of destroying them so that they will not stand in the way of progress are shared by *both democratic and totalitarian societies;* and the core issues of the capacity of the human mind and of human society to turn monstrously against victim peoples must be addressed when genocide erupts, whatever the political definitions of government.

Nonetheless, Rummel's point is that the capacity for difference, dissension and protest, the inherent system of political checks and balances that are present in democracies, and the far greater commitment to freedom and justice for all do represent major "stops" against the genocidal process, and as indicated there is no faulting his excellent statistical proofs.

—*Israel W. Charny*

References and Recommended Reading

Rummel, R. J. (1997). *Power Kills: Democracy as a Method of Nonviolence.* New Brunswick, NJ: Transaction Publishers.

Rummel, R. J. (1999). *Statistics of Democide: Genocide and Mass Murder since 1900.* New Brunswick, NJ: Transaction Publishers.

DENIALS OF GENOCIDE

DENIAL OF GENOCIDE, PSYCHOLOGY OF

Denial of genocide may reflect a variety of motives. Deborah Lipstadt concluded from her comprehensive survey of Holocaust deniers that most "are antisemites or bigots" (p. 206), but there are many other motives for denial.

One effect of denial is that perpetrators of past genocides are absolved from responsibility for their actions. Denial also, according to Israel Charny, constitutes "an attack on the collective identity and national cultural continuity of the victim people" and "places further burdens on their recovery." Furthermore, by obscuring the reality of genocide as a widely practiced form of state policy in the modern world, denial may increase the danger of future outbreaks of genocidal killing.

Deliberate denial of a known genocide is a harmful act that deserves to be included in the same moral domain as actual contributions to a genocide—indirect and direct. Indeed, denial may be appropriately regarded as the last stage of genocide, one that can continue long after the actual killing has ended.

Another motive for denying that a case of mass killing constitutes genocide is to avoid responsibility for doing something about it. Thus, the Clinton administration resisted labeling the Rwandan genocide of 1994 as "genocide" in order to avoid having to become directly involved in trying to stop it or punish the perpetrators [Jehl, Douglas. Officials told to avoid calling Rwanda killings genocide. *New York Times,* June 10, 1995, A8].

Roger Smith, Eric Markusen, and Robert J. Lifton in a now-classic article that exposed some of the machinery of Turkish government efforts to deny the Turkish genocide of the Armenians in 1915, suggest that desire to advance one's career may motivate genocide denial. They identify two forms of such careerism, one that is oriented toward material rewards, and one that involves the satisfactions that go with association with power.

Charny has proposed a wide-ranging classificatory system for distinguishing different types of denials. He notes that some deniers are genuinely ignorant that a certain genocide occurred and suggests that these be considered "innocent denials." He proposes that denials can be scaled along two dimensions: the first ranges from when the denier truly does *not* know the facts of the genocide, to increasing and full knowledge of the facts while denying them; the second, the extent to which the denier consciously and sincerely disavows—condemns, criticizes, regrets—the violence of a genocide, to increasing and malevolent celebrations and encouragement of genocidal violence as a thinly disguised or even more blatant accompaniment of the "denial" of the genocide. Charny suggests that there is much more "innocent denial" than we have realized, and that in effect it reflects the readiness of large numbers of people to acquiesce to and/or play facilitating roles in genocides when they take place in their society, without realiz-

20 Percent in US Think It Possible There Was No Holocaust

In April 1993, a Roper poll found that 20 percent of the United States high school students and 22 percent of adults think it seems "possible" that the Holocaust never happened.

Five Characteristics of the "Logic" of Denials of Genocide

1. Innocence and Self-Righteousness

The respondents claim that they only want to ascertain the truth. Moreover, they do not believe that human beings could have been as evil as the descriptions of the genocide imply.

2. Science in the Service of Confusion

We do not know enough to be certain of the facts of history. Rather than condemning anyone we should await the ultimate verdict of research. This is a manipulative misuse of the scientific principle that demands that facts be proven before they are accepted in order to obfuscate facts that are indeed known and to confuse the minds of fair-minded people.

3. Practicality, Pragmatism and Realpolitik

Dealing with ancient history is impractical; it will not bring peace to the world in which we are living today. One must be realistic and mindful of realpolitik, to the practical interests of our times.

4. Distorted Linkages and Temporal Confusions

A dishonest linkage of different ideas pulled out of their temporal contexts in order to excuse denial of the facts. *Current or recent* Armenian terrorism against Turks will be exonerated and encouraged if Turkey admits to the Armenian Genocide in the *past.* The apparent needs of the present and future are taken as reasonable grounds for the censoring or changing the historical record.

5. Indirection, Definitionalism, and Reversal

Responses which avoid the essential issue—whether or not the genocide occurred—by failing to reply, or by going off on tangents about trivial details. *Definitionalism* refers to a maddening form of resistance to acknowledging a known genocide commonly used by academics who enter into definitional battles over whether or not a given event fits a particular definition of genocide. It is like the family of a murdered person having to listen to lawyers argue about whether the victim's death can be proven. The ultimate maddening form of denial is a full scale reversal of the roles so that it is the victims who are cast as the murderers, and the murderers become the poor victims.

—Israel W. Charny and Daphna Fromer,
Internet on the Holocaust and Genocide

ing or acknowledging the full meaning of the genocidal process they are tacitly or actively supporting. Another form of "innocent denial" is the insistence on unlimited free speech to allow revisionists full access to university campuses, publication and so on. However, serious caution is called for because there are also entirely purposeful denier propagandists who pose as 'innocent,' for example those claiming the rights of free speech and the right to present the 'other side' of an issue as a contrived way of infiltrating denials into academic circles.

Another proposed category of denial is "definitionalism," which refers to the practice of defining genocide in such a narrow way that certain cases of mass killing are excluded. Charny also labels as a form of denial "the insistent refrain of any people that the genocide that befell them is the only true and ultimate form of genocide, while the mass murders of other people have to be defined as some lesser crime and tragedy."

—Eric Markusen and Israel W. Charny

References and Recommended Reading

Charny, Israel W. (1991). The psychology of denial of known genocides. In Charny, Israel W. (Ed.), *Genocide: A Critical Bibliographic Review. Volume 2.* London: Mansell Publishing; and New York: Facts on File, pp. 3–37.

Charny, Israel W. (1997). Commonality in denial: Classifying the final stage of the genocide process. *International Network on Holocaust and Genocide,* 11(5), 4–7.

Lipstadt, Deborah (1993). *Denying the Holocaust: The Growing Assault on Truth and Memory.* New York: Free Press.

Smith, Roger, W.; Markusen, Eric; and Lifton, Robert Jay (1995). Professional ethics and the denial of Armenian Genocide. *Holocaust and Genocide Studies,* 9(1), 1–22.

DENIALS OF THE ARMENIAN GENOCIDE

Those who initiate or otherwise participate in genocide typically deny that the events took place, that they bear any responsibility for the destruction, or that the term "genocide" is applicable to what occurred. But denial can enter into the very fabric of a society, so that those who come after sustain and even intensify the denial begun by perpetrators. The most strident and elaborate denial of genocide in history follows this pattern. The Turkish Republic, because it was established in 1923, is not formally responsible for the genocide against Armenians, but it continues to this day to deny that the Young Turk government of its predeces-

Senator Robert Dole: The Inaccessible Turkish Archives

The Ottoman archives from 1915 to 1923 should contain important documents on the Armenian Genocide. Usually, archives are opened 50 years after the events, but the Turkish government historically resisted opening the 1915–1923 archives. Today, Turkey claims it has opened the relevant archives, and some of those opposed to the resolution will argue the Senate should await analysis of these archives before approving the Armenian Genocide resolution. This argument is specious because: First, the evidence of the genocide is already overwhelming; second, Turkey does not even own all the relevant Ottoman records—they are scattered in the USSR, Vatican, Jerusalem, France, and England; third, according to Turkish sources, government officials have, for fifty years, combed through and destroyed damaging records; fourth, Turkey, in fact, has not opened all the relevant archives, only the catalogued or the records of these agencies which were not involved in the genocide—War Ministry, Interior Ministry, and Committee of Union and Progress; fifth, the Turkish government has been using the archives argument as a delaying tactic for years.

Nothing in the Turkish-held archives will change whether a 2,100,000 Armenian population went down to less than 100,000 between 1915 and 1923. Nothing in the archives can change the existing verified government orders, admissions, third-party observances, and other documents which conclusively establish a government-ordered program to annihilate the Armenians. Nothing in the Turkish-held archives will change the overwhelming evidence of the genocide.

—US Senator Robert Dole (Congressional Record)

30,000 Armenians Were Deported from Constantinople

A leading scholar of the Armenian Genocide, Vahakn Dadrian, has shown in a paper in *Holocaust and Genocide Studies* that 30,000 Armenians had been deported from Constantinople, and the deportation of the remaining 80,000 Armenians was being planned. According to Dadrian, "German ambassador Metternich, on 7 December 1915, informed Berlin that 4000 Armenians had recently been removed from Constantinople, that the total number of those deported from the Ottoman capital up to that time had reached 30,000, and that 'gradually a clean sweep will be made of the remaining 80,000 Armenian inhabitants of the Ottoman capital.'"

sor state, the Ottoman Empire, engaged in massive destruction of Armenians from 1915–1917, resulting in the deaths of over one million men, women, and children.

Despite the vast amount of evidence that points to the historical reality of the Armenian Genocide, denial of this genocide by successive regimes in Turkey has gone on from 1915 to the present. Unlike the Holocaust, which has been denied by individuals, the Armenian Genocide has been continuously denied by Turkish *governments* for eighty years. Out of political expediency, other governments, including that of the United States, have aided and abetted Turkey in its rewriting of history.

The basic argument of denial has remained the same—it never happened, Turkey is not responsible, the term "genocide" does not apply. The current emphasis is on removing the label "genocide" from the Armenian experience. This is done in part by describing the genocide as a civil war within a global war. Paradoxically, it also attempts to deny the Armenian Genocide by acknowledging the Holocaust. In part this involved the claim that Turkey saved many Jews from the Nazis, the unstated premise being that a people who did that could not have killed a million Armenians. It also attempts to exploit the "uniqueness" argument to discredit the 1915 genocide; in this perspective, the Holocaust is the *only* example of genocide. Moreover, Turkey has also gone to extraordinary lengths, including threats and disruption of academic conferences, to prevent Jews from learning about the Armenian Genocide. It is important for Turkey to stifle awareness among Jews, because for victims of Nazism to state publicly that Armenians and Jews have both been subjected to genocide carries

Ambassador Morgenthau: "The Whole History of the Human Race Contains No Such Horrible Episode"

When the Turkish authorities gave the orders for these deportations, they were merely giving the death warrant to a whole race; they understood this well, and, in their conversations with me, they made no particular attempt to conceal the fact. . . . I am confident that the whole history of the human race contains no such horrible episode as this. The great massacres and persecutions of the past seem almost insignificant when compared to the suffering of the Armenian race in 1915.

—Henry Morgenthau, Sr.,
US Ambassador to the
Ottoman Empire, 1919

COMBATTING DENIALS OF THE ARMENIAN GENOCIDE IN ACADEMIA

It is important to understand the immorality and the harmful consequences of denying genocide. As prominent scholars of genocide such as Israel Charny, Robert Jay Lifton, Deborah Lipstadt, Eric Markusen, and Roger Smith have noted: the denial of genocide is the final stage of genocide; it seeks to demonize the victims and rehabilitate the perpetrators; and denying genocide paves the way for future genocides by making it clear that genocide demands no moral accountability or response.

The first major example of Armenian Genocide denial in the United States occurred in 1935 when the Turkish government prevailed on the US Department of State to stop the Hollywood film company MGM from making a film from Franz Werfel's best-selling novel about the Armenian Genocide, *The Forty Days of Musa Dagh*. That a country with a horrible human rights record such as Turkey could succeed in censoring a film in the United States remains a black mark in US history.

During the beginning of the Cold War, Turkey exploited its NATO client relationship with the United States and began pushing certain Turkologists to deny the Armenian Genocide in their scholarship. Lewis V. Thomas, at Princeton University in the 1950s, was one of the first scholars to have collaborated with Turkey. By the 1970s a handful of scholars emerged in US universities who were working in some capacity or other with the Turkish government in order to help Turkey absolve itself of responsibility for the extermination of the Armenians. Bernard Lewis (Princeton University), Justin McCarthy (University of Louisville), Stanford Shaw (UCLA), and most recently Heath Lowry (Princeton University) are among the most vocal genocide deniers. Lewis had reversed his position on what he termed in his book *The Emergence of Modern Turkey* (1962) "the holocaust of the Armenians which took the lives of 1.5 million Armenians." Shaw and McCarthy have published shoddy and desperate books and articles claiming there was no genocide and that the Turkish government really treated the Armenians nicely while they were deporting and killing them. McCarthy revises demography to suggest that there really weren't many Armenians in historic Armenia.

The most celebrated case of Armenian Genocide denial involves Heath Lowry. Lowry had worked for the Turkish government in Turkey in the 1970s, and in the 1980s as director of the Turkish government funded Institute of Turkish Studies in Washington DC. He has devoted much of his career to denying the Armenian Genocide. In 1985 he was involved in the dissemination of a petition signed by Turkologists denying the Armenian Genocide by questioning whether all the research on the subject had been completed. Shortly thereafter, Israel Charny conducted a survey among the signers and several of them confessed to having regretted signing the petition. In 1990 Lowry was exposed as having worked closely with the Turkish ambassador to the US, Kandemir, to persuade the distinguished genocide scholar Robert Jay Lifton [illegible] Lifton made references to the role of Turkish physicians in the Armenian Genocide in his 1986 book, *The Nazi Doctors*. A three-page memorandum Lowry had written to the Turkish am-

continues

continued

bassador about Lifton's book was sent to Lifton inadvertently along with a ghost-written letter drafted by Lowry for Ambassador Kandemir to send to Lifton. In 1994 Lowry, who had never held a full-time teaching job in the United States and has a dramatically inadequate scholarly record, was awarded the Ataturk Chair in Turkish Studies at Princeton University. The chair was funded by the Turkish government and by the wealthy Turkish-American businessman Ahmet Ertegun, the son of the Turkish ambassador who was instrumental in quashing the film *The Forty Days of Musa Dagh* in 1935.

The Lowry-Turkish ambassador correspondence prompted Lifton to coauthor with genocide scholars, Roger Smith (College of William and Mary) and Eric Markusen (Southwest State University, Minnesota) what became a major article, "Professional Ethics and the Denial of Armenian Genocide" (1995). The article describes the Lowry-Turkish Ambassador denial strategies and publishes a facsimile of the Lowry memorandum and the ghost-written letter. The article explores the reasons "scholars" engage in genocide denial.

In the wake of the Lowry scandal, several scholars formulated a petition opposing the Turkish denial and Lowry's appointment at Princeton. "Taking a Stand against the Turkish Government's Denial of the Armenian Genocide and Scholarly Corruption in the Academy" was a petition signed by over 150 major scholars and writers around the United States and in Europe and the Middle East, and constituted perhaps the most powerful coalition of intellectuals to ever oppose Turkish denial. It was published in *The Chronicle of Higher Education* in February 1996. Among the signers were Raul Hilberg, Yehuda Bauer, Israel Charny, William Styron, Rose Styron, Susan Sontag, Kurt Vonnegut, Robert Jay Lifton, Seamus Heaney, Derek Walcott, Arthur Miller, Henry Louis Gates, Jr., and Cornel West. The Lowry scandal was covered by the *New York Times, Boston Globe, Chronicle of Higher Education* and other prominent publications. Although Princeton refused to act responsibly and face the harmful meaning of genocide denial, the Lowry scandal has generated significant consciousness about the Armenian Genocide and Turkish denial, and it has reflected poorly on Princeton.

In the fall of 1997, major scholars and writers in the United States once again signed a petition protesting the Turkish government's funding of chairs in Turkish studies at seven American universities (Princeton, Harvard, Indiana, Chicago, Portland State, UCLA, and Georgetown). They vehemently opposed these chairs because the Turkish government was making stipulations that the chairholders had to do work in the Turkish archives, and because of Turkey's egregious human rights record, which includes a long history of human rights abuses and anti-intellectual repression. In addition to denial of the Armenian Genocide, Turkey has been targeted by Amnesty International and Human Rights Watch for numerous human rights abuses, including imprisoning more writers than any country in the world, banning books, torturing children, requiring virginity tests of women, and other repressive and violent acts against civilians and free expression. The petition "We Oppose Tainted Chairs Funded by the Turkish Government at American Uni-

continues

continued

versities" was instrumental in defeating the proposal for a Turkish Chair at UCLA and was the subject of feature stories in the *Los Angeles Times* and *The Chronicle of Higher Education.* In its meeting in Montreal in June, 1997, the Association of Genocide Scholars voted unanimously to confirm the validity of the Armenian Genocide, and to underscore that the Armenian Genocide conforms to all of the definitions of genocide stipulated in the United Nations Convention on Genocide.

—*Peter Balakian*

References and Recommended Reading

Lewis, Bernard (1962). *The Emergence of Modern Turkey.* New York: Oxford University Press.

Lifton, Robert Jay; Markusen, Eric; and Smith, Roger W. (1995). Professional ethics and the denial of Armenian Genocide. *Holocaust and Genocide Studies,* 9(1), 1–22.

a kind of moral persuasiveness that non-victims may lack.

Denial is argument, but it is also a set of tactics that in the Turkish case has shifted over the years. In the period immediately after World War I the tactic was to find scapegoats to blame for what was said to be only a security measure gone awry. This was followed by an attempt to avoid the whole issue, with silence, diplomatic efforts and political pressure used where possible.

In the 1960s efforts were made to influence journalists, teachers, and public officials by telling "the other side of the story." Foreign scholars were encouraged to revise the record of genocide, presenting an account largely blaming the Armenians or, in another version, wartime conditions. In the 1970s Turkey was successful in its efforts to prevent any mention of the genocide in a report of the United Nations (which in later years did acknowledge the Armenian Genocide), and in the 1980s and 1990s in its pressure on the Reagan and Bush administrations to defeat Congressional resolutions that would have authorized a National Day of Remembrance of the Armenian Genocide in the United States. The Turkish government has also attempted to exclude any mention of the genocide in textbooks, and to prevent its inclusion in Holocaust and human rights curricula.

The Turkish government has attempted to disrupt academic conferences and public discussions of the genocide, notably a conference in Tel Aviv in 1982 with demands backed up with threats to the safety of Jews in Turkey. The US Holocaust Memorial Council reported similar threats over plans to include references to the Armenian Genocide within the interpretive framework of the Holocaust Memorial Museum in Washington.

Finally, since the 1980s the Turkish government has supported the establishment of "institutes" whose apparent purpose is to further research on Turkish history and culture but which also tend to act in ways that further denial.

Despite its past success, Turkey's denial of the genocide has come under increased scrutiny. It continues to spend millions of dollars trying to protect its image and, even though most Armenians would be satisfied with Turkey's acknowledgment of the genocide, to fend off any demands for reparations or restitution of property. On the other hand, as scholarship on the Armenian Genocide has expanded dramatically, the genocide has been officially recognized by, to mention only a few, the European Parliament, the United Nations, various agencies of the governments of France, Israel and Russia, and the US House of Representatives, which in 1996 voted overwhelmingly to withhold three million dollars of foreign aid to Turkey as long as it refuses to acknowledge the genocide.

The facade of denial has cracked, but much remains to be done: scholars, journalists, and teachers, in particular, have vital work ahead of them. In part, it is a matter of answering, and exposing, the denials, but more fundamentally of placing the Armenian Genocide as fully and truthfully on record as possible. Turkey may continue to deny that the genocide took place, but the world will know. Denial keeps open the wounds of genocide, but through solidarity with the victims and the restoration of a people's history, a process of healing can begin.

—Roger Smith

References and Recommended Reading

Smith, Roger W. (1991). Denial of the Armenian Genocide. In Charny, Israel W. (Ed.), *Genocide: A Critical Bibliographic Review. Volume 2.* London: Mansell Publishing; and New York: Facts on File, pp. 63–85.

Smith, Roger W.; Markusen, Eric; and Lifton, Robert Jay (1995). Professional ethics and the denial of Armenian Genocide. *Holocaust and Genocide Studies,* 9(1), 1–22.

DENIALS OF THE GENOCIDE OF NATIVE AMERICANS

The concept of an American holocaust has been set forth by Native American scholars and activists in their effort to understand the history of the United States as heir to the European legacies of colonialism, genocide, and racism. The history of atrocities, massacres and genocide in the Americas in general and the United States in particular is well documented in many sources, beginning as early as 1542 with Bartolomé De Las Casas' brief account of the devastation of the West Indies by the Spaniards.

Various forms of denial can be seen in what the perpetrators and their collaborators have said and done in regard to these events. For example, in the California gold rush of the 1850s, whole tribes of Native Americans were massacred in what Deloria called "systematic genocide" in order to gain access to their lands that were supposed to be off-limits to the miners under preexisting federal treaties. Through intense political pressure in Washington, DC, "the California Indian treaties . . . never ratified by the US Senate . . . were conveniently buried in the Senate archives where they remained as classified documents for half a century. The whites of California did not even want the description of the Indian reservations known" (Deloria, 1973, pp. 23–24).

In another case, the Colorado Volunteers massacred hundreds of Cheyenne and Arapaho Indians at Sand Creek in 1864. Afterwards, David Nichols, one of the volunteers and later a regent of the University of Colorado "participated fully in a systematic effort to falsify the circumstances that prevailed . . . claiming huge numbers of warriors had been present when in fact there were almost none, denying that the victims were almost exclusively women, children, and old men (as the record so clearly demonstrated they were), insisting that wanton mutilation of the corpses had not occurred despite overwhelming evidence to the contrary . . . [and] sought . . . not only to justify his deeds but to glorify them in the context of a 'battle'" (Jaimes, 1992, p.2).

There are many other examples of denial by perpetrators who wish to escape negative reactions to their deeds. More troubling are the later denials by people not directly involved in the genocidal events but who appear to have ideological reasons for their denials. One way to deny genocide is simply to ignore it in a context where it would be relevant. Thus, Massachusetts School Superintendent Wilbur Gordy in 1909 argued that to promote a peace-loving spirit among school children, teachers of American history should emphasize the destructive effects of war. But he apparently did not think it important to emphasize destructive effects of the genocidal wars against native peoples. In citing "facts" to illustrate the "peaceful" evolution of American institutions, he asserted that in settling America, "European life entered the new world, received large modifications from *physical influences* [my emphasis], and then reacted upon the social and political life of the old world . . . in the end, [European] man mastered the wilderness and brought under his control a continent." What better way to deny genocide than to ignore the existence of the human residents of the "wilderness?"

A more general pattern of denial is evident in response to criticisms of US policies toward Native Americans, such as the many criticisms of the Columbian Quincentenary celebrations, and to the UN Year of Indigenous Peoples. Many historians deny not only that Columbus was responsible for the genocide and other crimes against humanity perpetrated by his successors, but also that the United States' campaigns against the Indians were in fact genocidal (Jaimes, 1992). On the other hand, in October of 1992, an International Tribunal of Indigenous Peoples and Oppressed Nations in the USA unanimously found the US Government guilty of numerous violations of international law in its treatment of Native Americans and other groups, including several violations of the 1948 Genocide Convention [*Verdict of the International Tribunal of Indigenous Peoples and Oppressed Nations in the USA.* San Francisco, CA: American Indian Movement, October 4, 1992]. To the extent that open-minded debate of these charges and denials can be generated, there is reason to hope that a deeper understanding of the fundamental causes of genocide can be gained.

—Clinton F. Fink

References and Recommended Reading

Deloria, Jr., Vine (1973). *God is Red.* New York: Grosset and Dunlap.

Jaimes, M. Annette (1992). Introduction: Sand Creek the morning after. In Jaimes, M. Annette (Ed.), *The State of Native America: Genocide, Colonization and Resistance.* Boston, MA: South End Press.

DENIALS OF THE HOLOCAUST

Of all the intellectual monstrosities of the late twentieth century, one of the most vicious and factually indefensible has been that school of historical revisionism known as Holocaust denial. Its proponents purport to have "proven" that the systematic Nazi extermination of somewhere between five and six million Jews did not occur. Such genocidal dimensions were never really part of the Nazi character, they argue. Rather, the whole idea of a Holocaust perpetrated by the Third Reich is, instead, a colossal and sustained propaganda myth contrived for purposes of gaining moral advantage by Germany's politico-military adversaries, in combination with an "international Jewish conspiracy" during and after World War II.

Probably the first purveyor of such tripe was Paul Rassinier, a former French Communist Party member turned virulent anti-Communist cum Nazi apologist, who published his seminal work on the topic, *Le Passage de la Ligne (Crossing the Line),* in 1948. In the main, his position can be reduced to a simple duality: first, that much of what the Nazis are accused of accrues from "the natural tendency of its victims to exaggerate"; second, that to the extent atrocities happened at all in the Nazi death camps, they were more the responsibility of the victims—who, Rassinier claimed, had been placed "in charge" by their SS keepers—than of the SS or nazism more generally.

Rassinier's themes were quickly picked up by pro-Nazi/antisemitic figures in the United States, such as the evangelical "Christian" publicist, W.D. Herrstrom (*Bible News Flashes*); white supremacist publisher, James Madole (*National Renaissance Bulletin*); national

Templates for Gross Denial of a Known Genocide: A Manual

"The Holocaust Is the Hoax of the Twentieth Century"
"There Never Was an Armenian Genocide"

1. Question the statistics so that you claim only a smaller number were involved.
2. Move from the absolute facts of deaths of countless innocent people to a relativism that mitigates the horror.
   - The deaths that took place were inadvertent, because of wartime/famine/migration etc., not because of willful murder.
3. Emphasize that the victims were strangers to whom we cannot feel naturally close, in order to deflect the identification with them and their fate. Regard the victims as a problem ("the Jewish problem," "the Armenian issue") and not as people.
   - "Lord Moyne of Great Britain, when made to negotiate with the Nazis release of Jews during the Holocaust: "What shall I do with a million Jews?""
4. Rationalize the deaths as coming to the victims out of the inevitability of their history of relationships.
   - The Armenian uprising at Van proved they supported the Russians, and the Armenian threat had to be eliminated.
   - The Jews were always obnoxious. There is a reason they are always hated.
5. Distance the event timewise: It all happened so long ago, there is a new generation of the victimizer people today. Why bring it all up again? Let the wounds heal.
6. Justify by the realpolitik of today not antagonizing the people (and their successors) who committed the genocide. They are our allies. Whoever brings up this issue is weakening the alliance.
7. Justify putting aside the past in favor of current economic interests.
8. Be sure to deny outright the claims of genocide, and at the same time advance the counter-claim that the victims received good treatment at the hands of the perpetrators.
   - The Armenians were moved to a hospitable climate like California and every measure was taken to protect them.
   - At Auschwitz the Jews dined to orchestral music, and swam in an Olympic pool.

[These templates were developed in a dialogue with Vartan Gregorian, then president of the New York Public Library, and were also based on joint research with Marjorie Housepian Dobkin.]

—Israel W. Charny, Internet on the Holocaust and Genocide

socialists like George Lincoln Rockwell and Gerald L.K. Smith *(The Cross and the Flag);* and eminent Smith College historian, Harry Elmer Barnes. The latter, with the release of his *The Struggle Against Historical Blackout* in 1947, set down the ideological/theoretical framework within which Rassinier, Smith, Herrstrom and their ilk could pretend to at least marginal "scholarly" credibility.

By the late 1950s, the emerging "field" of Holocaust denial in the US had produced its first genuine "academic specialist," Austin J. App, professor of English

Auschwitz: A Response to Holocaust Denials on the Internet

After having visited Auschwitz, a group of students at the University of Linz, Austria, organized an exhibition that was subsequently shown at several locations in upper Austria. These young people also had the idea of trying to counterbalance the increasingly aggressive offerings of neo-Nazi propaganda on the Internet. They thus created an electronic page about Auschwitz supporting it with illustrational materials and factual data, and asked Simon Wiesenthal to provide an introductory text. They brought a laptop and software to the Documentation Center to demonstrate their presentation, and Mr. Wiesenthal subsequently wrote the following words of introduction:

Auschwitz has become synonymous with the greatest crime in the history of mankind, and it has been very well documented. Auschwitz is the place where the planned and carefully organized genocide was translated into action. The victims were not buried but burned, and their ashes were scattered over the surrounding fields as fertilizer. Auschwitz was the place of death of one and one-half million people of various nationalities; 90 percent of them were Jewish. Human language lacks the words to describe the atrocities to which innocent men, women, and children were exposed in this place of horror. Many were bestially murdered outright, while thousands of others were left to die of starvation or made to perform excruciating work under inconceivable conditions until they died of exhaustion. For years Auschwitz represents the realization of an inhuman ideology with individuals selected on racial principles being exterminated by industrial methods. What today remains of the camp and its facilities can convey only a very limited impression of what hundreds of thousands were made to suffer there. People of today who were never in a German concentration camp can hardly believe, much less understand, the atrocities committed by the Nazis in Auschwitz and in many similar places; these are unimaginable both in their extent and in their brutality—but they are nevertheless true!

—*Simon Wiesenthal*

literature at the University of Scranton and later at LaSalle College. App's tactic was to place Rassinier's form of "logical" denial on tentatively "scientific" footing, developing an obfuscatory "statistical profile" of pre- and postwar European demography through which conventional estimates of six million Jewish victims of Nazi extermination might be challenged as "grossly inflated."

During the second half of the 1960s and throughout the 1970s, App's sort of "scholarship" began to take hold on North America's extreme right and, increasingly, to cross-pollinate with European strains. In the US, 1969 saw the anonymous release of *The Myth of the Six Million,* a book actually written by a Harvard-trained history professor named David Leslie Hoggan, published by Willis Carto, founder of the neo-Nazi Liberty Lobby and owner of the openly fascist Noontide Press, and introduced by E. Anderson, a contributing editor for what was then Carto's main periodical publication, *American Mercury.* In England, Richard Verrall (a.k.a., Richard Harwood), leader of the British National Front and publisher of a neo-Nazi tabloid, *Spearhead,* followed suit with the 1974 publication of a booklet entitled, *Did Six Million Really Die?*

Jean-Marie Le Pen Fined for Dismissing Gas Chambers as a "Detail in History"

Jean-Marie Le Pen, the leader of the extreme right National Front party in France, was convicted of crimes against humanity for dismissing the gas chambers of World War II as a "detail in history" at a news conference in Munich. Le Pen had used almost identical words in 1987 and was fined and convicted then by a French court; he also repeated them in an interview with the *New Yorker* magazine. French civil-rights groups filed a complaint against him after the Munich episode and won a court judgment that required him to pay 300,000 francs ($50,000) to publish the ruling in a dozen French newspapers.

Le Pen called a Jewish government minister, Michel Durafour, "Durafour-Crematorium" in 1988, and another time said of another minister, Simone Weil, who survived one of the camps, "When I speak of genocide, I always say that in any case they missed old lady Weil."

A 1990 French law has made it a crime to deny the Holocaust.

—*Press Reports*

A couple of years later in the US, an MIT/University of Minnesota graduate named Arthur R. Butz, employed at the time as a professor of electrical engineering at Northwestern University, moved things forward by publishing *The Hoax of the Twentieth Century: The Case Against the Presumed Extermination of European Jewry.* In this book, it is argued on a supposedly technical basis that the mass gassings and cremations of Jews and others, documented during the Nuremberg Trial as having taken place at locations like Auschwitz (Oswiecim) and Treblinka, "simply could not have occurred" given "the rather obvious technological limitations" of the equipment used. At this point, it is fair to say that all of the cornerstones for a comprehensive "rebuttal" of the Holocaust as an historical fact had been laid.

The Institute for Historical Review

In 1978, the various international strands of Holocaust denial began to be consolidated under the rubric of the Los Angeles-based Institute for Historical Review (IHR), funded by Willis Carto and headed by a former British National Front officer named William David McCalden. In addition to unrestricted access to what had become Carto's own primary periodical publication, *The Spotlight,* and Noontide Press, his book-publishing concern, the IHR quickly established its own "academic" organ, the *Journal of Historical Review,* and a book publishing operation under its own imprimatur. Moreover, in 1979, it initiated a series of "scholarly conferences" known as International Revisionist Conventions—to bring together and coordinate the activities of deniers the world over.

These were concretized to a considerable extent during the 1980s via the case of Ernst Zundel, a German immigrant to Canada and ardent Nazi, who was charged by Crown Counsel with instigating social and racial intolerance through his publishing house, Samisdat Press. During his first trial, in which the IHR arranged for him to be represented by attorney Douglas Christie and otherwise assisted by an "expert" witness, French Holocaust denier, Professor Robert Faurisson, Zundel was convicted and sentenced to serve 15 months in prison. He was then able to win an appeal on procedural grounds and was retried in 1988.

During the second trial, Christie and Faurisson brought in yet another expert, prominent British denier, historian

David Irving. Between the three, a strategy was hatched—presumably under a variation of the theory that "the truth is the best defense" wherein the thesis advanced by Arthur Butz would be "scientifically" corroborated. For this purpose, they retained the services of Fred A. Leuchter, reputedly "an engineer, skilled in the functioning of gas chambers," who, as a consultant to prison administrations across the US "specialized in constructing and installing execution apparatus." Leuchter, having been dispatched to Auschwitz/Birkenau and Majdanek on "site visits," submitted a detailed report that it was "chemically and physically impossible for the Germans to have conducted gassings" in those camps. Although it was quickly established in court that Leuchter lacked even the most rudimentary engineering credentials—his sole degree turned out to be a BA in history from Boston University—his "findings" had already caused something of an international media sensation. Although these were debunked almost as rapidly as their author, with the result that Zundel was convicted and sentenced to serve 15 months in jail (the conviction was later overturned because of procedural considerations), the IHR immediately launched an intensive cam-

President Ronald Reagan: I'm Horrified by People Who Say the Holocaust Was Invented

I'm horrified today when I know that there are actually people now trying to say that the Holocaust was invented, that it never happened, that there weren't six million people whose lives were taken cruelly and needlessly in that event, that all of this is propaganda.

In World War II, I was in the military and I remember April 1945. I remember seeing the first film that came in when the war was still on. Our troops had come upon the first camps and had entered those camps. And you saw, unretouched—and no way that it could have ever been rehearsed—what they saw—the horror they saw.

"I Felt Nauseous" in a Mob of Neo-Nazis

"I felt nauseous and chilled when I stood unidentified as a Jew or a newspaperman in a mob of stupid and evil Germans who, with mass murder in their eyes shouted, laughed and cheered, 'Auschwitz, Auschwitz!'" Thus Shlomo Shamgar, an Israeli newspaperman for the daily *Maariv* said after attending incognito an "International Revisionist Congress" in Munich. "They were obviously ready to finish then and there the remaining destruction of the Jews that, according to them, they had never done at all in the past."

The conference was convened in honor of Fred Leuchter, an American of German origin who is an "expert" on gas ovens, who reported that he traveled to the sites of the Nazi death camps in Poland and didn't smell any traces of zyklon-B. Leuchter, who was received with an ovation, asked rhetorically, "Until when will the persecuted German people pay for a sin they did not commit? Enough with the alleged Holocaust!" Robert Faurisson spoke briefly and said he was prepared to go to jail. He concluded his remarks with a prayer for the restoration of the Third Reich in its historic boundaries.

—*Press Report*

COMBATTING DENIALS OF THE HOLOCAUST IN A SOUTHERN US COMMUNITY

Huntsville, Alabama, population approximately 164,470 persons, is home to resident Holocaust/Shoah denier, Dr. Robert Countess, Co-Director with Bradley R. Smith of the Committee for Open Debate on the Holocaust (CODOH), and Member, Editorial Board, *Journal of Historical Review* based in Torrance, California.

On two separate, but related occasions—the Fall of 1993, and, again, the Fall of 1994—Countess arranged for lectures of three of the leading international Holocaust/Shoah deniers—David Irving of England, Robert Faurisson of France, and Ernst Zundel of Canada—on the campus of the University of Alabama in Huntsville (UAH), taking full advantage of the nondiscriminatory public service policy of campus facilities rental, subject to no calendar conflict and/or use by legitimately recognized faculty and student campus groups. Because of a particular clause in its policies regarding use of facilities and Countess's apparently deliberate attempts at deception, the local Public Library was able to deny him the use of its facilities for a presentation by Faurisson. After 1994, Countess made it clear that it was his intention to bring to Huntsville and UAH other Holocaust/Shoah deniers as well as return visits by the aforementioned Irving, Faurisson, and Zundel.

University forums have not been the only venue at which Countess has paraded his Holocaust/Shoah denial. Also preoccupied with every seeming moral, ethical, and military infringement of human rights by the State of Israel against the seemingly innocent Palestinians, not to mention US foreign aid to Israel, he has pontifically utilized the "Letters to the Editor" sections of both the morning *Huntsville News* (now defunct) and the afternoon and weekend *Huntsville Times,* publishing more than *fifty* letters since 1988 as well as several book reviews of works critical of Israel.

Countess originally tried to secure the sponsorship of the student organization, Association for Campus Entertainment (ACE), but after presentations by the Jewish Student Organization (JSO) as well as representatives of the Jewish Community Council of North Alabama (JCCNA), sponsorship was withdrawn. Countess then chose to accuse the media, both in print and radio and television, of censorship and denial of free speech, thus opening the door to full coverage of these events, including the national *USA Today* and Alabama's state-wide Jewish newspaper, *The Southern Shofar.* In addition, Countess was able to arrange coverage on two local radio talk shows, one of which was already favorable to him and other deniers, and to *purchase* thirty minutes of local public access cable television time in the form of an uninterrupted interview, which gave him free rein for the presentation of his ideas.

The university itself chose to distance itself not only from Countess and his presenters but from Holocaust/Shoah denial as well. Both the President of the university and its Director of Public Relations, as well as the Dean of the College of Liberal Arts, himself a French historian, issued formal statements denying endorsement or sponsorship as well as expressing regret that such events were taking place on their campus. Significantly, History

continues

continued

Club students and History Honor Society students, non-Jews, publicly protested the presentations, passed out informational leaflets and bibliographies on the Second World War, and arranged for the showing of the film *Schindler's List* to coincide with David Irving's scheduled appearance. In the Spring of 1995, the first course on the history of the Holocaust/Shoah was taught at the university, an academic response to the affair, and a Holocaust/Shoah literature course was scheduled for Spring, 1998.

The Christian clergy and Christian community were largely silent. The only public exception was the passage of a resolution by the North Alabama Presbytery of the Presbyterian Church USA condemning both antisemitism and Holocaust/Shoah denial without, however, mentioning Countess (who was originally ordained within the Orthodox Presbyterian tradition) by name. Through its Jewish Community Council and the person of the Rabbi of one of the two local Congregations, the Jewish community chose to respond by *networking* with the university and the media.

Suggested Additional Responses to Combat Denial

1. The role of the media—both print and radio and television—must be understood by all involved as *allies* in the cause of combatting Holocaust denial. Collectively, they must be urged to provide in-depth coverage of the nature of Holocaust denial and its affiliated network of antisemitic and racist institutions as was done in this particular case.
2. Civic and religious groups, especially non-Jewish ones, must be enlisted in the fight against denial of the Holocaust, hopefully with more success than was the case with the clergy and religious institutions of Huntsville, Alabama.

—*Steven L. Jacobs*

References and Recommended Reading

Lipstadt, Deborah (1990). *Denying the Holocaust: The Growing Assault on Truth and Memory.* New York: Free Press.

Stern, Kenneth (1993). *Holocaust Denial.* New York: American Jewish Committee.

Vidal-Naquet, Pierre (1993). *Assassins of Memory: Essays on the Denial of the Holocaust.* New York: Columbia University Press.

paign to capitalize on the popular first impression it had achieved. In this, the institute has relied primarily on the talents of a California-based publicist named Bradley Smith who packaged and promoted Leuchter's discredited material as if it were the very essence of scientific research—or at least a tenable point of view, which is intrinsically worthy of inclusion in the academic agenda—while concentrating his energy on obtaining advertising space trumpeting this notion in campus newspapers across the country. By 1992, the IHR had managed to shift the sordid fabrications comprising Holocaust denial from the outermost lunatic fringe of social discourse into the vastly more legitimate areas of First Amendment debate and scholarly dialogue.

Deborah Lipstadt's Contribution to the Study of Denial

Comes now Deborah Lipstadt, Dorot Chair in Modern Jewish and Holocaust Studies at Emory University, with what is probably the first comprehensive public effort at analyzing and resisting the rising tide of Holocaust denial. Her book, *Denying the Holocaust: The Growing Assault on Truth and Memory,* is thus a milestone of sorts, trying as it does not only to rebut the deniers' arguments, but to place their activities in the broader sociopolitical panorama that gives them potency.

The weight of Lipstadt's presentation rests on providing information that thoroughly debunks the sort of intentional misinformation by which deniers have adorned themselves with a veneer of superficial plausibility. When Lipstadt trains her guns on recent pseudoscientific postulations of others, such as Butz, Faurisson, and Leuchter, the sheer extent and solidity of the base of technical literature available to her are devastating. By the time she is finished, the author has dismembered every known variation of such shopworn revisionist themes as zyklon-B being a chemical appropriate only for delousing rather than exterminating human beings, the gas chambers at Auschwitz and elsewhere being "ill designed" to serve the purpose ascribed to them, and the crematoria at such facilities being "inadequate" to handle the volume of corpses "allegedly" run through them.

In framing her responses, Lipstadt does a great service by setting out a sort of typology of Holocaust revisionism. Not everyone involved, she maintains, is as crude as the outright deniers like Butz, Faurisson, Leuchter, Carto, Irving, and Zundel. Others, like Rassinier, Barnes, Hoggan, and App might be better understood as "minimizers"; that is, those who engage in a range of sophistries designed to make the magnitude of the Holocaust appear less than it was. From there, by carefully mixing known facts with their fictions, the latter group advances false sets of moral comparisons—e.g., the Nazi extermination center at Auschwitz was "really no different" than the concentration camps at Dachau; and Dachau wasn't that different from the camp at Manzanar where Japanese-Americans were interned by the US government during the war. Therefore the Nazi treatment of *untermenschen* (subhumans) was "no worse than" that accorded by the US to its "Jap" minority—which the author rightly describes as being "immoral equivalencies."

It is the more diffuse, institutionalized, and ubiquitous symptomologies of denial, rather than the blatant crudities of Rassinier and Butz, that we must address, Lipstadt contends, if we are ever to rid ourselves of the hideous implications represented by the deniers. "If Holocaust denial has demonstrated anything," she observes, "it is the fragility of memory, truth, reason, and history." The object, of course, is to affirm and reinforce each of these as natural societal barriers against repetition of that which is being denied and forgotten. "When we witness assault on truth," she says, "our response must be strong, though neither polemical nor emotional. We must educate the broader public and academe about this threat and its historical and ideological roots. We must expose these people for what they are."

—*Ward Churchill*

References and Recommended Reading

Churchill, Ward (1997). *A Little Matter of Genocide: Holocaust and Denial in the Americas 1492 to the Present.* San Francisco, CA: City Lights Books.

Lipstadt, Deborah (1993). *Denying the Holocaust: The Growing Assault on Truth and Memory.* New York: Free Press.

DENIALS OF OTHER GENOCIDES OF NON-JEWISH PEOPLE IN THE HOLOCAUST

As stated in the entry DENIALS OF THE HOLOCAUST, of all the intellectual monstrosities arising during the course of the late twentieth century, one of the most vicious and factually indefensible has been that "school of historical

China Gives Contemporary Example of Governmental Denial of Genocidal Massacre

The government of China has given a vivid contemporary example of how government power and policy can be mobilized to deny a genocidal massacre—even when it was undeniably observed and recorded by scores of people, and news of the events has been broadcast by modern news media around the world.

At the end of June 1989, news sources reported that Chinese troops, backed by tanks, fired on unarmed civilians and drove thousands of protesters from Tiananmen Square. Western intelligence reports said the toll was as high as 3,000. The Chinese government says 200 to 300 people, most of them soldiers, were killed in the confrontation. Subsequently the authorities arrested thousands and are known to have executed scores of the arrestees.

"We're looking at a fantastic propaganda campaign that's beginning to work—the seed of doubt has been sown," said one of the Western military experts who collected and analyzed the evidence. Western experts cited an example of the Chinese propaganda approach. A videotape of one incident begins with a Chinese soldier firing his assault rifle into a crowd, killing a student, a woman and another bystander before running out of ammunition, and then being overrun by the crowd of civilians who killed him. "The Chinese use the tape only from the point where the mob attacks," a Western military source said, "to the point that even some people in the West who were sure there was a massacre began saying, 'Well, now I don't know.'"

—*Press Reports*

revisionism" known as "Holocaust denial." *But those who deny all holocausts other than that of the Jews have the same effect.*

The costs of these systematic assaults on truth and memory by those who argue the uniqueness of Jewish victimization have often been high for those whose suffering is correspondingly downgraded or shunted into historical oblivion. This concerns not only the victims of the many genocides occurring outside the framework of nazism, but non-Jews targeted for elimination within the Holocaust itself.

Holocaust exclusivists contend that the Gypsies stand apart from the Holocaust because, unlike the Jews, they were "not marked for complete annihilation." According to Richard Breitman, "The Nazis are not known to have spoken of the Final Solution of the Polish problem or the Gypsy problem." Or as Yehuda Bauer put it in his three-page entry on "Gypsies" in the *Encyclopedia of the Holocaust*—that's all the space the Sinti and Roma are accorded in this 2,000 page work, the editor of which did not have a Gypsy write the material filling it—"[The] fate of the Gypsies was in line with Nazi thought as a whole; Gypsies were not Jews, and therefore there was no need to kill them all."

As concerns the Gypsies, the argument amounts to a boldfaced lie. This is readily evidenced by Himmler's "Decree for Basic Regulations to Resolve the Gypsy Question as Required by the Nature of Race" of December 8, 1938, which initiated preparations for the *complete extermination* of the Sinti and Roma (emphasis added)." Shortly after this, in February 1939, a brief was circulated by Johannes Behrendt of the Nazi Office of Racial Hygiene in which it was stated that "all Gypsies should be treated as hereditarily sick; the only solution is elimination. The aim should be the elimination without hesitation of this defective population."

Indeed, Gypsies were automatically subject to whatever policies applied to Jews during the entire period of the Final Solution, pursuant to a directive issued by Himmler on December 24, 1941 (i.e., prior to the Wannsee Conference that set the full-fledged extermination program in motion). Hence, there is no defensible way the fate of the Gypsies can be distinguished from that of the Jews.

All during the 1930s, while Gypsies as well as Jews were subjected to increasingly draconian racial oppression, first in Germany, then in Austria and Czechoslovakia, a certain amount of international outrage was expressed on behalf of the Jews. Foreign diplomatic and business pressure was exerted, resulting in an at least partial and transient alleviation in Jewish circumstances, and facilitating Jewish emigration to a degree (150,000 left by 1938). From then until the collapse of the Third Reich, the Nazis displayed a periodic willingness to broker Jewish lives for a variety of reasons, and diplomats like Sweden's Count Folke Bernadotte made efforts to effect their rescue. None of this applies to the Sinti and Roma.

Another case concerns the Slavic populations in the Soviet Union. A gross estimate of the results of Nazi genocide against the Slavs comes to somewhere between 15.5 and 19.5 million in the USSR, between 19.7 and 23.9 million when the Poles, Slovenes, Serbs, and others are added in. As Simon Wiesenthal, a survivor of Auschwitz, long ago observed, "The Holocaust was not only a matter of the killing of six million Jews. It involved the killing of eleven million people, six million of whom were Jews." Wiesenthal spoke on the basis of what was then the best available evidence. Today, some 50 years later, the only correction to be made to his statement lies in the fact that we now believe his estimate of 11 million was far too low. The true human costs of Nazi genocide may come to 26 million or more, 5 to 6 million of whom were Jews, a half-million to a million or more of whom were Gypsies, and the rest mostly Slavs. Only with these facts clearly in mind can we comprehend the full scope of the Holocaust and its real implications.

Deniers of the Holocaust must, of course, be confronted, exposed for what they are, and driven into the permanent oblivion they so richly deserve. But so, too, must those who choose to deny holocausts more generally.

Only in this way can we hope to arrive at the "universality" called for by Michael Berenbaum, former executive director of the US Holocaust Memorial Museum Research Institute, when he suggested that the "Holocaust can become a symbolic orienting event in human history that can prevent recurrence." Undoubtedly, this was what the executive director of the Institute on the Holocaust and Genocide in Jerusalem, Israel Charny, had in mind when he denounced "the leaders and high priests" of different cultures who insist on the uniqueness, primacy, superiority, or greater significance of the specific genocide of their people," elsewhere adding that: "I object very strongly to the efforts to name the genocide of any one people as the single, ultimate event, or as the most important event against which all other tragedies of genocidal mass death are to be tested and found wanting . . . For me, the passion to exclude this or that mass killing from the universe of genocide, as well as the intense competition to establish the exclusive 'superiority' or unique form of any one genocide, ends up creating a fetishistic atmosphere in which the masses of bodies that are not to be qualified for the definition of genocide are dumped into a conceptual black hole, where they are forgotten."

In every instance, the particularities of these prior genocides serves to inform our understanding of the Holocaust. Reciprocally, the actualities of the Holocaust serve to illuminate the nature of these earlier holocausts. No less does the procedure apply to the manner in which we approach genocides occurring since 1945, those in Katanga, Biafra, Bangladesh, Indochina, Paraguay, Guatemala, Indonesia, Rwanda, Bosnia, and on and on. Our task must be to fit all the various pieces together in such a way as to obtain at last a comprehension of the whole. There is no other means available to us. We must truly "think of the unthinkable," seriously and without proprietary interest, if ever we are to put an end to the "human cancer" (see title of book by Charny in References) that has spread increasingly throughout our collective organism over the past five centuries. To this end, denial in any form is anathema.

—*Ward Churchill*

References and Recommended Reading

Charny, Israel W. (1982). *How Can We Commit the Unthinkable?: Genocide, The Human Cancer.* Boulder, CO: Westview Press. Republished in Portuguese with a new Introduction and Bibliography as *Anatomia do Genocídio: Uma Psicologia da Agressão Humana.* Rio de Janeiro: Editora Rosa dos Tempos, 1998.

Churchill, Ward (1997). *A Little Matter of Genocide: Holocaust and Denial in the Americas, 1492 to the Present.* San Francisco, CA: City Lights Books.

DENIERS OF THE ARMENIAN GENOCIDE

In the last third of the twentieth century, the Turkish Republic's official denials gained the support of a coterie of academic deniers who, under the guise of revisionist scholarship, began to expunge the facts of the Armenian Genocide from history texts. The growth of area studies in Europe and, especially, the United States, which since World War II had fostered the advancement of research about the Middle East, also contributed to the emergence of specialists on the Ottoman Empire. Recasting Turkish history in light of the Turkish Republic's integration into the Western military alliance against the Soviet Union, they also refurbished the disputed chapters of the Ottoman period. This trend was spawned in

Professor Bernard Lewis Found Guilty of Denial of Armenian Genocide

In June 1995, Professor Bernard Lewis of Princeton University was found guilty by a court in Paris on civil charges that had been brought against him, as per the headline in *Le Monde,* "for denying the reality of the Armenian Genocide." This court, which was hearing a second *civil* case against Lewis following an earlier *criminal* case, found Lewis guilty of a "fault" and causing damage to another party because of his dereliction of responsibility as a scholar. The court ruled that in his denials of the genocide, Lewis calculatedly ignored and did not relate to major evidences and judgments by serious bodies, such as the UN Whitaker Commission in 1985 and the European Parliament in 1987, which have attested to the Armenian Genocide. Lewis was therefore convicted for "hiding elements which go against his thesis . . . [that] the reality of the Armenian Genocide results from nothing more than the imagination of the Armenian people." He was ordered to pay a fine of 10,000 francs, punitive damages of one franc and all court costs. *Le Monde,* in which Lewis had denied the Armenian Genocide, was ordered by the court to report the sentence.

—*Press Reports*

1952 by Lewis V. Thomas of Princeton University who intellectually legitimated the racial homogenization of Turkey by arguing that despite the violence, the process contributed to the development of a stable nation friendly to the United States.

This rationalization of the Armenian Genocide began to take root in Western academic circles, and was further strengthened by the hiring of Bernard Lewis at Princeton. One of the most prominent English specialists on the Middle East, Lewis's stature provided a lofty cover for the Turkish national agenda of obfuscating academic research on the Armenian Genocide. He was joined by Stanford Shaw, the most flagrant academic denier of the Armenian Genocide, who introduced into scholarly literature the full arguments of the Turkish state by displacing the entire episode of the Armenian massacres from Ottoman history. At the University of California, Los Angeles (UCLA), Shaw trained two students who transformed the academic denial of the Armenian Genocide into a profession. Justin McCarthy of the University of Louisville, Kentucky, a demographer, presumed to demonstrate that the Armenian losses were the result of interethnic and civil warfare and not the consequences of deportations and massacres. Heath Lowry produced tracts seeking to undermine the veracity of the main historical documents that were authored in the wake of the Armenian massacres and began challenging Holocaust specialists engaged in comparative genocide studies. He carried out his program of academic intimidation under the direct auspices of the Turkish Embassy by ghost-writing correspondence for the Turkish Ambassador challenging Holocaust specialists studying the Armenian Genocide.

With the founding in 1982 of the Institute of Turkish Studies (ITS) in Washington, DC, an organization fully funded by the Turkish government, the rationalizing current gained ascendancy in the field of Middle East Studies. ITS became the principal agency in the United States promoting research on Turkey and the Ottoman Empire. Under the directorship of Heath Lowry, ITS's and the Turkish government's true intention of purchasing legitimacy and silencing critics became fully apparent. The Turkish state's academic agenda registered its moment of greatest success in subordinating the discipline to its political interests when in 1993 Lowry was appointed to a newly founded chair of Turkish and Ottoman Studies, also funded by the Turkish government, at Princeton University.

While the field of Middle East Studies became permeated with denialist views, genocide specialists and the Armenian community mounted an effort to respond. In 1995, a French court found Bernard Lewis liable for denying the Armenian Genocide. In the same year evidence corroborating the close cooperation of Lowry at ITS with the Turkish ambassador in Washington became public, further demonstrating the coordinated efforts of academic deniers and the Turkish political agenda of obliterating the facts of the Armenian Genocide from modern historical literature.

—Rouben Paul Adalian

References and Recommended Reading

Adalian, Rouben (1992). The Armenian Genocide: Revisionism and denial. In Dobkowski, Michael N., and Wallimann, Isidor (Eds.), *Genocide in Our Time: An Annotated Bibliography with Analytical Introductions.* Ann Arbor, MI: Pierian Press, pp. 85–105.

Adalian, Rouben P. (1997). The ramifications in the United States of the 1995 French Court decision on the denial of the Armenian Genocide and Princeton University. *Revue du monde arménien moderne et contemporain,* 3, 99–122.

Smith, Roger W.; Markusen, Eric; and Lifton, Robert Jay (1995). Professional ethics and denial of Armenian Genocide. *Holocaust and Genocide Studies,* 9(1), 1–22.

DENIERS OF THE HOLOCAUST

HISTORICAL REVISIONISM VERSUS HOLOCAUST DENIAL

Historical revisionism is the *legitimate* understanding of historical research that mandates rethinking and rewriting our understanding of specific historical events as more material and interpretations become available. It is the very substance of scholarly and academic dialogue and responsibility. However, *Holocaust revisionism* is none of the above. It is instead an attempt, often by an antisemitic fringe minority that is well-financed and internationally-networked, to raise doubts and questions in the unsuspecting and unaware minds of the

Denying the Holocaust: The Growing Assault on Truth

A lone denier, Bradley Smith, has garnered incredible amounts of attention with a tactically brilliant but devious maneuver: the placing of advertisements in student newspapers arguing that there was no Holocaust.

But Bradley Smith's attempt to place these ads is not the only new development. In recent years, Holocaust denial has made a subtle shift in its modus operandi. No longer are the deniers publishing their pseudo-research articles in neo-Nazi and Klan-like publications. In the 1980's, they began to produce material that had the form of academic articles. This material appears at first glance to be the product of serious research. A few years later, they took another step forward in their effort to convince people that there had been no Holocaust. They began to conduct "scientific" studies which purported to "prove" their point. The best known of these was the infamous Leuchter Report which claimed to establish scientifically that the gas chambers at Auschwitz were not death chambers. Leuchter's supposed credentials as an electrical engineer have been proven false—he has a B.A. in history. [The Massachusetts courts have enjoined him from trying to pass himself off as an engineer.] His "research" has been shown to be fundamentally flawed.

Leuchter's efforts reflect another shift in the deniers' tactics. Today, some deniers argue that they do not "deny" the Holocaust, they only deny that there were gas chambers. They argue that the gas chambers were really "delousing" chambers. Deniers' literature—including the infamous ads by Bradley Smith—turn the horror of the gas chambers on its head by claiming that this was a "life-saving procedure."

If there were no gas chambers in Auschwitz, one has to wonder what were the Jews doing there? Where did the millions of Jews, who were transported to Auschwitz and other camps go? Documents abound indicating that this was a murder operation, not a "fumigation" effort. Trying to deny the existence of the gas chambers is the first step in an attempt to deny the Holocaust altogether. Once they can deny the existence of gas chambers, then it is relatively simple to deny the rest of the Holocaust. Bradley Smith and his small group of followers have clouded the issue by wrapping themselves in the flag of free speech. They accuse "Zionist" establishment groups of subverting their right to speak the truth. Using this tactic slyly plays on the controversy about political correctness.

continues

continued

Astonishingly some campus presidents (Duke University) and student editors (Ohio State and Rutgers) believe that they cannot deny Smith room to run his ads or his op-ed piece because that constitutes a limit on his freedom of speech. Such an argument is reminiscent of the observation that "some people's minds are so open that their brains have fallen out." At Ohio State University, Smith tried to place one of his ads in the student newspaper, *The Lantern.* After the journalism school committee that oversees the newspaper voted not to publish the ad, the editor, convinced that not to run the ad was a violation of the ethic of freedom of the press, used it as an op-ed piece. She argued that, although the information in the ad was totally incorrect, her fellow students had a right to know what the controversy was all about. A powerful editorial appeared the same day condemning Smith and his committee as " . . . racists. Pure and simple." Despite the strength of the condemnation, by choosing, as was done at Rutgers to run the ad as an op-ed piece with other articles answering it, the editors fell right into Bradley Smith's hands. They set up Holocaust denial as one side, however controversial, in a debate. This is an essential part of the deniers' strategy: presenting themselves as a legitimate historical alternative. When Smith called her to congratulate her for "being true to her principles," she acknowledged to a CBS crew that was filming the interchange that she felt like she had been "had." She and her colleagues may have seen the light. The problem was that it was just a little late.

The editors who have chosen to publish this ad have made another critical mistake. They present this as a first amendment issue. But this is not a matter of free speech. Editors reject ads and op-ed pieces all the time if they do not conform to their paper's code of ethics and advertising. Some who defend the ad cite Justice Louis D. Brandeis' 1927 argument in *Whitney v. California* that "to expose . . . falsehood and fallacies is more speech, not enforced silence." But Brandeis was talking about government enforced silence. This is not an issue of enforced silence. The Ohio State paper argued that "No matter how repugnant, we must let Bradley Smith have his public say." Wrong. Bradley Smith does have a right to public say. "We," however, are not required to provide him with the forum, especially when space is limited. Bradley Smith and his cohorts have an absolute right to stand on the most heavily trafficked corner on the campus—or anywhere else—and proclaim their insidious theories. If they wish to distribute booklets advocating their beliefs, they have the right to do so. Giving them unlimited editorial space in a newspaper is not an issue of censorship but one of differentiating between an opinion—however controversial—and obvious falsehoods designed to stimulate prejudice and antisemitism.

Neo-Nazis and other antisemites have pounced upon denial with great enthusiasm. Today, neo-Nazis in Germany and Austria no longer try to justify all that Hitler did, including the Holocaust. Now they proclaim that Hitler was a great man who has been unfairly accused of having committed this heinous crime.

Combatting this pernicious trend is of the utmost importance. It is not just a threat to Jews and their history, but a threat to all who believe in the ultimate power of truth.

—Deborah E. Lipstadt, Internet on the Holocaust and Genocide

naive and those whose knowledge of the period is limited regarding the *facts* of the Holocaust/Shoah. A better term, therefore, to describe such persons and/or organizations is that of *Holocaust* or *Shoah deniers.*

The rationale behind their position is relatively simple: For one thing, their attack on the validity of the Holocaust/Shoah often is part of an attack on the State of Israel, which they claim has orchestrated the entire myth of the Holocaust and in general continues to control and dominate American and world-wide public opinion for economic and political gain. By extension, Shoah denial of course can be equally an attack on the world-wide community of Jews, indeed on all people of good will, Jews and non-Jews alike, who fought and died during the Second World War, for it dishonors the dead and denigrates the efforts of the Allies to stop the spread of National Socialism (i.e., nazism).

Scholars will continue to debate various points regarding the facts and interpretations of many specific events associated with the Second World War and the Holocaust. They will continue to differ regarding numbers, key personnel, and reasons for events. But no credible scholar of the Second World War will deny that part of the overall agenda of Hitler and his minions was the destruction of European Jewry. Equally, no scholar worthy of that appellation will deny that the path to achieving that end was the murdering of millions of Jews in ghettos, concentration and death camps by liquidation, shootings, gassings, starvation, beatings, and the like.

Holocaust revision/Shoah denial is the implementation of the so-called "Big Lie" first suggested by Hitler's Propaganda and Culture Minister, Joseph Goebbels: If you tell it long enough and loud enough and dress it up in the sophisticated apparatus of slickly-produced publications presented by individuals with seemingly legitimate credentials, there will be those who will begin to believe it.

The following sections include biographical notes on several leading Holocaust/Shoah revisionists.

—Steven L. Jacobs

HOLOCAUST/SHOAH REVISIONISTS

Arthur Butz

Revisionist-denier Arthur R. Butz was born in and grew up in New York City. He received his Bachelor of Science and Master of Science degrees in Electrical Engineering from the Massachusetts Institute of Technology and his Doctor of Philosophy in Control Science from the University of Minnesota in 1965. Presently, he is Associate Professor of Electrical Engineering and Computer Sciences at Northwestern University in Evanston, Illinois, having joined that faculty in 1966.

Butz's infamy is based primarily on his legitimate academic standing and on the guise and thin veneer of pseudoscholarship in the publication of his book, *The Hoax of the Twentieth Century,* originally published by the revisionist publishers, Historical Review Press in England in 1976, and thereafter by the Institute for Historical Review in Torrance, California (first American printing in May 1977).

The uniqueness of Butz's approach to Holocaust/Shoah denial as presented in this book stems from the following: (1) the physical attractiveness of the volume itself, replete with copious footnotes and extensive bibliography; (2) his apparent confrontation with the major works of Holocaust scholarship (e.g., Lucy Dawidowicz, Raul Hilberg, Nora Levin, etc.); (3) his supposed examination of actual first-hand source material, including the Nuremberg Trial records; (4) his seeming willingness to reject other deniers as faulty scholars; and (5) his willingness to grant that as many as 1,000,000 Jews *may* have died during the Second World War as a result of German persecutions. But the bottom line is that Butz emphatically and categorically rejects the fact of the Holocaust. He bases his conclusions on the "facts" that *all* written accounts of the Holocaust are either doctored or fabricated, and all personal testimonies that affirm that such things happened are the direct result of intense political pressure. Additionally, he uses his scientific and engineering background and training to "refute" the use of zyklon-B gas at Auschwitz as anything other than a disinfectant, and claims the use of crematoria was to prevent the spread of disease, primarily typhus.

Repeated attempts by organized groups, Jewish and other, to have Butz ousted from the Northwestern faculty, which continues to uphold his right of "free speech" and publishing, have been unsuccessful. This is a case that for many raises serious questions about the proper limits of "academic freedom" and "free speech," and whether democracies can and should create defenses and set limits on totalitarian statements and campaigns of prejudice that ultimately can threaten to topple democratic institutions.

Robert Faurisson

Professor Robert Faurisson, formerly of the University of Lyon II, France, continues to be a leading French and international Holocaust denier. Faurisson was born in London in 1929 to a French father and Scottish mother. He studied and taught at the Sorbonne in Paris from which he received his doctorate in comparative literature and linguistic analysis. Beginning in the 1960s he began to question the historicity of various aspects of the Holocaust/Shoah using his own methodological approach. His published writings include *The Rumor of Auschwitz; Is the Diary of Anne Frank Genuine?; Treatise in Defense Against Those Who Accuse Me of Falsifying History* [which includes a Preface defending his right to free speech by American Jewish Professor at MIT, Noam Chomsky]; *The 'Problem of the Gas Chambers'; A Prominent False Witness: Elie Wiesel;* and *Confessions of SS Men Who Were at Auschwitz,* among others.

Faurisson was first brought to trial in 1983 and was fined and sentenced to a three month suspended sentence for defamation. In September of 1989, he was severely beaten by three youths claiming to represent "The Sons of the Memory of the Jews," an unknown organization that has never been found. He was again brought to trial in 1991, and in April of that year found guilty and fined 250,000 francs, 100,000 francs of which were suspended. He does, however, continue his active schedule of writing and lecturing, not only in France but in the United States as well.

Among his principal contentions have been the physical impossibility of gas chambers being used at Auschwitz and other death camps to murder large numbers of Jews; that Hitler himself never ordered the genocide of the Jews since no document stating such has ever been found (a la David Irving); the numbers of dead as a result of the so-called Nazi persecution of the Jews are highly inflated; and that Jews themselves share a measure of responsibility for the Second World War.

David Irving

David Irving, considered by many Holocaust commentators to be a Holocaust/Shoah denier/revisionist, is perhaps the best known due to the sheer quantity of his published works, which include *The*

A Survivor Debates Arthur Butz

In *The Hoax of the Twentieth Century,* Arthur R. Butz attempts to reconstruct the knowledge with regard to the gas chamber atrocities, which in his opinion is based solely on propaganda of the Nuremberg Trial in 1946. He states that no German documents from Auschwitz mention a gas chamber. He cites a document from the construction firm of Topf and Sons in Erfurt which makes reference to a *Fergasungskeller* (gassing cellar). However, with his knowledge of engineering, he tries to explain this as a "gas generation cellar" for igniting the crematoria used for disposing of those who had died in the camps from presumably natural causes. To the great delight of German neo-Nazis, a German translation of this book is on the market.

On April 30, 1981, I had the singular opportunity of challenging Butz to his face on the "Freeman Reports," a television program carried by Cable News Network (CNN) and broadcast to hundreds of thousands of viewers. I conversed by phone with him from the studios of CNN in Hollywood, California. I pointed out to Butz that his skillfully constructed lies collapse readily in the face of evidence offered by the following primary sources:

- Testimonies of hundreds of former Auschwitz prisoners, especially Sonderkommando survivors, as well as SS officers, taken during the Auschwitz Trial before the court in Frankfurt am Main.
- Notable memoirs by SS officers, including those of the Auschwitz commandant Rudolf Höess, Perry Broad of the SS Political Department, and the diary of Dr. Kremer.
- Published manuscripts of Sonderkommando prisoners which were buried and found on the grounds of Auschwitz-Birkenau crematoria.
- About two hundred authentic photographs made by the SS Erkennungsdient (SS photographers) in Auschwitz-Birkenau, recording the arrivals, selections, and marches towards the gas chambers of Jews deported in 1944 from Hungary.
- Three photos made by the Auschwitz resistance movement showing Sonderkommando members at work.
- Reprints of the authentic detailed ground plans of the four crematoria with eight gas chambers in Birkenau.

I had scarcely finished this list when Butz said, "I don't want to hear any more of this." Pointing my finger at him, I said, "Dr. Butz, you are a liar. Sue me!" He only answered, "I'm hanging up now," and broke our conversation without responding to the challenge. I feel that such open and direct confrontation is for now the best way to expose these fabricators of "facts."

In the same broadcast, I stated that—except for the Sonderkommando—I am, to my knowledge, the only person to be brought regularly (in 1943 and 1944) into the old Auschwitz crematorium. My presence in the crematorium was kept very secret and I was always threatened with death if I would tell anybody where I have been. I had to fill directly from the ovens—the urns for German inmates (non-Jews) who had died and whose family had paid for the urns. I was brought there by my boss, Unterscharfüehrer Albrect, then head of the Auschwitz crematorium, from the Registrar's Office where I worked as a typist. Thus I had direct personal knowledge of the gas chamber. *I had been there!*

—*Lilli Kopecky, Internet on the Holocaust and Genocide*

Trail of the Fox (1977); *Hitler's War* (1977); *The War Path* (1978); *Goering: A Biography* (1989), among others. All of his works reveal a prodigious amount of research into actual textual materials together with faulty conclusions seemingly aimed at whitewashing the crimes of the Nazis, including Hitler himself.

The son of a British Royal Navy Commander, Irving studied at both the Imperial College of Science and Technology and University College London, but failed to receive a degree from either institution. Curiously, this self-styled historian holds no academic degree whatsoever beyond the equivalent of a United States high school diploma. His antisemitism and his identification with both neo-Nazi groups and denial/revisionist groups such as the Institute for Historical Review, in Torrance, California, where he appeared at their Ninth Annual Conference (1989) have led to his being banned from Canada, Germany, and Australia.

Among his principal arguments, supposedly based upon his "findings" are the following: That the supposed gas chambers of Auschwitz did not exist; that Hitler himself, whom he characterizes as weak, ineffectual and vacillating in decision-making, gave no order for the destruction of the Jews, that no document has ever been found to support the claim that he did so; that Allied atrocities, such as the bombing of the civilian population of Dresden, Germany, were on par with or worse that those committed by the Nazis; and that Winston Churchill of Great Britain and Franklin Delano Roosevelt of the United States were corrupt leaders whose own agendas for the total destruction of Germany were for self-serving ends.

Irving's pseudohistorical work has been discredited by many leading scholars including Professors Walter Laqueur and John Lukacs of the United States, Alan Bullock of Great Britain, and Eberhard Jäckel of Germany. On the other hand some of his work is honorable. To his credit, for example, Irving was among the first to discredit the so-called "Hitler Diaries" as fakes, both in newspapers in England and Germany. Overall, however, there is no doubt that in denying that gas chambers ever existed, Irving is a manifest denier; yet incredibly, but also tellingly, Irving *denies being a denier.* He seems to thrive on public uproar and has been known to bring suit against a bookstore that does not carry a book by him. Recently, he has sued Deborah Lipstadt, professor at Emory University and author of *Denying the Holocaust: The Growing Assault on Truith and Memory* (see DENIALS OF THE HOLOCAUST) in England, and the trial may develop into another important precedent in law against denial, like the conviction of Professor Bernard Lewis in Paris for denial of the Armenian Genocide (see DENIERS OF THE ARMENIAN GENOCIDE).

In 1995/1996 a major controversy arose in the United States over St. Martin's Press's agreement to publish Irving's book, *Goebbels: Mastermind of the Third Reich.* After protests by Jews and many other scholars and writers, the offer was withdrawn, allowing Irving to claim both censorship and Jewish conspiracy. The book has since been published in England and Irving continues to write, publish, and lecture on World War II.

Ernst Nolte

Professor Ernst Nolte is a German historian and philosopher who teaches at the Free University of Berlin. He remained at the center of the so-called *Historikerstreit* ("Historians Fight") of the 1980s, along with Andreas Hilgruber, Michael Sturmer, Jurgen Habermas, Eberhard Jäckel, Hans Mommsen, Martin Broznat, Thomas Nipperday, Klaus Hildebrand, and others. His own *cause celebre* was the response engendered by two articles that purported to "rehabilitate" National Socialism in the larger context of German history. The first, "Between Historical Legend and Revisionism: The Third Reich in the Perspective of 1980," was later published in the *Frankfurter Allegemeine Zeitung,* July 24, 1980. The second, "The Past That Will Not Pass: A Speech That Could Be Written But Not Delivered" was published in that same newspaper, June 6, 1986.

Essentially, Nolte's arguments can be reduced to three: (1) The "excesses" of the Third Reich are not singularly unique to it but follow patterns already long established in history, for example, both the French and Russian Revolutions and the practices of the Stalinist collectivization; (2) Hitler himself should not be viewed as unique, but rather as one who took Josef Stalin as his behavioral model; (3) The most controversial of his arguments, which is more philosophical than historically supportable, is that *negative* mythologizing of the past—to view *all* events as bad—especially the immediate past, has disastrous overtones both for the world of scholarship and the world of politics. Thus, there is a need in the 1980s for a reassessment and revision of our historical understanding of the years of the "Hitler era."

By arguing as he did, Nolte essentially attempted to rob the Holocaust, as well as the phenomenon of National Socialism, of *any* claim to historical uniqueness whatsoever—which evoked cries of protest of non-neoconservative historians, not only in Germany but throughout the Western world.

Paul Rassinier

Rightly regarded as the "Father" of French, and thereby international Holocaust/Shoah denial/revisionism, Paul Rassinier was born on March 18, 1906, at Beaumont, in central France, where he was later to qualify and teach both history and geography at the high school level in that same region. A Socialist and pacifist, he originally engaged in resistance activities after the Nazis overran France in the early 1940s. Coming to the attention of the Gestapo, he was arrested in October of 1943 and interned in both Buchenwald and Dora concentration camps where he suffered brutally. Liberated in 1945, he ran successfully for a Socialist seat in the National Assembly, served for one year, due to ill health retired on a pension, and was later awarded a medal for his Resistance work. He died on June 29, 1967. His two major denial volumes were *Le Passage de la Ligner,* 1948 *(Crossing the Line),* and *Le Mensonge d'Ulysses,* 1950 *(The Lie of Ulysses),* later published in English together with his shorter writings by the revisionist publishers Noontide Press, Newport Beach, CA, under the title *Debunking the Genocide Myth* (1977). No one is certain, based on his experiences during the Second World War, what turned him toward denial/revisionism. According to Professor Pierre Vidal-Naquet, Rector of the L'École des Hautes Études en Sciences Sociales in France:

"Rassinier is defined as a Holocaust denier because of his bold assertion that the gas chambers were not part of a well-organized comprehensive program aimed at annihilating the Jewish people. . . . Rassinier's importance lies in his being the father of French revisionism and a person of great influence in the anarchist camp in France, both in his own time and to this day. . . . The originality of Rassinier's revisionism lies in his contribution to forming a unique synthesis of elements from the far left with the ideas of the far right, combining anticapitalist, anti-Communist, anti-Semitic, and anti-Zionist elements with libertarian pacifism and anarchism—in short, an ideological synthesis serving those groups that do not identify themselves politically with the establishment on the left or the right" [Vidal-Naquet, Pierre and Yagil, Limor (1994). *Holocaust Denial in France: Analysis of a Unique Phenomenon.* Tel Aviv: Tel Aviv University, Project for the Study of Antisemitism, pp. 32, 37–38].

Rassinier's primary arguments denying the Holocaust may be summarized as follows: (1) That the communists are primarily responsible for spreading the lies of extermination camps throughout Western Europe; (2) The *accuracy* of the testimony of the various witnesses may be called into question; (3) Even the testimony of Rudolf Höess, Commandant of Auschwitz from 1941–1943 is seriously suspect; (4) Even the works of many of the scholars of the Holocaust, especially Raul Hilberg, are seriously flawed because of their Jewish identities; (5) The actual number of Jewish dead is considerably less than 6,000,000, which is a preposterous figure; (6) No documents attributed to Adolf Hitler, Heinrich Himmler or Reinhard Heydrich implicating them in the supposed plot to annihilate the Jews have been found because none existed and because there was no such plot.

Bradley Smith

Revisionist-denier, Bradley R. Smith, of Visalia, California, is co-director with Robert R. Countess of Huntsville, Alabama, of the *Committee for Open Debate on the Holocaust* (CODOH), and author of the pamphlet, "The Holocaust Controversy: The Case For Open Debate," published by the revisionist Institute for Historical Review, Torrance, California, where Smith was Media Director. The "Committee" is the source for Smith's campaign to publish revisionist articles as advertisements in college and university newspapers throughout the United States and Canada. The actual number of members of the "Committee" is unknown.

Under the guise of free speech and contra-censorship, Smith's technique is to pay for a full-page advertisement in any college or university newspaper willing to accept it, challenging accepted historical understandings of the Holocaust. The majority of colleges and universities have rejected his advertisements as historically inaccurate and seriously methodologically flawed, including the University of Chicago, Dartmouth College, Emory University, Georgetown University, Harvard and Yale Universities; but many other institutions of higher learning have published his advertisements, oft-times with disclaimers, but with affirmations about "free speech" and the "true spirit of inquiry" in "the open market-place of ideas," including Queens College, New York, the University of Maryland, Duke University, Northwestern University, Cornell University, Vanderbilt University, Louisiana State University, and Brandeis University.

Little is known of Smith's background and he seems to have taken great personal care to obscure it. It is known, however, that he was born in 1951, completed his high school education in a Jesuit school in Portland, Oregon, and has allied himself with right-wing and white racist groups while seemingly distancing himself from overtly antisemitic ones.

Ernst Zundel

Born in Germany in 1939, Holocaust denier, Ernst Christof Friedrich Zundel, emigrated to Canada in 1957, presumably to study photoretouching and graphic arts. Originally granted landed immigrant status, he became a permanent resident of Canada in 1958, but has consistently been denied citizenship. Early on he came into contact with and under the influence of Adrien Arcand, Canada's leading fascist, someone whose antisemitic views were compatible with his own. Moving to Toronto, he quickly became a major supplier, publisher, and distributor of both antisemitic and Holocaust denial literature under his own imprint of Samisdat Publishers. Among his publications are *The Hitler We Loved and Why; UFO's, Nazi Secret Weapon?;* and Richard Harwood's [pseudonym], *Did Six Million Really Die?*

First brought to trial in 1985 for publishing "false news,'" he was subsequently convicted, sentenced to fifteen months in jail, three years probation and prohibited from any publishing activities during that time. In June of 1987, his conviction was overturned and a new trial was ordered. His second trial saw such Holocaust denial "luminaries" as David Irving of Great Britain, Fred Leuchter and Bradley Smith of the United States, and Ditlieb Felderer of Sweden rush to his defense and testify in court. Again convicted, the Supreme Court of Canada in 1992 struck down the law against the spreading of so-called "false news" as too vague, thus again overturning his conviction.

Ever the showman, Zundel has been seen in public wearing a construction hardhat with the words "Freedom of Speech" stamped on it, as well as carrying an eleven-foot cross with the same words up the courthouse steps to his trial. Likewise, he is not above wearing the "uniform" of a concentration camp inmate, arguing that he is a wrongly condemned political resistance fighter.

Zundel has continued to make disturbingly effective use of the Internet to publish and disseminate his materials, and thus far has been successful in fending off limitations of his right to do so, including that of the German government, which has regularly denied his visa requests for visits to the place of his birth.

—*Steven L. Jacobs*

References and Recommended Reading

Kulka, Erich (1991). Denial of the Holocaust. In Charny, Israel W. (Ed.) *Genocide: A Critical Bibliographical Review. Volume 2.* London: Mansell Publishing; and New York: Facts on File, pp. 38–62.

Lipstadt, Deborah (1993). *Denying the Holocaust: The Growing Assault on Truth and Memory.* New York: Free Press.

DIMENSIONS MAGAZINE: WRESTLING WITH MEMORY

Dimensions is an Anti-Defamation League periodical begun shortly after the inauguration in 1984 of its Holocaust Studies Center and my appointment as director. The intellectual atmosphere in Europe and America during that time was quite unlike what existed before. Not only scholars and survivors, but also filmmakers, journalists, educators, and theologians were exploring for the first time, and with irrepressible fascination, the Western world's responses to the Holocaust era.

The only periodical then in circulation dedicated to charting this remarkable growth of popular interest in the Holocaust era was *Shoah,* but its publisher, Rabbi Irving Greenberg of the New York-based Zachor: The Holocaust Resource Center of the National Jewish Resource Center, decided to end its eight-year run, paving the way for *Dimensions.* I became *Dimensions'* Founding Editor-in-Chief.

From the beginning *Dimensions* was deeply involved in exploring the surprising extent and range of responses to European Jewry's sustained wartime terror and persecution: Why did most of the free world acquiesce in Nazi mass murder? Why did the medical profession in Nazi Germany so eagerly embrace the tenets and practice of "racial hygiene"? How did some Jewish children manage to survive? Who were the men and women who saved Jews from certain destruction? The magazine also became a

A cover of Dimensions *magazine, published by the Anti-Defamation League's Braun Center for Holocaust Studies. (Courtesy of Dennis B. Klein, Editor-in-Chief)*

forum of debate over memory itself; that is, over what our own world chooses to remember or forget: How are the Europeans today dealing with the Nazi past? Are Americans merely finessing discussion of America's wartime behavior?

As its name implies, the magazine defines dimensions of a problem that previous generations ignored, for it expresses a desire to discover something about our time—an era spanning most of the twentieth century that has produced such evil as well as considerable indifference and even hostility to understanding it. *Dimensions* was also determined to capture the quality of fevered debate. We wanted writers who could write with conviction rather than with cold dispassion. Frequently, we commissioned essays written by nonspecialists who rarely or never before explored the questions of moral responsibility. These included Don DeLillo, Norman Cousins, Wladyslaw Bartoszewski, Peter Rushforth, Anne Roiphe, Stephen Ambrose, Irvin Faust, Russell Hoban, Nathan Glazer, Alfred Kazin, Anthony Storr, Stanislaw Baranczak, and Robert Coles.

Dimensions consistently commissioned evocative illustrations for the magazine's covers—a feature that has garnered distinguished awards from the International Society of Illustrators (1988) and the Visual Club of New York, an American Competition (1995). The magazine also provided occasional documentary discussion guides for the classroom and other formal and informal settings. Among them were inquiries into Kristallnacht and its exposure of Nazism's violent underpinnings, the Warsaw Ghetto uprising's paradoxical blend of resistance and despair, the Danish rescue's singular example of national, collective rescue, the camps' liberation and the survivors' (and witnesses') still-incomplete transition to normal life, and the best and the worst books on the Holocaust era.

A magazine devoted to a single issue—one, moreover, so dismal—has raised doubts about how it could last: How many dimensions of the Holocaust could there possibly be? But it has become amply clear over time that discussion of the subject is a work in progress. The subject seems to provoke new debates and public concerns: the opening of museums and the codification of memory, the Holocaust denial movement and the obliteration of memory, state teaching mandates and the Americanization of memory, and such public sensations as *Schindler's List,* the Goldhagen affair, and the Vatican's 1998 document about the Holocaust. For the foreseeable future, there will be no dearth of new material or new, engaged writers seeking to discover how the Holocaust is changing the way we think about our society and culture

For further information, consult the website http://www.adl.org. For a list of essays that have appeared in the magazine or for further inquiries, send an E-mail message to dbkleinl@juno.com.

—Dennis B. Klein

EAST TIMOR, GENOCIDE AND DENIAL IN

Hundreds of thousands of people have been killed in East Timor since 1976. Some have been murdered by the occupying Indonesian forces, some have died as a result of malnutrition and some from illnesses. There are estimates of the numbers of dead reaching some 200,000 people—which constitutes about a third of the population.

For 300 years, the eastern part of the small island of Timor was a Portuguese colony. Following the revolution in Lisbon in 1974, there began a process of decolonization in all of the former colonies in Portugal, and in East Timor too there developed political parties. Some of these political parties wanted to unite the primarily Catholic territory of East Timor with Indonesia, which is its large Muslim neighbor. Other parties sought autonomy under a Portuguese confederation. Still others, and especially the movement known as "Fretilin"—the Revolutionary Front for East Timor Independence, sought absolute independence. The political differences became extreme, and in 1975 became an actual civil war. The Fretilin fighters defeated their enemies, but at the expense of a large number of casualties, and a further price of the flight of many thousands to the west in Indonesia. In November 1975, Fretilin declared East Timor independent, but then Indonesia sent in

Bishop José Ramos-Horta: East Timor Lost about One-Third of Its Population

The toll has been enormous. East Timorese have experienced brutality of genocidal proportions, with the loss of about one-third of the population. Our culture has been severely damaged, our people marginalized by Indonesian immigrants, their land taken and the environment destroyed.

Although the invasion was probably the most serious political and military mistake of Mr. Suharto's long rule, we East Timorese leaders must have the courage and humility to acknowledge our share in the tragedy.

East Timorese leaders, too, sometimes acted with understandable immaturity and at other times with reckless irresponsibility. We were the ones who unleashed a civil war that caused the deaths of hundreds of our own people. Some in Fretilin were particularly violent during that period.

East Timorese resistance fighters must cease their activities and pursue a nonviolent strategy inspired by the great men of this century, Mahatma Gandhi, Martin Luther King and the Dalai Lama.

—*Press Report*

That Body on the Water Spring

Fatima Gusmao is a beautiful woman whose tranquil life was utterly changed by the Indonesian invasion. We spoke in English in August 1989 and Fatima re-enacted some experiences as she spoke.

> In 1976 we went to a small village outside Ainaro, in the mountains; we call it *suco,* usually about ten families together. We heard the Javanese would be coming through there. In one house there was a pregnant woman and some children, three or four, and those people did not want to come with us. The man says they have no guns, why would the Indonesians harm them, it is their house, why would they leave it to run away, how would they get food running? He says he is responsible, has to look after the woman who will soon give birth, that is not a time to move. We say of course it is your decision, we cannot stay any longer trying to convince you. We want this lady to have her baby in a secure place. If you think this place is secure we do not, so we will leave you.
>
> It is about an hour since the soldiers go. Some of us go to see how those people are.
>
> When we get closer we see it is the pregnant woman outside. She is naked. She holds herself, all her stomach is cut open, the baby and everything coming out, the blood has started to dry black. She is just alive and I think she knows us. She tries to speak but no sound comes out. Tears run from her eyes all over her face. We can do nothing for her. We cannot fix a wound like that. We try to take the baby out but it is dead, cut by the knife.
>
> The other people inside the house are all dead, cut completely in pieces by very sharp knives. The arms chopped here [shoulder], here [elbow] and here [wrist], heavy strokes falling on them. The small children are broken, torn apart by their legs, like you tear paper. It is so horrible we can hardly believe. Those with us who had not seen them before understand then that the Indonesians come just to kill us all.
>
> These things I saw with my own eyes. They are not a dream or what others tell me, and I can never forget.

—James Aubrey

troops to "make order." In July 1976 Indonesia annexed East Timor to its territory as its twenty-seventh state, and since then Indonesia has ignored calls of the United Nations and the Security Council to withdraw from the territory. Through the years, Indonesia has ruled with an iron hand, with many executions, imprisonments and denials of human rights to the point where Amnesty International reported a negative birth rate on the island. *[As this encyclopedia goes to press, following the fall of the longtime ruler of Indonesia, Suharto, there is consideration for the first time of possible autonomy or freedom for East Timor.—Ed.]*

According to Loong Wong of Dearborn University in Australia: "Official Indonesian figures similarly leave 133,000–170,000 East Timorese unaccounted for. Indonesia claims this massive loss was due to a famine in 1978–1979. This is to avoid acknowledgment that the famine was provoked by the military measures Indonesia adopted. Throughout Indonesia's occupation, human rights abuses have been rampant. Year after year, Amnesty International has chronicled detentions without trial and torture. For example, in 1985, Amnesty reported "the systematic execution and 'disappearance' of people" in East Timor. This has not only been denied by the Indonesian authorities, but also rationalized away. Vice-President Adam Malik was reported to have claimed that "only 50,000 to 80,000 died. It is war. What is the big fuss?" These military measures were often accompanied by destruction of food resources; invariably, defoliants and other associated chemicals are used. Beyond the outright display of force, additional restructuring measures were initiated. Mass sterilization of Timorese women occurred without consent during surgical operations to decrease the Timorese population. Accompanied by a state-sponsored program of mass migration of Indonesians to East Timor, the East Timorese have been rendered a minority in their own country. Supporters of the Indonesian government often assert that the atrocities committed can be attributed to unfortunate breakdowns in discipline amongst units of the Indonesian forces and that these units were subsequently withdrawn and punished. In November 1991, following a televised massacre of East Timorese in Dili, the Australian government similarly offered such a rationalization. Its foreign minister, Gareth Evans, described the killings as "an aberration of a section of the Military." Not surprisingly, Indonesia similarly voiced such a view. In response to the televised massacre and expressions of worldwide protests, Indonesia initiated a Commission of Inquiry into the Dili shootings. In its report, the Commission found that the number killed was 50 and far greater than the official military figure of 19; it exonerated the military of responsibility for the killings and other violations. It instead incriminated the East Timorese "instigators" of the demonstration. The commission ignored substantive evidence supporting the systematic nature of military action during and after the incident. Indonesia has consistently claimed that the Timorese people agreed to independence through integration with Indonesia in 1976. Despite being discredited, this fiction persists. The myth and denials of genocidal acts and intent against the Timorese remain."

In 1996 the Nobel Peace Prize was awarded to Bishop Carlos Bello and José Ramos-Horta. The Nobel Committee stated: "In 1975, Indonesia captured East Timor and began a program of methodical suppression of the inhabitants. It has been estimated that since then about a third of the residents of East Timor have lost their lives because of hunger, infectious epidemics, war and terror . . . In awarding the Nobel Peace Prize this year to Bello and Ramos-Horta, the Norwegian Nobel Committee seeks to express its appreciation for their continuing contributions, including their self-sacrifice, for a small but beleaguered nation. The Nobel Committee hopes that this prize will increase the efforts made to find a diplomatic solution to the conflict in East Timor that will be based on the rights of the people of East Timor for self-definition."

According to Australian scholar, James Dunn, "The experience of East Timor, following the invasion of the Portuguese colony by Indonesia in 1975, possesses unique characteristics as a case of genocide in a contemporary setting, in the terms of Article II of the UN Convention on Genocide. The annexation of the former Portuguese colony by Indonesian armed forces resulted, in relative terms, in one of the heaviest losses of life in modern history. As far as the Timorese are concerned there is another, historical, dimension to their case. In 1942, the Timorese rallied to the Allied cause, and their generous assistance enabled an Australian commando force to contain thousands of Japanese troops at a time when invasion of Australia seemed imminent. However, when the Australians withdrew, the Japanese turned on their supporters, imposing a harsh occupation that cost the lives of more than 10 percent of the population. Thus, for the second time within half a century the unfortunate people of East Timor faced another ordeal of indiscriminate killing,

One of the Worst Cases of Genocide

The annexation of East Timor was not just a violation of the UN Charter and the later UN resolutions and other instruments enshrining the right to self-determination: It resulted in such a catastrophic loss of life that it must stand as one of the worst cases of genocide in modern times, in the terms of the 1948 Convention. In a way it provides the ultimate test of the commitment of the international community to the upholding of human rights—our readiness to rally in support of the rights of the small, the weak and the vulnerable.

—*James Dunn*

torture and destruction of their villages. The regime may have been different, but many of its methods were similar, and the loss of life in East Timor has turned out to be even greater."

Following the fall of the regime of President Suharto in 1998, Indonesia and Portugal announced that they had reached agreement on the outlines of an autonomy plan for the disputed territory of East Timor that would give the Timorese the right to self-government except in foreign affairs and defense. The agreement is a major diplomatic break following two decades of standoff between Portugal, which abandoned the territory after its 1974 revolution, and Indonesia, which invaded the following year. Internationally, East Timor has never been recognized as part of Indonesia.

—*Assembled from Articles by Loong Wong and James Dunn and Additional Press Reports*

References and Recommended Reading

Dunn, James (1994). The East Timor genocide. In Charny, Israel W. (Ed.), *The Widening Circle of Genocide. Volume 3 in the Series, Genocide: A Critical Bibliographic Review.* New Brunswick, NJ: Transaction Publishers, pp. 192–216.

Turner, Michelle (1992). *Telling: East Timor, Personal Testimonies 1942–1992.* Sydney: New South Wales University Press.

Wong, Loong (1993). Denial of genocide in East Timor. *Internet on the Holocaust and Genocide,* Issue 44–46, 17.

EDUCATION ABOUT THE HOLOCAUST AND GENOCIDE

EDUCATION ABOUT THE HOLOCAUST IN THE UNITED STATES

For over twenty years in the aftermath of World War II, study of the Holocaust in US public schools was minimal to almost nonexistent. There were many reasons for this, including but not limited to the following: a lack of knowledge and/or interest by teachers about the Holocaust; a lack of attention to the Holocaust in school textbooks; the absence of the mention of the Holocaust in school, district, county and state curriculum guidelines; and a dearth of curricular resources. If the Holocaust was taught at all, it was by individual teachers who perceived the need to do so and/or had the interest in doing so. Most of the initial pedagogical efforts were by educators in Jewish day-schools. If students were even introduced to the Holocaust in the public schools, it was generally through *The Diary of Anne Frank,* most often using a long excerpt in literature anthologies.

As various universities began to teach about the Holocaust and as researchers and survivors published research and first-person testimonies, an ever-increas-

Teaching How States Destroy Citizens Rather than Represent Them

Genocide can be related to the liberal arts curriculum as the worst example of how states destroy subjects and citizens rather than liberate and represent them. We need to understand how genocide occurred and what it reflects about where we are at.

Genocide can be taught through case studies and survey courses in the social sciences, literature and philosophy. In teaching about genocide, your choice of cases and focus may depend not only on whether you prefer intense study of one case or a survey of several cases but on your audience; you may choose different foci in Berlin, Birmingham, Brooklyn or Brookline. When teaching in Berlin, I focused on the so-called bystanders in order to get students to examine the responsibility of all of German society rather than just the machinery of destruction. In education about genocide, one must stress that to understand is not to forgive or to accept all. But it is essential to understand before we evaluate and judge.

Because of its embeddedness in western civilization and in Christianity, it seems likely that the Holocaust will continue to be the case most chosen. My thesis is that genocide was the Nazi locomotive of history or vehicle of social change rather than simply an unanticipated outcome of search for a solution to "the Jewish Question"—nor was it restricted to Jews. In this perspective, the aim is to understand the development of the criminal state and the evolution of a chain of murders and genocides.

The question always recurs: How do we understand the Final Solution in relation to other Nazi crimes against humanity during the same period? The latter includes (1) the categorical murders of defective "Aryan" children and institutionalized adults in 1939; (2) the totalistic genocide of the Gypsies (with little publicity) throughout German-occupied Europe; (3) the mass starvation of captured Russian soldiers; (4) the selective killings of the Polish intelligentsia and significant groups of other Slavic peoples; and (5) the incarceration and often consequent deaths of political prisoners and German homosexuals in German concentration camps. The second, third and fourth can be classed as genocide under the United Nations Genocide Convention and were so regarded by Lemkin (1944) prior to the Convention. Although the Final Solution was a singular genocide which cannot be comprehended without explaining the role of antisemitism in European history and politics, it was one of a train of murders which needs to be understood in the context of Nazi ideology (including its bio-sociology as well as its race myth) and war goals.

—Helen Fein

ing interest was generated among educators at the public school level in the subject matter. Various school districts, including those in New York City, Philadelphia, and Los Angeles, developed curricula and mandated that their schools teach about the Holocaust. By the mid- to late 1970s there was an explosion of activity in regard to teaching about the Holocaust. Such efforts have been carried out by eclectic groups including individual teachers and professors, state departments of education, school district and/or individual school committees, community-based Holocaust education steering committees, nonprofit educational organizations, Holocaust resource centers, and specialized museums.

It was also in the mid-1970s that the noted Holocaust education organization, Facing History and Ourselves, was established. Over the years, its activities have provided numerous teachers and school districts the support, staff development and materials they have needed to develop Holocaust education programs.

Indeed, since the mid-1970s a wide range of curriculum units, teaching materials, professional publications and conferences have been produced to assist educators in the development of instructional units on the Holocaust. Some of these materials have been created as part of self-contained curricula focused solely on the Holocaust, while others have focused on the relationship of the Holocaust to contemporary social problems such as intolerance, prejudice and hate crime.

As of 1995, five states (California, Florida, Illinois, New Jersey, and New York) had mandated the teaching of the Holocaust in their public schools. Ten other states (Connecticut, Georgia, Indiana, North Carolina, Ohio, Pennsylvania, South Carolina, Tennessee, Virginia and Washington) either recommend or encourage their public school personnel to teach about the Holocaust. In 1995, the state of Nevada created a Council to develop resources and teacher training programs on the Holocaust. Among these states, some have either developed state guidelines (California), a curriculum on the Holocaust and/or genocide (Connecticut, Florida, New Jersey, New York, Ohio, Pennsylvania, South Carolina, Vir-

Lego Concentration Camp, *one of seven boxes by Polish artist Zbigniew Libera, 1996.* [Some educators have cautioned strongly against the use of models that may constitute the "gimmicks" that result in a play-like atmosphere rather than real historical understanding.—Ed.] *(Courtesy of Zbigniew Libera, with the kind assistance of Stephen Feinstein)*

ginia), or a study guide (Georgia). Employing a different approach, Tennessee has established a Holocaust Commission whose charge is to commemorate the Holocaust through education.

Each state approaches Holocaust education differently. In New York, for example, the study of the Holocaust is viewed as part of a larger, more encompassing examination of human rights issues in the high school curriculum. In New Jersey, the study of the Holocaust and other genocides is stipulated for students in both elementary and secondary schools, leaving the exact design and placement of the instructional program up to local districts. In California, the Holocaust, other genocidal events, and human rights violations have been incorporated into the state's curriculum standards with the understanding that teachers will address these concerns in their curriculum at certain points in the study of history and other social sciences. The exact design and amount of time spent on the issues is at the discretion of individual teachers. All of these efforts have "legitimized" the teaching of the Holocaust for many educators by providing them with important institutional support to teach about the Holocaust; and thus, have paved the way for teachers to spend more classroom time on this history.

Two major Holocaust museums and research centers—the United States Holocaust Memorial Museum, and the Beit Hashoah Museum of Tolerance (established under the auspices of the Simon Wiesenthal Center in Los Angeles)—opened in the 1990s, and a major function of both is educating about the Holocaust.

Indeed, the opening of the United States Holocaust Memorial Museum (USHMM) in 1993 marked a new stage in the growth of Holocaust education. This federal institution's mandate is overtly educational, and the USHMM provides services to a national audience via publications, a national student art and essay contest, support for site visits to the Museum by schools, outreach conferences, development of curriculum materials and electronic on-line resources, including e-mail and Internet learning resources on the World Wide Web. In its first year, the Museum received 30,000 inquiries from educators for assistance, a pace that has not diminished over time.

The Association of Holocaust Organizations, formed in the early 1980s has also encouraged broad dissemination of Holocaust programming, materials and scholarship through its annual conferences and publications. Indicative of the burgeoning grassroots interest in Holocaust education, the organization's membership consists of institutions as large as the USHMM to those serving individual communities primarily throughout North America. Parallel to this trend is the development in various states of school and university Holocaust centers offering teacher support and training programs, often associated with higher education coursework or research activities about the Holocaust and related issues.

As of December 1996, there were approximately fifty Holocaust resource centers, twelve memorials, and nineteen Holocaust museums in the United States. The express function of many of the centers and museums is to conduct public outreach programs on various aspects of the Holocaust and/or support the teaching of the Holocaust in local and regional school districts. Many centers assist schools in developing curricula, provide inservice programs to teachers in private and public schools, and assist teachers and students in locating speakers (including survivors and liberators), films, and adjunct materials. Many have also developed their own curricula.

The formative years for Holocaust education have passed. As a field, the study of the Holocaust is interdisciplinary, drawing upon insights and research from disciplines as disparate as theology, history, the social and behavioral sciences, literature, the fine arts, medicine, law and others. The burgeoning scholarship on the Holocaust shows no signs of abating, and interest in both the history of the period 1933–1945 and its implications for contemporary society and government policies shows no signs of waning.

Since no systematic study has yet been undertaken to assess how widespread Holocaust education is in the United States, it is impossible to state with certainty how many teachers, schools, or school districts are involved in educating about the Holocaust, let alone to definitively comment on the quality of such work. It is safe to say that due to certain special Holocaust education programs (e.g., Facing History and Ourselves, and the Holocaust and Jewish Resistance Summer Teachers' Seminar, which is sponsored by the Jewish Labor Committee in New York City and directed by former resistance member, Vladka Meed), the establishment of the two major Holocaust museums, the support and assistance of Holocaust resource centers and memorials across the United States, and various state recommendations and mandates to teach about the Holocaust, thousands of teachers from the elementary grades through higher education are involved in teaching, at least to some extent, about various facets of the Holocaust.

The positive nature of the growing interest among educators in teaching about the Holocaust is not without its drawbacks. It is one thing to mandate that a topic be taught, and an altogether different situation to actually teach it effectively (i.e., accurately, comprehensively, thought-provokingly, meaningfully). In fact, some decry any mandatory study of the Holocaust, claiming that such mandates endanger the quality of such educative endeavors. Such critics assert that this is based on the fact that many educators are not conversant with, let alone well versed in, the history of the Holocaust, and to "force" them to teach the Holocaust is counterproductive.

In his 1979 essay, "Toward a Methodology of Teaching About the Holocaust," historian and Holocaust survivor, Henry Friedlander, warned that both the popularization and the proliferation of pedagogical activity on the Holocaust could prove to be detrimental. He asserted that a lack of focus and attention to detail (e.g., accurate content and sound teaching methodologies) can easily result in "dilettantism." Such dilettantism, he feared, would lead to a watering down of the subject matter and, ultimately, lead to a simplistic understanding of such complex subject matter by both teachers and students. Unfortunately, many of the current curricula and teacher guides on the Holocaust contain weak curricular rationales and/or pedagogical components (e.g., objectives, readings, learning activities). Likewise, in certain cases various aspects of the proposed content is bereft of accurate and recent scholarship and, at times, adequate breadth and depth to address the complexity of this history.

For the field to attain maturity, greater attention in the areas of theory, research, and evaluation of curriculum and instruction are required. Currently, curriculum and instruction on the Holocaust lack (1) a coherent structure that sets priorities for the selection and organization of content, (2) a grounded body of research vis-à-vis the efficacy of effective instruction, and (3) a set of broad themes to facilitate connections among historical events and patterns of change and contemporary or future social issues.

Evaluation of educational outcomes has only received minimal attention, primarily through reports completed for programs affiliated with the federal National Diffusion Network, a US Department of Education project that selects and disseminates exemplary educational programs. Two Holocaust projects, Facing History and Ourselves and Life Unworthy of Life, a curriculum developed by the Center for the Study of the Child in Michigan, were chosen for national diffusion. Little is known about the degree to which students learn either at higher levels of cognition concerning Holocaust history and related issues, or at the moral level as to how such instruction affects student attitudes and values dealing with prejudice, intolerance and stereotyping. Much more research on the impact of specific curricular and instructional programs as well as standardized assessment instruments are needed to ascertain the impact of Holocaust education on learners from the middle grades through higher education. Efforts to develop an evaluation instrument for Holocaust curricula have resulted in the generation of lists of relevant concepts and content topics, but little clarity on their relative significance or their capacity to illuminate essential ideas and themes about the Holocaust. This is a major area that needs the attention of historians, curriculum theorists, and experts in evaluation.

As the field matures, it is likely that all of the above concerns will be addressed; and hopefully, this will be done collaboratively by teachers, researchers, as well as historians and other Holocaust scholars.

—Samuel Totten and William R. Fernekes

References and Recommended Reading

Friedlander, Henry (1979). Toward a methodology of teaching about the Holocaust. *Teachers College Record,* 80(3), 519–542.

Parsons, William S., and Totten, Samuel (1993). *Guidelines for Teaching about the Holocaust.* Washington, DC: United States Holocaust Memorial Museum.

Shimoni, Gideon (1991). *The Holocaust in University Teaching.* Elmsford, NY: Pergamon Press.

Totten, Samuel, and Feinberg, Stephen (in press). *Teaching about the Holocaust: Critical Essays.* Needham Heights, MA: Allyn and Bacon Publishers.

EDUCATION ABOUT OTHER GENOCIDES

The study of genocide and specific genocidal acts (with the exception of the Holocaust) is extremely limited in secondary school grades (7–12), colleges and universities of US schools.

There are numerous reasons for this: at the secondary levels the subject matter is both extremely complex, and many teachers and school districts shy away from controversy; teachers have not been prepared to teach about this difficult subject; there is scant coverage of the topic in most textbooks, and texts generally drive the curriculum; teachers already face an overcrowded mandated curriculum; there is a lack of well defined support to teach the subject, for example, there is a failure to provide well-planned and thorough in-service training for those teachers who are interested in and/or expected to teach these issues; and in some cases there is possibly also a lack of interest or care on the teachers' parts.

Noted genocide scholar Leo Kuper observed in 1989 that while courses in various disciplines at the university level do address specific genocidal acts—though the number of courses in 1997 is still relatively small—few courses focused on the comparative study of genocide.

A major concern all educators face when tackling a subject as torturously complex, controversial and horrific as genocide and genocidal acts is what should be taught. Other than the centrality of the Holocaust, there is little to no consensus on this significant issue. More often than not, the "other genocides" that are addressed at the high school level are the genocide of the Armenians

Illustrative Student Assignments in Courses on Genocide

The following are examples from two courses on genocide of student assignments:

Prof. Colin Tatz, Director, Centre for Comparative Genocide Studies, Macquarie University, Sydney, Australia

Essay: Choose one case study to illustrate the seven major themes. Note: These points must be considered in addressing the topic of your choice. But not all themes may be applicable; where they are inapplicable, you should say so.

1. The ideological basis for the genocide
2. The socio-political basis for the genocide
3. The techniques/technologies used
4. The question of legal/moral responsibility, especially the role of the state, and which areas of the state, which bureaucracies and which professions were involved
5. The interest or indifference of neighbors and nations during the events
6. The nature of the genocide (its 'classification,' scale, dimension in comparison with the two major genocides—the Holocaust and the Armenian Genocide)
7. The punishment (if any) for genocide and world reaction to it? It is important that you always bear in mind, at the very least, the UN definition of genocide when discussing your case choice.

Choices: (1) The treatment of Gypsies (the Roma or Romani people) in World War II. (2) The atomic bombing of Hiroshima and Nagasaki: was this genocide? (3) Mass killings of Communists in Indonesia 1965–66. (4) Mass killings in Cambodia (Kampuchea) 1976–81—a case of "autogenocide"? (5) The case of East Timor. (6) Genocide in Rwanda and Burundi (the 1970s and the 1994 events). (7) The treatment of the Jehovah's Witnesses in Central Africa. (8) The position of the Kurds in the Middle East during the 1990s. (9) The "Disappeared" People in Argentina. (10) The man-made famine in Soviet Ukraine. (11) The "wreckers" and "the enemies of the Soviet Union" during Stalin's purges. (12) The secession of Biafra from Nigeria. (13) The creation of Bangladesh, involving three million dead, 1971. (14) The treatment of the Baha'i in Iran. (15) The Aché Indians in Paraguay. (16) South Africa: Was apartheid genocide? (17) Genocide in Equatorial Guinea—the trial of dictator Macias. (18) The Chmielnicki pogroms against Jews in 1648: Was this genocide? (19) The case of Brazil's Indians. (20) The black Jews of Ethiopia. (21) Australia's Aborigines: What aspects of our treatment amount to genocide? (22) The annihilation of Aborigines in Tasmania (is this a clear case? Compare the Aborigines' mainland experience). (23) The massacre of the Acholi soldiers in Amin's Ugandan army. (24) 'The genocide that is rife in Algeria'—Franz Fanon, writing in 1959. (25) Russian treatment of Chechens, Ingush and Crimean Tatars in the 1940s. (26) The Nazi genocide against Russian prisoners of war. (27) Violence and massacres in Northern Ireland: a case of what? (28) Tibet under China: a case of what? (29) The annihilation of the people of Melos in 416 B.C.E. (30) The Roman destruction of Carthage. (31) "Ethnic cleansing" in what

continues

continued

was Yugoslavia. (32) The contention that organized rape has been an instrument of genocide in Bosnia. (33) Witches in Europe in the Middle Ages. (34) The fate of the Pontian Greeks in Smyrna in 1923.

Prof. Margi Nowak, University of Puget Sound, Tacoma, Washington

Arendt acknowledges the inevitability of moral relativism and its attendant problems "once the absolute and transcendent measures of religion or the law of nature have lost their authority" (299). She furthermore states that "nothing perhaps distinguishes modern masses as radically from those of previous centuries as the loss of faith in a Last Judgment . . . the idea of an absolute standard of justice combined with the infinite possibility of grace" (446–447).

In a parallel vein, Des Pres writes of the nihilism that results "when mythic structures collapse and symbolism fails" and the choice becomes one of "ourselves or nothing" (207). In the final chapter of his book, however, he nevertheless does employ the vocabulary of myths and symbols. He terms the death camps "the realized archetypes of eternal victimhood, of evil forever triumphant" (177), and he also states that "once we see the central fact about the survival experience—that these people passed through Hell—the archetypes of doom are, if not cancelled, at least less powerful in their authority over our perceptions" (ibid.).

At the end, however, he explicitly recognizes a non-transcendent basis for existence: "Life has no purpose beyond itself; or rather, having arisen by chance in an alien universe, life is its own ground and purpose, and the entire aim of its vast activity is to establish stable systems and endure" (193–194).

In relation to the ideas expressed above:

a. Contrast and compare Arendt's and Des Pres's thoughts concerning moral consciousness and social action.
b. Clarify which parts of either or both interpretations you personally find most viable and most problematic for:
   1. modern society in general;
   2. yourself in particular.

Sources

Arendt, Hannah (1951/1973). *The Origins of Totalitarianism.* New York: Harvest/Harcourt Brace Jovanovich.

Des Pres, Terrence (1973). *The Survivor: An Anatomy of Life in the Death Camps.* New York: Oxford University Press.

and/or the Cambodian genocide. This is due, in part, to the attention given those genocides by certain state curricula (e.g., California, Connecticut and New York), as well as the fact that resources for teaching such genocides are more readily available than others.

To provide a through understanding of such a complex topic, students need to wrestle with a tangle of complex historical, political, philosophical, sociological and moral issues. At a minimum, the study needs not only to address what, how, where and when a genocide happened, but also the why. Too many current curricula, including those on the Holocaust, neglect to address the "why."

Any meaningful study of genocide must also focus on the "human." Study of the "human" dimension means that there should be ample opportunity for the students to examine what the genocide meant to the individual(s) who were caught up in such a convulsion of brutality, including their "roles" as victims, perpetrators, accomplices, resisters, or bystanders—not all of which are mutually exclusive. It also means dealing with a host of issues about power and the abuse of power, individual responsibility, and collective responsibility. Such an approach would also focus on what some refer to as the relations of "ourselves" to discrimination, ethnicity, nationality, obedience, prejudice, racism, scapegoating, etc.

At some point in the study, the concept and definition of genocide needs to be addressed. More often than not, most current curricula define genocide in an unsatisfactory and loose manner. Too often genocide is simply defined as yet another human rights violation, which is unacceptable and constitutes poor pedagogy.

While most scholars and educators agree that the historical antecedents leading up to and culminating in a genocidal act (i.e., the genocidal process) should be taught, this too is often done in a perfunctory manner. Instead of studying the "messy" affair that history is, events are often portrayed in a "clean" linear and simplistic fashion. Many times, the key philosophical, political, sociological, and moral issues are treated in a similar fashion.

Assuming one masters the above concerns, there is still the problem of how to teach about genocide in an efficacious manner. A major flaw endemic to much of current curricula on genocide, at least at the secondary level, is that the suggested teaching methods are routine and predictable, many of the learning activities are comprised of memorizing facts and pencil-and-paper exercises that call for answers to lower level cognitive questions, and many include simplistic and historically inaccurate simulations and other gimmicky activities.

At the very least, the study of genocide should be one that provides ample opportunity for students to think in truly critical and creative ways, explore the significance of what they are learning, and reflect on what their learning means to them as individuals, citizens in a democracy, and citizens in an interdependent world. In light of the complexity of the subject matter as well as the horrific nature of the crimes, it is imperative that students be given ample time to raise questions and share and explore their feelings and insights.

Numerous critical challenges and issues vis-à-vis educating about genocide exist, and among the most significant are: the need for the development of more sophisticated curricula (both content and methodology-wise) on not only the Armenian Genocide, the Ukrainian Famine, the Holocaust, and the Cambodian genocide but other genocidal acts; the development of textbooks that address the issue of genocide and genocidal acts in more depth; the need for school districts to provide in-depth in-service training for their teachers who are expected to teach about genocide; and serious research in regard to what content is most appropriate for various grade levels and student abilities, as well as what teaching strategies are most effective in teaching this material.

The development of effective curricula/teacher guides will demand more and serious collaboration between scholars of genocide, experts in the areas of curriculum and instruction, and teachers. By combining the expertise of the various professionals, the resulting curriculum will more likely be factually and conceptually correct as well as pedagogically sound.

Field testing is a vital component in the process of developing a sound curriculum, and it is a component that is often ignored. Once a curriculum has been developed by a battery of experts and practitioners, it should be field tested in the type of classrooms in which it will be used upon completion. After an instructor and his/her class have actually used a section of the curriculum, they should be asked to critique it, and the curriculum developers should take these critiques and revise the curriculum. This process should be repeated several times until a curriculum is ready for use in a classroom.

The history of curriculum is fraught with examples of one curriculum program after another meeting a quick death due to the fact that the individuals who were supposed to teach the curriculum were either not conversant or comfortable with the new information and concepts, or did not know how to effectively teach the material. If this subject matter is to be taught in an effective way, it is imperative that teachers receive thorough and well-planned instruction in regard to both the content as well the teaching strategies that are known to engage the students and to lead to in-depth learning.

—Samuel Totten

References and Recommended Reading

Freedman-Apsel, Joyce, and Fein, Helen (Eds.) (1998). *Teaching about Genocide: A Guidebook for College and University Teachers: Critical Essays, Syllabi and Assignments.* Washington, DC: American Sociological Association. (Originally published for the Institute for the Study of Genocide in 1992 by *Human Rights Internet.*)

Parsons, William S., and Totten, Samuel (1994). *Guidelines for Teaching about the Holocaust.* Washington, DC: United States Holocaust Memorial Museum.

Totten, Samuel (1991). Educating about genocide: Curricula and inservice training. In Charny, Israel W. (Ed.) *Genocide: A Critical Bibliographic Review. Volume 2.* London: Mansell Publishing; and New York: Facts on File, pp. 194–225.

Totten, Samuel (Ed.) (1994). Educating about genocide. Special Triple Issue of *Internet on the Holocaust and Genocide,* Issues 51/52/53, 1–30.

Totten, Samuel, and Parsons, William S. (Eds.) (February 1991). *Teaching about Genocide,* Special Issue of *Social Education,* 55(2), whole issue.

THEMES IN GENOCIDE EDUCATION IN NORTH AMERICAN COLLEGES

Courses in the Holocaust and genocide are more likely to be taught in colleges and universities in the United States and English-speaking Canada than in any other region or country. However, two surveys of genocide courses have found that only a minority were comparative courses, but also that those offering courses on the Holocaust explicitly or implicitly linked the Holocaust to a broad conception of genocide [Clive Foss in Freedman-Apsel and Fein, 1998].

Courses on genocide are critical to the traditional western liberal arts curriculum, which explores the development and assumptions of civilization. Genocide is an issue that not only deserves explanation for its own sake but to probe our assumptions about civilization, rationality and modernity.

The Holocaust will probably continue to be the focus of most genocide courses in North America because of how it is embedded in Western civilization, its effects on modern history, the plethora of records from different sources documenting it, and the revival of neo-Nazi and racist movements that deny the mass murder of the Jews in order to legitimate antisemitism. Further, many teachers prefer to concentrate on one historical case in depth and have not mastered the range of sources needed to teach a comparative course. But new works make framing such a course much simpler. [For a sourcebook of case studies throughout history, see Chalk and Jonassohn, 1990; for a compilation of case studies and oral histories of twentieth century genocides, see Totten, Parsons, and Charny, 1997; for

Teaching about Genocide: A Guidebook for College and University Teachers

Teaching about Genocide: A Guidebook for College and University Teachers: Critical Essays, Syllabi, and Assignments. Editors: Joyce Freedman-Apsel and Helen Fein. Human Rights Internet on behalf of the Institute for the Study of Genocide, John Jay College of Criminal Justice, 1992, 103 pp. (A new edition, dedicated to Hilda and Leo Kuper, published by the American Sociological Association in 1998, adds an introductory essay by Helen Fein with reflections and new suggestions for teaching about genocide.)

This is the first teaching guide on teaching about genocide at the college level with actual syllabi, class exercises, test questions, and research projects from college and university teachers of anthropology, history, literature, political science, psychology, and sociology.

Contents:

continues

continued

History of 20th Century Genocide
Joyce Freedman-Apsel (Sarah Lawrence College)

Literature
Literature of the Holocaust and Genocide
Thomas Klein (Bowling Green State University)

Political Science
Human Destructiveness and Politics
Roger Smith (College of William & Mary)

Government Repression and Democide
R.J. Rummel (University of Hawaii)

The Politics of Genocide
Colin Tatz (Macquarie University, Sydney, Australia)

Psychology
Genocide and "Constructive" Survival
Ron Baker (Richmond Fellowship College)

Sociology
Selected Topics in Sociology—Human Rights and Genocide
Rhoda Howard (McMaster University, Hamilton, Ont., Canada)

Kindness and Cruelty—The Psychology of Good and Evil
Ervin Staub (University of Massachusetts, Amherst)

The Comparative Study of Genocide
Leo Kuper and Richard Hovannisian (UCLA)

Moral Consciousness and Social Action
Margi Nowak (University of Puget Sound)

Order from: American Sociological Association, 1722 N. St. N.W., Washington, DC 20036-2981, USA, $25 non-members; $19 members—Stock No. 366.T92

a review of the literature and of controversies in the field, see Fein, 1993; for examples of course offerings and syllabi in different fields, see Freedman Apsel and Fein, 1998.]

Courses on the Holocaust are most often taught in the history department; departments of political science, literature, sociology, philosophy, anthropology and religion also offer courses. The sources and analytic methods used often overlap fields.

We may observe the kinds of questions behind the syllabi by noting the themes of three "generations" or successive periods of Holocaust scholarship: explaining (1) the perpetrators; (2) the victims; and (3) the bystanders.

Focusing on history and social sciences, the critical initial question starts

Genocide in World History Textbooks

The following is a description of how seven world history textbooks selected from the Virginia state-approved list of texts address the issue of genocide. These textbooks are used widely throughout the United States. The books reviewed are:

Beers, Burton F. (1990). *World History: Patterns of Civilization.* Englewood Cliffs, NJ: Prentice Hall.

Dunn, Ross E., et al. (1988). *A World History: Links Across Time and Place.* Evanston, IL: McDougal, Wittell.

Farah, Mounir, and Karls, Andrea B. (1990). *World History: The Human Experience.* Columbus, OH: Merrill Publishing.

Greenblatt, Miriam, and Lemmo, Peter S. (1989). *Human Heritage: A World History.* Columbus, OH: Merrill Publishing.

Jantzen, Steven H., et al. (1990). *World History: Perspectives on the Past.* Lexington, MA: D.C. Heath.

Perry, Marvin, et al. (1990). *History of the World.* Boston, MA: Houghton Mifflin.

Stearns, Peter N., et al. (1989). *World History: Traditions and New Directions.* Menlo Park, CA: Addison-Wesley.

The first dilemma encountered in reviewing these textbooks was finding an accurate definition of genocide. Six of the seven texts had a very similar definition: "the systematic killing of an entire people." One textbook, *World History: The Human Experience,* by Farah and Karls, gave a more specific definition of "a planned and deliberate destruction of a social, political or cultural group."

Four examples of genocide were reviewed. By far the most attention was given to the Holocaust. All the texts stated six million Jews were murdered and six of the seven commented that millions of non-Jews were killed as well. Seven books mentioned Slavs, three Gypsies, one handicapped, and one clergy and intellectuals. No texts included homosexuals as a targeted group of the Nazis.

One and one-half pages represented the average space devoted to the Holocaust, with six of the seven including at least one photograph primarily of people in camps such as Auschwitz. Overall, the coverage of the Holocaust was bland and lacking descriptions that truly indicated the horror of the Holocaust.

A second example of genocide addressed in the texts was that of the massacre of Armenians living in Turkey. Two of the seven introduced genocide at this point. Very little detail was presented in four of the seven books, and accounts of the deaths in Armenia ranged from one million to several million. Three texts said the deaths occurred over a thirty-year period and one text stated they took place during World War I.

A third genocide addressed was the Soviet executions and manmade famine under Stalin in the early 1930s. This topic received the second largest amount of coverage behind the Holocaust. The accounts varied greatly. All agreed that people had been killed, but the estimates of numbers of those killed ranged from thousands to 10 million. Two texts said "rural people" or "peasants" were killed, and five offered an explanation that Kulaks, wealthy peasants opposing collectivism, were Stalin's target. Six of the seven mentioned the great famines of 1932 and 1933, with three stating that millions died from these famines. Only one pointed out that Stalin deliberately withheld aid from those starving because they resisted his policies.

continues

continued

The fourth incident addressed was the reign of terror under Pol Pot and the Khmer Rouge in Cambodia (Kampuchea). All seven texts mentioned the genocide in Cambodia, but the coverage was a paragraph or less in four of the seven texts. Two texts pointed out that from one-sixth to one-fourth of the entire population died as a result of outright murder, disease, or starvation as a result of government actions.

Based on the examination of the seven texts, it is clear that they vary considerably in their detail, accuracy and consistency of coverage. I found virtually no change in the pattern of coverage of genocide in these seven texts from an earlier review I conducted in 1987. Overall, the concept of genocide and the similarities between these terrible actions are not presented. Rather than having students memorize all the acts of genocide throughout history, including body counts for each, they need to examine the causes of genocide and ways to prevent it from taking place in the future. Recent events in Bosnia point out the moral dilemmas of nations of the world in responding to acts of genocide. This dilemma is ignored in the texts reviewed.

—*Dan B. Fleming*

with the design of the perpetrators; how can we understand the origin of the "Final Solution of the Jewish Question?" We can answer in terms of three contexts: (a) the history of antisemitism and the place of the Jews in Western civilization; (b) the rise of the Nazi criminal state; and (c) the portents and preconditions, including the assumptions of members of the international system (i.e., the "bystanders") that enabled Nazi Germany to annihilate the Jews, Gypsies and to commit selective genocide against Soviet prisoners of war and against Poles and Slavic peoples.

One could not understand the preconditions without acknowledging the impact of the Armenian Genocide of 1915 on Hitler's understanding of what could be done. He made plans in 1939 for widespread slaughter of Polish civilians—a crime aborted by German military resistance. Hitler said: "Only thus shall we gain the living space [*Lebensraum*] we need. Who, after all, speaks today of the annihilation of the Armenians?" The comparisons between the Armenian Genocide and the Holocaust offer the teacher the possibility to enrich a Holocaust course by deepening explanation of its origin and to show what are the consequences of tolerating genocide.

Were one to begin with a comparative approach, one has a wide range of questions to begin with indicated by course titles including "The Comparative Study of Genocide," "Government Repression and Democide," "Human Destructiveness and Politics," "The Politics of Genocide"—all the above were in political science; "Genocide and 'Constructive' Survival," "Kindness and Cruelty: The Psychology of Good and Evil" and "Moral Consciousness and Social Action"—in psychology and sociology departments.

What most distinguishes genocide education from other subjects in liberal arts is its dimensionality; it is moral, cognitive, and often emotional learning. Whether because of their own background or their empathy, teachers electing to focus on genocide reflect on the unbearable because they believe genocide to be intolerable but not inconceivable. We need to conceive of it as a human phenomenon to stop it.

—Helen Fein

References and Recommended Reading

Chalk, Frank, and Jonassohn, Kurt (1990). *The History and Sociology of Genocide: Analyses and Case Studies.* New Haven: Yale University Press.

Fein, Helen (1993). *Genocide: A Sociological Perspective.* London: Sage Publications.

Freedman-Apsel, Joyce; and Fein, Helen (Eds.) (1998). *Teaching about Genocide: A Guidebook for College and University Teachers: Critical Essays, Syllabi and Assignments.* Washington, DC: American Sociological Association.

Totten, Samuel; Parsons, William S.; and Charny, Israel W. (Eds.) (1997). *Century of Genocide: Eyewitness Accounts and Critical Views.* New York: Garland Publishing. Paperback, expanded, with title change of original hardcover, *Genocide in the Twentieth Century: Critical Essays and Eyewitness Accounts,* 1995.

EICHMANN, ADOLF: THE FUNCTIONARY AND THE SYMBOL

BIOGRAPHY OF ADOLF EICHMANN

Adolf Eichmann was born on March 19, 1906 in Solingen, Germany. He was the son of a middle class Protestant family that moved to Linz, Austria where Eichmann spent his youth. After failing to finish his engineering studies, he worked briefly as a laborer in his father's mining business and then in the sales department of an Upper Austrian electrical construction company. Between 1927 and 1933, Eichmann worked as a traveling salesman for the Vacuum Oil Company.

Eichmann's rise to infamy in the ranks of Nazi Germany began on April 1, 1932 when, at the behest of a friend, Ernst Kaltenbrunner, he joined the Austrian Nazi Party. In September 1934, after a period of unemployment, Eichmann found a position in Himmler's Security Services (SD). This job provided Eichmann with the opportunity to utilize his bureaucratic skills that eventually enabled him to be entrusted with coordinating the "Final Solution."

From the first months of 1935, Eichmann was officially responsible for "Jewish questions" at the Berlin Office of the SD specializing in the Zionist movement. In 1937 he actually made a trip to Palestine in order to study the developing Jewish community there and in the process acquired a rudimentary knowledge of Hebrew and Yiddish. In March 1938, following the annexation of Austria to Germany, Eichmann was sent to Vienna to organize the emigration of the Jews. This period in Vienna afforded Eichmann the opportunity to perfect his organizational skills with regard to the "Jewish Question." He developed a method of forced emigration that included confiscation of Jewish property, putting fear into the Jewish population and destroying their economic wellbeing. All of these principles were utilized throughout Nazi controlled territory in their genocidal policies toward the Jewish population.

Between 1938–1939, Eichmann's role continued to grow as he was appointed head of the Jewish section in the Gestapo. This position enabled Eichmann to play the central role in the expulsion of Polish Jewry between 1939 and 1940. Starting in 1941, Eichmann partook in preparations to execute the mass murder of European Jewry. By this time, Eichmann was promoted to the rank of *Obersturmbannfüher* (lieutenant colonel) with the responsibility of transporting European Jewry to extermination camps. Eichmann also organized the Wannsee Conference, which finalized the plans to exterminate the Jews of Europe.

Following the defeat of Nazi Germany, Eichmann fled to Argentina with the help of the Vatican. He lived there until May 1960, when he was captured by the Israeli Secret Service and brought to Israel. His trial began in April 1961 and lasted until August 1961. Israel does not allow the death penalty with the exception of crimes of genocide. On December 2, 1961, Eichmann was sentenced to death for crimes against the Jewish people and crimes against humanity, and he was executed on June 1, 1962.

—*Marc I. Sherman*

References and Recommended Reading

Wistrich, Robert (1982). *Who's Who in Nazi Germany.* London: Weidenfeld and Nicolson.

PSYCHOLOGY OF ADOLF EICHMANN

Adolf Eichmann was a major bureaucrat in the administration of the Nazi death camp system who was responsible for the transport of millions of victims to their grim fates. In his personal manner, he exemplified the drab drone who was committed to industriousness and efficiency, and especially to obeying and carrying out assigned duties and orders. There is little to link Eichmann with the florid or charismatic antisemitic expressions of other major German leaders, nor did he exemplify in his known utterances and style any involvement with thunderous bloodlust and passion for killing. Eichmann was present at many executions. He expressed amazement at the courage shown by Jews being led to their deaths. On one occasion watching the gassing of 80 to 100 Jews in a truck, he wrote that he couldn't look because "I was simply afraid. I tried to force myself but I saw a grasping hand . . . I wanted to get off." On another occasion when Jews were lined up to be shot, he wrote that he "wanted to jump into the grave so as to save [a] child," who was being protected by his mother, "but it was too late . . . the child was hit by a bullet in his head." Later he requested that a more "humane method" be developed. But despite these seeming moments of human reactions, he clearly persevered and excelled in his work as the chief administrator of the mass killing. Following the defeat of the Nazis, Eichmann escaped to Argentina where he was abducted by Israeli secret service agents and brought to trial in Jerusalem. This trial, twenty years after the Holocaust, constituted an intense experience for many survivors of the Holocaust by providing for them both an opportunity to tell anew the story of their terrible persecution and a symbolic triumph in their new land of freedom over one of the arch functionaries of the death system. Although the State of Israel has rejected the death penalty in its overall judicial system, the one exception that was retained was for the high crime of genocide, and having been found guilty, Adolf Eichmann was executed.

For many, the larger significance of Eichmann goes beyond his individual story or the triumph of retributive justice. Eichmann has emerged as an important prototype of one kind of overwhelmingly dangerous human being. He does his duty slavishly without conscience of a higher cause of commitment to human life. During the course of his imprisonment in Israel, Eichmann was examined by a husband-wife psychiatrist-psychologist team of Drs. Shlomo and Shoshana Kulcsar. The results of their studies, including extensive psychological testing, emphasized Eichmann's inability to experience humanness—connection and feeling for people. People were organized as *things* for him. The warm human sentiments of needs for closeness, connection and sympathy were nonexistent; correspondingly, even if surprisingly, the passions of anger and aggression were unacceptable inside of Eichmann's personality.

These findings about Eichmann are consistent with a great deal of other evidence in psychology that one major group of killers and destroyers in everyday human life involves people who do not experience the humanness of others, but who treat others as things or instruments serving whatever needs, obligations or ambitions that are important to them. Psychologist George Bach suggested the concept *thinging.* Alongside of this group, there is a contrasting group of dangerously violent people who are characterized by explosive, uncontrolled and deranged emotions of hate, aggression and contemptuous disregard of the value of other living beings.

Also similar to the first group represented by the character of Eichmann are the many people who disconnect themselves from the meanings of events of destruction of others by continuing to go about their own lives unknowingly, remaining *bystanders* who take no active steps to protest the killings or to rescue possible victims, because it is not in their self-interest to risk their own selves.

The legacy of the meaning of Eichmann was given prominence by Hannah Arendt in her major work on *Eichmann in Jerusalem: A Report of the Banality of Evil* where she underscored the considerably bureaucratic nature of the destruction in the Holocaust—perpetrators doing what they were ordered to do and expected to do without being personally involved, committed or that aware of the terrifying destruction they were executing.

—Israel W. Charny

References and Recommended Reading

Arendt, Hannah (1987). *Eichmann in Jerusalem: A Report of the Banality of Evil.* Revised and Enlarged Edition. New York: Penguin Books (originally published in New York: Viking Press, 1963).

Kulcsar, I. Shlomo (1978). De Sade and Eichmann. In Charny, Israel W. (Ed.), *Strategies against Violence: Design for Nonviolent Change.* Boulder, CO: Westview Press, pp. 19–33.

EICHMANN IN JERUSALEM: A REPORT ON THE BANALITY OF EVIL

The most explosive statement on the trial of Adolf Eichmann that was held in Jerusalem in 1961 after his capture by Israeli security forces in Argentina was unquestionably the book written by Hannah Arendt entitled *Eichmann in Jerusalem.* The work originated in commission by *The New Yorker* magazine to cover the trial, and was finally written up in the summer and fall of 1962 while Arendt served as a Fellow of the Center for Advanced Studies at Wesleyan University. The book itself was published in 1963, with a 1964 version that carried a postscript and reply to critics.

The work has been subject to such repeated and withering assaults and no less fatuous praise from sources remote to Hannah Arendt's way of viewing and thinking that it is not amiss to harken back to the text itself. The biggest surprise in store for the viewer is that the overwhelming burden of the book is a straight, legal narrative of the trial of one man in one courtroom for specific crimes against one people—the Jewish people. The Arendt volume shares the position of the Israeli judicial system: that Eichmann was guilty of heinous war crimes, and that Israel, as the representative of the Jewish state and its people, had every right to execute the culprit.

The largest portion of *Eichmann in Jerusalem* is taken up with exposition and narrative: moving from the character of the German judicial system and its corruption under Nazism, to a biographical profile of Eichmann, on to the stages in the development of the Nazi plan for the genocide of the Jewish people leading up to the Wannsee Conference. The next large portion of the work is taken up with a series of brilliant historical sketches of deportations. The first wave came from Germany, Austria and the Protectorates. The second wave came from Western Europe, France, Belgium, Holland, Denmark and Italy. This was followed by a third wave of deportations, from Central Europe, especially Hungary and Slovakia. At the level of historical sweep, the Arendt volume stands side by side with the works of Lucy Dawidowicz and Raul Hilberg.

The controversial elements are actually restricted to the *Epilogue* and *Postscript.* Indeed, even Arendt's description of the Nazi killing centers at Auschwitz, Bergen-Belsen, Theresienstadt, and recitation of the evidence and eyewitness accounts of the Holocaust follow a familiar path. There is no effort to dismiss, denigrate or become disingenuous about the existence of the Holocaust, or even that it was a warfare aimed at the specific liquidation of the Jewish people. To be sure, it was the very specificity of the Nazi crimes against a specific subset of humanity that permits Arendt to reason that Israeli courts had full jurisdiction in the matter of the disposition of Eichmann, no less than the precedent set by the Allied courts after World War II in the Nuremberg Trials. So we must look at the ethical and psychological aspects of the Arendt volume for an answer as to why her work aroused such passions among scholars, politicians and Jewish communities the world over.

The problem inheres in the subtitle *A Report on the Banality of Evil,* rather than the title. The choice of words was not casual nor accidental. Arendt was in search of the *why* of the Holocaust even more than operational details. She aimed to understand how this colonel in the Nazi Wehrmacht could perform such a hideous role in modern history, show little remorse, yet also display keen analytical insight into the trial processes no less than the killing fields he helped organize and supervise. Arendt located the problem and her answer in terms of *the nature of the bureaucratic mind—a world of operations without consequences, information without knowledge.* In this strict sense, she felt that *banality* was the most appropriate single-word description of Adolf Eichmann.

And while not even Arendt's most bitter opponents would accuse her of being a Holocaust denier, there is a problem with the word *banality.* It strongly implies the mundane, the ordinary, the everyday vulgarities given to all creatures—great and small. To use such a term to describe Eichmann thus appeared as a form of clever apologetics making him into an everyday functionary—interchangeable with other unimportant people and their passive followers. At the same time, one might point out that for Arendt there is also a banality of goodness. In this category one might easily place Oskar Schindler—womanizer, profiteer, Nazi Party member, and savior of one thousand Jews from the ovens of Auschwitz. It was Arendt's special ability to appreciate the mixed motives from which human beings operate that accounts for good and evil alike. In this sense, her Kantian philosophical roots served her well as a student of the Holocaust.

The question thus arises, and Arendt admits to it, whether the trial was actually intended to punish a single person for his specific crimes, or a symbolic assault on the totalitarian regime that existed in Germany between 1933–1945. In response, Arendt argued that the use of the word *banal* meant nothing more or less than a factual description of an evil man, but not a deranged one, an ambitious bureaucrat rather than a dedicated ideologue. Arendt observed of the judges in the Eichmann trial, "a conspicuous helplessness they experienced when they were confronted with the task they could least escape, the task of understanding the criminal whom they had come to judge." As might be imagined, this only rubbed salt into a wound—one that still has not healed nor even abated.

Arendt placed her finger on the soft underbelly of the trial, not only of Eichmann but of his likeness: to single out on the one hand the most monstrous of perverted sadists, and yet claim that he was intrinsically little else than a cog in the Nazi war machine, a figure representing the entire Nazi movement and antisemitism at large. While this might have passed with a disturbing nod, Arendt's further claim was that the physical extermination of the Jewish people was a crime against humanity perpetrated upon the body of the Jewish people, so that it was not the crime against that specific people that was subject to punishment. But again, the issue was joined between Arendt and her critics, since there was a subtle denial of the uniqueness of the Holocaust in the long history of human savagery.

Arendt's careful outline of how the Wannsee Conference produced decisions to exterminate the Jews, to make Europe *Judenrein* or Jew-Free, is chilling and numbing. It is among the best writing she was able to muster. And if there were strange elements, such as linking Eichmann to the Kantian precept of obedience to the law and a moral obligation, the actual savagery and fury of the Nazis and their more than willing helpers among the occupied nations can hardly fail to elicit a powerful response in readers even now.

The onc element that did arouse additional anger was a subtle equation of the victims with the victimizer. The participation of Jews in all sorts of Jewish Councils and Zionist emissaries (exempt from the normal victimization) in bad bargaining—and at times even in bad-faith efforts to save Jewish souls by trafficking in monetary and commodity bribes to the Nazis—which, while not condemned by Arendt, are dealt with in less than sympathetic terms. That transport lists to concentration camps were often put together by Jews that sent many to their deaths and preserved the lives of some, has been well documented. But in Arendt's hands, such acts of complicity only deepened the notion of *banality* as a common feature of the tormentors and the tormented.

One can say that Arendt's book is a landmark in the psychology of the Holocaust. *Eichmann in Jerusalem* provides a foundation that makes possible a political psychology of Nazism far beyond earlier works—even of her own efforts to study the nature of totalitarian power and mass movements. If *Eichmann in Jerusalem* was found even by its admirers such as Stephen Spender as "brilliant and disturbing," and Hans Morgenthau as "troubling our consciences," it is because *the psychological profile makes the Holocaust not a special event but a common human failing of civility and decency.* Arendt wrote a work on Jews worthy of a German scholar and a Classical Greek humanist. Whether the work captured the ultimate tragedy of the Jewish people in the twentieth century, or even the imagination of the Israeli citizens at the time, remain open issues. But whatever turns out to be the ultimate judgment, this is clearly one of those rare works in which the object of the discourse is of great significance along with the subject of investigation.

—*Irving Louis Horowitz*

References and Recommended Reading

Arendt, Hannah (1987). *Eichmann in Jerusalem: A Report on the Banality of Evil.* Revised and enlarged edition. New York: Penguin Books (originally published in New York: Viking Press, 1963).

Bracher, Karl Dietrich (1970). *German Dictatorship: Origins, Structure, and Effects of National Socialism.* New York: Praeger Publishers.

Weitz, Yechiam (1996). The Holocaust on trial: The impact of the Kasztner and Eichmann trials on Israeli society. *Israel Studies,* 1(2), 1–26.

ENVER, ISMAIL

Ismail Enver Pasha (1881–1922) was an instigator of the Armenian Genocide. A military officer, Enver was the principal proponent of Germanophile policies in the Young Turk government. Enver demonstrated organizational and leadership skills at an early age. He was one of the organizers of the 1908 Young Turk Revolution. In 1911 he organized the defense of Libya against Italy and in 1913, after leading the January 23 coup that installed the Committee of Union and Progress (CUP) in power, he reversed the Ottoman defeat in the First Balkan War by recapturing Edirne (Adrianople) from the Bulgarians. By 1914 he was married into the Ottoman imperial family and was Minister of War. He steered the Ottoman state into war on the side of the Central Powers by entering into an alliance with Germany. While nominal command of the Ottoman armies was exercised by Turkish officers, planning, strategizing, and financing devolved to the large German military mission serving out of the War Ministry. In pursuit of his quest for a Pan-Turkic empire stretching to Central Asia, Enver personally led the first major campaign against Russia, which resulted in a disastrous defeat at the border outpost of Sarikamish in the Armenian highlands.

Enver played a major role in the Armenian Genocide. He took the first steps to implement the CUP blueprint for genocide by ordering the Armenian recruits in the Ottoman forces to be disarmed and reassigned to labor battalions before their summary executions. While these instructions were explained on the basis of accusations of treasonous activity, the defeat of his army only provided the pretext for escalating a campaign of extermination whose instruments had already been forged and which now were unleashed against the civilian population also. Within the Ministry of War, Enver had at his disposal a secret outfit called the Special Organization (SO), *Teskilâti Mahsusa* in Turkish. The SO was led by Behaeddin Shakir, a medical doctor, and its cohorts in the field were commanded by CUP confidants whose singular assignment was the execution of the Armenian population. These mobile killer units carried out the systematic massacres of the deported Armenians. Upon the collapse of the Russian front in 1918, the advance of the Ottoman armies into the Caucasus, under the command of Enver's brother, Nuri, provided further opportunity for the SO operatives to instigate atrocities against Armenians in Azerbaijan.

At the end of the war Enver took refuge in Germany. A postwar tribunal in Constantinople tried him in absentia and condemned him to death. Many officers of the Special Organization were arrested by the British occupation authorities after the Ottoman surrender. While some were eventually put on trial and found guilty of crimes, most eluded justice when Mustafa Kemal negotiated their release in exchange for British prisoners. As for Enver, in 1920 he traveled to Russia and offered his services to the new Soviet regime, which sent him to quell rebellion among the Muslims of Central Asia, only to see him join the Basmaji revolt as soon as he arrived in Bukhara. He was killed in action by Soviet forces.

—Rouben Paul Adalian

References and Recommended Reading

Dadrian, Vahakn N. (1993). The role of the Special Organisation in the Armenian Genocide during the First World War. In Panayi, Panikos (Ed.), *Minorities in Wartime: National and Racial Grouping in Europe, North America, and Australia during the Two World Wars.* Oxford and Providence, RI: Berg Publishers, pp. 1–39.

ETHIOPIA, GENOCIDE IN

Genocidal Killing of Political Opponents in Ethiopia, 1974–1979

After seizing political control over Ethiopia on September 12, 1974, the Provisional Military Administrative Council (PMAC) instituted a policy of threats, arrests, torture, and extrajudicial killing to repress any opposition to it. Such repression only provoked greater resistance by a variety of ethnic and political factions. For example, in 1975, the Tigray Peoples Liberation Front began armed opposition to the military government. The new regime also faced threats from the Western Somalia Liberation Front and from the Eritrean Peoples Liberation Front, both of which supported the right of ethnic groups to secede from Ethiopia. Beginning in 1975, the Ethiopian Peoples Revolutionary Party (EPRP) sought to integrate the diverse ethnic-based opposition in demands for a more radical socialist transformation of Ethiopia under civilian control. By February 1977, armed conflict between and among the various groups vying for control of Ethiopia escalated to the point of mutual annihilation. The EPRP began assassinating leaders of the PMAC in what came to be known as the "white terror." The government forces responded with the so-called "red terror," and by the end of 1977 had killed, tortured, or jailed so many members and supporters of the EPRP that it was practically eliminated as a political force.

Genocidal Killing by Resettlement in Ethiopia, 1984–1986

Between 1984 and 1986, the government of Ethiopia conducted a program designed to forcibly resettle hundreds of thousands of peasants from arid environments to more fertile areas. Although resettlement had been employed in Ethiopia since 1950, the Revolutionary Government in power during the 1980s lacked the necessary resources, including malaria prevention measures. Moreover, the Revolutionary Government used resettlement as a political tool, placing its supporters in key areas and moving political opponents to distant provinces. Those who refused to move were forced to do so. Government soldiers seized people including the sick and elderly from the streets, markets and farms and resettled them. By the end of 1986, about 700,000 people had been resettled. Conflicts between the resettled people and those indigenous to the areas, as well as government attacks against resettlement camps, added to the death toll created by diseases and hunger.

—Edward Kissi and Eric Markusen

References and Recommended Reading

Clay, Jason W., and Holcomb, Bonnie K. (1986). *Politics and the Ethiopian Famine, 1984–1985.* Cambridge, MA: Cultural Survival.

Giorgis, Dawit Wolde (1989). *Red Tears: War, Famine, and Revolutions in Ethiopia.* Trenton, NJ: Red Sea Press.

Halliday, Fred, and Molyneux, Maxine (1981). *The Ethiopian Revolution.* London: NLB.

Kissi, Edward (1998). Famine and the politics of food relief in United States relations with Ethiopia: 1950–1991. Ph.D. dissertation, Department of History, Concordia University, Montreal, Canada.

ETHNIC CLEANSING AND GENOCIDE

Ethnic cleansing is the deliberate, systematic, and forced removal of a particular ethnic group from a specified territory. The "cleansed" group is forced to move because it is regarded as undesirable or dangerous by a more powerful group with designs on the territory. In his 1996 book, *Ethnic Cleansing,* Andrew Bell-Fialkoff emphasizes that "cleansing" has not been limited to ethnic groups and prefers the broader term "population cleansing" to reflect the fact that groups defined by religion, race, class, political beliefs, and sexual preference have also been forcibly removed from their homes. He places population cleansing on a continuum between genocide, in which groups are targeted for outright destruction at one extreme, and "subtle pressure to emigrate" at the other (pp. 1–4).

Although the term *ethnic cleansing* is of recent origin, the practice is ancient. In his historical overview of population cleansing, Bell-Fialkoff identifies the Assyrians between 745 and 727 BC as the first known perpetrators. The contemporary case that brought the term into common parlance took place in Bosnia and Hercegovina between 1992 and 1995, when Bosnian Serbs used murder, rape, destruction of homes, economic deprivation, and terrifying propaganda to compel Bosnian Muslims to flee to areas outside of Serb control.

—*Eric Markusen*

References and Recommended Reading

Bell-Fialkoff, Andrew (1996). *Ethnic Cleansing.* New York: St. Martin's Press.

EUGENICS AND GENOCIDE

EUGENICS AND THE HOLOCAUST

The science of eugenics (the improvement of the human species) provided a scientific rationale that ultimately led to the Holocaust. Originating in late nineteenth century England, eugenics received its initial acceptance and application in the United States. The American eugenics programs included a federal program of selective immigration and state programs of enforced sterilization of institutionalized people defined as intellectually and mentally handicapped.

Eugenics, the American experience in particular, provided a "legitimate" scientific foundation for the racial policies of the Hitler regime. The subject of eugenics was taught throughout the German education system. Universities and medical schools played a key role in the promulgation of Nazi eugenic and racial thought. Prestigious institutes including the Kaiser-Wilhelm organization (now known as the Max Planck Society) sponsored eugenic and racial research. Classes and clinics on eugenics, genetics and racial hygiene (terms used synonymously at that time) became part of the basic compulsory curriculum in every medical school in the Reich.

The first major eugenics program of the Hitler-state was that of enforced sterilization established under a law passed in July 1933. This massive eugenic program resulted in the surgical steril-

Professor Eduard Pernkopf, an ardent supporter of the Nazis and newly appointed Dean of Medicine at the University of Vienna, addressing the Vienna Faculty of Medicine on 25 April 1938. (Courtesy of Professor Gustav Spann, Institute für Zeitgeschichte, Vienna, through the good offices of Professor William E. Seidelman, M.D.)

ization of an estimated 400,000 German men and women diagnosed as having (or considered to be at risk of transmitting) conditions that were thought to be hereditary and undesirable. The sterilization program legitimized state-enforced selection on the basis of "scientifically" determined characteristics that were defined by medical science as hereditary and by the state as undesirable. The 1935 Nuremberg racial laws extended eugenic thinking to include race and ethnicity. Selection of the "unfit" under the sterilization law eventually included the selection of handicapped children for killing. The murder of handicapped children was followed by the selection and killing of mentally ill adults from psychiatric institutions in an operation known by the code-named *Aktion T-4*.

At the infamous Wannsee Conference of January 1942 the methods considered for addressing the "problem" of the procreation of Jews captured in the Eastern Territories included mass sterilization. When sterilization was deemed impracticable, the method decided upon was that of liquidation using the experienced personnel and equipment of the *T-4* killing program. SS doctors chosen for the selection of detraining prisoners at Auschwitz/Birkenau were required to have special qualifications in genetics and eugenics.

The basic paradigm of medical practice during the Hitler period was that of the physician as a "selector" acting on behalf of the state in order to improve the health

Anatomy Text at University of Vienna from Nazi Era

As of February 1997, the University of Vienna began to examine whether the illustrations in a famous book on anatomy were based on drawings of victims of the Nazis. The investigators also looked at thousands of numbered containers which contain parts of bodies that were used for research to see if these included victims of the Nazi regime. The Rector of the University who announced the investigation said: "I am ashamed as a human being and as a representative of the University of Vienna in the shameful involvement of the University in the Nazi atrocities. I regret that for fifty years so little was done to throw light on this dark chapter in the history of the University of Vienna."

The atlas of anatomy in question was first published in 1937 and has undergone 415 printings with a large number of revisions and has become one of the bibles of anatomy among medical students and art students all around the world. Its author, Eduard Pernkopf was an ardent supporter of the Nazi party, was appointed Dean of the Faculty of Medicine in 1933, and was the university's Rector between 1943 and 1945. At the time when he was appointed a member of the Austrian Academy of Sciences, he wore a Nazi uniform. Alongside of some of the illustrations in the atlas, accompanying the signature of the artist, there appear Nazi swastikas.

A spokesman for the university said, "Bodies of criminals were delivered for research purposes to the university which received the bodies from the District Court. From 1942 on, there was no shortage of bodies." The spokesman noted that most of the victims were, most probably, non-Jewish members of the Austrian underground, because it is not logical to believe that the scientists made use of bodies from the concentration camps.

The Vienna Psychiatric Hospital revealed that it has the brains of hundreds of children that were murdered by the Nazis.

—Press Report 1997, with corroboration by William Seidelman

of the nation (*volksgesundheit*). Having defined people as an underclass or a risk to the genetic or racial health of the population, medical science deemed the so-called "inferiors" to be appropriate "subjects" who could be selected for enforced sterilization, incarceration and, ultimately, extermination. The "scientific" foundation was eugenics.

—William E. Seidelman

References and Recommended Reading

Burleigh, Michael (1994). *Death and Deliverance: "Euthanasia" in Germany c. 1900–1945.* Cambridge: Cambridge University Press.

Burleigh, Michael (1997). *Ethics and Extermination: Reflections on Nazi Genocide.* Cambridge: Cambridge University Press.

Lifton, Robert Jay (1986). *The Nazi Doctors: Medical Killing and the Psychology of Genocide.* New Haven, CT: Yale University Press.

Proctor, Robert (1988). *Racial Hygiene: Medicine under the Nazis.* Cambridge, MA: Harvard University Press.

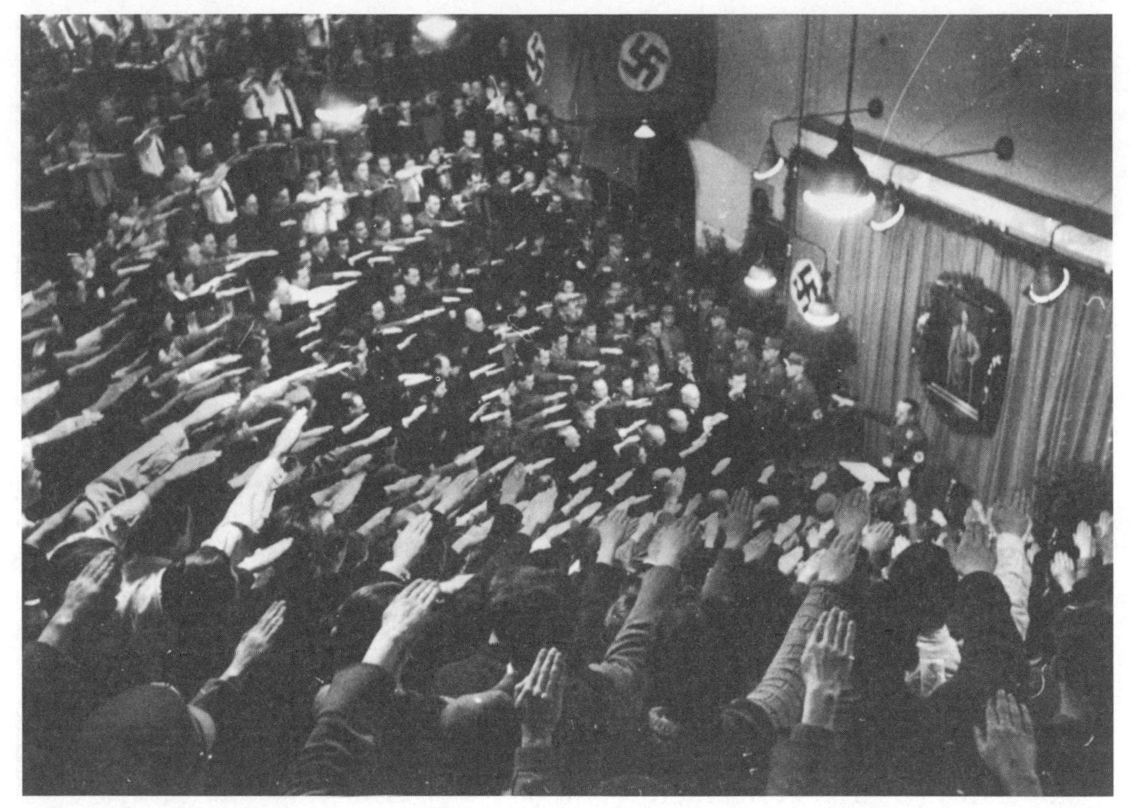

Again, Professor Pernkopf addresses the Faculty of Medicine at the University of Vienna on 25 April 1938. (Courtesy of Professor Gustav Spann, Institute für Zeitgeschichte, Vienna, through the good offices of Professor William E. Seidelman, M.D.)

EUGENICS AND THE DANGERS OF ACADEMIC RACISM

Eugenics is a term coined in 1883 by Francis Galton (1822–1911), an English scientist and half-cousin of Charles Darwin. Galton (1907) defined eugenics as a "science" that would "give the more suitable races . . . a better chance of prevailing . . . over the less suitable . . ." (p. 17). Galton came close to justifying genocide asserting that "there exists a sentiment, for the most part quite unreasonable, against the gradual extinction of an inferior race" (p. 200). Eugenicists would be strong supporters of Nazi racial policy, and many contemporary eugenics advocates continue to justify genocide.

Webster's Third International Dictionary defines racism as "the assumption that psychocultural traits and capacities are determined by biological race and that races differ decisively from one another which is usually coupled with a belief in the inherent superiority of a particular race and its right to domination over others."

Eugenics can be *seen* as a kind of "generic" racism that divides the human race into the genetically superior and inferior. The inferior usually turn out to be the traditional targets of racism. In 1865, for example, Galton (1976) wrote that the Negro, Hindu, Arab, Mongol, and Teuton all have "their peculiar characters," which "are transmitted, generation after generation, as truly [sic] as their physical forms."

Antisemitism has also been common among eugenicists. In 1884 Galton wrote to the distinguished botanist, Alphonse

"Euthanasia"

[In Nazi Germany, the first mass murders were of the mentally ill and retarded and the physically disabled, and these were euphemistically described by the regime as euthanasic measures. Whether one does or does not agree with individual euthanasia, any program of mass euthanasia is inevitably genocidal.—Ed.]

Euthanasia, the practice of ending a life to release an individual from disease or suffering, originated at least as early as the Greeks. Since ancient times euthanasia has been associated with both infanticide and the killing of the elderly and infirm. Plutarch commented on the Spartan practice of "euthanasia" of weak or deformed children. Both Plato and Aristotle approved of euthanasia for the elderly. Voluntary euthanasia involves deliberate action in ending a life at the request of the dying patient or that person's legal representative. For many modern people, euthanasia is merciful and loving relief for the terminally ill. A modern movement promoting the right to die has taken up the cause of euthanasia – in the form of doctor assisted suicide. Historically, euthanasia has always been seen as immoral by monotheisitic religions and associated with murder.

—Barry Mehler

de Candolle: "It strikes me that the Jews are specialized for a parasitical existence upon other nations . . ." Karl Pearson, Galton's disciple and biographer, echoed this opinion 40 years later. Attempting to prove Jewish immigrants undesirable, he argued that "there should be no place" for the Jews because they "will not be absorbed" into British society and would become "a parasitic race" [Hirsch, J. (1976). Behavior-genetic analysis and its biosocial consequences. In Bloch, Ned. J., and Dworkin, Gerald (Eds.), *The IQ Controversy: Critical Readings,* New York: Pantheon, p. 161].

Thus, from its very beginnings, eugenics assumed a hierarchy of races and fostered discrimination based on that assumption. The genocidal intent of contemporary eugenics is quite clear. Eugenics advocates believe that social policy must be aimed at making room for "better humans," the obsolete and incompetent must "make way . . . Evolutionary progress means the extinction of the less competent. To think otherwise is mere sentimentality" [Lynn, R. (1974). Review of *A New Morality from Science* by R.B. Cattell (1972), *Irish Journal of Psychology* (2), p. 207].

Although eugenics was also supported by communists, American liberals, and even Catholics, fascists and neo-Nazis have been uniquely and centrally involved in the development of eugenics. Eugenics was an essential part of fascism. As the French fascist Déat wrote in 1944, "Race is not just something to be preserved, it *is* the point of departure for the conquest of the future." To purify the racial identity of the state, "preserve its spirit and maintain its historical role."

Eugenics advocates were important promoters of both the Nazi eugenics program and the Holocaust. In Gemany, a eugenics enthusiast such as Otmar Freiherr von Verschuer, Director of the Kaiser Wilhelm's Institute of Anthropology, Human Genetics and Eugenics, supervised Josef Mengele's dissertation at the Kaiser Wilhelm and stayed in close touch with him during his "research" at Auschwitz. Verschuer would later join a new postwar generation of eugenics enthusiasts associated with the *Mankind Quarterly* and the Pioneer Fund. American eugenicists also were Hitler's cheering squad when it came to eugenics, and

Outstanding Leaders in American Intelligentsia Were Avid Supporters of the Eugenics Movement in the 1930s

[Well-known and outstanding leaders in American intelligentsia were among the avid supporters of the eugenics movement in the 1930s. The following reproduces a letterhead of the Eugenics Committee of the United States of America, and an excerpt from one of its flyers.—Ed.]

INTERNATIONAL COMMISSION ON EUGENICS

EUGENICS COMMITTEE OF THE UNITED STATES OF AMERICA

Irving Fisher, Chairman
Madison Grant
C. C. Little

Henry E. Crampton, Secretary-Treasurer
Barnard College, Columbia University
New York City

Charles B. Davenport, Vice-Chairman
Harry Olson
Henry Fairfield Osborn

ADVISORY COUNCIL

Miss Grace Abbott
Prof. W. S. Anderson
Mr. Frank L. Babbott
Dr. Lewellys F. Barker
Mr. Frederick S. Bigelow
Dr. Harold Bowditch
Dr. Philip K. Brown
Pres. W. W. Campbell
Prof. Walter B. Cannon
Prof. T. N. Carver
Prof. W. E. Castle
Prof. Edwin G. Conklin
Rev. John M. Cooper
Sen. Royal S. Copeland
Mr. Alexander B. Cox
Surg. Gen. H. S. Cummings
Prof. C. H. Danforth
Dr. Oscar Dowling
Dr. Knight Dunlap
Prof. Edward M. East
Dr. Charles W. Elliot
Dr. Haven Emerson
Dr. Arthur H. Estabrook
Dr. David Fairchild
Pres. Livingston Farrand
Dr. Walter E. Fernald
Dr. Eugene L. Fisk
Mr. Homer Folks
Rev. Harry E. Fosdick
Mr. Raymond B. Fosdick
Mr. Robert Garrett
Prof. Franklin H. Giddings
Dean Virginia C. Gildersleeve
Prof. Henry H. Goddard
Mr. Charles W. Gould
Prof. William K. Gregory
Prof. Michael F. Guyer
Prof. Winfield Scott Hall
Prof. Ross G. Harrison
Dr. C. Floyd Haviland
Prof. Samuel J. Holmes
Dr. Earnest A. Hooton
Dr. Lucien Howe
Dr. Alcs Hrdlicks
Mr. Arthur Hunter
Prof. Ellsworth Huntington
Dr. John N. Hurty
Dr. Walter B. James
Mrs. Helen Hartley Jenkins
Prof. H. S. Jennings
Hon. Albert Johnson
Prof. Roswell H. Johnson
Dr. David Starr Jordan
Prof. H. E. Jordan
Mrs. Otto Kahn
Dr. W. W. Keen
Prof. Truman Lee Kelly
Dr. John H. Kellogg
Dr. Vernon Kellogg
Dr. Helen Dean King
Prof. Charles A. Kofold
Dr. Daniel W. LaRue
Dr. H. H. Laughlin
Bishop William Lawrence
Prof. Frank R. Lillie
Rev. Frederick Lynch
Rabbi Louis Mann
Prof. C. E. McClung
Dr. William McDougall
Pres. J. C. Merriam
Prof. Maynard M. Metcalf
Prof. Adolf Meyer
Prof. Ann Haven Morgan
Pres. Lemuel H. Murlin
Prof. Henry F. Nachtrieb
Pres. W. A. Neilson
Prof. George H. Parker
Dr. Stewart Paton
Pres. E. F. Pendleton
Mr. Paul Popenoe
Mrs. John T. Pratt
Dr. W. S. Rankin
Dr. Aaron J. Rosanoff
Prof. E. A. Ross
Mrs. C. C. Rumsey
Prof. C. E. Seashore
Dr. Florence Brown Sherbon
Dr. William F. Snow
Prof. Charles R. Stockard
Mr. Lothrop Stoddard
Prof. Lewis M. Terman
Prof. Robert J. Terry
Prof. Edward L. Thorndike
Dean Victor C. Vaughan
Prof. Herbert E. Walter
Prof. Robert Dec. Ward
Dr. William H. Welch
Prof. William M. Wheeler
Pres. Ray Lyman Wilbur
Prof. Harry H. Wilder
Prof. Walter F. Willcox
Dr. Clark Wissler
Dr. Frederick A. Woods
Dr. Robert S. Woodward
Dr. Robert M. Yerkes

The Eugenics Committee invites you to become a member of the Eugenics Society of the United States of America.

The time seems ripe for a strong public movement to stem the tide of threatened racial degeneracy following in the wake of the War. America in particular needs to protect herself against indiscriminate immigration, criminal degenerates and the race suicide deplored by President Roosevelt.

Eugenics stands against forces which work for racial deterioration, and for progressive improvement in vigor, intelligence, and moral fiber in the human race. It represents the highest form of patriotism and humanitarianism, while at the same time it offers immediate advantages to ourselves and to our children. By eugenics measures, for instance, our burden of taxes can be reduced by decreasing the number of degenerates, delinquents and defectives supported in public institutions; such measures will also increase safeguards against our persons and our property.

Stefan Kühl has shown just how valuable that service was to Hitler's killing machine.

Confusion has arisen regarding the "positive" value of eugenics for disease control in societies that provide proper safeguards against fascist and totalitarian extremism. There has arisen considerable confusion between genetics and eugenics. Genetic counseling, genetic engineering, the human genome project and other scientific endeavors in the field of genetics certainly hold promise for legitimate health care uses. Eugenics *should* not be confused with any of these sciences. Eugenics is not a science, it is a political movement aimed at using genetic technology to control human reproduction. There is no positive side to "eugenics." Eugenicists' support of Nazi genocide was the most striking example of the relationship between eugenics and genocide. Eugenicists today suggest that First World countries allow Third World countries "to go to the wall" when they collapse into chaos, mass famine and genocide. For them, foreign aid to underdeveloped Third World countries is a mistake. Thus, distinguished psychologist Raymond Cattell has written [Cattell, Raymond (1972). *A New Morality from Science: Beyondism.* New York: Pergamon Press], "A condition of birth of the new is the disappearance of the old. However, . . . newer and more humane methods must prevail . . . Wherever a question of relative reduction of a population is concerned the word 'genocide' is bandied about as a propoganda term. Nature constantly commits both homicide and genocide."

—Barry Mehler

References and Recommended Reading

Galton, Francis (1907). *Inquiries Into Human Faculty and its Development.* London: Dent. (Original work published in 1883.)

Galton, Francis (1976). Hereditary talent and character: I. II. In Bajema, Carl J. (Ed.), *Eugenics: Then and Now.* Stroudsburg, PA: Dowden, Hutchinson and Ross. (Original work published in *Macmillan's Magazine,* 1865, 12 (68), 157–166; 12 (71), 318–327.)

Kuhl, Stefan (1994). *The Nazi Connection: Eugenics, American Racism, and German National Socialism.* New York: Oxford University Press.

EUROPEAN CONVENTION ON THE NON-APPLICATION OF STATUTORY LIMITATIONS TO CRIMES AGAINST HUMANITY AND WAR CRIMES (1974)

The European Convention on the Non-Application of Statutory Limitations to Crimes Against Humanity and War Crimes opened for signature at Strasbourg on January 25, 1974. The Convention's primary goal, as stated by its title, was to prevent those accused of committing crimes against humanity and/or war crimes from benefitting from any statute of limitations. State signatories include Canada, France, the Netherlands and the United States. The Convention was modeled after the United Nations Human Rights Commission's Convention of the Non-Applicability of Statutory Limitations to War Crimes and Crimes Against Humanity.

—Michael J. Bazyler

FACING HISTORY AND OURSELVES

Facing History and Ourselves is an educational and professional development organization that engages students and the community at large in an examination of racism, prejudice, and antisemitism in order to promote the development of a more humane and informed citizenry. By studying the historical development and lessons of the Holocaust and other examples of genocide, participants in Facing History programs make the essential connection between history and the moral choices they confront in their lives.

Facing History applies the methods of the humanities—inquiry, analysis, and interpretation—to teaching about the human capacity for both monumental evil and extraordinary courage. Program participants confront the moral questions inherent in a study not only of violence, racism and antisemitism, but also of courage, caring and compassion as they explore the root causes of hate and ways to combat prejudice.

Facing History and Ourselves uses a concept of education in which students "construct" knowledge—make meaning of what goes on in the world by connecting new subject matter to what they already know. Readings and activities in the principal resource book, *Facing History and Ourselves: Holocaust and Human Behavior,* as well as other written resources, audiovisual materials, and resource speakers, encourage students to understand the complexities of history and to enter into constructive dialogue with others.

Facing History and Ourselves provides insight into the meaning of morality, law, citizenship, and human behavior. Following a sequence that begins with reflection, moves to judgment, and ends with participation, it confronts these issues and others like them with materials grounded in concrete historical content, in particular a rigorous study of the failure of democracy in Germany in the 1920s and 1930s that led to the Holocaust. Supported by conferences, scholarly research on history and education, and continuous program evaluation, Facing History has offered for more than two decades a dynamic, long-term intervention that has a lasting effect on adolescents, educators, and communities. Based on Facing History's unique approach to citizenship and democracy, students and other participants in its programs understand how the history they learn in the classroom relates to their own lives, their nation, and what it takes to preserve and nurture a democracy.

Through the Facing History and Ourselves program, participants move from "thinking about their own thinking" to contemplating how they can play a constructive role in their schools, neighborhoods, and the larger community. In

1997, a new national initiative, *Choosing to Participate: Courage, Community, and Civil Society,* began to bring together and extend the many strands within Facing History that directly address the question: "How can I make a difference?" Culminating in 2001, this five-year national multifaceted project is creating arenas for discussing and acting upon key issues that confront us all as we enter the next millennium.

Included in this initiative will be a conference and the publication of new resource materials developed through the Harvard/Facing History and Ourselves Project, which develops, evaluates, and disseminates new educational resource materials and approaches for encouraging responsible participation in a democratic society. Facing History's 1999 Annual National Human Rights and Justice Conference, *Participating in Democracy,* and the new resource materials entitled, *Courage, Community, and Civil Society in America,* examined the concept of membership in a democracy.

The approach of Facing History and Ourselves is well tested and extensively used. Over the past two decades, 11,000 teachers have participated in Facing History workshops and institutes; the program reaches approximately 1,000,000 students annually. It is used in public, independent, and parochial middle schools and high schools; colleges and universities; technical vocational schools; and adult education programs in the United States, Canada, and Europe.

Headquartered in Boston, the Facing History and Ourselves National Foundation has regional offices in Chicago, Cleveland, Los Angeles, Memphis, New York, and San Francisco. A program associate, based in Davos, Switzerland, offers Facing History and related programs in Europe. A National Advisory Board composed of distinguished academicians brings Facing History and Ourselves additional rigor on such topics as scholarship, education, pedagogy, history, and theology.

Professional Development: Modeling the Pedagogy

Educators learn the Facing History approach by experiencing it themselves through introductory sessions, week-long institutes, and two-day follow-up workshops. These settings provide in-service and preservice teachers with opportunities to meet scholars who challenge their thinking not only about ethics and history but also about the process of education and membership in a democratic society. Teachers consider methods for developing critical reading, viewing, writing and thinking; techniques for approaching difficult topics with students; evaluation and assessment issues; and suggestions for integrating multicultural literature into classes.

Whether in shorter workshops or more intensive institutes, participants respond to their own learning and at the same time discuss strategies for raising the same issues with students. In format, content and methodology, these professional development activities provide educational models that teachers can use, often engaging participants in designing lessons based on *Facing History and Ourselves: Holocaust and Human Behavior.* In addition, the organization supports continuous professional development through ongoing workshops and conferences, intensive follow-up support from program staff based at each of the Facing History offices, and participation in a national and international network of educators.

Through its long-term relationships between program staff and classroom teachers, Facing History and Ourselves bridges research and practice, scholars and teachers. Staff and advisors incorporate the latest historical scholarship and research on learning into models and materials for teachers in the classroom.

The bridge goes the other way too, as Facing History's network of teachers challenges researchers with feedback from classrooms. This keeps the program timely and innovative, in particular as students ask how the history they learn in the classroom relates to their nation and democracy.

Since 1994, the Harvard/Facing History and Ourselves Project, a partnership with Harvard University, has extended the organization's scholar-teacher connection. Bringing together Facing History staff with educators from Harvard and many other institutions of higher learning, the project links theory and classroom practice as it develops resource materials and programs for preservice and in-service teachers. Examining threats to democracy that are often expressed in apathy, rage or prejudice, it focuses on the relationship of the individual to society, the origins and dangers of violence and group hatreds, and avenues for working out conflict and promoting compassion.

Extensive validation of the effectiveness of Facing History and Ourselves has been provided by independent scholars who have rigorously examined specific aspects of the program. Panels convened by the US Department of Education have consistently recognized Facing History as a model for educational intervention and national replication. According to various research efforts, Facing History provides a vocabulary for discussing critical issues while expanding students' perspectives. It increases empathy, creates an awareness of choices, and prepares students for responsible citizenship in a democracy. Pre-, post-, and follow-up surveys have shown that teachers who participate in Facing History's professional development programs can utilize the methodologies and resources provided to create courses that address history and its meaning for today. Currently, Facing History is expanding its assessment efforts as it contributes to the national dialogue about effective educational interventions. For example, under a grant from the Carnegie Corporation of New York, Facing History and Harvard scholars are assessing the ways its program helps young people become active, thoughtful citizens who interact positively with people of diverse ethnic and racial backgrounds.

Some Examples of Resources from Facing History and Ourselves

Facing History and Ourselves: Holocaust and Human Behavior (Facing History and Ourselves National Foundation, 1989; original edition, 1982). This resource book provides an interdisciplinary approach to citizenship education. Readings and activities explore the consequences of discrimination, racism, and antisemitism by holding up "the tarnished mirror of history" to one of the most violent times of the recent past—the 1930s and 1940s.

Elements of Time (Facing History and Ourselves National Foundation, 1990). The result of a five-year collaboration with the Fortunoff Video Archives for Holocaust Testimony at Yale University, this manual includes transcripts, background information, and suggestions for using the archive's materials.

I Promised I Would Tell, by Sonia Weitz (Facing History and Ourselves National Foundation, 1993). Weitz, poet and survivor of the Holocaust, has created a vivid tapestry of her years in Poland, including her childhood in Krakow and the years she spent in concentration camps and a camp for displaced persons.

The Jews of Poland (Facing History and Ourselves National Foundation, 1997). This book describes Jewish life in Eastern Europe before, during, and after the Holocaust. Through the reading of excerpts from autobiographies, diaries, official documents, and literary works, this book examines the ways the Jews of

Poland and their non-Jewish neighbors responded to questions of identity, membership, and difference at various times in their shared history.

Study Guides and Videos

Participating in Democracy: Choosing to Make a Difference (Facing History and Ourselves National Foundation, 1995). This videotape and study guide, highlighting recipients of Reebok Human Rights Awards, illustrate a variety of nonviolent ways for expressing both outrage and compassion.

Memphis: Building Community (Facing History and Ourselves National Foundation, 1996). Focused on the theme of identity and democratic citizenship, this study guide recalls the courageous individuals who tried to promote democracy by shattering the barriers dividing the people of Memphis and the nation.

The New England Holocaust Memorial: A Study Guide (Facing History and Ourselves National Foundation, 1996).

A Discussion with Elie Wiesel: Facing History Students Confront History and Violence (Facing History and Ourselves National Foundation, 1993). In this video, six students talk with Nobel Prize winner Wiesel about their experiences with hatred and violence.

For further information, contact Facing History and Ourselves National Foundation, 16 Hurd Rd., Brookline, MA 02146 USA, tel: 617–232–1595; fax: 617–232–0281, e-mail: info_boston@facing.org; website: http://www.facing.org.

—*Margot Stern Strom*

FAMINE AS A METHOD OF GENOCIDE

Throughout most of history the great majority of people were considered successful if they were able to provide adequate food, clothing and shelter for their dependents and themselves. But hunger, starvation, and famine have, in all ages and in all parts of the world, been the source of the greatest suffering. The original meaning of "famine" in English was hunger or dearth. Its current meaning as mass death produced by starvation originated with Malthus who used it not as a description of empirical fact, but as a logical last step in his theory of checks on population growth. Famines, in the sense of mass deaths, are unlikely to occur as a result of massive crop failures, but they commonly do occur as the result of man-made starvation regimes leading to famines in the Malthusian sense of the term.

While there exists a vast literature on natural events that affect food supplies, there is a much more limited literature on such man-made famines. These are of two kinds: The first kind of man-made famine occurs as the result of the unintended consequences of economic, political, and social processes that aggravate rather than ameliorate an existing shortage of food caused by natural events.

The second kind of man-made famine is the result of age-old intentional use of hunger as a means of conflict and warfare. The fact that human beings need food and water in order to survive has been a crucial element in the conduct of conflict since the earliest times. From the 'to bed without supper' punishment inflicted by some parents on their misbehaving offspring, to the starvation imposed on beleaguered towns, the deprivation of nourishment has always been perceived as a method of enforcing superior demands.

The use of deliberate starvation in the conquest of fortified towns and cities was largly superceded by more modern technologies of bombarding from the ground and from the air, which made the defense of towns impossible. However, the use of deliberate famine as a method in the conduct of conflicts has not disappeared entirely because its basic appeal has remained unchanged: it acts on the basic survival needs of the enemy, it is a low technology method that is easy to administer, and it is cost effective.

For these reasons famine and starvation have been and continue to be among the methods used by the perpetrators of genocide. However, famine as a method of genocide does have one disadvantage: it is almost impossible to target specific subgroups among the victims.

One arena of conflict where starvation has been used with deliberate intent is in the confrontation between indigenous peoples and their imperial colonizers. For example, in the late nineteenth century the US encouraged hunting to extinction of the bison in order to control the Indians of the northern Plains. By 1910 this policy had been so successful that only ten bison, out of an estimated mid-nineteenth-century population of 60 million, remained. Since the bison was the mainstay of the Indians' diet, its disappearance played a major role in their submission to the government's wishes. Impressed by their own success, the government continued to use the withholding of rations from recalcitrant Indians even after they had been confined to reservations.

The colonial policies of Germany in Southwest Africa at the beginning of this century were even more crudely stated and documented, and included depriving the Hereros of food and especially of water. When it finally came to a decisive battle, the Hereros were deliberately allowed to escape into the Omaheke Desert where they were condemned to die of thirst.

During the 1930s Stalin performed a carefully planned and large scale famine that killed five-seven million Ukrainians. He wanted to collectivize agriculture not only to eliminate the Kulaks, but also to increase agricultural production. He also wanted to accelerate industrialization. To pay for the import of the required technology, he exported the agricultural surpluses produced by strict production quotas and confiscation of all foodstuffs. The resulting famine was hidden from the outside world and denied when information leaked out. Even offers of food shipments by humanitarian organizations were refused.

During World War II the differential rationing of food by the Germans divided the population of Europe into the well-fed, the underfed, the hungry, and the starving. The Germans were the only well-fed people with progressively smaller amounts going to less valued populations and the least going to the Jews. The latter's rations were intended to starve them to death and survival was only possible for those who found underground ways of supplementing their rations.

The World Food Conference held in Rome in 1974 passed resolutions to outlaw starvation as a means of warfare, but available data provide no evidence that these resolutions have been respected during recent conflicts. During the well-publicized 1980s famine in Ethiopia, food shipments were distributed only to supporters of the regime while food exports continued to flourish. By comparison, Kenya, which experienced the same climatic conditions, did not suffer a famine. In Bosnia, the victims of ethnic cleansing were starving while Serbia was exporting food to Russia in exchange for technology and weapons. In the Sudan, the government destroyed field crops and periodically refused entry to humanitarian aid shipments while at the same time exporting wheat. It has also been reported that the government misappropriated humanitarian aid funds in order to pay for the import of armaments.

Control and withholding of food and water continue to be important weapons in most conflicts, and play a special role in genocides. When a conflict is between contending countries, the control of food affects the opponents. When the control of food is used in the performance of a genocide within the perpetrator's country, it victimizes a constituent population. When that country continues at the same time to export foodstuffs, this becomes the easiest ways of documenting that a famine is man-made.

—*Kurt Jonassohn*

References and Recommended Reading

Golkin, Arline T. (1987). *A Heritage of Hunger: A Guide to Issues and References.* Claremont, CA: Regina Books.

Newman, Lucile F. (Ed.) (1990). *Hunger in History.* Cambridge, MA: Basil Blackwell.

FILMS OF THE HOLOCAUST, GENOCIDE, AND FUTURISTIC DESTRUCTION

FILMS OF THE HOLOCAUST

Film has figured prominently in documenting and responding to the Holocaust since the final days of the Third Reich. The number of films and telecasts dealing with this subject has burgeoned in the decades since the war's end, and these media are unrivaled in their extensive influence on how people understand the Holocaust.

Footage documenting Nazi deportations, concentration camps, and mass executions was recorded sporadically by German officers and, more rarely, by their victims during the early 1940s. Nazis used propaganda films to champion sterilization and euthanasia for the mentally ill (e.g., *Existence without Life,* 1939), to promote German antisemitism (*The Eternal Jew,* 1940), and to camouflage the concentration camp Terezin (*Hitler Presents a Town to the Jews,* 1944).

The first public displays of films documenting Nazi genocide took place in late April-early May 1945 as American and British newsreels reported the Allies' liberation of concentration camps. These films were widely credited as watershed proof of Nazi atrocities. *Nazi Concentration Camps* (1945), a US government compilation of liberation footage, played an unprecedented role as evidence during the Nuremberg war crimes trials. Similar footage was used in propaganda films shown during the late 1940s to Allied troops stationed in postwar Europe and Germans in de-Nazification programs (e.g., *Nuremberg,* USA, 1948). The significance of this documentary footage as constituting a morally charged act of "witnessing" the Holocaust continues to be invoked in numerous films and telecasts.

A small number of documentary films and telecasts made during the late 1940s and 1950s dealt with aspects of what has since come to be known as the Holocaust. Of these, Alain Renais' *Night and Fog* (France, 1955) remains the most celebrated, as widely admired for its artful juxtaposition of vintage and contemporary images, its probing, poetic text and affective score as for its chronicle of genocide. At the same time, the film is often faulted for not mentioning the centrality of Jews as victims of Nazi genocide. While early documentaries on Nazism are centered on perpetrators, others deal primarily with their victims, focusing on survivors and their postwar future. These include Henri Cartier-Bresson's *Reunion* (France, 1946); *We Who*

Are Still Alive (Poland, 1947, dir. Natan Gross) on Jewish life in postwar Poland; and *Placing the Displaced* (USA, 1948, dir. Martin A. Bursten), a HIAS (Hebrew Immigrant Aid Society) docudrama on DPs (Displaced Persons).

Features made in postwar Europe, often involving Holocaust survivors in their production, are among the earliest dramatic portrayals of Jewish persecution, resistance and survival during the Nazi era. *The Last Stop* (Poland, 1947, dir. Wanda Jakubowska) reenacts the torments of Auschwitz in situ; *Long is the Road* (Germany, 1948, dir. Herbert B. Fredersdorf and Marek Goldstein) follows a young couple of survivors who fall in love in a DP camp. Set in a postwar orphanage, *Our Children* (Poland, 1948, dir. Natan Gross) is tellingly self-conscious of the challenge of dramatizing Holocaust experiences. *Border Street* (Poland, 1948, dir. Aleksander Ford) examines Polish-Jewish relations during the resistance against Germany. Andrzej Wajda's war trilogy—*A Generation* (Poland, 1955); *Canal* (1957); *Ashes and Diamonds* (1958)—revisited this subject a decade later. Czech filmmakers also addressed the Holocaust in a number of early postwar dramas, beginning with Alfred Radok's *Distant Journey* (1948). Holocaust survivors are an important presence in films made in postwar Palestine, notably the work of Meyer Levin (*My Father's House,* 1946; *The Illegals,* 1947).

Though Hollywood seldom dealt with the Holocaust during this period, two films—*The Diary of Anne Frank* (1959, dir. George Stevens), and *Judgment at Nuremberg* (1961, dir. Stanley Kramer)—were widely seen internationally. Both were anticipated by American television versions; indeed, during the 1950s, prime-time drama anthologies and Sunday ecumenical series presented several original teleplays exploring America's relationship to the Holocaust by such writers as Paddy Chayefsky, Ernest Kinoy, Reginald Rose, and Rod Serling.

In the 1960s television played an increasingly important and distinctive role in portraying the Holocaust. In 1961 the war crimes trial of Adolf Eichmann in Jerusalem was televised internationally, contributing to the case's impact as a landmark of international Holocaust remembrance. In the ensuing years the causes and consequences of the Holocaust were addressed in a growing number and variety of dramatic films made for general audiences. These include adaptations of Holocaust literature (*The Pawnbroker,* USA, 1965, dir. Sidney Lumet; *The Garden of the Finzi-Continis,* Italy, 1970, dir. Vittorio DeSica); as well as the thriller, *The Boys from Brazil* (USA, 1978, dir. Franklin J. Schaffner); the sexually charged drama, *The Night Porter* (Italy, 1974, dir. Liliana Cavani); the postmodern Wagnerian epic, *Our Hitler* (Germany, 1978, dir. Hans-Jürgen Syberberg); the musical, *Cabaret* (USA, 1973, dir. Bob Fosse) and the comedy, *The Producers* (USA, 1967, dir. Mel Brooks). Some of these films provoked considerable critical ire as "exploitations" of the Holocaust. Israeli cinema paid renewed attention to Holocaust survivors following the Eichmann trial as well (e.g., *The Glass Cage,* 1964, dir. Phillippe Arthuys), and a number of films analogized Nazis and Arabs. At this time the Holocaust became more widely recognized as a powerful moral paradigm and was invoked, sometimes obliquely, in the work of leading international directors: Ingmar Bergman (*Persona,* Sweden 1966; *The Serpent's Egg,* 1970), Rainer Werner Fassbinder (*The Marriage of Maria Braun,* Germany, 1978), Luchino Visconti (*The Damned,* Italy, 1969), and Lina Wertmuller (*Seven Beauties,* Italy, 1975). As its master narrative became increasingly familiar, the Holocaust figured more prominently in documentary films and telecasts on

World War II, notably the work of Marcel Ophuls (*The Sorrow and the Pity,* France 1970; *The Memory of Justice,* 1976) and the "Genocide" episode of the televison series *The World at War* (England, 1975, dir. Michael Darlow).

Telecasts of the popular American miniseries, *Holocaust* (dir. Marvin Chomsky) in 1978–1979 generated an unprecedented public discussion in the United States and Europe, especially West Germany, of both the subject and the nature of its mediation. Reponses to the miniseries, often critical, engendered new films and telecasts (e.g., *The Boat is Full,* Switzerland, 1981, dir. Markus Imhoof; *Homeland,* Germany, 1984, dir. Edgar Reitz) as well as the initiation of American efforts to videotape Holocaust survivors' testimony, notably the Fortunoff Video Archive at Yale University.

Documentaries increasingly centered on the recollections of survivors (*Kitty: Return to Auschwitz,* England, 1980, dir. Peter Morley; *Robert Clary A5714: A Memoir of Liberation,* USA, 1985, dir. Bud Margolis) and to the process of remembering the Holocaust. Distinguished among such films is Claude Lanzmann's *Shoah* (France, 1985), which explores the ordeal of confronting survivors and bystanders with memories of mass murder as the film challenges the formal conventions of documentary-making in its length (nine-and-a-half hours) and relentless style of interviewing. As the postwar generation came of age, the children of survivors became the subject of self-reflexive documentaries (*In Dark Places,* USA, 1978, dir. Gina Blumenfeld; *A Generation Apart,* USA, 1984, dir. Jack and Danny Fisher). Other films investigated hitherto unexplored aspects of the Holocaust narrative, from the *Judenrat* (*Chaim Rumkowski and the Jews of Lodz,* Sweden, 1982, dir. Peter Cohen) to righteous Gentiles (*Weapons of the Spirit,* France, 1987, dir. Pierre Sauvage). A number of more recent documentaries have been the subject of controversies over their factuality or propriety: *Liberators* (USA, 1992, dir. William Miles and Nina Rosenblum), *Balagan* (Israel, 1993, dir. Andres Veiel), *Profession: Neo-Nazi* (Germany, 1994, dir. Winifred Bonengel).

During the last decades of the twentieth century the Holocaust has been a regular, prominent and sometimes contentious presence in international film and television dramas: these include *The Last Metro* (France, 1980, dir. François Truffaut); *Playing for Time* (USA, 1980, dir. Daniel Mann); *Mephisto* (Hungary, 1981, dir. István Szábo); *Sophie's Choice* (USA, 1982, dir. Alan Pakula); *Goodbye Children* (France, 1987, dir. Louis Malle); *Commissar* (USSR, 1988, dir. Aleksander Askoldov); *The Nasty Girl* (Germany, 1990, dir. Michael Verhoeven); *Europa, Europa* (Germany, 1991, dir. Agnieszka Holland); *Korczak* (Poland, 1991, dir. Andrzej Wajda); *Genghis Cohn* (England, 1993, dir. Elijah Moshinsky); *Mendel* (Norway, 1997, dir. Alexander Rosler). In 1993, Steven Spielberg's *Schindler's List* (USA) received unprecedented international attention. This Academy Award-winning film elevated the filmmaker to the status of a spokesman for the Holocaust. Spielberg has used profits from this film to support the Shoah Visual History Project, a large corpus of filmed survivor interviews inventoried in a computer database. The extensive response to this film, including "*Schindler's List* tours" of Kracow and environs, exemplifies the unrivaled impact the medium now has on Holocaust representation.

Selected Films on the Holocaust

Nazi Concentration Camps (USA, 1945, 59 min., B&W). Compiled by the US Counsel for the Prosecution of Axis Criminality, this documentary was presented as evidence at the first international Nuremberg war crimes trial. The film presents footage recorded at POW

Brutal SS Commandant Arnon Goeth (Ralph Fiennes) selects a fearful Helen Hirsch (Embeth Davitdz) to be his housemaid in the feature film Schindler's List *by Universal Pictures. (© 1993 by Universal City Studios, Inc. With the kind assistance of the office of Michael Berenbaum, President of the Survivors of the Shoah Visual History Foundation, created by Stephen Spielberg)*

and concentration camps liberated by Allied forces, including Leipzig, Penig, Ohrdruf, Hadamar, Breendonck, Hanover, Arnstadt, Mauthausen, Buchenwald, Dachau and Bergen-Belsen.

Night and Fog (*Nuit et Bruillard;* France, 1955, 30 minutes, color/B&W). Directed by Alain Resnais, with script by Jean Cayrol and score by Hanns Eisler, this was the first widely seen documentary that traces the chronology of the "Final Solution." The film makes pointed use of cross-cutting between vintage images of the Nazi era and footage shot in the present, calling the viewer's attention to the challenges of remembering the Holocaust era.

Judgment at Nuremberg (USA, 1961, 186 min., B&W). Originally scripted by Abby Mann as a drama telecast live on CBS' *Playhouse 90* in 1959, this feature film dramatizes one of the later Nuremberg war crimes trials conducted by the US military, in which the defendants were German jurists who carried out Nazi laws that persecuted Jews and dissidents. The film's climax centers around the screening of concentration camp footage as a morally galvanizing moment.

Holocaust: The Story of the Family Weiss (USA, 1978, 450 min., color). First telecast as a four-part miniseries on NBC, this dramatic epic has been seen by hundreds of millions of viewers around the world. Gerald Green's drama traces the narrative of the Holocaust through the experiences of members of one middle-class German-Jewish family. The miniseries was both very popular and widely criticized as a "trivialization" of its subject in the first extended public discussion of the challenges of mediating the Holocaust.

Shoah (France, 1985, 563 minutes, color). Claude Lanzmann's documentary challenges the conventions of documentary filmmaking as it explores the phenomenon of Nazi death camps in Poland. Eschewing vintage footage, the film consists primarily of extensive interviews with eyewitnesses to the Nazi genocide. The film's unusual length and the filmmaker's uncompromising demands of his informants have received both critical admiration and condemnation.

Schindler's List (USA, 1993, 197 minutes, B&W). Filmmaker Steven Spielberg's adaptation of the historical novel by Thomas Keneally about Oskar Schindler's efforts to rescue over a thousand Jews from Nazi persecution attained unprecedented critical acclaim and public response for a popular film on the Holocaust and won an Academy Award. Cinematographer Janusz Kaminski shot the film in black and white, emulating period documentary footage and Roman Vishniac's photographs of prewar Polish Jewry.

—*Jeffrey Shandler*

References and Recommended Reading

Avisar, Ilan (1988). *Screening the Holocaust: Cinema's Images of the Unimaginable.* Bloomington, IN: Indiana University Press.

Doneson, Judith E. (1987). *The Holocaust in American Film.* Philadelphia, PA: Jewish Publication Society.

Insdorf, Annette (1989). *Indelible Shadows: Film and the Holocaust.* 2nd ed. New York: Cambridge University Press.

Shandler, Jeffrey (1999). *While America Watches: Televising the Holocaust.* New York: Oxford University Press.

FILMS OF OTHER GENOCIDES

There are numerous films about various genocidal acts, but they are still far fewer in number than those that address the Holocaust. Most of the small number of films are about the Turkish genocide of the Armenians, the Cambodian genocide, and the genocidal actions and so-called "ethnic cleansing" in the Former Yugoslavia in the early 1990s, and the genocide of the Tutsis in Rwanda in 1994. One may safely assume that as an ever-increasing number of people become concerned about the perpetration of genocide, along with the ongoing development of relatively inexpensive and easy to convey and use video technology, more and more films will be produced on various genocides.

The genocidal acts that are addressed in these films are of both a physical and cultural nature. They include the near-absolute extermination of the people of Tierra del Fuego (*The Ona People,* Documentary Educational Resources); the genocide of the Tasmanian aborigines in Australia (*The Last Tasmanian: Extinction,* McGraw-Hill Films); the Turkish slaughter of the Armenians (*The Forgotten Genocide* and *The Armenian Genocide,* Atlantis Productions); the Soviet, man-made famine in the Ukraine (*Harvest of Despair: The Unknown Holocaust,* International Historic Films); the forced exile of the Estonian people from the USSR beginning in 1939 (*The Estonians: For the Record,* Esto Film/Canada); the purges in the Soviet Union under Stalin (*Diary for All My Children,* New Yorker Films); the cultural genocide committed against the tribal Igorot people of the northern Philippines by the Marcos government (*Seasons of Thunder,* Philippine Resource Center); the genocide of the Tibetan people by China (*Tibet: A Case to Answer,* Special Broadcasting Service of Australia); the genocidal acts committed by the Guatemalan government against its indigenous population (*Guatemala: Personal Testimonies,* First Run/Icarus Films, and *Guatemala: Roads of Silence,* The Cinema Guild); the mass killing of the Cuiva people in Colombia (*The Last of the Cuiva,* Michigan Media); the cultural and actual genocides of various indigenous populations of the Amazon region (*Amazonia: Voices from the Rainforest,* The Video Project); the genocidal acts committed by the Khmer Rouge against the Cambodian people (*Cambodia: Year Zero: Year One,* Active Home Video); the mass murder of the Shia Marsh Arabs by the Iraqi regime of Saddam Hussein (*Saddam's Killing Fields,* Landmark Media Inc.); the genocidal actions and "ethnic cleansing" perpetrated in the former Yugoslavia by various factions (*The Ethnic Cleansers and the Cleansed: The Unforgiving,* Films for the Humanities and Sciences, and *Bosnia and Serbia: Yellow Wasps,* Chip Taylor Commuications); and the 1994 genocide of the Tutsis in Rwanda (*Rwanda: How History Can Lead to Genocide,* Filmakers Library, and *Chronicle of a Genocide Foretold,* First Run/Icarus Films).

In addition to focusing on the specifics of an account of genocide, a small number of films produced in the 1990s also focus on the passivity of western nations in regard to ignoring early warning signals of genocide and/or political evasion, apathy, and hypocrisy while genocide was being perpetrated. A classic example of such a film is *From Yugoslavia to Bosnia* (Landmark Media Inc.). Others focus on how certain Western nations actually support former genocidal regimes in the years following a genocidal tragedy, thus highlighting the despicable nature of realpolitik. A good example of the latter is *Cambodia: The Betrayal* (Filmakers Library).

The vast majority of the aforementioned films are either documentaries and/or were produced especially for classroom use. The most notable of the feature films on genocide is *The Killing Fields,* an outstanding film that tells the true story of one man's struggle to hold on to life during the period when the Pol Pot government slaughtered up to three million Cambodian people, and his friend's frantic attempts to save him.

Ultimately, the fact remains that many incidents of genocide have not been addressed by filmmakers. The exact reason is unclear. It is possible that filmmakers may not be cognizant of some genocidal acts or may prefer to key in on better-known or more recent atrocities.

Selected Films on Genocide

The Armenian Case (45 min., color, videocassette). Available from Atlantis Productions, 1252 La Granada Drive, Thousand Oaks, CA 91362. In this film, survivors of the Armenian Genocide and European and American eyewitnesses recall the historical events that were to shape the destiny of the Armenian people. It includes documentary sequences on World War I, and the establishment of the Republic of Armenia and Soviet Armenia.

The Forgotten [Armenian] Genocide (29 min., color, videocastte). Available from Atlantis Productions, 1252 La Granada Drive, Thousand Oaks, CA 91362. This film presents the story of the genocide of the Armenian people committed by the Turks in 1915.

Forsaken Cries: The Story of Rwanda (35 min., color, videocassette). Available from Amnesty International-USA, 322 Eighth Avenue, New York, NY 10001. This documentary, which examines Rwanda as a case study of the human rights challenge of the twenty-first century, incorporates historical footage, interviews, and analysis of the genocide that resulted in the deaths of up to one million people in 1994.

From Yugoslavia to Bosnia (50 min., color, videocassette). Available from Landmark Media, 3150 Slade Run Drive, Falls Church, VA 22042. This video relates the story of the war in the Former Yugoslavia from its inception up to events in 1994. The narrator discusses the atrocities/genocide and "ethnic cleaning" as well as European and US political evasion and apathy. The film features

President Bill Clinton, Prime Minister Margaret Thatcher and two historians who contradict accepted opinion on the causes of the situation.

Guatemala: Personal Testimonies (20 min., color, videocassette). Available from Icarus Films, 200 Park Avenue South, Suite 1319, New York, NY 10003. This series of testimonies from Guatemalan Indians clearly bears witness to the widespread abuse of human rights and genocidal actions committed by the government of General Rios Montt.

Harvest of Despair: The Unknown Holocaust (55 min., color with black and white sequences, videocassette). Available from the Ukrainian Research Centre, St. Vladimir Institute, 620 Spadina Ave., Toronto, Ontario, Canada M58 2HY. A documentary of the Ukrainian "terror famine" of 1932–1933. It includes interviews with survivors and scholars about various aspects of the genocide, and rare photographic evidence.

The Killing Fields (137 min., color, videocassette). Available from Swank Film Programmer, 6767 Forest Lawn Dr., Hollywood, CA 90068. This moving film tells the horrific and true story of one man's (Dith Pran, an interpreter for *New York Times* reporter, Sydney Schanberg) traumatic experiences in Cambodia during the mid- to late–1970s during which the Khmer Rouge killed 3 million out of its 7 million fellow citizens in an attempt to create a "new society."

Saddam's Killing Fields (52 min., color, videocassette). Available from Landmark Media, 3450 Slade Run Drive, Falls Church, VA 22042. In this film, historian and presenter, Michael Wood, presents evidence of the Saddam Hussein's regime's sustained and murderous destruction of the Shia Marsh Arabs, whose way of life goes back 5,000 years.

Year Zero (53 min., color, videocassette). Available from American Friends Service Committee, Pacific Southwest, Region, 980 N. Fair Oaks Ave., Pasadena, CA 91103. Produced in Cambodia in September 1979 for Britain's Associated Television, this film presents gruesome evidence of the genocide committed between 1975 and 1979 when up to three million people were murdered, worked and starved to death by the Khmer Rouge.

—*Samuel Totten*

References and Recommended Reading

Totten, Samuel (1988). The literature, art, and film of genocide. In Charny, Israel W. (Ed.), *Genocide: A Critical Bibliographic Review.* London: Mansell Publishing; and New York: Facts on File, pp. 232–240.

Totten, Samuel (1991). *First-Person Accounts of Genocidal Acts Committed in the Twentieth Century: An Annotated Bibliography.* Westport, CT: Greenwood Press.

FILMS OF NUCLEAR, CHEMICAL, AND BIOLOGICAL DESTRUCTION

Nuclear, chemical and biological destruction are all real possibilities in a world where arrogance, atavism, nationalism, and one-upmanship seem to be the rule rather than the exception.

For close to fifty years the world community has faced the threat of nuclear annihilation. With the end of the Cold War and the break-up of the Soviet Union, there was hope that nuclear tensions would diminish significantly. That hope was short-lived when a nuclear crisis between India and Pakistan erupted, and in 1998 both countries exploded several nuclear test bombs, including one hydrogen bomb. Many political analysts claimed that the world had not faced such a dangerous "nuclear situation" since the Cuban Missile Crisis in 1962. Speculation arose that not only might the crisis result in a nuclear arms race in the region but that other countries such as Iran, Iraq, Syria, Libya, and North Korea, all of whom have sponsored terrorism across the globe, may demand the same technology.

Many experts have been of the opinion that there would be nations who would settle for what has been deemed the "poor man's nuclear bomb," meaning chemical and biological weapons. In fact, Iraq, which has attempted to develop its own nuclear capability, already used chemical weapons against its Kurdish population in the late 1980s. Still, it appears that the "prestige" of being in "the nuclear club"—that is, actually developing a nuclear capability—is so great, that certain countries are intent on developing nuclear arsenals.

The Cold War super powers have also used chemical weapons in their own inimitable ways—the United States used Agent Orange as a herbicide in Vietnam, which caused untold grief against both the native population and its own soldiers, and the former Soviet Union is suspected of having used chemical weapons in its war in Afghanistan.

Hundreds of films, videos, and television programs have been produced on various aspects of nuclear weapons and nuclear war. The vast majority of such films were produced in the 1950s during the outset of the "atomic age" and throughout the 1980s when antinuclear activists across the globe protested the nuclear arms race and the threat of nuclear annihilation. Far fewer were produced in the 1960s and 1970s. The fewest have been produced in the 1990s. With the end of the Cold War and a less bellicose stance among the five acknowledged nuclear powers, many filmmakers may have seen little point in producing films on a subject that was apparently no longer of wide public concern. However, with increasing speculation about a nuclear arms race between India and Pakistan along with the possible proliferation of nuclear weapons to other states, the quiescence of filmmakers may end.

Hundreds of films have been made about various aspects of the atomic bombings of Hiroshima and Nagasaki. These have included archival footage of the devastation wrought by the atomic bomb, documentaries, Hollywood dramas and other feature films, and science fiction movies. Many of the documentaries use stock footage of the aftermath of the atomic bomb and/or include interviews with survivors. Among the subject matter covered in such films are the reasons behind the decision by the United States to drop the atomic bombs; the suffering of the victims in the immediate aftermath of the bombings; the long-term impact, psychological and physical, of the atomic bombings on the survivors; the insights, feelings, and memories of the survivors; the effects of the atomic bombings on buildings as well as vegetation; art created by the survivors; and the comments of survivors about their fears that the leaders of the world will not heed their warnings about the horror of nuclear war.

Far fewer feature (fiction) films have been produced about nuclear war. There are numerous reasons for this, but certainly one of the foremost is the fact that in the US during the 1950s, the activities of Senator Joseph McCarthy and the House Un-American Activities Committee virtually put a halt to the production of controversial films, especially those that could be perceived as "unpatriotic." Thus, according to Robert Musil, during "much of the 1950s nuclear war went untreated in Hollywood with the exception of films . . . that closely resembled official government positions." Once the McCarthy period was on the wane, numerous films were made. However, the "Bomb" and the subject of nuclear war often served merely as a plot situation for poorly written and easily forgettable movies. This was particularly true of a profusion of science fiction films. A classic exception was Stanley Kubrick's satire, *Dr. Strangelove, or How I Learned to Stop Worrying and Love the Bomb.* Then in the 1980s, following huge antinuclear rallies both in Europe and the United States, numerous feature films and television movies were made about the dangers of nuclear weapons and nuclear war. Many were criticized for either having weak plots, being melodramatic, or being technically incorrect with regard to nuclear technology or the effects of nuclear weapons. Still, it must be acknowledged that several of these films prompted debate in the United States and beyond between political officials, military personnel, and members of the public. A prime example was *The Day After,* a made-for-television movie about the aftereffects of nuclear war and the horrendous impact on the citizens of Kansas. It garnered a wide audience and engendered considerable debate among members of the public and their political representatives.

Of the numerous documentaries produced about the dangers of nuclear weapons and war, many are extremely informative. Among the topics covered in these films are the following: all-out nuclear war scenarios; an examination of the possible ways that nuclear war might erupt; the devastation that would be caused by a nuclear war; the power of the hydrogen bomb in comparison with the atomic bombs that were dropped on Hiroshima and Nagasaki; various nations' preparations for nuclear war; the possibility and consequences of a preemptive nuclear strike by one nuclear power against another; the impact of a single nuclear bomb on a city; the problems of vertical and horizontal nuclear proliferation; pros and cons of a space-based nuclear "defense"; the efficacy of civil defense in the event of nuclear war; medical problems that would be incurred in a nuclear war; psychological effects of the threat of nuclear war on the citizens of nuclear powers; children's' fears of the threat of nuclear war; points of view of citizens in countries stockpiling nuclear weapons; views of nuclear critics; and antinuclear protests.

Numerous areas still need to be addressed: the direct link between the so-called "peaceful atom" and the "military atom"; the problems and dangers of horizontal nuclear proliferation; the intransigence of the members of the so-called nuclear club to seriously cut back and/or eliminate their nuclear arsenals; the secret and not-so-secret trade between nations of nuclear knowledge and technology; actual cases in which the United States or the former Soviet Union went on nuclear alert or contemplated the use of nuclear weapons; an examination of the many proposals that have been explored over the past forty years to reduce the threat of nuclear war; and an examination of the concepts of "nuclear winter" and "nuclear fall," as well as their highly significant ramifications for humanity and the planet.

Far fewer films have been produced about chemical and biological weapons and warfare. As far as nonfiction is concerned, unlike the hundreds of their nuclear counterparts, some tens of films have been made about chemical and biological warfare. Interestingly and tellingly, however, more films about these topics have been produced in the late 1980s and the 1990s than on the issue of nuclear weapons and nuclear warfare. Among the topics addressed vis-a-vis chemical weapons and warfare are: the use of napalm by the United States during the Vietnam War; the political, legal, and military and medical aspects of the Agent Orange controversy; the suffering that US military personnel experienced due to LSD experiments in the 1950s, Agent Orange during the Vietnam War, and unexplained illnesses among veterans of the

Gulf War; the suspicion that Iraq used chemical warfare against Iran's civilians during the Iran/Iraq war in the 1980s; the US military's plan to combat chemical weapons; the alarming proliferation of chemical weapons; the way in which chemical warfare might be conducted; and the problem of disposing of existing, older chemical weapons. Films that address biological weapons and warfare address such issues as: Japan's experiments in germ warfare during World War II; the impact of biological warfare on the average citizen and the planet; the interests of smaller states and terrorist groups in obtaining biological weapons as a cheap alternative to nuclear weapons; and the debate over whether there is any effective defense against biological weapons.

With the increase in nuclear tensions and as more and more nations attempt to build, stockpile and/or threaten or actually use chemical or biological weapons on their enemies, filmmakers are bound to begin to explore such critical issues in an ever increasing number of films.

Selected Films on Nuclear, Chemical, and Biological Weapons and Warfare

The Day After (150 min., color, videocassette). Available from Social Studies Service, 10,000 Culver Blvd., Dept. A4, P.O. Box 802, Culver City, CA 90232–0802. This made-for-television movie is about the aftereffects of nuclear war as Kansas citizens attempt to cope with myriad horrors. Some critics have asserted that the movie presents a hysterical view of a complex situation, while others contend that the horrors it portrays are limited and less severe than those that would result should a nuclear war occur.

Fighting the Poor Man's Atom Bomb (28 min., color, videocassette). Available from Carousel Film and Video, 260 Fifth Ave., Suite 905, New York, NY 10001. This documentary explores the methods and equipment used by the US military to protect against the dangers of toxic chemicals and biological weapons.

The Germ Genie (44 min., color, videocassette). Available from Films for the Humanities, and Sciences, PO Box 2053, Princeton, NJ 08543–2053. This video traces the history of biological warfare from the Middle Ages through the 1990s. In doing so, it examines the latest biological weapons research under way in laboratories in the United States and Great Britain. It includes a debate between military experts and skeptical scientists about whether defense against germ warfare is possible.

Ground Zero (52 min., B&W, videocassette). Available from CBS News, 524 57th Street, New York, NY 10019. This initial section of the CBS series, entitled "The Defense of the United States," examines the prospects, preparation, and consequences of a nuclear war. It includes a detailed description of the effects of a 15-megaton nuclear bomb on the Strategic Air Command headquarters in Omaha, Nebraska.

Hiroshima/Nagasaki, August 1945 (17 min., B&W, videocassette). Available from Circle Film Programs, 11 West 53rd Street, New York, NY 10019. This film presents actual footage of the aftermath of the atomic bombing of Hiroshima and Nagasaki as well as comments by numerous survivors.

Legacy of Hiroshima (60 min., color, videocassette). Available from the Wilmington College Peace Resource Center, Hiroshima/Nagasaki Memorial Collection, Pyle Center, Box 1183, Wilmington, OH 45177. This documentary presents the insights, feelings, and memories of survivors of the atomic bombing of Hiroshima.

Missiles of October (155 min., color, videocassette). Available from Audio/Brandon Films, 34 MacQuestion Parkway, South, Mt. Vernon, NY 10550. This is a feature-length dramatization of the Cuban missile crisis.

Nuclear Nightmares (90 min., b/w, videocassette). Available form Corinth Films, 410 East 62nd Street, New York, NY 10021. Peter Ustinov examines four possible ways that nuclear war might erupt: escalation, proliferation, accident, and preemptive first strike. Each sequence culminates in a fallout shelter where Ustinov reveals what happened. It has been called irreverent and cynical.

Poisoned Winds of War (58 min., color). Available form Coronet Film and Video, 108 Wilmot Rd., Deerfield, IL 60015–5196. Produced in 1991, this is a segment from the public television series, *Nova,* which examines the disturbing proliferation of chemical weapons. In doing so, it discusses the fact that although official US policy bans first use of chemical weapons, the 1986 Defense Authorization Act approved the production of binary chemical weapons. It also explores how military personnel are being trained to operate in a "chemically-secure" environment.

Dr. Strangelove, or How I Learned to Stop Worrying and Love the Bomb (93 min., B&W, videocassette). Available from Columbia Cinematheque, 711 Fifth Ave., New York, NY 10022. This scathing satire and feature film submits that the mechanisms the US and USSR rely on to prevent war—nuclear deterrence, technological advances, etc.—are the very things that could lead to nuclear destruction.

The War Game (50 min., videocassette). Available from Films, Inc., 1144 Wilmette Ave., Wilmette, IL 60091. This BBC film simulates the effect of a nuclear attack on a town in Kent, England, in which a large proportion of the population is killed. It shows the survivors trying to evacuate while experiencing widespread chaos. The film, which is extremely graphic, is reportedly based on information supplied by experts in the areas of nuclear defense, economics, and medicine. Aside from the actual footage from Hiroshima and Nagasaki, It is one of the most powerful and devastating films on the effects of nuclear war.

—*Samuel Totten*

FILMS OF FUTURISTIC DESTRUCTION

From *War of the Worlds* to *On the Beach* to *Independence Day,* film has explored the fears and tensions that the world has of nuclear destruction or invasion by aliens. Film theory, the scholarly analysis of filmic themes, involving movies of the 1940s and 1950s never mention the Holocaust and rarely the word genocide, but the issues are there subtextually, just beneath the surface.

There have been two major defining metaphors or subtexts of futuristic destruction: Hiroshima or atomic bombing and McCarthyism/Communism.

Hiroshima films are also of two kinds: the first is the *Godzilla* films directed by Tomoyuki Tanaka, beginning in 1954. These are films in which a strange dinosaur-like monster emerges from the ocean, after atomic testing has taken place. Godzilla almost destroys Japan and by extension the world before he is himself destroyed. The *Godzilla* films emerged out of Japanese fantasies of strange creatures under the rubble of the Hiroshima bombing. The message is clear: uncontrolled nuclearism will destroy the universe. At the same time, a theme of the biological unknown is also invoked, as humankind faces unknown awaiting forms of mass death resulting from biological transformations such as nature continuously shows itself capable of producing to kill literally millions of human beings. Godzilla is the animal-like shape of this fear. The second kind is much more direct. In films such as *On the Beach* (1959) or *The Day After,* this genre deals with what happens to survivors after the "bomb" is dropped, the desolation of survivors and the near impossibility of survival in the long run. This subtextual genre is quite simple and straighforward.

Today, this genre is more popular than ever, though it has been sanitized and secularized. *Godzilla* becomes *The Blob, Jaws, Piranha,* or *Anaconda.* Such 50s and 60s variations as *Day of the Triffids, Panic in the Streets,* or *La Peste* emerge in the 90s as *Typhoon, Earthquake,* and *Arachnophobia.* The message is that nature has gone beserk, deranged, due to environmental tampering and man's insensitivity to the balance of life.

The second genre is based on the McCarthyism/Communism fear, the so-called "Red Scare." McCarthy was a US Senator in the 1950s who intimidated President Dwight D. Eisenhower and the entire USA with his fantasies and fears of a Communist "take-over" of America. It led to great paranoia, crushed careers and destroyed families. McCarthyism was fed by the fear that Soviet Russia would use the "bomb" to annihilate the American way of life and would also burrow within its system and kill it from inside. These political fears manifested themselves in some movies that combined the theme of supernatural monsters with a metaphor of a danger burrowing from within such as *The Thing,* about a monster under ice who emerges due to nuclear pollution; *The Creature from the Black Lagoon;* or the best example of all, *The Invasion of the Body Snatchers,* wherein aliens enter the skin of mortals and take over their bodies, looking like ordinary Americans but with sinister ambitions to take over the entire country. A more recent update of this theme, but much more humorous (which indicates less fear), is *Men in Black* (1997).

The fear of nuclear destruction has diminished somewhat in the 1990s and the Communist empire has vanished, but nuclear terrorism is still a threat. As Joseph Rotblat, a Manhattan Project scientist, professor of physics at the University of London, and winner of the 1995 Nobel Prize in Peace, has said: "I believe we have made significant progress (in eliminating nuclear weapons) . . . but I am disappointed that the progress is not greater, particularly that the nuclear powers still stick to the same way of thinking as they did during the Cold War—that nuclear weapons are needed for security."

However, in the 1970s and 1980s, as the Communist fears of the Cold War wound down, film directors such as Steven Spielberg and George Lucas made films like *E.T.* and *Star Wars* in which the "aliens" are far from dangerous; they are downright friendly, even cuddly, like teddy bears. It would be interesting to ask Spielberg how the Holocaust intertwines with aliens from other planets. Does he see a connection between these two forms of destruction—man-made evil on earth and alien-evil from Mars? Presumably he would answer that man-made evil is much worse. Mars may be friendly. Outer space may be entertaining.

A third wave of films has also arisen that is *both* humorous and brooding. Here aliens are evil, even difficult to destroy, but wit, caprice, and concentrated energy, plus a winning Afro-American or two will prevail. Examples include *Men in Black* and *Independence Day,* both starring the black comic, Will Smith. Some of the *Star Trek* and *Star Wars* series are also darker, pessimistic, yet ultimately victorious. There will be a happy ending amidst great loss.

In conclusion, films of futuristic destruction, whether of nuclear omnicide or environmental destruction (such as *Soylent Green, Planet of the Apes,* and *Blade Runner*) reflect the underlying fears of our generation. Such fears have abated somewhat as we have undertaken the task of reducing nuclear stockpiles and environmental threats; however, as we approach the millenium, these fears resurface. These fears of environmental catastrophe can also be seen as a result of man's purposeful neglect of the planet that can be viewed as a form of ecological genocide.

—*Jack Nusan Porter*

References and Recommended Reading

Goin, Peter (1991). *Nuclear Landscapes.* Baltimore, MD: Johns Hopkins University Press.

Nuclear Age Peace Foundation (1997). *Waging Peace World Wide. Journal of the Nuclear Age Peace Foundation,* Special Issue, 7(3).

FINAL SOLUTION

The Final Solution (*Die Endlösung*) of the "Jewish Problem" involved the systematic annihilation of European Jewry. This "solution" differed radically and fatally from two earlier European attempts to "solve the Jewish problem." For example, in Western Europe, the "Enlightenment" ushered in by Napoleanic reform, assumed that given the opportunity of political emancipation all Jews would assimilate. In Eastern Europe, Konstantin Pobedonostsev, appointed by Czar Alexander III to solve Russia's "Jewish problem," conceived his "infamous formula," one-third will convert, one-third will starve and one-third will emigrate. In both Eastern and Western Europe, there was a prevailing and diffuse cultural antisemitism. However, Nazism sought the extermination of the Jewish people. The Hitlerian "solution" was an attempt to create a new, *Judenrein* (Jew-free) world. Achievement of this apocalyptic goal involved all segments of German society and the pursuit of Jews throughout Europe. Some fifteen million people were murdered by the Nazis, but the purpose of the Holocaust was to murder all Jews. In Elie Wiesel's telling formulation: "Not all victims were Jews, but every Jew was a victim."

—*Alan L. Berger*

References and Recommended Reading

Browning, Christopher R. (1992). *Ordinary Men: Reserve Police Battalon 101 and the Final Solution in Poland.* New York: HarperCollins.

Hilberg, Raul (1985). *The Destruction of European Jewry.* Three volumes. Revised and Definitive Edition. New York: Holmes and Meier.

Source Document

FROM A SPEECH BY HIMMLER BEFORE SENIOR SS OFFICERS IN POZNAN, OCTOBER 4, 1943

I also want to speak to you here, in complete frankness, of a really grave chapter. Amongst ourselves, for once, it shall be said quite openly, but all the same we will never speak about it in public. Just as we did not hesitate on June 30, 1934 *[The reference is to "the Night of the Long Knives" when the SA leader Röhm and his troop were murdered.—Ed.]* to do our duty as we were ordered, and to stand comrades who had erred against the wall and shoot them, and we never spoke about it and we never will speak about it. It

continues

continued

was a matter of natural tact that is alive in us, thank God, that we never talked about it amongst ourselves, that we never discussed it. Each of us shuddered and yet each of us knew clearly that the next time he would do it again if it were an order, and if it were necessary.

I am referring here to the evacuation of the Jews, the extermination of the Jewish people. This is one of the things that is easily said: "The Jewish people are going to be exterminated," that's what every Party member says, "sure, it's in our program, elimination of the Jews, extermination—it'll be done." And then they all come along, the 80 million worthy Germans, and each one has his one decent Jew. Of course, the others are swine, but this one, he is a first-rate Jew. Of all those who talk like that, not one has seen it happen, not one has had to go through with it. Most of you men know what it is like to see 100 corpses side by side, or 500 or 1,000. To have stood fast through this and—except for cases of human weakness—to have stayed decent, that has made us hard. This is an unwritten and never-to-be-written page of glory in our history, for we know how difficult it would be for us if today—under bombing raids and the hardships and deprivations of war—if we were still to have the Jews in every city as secret saboteurs, agitators, and inciters. If the Jews were still lodged in the body of the German nation, we would probably by now have reached the stage of 1916–17.

The wealth they possessed we took from them. I gave a strict order, which has been carried out by SS *Obergruppenfrürer* Pohl, that this wealth will of course be turned over to the Reich in its entirety. We have taken none of it for ourselves. Individuals who have erred will be punished in accordance with the order given by me at the start, threatening that anyone who takes as much as a single Mark of this money is a dead man. A number of SS men—they are not very many—committed this offense, and they shall die. There will be no mercy. We had the moral right, we had the duty towards our people to destroy this people that wanted to destroy us. But we do not have the right to enrich ourselves by so much as a fur, as a watch, by one Mark or a cigarette or anything else. We do not want, in the end, because we destroyed a bacillus, to be infected by this bacillus and to die. I will never stand by and watch while even a small rotten spot develops or takes hold. Wherever it may form we will together burn it away. All in all, however, we can say that we have carried out this most difficult of tasks in a spirit of love for our people. And we have suffered no harm to our inner being, our soul, our character.

Source: Arad, Yitzhak; Gutman, Yisrael; and Margaliot, Abraham (Eds.) (1981). *Documents on the Holocaust: Selected Sources on the Destruction of the Jews of Germany and Austria, Poland and the Soviet Union.* Jerusalem: Yad Vashem.

FIRST-PERSON ACCOUNTS OF GENOCIDE

A uniquely valuable source for probing into the myriad complexities and horrors of genocide is that of first-person accounts. The strongest accounts provide a personal perspective that powerfully depicts what the ever-increasing deprivation of human rights and, ultimately, the horrors of genocide mean to the individual. "First-person accounts" refer to any written, oral or videotaped account by survivors and other individuals who witnessed any aspect of a genocidal event. Such accounts may appear in any of the following forms: memoirs; autobiographies; diaries, interviews, oral histories, testimony at trials and other official and unofficial hearings; statements in texts, journals, and other periodicals; audiotapes; and videotapes/films.

The greatest number of personal accounts is available on the Holocaust.

These number in the tens of thousands. There is a dearth of accounts concerning the fate of the Gypsies during the Holocaust years. A much smaller but still relatively large amount (when compared with what is available in regard to still other genocides) is available on the Armenian Genocide and the Soviet manmade genocidal famine in the Ukraine. An even smaller number of accounts exist on the Soviet deportations of whole nations, the Bangladesh genocide, and the Cambodian genocide. Finally, a minute number of accounts are available about the slaughter of the Hereros, the Tibet genocide, the slaughter of the Ibos in Nigeria, the genocidal acts in Uganda under Idi Amin and Milton Obote, the genocide in East Timor, the slaughter of the Guatemalan Indians, the slaughter of the Aché Indians in Paraguay, the genocide of the Brazilian Indians, and the Rwandan genocide in 1994.

Survivors have written and/or spoken about their personal experiences for various reasons, including bearing witness to: the humiliation, degradation, brutality, and atrocities to which they and others were subjected; the way of life of their people that was either wholly or partially eliminated; their efforts to retain a sense of self and humanity under conditions of horrific duress and brutal conditions; acts of resistance; the altruism of those who risked their own lives in order to hide and/or rescue the victimized; the depressing fact that the world looked upon their plight with resounding silence and indifference; the memory of the dead; and, in many cases, a life-affirming hope that present and future generations will learn to live in harmony.

First-person accounts also contribute to the corroboration of key points and facts in the historical record of a genocide, and also add new and unique information to the existing storehouse of historical data. Likewise, they help to refute the insidious attempts by so-called "historical revisionists" who attempt to minimize or deny the occurrence of a genocidal act. Finally, they become key sources for research and educative purposes.

Some scholars question the validity of using first-person accounts as key sources in the study of historic events, asserting that such accounts lack the desired objectivity, are extremely difficult to test for reliability, may present inaccurate information or hearsay as facts, and/or fail to cast information in a sufficiently broad historical context. Other scholars, however, assert that first-person accounts are valuable historical sources in that they provide unique personal insights into the genocidal process, the consistency of information found in various accounts about the same incident(s) provide valuable corroboration of facts, and that there are certain issues and events about which information can only be gleaned from first-person accounts.

As valuable as first-person accounts of genocide are, they are not without certain significant limitations, including: the accuracy of the witnesses' memory; the individuality of experiences encountered; a general lack of attention in the accounts to sociopolitical factors that led up to and culminated in the genocide; problems of self-censorship of unwelcome behaviors; and, in certain cases, the format used to relate his/her story (e.g., the use of the third-person or those that are ghost-written).

With the main exception of diaries, many first-person accounts of genocide have been written, recorded, or filmed at least five years or more after the conclusion of the events. Memoirs, oral histories, and interviews that were either written or conducted a year or more after the fact are frequently not as accurate in their presentation of events as those found in diaries. As memory fades, subtle but significant details may become garbled or lost. Certain perceptions may be influenced by later experiences and ideas, and some witnesses may confuse rumors with reality. Some may inadvertently embellish certain details and then accept the latter as facts. Verification of the accuracy of information found in these accounts becomes imperative. That is fairly easy to do in regard to the more general events in which large numbers of people were involved (e.g., the discriminatory practices put into effect by a genocidal government, deportations, or methods of killing), but it is more problematic when testimonies address little known and/or isolated events that involved a small number of people or sole individuals. Thus far, a much greater emphasis has been placed on collecting survivors' accounts than scrutinizing the information for accuracy.

Most genocidal acts in this century have lasted several years, taken place over enormous expanses of land, and involved hundreds of thousands if not millions of people. In fact, therefore, no single person or group is capable of providing a comprehensive picture of a genocidal act based on their experiences and observations because it is not humanly possible to do so. By their nature, first-person accounts provide uniquely personal views of specific aspects of the larger genocidal crime.

Some accounts suffer from self-censorship of distasteful or loathsome behavior either committed by the witness, family members of the witness and/or fellow victims. Such actions may involve collaboration with the perpetrators, denying assistance to family members or others in dire need, mistreating other victims, etc. Though speaking of memoirs of survivors in general, Aharon Appelfeld's observation is especially apropos to the issue of self-censorship: "If you read the many collections of testimony written about the Holocaust, you will immediately see that they are actually repressions, meant to put events in proper chronological order. They are neither introspection nor anything resembling introspection, but rather the careful weaving together of many external facts in order to veil the inner truth" [Appelfeld, Aharon (1994). *Beyond Despair: Three Lectures and a Conversation with Philip Roth.* New York: Fromm International Publishing, p. 14].

There is a critical need to collect as many accounts as possible from the aging survivors of genocidal acts. There is also a dire need to collect as many accounts as possible of the least documented and from more recent genocidal acts in this century (e.g., those that took place in Bangladesh, Burundi, East Timor, the Former Yugoslavia and Rwanda). Likewise, there is the need to translate accounts into various languages so that more scholars will have greater access to the information. The information in all accounts must be analyzed, checked and cross-checked in order to glean additional information about little-known aspects of the genocidal acts, to cull the key information and to corroborate the facts, statements, and assertions in each of them, and/or to note any discrepancies and factual errors. The accounts also need to be catalogued in a systematic manner in order to facilitate their use by scholars and others.

—Samuel Totten

References and Recommended Reading

Hovannisian, Richard G. (1980). *The Armenian Holocaust: A Bibliography Relating to the Deportations, Massacres, and Dispersion of the Armenian People, 1915–1923.* Cambridge, MA: Armenian Heritage Press. 43 pp.

Totten, Samuel (Ed.) (1991). *First-Person Accounts of Genocidal Acts Committed in the Twentieth Century: An Annotated Bibliography.* Westport, CT: Greenwood Publishers. 351 pp.

Totten, Samuel (1991). First person accounts of genocidal acts. In Charny, Israel W. (Ed.), *Genocide: A Critical Bibliographic Review. Volume 2.* London: Mansell Publishing; and New York. Facts on File, pp 321–362.

Totten, Samuel; Parsons, William S.; and Charny, Israel W. (Eds.) (1997). *Century of Genocide: Eyewitness Accounts and Critical Views.* New York: Garland Publishing. 488 pp. Paperback, expanded, with title change of original hardcover, *Genocide in the*

Twentieth Century: Critical Essays and Eyewitness Accounts, 1995.

FORTUNOFF VIDEO ARCHIVE FOR HOLOCAUST TESTIMONIES

I cannot teach this book. Instead,
I drop copies on their desks,
like bombs on sleeping towns,
and let them read.
—Thomas E. Thornton, "On Wiesel's Night"

The Fortunoff Video Archive for Holocaust Testimonies at the Yale University Library presently holds more than 3,800 videotaped testimonies of Holocaust witnesses. The videotaping of these first-person accounts began in 1979 as a grassroots project in New Haven, Connecticut. When almost 200 testimonies had been completed, the collection was deposited at Yale. Since then affiliated taping has been initiated by twenty-three North American projects as well as in Athens, Buenos Aires, Belarus, Belgrade, Berlin, Bratislava, Brussels, Israel, London, Paris, Poland, Ukraine, and Thessaloniki.

Other repositories contain substantial collections of written or audiotaped testimonies. However, the television image, using an open ended, free-flowing interviewing process, discloses expressive details about the day-to-day experiences of the witnesses with a force that can hardly be exaggerated. The witnesses discuss their earliest memories and postwar experiences, as well as what happened to them during the Holocaust. Among our aims are making the testimonies intellectually accessible to researchers and scholars, preserving them, and creating educational programs available on a loan basis to schools and community groups.

Records for 1,500 testimonies have been entered into the RLIN's (Research Libraries Information Network) international bibliographic catalog and in Yale's online public access catalog, which is available on the World Wide Web. In 1990 a *Guide* was published containing 255 testimony records. A second *Guide* containing records for the 572 testimonies was published in 1994. The *Guide* and the database contain a subject index that includes topical and geographic headings, and a two hundred word summary of each testimony. Through the use of the database and/or the published *Guide,* researchers have intellectual access to the video testimonies that are available for viewing at the Fortunoff Archive.

A descriptive list of programs is available from the Fortunoff Video Archive and on the Video Archive's homepage. It includes edited testimonies and composites of several witness accounts. The programs can be borrowed for periods from two weeks to five years. They often provide students with the only opportunity they will have to "meet" a survivor. They convey not only the words of the witnesses, but their images—persons with whom viewers can identify and from whom they do not have to distance themselves. Through these living portraits students do not see the survivor as "the other," which can happen when they look at horrific photographs or documentary footage of the camps and liberation. The telling includes tears, facial expressions, and body-language, nuances that cannot be conveyed in any other genre.

Researchers, educators, documentary producers, museum personnel and students of all ages have visited the Fortunoff Video Archive and incorporated its materials into their work. It is the hope of the Archive that the testimonies will assist educators to "teach this book," supplementing written texts and personalizing Holocaust history.

Additional information about the Fortunoff Video Archive is available through the Internet.

For further information, contact Fortunoff Video Archive for Holocaust Testimonies, Yale University, P.O. Box 205240, New Haven, CO 06520–8240, tel: 1–203–432–1879, website: http://www.library.yale.edu/testimonies.

—Joanne Weiner Rudof

References and Recommended Reading

Hartman, Geoffrey H. (1996). *The Longest Shadow: In the Aftermath of the Holocaust.* Bloomington, IN: Indiana University Press.

Langer, Lawrence L. (1991). *Holocaust Testimonies: The Ruins of Memory.* New Haven, CT: Yale University Press.

G

GAS CHAMBERS

Gas chambers were crucial in nazism's death camp universe. While German troops had used poison gas in World War I, *the systematic gassing of noncombatant civilians in chambers especially constructed for this purpose was new in the annals of human history.* The German use of gas to kill Jews and other unarmed civilians evolved in three stages. Initially (1940–1941) mobile vans were employed. This consisted of directing the van's exhaust fumes into the packed "cargo" area. Those inside died of suffocation. The method was apparently used first against the mentally ill and retarded and physically disabled (who were generally killed either by lethal injection or by gassing in vans, until these killings were stopped in response to protests by family, friends and pastors). When next applied by the *Einsatzgruppen* military squads to Jews, army commanders complained that this method was too slow and was exacting a high emotional cost on the men under their command who had to remove the bodies. The second stage occurred with construction of the first stationary gas chamber at Chelmno (Kulmhof), the first operational killing center (8 December 1941). The third stage was ushered in by the construction of enormous gas chambers at Auschwitz, Treblinka and other death camps (1943).

—*Alan L. Berger*

References and Recommended Reading

Ehrenberg, Ilya, and Grossman, Vasily (1981). *The Black Book: The Ruthless Murder of Jews by German-Fascist Invaders, throughout the Temporarily-Occupied Regions of the Soviet Union and in the Death Camps of Poland, during the War of 1941–1945*. Translated by John Glad and James S. Levine. New York: Holocaust Library.

Reitlinger, Gerald (1953). *The Final Solution: The Attempt to Exterminate the Jews of Europe 1943–1945*. New York: Beechhurst Press.

GENGHIS KHAN

Born the son of a Mongolian tribal leader in 1167 and originally named Temujin, Genghis Khan was the greatest military leader of his generation whose empire ultimately extended beyond the borders of his native Mongolia to include both Russia and China. After his own father was poisoned when he was only ten years old, Temujin entered the service of the then-leader of Mongolia, Toghril Khan, and quickly became known for his intelligence and fearlessness in the face of the enemy. By the time he was thirty-nine, he had himself become Genghis Khan or "Ruler of All Mongol Chiefs." One year later, in 1207, he launched his first military offensive against his enemies on the Asian mainland. Continuing his forays against the Northern Chinese empire, by 1215 he had successfully established himself in Beijing; and by 1223 he had defeated the Russian army as well as the armies of Turkistan, Afghanistan, much of Persia and large parts of Eastern Europe. He is believed to have died in 1227 in the midst of yet another military campaign.

Khan's success was not only based on his military and organizational genius but on his brutalization of those he defeated, putting to death not only those he defeated in battle, but vast numbers of men, women, and children who found themselves in conquered territories. The actual numbers of dead are said to be in the several hundreds of thousands, though the actual numbers will never be accurately known.

—Steven L. Jacobs

GENOCIDAL MASSACRES

There is consensus among genocide scholars that a case of mass killing can be genocidal even if it does not constitute a genocide as strictly defined. Henry R. Huttenbach has suggested that, "In the process of categorizing acts of genocide, a secondary category ought to be included under the rubric "genocidal," indicative of events that can be clearly identified in character even though the crime was not consummated *in toto* . . ." [Huttenbach, Henry R. (1988). Locating the Holocaust on the genocide spectrum: Toward a methodology of definition and categorization. *Holocaust and Genocide Studies,* 3(3) p. 294.] Leo Kuper proposed the concept of genocidal massacre to characterize acts of mass killing that do not conform strictly to the criteria of the Genocide Convention, but have some features that do fit it. Helen Fein used the term for "massacres that are not part of a continuous genocide but are committed by an authority or other organized group against a particular ethnic or other distinguishable group." Israel Charny used the term for "events of mass murder that are on a smaller scale" than genocide, and points out that this concept describes "many pogroms, mass executions, and mass murders that are, intrinsically, no less vicious and no less tragically final for the victims."

—Eric Markusen

References and Recommended Reading

Charny, Israel W. (1994). Toward a generic definition of genocide. In Andreopolous, George L. (Ed.),

Genocidal Massacres in Algeria

As of November 1998, an estimated 70,000 people, many of them women and children, have been killed in armed clashes and outright massacres since the military government voided elections in 1992 that probably would have been won by militant Islamic fundamentalists. Prevented from attaining power by the ballot, the fundamentalists have attempted to seize it through terror. According to one observer, "The violence has been so barbaric, so extensive, so extreme, that it is taking the shape of genocide. These are crimes against humanity, and we need to hear, from everywhere, the firm condemnation of those who are responsible."

A characteristic style of massacre has been when members of the Armed Islamic Group, equipped with shotguns, knives, swords and axes, invade a village. The invaders take attractive women and girls with them as sexual captives and slaughter the rest of the villagers unmercifully. The majority of the panicked victims have been women and children. Many of the bodies are burned and some are decapitated, in some cases, the heads of victims were left on doorsteps, reported one veteran journalist.

—Press Reports

Genocidal Massacre in a Church in Liberia

In August 1990, Liberian government troops were responsible for the massacre of at least 600 refugees, including babies, sheltering in a church in the Liberian capital Monrovia. Survivors of the attack said government troops burst into St. Peter's Lutheran church on the outskirts of the city about 2 A.M. Monrovian time and butchered men, women, children, and babies with knives, guns and cutlasses. They said a group of 30 soldiers with machine guns broke down the church door and fired point blank at some of the 2,000 refugees who had taken shelter. Soldiers then went to the upper floor and shot at hundreds of refugees sleeping there. The survivors said soldiers butchered men with knives and shot women and children with machine guns. Soldiers asked women who tried to flee with their children to stand aside. Other soldiers then fired on them. "We thought they had come to ask us questions. Then they started killing and everyone began screaming and trying to hide," said one man who hid in the church roof during the massacre.

The entire floor of the church was thick with bloodstains and bodies were huddled under pews where people had tried to hide. The bodies of boys aged seven or eight were draped on the church altar and a pile of bodies was half-hidden in a dark corner beside the altar. Dead women lay on the floor with children still wrapped in shawls on their backs. The church crucifix had been thrown to the ground and bullet holes riddled the ceiling.

—*Press Reports*

Genocide Knows No Borders

A news story from Borneo contained a small reminder that Hitler wasn't the only person who believed in exterminating his enemies. Residents of Mandor, a city on the island, are troubled because someone changed a sign on a memorial for civilians who were slaughtered during the Japanese occupation of the island during World War II. The original sign identified the spot as "The Massacre Place." The new sign calls it "The Place of Mass Burial." Residents of the area said they suspect the provincial government changed the wording to make it less offensive to Japanese visitors.

The memorial marks a killing field where civilians were slaughtered by Japanese troops. Some residents of the area have put the number of victims at 20,000, including scholars, doctors, officials and business leaders who might have posed a threat to Japanese rule. A man whose parents died at the spot and who is trying to keep the memory of the atrocity alive said: "In a few years, the Japanese tried to kill all they thought would oppose them."

The evil that is genocide can't be measured simply by counting the victims. For the survivors of the Massacre Place who are trying to keep the story from being toned down, what happened near Mandor constitutes their own terrible version of a holocaust.

—*Excerpted from an editorial in the Omaha Morning World-Herald*

Genocide: Conceptual and Historical Dimensions. Philadelphia, PA: University of Pennsylvania Press, pp. 64–94.
Fein, Helen (1993). Discriminating genocide from war crimes: Vietnam and Afghanistan reexamined. *Denver Journal of International Law,* 22(1), 29–62.
Kuper, Leo (1981). *Genocide: Its Political Use in the Twentieth Century.* London: Penguin Books; and New Haven, CT: Yale University Press (1982).

GENOCIDAL MENTALITY

In their 1990 comparative study of the psychological and social processes involved in both the perpetration of the Holocaust and the preparations for nuclear warfare, psychiatrist Robert Jay Lifton, and sociologist Eric Markusen, defined the "genocidal mentality" as "a mind-set that includes individual and collective willingness to produce, design, and, according to certain standards of necessity, use weapons known to destroy entire human populations—millions, or tens of millions, of people" (p. 3). In a broader sense, the genocidal mentality refers to the willingness of governments, and their citizens, to engage in the mass killing of innocent people. The motives for such slaughter vary from case to case, but genocide scholars Frank Chalk and Kurt Jonassohn have identified four of the most common rationales: to eliminate a group perceived by the killers as a threat; to spread terror among enemies; to accumulate economic wealth; and "to implement a belief, a theory, or an ideology."

Lifton and Markusen found that both the Holocaust and the nuclear arms race emerged out of periods of psychological and social trauma that led to the ideological embrace of mass killing as a means of "curing" the trauma. In the Nazi case, the psychosocial trauma stemmed from defeat in the First World War followed by economic hardship and political instability; whereas in the nuclear case it reflected the terrifying reverberations of the atomic bombings of Hiroshima and Nagasaki and the post–World War II rise of the Soviet Union as a totalitarian superpower that soon developed its own nuclear arsenal. In the Nazi case, the mass killing was actual, while in the nuclear case the mass deaths were followed also by slow sequences of further deaths for those who experienced fatal radiation-associated illness through being exposed to the bombs or to nuclear tests in various countries. During the Cuban Missile Crisis of 1962, the United States and the Soviet Union came dangerously close to crossing the threshold into actual nuclear conflict.

Among the psychological and social processes Lifton and Markusen found contributing to the genocidal mentality in both cases were such factors as the extensive employment of euphemistic language that muted the deadly reality; professional socialization whereby incoming participants were coached and assisted by more deeply implicated participants; the capacity of the human mind to numb itself to disturbing thoughts and images; the conviction that killing (or being willing to kill) members of another group of people was necessary for the safety and security of one's own group; the legitimation of both projects by the highest governmental authorities; and the involvement of participants in vast bureaucracies in which division of labor and hierarchical authority diminished a sense of personal responsibility.

At the conclusion of their study, Lifton and Markusen urged the recognition and nurturing of a "species mentality" as an antithesis and alternative to the genocidal mentality. Such a species mentality entails an expansion of collective awareness, an altered sense of self that embraces our reality as members of a single, endangered species. The species mentality repudiates, on moral and empathic grounds, the resort to genocide and other egregious violations of human rights.

—Eric Markusen and Robert Jay Lifton

References and Recommended Reading
Chalk, Frank, and Jonassohn, Kurt (1990). *The History and Sociology of Genocide: Analyses and Case Studies.* New Haven, CT: Yale University Press.
Lifton, Robert Jay, and Markusen, Eric (1990). *The Genocidal Mentality: Nazi Holocaust and Nuclear Threat.* New York: Basic Books.

GENOCIDE: A CRITICAL BIBLIOGRAPHIC REVIEW

The series entitled *Genocide: A Critical Bibliographic Review* brings together scholars from different disciplines to summarize the work that has been done in their subject areas in a comprehensive encyclopedic essay accompanied by a critical bibliography that provides annotative summaries and evaluative remarks on the most important and useful books, articles and other materials in that specific area of the study of genocide.

Four volumes have been published to date:

Charny, Israel W. (Ed.) (1988). *Genocide: A Critical Bibliographic Review.* London: Mansell Publishing; and New York: Facts on File. 273 pp.
Charny, Israel W. (Ed.) (1991). *Genocide: A Critical Bibliographic Review. Volume 2.* London: Mansell Publishing; and New York: Facts on File. 432 pp.
Charny, Israel W. (Ed.) (1994). *The Widening Circle of Genocide. Volume 3 in the Series, Genocide: A Critical Bibliographic Review.* New Brunswick, NJ: Transaction Publishers. 375 pp.
Krell, Robert, and Sherman, Marc I. (Eds.) (1997). *Medical and Psychological Effects of the Concentration Camps on Holocaust Survivors. Volume 4 in the Series, Genocide: A Critical Bibliographic Review.* Series Editor: Israel W. Charny. New Brunswick, NJ: Transaction Publishers. 365 pp.

The initial volume in the series, published in 1988, was the first bibliography to address not only certain specific cases of genocide, such as the Holocaust and the Armenian Genocide, but also the study of genocide as a process, the development of the field of genocide studies, and thinking about possible steps that could be taken to intervene in cases of genocide and to prevent the eruption of genocide. The contributors to the series are drawn from a wide range of fields, including political science, international relations, law, psychology, sociology, education, and more. Throughout there is a clear overriding message that the genocides of each and every victim people are to be regarded reverently, let alone that all genocides are manifestations of a larger process of the readiness of human beings, individually, in mob or group actions, and as racial/ethnic/political entities, to resort to genocidal killings of groups of human beings.

The initial volume in the series was recognized by the American Library Association as an Outstanding Reference Work, and each of the volumes has earned major positive reviews as "indispensable" and "vital" for students and researchers of genocide. For additional information, consult the entry BIBLIOGRAPHIES ON THE HOLOCAUST AND GENOCIDE.

—*Israel W. Charny*

GENOCIDE AS A PROCESS

Genocide is usually the result of an evolution. A number of influences join to start this evolution. Difficult social conditions in a society greatly impact members of the group. They respond to this by turning against a subgroup of society. As they take action against this subgroup, the perpetrators, the rest of society (the bystanders) and the norms and institutions of society change, making increasing violence against the victims possible. The passivity of internal and external bystanders (outside nations) allows the unfolding of this evolution.

Difficult social conditions are frequently the starting point for genocide. They have varied forms: intense economic problems; or intense political con-

Inevitabilism: A Concept for Understanding the Process of Genocide

Colin Tatz's concept of "inevitabilism" tries to move away from the dichotomy of intentionalist and functionalist lines. Tatz argues that in the Jewish case all the ingredients necessary for genocide were in place. He likens the ingredients to the parts of an engine: What was "needed" in Germany was the radical driver, Hitler, to switch it on. As applied to the Armenian case, the "ingredients" include: the "ideas [Pan-Turkism] and acts of various designers and engineers [Enver, Talaat, and Jemal], fuel makers and fuel injectors [Special Organization]."

While the term is not an end in itself, and therefore should not be used loosely, it at least tries to put some light on this complex, chilling and perhaps unexplainable part of human behavior.

Tatz would readily admit that universal labels, universal explanations do not fit all genocides. In the end, there is only mass destruction of life.

—*International Network on Holocaust and Genocide*

flict within a society, including conflict between dominant groups and subordinate ones that are poor and have limited rights; or very great and rapid social changes; or their combination. These conditions create social chaos and disorganization and have great psychological impact.

Under such conditions people often turn to their group for support. They join together in *scapegoating* some other group for the life problems, or in creating ideologies that promise a better life but are destructive in that they identify some group as an enemy that stands in the way of the fulfillment of the ideology. Scapegoating and ideologies help people feel better about themselves, provide a new, hopeful view of reality in the midst of chaos, and create connection among those who scapegoat or join an ideological movement.

As the group or its members begin to harm the scapegoat or ideological enemy, they begin to change. As they persecute, abuse, torture or kill, individuals and groups "learn by doing." They change as the result of their own actions and become more committed to violence. Perpetrators justify their actions as a response to the actions or character of their victims. They further *devalue* and *dehumanize* their victims and in the end often exclude them from the human and moral realm. *Moral values and rules become inapplicable* to them. Institutions and organizations are created to harm or kill the victims. Norms of conduct profoundly change with regard to the victims.

All this is more likely to happen in cultures with certain characteristics. One of these is a history of devaluation of one group by another. Such cultural devaluation is usually deeply set and becomes especially influential when life conditions are difficult, as in the case of antisemitism in Germany. At times, in addition to devaluation by one group of another, there is a history of conflict and violence between two groups and intense mutual antagonism, as in the case of Rwanda and Bosnia. In other cases, even a period of peaceful coexistence and considerable intermingling between peoples, such as was true of a large number of Serbs, Croats, and Muslims in some cities in the Former Yugoslavia, can break down in the face of a re-eruption of historical hatreds and memories of past genocidal killings.

Other characteristics of culture that make the genocidal process probable include strong respect for authority in a society, a monolithic rather than pluralistic society, unhealed wounds due to past violence against the group, certain cultural self-concepts (belief in the group's superiority, often as a mode of overcoming fears of weakness-inferiority), and a history of violence in dealing with conflict. As Rummel has shown, totalitarian societies are far more likely to commit genocide than are democratic societies. Democratic states are especially unlikely to turn violently against a group when democracy is well-established and deep-seated rather than superficial.

The increasing violence against victims is made more likely by the *passivity of internal and external bystanders.* They tend to remain passive and they too change as they do so. They distance themselves from the victims, often by justifying the violence against them. The passivity of bystanders affirms the perpetrators. Early strong reactions by the bystanders, before perpetrators have developed strong commitment to their ideology and murderous course, could inhibit the evolution toward genocide.

—*Ervin Staub and Israel W. Charny*

References and Recommended Reading

Charny, Israel W. (1982). *How Can We Commit the Unthinkable?: Genocide, the Human Cancer.* Boulder, CO: Westview Press. Republished in Portuguese with a new Introduction and Bibliography as *Anatomia do Genocídio: Uma Psicologia da Agressão Humana.* Rio de Janeiro: Editora Rosa dos Tempos, 1998.

Staub, Ervin (1989). *The Roots of Evil: The Origins of Genocide and Other Group Violence.* Cambridge: Cambridge University Press.

GENOCIDE EARLY WARNING SYSTEMS

[In 1999, US President Bill Clinton announced a proposal to create a national Genocide Warning Center.—Ed.]

GENOCIDE EARLY WARNING SYSTEM (GEWS)

After genocide has occurred, many people around the world care very much about the victims, the unbearable pain of the survivors and their extended families, and the survival of their nationality, ethnic or religious groups. However, human society has thus far failed, almost completely, to take strong and effective stands against *ongoing* events of genocide or genocides that threaten to occur in the *foreseeable* future.

Some or perhaps even much of the Holocaust might have been prevented had the free world taken notice of the abundant information about the incredible murders of the Jews that were taking place. To this day many are critical of both the United States and British governments for failing to commit military resources to bomb the supply lines to Auschwitz itself—as Jews had requested of the Allied governments at the time. Similarly, the International Red Cross has received much criticism because it remained silent about its knowledge of Hitler's death camps. Even Zionist organizations in the United States and in the Jewish community of then-Palestine have been criticized for failing to take sufficient actions against Hitler. In each of these cases, the parties who *could* have helped had their own "good reasons" for not offering the help they could have given. In each case, there was a "reasonable" argument why Hitler could not be opposed more openly because of what it would have "cost" to do so.

The purpose of a Genocide Early Warning System (GEWS) is to develop an information system that will not only receive, house, and make available on a continuous basis information of ongoing

Israel Charny: On the Development of the Genocide Early Warning System (GEWS)

Sometime around 1966, I came to feel very deeply that I wanted to understand more of how human beings could have committed the terrible acts of the Holocaust. I was, after all, a practicing clinical psychologist working with my fellow human beings in their personal, marital and family hells and forebodings day after day; and presumably I knew something about the underlying nature of creatures of our species, both the better and the worse. Or did I? I heard the "Jew" in me cry out—from all the hurt and suffering in my own life; from my deep identification with my people; and from all in me that searched for greater justice in a world where the lives of so many people are often held in callous disregard. What in the name of God did we psychologists really understand of the men who conceive, build and staff the Auschwitzes of our times? Did we even really understand the small events of deceit and betrayal that are everyday occurrences in family life, friendship, and business and collegial relationships? Had we ever really accounted in our psychology of the normal personality for the incredible readiness of human beings to incinerate the last skeletons of humankind's claim to decency? I realized that I, for one, knew nothing. In all the excellent training I had enjoyed in a fine American doctoral program in clinical psychology some years earlier, I had hardly encountered this member of our species who, day in and day out, in large events and small, malevolently destroyed his fellow humans in body and spirit. It struck me as absurd that I should be treating this same person in his everyday despairs and anguish when I really did not understand how people could descend to such monstrous levels of madness far beyond any of the traditional clinical conditions I had been taught. I resolved to read and study everything I could get my hands on about how people could perpetrate the worst ugly hells and deaths on fellow human beings, and ultimately on themselves as well.

It seemed obvious that one place I should turn was the memorial authority of the Holocaust, Yad Vashem, in Jerusalem. So I wrote to them to ask where I could get a bibliography of studies of how it is that humans "born in the image of God" could execute the horror of the Holocaust and other genocides. The reply I received proved instructive but not in the way I had hoped: my correspondent at Yad Vashem advised me courteously that they had no material on the subject!

Some ten years later, I was in the Yad Vashem library with my colleague, Dr. Chanan Rapaport. We were looking for pictures of the Holocaust to use in our forthcoming book about genocide to portray the universal tragedy of men, women and children as they are led to their deaths by their fellow human beings. While we were awaiting material from the archives, I began browsing idly in the catalogue. I decided to pursue my question of some years back by looking up recent works about the sources of humankind's destructiveness and violence, from varied points of view: the social sciences, philosophy, theology, political science, international relations, art and literature. As I was not having much success locating various well-known works, I asked assistance of one of the librarians who had been very helpful to us.

"Are the books you are looking for about the Holocaust?" she asked a bit suspiciously.

continues

continued

"No, these books are about humanity's ability to commit genocide," I replied.

"Well, we don't carry books on any of that," she replied somewhat uncomfortably and, I thought, with some annoyance. "That's not our subject," she explained. "All we're concerned with is the Holocaust."

Yet, obviously, the story of the Holocaust of my own Jewish people is the universal story of humanity everywhere on our idiot, blood-soaked planet. The tragedies and outrages of the Holocaust to my people are, at one and the same time, the never-ending tragedies and outrages to *all* peoples who have been decimated since the dawn of the human race or who may yet suffer this fate in unmarked dawns to come.

Psychiatrist Fishel Schneerson was a psychologist in Tel Aviv who called out in deadly 1943: "We must alert the peoples of the entire world that the destruction of millions in Europe is not the tragedy of those millions alone, nor of the Jewish People mourning its sons, but this is a world-wide epidemic, in the fullest sense, that threatens death and destruction to the existence of humanity itself. Although everyone knows that the Jewish People are indeed the first victims of the Nazi destruction, they are neither the only ones nor the last. It is enough to recall the slaughter of the Gypsies that the Nazis are conducting in Europe according to their plan for eliminating inferior races, as well as the mass destruction of Soviet prisoners. This is the way of epidemics, the surest victims are the weak, but in the course of time none are spared and more and more victims are added."

—Israel W. Charny

massacres in the world, but to constitute a center that is an international agency on behalf of humankind in caring about and protecting human life. The information to be delivered to society by the Genocide Early Warning System not only is to maintain updated factual information but to convey that a humane society intends to keep a spotlight on the wrongdoings of mass murder. The real purpose of early warnings of genocide is to help the world develop new energies and new forms for attacking mass murder long before the murderers have completed their horrible task (essentially, the millions of words written about genocides to date represent crying *after* the deed was done).

The GEWS is to collect information on three levels. First and foremost, it is to assemble information of ongoing genocides and massacres in the world on a regular, authoritative basis. Second, it is to continuously monitor information on violations of human rights. Third, it is to form the basis for a series of research efforts to understand the patterns through which massacre, mass murder, and genocide build up in a society, so that we will learn how to predict and alert people to the increasing dangers of mass murders in different societies long before they occur.

GEWS is built on a conceptual structure that assembles information over a long term about the basic processes in each society that *support human life* and those that are moving toward the *destruction of human life*. Both processes are present in all societies. A balance of the processes in favor of the protection of human life is the desired hallmark of a society that will be less available to engage in mass murder. Clearly, societies

David Scheffer: "'Neutrality' in the Face of Genocide Is Unacceptable"

"Neutrality" in the face of genocide is unacceptable and must never be used to cripple or delay our collective response to genocide. The international community must respond quickly to confront genocidal actions. The consequences of genocide are not only the horrific killings themselves but the massive refugee flows, economic collapse, and political divisions that tear asunder the societies that fall victim to genocide. The international community can pay a far higher price coping with the aftermath of genocide than if it were prepared to defeat genocide in its earliest stages.

—David Scheffer, US Ambassador at Large for War Crimes Issues (Press Report)

exist in which, long before the mass murder was executed, the balance was very much tipped toward the destruction of human life.

GEWS identifies *ongoing processes* as differentiated from *critical incidents* that are also recorded; the first refer to less dramatic but steady patterns or processes in a society such as the degree of discrimination of minorities; whereas the second refers to dramatic events such as a major turn in policy as a result of the emergence of going to war or of economic breakdown.

At another level of analysis, GEWS assembles information about general *societal processes* such as a free press, or the role of law, along with *the roles of leaders* or the decisive decisions and implementations by heads of states or cultures such as presidents, prime ministers, dictators, and religious leaders.

These levels of information are studied along a time continuum that begins with the ongoing situation in a culture long before there may have developed what we call *the genocidal fantasy or ideology* in that culture. The monitoring continues by tracking when an idea of genocide begins to be widely proposed and approved in a society, and when it gains political support of groups of people who actually seek to organize and implement the genocidal plan. The early warning system is responsive to any ideas that refer to keeping other groups of people "in their places," "kicking out" or "cleansing" an ethnic, national, religious, political or any other group from the society, and certainly any ideas about eliminating them in a "final solution."

The GEWS continues by observing any events in a society that can become triggers or precipitants for further escalations of the destructive trends and genocidal fantasies present in that society. Often these involve rumors of terrorist events that have been directed at one's people, which understandably fan the retaliatory instincts of the population. This is the classic prescription of pogroms throughout history, for example, rumors that Jews killed a Christian sparked many violent massacres of Jews. What are natural feelings of revenge are taken as a basis for unleashing the virulent genocidal mentality that has been awaiting in the society—as ultimately it awaits in *all* human societies at this point in our evolution as a species.

Finally, the GEWS tracks those situation and events where actual legalization and institutionalization of genocide in a given society begins to take place, the military gives orders to kill the targeted group, the legal system justifies those who do the killing, the church system ignores or rationalizes the killings, the educational system ignores or trains students to applaud the killing, and so on of the various institutions of society as they are co-opted and corrupted as supporters of the genocide.

The GEWS identifies ten major early warning processes that define a series of natural psychocultural processes with which all groups (and individuals—see the original work for how this system of *societal* indicators derives from and extends a model rooted in *individual* psychology and how every human being must deal with these same issues). These processes may be turned by society toward support of life, or they may be turned toward momentums of increasing violence toward human life, culminating in genocide.

Genocide Early Warning Processes

Following are the ten major early warning processes.

Early Warning Process 1. The Valuing of Human Life

The valuing of human life refers to the basic norms in any given society regarding the degree to which it values or devalues human life. Life is cheap in totalitarian societies. It can be seen as held cheaply in other societies that provide medical and rehabilitative services indifferently or callously after an ecological or nuclear accident. The respect and value placed on human life are one of the important aspects of a culture when the time comes that the society is faced with a possibility of being drawn into committing mass murders of a target group.

Early Warning Process 2. Concern with the Quality of Human Experience

The second indicator is the concern that a society shows for the quality of human experience, and whether and to what extent the norms of society are that people should be given the opportunity to live their lives as comfortably as possible with respect to basic shelter, food, medical treatment, opportunity to work, freedom from oppression, free speech, and so forth. Societies that do not care about their own people are hardly likely to care about others.

Early Warning Process 3. The Valuing of Power

This indicator refers to the ways in which power is valued in a society. Power in the sense of self-affirmation is necessary in order to fulfill the energies of life of both individuals and groups, but when the goals of power are to control, dominate, enslave, and exploit people, such a power orientation is inherently a harbinger of the development of policies of torture, disappearance, execution and genocidal massacres.

Early Warning Process 4. Machinery for Managing Escalations of Threat

This process refers to the development of a machinery for responding to threats and managing unfolding escalations of threat. Objective threats are omnipresent in human life, but there are also dangers of subjective exaggerations and distortions in the human experiences of threats, so that a serious need exists to cross-check information and impose checks and balances on the powers of decision makers who formulate the policies for responding to dangers. Thus, some American military and political leaders called earnestly for preemptive nuclear strikes against the population centers of the Soviet Union in the years before *Glasnost* and *Perestroika*. What a tragedy that would have been!

Early Warning System 5. Orientation toward Force for Self-Defense and Solution of Conflicts

A society's orientation toward force for self-defense in its solution of conflicts is the next early warning process. It is, of course, a continuation of the previous indicator since the question now is how

Outline of Genocide Early Warning System (GEWS)

I. MANIFEST DATA

I-1. EVENTS. Reports of Genocide and Other Major Human Rights Violations.

Information is to be collected on current acts of genocide all around the world, as well as on other major human rights violations including: torture, detention in concentration camps, imprisonment without due process, slavery, denial of the right to emigrate freely, denial of free speech, and so on, according to categories from the United Nations Universal Declaration of Human Rights.

I-2. PEOPLES. The above events are to be recorded as to the nations or peoples involved, both as initiators and as targets. The classification scheme includes religious categories such as Jew, Christian, Hindu, Arab, etc., ideological groupings, nationalities, etc.

I-3. STAGES. Events are to be classified according to the sequences or stages in which they occur, as reported by news sources.

I-4. REPORTED CAUSES. The overt causes or precipitants and the background causes and processes presumed to have led to the above events are classified following the concepts used by the reporting source; e.g., dictatorial fiat, attempt to divert attention from internal problems, desire to appropriate economic resources of a victim people, religious ideology, etc.

I-5. DATA SOURCE. The data sources are news gathering agencies around the world which are judged as attaining relatively high levels of objectivity and accuracy in their reports. We also utilize data from specialized agencies which investigate and report various cases of genocide and human rights violations that are brought to their attention.

II. SOCIAL INDICATORS OF POTENTIAL GENOCIDE

Each event is to be classified according to social indicators such as the value placed on human life, attitudes toward target peoples, the level of violence in the society and other psychosocial and institutional processes. An attempt is made to identify patterns among these indicators associated with increasing violations of human rights and momentums toward genocide.

Entries of social indicators are further classified as to whether they represent critical incidents in the history of a people or larger ongoing processes within the society, and as to whether they stem primarily from the decision of a leader or leaders or from more general societal processes.

III. COMPUTERIZATION: DATA ENTRY

Information is to be entered into a computer databank to be processed, sorted and correlated for periodic reports and testing of theories.

IV. INFORMING THE WORLD COMMUNITY

The final objective is to disseminate the information of the genocide and human rights databank to the world via international television and radio, press reports, periodicals and magazines, reports to national governments, reports to various international organizations, reports to scientific organizations, publications, academic instructional programs and so on.

much force should be used in response to varying degrees of threat aimed toward one's people. It is human to want to destroy one's enemies, but societies can dangerously misjudge threats, use excessively brutal and destructive force in self-defense, and turn self-defense into an exercise of brutality, sadism and murder (which is what has happened to many well-intentioned nations). The preservation of life is no less a continuing moral goal when one has to use force in self-defense.

Early Warning Process 6. Overt Violence and Destructiveness

This process is also concerned with a society's use of violence and destructiveness. Some societies are concerned that their police, army, and population at large not be inherently violent, for example, that police not kill even when they are doing their duty to stop criminals and enemies. The unarmed English bobby with his night stick was a symbol for many years of a kind of police power intended to minimize undue use of violence and escalations of violence. The degree to which violence is heralded, rehearsed and taught in American television is obviously connected to the very real dangers many Americans face from assault and murder in many cities across their great continent. A society that limits exposure to violence in its media, and develops mature attitudes in its journalistic reports of actual events of violence, can also be expected to be less susceptible to being drawn into genocidal processes toward others.

Early Warning Process 7. Dehumanization of a Potential Victim Target Group

This early warning process refers to dehumanization of a potential victim target group. "Polack jokes" and "nigger jokes" that may seem like innocuous humor can become the basis in strained times for assigning targeted groups of peoples a status as *less-than-human* or *nonhuman,* therefore not deserving of the protections that human society gives to its bona fide members. Every person and every society must decide how much to curtail the natural humor of ethnic differences, especially when these become manifestly prejudicial statements openly devaluating and degrading another group. When an actual choice develops in a society whether to attack and exterminate a given minority group, the extent to which that minority previously has been assigned a role of subhuman or nonhuman will play an important role even in the readiness of the soldiers on the front line to execute such a policy.

Early Warning Process 8. Perception of Victim Groups as Dangerous

This early warning process is the perception of the potential victim group as dangerous. Strangely, many of the minority groups who have been targeted as less than us or not human at the same time are treated as if they are a most dangerous force that threatens to wipe out one's entire society. In other words, the dehumanized are also invested with "super powers" as groups that have physical, economic, religious, racial or other powers to destroy us. The combination of dehumanization and attribution of danger evokes a self-defense mechanism against the other people to seek to destroy them before they destroy us. The fact that these people also have been defined as not human then allows one to be cruel and brutal to them. Genocide is now fully possible.

Early Warning Process 9. Availability of Victim Group

The early warning system continues with a dimension of the availability of the victim group. This is a very difficult topic to speak about. There is no justification for any degree of excusing victimizers as if their victims were "asking for it" or were in any way to blame for being available to be victimized. Responsibility for the victimization by the perpetrator stands in its own right and must be completely condemned. However, without losing respect for the victims or empathy for their plight, groups and nations who are, to begin with, too defenseless, weak, naive, and susceptible to being bullied and terrorized tend to make the victimization process possible. Thus, the State of Israel represents a necessary historical corrective process by the Jewish people to move from being naive scholars of the Bible and romantic believers in the goodness of God into being a strong nation with an excellent army that will, legitimately, never again allow Jews to be killed en masse. The fact also is that when former victim-peoples become strong, they must learn also not to overuse their power as other nations have done to them.

Early Warning Process 10. Legitimization of Victimization by Leadership Individuals and Institutions

This indicator refers to an advanced stage in the development of genocide when a society's leadership actually endorses and ratifies the mass destruction. The strong-men of the government authorize and praise the killing of the targeted victim-people, the courts dismiss or simply do not bring charges against perpetrators, the churches bless in the names of their gods, and so on.

Theoretical Model

The basic principle of a Genocide Early Warning System is that of an information feedback system. Laszlo described this principle in his discussion of a more general "World System Research and Information Bureau": "The theoretical principle . . . is an analogue of the technique known as biofeedback. It has become known in the last few years that the human being can exert unsuspected control over his or her body when informed of its relevant states and told what kind of states to strive for. The lesson to be learned is to apply the analogue of biofeedback to the world's human population."

At the least, a Genocide Early Warning System would substantially prevent genocides from going undetected. Of course, although public opinion can be a powerful tool, it does have its limits as well. A megalomaniac will not easily open the doors of extermination camps to visiting investigators. (The Nazis, for example, maintained for some time a "demonstration camp" at Theresienstadt for the benefit of International Red Cross officials.) Nor would genociders necessarily stop determined plans to kill their victims just because an international agency makes inquiries. Ultimately, what is needed is a system of world institutions with the authority of law to intervene and put an end to mass killings. A Genocide Early Warning System would be an invaluable tool and transitional step. Under a world spotlight, a momentum of some genocidal processes might at least be slowed. As many observers have pointed out, genocidal campaigns usually do not reach their zenith until it becomes clear that it is possible to "get away with it."

At this point, there is no question but that a variety of people and institutions are groping toward articulating a new worldwide awareness of human rights and genocide, but most of these initiatives are in their infancy, and are highly irregular, relatively unsupported, and unsystemized. It is not yet clear if any of them will be able to generate a momentum that will support the development of a permanent system for monitoring genocide in this world.

History of GEWS

The proposal for a GENOCIDE EARLY WARNING SYSTEM (GEWS) was

originally formulated by Israel Charny and was developed in collaboration with Chanan Rapaport. The first publication, jointly authored, appeared in 1977. Although several pilot studies were run, the GEWS never secured sufficient funding to be activated. However, the theoretical model of GEWS has also been applied to the reconstruction of other genocides including the following:

Astourian, Stephan (1990). The Armenian Genocide: An interpretation. *The History Teacher,* 23(2), 111–160.

De Champs, Elisabeth, and De Champs, Phillipe (1996). Le Génocide Rwandais—Deux Ans Après: Le Modelle d'Israel W. Charny. *Dialogues (Brussels),* No. 190 (April–May), 10–32. (French)

The proposed Genocide Early Warning System was hailed by Willie Brandt of Germany, Pierre Mendes-France of France, and by Roberta Cohen, Human Rights Officer of the US Department of State. It was described in *Choice,* a library review magazine, as "brilliant," and in the *New York Times Book Review* as a "noteworthy contribution to thinking about the condition of humanity on the earth"; and it was recognized by a United Nations study on genocide that stated: "Many welcome the establishment of early warning systems for potential genocide situations in order to prevent recurrence of the crime. Intelligent identification of potential cases could be based on the databank of continuously updated information, which might enable remedial, deterrent overt measures to be planned ahead. Reliable information is the essential oxygen for human rights: this could be facilitated by the development of the United Nations satellite communications network. The Institute on the Holocaust and Genocide in Israel has proposed such a body."

—Israel W. Charny

References and Recommended Reading

Charny, Israel W., in collaboration with Rapaport, Chanan (1982). Toward a Genocide Early Warning System. In Charny, Israel W. *How Can We Commit the Unthinkable?: Genocide, the Human Cancer.* Boulder, CO: Westview Press, pp. 283–331. Republished in Portuguese with a new Introduction and Bibliography as *Anatomia do Genocídio: Uma Psicologia da Agressão Humana.* Rio de Janeiro: Editora Rosa dos Tempos, 1998.

Charny, Israel W. (1992). Early Warning, Intervention, and Prevention of Genocide. In Dobkowski, Michael N., and Wallimann, Isidor (Eds.), *Genocide in Our Time: An Annotated Bibliography with Analytical Introductions.* Ann Arbor, MI: Pierian Press, pp. 149–166.

EARLY WARNING SYSTEM (EWS)

The Early Warning System (EWS) is a scientific method for performing two services. First, by use of the designed questions it is possible to identify a potentially genocidal movement. Second, by use of a parallel set of designed questions it is possible to discern when a legitimate government is becoming vulnerable to replacement by a populist elite practicing terror as a weapon of ideological warfare.

We do not have a science when an epidemic of some deadly disease is reported. We have a science when a group of specialists can sit together and from their research predict that when certain factors continue unchecked *there will be an epidemic.* Predictability is the test of a scientific method, and we now have the capacity to predict what movements will commit genocide if they have the power to do so. We can also predict when and where genocides may be committed, if a legitimate government fails to defend its constitution and protect the rights of its loyal citizens from enemies both foreign and domestic.

EWS is directed toward the goal of strengthening legitimate governments,

Franklin Littell's Writings on Early Warnings of Genocide

[Franklin Littell is an ordained Methodist minister and professor of theology.—Ed.]

Over the decades after I returned from work in Germany (1958), I have taught graduate seminars and given hundreds of lectures, sermons and public speeches on the threat of totalitarian movements and regimes to peace and human rights.

My first published articles, both academic and popular, were concerned with distinguishing dangerous and disloyal movements (fascist and communist and American nativist) from movements of affirmation or dissent ("loyal oppositions") functioning in good faith in the public forum. I moved from concern about "extremism" and "prejudice" to identifying objective factors such as use and misuse of power in civic posts, style of internal organization and command tone of public discourse ("The Language of Assault" in contrast to "The Language of Dialogue"), and the record of behavior toward fellow citizens (especially violence against Jews and Negroes).

Following my move to Perkins School of Theology at Southern Methodist University in 1960, I found myself caught up in a swirling attack on my denomination and also the university. Until the assassination of President Kennedy, the John Birch Society and other populist/nativist organizations were riding high. At the request of the Methodist bishops and superintendents, I gave dozens of speeches, crisscrossing the region from El Paso to Corpus Christi, from Rio Grande Valley to Marshall and Denison—warning against Nazi-type answers to communism. I also had to take an unlisted telephone number because of threats on my life made to my wife and children. In the urgency of this Texas experience, I began to talk about the importance not only of identifying anti-democratic movements but of stopping them before they grew strong enough to destroy democratic alternatives. I worked up a Study Manual which was published by Macmillan (1969) as *Wild Tongues: A Study in Social Pathology*. In this book there appeared a "grid" of 15 points on "How to Identify Totalitarian Movements," and a "grid II" of practical measures to be taken to inhibit their growth. In the book I did not use the phrase, "Early Warning System," although the scheme for identification and sense of urgency were there. "The earlier effective action is taken, the less violence will be necessary" (p. 72).

The first published titles by me using the phrase "Early Warning System" that I have been able to find came in the report of my two major addresses at the 1988 Oxford/London International Conference "Remembering for the Future." One of these papers also appeared in *Holocaust and Genocide Studies* [1988, (3)4, 483–490]. I also gave a paper on Early Warning which was published in Peter Hayes' edition of the conference report: *Lessons and Legacies* [Northwestern University Press, 1991]. By then it was constant in my teaching, preaching and writing.

Someday someone may dig the answer out as to when I first used that phrase. I don't have the time. To illustrate the problem: between November 1978 and the present I have published hundreds of columns of commentary in a number of newspapers and the phrase appears frequently in the columns. The main thing is that it's a very good way of helping students and other listeners remember that the issue is existential in democratic countries, and not just of academic interest. I think it's like one of those scientific solutions we hear about in hard sciences, where teams in two or three different countries come to a formula or a solution of a problem at the same time—apparently working independently, but of course in fact reading the same journals and corresponding with the same people for years.

—Franklin H. Littell

by which we mean republics, constitutional monarchies or simple democracies. EWS does not apply to the situation in old-fashioned despotisms; it applies only to those modern dictatorships that are the matured expression of genocidal movements and elites.

When concepts of international law first emerged, during the time when kings ruled by divine right, there were two tests of legitimacy in government. First, has the ruler succeeded in establishing his authority and maintaining order over a certain area? Second, has his rule been recognized by a critical mass of other regimes?

Neither of the traditional tests is applicable in the age of populist movements and popular sovereignty. Rather, two quite different tests of legitimacy apply. First, with the appropriate safeguards to check overhasty actions, do public policies finally reflect the will of the people? Second, and equally as important, are the rights and liberties of "loyal oppositions" protected by the full force of the laws? A footnote to this second question concerns the responsibility of a legitimate government to inhibit and suppress movements that are not in good faith in the public forum—for example, terrorist, potentially genocidal movements that by violence threaten loyal citizens and the general welfare.

We are brought back to the task at hand, which is to define the defense of a legitimate government against disciplined cadres that —sometimes operating behind the facade of parliamentary politics—in fact have enlisted in a specialized branch of modern war. Although governments such as the Israeli and the German have long been confronted by the challenge of terrorist, potentially genocidal movements, only recently have Americans suffered major assault. The murderous attacks on the World Trade Center in New York and the Federal Building in Oklahoma City remind us that assaults may be sponsored internationally or may be indigenous in planning and execution.

The "grids" here presented were developed in the course of the writer's decade of duty in the American occupation of postwar Germany. They have been improved by insights gained in graduate seminars (1958–86) and in discussions following public addresses. They were published in much their present form in Chapters 2 and 3 of *Wild Tongues* in 1969, and in improved form in *Holocaust and Genocide Studies* in 1988. *Wild Tongues* was prepared as a critical guide to American nativist, populist and racist movements for study and use by local action groups sponsored by local church and community organizations. Using the German Nazi movement as a test case, the nature and structure of American right-wing movements was analyzed and specific counteractions recommended.

The task is to distinguish a potentially genocidal movement from other movements operating in good faith in the public forum. Under the American Bill of Rights this cannot be done on the basis of ideas or advocacy, but must be related to overt action(s).

The following designation points are pertinent for identifying terrorist, potentially genocidal cadres.

1. The cadre prints, distributes, and uses antisemitic or other prejudicial material for attracting sympathizers and recruiting members.
2. The cadre makes antisemitic or other prejudicial appeals through the media or in mass meetings.

3 and 4. Actions such as those itemized in #1 and #2 are used as weapons against any other ethnic, religious or cultural community.

5. Members cultivate the politics of verbal assault and physical

violence—publishing slanderous charges, bombing meeting places and homes and media, beating and assassinating opponents.

6. The cadre pursues the politics of polarization, scorning the middle ground of compromise or consensus, rejecting the politics of moderation and orderly change. If it becomes numerous enough, instead of functioning as a parliamentary opposition it builds the structures of "a state within a state."
7. The cadre uses the *Language of Assault* toward political opponents, rather than using the *Language of Dialogue* and participating in good faith in the political forum.
8. The cadre deliberately drives a wedge between the generations, creating youth groups hostile to their parents' generation and to their heritage.
9. The cadre maintains camps for paramilitary training, including the use of antipersonnel weapons, outside the control of public officials (either Police or Military).
10. The cadre trains and maintains private armies, demonstrating in public in uniform, parading and marching to intimidate loyal citizens.
11. Leaders of the movement elaborate a quasi-religious structure of authority and sanctions, with political hymns, shrines, martyrs, liturgies.
12. Archaic tribal, clannish or religious symbols are worn by members as recognition signs; secret passwords, handshakes, and other in-group signals are used to identify cobelievers in public situations.
13. Induction and termination of membership are observed as quasi-religious rites. Straying members are treated as "heretics"—subject to exorcism, with intensive group confession techniques applied in attempts at "rescue."
14. The movement's basic unit is the closed cell, with three to seven the standard number. This is the classic unit of a revolutionary party or intelligence operation, but it lies outside the style appropriate for loyal citizens to use in exercising influence upon a legitimate government.
15. The movement practices deception and confuses public opinion by launching one-issue "fronts" —without clear identification of sponsorship, financing and control. A great deal of money is raised this way, ostensibly for some good public purposes—but actually to serve the party's internal interests in the pursuit of power. These devices are known as "the large net" within which "innocents" are caught.
16. The cadre's studied tactics include infiltration and subversion of public institutions and voluntary associations, turning their direction from public service to bolstering the movement's drive for power. (The history of subversive initiatives in Europe as well as America indicates that there are two prime targets of totalitarian cadres: one, control of education and schools; two, control of the police and public safety.)

No single point in the grid is enough to define the problem, but a *kairos* or pattern of 8 or 10 should be enough to start red flags waving and alarm bells ringing. By applying the grid it can be established that behind the facade of a political movement in good faith there is a power center that is a potentially genocidal conspiracy.

What is needed of legitimate governments at the threshold of the twenty-first century is the applied will and intelligence to move beyond nineteenth-century slogans, to internalize the costly lessons of the twentieth century "Age of Genocide," and to carry to its conclusion the suppression of genocide and the punishment of those who engage in it—or even lay plans to do so.

—*Franklin H. Littell*

References and Recommended Reading

Littell, Franklin H. (1969). *Wild Tongues: A Handbook of Social Pathology.* New York: Macmillan.

Littell, Franklin H. (1988). Early warning. *Holocaust and Genocide Studies,* 3(4), 483–490.

FORUM FOR EARLY WARNING AND EMERGENCY RESPONSE (FEWER)

Internal armed conflict is the scourge of the late twentieth century. Today wars within states far outnumber those between nations, and pessimism often characterizes the international community's response to them. What can be done to resolve seemingly intractable disputes? How can conflicts with such deep-rooted causes stretching back over decades, even centuries, be brought to a peaceful conclusion? Will the years of violence and hatred ever permit warring peoples to live together side by side in the same land? The answers to such questions have been sought with increasing urgency in recent years and resulted in an explosion of interest in the concept of conflict prevention. This in turn has led to a growing realization that successful conflict prevention is heavily dependent on the development of an effective early warning system. Without adequate forewarning of an impending crisis, the task of preventing the dispute from escalating into armed conflict becomes that much more difficult.

Despite the large amount of research that has gone into the subject of developing such a system, however, few concrete proposals have emerged. Although in recent years a number of intergovernmental (IGO) and nongovernmental (NGO) organizations have initiated policies on early warning and early action, there is little coordination between information gatherers, policy makers and the relevant actors, both external and internal. In an attempt to address the manifold difficulties of establishing an effective early warning system that can provide reliable information in a coherent and accessible way, a coalition of IGO representatives, UN agencies and NGOs, including International Alert, have developed the FEWER project (Forum for Early Warning and Emergency Response).

FEWER distinguishes itself from other early warning initiatives in a number of important ways. Firstly, it is highly action-oriented, directly linking conflict early warning to early action. Secondly, it works to provide decision makers with balanced, timely and reliable information and analysis on conflict-threatened countries and regions as well as possible policy responses based on and tailored to local needs and capacities for peace. Finally, and perhaps most significantly, FEWER is a collaborative effort on a global scale encompassing existing early warning projects and capitalizing on expertise drawn from both the Northern and Southern Hemispheres. Ultimately, its objective is to develop a single, coherent system of conflict indicators, analysis and policy recommendations in order to identify opportunities for conflict prevention and provoke constructive responses from the international community.

Although still in the developmental stage (it was only launched as a concept in September of 1996), FEWER is currently supported by a core of eight partner organizations, IGOs, including the United Nations Department of Humanitarian Affairs (UNDHA) and United Nations High Commission for Refugees (UNHCR), NGOs and academic institutions from six countries. An additional nine organizations have expressed an interest in becoming FEWER Partners and a strong relationship has been built up with governments and the European Commission. In June 1997, the Secretariat moved to London to be hosted by International Alert for approximately one year, and an independent, full-time coordinator was appointed to develop and implement a strategy for the forthcoming year.

Essentially, the broad strategic aims and objectives during this formative period will be to provide an understanding of the relevance of FEWER to producers and users of conflict early warning, launch field-based early warning projects supported by operational working groups and establish an independent Secretariat able to coordinate and support FEWER early warning activities.

For the first year, FEWER will focus on two pilot projects in the Caucasus and Great Lakes region of east/central Africa. Its primary activities will be threefold:

1. Regional early warning:
   - the provision of risk assessments and policy recommendations that are (a) balanced and reliable; (b) systematic and timely; (c) meet high standards of quality and rigor; and (d) meet user demand.
2. Complementary research:
   - the provision of a series of contextual studies providing the framework for early warning reports; (a) best practice studies; (b) policy/user studies; and (c) thematic studies.
3. Direct engagement with decision-makers:
   - regular presentation of information to key decision-makers;
   - regular information exchange and dialogue among key actors in crisis areas.

In addition, a standard formatting of reports and common terminology and an agreed list of indicators are being developed to ensure coherence and uniformity. Indicators currently in use are those provided by the organization PIOOM [see HUMAN RIGHTS AND GENOCIDE] at the University of Leiden, Holland, and are based on the study of a variety of situations within a given country or region, including the political, minority, labor and religious/ideological situations, a detailed analysis of which give indications of the possibility of tensions escalating into violence within the region. A study of Zaire toward the end of 1994 using these indicators illustrated the country's deep social, economic and political deterioration. Three-quarters of all hospitals had been closed and disease was widespread. Government ministries had ceased functioning, Mobutu constantly played ethnic politics, and the security forces had become a law unto themselves. The economy had shrunk by 40 percent, incomes had collapsed and refugees from the surrounding region were contributing to the country's rapid decline resulting ultimately in the overthrow of Mobutu.

Close relations with UN agencies and the EU and regular communication between different types of NGOs, IGOs and governments are required to further enhance cooperation on policy planning, development and implementation. A greater exchange of information and increased awareness of the factors that can lead to the outbreak of conflicts would be a significant step on the path toward establishing a genuinely global network that has the capacity to warn of impending crises and provoke an early and effective response from the international community.

—*Kumar Rupesinghe*

References and Recommended Reading

Jongman, Albert J., and Schmid, Alex P. (1994). *Monitoring Human Rights: Manual for Assessing Country Performance.* Leiden, The Netherlands: Leiden University, PIOOM (Interdisciplinary Research Program on Root Causes of Human Rights Violations) [Wassenaarsweg 52, 2333 AK Leiden, The Netherlands].

Rupesinghe, Kumar, and Kuroda, Michiko (Eds.) (1992). *Early Warning and Conflict Resolution.* London: Macmillan, and New York: St. Martin's Press.

Schmeil, Susanne (1997). The continuing quest for early warning and early response. *Refuge,* 16(1), 1–3.

MINORITIES AND GENOCIDE: EARLY WARNING AND MINORITIES AT RISK AROUND THE WORLD

Nearly 80 distinct ethnic and religious groups were victimized as a result of deliberate government policies between 1980 and 1997. Table 1 lists the groups identified in a global survey of politically active minorities and national peoples by the Minorities at Risk Project and provides profiles of their victimization. Discriminatory policies are the most common source of victimization, genocide is the least common.

Discrimination against minorities and national peoples has many origins. Recent immigrants and the descendants of slaves often are subject to discriminatory policies. So are religious minorities, especially in Islamic states. Conquered indigenous peoples and ethnonationalists like the Kurds and Palestinians may be targets of discrimination because dominant groups see them as culturally inferior or as security threats. When minorities and national peoples riot or rebel against authorities, discriminatory policies often are tightened. Table 1 identifies 11 minorities subject in the mid-1990s to two or more of these three kinds of discriminatory policies: (1) restrictions on their rights to organize and participate in politics on an equal footing with other groups; (2) restrictions on their material well-being (such as discrimination in employment, land-holding, access to higher education); and (3) restrictions on their cultural rights (such as religious practices and use of their language).

A more life-threatening kind of victimization occurs during armed conflicts when civilian members of minorities are targeted by government forces or rebel factions. An extreme case is the civil war in Sudan, where hundreds of thousands of noncombatant Dinka, Nuba, Shilluk, and others have died since 1983 in massacres, executions, shelling, and starvation inflicted by government forces, militias, and rival rebel factions. The table shows that 40 of the 77 victimized groups have been targeted during warfare since 1980.

Also common is forcible resettlement of members of a minority or dispossession of their land or property: 37 groups were seriously victimized in this way between 1980 and the mid-1990s. Such policies may be taken for security reasons, for example when governments in Guatemala and Nicaragua forced native peoples suspected of supporting rebels into army-controlled resettlement camps. The Iranian government's religiously-motivated confiscation of property of the Baha'i faith during the 1980s is a second example. The use of force or terror to "cleanse" an area of a particular group, a policy followed by contending groups in the Former Yugoslavia, is a more extreme example.

TABLE 1
Minorities Victimized by Discrimination, Ethnic Warfare, Repression, and Genocide 1980–1997

			*Type of Victimization**					
Europe	*Groups*	*Period of Victimization*	*Discrim*	*War Victims*	*Displaced*	*Repress*	*Geno/Pol*	*Risks of Increased Victimization*
France	Muslims	ongoing	X					+
Germany	Turks	ongoing	X					–
Albania	Greeks	ongoing	X					0
Latvia	Russians	1990–present	X					–
Romania	Roma	ongoing	X					–
Yugoslavia	Kosovar Albanians	1988–present	X			X		++
Yugoslavia	Hungarians, Sandzak Muslims	1991–present	X					–
Azerbaijan	Armenians	1988–1994	X	X				–
Croatia	Serbs	1991–present	X	X	X			0
Croatia	Roma	ongoing	X					0
Georgia	Abkhaz	1991–1993	X					– –
Bosnia	Muslims	1992–1995		X	X		X	+
Bosnia	Croats, Serbs	1992–1994		X	X			– –
Russia	Chechens	1994–1996		X		X		–

			*Type of Victimization**					
Middle East	*Groups*	*Period of Victimization*	*Discrim*	*War Victims*	*Displaced*	*Repress*	*Geno/Pol*	*Risks of Increased Victimization*
Iran	Turkmen	ongoing	X					0
Iran	Christians	ongoing	X					0
Israel	Arabs	ongoing	X					0
Saudi Arabia	Shi'i	ongoing	X			X		0
Iraq	Kurds	1961–present	X	X	X	X	X	++
Iraq	Shi'i	1975–1992	X	X	X	X		+

(continues)

TABLE 1
(continued)

Middle East	*Groups*	*Period of Victimization*	*Type of Victimization**					*Risks of Increased Victimization*
			Discrim	*War Victims*	*Displaced*	*Repress*	*Geno/Pol*	
Israel-Occupied Territories	Palestinians	1967–present	X		X	X		+
Lebanon	Palestinians	1967–1991	X	X	X			0
Morocco	Saharawis	1975–present	X		X			0
Iran	Kurds	1979–1992	X	X	X	X		0
Iran	Bahai's	1979–1992	X		X	X		0
Turkey	Kurds	1984–present	X	X	X	X		+

Asia	*Groups*	*Period of Victimization*	*Type of Victimization**					*Risks of Increased Victimization*
			Discrim	*War Victims*	*Displaced*	*Repress*	*Geno/Pol*	
Burma	Kachin, Karen, Shan, Mon	1961–present	X	X		X		0
Burma	Royhinga Muslims	1993–1994	X		X			0
Bhutan	Lhotshampas	1988–present	X		X			–
Cambodia	Vietnamese	ongoing	X		X			–
China	Tibetans	1953–present	X		X	X	X	+
China	Uighers (East Turkomen)	1980–present	X		X	X		++
India	Nagas	1950s–present		X	X			0
India	Tripuras	late 1970s–present		X				0
India	Sikhs	1982–present	X	X				–
India	Bodos, Assamese	1989–present		X	X			+
India	Kashmiris	1990–present	X	X		X		0
Indonesia	Papuans	1963–present	X		X			0

(continues)

TABLE 1
(continued)

Asia	*Groups*	*Period of Victimization*	*Type of Victimization** *Discrim*	*War Victims*	*Displaced*	*Repress*	*Geno/Pol*	*Risks of Increased Victimization*
Indonesia	East Timorese	1975–present	X	X	X	X	X	0
Pakistan	Ahmadis, Hindus	ongoing	X					0
Pakistan	Shi'i	ongoing	X					+

Africa South of the Sahara	*Groups*	*Period of Victimization*	*Type of Victimization** *Discrim*	*War Victims*	*Displaced*	*Repress*	*Geno/Pol*	*Risks of Increased Victimization*
South Africa	Blacks	1950s–1990			X	X		– –
Ethiopia	Eritreans, Tigreans	1960–1991		X	X	X		– –
Ethiopia	Oromo, Somali	1960s–present		X	X	X		+
Ethiopia	Afar	1975–1985		X	X			–
Angola	Ovimbundu	1975–1994		X				–
Zimbabwe	Ndebele	1980–1987		X		X		0
Nigeria	Ogoni	1980s–present	X			X		0
Sudan	Dinka, Nuba, Shilluk	1983–present	X	X	X	X	X	++
Chad	Southerners	1985–1994		X		X		0
Liberia	Gio, Mano	1985–1990		X		X		– –
Somalia	Isaaq clan, northerners	1988–1991		X			X	0
Mali	Tuareg	1990–1995	X	X		X		–
Niger	Tuareg	1991–1995	X	X				–
Kenya	Kikiyu, Luo, Luhya, Kisii	1991–1993	X		X	X		0
Congo-Kinshasha	Banyamulenge (Tutsi)	1991–present	X			X		+
Rwanda	Tutsi	1993–1994	X			X	X	– –
Burundi	Hutu	1993–present	X	X		X		++

(continues)

TABLE 1
(continued)

Latin America	*Groups*	*Period of Victimization*	*Type of Victimization**					*Risks of Increased Victimization*
			Discrim	*War Victims*	*Displaced*	*Repress*	*Geno/Pol*	
Dominican Republic	Haitians	ongoing	X					0
Guatemala	Mayans	1966–1995	X	X	X	X	X	–
Nicaragua	Miskito	1981–1990		X	X			– –

Source: Compiled from information in the files of the Minorities at Risk Project, University of Maryland at College Park, available on a World Wide Web site, address http://www.bsos.umd.edu/cidcm/mar.

*Principal types of harm suffered by members of the group:

Discrim: Group was subject to explicit policies of political, economic, or cultural discrimination in the mid-1990s.

War victims: Civilian members of the group were targeted during warfare between rebel and regime forces.

Displaced: Some of the group was forcibly resettled or dispossessed of their lands and property.

Repress: Many civilian members of the group were subject to repressive policies, or were at risk of violent attacks and deprivation of freedom and property by security forces or vigilante groups acting with tacit approval of state officials.

Geno/pol: The group was the target of deliberate, sustained policies aimed at its collective destruction.

Repression refers to government policies in which force and threats are widely used to restrict the movement and political activities of members of a minority or national people. The table identifies 39 groups that have been victimized in a substantial way by repression. Also included in this category are groups subject to recurring acts of state terrorism, that is, deadly attacks and abductions by security forces or vigilante groups. State terror usually aims to discourage members of a minority from actively supporting political opposition movements and rebellions.

The most severe forms of victimization are genocide and politicide (political mass murder). Ten of the 77 groups in the table were systematically targeted by such policies, including Muslims in Bosnia (1992–1995) and Tutsi in Rwanda (1994). Russian forces in the breakaway republic of Chechnya in 1995–1996 used widespread and indiscriminate violence against civilians that came close to the threshold of genocide.

Half of the episodes of conflict and victimization listed were still occuring in 1997. So long as open conflicts continue, some forms of victimization are likely to persist. For some fortunate groups, like Mayans in Guatemala, black South Africans, and Bosnian Muslims, conflict has led to settlements, political reforms, or international responses that have ended or checked abuses. The table's last column assesses the risks that each group's victimization will increase in the late 1990s as a result of escalating conflict and repression, or decrease as a result of reforms and peace settlements. The gravest concern is that ongoing policies of discrimination and repression in authoritarian states may escalate into genocides and politicides.

Groups at high risk should be subject to intensive international scrutiny and preventive efforts. Work is underway in the UN system, the US government, the European Union, and by academic researchers to establish systems that can provide policy makers and activists with more timely and reliable alerts of impending humanitarian disasters. Effective early warning systems would enable observers to differentiate among impending conflicts and to monitor on a daily basis the turning point events (accelerators) that lead to rapid escalation.

—Ted Robert Gurr
with Barbara Harff

References and Recommended Reading

Gurr, Ted Robert, and Harff, Barbara (1996). *Early Warning of Communal Conflicts and Genocide: Linking Empirical Research to International Responses.* Tokyo: United Nations University Press, Monograph Series on Governance and Conflict Resolution, No. 05.

Harff, Barbara, and Gurr, Ted Robert (1996). Victims of the state: Genocides, politicides and group repression from 1945 to 1995. In Jongman, Albert J. (Ed.), *Contemporary Genocides: Causes, Cases, Consequences.* Leiden, The Netherlands: Leiden University, PIOOM (Interdisciplinary Research Program on Root Causes of Human Rights Violations), pp. 33–58.

GENOCIDE IN ANTIQUITY

No history of genocide can afford to ignore the ancient past.

What one might call "genocidal consciousness" can be seen in antiquity. Dicaearchus, a Greek writer of the third century B.C.E., wrote a work entitled *de interitu hominum (On the Destruction of Human Life),* in which he collected causes of mass deaths and concluded that a greater number of human lives had been taken by human design than by natural disaster. Included in this catalogue was the destruction of entire groups *(quaedam genera hominum).* His testimony makes it clear that, even if the word "genocide" is of recent coinage, such a "genocidal consciousness" can be seen in antiquity.

Any study of the past reveals it to have been littered with cultures that have disappeared. Hittites, Lydians, Medes, Hurrians, Etruscans, Minoans, Parthians, and many others have all left significant traces in the archaeological record and literary tradition. Nevertheless, their languages, cultures and experiences are only recordable through the exhumation of their remains. This does not mean that every culture in history that has ceased to exist has been the victim of a genocide. The possibility must nevertheless be entertained.

Genocidal rhetoric can certainly be found in the foundation texts of antiquity. In the *Iliad,* for example, Agamemnon, the High King of the Greeks tells his brother, the king of Sparta, that their purpose in the Trojan War is the utter destruction of Troy, down to the tiniest child. "My dear Menelaus, why are you so chary of taking men's lives? Did the Trojans treat you as handsomely as that when they stayed at your house? No, we are not going to leave a single one of them alive, down to the babies in their mother's wombs. Not even they must live. The whole people must be wiped out of existence, and none be left to think of them or shed a tear." In the myth cycle, when Troy finally falls, Agamemnon's intentions are carried out. The city is burned, its men all slain along with the boy children. The women and girls are taken as slaves by their conquerors.

The Greeks were not alone in this rhetoric. In the *Book of Joshua,* the Israelites are portrayed as annihilating towns in fulfillment of the divine injunction to kill the peoples of Canaan; likewise, the *First Book of Samuel* promises the annihilation of the Amalekites. This is within a tradition of genocidal discourse existing among the ancient cultures of the region. Both the Egyptians and Assyrians claimed the utter destruction of their foes. Although these reflect a rhetorical tradition rather than historical reality, there is nevertheless a point to be made here. It is an interesting detail that in the archaeological record of Israel, there is little evidence of massacre, city-destruction or depopulation of any time associated with the Exodus period (i.e., between 1200 and 1000 B.C.E.). At Ai, for example, which the *Book of Joshua* states was burned to the ground, there is no trace of burning in the relevant strata. Likewise, Assyrians and Egyptians will boast about having slaughtered all of their foes, but that doesn't mean that they actually did it. It tends to mean that they killed a lot of people by way of terrorizing local populations into submission, and that they wanted posterity to know what mighty warriors they were. It may seem strange to us that a politician would boast of the accomplishment of mass murder, and exaggerate his deeds to this effect. Yet it is sitting there, large as life in the *Book of Joshua,* or in the *Annals of the Assyrian Kings.* Such discourse proclaims the possibility of genocide by the assertion of its desirability.

The most frequently cited case of genocide perpetrated in antiquity is the destruction of Melos by the Athenians in 416 B.C.E. This is more probably because modern scholars have read Thucydides' celebrated "Melian Dialogue" which sets out a rationale of sorts for ancient imperialism than because of their familiarity with antiquity. Other cases are known: Sybaris, Skione, Asine, Torone, Askra and, perhaps, Pisatis. These are all genocides perpetrated by Greeks upon other Greek communities.

Of the primary conditions for the perpetration of genocide, the exclusion of a group from a community of obligations is perhaps the most basic. But at first glance, it would seem that classical Greeks had a very wide "universe of obligation," sharing language, customs, deities, sacred places, culture, even a form of sacral international law. The killing of other Greeks could horrify them. A play on the massacre of Greek Milesians by the Persians in 495/4 by the Athenian writer Phrynikos aroused such horror in Athens that it was suppressed. Thucydides records an anecdote of the aftermath of a battle during the Peloponnesian War. When the representative of the vanquished people saw how many of his folk had been slain in a battle with Athenians, he could say nothing, but returned home in weeping silence.

While the boundaries of this apparent universe of obligation seem linguistic (Hellenes and *Barbaroi,* those ignorant of the Greek language), this dichotomy oversimplifies Greek social relationships. They had few qualms about enslaving one another, and slaves were outside the universe of obligation. They viewed the enslaved as no longer human (let alone Greek), but as commodities. Enslavement *(andrapodismos)* was a primary vehicle of dehumanization and more to the point, deculturation, and therefore an effective weapon of genocide in antiquity.

Politics also formed a boundary of the universe of obligation. An Athenian political writer, the Old Oligarch, makes a clear social distinction between the *aristoi* and the common herd, the *poneroi.* Political massacre was not especially uncommon in periods of civil conflict. The populist dictators who dominated Greek *poleis* in the seventh and sixth centuries (the *tyrannoi* or tyrants) were noted for it. One anecdote, ascribed to a number of tyrants (in the case of Herodotos to Thrasyboulos of Miletos), describes one tyrant advising another, during a stroll in a wheat field, on how to secure power. Wordlessly, the tyrant flicks the heads off the tallest stalks of corn, a message plainly interpreted as "the murder of all of the people in the city who were outstanding in influence or ability."

Analysis of the way in which Greek states related to one another demonstrates that conflict between *poleis* was a far more natural state than peace. Herakleitos called battle *(polemos)* the "father and king of everything." At the heart of the Greek aristocratic ideology was the *agon,* the struggle or competition for glory and success. This is no polite aristocratic contest. In the *Iliad,* Homer laid bare the consequences of the *agon:* not the mere return of Helen, nor even the conquest of Troy. It is the complete physical destruction of the city and its people. In sober reality, conflict does not have limits, and the specter of massacre always lurks in the shadows of war. This can be seen particularly in the late Archaic period when a number of Greek *poleis* were destroyed by their Greek neighbors, the best documented case being the destruction of Sybaris by the Crotoniates.

Flourishing by virtue of its exploitation of the local natural resources, Sybaris was so successful that the city extended its control over up to twenty-five other cities and was able to send out colonies of its own. Its coins, minted from the middle of the sixth century, characteristically feature a bull, perhaps symbolic of the agricultural wealth of the city. Trade links existed with the Etruscans in the north, and to the east with the Ionian Greeks, most notably the Milesians.

The southern Italian region of Bruttium exploited by Sybaris also attracted other colonists. Not long after the establishment of Sybaris, Croton was founded nearby, also by Achaean Greeks. Like Sybaris, it became an extremely successful community, perhaps assisted by nearby silver deposits. Both Sybaris and Croton became contenders for the leadership of the south Italian Greeks. Nevertheless, they joined together in about 530 B.C.E., against a common enemy, cooperating in the defeat of Siris, another nearby colony. Civil strife in Sybaris offered the Crotoniates an opportunity to take action against their powerful neighbor. In 510, political exiles from Sybaris incited the Crotoniates to attack their homeland. But the Crotoniates went further than expected. Not content merely to defeat the Sybarites, they took no prisoners, and slew all whom they found, even those retreating. A vast number of Sybarites perished, whereupon the Crotoniates plundered the city and laid it waste. According to one writer, the site was then obliterated by diverting the Crathis River over it.

The Crotonians were not content with simply destroying this Sybaris. Exiles and escapees from the destruction refounded the city some years later. In 476, the Crotoniates again destroyed it. The city was again refounded in 453, and again destroyed by the Crotoniates. Numismatic patterns have identified no fewer than four attempts to refound Sybaris. The reason for the repeated failure was the implacable hostility of Croton. Never again would they tolerate a Sybaris on their doorstep.

Is this genocide? It certainly looks a great deal like it. The Crotoniates had no intention of tolerating Sybaris. They did not destroy the place once, but four times. They killed every Sybarite they could find. This was policy, not impetuosity. A decision to take no prisoners might be seen as one taken in the heat of battle, but not one to obliterate a site, with all of its cultural, social and religious associations, by inundating it with the waters of a river.

The case of Sybaris is not isolated. It is the harbinger of the savage warfare of the [illegible], in which Greek states exhibited what Peter Green has called "the habit of genocide." Also it recalls the obliteration of Asine, Mycenae, Tiryns, Skione, Plataia and Melos. These in turn point to the many inhumanities of the Greek world; political massacres; the ongoing culture of terror, dehumanization and cultural destruction inflicted upon the Helots of Sparta; and the enforced deculturation of slavery.

The Greeks were not alone in such barbarity. The Romans were responsible for the destruction of entire communities at Carthage and Corinth, and sought to exterminate the Gallic Druids. The military practices of Julius Caesar in Gaul involved systematic depopulation, mass murder and enslavement. Such brutalities, however, were more typical than innovative.

While genocide is a modern term, it does have ancient antecedents that assist in developing its definition. The cases cited are some of the broad range of historical examples from antiquity that can be brought to bear on the question. *Modernity may have brought genocide to new ideologies and technologies, but the phenomenon may well be as old as civilization itself.* We would do well in any discussions of what genocide is, or how it has developed, to treat ways in which the ancient past both underlies and informs recent experience. If we are truly to understand what genocide is, and from whence the impulses arise that bring it into being, then the experience of antiquity must be taken seriously and examined accordingly.

—Bill Leadbetter

References and Recommended Reading

The Bible.

Carlton, Eric (1994). *Massacres: An Historical Perspective.* Aldershot, UK: Scolar Press.

Chalk, Frank, and Jonassohn, Kurt (1990). *The History and Sociology of Genocide: Analysis and Case Studies.* New Haven, CT: Yale University Press.

Ducrey, Pierre (1986). *Warfare in Ancient Greece.* Translated from the French by Janet Lloyd. New York: Schocken Books.

Homer. *Iliad.*

Leadbetter, Bill (1996). Genocide in antiquity. *International Network on Holocaust and Genocide,* 11(3), 4-7.

GENOCIDES DURING THE MIDDLE AGES

Throughout history genocides and genocidal massacres have been carried out for utilitarian ends motivated by lust for power and wealth. Perhaps the best known cases of genocide are those carried out in the thirteenth century by the Mongols under Genghis Khan. In the course of creating the largest empire in history up to that time, the Mongols performed several genocides. These illustrate the three major motives for performing utilitarian genocides. Some of them were meant to eliminate a threat; some of them were intended to spread terror; and some of them were carried out to acquire economic wealth. While these three motives were present in various proportions in all cases, one of them always predominated.

When the Mongol empire started to break up, the Chinese under the Ming dynasty took their revenge. They had long resented that their ancient culture had been subjugated by an illiterate nomadic tribe. They drove the Mongols out of China in repeated campaigns and eradicated all evidence of the Mongol's rule so thoroughly that they even destroyed all texts written in the Mongol's language.

Many other cases, though less well-known and less successful in their self-appointed missions, occurred in most parts of the world. Amir Timur, who entered literature as Tamerlane, was so impressed by Genghis Khan's successes that he had his court genealogists provide him with Mongol origins and claimed descent from Genghis Khan. However, while his irrational cruelty during raids into India destroyed the population of several cities, these campaigns achieved nothing except a reputation for lust for blood that went well beyond what was customary in the fourteenth century.

The incursions of Moslem invaders beginning in the late twelfth century and their establishment as rulers of several parts of India led to several genocidal massacres and even genocides. While these conflicts are often represented as being about ethnic and religious differences, it seems clear that they were really about the control of wealth and power. A case in point is Vijayanagar, a great and prosperous city in the Deccan (India). Over a period of over 250 years, it was conquered several times by Hindu or Moslem conquerors who each massacred much of the noncombatant population and looted the treasures of the city. Babur, who lived during the early sixteenth century, himself noted the important events of his reign and reported the massacres of women and children and the building of pyramids of human heads. However, in regions that were short of an adequate labor force or required skilled artisans, slavery became an alternative to genocide. The rulers in such regions eventually realized that captured slaves were much more valuable than massacred bodies. Documenting cases of genocide presents many difficulties. Evidence may be left by the victims or the perpetrators, but only rarely by both. The perpetrators and the bystanders usually had a greater interest in celebrating their victories, while the losers emphasized their suffering. Intent, which is such a crucial part of the precise definition of genocide, is hardly ever declared, and therefore can only be inferred from circumstantial evidence.

The period of the Crusades represents the beginning of the transition from utilitarian to ideological genocides. The Crusaders' religious motives have received much more attention than their utilitarian ones. While it may be difficult to decide which motive predominated, it is not at all difficult to decide that their methods amounted to genocide.

The Crusades were a series of military campaigns by Christians of Western Europe to "recover" Jerusalem and the Holy Land from infidels, or to Christianize pagan sections of Europe. While not all the Crusades were genocides, those listed here certainly can be categorized as such. The First Crusade (1096–99) was made up of two groups: (1) unorganized bands of peasants who on their march devastated the Jewish quarters of many cities, but most of whom were killed on the overland journey to Constantinople, and (2) organized companies of European knights and soldiers under the command of French nobles. The Crusaders were merciless and indiscriminate in their killing. In Antioch (1098), the Crusaders massacred everyone in the city, whether they were Muslim or Christian, never stopping to ask who was who. During the siege of Jerusalem (1099), the Crusaders spared no one—men, women and children were slaughtered. It is said that the city's streets ran ankle deep in the blood of the slain and when the killing ceased there were huge pyramids of bodies burnt outside the city walls.

The Fourth Crusade is a good example of a purely utilitarian genocide, as the Crusaders never intended to go to Jerusalem, but instead deliberately chose to kill off economic rivals and get rich in the process. The Fourth Crusade was largely composed of French and Italian (mostly Venetian) soldiers led by many nobles. The Venetians, who had constructed ships and who had assembled provisions, proposed that the French assist them in attacking the seaport of Zara (also called Zadar), a major port city on the Dalmatian coast, south of Zagreb. It was the greatest Adriatic rival of Venice during this period. The Crusaders attacked Zara in November 1202, thoroughly pillaging the city and killing all its inhabitants. Then the Venetians directed their efforts to Constantinople, their chief trading rival. On April 13, 1204 they captured Constantinople. The army was given permission to go on a three day rampage, which spared neither women nor children and was so widespread that rivers of blood flowed down the city's streets for several days. The Crusaders, afraid that the Greeks who had survived might try to attack them, deliberately set fire to the city. There are no exact figures with regard to the number of dead, but it is clear that few survived the slaughter. The city and its population were almost completely destroyed.

The Albigensian Crusade at the beginning of the thirteenth century ravaged the Languedoc in the south of France. It was organized against a heretical group that did not accept the guidance of Rome. While the group disappeared as the result of a brutal campaign that spared neither women nor children, the king of France was able to extend the borders of his realm.

—Kurt Jonassohn and
Karin Solveig Björnson

References and Recommended Reading

Chalk, Frank, and Jonassohn, Kurt (1990). *The History and Sociology of Genocide: Analyses and Case Studies.* New Haven: Yale University Press.

Jonassohn, Kurt, with Björnson, Karin Solveig (1998). *Genocide and Gross Human Rights Violations: In Comparative Perspective.* New Brunswick, NJ: Transaction Publishers.

GENOCIDES OF THE EARLY MODERN PERIOD

The literature provides several ways of distinguishing between the Middle Ages and the Early Modern Period, though often they overlap, as they do in the present treatment. For the purpose of the comparative study of genocide, it is useful to consider the appearance of ideological genocides and the gradual disappearance of utilitarian genocides as marking the advent of the Early Modern Period. However during this period these two types of genocide overlapped.

The establishment and expansion of the colonial empires of the European powers was marked by many genocides and genocidal massacres in all continents. Some indigenous people disappeared altogether while other were decimated. There are so many cases that only a few can be mentioned here.

The indigenous people of Tasmania completely disappeared, as did the Caribs of the West Indies. Genocidal massacres have characterized the conquests of Mexico, Peru, and most of the Americas. The Aztecs were an aboriginal people who settled in Mexico in the late twelfth century A.D. By the time the Spanish arrived in Mexico, the Aztecs had become a powerful people living in Tenochtitlan (Mexico City). Sources vary on the population of Tenochtitlan before the conquest, although 100,000 seems to be a generally accepted figure. Several hundred Spanish soldiers, led by Cortes and reinforced by many thousands of native allies, arrived at Tenochtitlan in the autumn of 1519. The emperor Montezuma greeted the Spaniards and welcomed them to his city. Soon after, he was taken prisoner, enabling Cortes to rule by using him as a puppet emperor. The Aztecs rose in rebellion and Tenochtitlan reverted to Aztec control in June of 1520. In the summer of 1521, the Spanish launched their final attack on Tenochtitlan, sparing neither the Aztecs nor their allies.

When Portuguese merchants sailed to Japan in order to establish a trading base, they also brought with them Catholic priests whose mission was to save the souls of the infidels. Their efforts proved too successful and led in the early seventeenth century to a series of expulsion orders that forced them to leave Japan. At the same time their converts were persecuted, forced to recant, or killed. The final event was a tax revolt by mostly Christian peasants, assisted by unemployed samurai who were also mostly Christian. It was their Christianity that was perceived as a special threat. In the ensuing battle they were all killed. This was clearly an early case of ideological genocide.

Ideological genocides are a modern phenomenon that is performed to implement a categorical imperative inherent in a belief, ideology, or theory. The persecution of the witches is often cited in this context, but their importance is often misunderstood. Firstly, it was not the case that individual witches were prosecuted for performing witchcraft. Rather, they were accused of being members of a conspiracy with the devil and were tortured in order to make them reveal their co-conspirators. Secondly, although these persecutions occurred sporadically throughout Europe, they are not genocides by our definition. Instead, their importance lies in the methods developed for identifying victims, extracting proofs and confessions, and conducting trials that were codified in the *Malleus Maleficarum* (sometimes translated as *The Witches' Hammer*) and have been in use ever since. This handbook was written by two Dominicans, and approved by the Pope over 500 years ago and it is still in print by several publishers and in several languages—which may or may not be an indication of its current influence.

Beginning in the sixteenth century, Europe was torn apart by many religious wars between Catholics and the newly formed Protestant faith. Protestant states persecuted Catholics and Catholic states continued, as they had for centuries, to persecute "heretics." The Thirty Years' War was characterized by many brutalities, and the conquest of Magdeburg can be considered a genocidal massacre. In France, the Saint Bartholomew's Day Massacre (24 August 1572) destroyed an entire generation of French Protestant (Huguenot) leadership. Tens of thousands of Protestants had come to Paris to celebrate the marriage of Henri of Navarre and Marguerite of Valois. They wore black clothing and were easily identifiable to the majority Catholic population. While historians are in agreement that King Charles IX ordered the execution of the Protestant leadership, they are still debating whether the massacres of Protestant civilians, which spread from Paris to various provinces within France and resulted in the murder of up to 100,000 men, women and children, was premeditated.

The wars of the Vendée (1793) spread rebellion throughout northern Vendée and Deux-Sèvres, and the southern regions of Maine-et-Loire and Loire-Inférieure. The term "Vendée" refers to all the regions in France that rose against the French Revolutionary regime. The constitutional decree of March 19, 1793 made it illegal to partake in counterrevolutionary activities or protests. On the 27th of the same month, a law was passed against all members of the nobility and anyone else deemed an "enemy of the Revolution." The penalty for being labeled as such was death. The idea to exterminate the population of the Vendée was already discussed by certain generals in April 1793. Jean Baptisté Carrier, the deputy from Nantes, repeated to anyone who would listen that he would rather turn France into a cemetery than fail the Revolution. On August 1, 1793, the government passed a decree prescribing a policy of total destruction *(terre brûlée)*. The same government became increasingly frustrated by the continued fighting and passed an order on October 1 to exterminate the people of the Vendée. It was at this time that the new word "populicide" (killing of people) was coined. In October 1793, the government declared that all Vendéan "brigands" would be exterminated before the end of October. The revolutionary army finally implemented these decrees in 1794 in a campaign that would claim the lives of more than 117,000 people, over 14 percent of the population. Men, women and children were massacred, often in their own homes. The army concentrated their efforts in the countryside, destroying everyone and everything in its path. Luckily, many of the towns escaped such widespread destruction.

—*Kurt Jonassohn and Karin Solveig Björnson*

References and Recommended Reading

Chalk, Frank, and Jonassohn, Kurt (1990). *The History and Sociology of Genocide: Analyses and Case Studies.* New Haven: Yale University Press.

Jonassohn, Kurt, with Björnson, Karin Solveig (1998). *Genocide and Gross Human Rights Violations: In Comparative Perspective.* New Brunswick, NJ: Transaction Publishers.

GOEBBELS, PAUL JOSEF

Paul Josef Goebbels was born in Reydt, Germany, in 1897, to a poor but devout Roman Catholic family. Unable to enlist in the German Army in World War I because of a birth defect of a club foot, he directed his energies toward the attainment of a doctorate in literature, history and philosophy from the University of Heidelberg in 1920. Unable to secure a newspaper position with the more liberal press, many of which were owned by Jews, he turned his attention toward the Nazi Party, which he joined in 1924, never forgetting his original failures. His antisemitism found its natural outlet in his talents at organization and propaganda.

In 1926 he was appointed *Gauleiter* or "District Head" of Berlin; and in 1928 was elected to the *Reichstag* or German Parliament. Two years later, Hitler appointed him chief of propaganda for the Nazi Party. Shortly after Hitler's appointment as Chancellor of Germany in January of 1933, he appointed Goebbels Minister of Propaganda and Public Information, thus giving him virtual control over Germany's communications media and cultural arts. On May 1, 1945, after the suicides of Hitler and his mistress-wife Eva Braun in the Chancellery Bunker, Goebbels committed suicide together with his wife, Magda, after first having arranged the deaths of their six young children, ages four to twelve.

Goebbels's "accomplishments" during his tenure as Minister of Propaganda and Public Information may be said to be three: (1) He was the architect of the infamous *Kristallnacht* ("Night of the Broken Glass") attack on the Jewish shops and synagogues in November 1938; (2) he was cocreator of *Der Fuhrerprinzip,* the so-called "Leadership Principle" by which the people of Germany swore total allegiance to Adolf Hitler in whom they were led to believe resided all goodness and truth for Germany's future and against whom resistance was to be equated with evil; and (3) he promoted his use of the so-called "Big Lie" by which falsehoods against a straw enemy (in this case, the Jewish People) were repeated over and over again in increasing exaggeration that he fully and correctly understood would make them believable to larger and larger numbers of people.

After the Second World War, his multi-volume *Diaries* were published in both German and English, revealing much about conditions in Germany during the Nazi hegemony and much about the Nazi hierarchy, including Hitler himself.

—*Steven L. Jacobs*

References and Recommended Reading

Reuth, Rolf-George (1994). *Goebbels.* Translated from the German by Krishna Winston. New York: Harcourt Brace.

GOVERNMENT AND GENOCIDE

There are at least eight basic types of societies that can be defined on a measurement scale of life and death. I place these broad types within a framework of political regimes rather than of cultural systems.

The following definitions of societal types should be viewed as political guidelines with near infinite shadings and not as rigid types.

1. *Genocidal Societies*—the state arbitrarily takes the lives of citizens for deviant or dissident behavior. But it must be emphasized that the distinction between genocidal and all other types of societies is qualitative: The genocidal society is the only form of rule that takes lives systematically.
2. *Deportation* or *Incarceration Societies*—the state either removes individuals from the larger body politic or in some way prevents their interaction with the commonwealth in general.
3. *Torture Societies*—people defined as enemies of the state are victimized short of death, returned to the societies from which they came, and left in these societies as living evidence of the high risk of deviance or dissidence.
4. *Harassment Societies*—deviants are constantly being picked up, searched, seized, or held in violation of laws that are usually remote from the actual crimes the state feels these individuals have committed. Since laws can be invoked against almost any behavior, the possibility of harassment of individuals through legal channels is infinite.

These four types of societies have in common the physical discomfiture and

We Should Apply Our Knowledge to Nations and Epochs

We should apply our knowledge of individual and group neurotic or psychotic behavior to the political scene, to peoples or whole generations. Such insights are reflected in significant works on group behavior, but statesmen have yet to apply these new insights to develop skills of diagnosis and policy to the political scene, to nations suffering from stress and catastrophe, or to critical epochs in history.

—*Eric H. Boehm*

dislocation of deviant, dissident individuals, brought about by means of everything from simple harassment for nonpayment of taxes, for example, to direct liquidation of the person. In order to avoid the undue softening of categories, it is important to appreciate that patterns of genocide involve physical actions and not just symbolic threat.

There are four other types of social systems that employ what might be called symbolic or noncoercive methods for gaining allegiance and adherence.

5. In *Traditional Shame Societies,* participation in the collective will is generated through instilling the individual with a sense of disapproval from outside sources and ensured by the isolation suffered as a result of nonparticipation in the normative system.
6. *Guilt Societies* are closely akin to shame societies but in guilt societies a sense of wrongdoing is internalized in the individual, causing persons of all persuasions to respond to normative standards.
7. *Tolerant Societies*—in many Western societies we observe tolerant systems, where norms are well articulated and understood but where deviance and dissidence are permitted to go unpunished; they are not celebrated, but neither are they destroyed. These can be described as a series of pluralisms operating within a large legal monism.
8. *Permissive Societies*—Finally, there are permissive societies in which norms are questioned and in which community definitions are transformed as needed rather than enduring as state definitions of what constitutes normative behavior. The decision-making process is itself subject to change. Such systematic alterations do not entail a loss of status or position within the society.

A major category left unresolved by such an interior or national model is the function of genocide due to imperial aggression or foreign intervention. Here we have the contradiction of upstanding European and American cultures being responsible for the liquidation of masses of native populations. Thus, there is the destruction of the Zulu people by the British; the decimation and virtual elimination of many Indian tribes by early European settlers in the American continent; and the impoverishment of the indigenous people in the former Belgian Congo. These are forms of genocide against foreign peoples rather than nationals.

Almost every society has all eight types present in one admixture or another. It becomes an analytic task to determine the essential characterization of the system and the point where quantity is transformed into quality: at what point the numbers of people involved in sanction by the state begin to define the character of that state.

—*Irving Louis Horowitz*

References and Recommended Reading

Horowitz, Irving Louis (1997). *Taking Lives: Genocide and State Power.* Fourth Edition, Expanded and Revised. New Brunswick, NJ: Transaction Publishers.

GUATEMALA, GENOCIDE IN

Various international human rights organizations, along with the United Nations, concur with the estimate that between 100,000 and 140,000 people, primarily impoverished indigenous Mayan people residing in small countryside villages, were the victims of terror, extrajudicial killings, hundreds of massacres and, ultimately, genocide perpetrated by Guatemalan government death squads in the 1980s and early 1990s.

Fearful of a leftist take-over as well as the actions of leftist guerrillas, the Guatemalan government, under the command of Efrain Rios Montt, a former army general who assumed power in a 1982 coup d'état, undertook a vicious campaign in which they ravaged whole villages, killings tens of thousands of innocent people. Leftist guerrillas fought and carried out an on-going insurgency, but the slaughter by government forces was indiscriminate, except for the fact that it was aimed at those of Mayan descent who eked out an impoverished existence in the highlands of the country. For many in the government, the slaughter was an ongoing attempt since the early 1960s to quell the desire by the *campesinos*—poor farmers—to scratch out more than a meager subsistence.

Governmental violence against the poor had its origins in the 1950s. Looking askance at the democratically elected government of Jacobo Arbenz Guzman, the United States Central Intelligence Agency organized a coup that overthrew Arbenz and replaced him with a right-wing government. In large part, Arbenz was considered anathema for he favored radical land reform and was viewed with suspicion by US-owned banana companies based in Guatemala, particularly the United Fruit Company. A subsequent series of US-supported right-wing governments and their policies resulted in a vicious cycle of government-sponsored repression and violence. In 1960 a military uprising failed but some rebel officers fled to the mountains where, inspired by the Cuban Revolution, they studied Marxism-Leninism and formed the initial guerrilla groups that would carry out the insurgency in the years ahead.

In 1966 the United States sent Green Berets to Guatemala and spent millions of dollars to train the Guatemalan Armed Forces. More than 8,000 people were killed in the subsequent counterinsurgency effort. It was during this period that army-organized death squads were formed and became active. Tellingly, after he became President in 1971, General Carlos Araña Osorio, who oversaw an increase of killing and disappearances, asserted that "If it is necessary to turn the country into a cemetery in order to pacify it, I will not hesitate to do so." For years on end the United States trained numerous Guatemalan military leaders at its School of the Americas. Many of these "leaders" went on to oversee the assassination, torture, terror, summary execution, and genocide of over a hundred thousand people, including the "disappearance" of approximately 40,000 others. They were also responsible for the destruction of over 440 villages. These actions resulted in more than 200,000 orphans, 80,000 widows, and the displacement of more than one million people from their homes.

The height of military counterinsurgency efforts were carried out in the early 1980s by government soldiers and paramilitary patrols. At this time, hundreds of Indian villages were destroyed in scorched-earth campaigns, thousands of people killed, and many driven from their homes and into exile. In *Unfinished Conquest: The Guatemalan Tragedy,* Victor Perera estimates that in one five-year counterinsurgency campaign (1978–1983) conducted by the Guatemalan army, almost one-third of Guatemala's 85,000 Ixil Maya Indians were wiped out.

In March 1994 the Guatemalan government and leftist guerrillas signed a human rights accord. In late December 1996, a peace treaty was signed between the leftists and the government. Part and parcel of the peace agreement was to be the implementation of earlier agreements to establish social equality via economic and agrarian reforms, the protection of human rights, and the establishment of a "Truth Commission" to investigate war crimes. It was also supposed to result in the resettlement of refugees, recognize Indian rights, reform election laws, disarm and demobilize rebels and ascertain the future of the Guatemalan military. A National Reconciliation Law was ratified and took effect in December 1996 that protected rebels from arrest. Concomitantly, in late 1996 the Guatemalan government issued a blanket amnesty for those involved in many crimes, but it is supposed to exclude those involved in torture, genocide, and forced disappearance. However, human rights workers have criticized the law, asserting that the vagueness in its language could prevent prosecution of those accused of atrocities throughout the 1980s and early 1990s. As of the late 1990s, prosecutions of the guilty have been rare and prosecutors seemed particularly reluctant to challenge the military. What is not rare is the exhumations of hundreds of mass graves—the Catholic Church in Guatemala has identified 422 massacre sites—where the victims' family members and friends retrieve the skeletons of the murdered and bury them in proper graves. Adding insult to injury, though, the notorious General Efrain Rios Montt was elected Speaker of Guatemala's Congress in December 1995. His ultimate aim was to be elected president of the country, but he was not successful in that effort.

In 1995 a United Nations Human Rights Commission in Guatemala sharply criticized the human rights record of the government of President Ramior de Leon Carpio. While not directly implicating the government, it presented extensive evidence of military involvement in human rights violations such as torture and cited complicity in cases of harassment, torture and murder. It particularly noted that authorities frequently and systematically failed to investigate such cases.

In June of 1996 a United States presidential panel, the Intelligence Oversight Board, issued a report based on a study that documented the fact the CIA "did not keep Congress adequately informed of its activities in Guatemala and was insensitive to human right abuses there." Further, the report asserted that "several CIA assets (agents) were credibly alleged to have ordered, planned, or participated in serious human rights violations such as assassination, extrajudicial execution, torture or kidnapping while they were assets—and that the CIA was contemporaneously aware of many of the allegations."

In February 1999 the Truth Commission (formally entitled the Commission for Historical Clarification), which was sponsored by the United Nations, issued a report on the tragedy that befell Guatemala over a period of some 36 years. In addition to concluding that more than 200,000 people were killed, more than 90 percent of them by government forces, it asserts that some of the state's counterinsurgency operations could be correctly deemed genocide. Further, the report dismissed the military's assertion that the massacres were the result of rogue soldiers, and it found there was a "strategy to provoke terror in the population" and that it was directed from the very top echelons of government. It further asserted that the state "had become an instrument to protect a racist and unjust economic order."

In the late 1990s the situation in Guatemala is still, at best, tenuous. Large landowners are wary of the outcome of the peace accords and some predict an apocalyptic turn of events involving land disputes between ranchers and landowners and indigenous groups. Many military personnel feel that they were slighted at the negotiating table, especially since their ranks and budget are to be cut by at least a third. Finally, in the mid to late 1990s, threats, terroristic actions and extrajudicial killings were still being reported in various areas.

—*Samuel Totten*

References and Recommended Reading
Perera, Victor (1993). *Unfinished Conquest: The Guatemalan Tragedy.* Berkeley, CA: University of California.

GULAG

The term *gulag* is a Russian language acronym, the best translation of which is "Chief Administration of Corrective Labor Camps." Established after the Russian Revolution in 1918, under the explicit orders of Stalin, this vast penal network was directly under the auspices of the dreaded KGB or Soviet State Secret Police. It is estimated that between the years 1934 and 1947, upwards of ten million men and women, both those suspected and those found guilty of "crimes against the State," were subject to forced labor in these camps. In addition to brutal treatment at the hands of the prison guards, the inmates were subjected to the brutality of Russian winters especially in the Siberian camps, disease, malnutrition and starvation, torture, and executions. No actual count exists as to the number either interned in these camps or who died as a result of their incarceration, but one can look at the work of R. J. Rummel for approximations. Though their administration by the KGB ceased with Stalin's death, the camps themselves continued to exist until the breakup of the Soviet Union in the 1990s.

The best known description of life in these Russian gulags is contained in the three-volume work by Aleksandr Solzhenitsyn, *The Gulag Archipelago 1918–1956: An Experiment in Literary Investigation.*

— Steven L. Jacobs

References and Recommended Reading
Conquest, Robert (1979). *Kolyma: The Arctic Death Camps.* New York: Oxford University Press.
Solzhenitsyn, Aleksandr I. (1974). *The Gulag Archipelago 1918–1956: An Experiment in Literary Investigation.* Three volumes. Translated from the Russian by Thomas P. Whitney. New York: Harper and Row.

THE GULAG ARCHIPELAGO, BY SOLZHENITSYN

The Gulag Archipelago by Aleksandr I. Solzhenitsyn is a trilogy on Soviet slave labor camps. Above all, it is an allegory on the trained capacity of dictatorship to eat its own, to destroy diversity and individuality in the name of collectivity, or at least the organic ideal of preserving the state at all costs.

While it can be considered as all one piece with his other works, *One Day in the Life of Ivan Denisovich, The Cancer Ward,* and *The First Circle,* this work is singular. The first volume of *The Gulag Archipelago* is a classic statement of social reality. It is widely acknowledged as the foremost contribution to the literature on power and powerlessness, and it will continue to contribute to that literature long after the biography of the author ceases to be a point of contention or argumentation.

Solzhenitsyn takes for granted that the Soviet Union as such was a total institution, a network of integrated agencies of coercion dedicated to the survival and promulgation of maximum state power over minimally empowered human beings no matter what the extent to the carnage. Few have been privileged to write from inside the whale; yet even those who have suffered similar outrages and tried to explain conditions or consequences to "outsiders" have been unable to create such a compendium of horrors.

The Gulag Archipelago brings to mind, with its documentary evidence of the slaying and imprisonment of tens of millions of Russians, comparison with the Japanese experience at Hiroshima and Nagasaki as recounted in Robert Jay Lifton's *Death in Life* and the Jewish experience of the Holocaust as recounted by Raul Hilberg in *The Destruction of the European Jews.* But the Soviet experience is unique, precisely because terror was self-inflicted, because Russians killed

Gulag prisoners breaking stones. Seen here using hammers, the prisoners had only the most primitive tools and did much of their work with their bare hands in the most arduous extremes of heat and cold. (Courtesy of David King)

and maimed other Russians, albeit often of different national backgrounds. In this sense, the banality of evil spoken of by Hannah Arendt is carried one step further; for the terror is not US airplanes over defenseless Japanese cities or the destruction of European Jews at the hands of the Nazi Gestapo. However awful these other holocausts may be, the enemy, for the most part, was external. In the Soviet case, the enemy was also for the most part, internal.

The Gulag Archipelago offers a special sort of Dostoyevskian nightmare in which Russian spies upon Russian, communist betrays communist, Red Army officers destroy Red Army officers. One of Solzhenitsyn's major contributions is to note how terrorism functioned as a structural feature of Soviet society rather than as an episodic moment in Russian time. That is to say, Solzhenitsyn does not simply speak about the Stalin era or about special quixotic moments in that era when terror was high but of the entire period of 1918–1956. The Gulag Archipelago existed because the need for terror replaced the practice of liberty within Russian life. Within this structural framework there were special eras, for example, 1929–1930, when 15 million peasants were either slaughtered, uprooted, or imprisoned; 1937–1938, when party personnel, intellectuals, and cadres of the military were entirely wiped out; and again in 1944–1946, when armed forces personnel, prisoners of war, and persons having contact with the West were similarly destroyed or disposed of.

It really matters little that *The Gulag Archipelago* is not an entirely balanced or fair-minded work, that it fails to recount properly and fairly the heroic events of Soviet development and of the Soviet people in the face of all sorts of foreign military adversity. The major accusation launched against Solzhenitsyn is of his emotivism and presumed mysticism. Underlying this charge is the most serious charge that he lacks adequate analytic categories; hence that his critique is one-sided, that it fails to take into consideration the positive achievements of Soviet industrialization. While it is doubtlessly correct that he uses emotional language, it is simply nonsense to claim that he preaches mysticism.

Solzhenitsyn's *Gulag Archipelago* has an implicit analytic scheme that deserves to be dealt with seriously, even profoundly. For in this towering statement of prison life in a totalitarian society there are "lessons" about twentieth century social systems as a whole. The political sociology of Soviet society illumines the contours of a future that indeed can "work"—at least in short bursts. *Herein lies its terrors for us all.*

—Irving Louis Horowitz

References and Recommended Reading

Horowitz, Irving Louis (1997). *Taking Lives: Genocide and State Power.* Fourth Edition, Expanded and Revised. New Brunswick, NJ: Transaction Publishers.

Solzhenitsyn, Aleksandr I. (1973). *The Gulag Archipelago, 1918–1956: An Experiment in Literary Investigation. Part I: The Prisons Industry;* and *Part II: Perpetual Motion.* Translated from the Russian by Thomas P. Whitney. New York and London: Harper and Row.

Solzhenitsyn, Aleksandr I. (1975). *The Gulag Archipelago, 1918–1956: An Experiment in Literary Investigation. Part III: The Destructive Labor Camps;* and *Part IV: The Soul and Barbed Wire.* Translated from the Russian by Thomas P. Whitney. New York and London: Harper and Row.

Solzhenitsyn, Aleksandr I. (1978). *The Gulag Archipelago, 1918–1956: An Experiment in Literary Investigation. Part V: Katorga; Part VI: Exile;* and *Part VII: Stalin Is No More.* Translated from the Russian by Harry Willets. New York and London: Harper and Row.

HAMIDIAN (ARMENIAN) MASSACRES

The Armenian Massacres in 1894–1896 were the first near-genocidal series of atrocities committed against the Armenian population of the Ottoman Empire. They were carried out during the reign of Abdul Hamid (Abdulhamit) II (1876–1909), the last sultan effectively to rule over the Turkish state. The massacres broke out in the summer of 1894 in the remote region of Sasun in southern Armenia, where the government relied on the excuse of Armenian resistance to Kurdish encroachment into the last recesses of the mountains to order the sacking of the alpine hamlets. The incident resulted in strong Armenian protests against the sultan's brutal policies and European interventions to quell further disturbances by persuading the Ottoman government to adopt reforms for the Armenian-populated provinces. The police responded to a demonstration held in Constantinople in September 1895 by Armenian political organizations that sought to pressure the government and the European Powers to implement the promised administrative reforms by letting loose a massacre in the capital city. Thereupon, beginning without provocation in the city of Trebizond on the Black Sea, and in a pattern indicating a premeditated plan, a series of massacres spread south through nearly every major Armenian-inhabited town of the empire. It culminated in the single worst atrocity in those months with the burning of the Armenian cathedral of Urfa (ancient Edessa) within whose walls some 3,000 Armenians had taken refuge during the siege of their neighborhood. To a last desperate attempt by Armenian revolutionaries to draw the attention of the world by seizing in Constantinople the European-owned Ottoman Bank in August 1896, the government responded by unleashing wholesale reprisals during which five to six thousand Armenians were killed in the space of three days within sight of the European embassies.

The massacres marked a new threshold of violence in the Ottoman Empire, especially because they occurred in peacetime with none of the exigencies of war invoked as justification for summary action. Their ferocity reflected the sultan's determination to dissuade the Armenians from entertaining any notions of seeing reforms introduced under Western pressure. They were also designed to strike a severe blow to Armenian efforts to organize politically by undermining their expectations and the sense of self-reliance they hoped to develop in order to cope with the aggravated disorder and misrule in the eastern provinces of the empire. Estimates of the dead run from 100,000 to 300,000. Tens of thousands fled the country. Thousands of others were forcibly converted to Islam. The associated plunder of homes and businesses economically ruined countless families, and the destitute counted in the hundreds of thousands. The conflicting interests of the European states, the steady support of the sultan by Kaiser Wilhelm II of Germany, and the reactionary policies of Tsar Alexander III in Russia, all adduced to neutralize the capacity of the Great Powers to hold in check the brutal autocracy of Abdul Hamid. Labeled infidels by their Turkish overlords and Muslim neighbors, the Armenians remained second class citizens expressly denied equal protection of the law. The impunity with which the entire episode of systematic massacres were carried out exposed the serious vulnerability of the Armenian population as the Ottoman Empire went into further decline. It also revealed the absence of resolve among the Western states for any kind of humanitarian intervention sufficient to remedy the problems described at the time as the Armenian Question.

Recalled by the Armenians as the "Great Massacres" and described in the literature of the time as the "Armenian Massacres," the atrocities of the 1890s are now often called the Hamidian Massacres to distinguish them from the greater atrocities associated with the 1915 Armenian Genocide. The Hamidian massacres verified the capacity of the Turkish state to carry out a systematic policy of murder and plunder against a minority population and to provide immunity to all parties associated with the crimes in the face of international protest. In retrospect, it had set a precedent all of whose elements, short of organized deportation, would be reproduced during the Armenian Genocide.

—Rouben Paul Adalian

References and Recommended Reading

Bliss, Rev. Edwin M. (1982). *Turkey and the Armenian Atrocities.* Fresno, CA: Meshag Publishing. [Reprint of the 1896 edition.]

Walker, Christopher J. (1980). *Armenia: The Survival of a Nation.* New York: St. Martin's Press.

THE HEREROS, GENOCIDE OF

The Herero people, like their neighbors, the Namas, were cattle-herding nomadic peoples living in South West Africa, a colony of Germany. At the beginning of the twentieth century, most of the approximately 4,500 German settlers in the country were cattle ranchers whose inland farms were connected to the seacoast by railroad lines. The railroad lines and the adjacent land were off limits to the native population, which disrupted their nomadic lifestyles. Moreover, under German rule the Hereros and the Namas were largely without civil or political rights and were frequently attacked by German settlers.

In 1903 the Hereros decided to rebel after learning of a German plan to concentrate them on reservations and build a major new railroad. On January 12, 1904, led by Chief Maharero, the Hereros launched a military campaign that killed approximately 100 Germans and captured most of Herero land. The Germans counterattacked, and by mid-August, had destroyed most of the Herero military forces. The surviving Herero, including many women and children, were driven by the Germans into the Omaheke Desert, where they died of thirst and starvation. The genocide of the Hereros has also become famous for one of the drastic devices used by German General Lothar von Trotha, in poisoning the water holes of the Hereros. The Germans also attacked all native villages, including the Namas. Approximately 80 percent of the Herero people, or 65,000, and approximately 50 percent of the Namas, or 10,000, perished.

According to Bridgman and Worley, there were many protests in Germany, including government agencies that refused to support the actions, and demands that the slaughter be stopped before all the Hereros were killed. The slaughter of the Hereros was recognized by the UN Whitaker Commission as one of the first genocides of the twentieth century.

—Torben Jørgensen and Eric Markusen

References and Recommended Reading

Bridgman, Jon, and Worley, Leslie J. (1997). Genocide of the Hereros. In Totten, Samuel; Parsons, William S.; and Charny, Israel W. (Eds.), *Century of Genocide: Eyewitness Accounts and Critical Views.* New York: Garland Publishing, pp. 3–40.

Dreschler, Horst (1980). *"Let Us Die Fighting": The Struggle of the Herero and Nama Against German Imperialism (1894–1914).* London: Zed Press.

HIBAKUSHA

Hibakusha are the survivors of the atomic bombings by the US of Hiroshima and Nagasaki in August 1945. Over the years, the several hundred thousand survivors suffered from disfiguration, radiation-induced illnesses including cancers, as well as genetic damage that affects future generations. A relatively early major and sensitively done study of the Hibakusha by Robert Jay Lifton introduced the concept of "psychic numbing" or psychological defenses against experiencing the unbearable horrors of the events that had taken place.

References and Recommended Reading

Lifton, Robert Jay (1967). *Death in Life: Survivors of Hiroshima.* New York: Random House.

HIMMLER, HEINRICH

Heinrich Himmler was born in 1900 in Munich, Bavaria, into a strict Roman Catholic family. His father was a schoolteacher. Graduating high school, he enlisted in the Army in 1917 but saw no action. After the First World War, he enrolled in the School of Technology in Munich where he studied both agriculture and economics without graduating, and worked at both chicken farming and sales in the 1920s until joining the Nationalist Socialist Party, which saw him become Assistant Propaganda Leader in 1926, one year after joining the SS. By 1929 he had become head of the SS, Hitler's personal bodyguard, and one year later was elected to the Reichstag.

With Hitler's ascent to power in 1933, Himmler became President of Munich and Chief of the Political Police for all of Bavaria as well as throughout the Reich, with the exception of Prussia, which was under the control of Hermann Goering. By 1936, he was *Reichsfuhrer-SS* for the entire Reich and Chief of the German Police, including being responsible for the network of concentration camps in Germany and later Poland.

He continued his rise to power by becoming Minister of the Interior in 1943 and Commander-in-Chief of the Reserve Army Group Vistula in 1944. By early 1945, realizing that the war was soon to be lost, he attempted to broker peace with the West rather than the Soviets by such tactics as transferring prisoners and ordering the termination of extermination, all to no avail. Captured by the Allies, after first attempting to disguise himself, he cheated the hangman's noose by committing suicide at Nuremberg prison on May 23, 1945.

Himmler's somewhat meteoric rise to power in the Nazi pantheon saw him becoming the second most powerful man in Nazi Germany directly behind Adolf Hitler. Supportive of Hitler almost until the very end, his mastery of organization and administrative procedures, coupled with a total lack of moral commitment to anything other than the so-called "Aryan ideal" of Nordic supremacy, enabled him to construct a system of terror and mass death and destruction not only against Jews primarily, but also against Sinti-Romani, Slavs, and Poles as well. The time-honored values of his boyhood within the Roman Catholic Church—namely those of obedience to authority, gentlemanly honor, and courage in the face of evil—were perverted by him in the organizational structure of the SS, and he gave himself over entirely to the antisemitic fantasy fueled by Hitler of the Jews as the enemies of all humankind as well as a direct threat to the racial purity of the Aryan race. Hitler's "Final Solution to the Jewish Problem" thus represented for Himmler the fulfillment of his own ideals and the means by which Aryan supremacy could be achieved.

—*Steven L. Jacobs*

References and Recommended Reading
Padfield, Peter (1990). *Himmler: Reichsfuhrer—SS.* New York: Henry Holt.

HIROSHIMA

Hiroshima was the first city to be attacked with a nuclear weapon. The nuclear weapon was dropped by the United States Army Air Corps over Hiroshima at 8:15 A.M. on August 6, 1945. It fell for 43 seconds before exploding at approximately 1900 feet above the city. The bomb that destroyed Hiroshima, "Little Boy," was a gun-type uranium bomb developed in the secret US nuclear project, the Manhattan Engineering Project. It had a yield of approximately 15 kilotons (equivalent to 15,000 tons of TNT).

The number of persons in Hiroshima at the time of the bombing is thought to have been approximately 400,000, of which some 40,000 were military personnel. The bomb destroyed most of the city, and resulted in the immediate deaths of some 90,000–100,000 persons. (There was no way to determine an exact number of deaths.) Deaths and injuries were caused by blast, heat, fire and radiation. By the end of 1945, approximately 140,000 peo-

On 5 December 1998, the UNESCO World Heritage Committee meeting in Merida, Mexico, decided to register the A-bomb Dome on the World Heritage List. A symbol of Hiroshima's pledge to abolish nuclear weapons and seek lasting peace, the A-bomb Dome will enter the twenty-first century as a legacy common to the entire human race. The steel skeleton of the dome, which at the time was the Industrial Promotion Hall, marks the epicenter of the blast of the atomic bomb, which burned away the dome's concrete covering. (Hiroshima Peace Memorial Museum)

The Children's Peace Monument in Hiroshima was unveiled on 5 May 1958 in honor of Sadako Sasaki, a young victim of leukemia caused by the A-bomb. (Hiroshima Peace Memorial Museum)

ple are thought to have died as a result of the Hiroshima bombing.

Survivors of the nuclear bombings of Hiroshima and Nagasaki are known as *hibakusha.* Officially recognized *hibakusha* from Hiroshima and the second atomic bombing at Nagasaki have numbered over 360,000. Many of these *hibakusha* have suffered from disfiguration and radiation-related illnesses, some of which have affected and will affect future generations. *Hibakusha* have lived not only with suffering, but with the fear that any illness could result in death. They have also faced discrimination and rejection.

The decision to drop nuclear weapons on Japan was made by US President Harry Truman and his close advisors, despite their knowledge that Japan was attempting to negotiate terms of surrender. On learning of the bomb's "success," Truman commented, "This is the greatest thing in history." The B-29 bomber that dropped the bomb on Hiroshima was named the *Enola Gay* after the mother of its pilot, Colonel Paul Tibbets.

In 1996, the International Court of Justice handed down an advisory opinion in which it found that the threat or use of nuclear weapons would "generally be contrary to the rules of international law applicable in armed conflict, and in particular the principles and rules of humanitarian law." The Court was unable to decide, however, whether or not such threat or use would be illegal in "an extreme circumstance of self-defense, in which the very survival of a State would be at stake." Since international humanitarian law was already in place at the end of World War II and the survival of the United States was not at stake, it can be concluded that the bombings of Hiroshima and Nagasaki were illegal acts of war. They violated international humanitarian law by attacking civilian populations and causing unnecessary suffering to combatants.

In Hiroshima Peace Memorial Park, among other buildings and monuments, there is a Peace Memorial Museum and a Memorial Cenotaph with this inscription: "Let all souls here rest in peace; for we shall not repeat the evil."

—David Krieger

References and Recommended Reading

Lifton, Robert Jay, and Mitchell, Greg (1995). *Hiroshima in America: A Half Century of Denial.* New York: Avon Books.

Sekimori, Gaynor (Translator) (1986). *The Legacy of Hiroshima, Its Past, Our Future.* Tokyo: Kosei Publishing. Introduction by Naomi Shohno. Foreword by George Marshall.

HITLER, ADOLF

Adolf Hitler was born in Upper Braunau, Austria, in April of 1889, the son of a petty bureaucratic customs official and a sickly mother. Adolf Hitler rose to become Chancellor of his adopted country of Germany, its unrivalled *Fuehrer,* head of the *Nationalsozialistiche Deutsche Arbeitspartei* (NSDAP, Nazi), and architect of the "Final Solution to the Jewish Question." Hitler was raised and grew to manhood at a time when antisemitism was rife throughout both countries, when its literature was all-too-prevalent and readily obtainable, and politicians were elected with clearly evident antisemitic positions.

As a young boy, Hitler was not a particularly good student, though he blamed

Adolf Hitler addressing the Reichstag in Berlin, 1944. (Corbis)

his teachers in *Mein Kampf* ("My Fight" or "My Struggle") for their failure to recognize his intellectual and artistic gifts. Remaining in Upper Braunau after his mother's death in 1907, four years after his father's death, he moved to Vienna where he failed the entrance examination to the Vienna Academy of Art's School of Painting and Architecture and supported himself by painting penny postcards and living in a flophouse. During his sojourn there he was influenced by the public politics and antisemitism of its Mayor, Karl Lueger ("I decide who is a Jew!").

Having relocated to Munich, with the outbreak of World War I, Hitler enlisted in the Bavarian Army, became a Lance Corporal, and was awarded the Iron Cross, First Class, in 1918. In October of that year, he was temporarily blinded in a gas attack and spent three months in a hospital. Upon his return to health, he remained in the military as a political indoctrination officer, attempting to learn of the many political parties springing up in Germany. He was assigned to visit the NSDAP, filed his report of its meeting, and received a short time later a membership card. In 1921 he was elected Chairman of the Party, and in 1923 attempted the infamous "Beer Hall Putsch" which landed him in Landsberg Prison, sentenced to five years, where he wrote volume one of *Mein Kampf.* He was released after serving only nine months of his sentence.

By the Reichstag elections of 1932, Hitler had become the leader of the largest political party in Germany, though the NSDAP never won a decided majority in any democratically held election. In January of 1933, he was appointed Chancellor of Germany and by 1939, the start of World War II, its undisputed *Fuehrer* or Leader. For the next two years, his military successes astounded the world as he subjugated Poland, France, Denmark, Norway, Austria, Belgium, and parts of North Africa. It is only with the ill-fated winter invasion of Russia in 1941, and America's entry into the war, that the tide began to turn. In the evening of April 30/May 1, 1945, as Soviet forces approached the underground bunker at the Chancellery in Berlin, Hitler along with his mistress-wife Eva Braun, whom he married the previous day, committed suicide, with the explicit instructions that their bodies were to be burned beyond recognition in the Chancellery garden.

Hitler Was a Disaster for the Germans as Well

Hitler provided the escape and ecstasy the people sought and needed, but at a terrible price. His image of the world was so completely false that his decisions contained the elements of the deranged. He committed so many irrational acts that the result could be only disaster, death, and misery for all the peoples under German sway, and for the Germans as well.

—*Eric H. Boehm*

While scholars continue to struggle and debate the specific sources of Hitler's antisemitism, his obsession with the Jews and his acceptance of the false myth of a Jewish world conspiracy as outlined in the notorious Russian forgery, *The Protocols of the Learned Elders of Zion,* one must always keep in mind the powerful antisemitic tenor of the times in which he lived, its political, economic, and religious thrusts, as well as the widespread belief in the truth of its biological and genetic manifestation (i.e., the racial identity of the Jews and their "willingness" to pollute and weaken the Aryan/Nordic race). Hitler came to his realization that the only solution was the total extermination and annihilation of the Jews and thereby set off and led one of the most far-reaching evil organizations of destruction seen in human history.

—*Steven L. Jacobs*

References and Recommended Reading
Bullock, Alan (1964). *Hitler: A Study in Tyranny.* New York: Harper and Row.
Kershaw, Ian (1998). *Hitler, 1889–1936: Hubris.* London: Allen Lane.
Lukacs, John (1997). *The Hitler of History.* New York: Knopf.

HOLOCAUST AND GENOCIDE BIBLIOGRAPHIC DATABASE

The *Holocaust and Genocide Bibliographic Database, Version 2.2* was developed at the Institute on the Holocaust and Genocide, Jerusalem in order to provide scholars with easy access to interdisciplinary material in the developing field of Holocaust and Genocide Studies. The database was largely funded through a grant from the US Institute on Peace in Washington, DC.

The database can be used through DOS on IBM-compatible personal computers using the Procite Bibliographic Database Manager. Procite offers a wide range of search possibilities as well as formatting capabilities to enable a user to print bibliographies to specific requirements.

Version 2.2 of the database contains over 9,750 unique bibliographic citations of books, chapters of books, book reviews, journal articles, film reviews and dissertations from 1980 through 1994 as well as a number of entries from earlier years. More then half the citations contain abstracts, with many including multiple abstracts. A unique controlled word list was developed to index each citation. This list can be used to search the database through specific fields or though free text searching. The subject areas in the database include: the Holocaust, Armenian Genocide, Cambodian Genocide, Ukrainian Famine, American Indians, Denial of Genocide, Genocide Prevention and Early Warning Systems, Nuclear Weapons, Altruism, Massacres, State Genocidal Tendencies, and Education and Curriculum Development for Genocide.

The database incorporates the first two volumes of the Institute on the Holocaust and Genocide, Jerusalem series, *Genocide: A Critical Bibliographic Review* (Charny, Israel W. [Ed.], Volume 1, 1988 and Volume 2, 1991 by Mansell Publishing in London and Facts on File Publications in New York). These citations were supplemented by material contributed by a group of "Distinguished Scholars of Holocaust and Genocide" selected specifically for the database. Finally, citations were incorporated into the database from various on-line sources and major works in the field.

Information on the database is available from the Institute on the Holocaust and Genocide, Jerusalem. Among the institutes at which the database can be accessed are the US Holocaust Memorial Museum in Washington, DC; the Simon Wiesenthal Center in Los Angeles; Yad Vashem in Jerusalem; the Wannsee Conference Museum in Berlin; and the Beth Shalom Holocaust Memorial Centre in Nottingham, England.

—*Marc I. Sherman*

References and Recommended Reading
Sherman, Marc I., and Charny, Israel W. (Eds.) (1994). *Holocaust and Genocide Bibliographic Database, Version 2.2.* Jerusalem: Institute on the Holocaust and Genocide.

HOLOCAUST AND GENOCIDE STUDIES

Holocaust and Genocide Studies first appeared in 1986, published by Pergamon Press in association with the United States Holocaust Memorial Council and Yad Vashem under the editorship of Professor Yehuda Bauer. Beginning with the spring 1993 issue, the journal is being published by Oxford University Press under the sponsorship of the United States Holocaust Museum. With Volume 10, Professor Richard D. Breitman became the journal editor. The journal appears three times a year and contains articles with abstracts, review essays, book reviews, letters to the editor, citations of recently published books on Holocaust and genocide studies, and a list of major research and resource centers on the Holocaust that appears annually in the last issue.

An editorial statement in the journal states that *Holocaust and Genocide Studies* is "an international, interdisciplinary journal, [that] promotes discussion on the implications of the Holocaust and of genocide, thus encouraging contemplation of the entire range of human behavior, of the moral dimensions of science and technology in society, and of methods of social and political organization. In addition to providing the major forum for work in the extensive body of literature and documentation of the Holocaust itself, the journal is the only publication to address the related study of how these insights apply to other genocides."

In fact, the journal has addressed primarily the Holocaust and only to a smaller extent other genocides. Jacobs (1998, p. 12) has done a critical analysis of the journal and writes that

> between 1986 and 1997, 208 articles were published: 189 articles dealing primarily with the Holocaust and only 19 or 10% dealing with "other genocides" or non-Holocaust concerns. They include: (1) Genocide—8; (2) Armenians—5; (3) Native Americans –1; (4) Religion and Theology—1; (5) Ukrainians—1; (6) Argentina—1; (7) Antisemitism—1; and (8) Israel—1. Turning to the reviews, the results were comparably similar: Between 1986 and 1997, 246 reviews were published: 208 dealing primarily with the Holocaust and only 38 or 16 percent with "other genocides" or non-Holocaust concerns. These include: (1) Genocide—7; (2) Armenians—5; (3) Antisemitism—4; (4) Religion and Theology—4; (5) Cambodia—4; (6) Israel—2; (7) Bosnia—2; (8) "Rightist Politics"—2; (9) Ukrainians—1; (10) Evil—1; (11) Human Rights—1; (12) Psychoanalysis—1; and (13) Yiddish Literature—1.

Jacobs concludes, "What this analysis confirms is that the Holocaust continues to dominate scholarly work in the journal and that the journal has been somewhat misnamed.... An expanded and more balanced agenda will *not* diminish the importance of 'Holocaust work,' but, again, redirect our collective energies to both present day genocides and future preventive concerns."

For further information, contact *Holocaust and Genocide Studies,* Oxford University Press, Great Clarendon Street, Oxford OX2 6OP, UK, tel: 44–1865–267907; fax: 44–1865–267485.

—Marc I. Sherman

References and Recommended Reading

Jacobs, Steven L. (1998). Holocaust and genocide studies: The future is now. *Center News: Center for Holocaust, Genocide and Peace Studies, University of Nevada, Reno,* 3(2), 10–13.

THE HOLOCAUST

THE HOLOCAUST: CONCENTRATION CAMPS AND DEATH CAMPS IN THE HOLOCAUST

CONCENTRATION CAMPS AND DEATH CAMPS IN THE HOLOCAUST

The German term *Konzentrationslager* or Concentration Camp is an "umbrella term" used to describe a variety of incarceration settings used by the Nazis both before and during the Second World War to imprison and ultimately exterminate Jews and those who were, for them, other asocial and apolitical elements, Sinti-Romani, Poles, Slavs, Russians, and even fellow Germans viewed as "enemies of the Reich." The Nazis utilized a number of camp structures. There were *Arbeitslagers* or Work or Labor Camps; *Kreigsgefangenlargers* or Prisoner-of-War Camps; *Durchgangslagers* or Transit Camps; and *Vernichtungslagers* or Extermination Camps or Death Camps. While originally found in Germany where they were primarily *Arbeitslagers* for German political prisoners and some Jews, by 1942 one or more kinds of *Konzentrationslagers* were also found in Poland and other occupied territories.

During the initial period of camp construction and incarceration, 1933–1936, the primary camps were *Dachau, Lichten-*

General (Later President) Eisenhower: If in the Future the Holocaust Is Denied

The same day I saw my first horror camp. It was near the town of Gotha. I have never felt able to describe my emotional reactions when I first came face to face with indisputable evidence of Nazi brutality and ruthless disregard of every shred of decency. Up to that time I had known about it only generally or through secondary sources. I am certain, however, that I have never at any other time experienced an equal sense of shock. I visited every nook and cranny of the camp because I felt it my duty to be in a position from then on to testify at first hand about these things in case there ever grew up at home the belief or assumption that "the stories of Nazi brutality were just propaganda." Some members of my visiting party were unable to go through the ordeal. I not only did so but as soon as I returned to Patton's headquarters that evening I sent communications to both Washington and London, urging the two governments to send instantly to Germany a random group of newspaper editors and representative groups from the national legislatures. I felt that the evidence should be immediately placed before the American and British publics in a fashion that would leave no room for cynical doubt.

I made the visit deliberately, in order to be in a position to give first-hand evidence of those things if ever, in the future, there develops a tendency to charge these allegations merely to "propaganda."

—General Dwight D. Eisenhower, Supreme Commander of the Allied Forces in Europe, 1945

Ethnic Cleansing of Germans by Czechs after World War II

In 1938 Hitler annexed the Sudetenland—parts of the provinces of Bohemia and Moravia—in Czechoslovakia with the broad support of the ethnic Germans, at the time the biggest ethnic group in the country. In March 1939 Nazi troops marched into Prague, occupying Czechoslovakia with known grim results including the deaths of 99 percent of the Jewish population. At the end of the war, Czech authorities perceived the Sudeten Germans collectively as a fifth column for the Nazis. In a series of decrees, the first post-war President, Edvard Beneš, sanctioned their expulsion, and granted amnesty to Czechs for the killing of between 15,000 and 240,000 ethnic Germans, depending on who is doing the counting. Czechs toting submachine guns loaded people onto freight trains—Czechs purged their land of three million Germans. According to some Sudeten Germans, 240,000 Sudeten Germans—almost a tenth of the population group—were killed by Czechs. People were given as little as two hours to leave, marched to railroad stations at gunpoint, stripped of their valuables and loaded on to freight trains.

Czech accounts put the figure between 15,000 and 40,000. Shortly before he became President of Czechoslovakia, Vaclav Havel said Czechs had a duty to apologize for the wrongs committed against ethnic Germans.

—*Press Reports*

berg, Sachsenberg, Esterwegen, Oranienburg, and *Columbia Haus.* Prisoners were primarily political; incarceration was of relatively limited duration and camp conditions were somewhat bearable.

During the second period, 1939–1942, which encompassed the start of the Second World War and included the rounding up of large numbers of Jews, the numbers and kinds of camps increased greatly and included *Sachsenhausen, Buchenwald, Mathausen, Flossenberg, Ravensbruck, Auschwitz-Birkenau, Natzwelier, Neuengamme, Gross Rosen, Stutthof, Chelmno, Treblinka, Sobibor, Belzec, Vught, Plaszow, Kaiserwald, Maidanek, Bergen-Belsen,* and *Mittelbau Dora.* In this phase, conditions deteriorated rapidly due both to overcrowding, disease, starvation, and the escalation of acts of cruelty and murder, and of course the crystallization of the ideology of the "Final Solution of the Jewish Problem." Several camps that had been less severe now made a transition into being *Vernichtungslagers* or Extermination Camps.

From 1942 until the end of the war in 1945, the primary task of all of the Konzentrationslagers was the deaths of more and more undesirables, primarily Jews, Sinti-Romani, Poles, and Russians, and also prisoners of all nationalities captured by the Germans. Even prisoners who were not specifically singled out for extermination were likely to find themselves the subjects of brutalities, medical experiments, and executions. In particular, however, the Jews were singled out for brutal and systematic extermination, increasingly by gassing with zyklon-B followed by burning the bodies in huge crematoria. The insecticide zyklon-B was delivered in a crystalline form and converted quickly to a noxious fatal gas upon exposure to air. Upon arriving at the Vernichtungslager after a journey of up to three weeks without benefit of food or water, crowded into cattle cars

The Fates of Non-Jewish Germans under the Nazis

Those who fought for human rights against Nazi injustice came to call themselves "the illegals." Where injustice had become law, normal standards and values were reversed, and those who stood for uprightness and humanity were lawbreakers in the Nazi state.

According to a Gestapo report of April 10, 1939, those charged with political crimes in the first six years under Hitler included 162,734 in "protective custody," the euphemism which usually meant concentration camp; 112,432 sentenced by trial; 27,369 awaiting trial. In one sample month, May 1938, 1,639 were executed after trial for political offenses of all sorts. Of the Wehrmacht 9,523 were executed on charges of mutiny and political work against the Nazis even before the coup d'etat of July 20, 1944, with its toll of additional thousands. Over a period of twelve years almost 3,000,000 Germans were in and out of concentration camps and penitentiaries for political reasons—sometimes for as little as a remark critical of the government. About 800,000 of these had been arrested for overt anti-Nazi acts; only 300,000 of them were still alive after the war—so that among the "illegals" alone 500,000 gave their lives.

—Eric H. Boehm

without adequate ventilation, those who survived, depending on their age and physical appearance, were directed either to labor barracks or directly to disguised "disinfectant showers" that were, in reality, preliminary gateways to large soon-to-be-sealed rooms housing upwards of 1,000 persons. Once sealed, these gas chambers received opened canisters of zyklon-B, usually poured from openings in the roof of the chamber. Within fifteen to twenty minutes the majority of those inside were dead; within thirty to forty-five minutes, all inside were dead. Doors were opened, fifteen minutes after further exposure to air the gas dissipated allowing sonderkommandos (specially assigned prisoners) to remove the dead, and after examining them and removing gold teeth and gold and other jewels secreted in various bodily orifices, to transport them either directly to large lime pits for burial or to ovens for incineration into ash.

A primary killing center was Auschwitz-Birkenau outside Krakow in southern Poland, where it is estimated that upward of one million prisoners, primarily Jews, perished. Other notorious Vernichtungslagers included Belzec, Chelmno, Treblinka, Sobibor, and Maidanek. But killings were also taking place regularly in many other camps, and some scholars include Buchenwald, Mauthausen, and Bergen-Belsen among the Death Camps. From 1942 until the end of World War II, all manner of Konzentrationslagers (Concentration Camps) continued to escalate the deaths of their prison populations regardless of their initial reasons for creation (i.e., political prisons, labor camps, prisoner-of-war camps, transit camps).

It is estimated that a minimum of two million persons, perhaps even four million persons, passed through all of the camps, with the largest number of deaths occurring at Auschwitz-Birkenau. By war's end the sites themselves were disease-ridden and starvation-laden to the point that many who survived until liberation were virtually unable to survive the transition to freedom.

After the war, those who were healthy enough to return to a reasonable state of normalcy found themselves beset with both medical and psychological problems.

The sections following describe several of the notorious camps in the Holocaust.

—Steven L. Jacobs

References and Recommended Reading

Gutman, Israel (Ed.) (1990). *Encyclopedia of the Holocaust.* Four volumes. New York: Macmillan.

Kogon, Eugen; Langbein, Hermann; and Rückerl, Adalbert (Eds.) (1993). *Nazi Mass Murder: A Documentary History of the Use of Poison Gas.* New Haven, CT: Yale University Press.

AUSCHWITZ

Auschwitz is the name of a specific death camp and an *archetypal symbol of the evil engendered by the Holocaust.* The gas chambers and crematoria of Auschwitz were the culmination of a process of assembly line killing, and stand as eternal witness to the convergence of religious and secular fantasies concerning the Jewish people and others deemed unfit to live. Located in southwest Poland, near Kracow, the Polish town Oswiecim was renamed by the Germans. Auschwitz was the site of World War I Austro-Hungarian military barracks and was located near a railroad line that linked many European cities. Established in June 1940 as a camp to punish Polish political prisoners, the site soon expanded its scope and physical size. In September of 1941, 600 Russian prisoners of war and 300 Jews were gassed using zyklon-B. Rudolf Höess was the commandant of Auschwitz from its inception until its capture by Russian troops in January 1944.

Auschwitz was divided into three main sections. Auschwitz I, the main

The barbed-wire fences of Auschwitz Concentration Camp. The barbed-wire fence has become one of the classic symbols of the Holocaust. (Yad Vashem, Jerusalem)

Israel Asks Poland to Remove Crosses

In August 1998, the Israeli government asked Poland to dismantle controversial crosses recently erected near the Auschwitz death camp. The Israeli cabinet secretary said the presence of 50 new crosses was inappropriate at a site where upwards of a million Jews were killed. Roman Catholics linked to a conservative radio station recently erected the 50 additional crosses around a cross put up a decade ago.

—*Press Reports*

camp, is where the Germans murdered approximately 150,000 people, the majority of whom were Polish, as well as Russians and Jews. The gate leading to this camp contains the cynical statement *Arbeit Macht Frei (Work Will Set You Free).* Auschwitz-Birkenau (Brezezinka), three kilometers from Auschwitz I, was completed in spring 1942. Approximately 1.33 million Jews, Roma (Gypsies), and some Russian prisoners perished at this location. The first Jewish deportees were gassed at Auschwitz-Birkenau in May 1942. Railroad tracks led straight into the camp where many perished almost immediately upon arrival. Auschwitz III, Monowitz or Buna, was the industrial section of the death camp where prisoners served as slave laborers for German companies such as I. G. Farben and Krupp. When prisoners were no longer able to work, they were sent to the gas chambers, and the industrialists purchased additional slaves from the SS.

Auschwitz was a vast necropolis. It was the largest killing center of Jewish people in Europe, and the only death camp in the enormous Nazi system where prisoners were tattooed. Death was administered efficiently in a variety of ways. First of all, there was the process of selection. Upon arrival, prisoners were selected either for immediate death—the elderly, sick, cripples, small children, pregnant women—or for slave labor. Dr. Josef Mengele, the infamous "Angel of Death," arrived in Auschwitz in May 1943 and directed at least seventy-four selections. Furthermore, Mengele also turned his attention to performing cruel experiments on twins and dwarfs. Selections were also carried out periodically, both in barracks and the so-called infirmary, in order to make room for additional prisoners. Death also came as a result of starvation, punishing physical labor, torture, and random acts of sadism.

Auschwitz was distinguished for its conveyor assembly-line techniques of producing and exploiting corpses. It had four gas chambers. After having been gassed, corpses were dragged to crematoria by the *Sonderkommando* (special-action squads of inmates) who, if they refused to participate, were shot on the spot. The average life expectancy of a *sonderkommando* was three months, after which time they would be gassed and burned. Corpses provided wealth for Germany. For instance, gold teeth were extracted, watches, jewelry and other valuable were looted and shipped back to the Reich, human hair was used for mattress stuffing, bones were ground and used for sprinkling on frozen road surfaces. Nevertheless, and in spite of disease, malnutrition and lack of organized outside support, Jewish prisoners staged a revolt on October 7, 1944, and partially destroyed Crematorium IV. Both men and women participated in this revolt whose leaders included Zalmen Gradowski, Josef Deresinski, Ala Gertner, and Roza Robota.

The State Museum of Auschwitz-Birkenau was established by former inmates of the camp. They wished to bear

The sign "Arbeit Macht Frei" decorated the entrance not only to Auschwitz but also to various other Nazi concentration camps. This photograph was taken from the entrance to Sachsenhausen Concentration Camp. (Photographed by Israel W. Charny)

witness for those who perished and to warn the world against the evils of nazism. In 1979 UNESCO officially designated Auschwitz-Birkenau as a "world heritage site." Consequently, Poland committed itself to preserve the site for posterity. The State Museum is responsible for maintaining the camps; housing various exhibits including human hair, shoes, artificial limbs, suitcases, eyeglasses, toothbrushes, and other belongings of the victims; and maintaining an archive. It has also been an active participant in the crisis that emerged concerning the placing of religious symbols near and in Auschwitz.

Reflecting the competing memories of Auschwitz held by non-Jewish Poles and by Jewish Poles and other Jews, controversy erupted over religious symbols at Auschwitz. The controversy initially arose in 1985 when a Carmelite Convent assumed the building formerly occupied by the commandant of the camp, and erected a thirty-foot high cross. After much delay and bitterness the convent was moved, but not the cross. In 1986, inside Auschwitz-Birkenau, Polish Boy Scouts placed crosses and Stars of David in memory of the victims. The Auschwitz Museum, which controls space within the camp's barbed wire fences, removed these symbols in December, 1997.

In 1998, over fifty years after Auschwitz ceased operating, divisiveness remains. Groups of right-wing Polish nationalists continue to place crosses near Block 11, the notorious wall of death where inmates were shot, to commemorate the murder of their countrymen. But this movement has been condemned by other Poles, including Jan Karski, as sacreligious. While it is true that for Polish Catholics the cross is a primary religious symbol, its use by the extreme right is politically motivated. For Jews, the cross stands as a symbol of the murderers. Thus, Auschwitz, which should serve to unite humanity in its fight against antisemitism, prejudice and hatred, may in fact cause more divisiveness. On the other hand, some signs of hope may emerge from an interfaith center currently being completed adjacent to Auschwitz. This may serve to bring people together. In any event, the controversy over the crosses at Auschwitz itself stands in stark contrast to the admonition chiseled on the memorial at Auschwitz-Birkenau:

> FOR EVER LET THIS PLACE BE
> A CRY OF DESPAIR
> AND A WARNING TO HUMANITY
> WHERE THE NAZIS MURDERED
> ABOUT ONE AND A HALF MILLION
> MEN, WOMEN, AND CHILDREN
> MAINLY JEWS
> FROM VARIOUS COUNTRIES
> OF EUROPE
> AUSCHWITZ-BIRKENAU
> 1940–1945

—Alan L. Berger

References and Recommended Reading

Dwork, Deborah, and Pelt, Robert Jan van (1996). *Auschwitz: 1270 to the Present.* New York: W.W. Norton.

Gilbert, Martin (1985). *The Holocaust: A History of the Jews During the Second World War.* New York: Holt, Rinehart and Winston.

BUCHENWALD

Built as a criminal and political prisoner camp, Buchenwald opened its doors on July 19, 1937. Located on the northern slope of the Ettersberg Mountain, approximately five miles north of Weimar, it consisted of more than 130 satellite camps, and was one of the largest concentration camps on German soil. The main camp itself consisted of three parts or subdivisions: the so-called "large camp" whose prisoners were housed there from the very beginning; the so-called "small camp," whose prisoners were isolated from the rest of the camp population; and the so-called "tent camp," primarily for Polish prisoners who arrived there after Germany's invasion of Poland in September of 1939.

Jewish prisoners began arriving at Buchenwald prior to the beginning of the Second World War. In the summer of 1938, 2,200 Austrian Jews were transferred to Buchenwald from Dachau; and, after *Kristallnacht* (November 9–10, 1938), more than 10,000 Jews were housed there. As was the case throughout the concentration camp system, Jews were treated far worse than their fellow prisoners, with the possible exception of Soviet Russians who were almost always sent immediately to their deaths.

From its beginning until the liberation of its prisoners, Buchenwald was administered by only two commandants: Karl Koch (1937–1942) and Herman Pfister (1942–1945). By 1944, its prisoner population reached a peak of almost 90,000 prisoners. By its liberation in 1945, more than 238,000 prisoners from more than thirty countries had passed through its gates, with more than 55,000 killed or murdered. Resistance activities were in evidence almost from the very beginning and consisted mainly of small acts of sabotage and the smuggling of small arms and munitions.

Two years after the liberation of Buchenwald, only six members of the camp administration were brought to trial; two were sentenced to death and four were sentenced to life imprisonment.

—*Steven L. Jacobs*

References and Recommended Reading
Hackett, David A. (Translator and Ed.) (1995). *The Buchenwald Report.* Boulder, CO: Westview Press.

DACHAU

Dachau was the site of the *first* Nazi concentration/death camp, operating from March of 1933 until April of 1945. It was located 10 miles northwest of Munich in Bavaria. All told, more than 200,000 prisoners passed through its electrified fences beneath the perennial welcoming sign of many subsequent concentration camps, *Arbeit Macht Frei.* It is estimated that more than 70,000 prisoners, the majority of them Jews, died at Dachau, though accurate totals are impossible to assess. Thirty percent of those still alive at liberation were estimated to be Jews.

Site of a World War I munitions factory, Dachau was initially a political camp for Communists, Social Democrats, and others opposed to the Nazi regime, including Jewish political opponents, and remained so throughout the war. After *Kristallnacht* in November of 1938, more than 10,000 Jews found themselves imprisoned at Dachau; only those who could give evidence of intent to leave Germany were then freed.

The first Kommandant of Dachau was Theodore Eicke who would later become Inspector-General of the entire camp system. Taking over in June of 1933, he very quickly established a system of rules and regulations—including electrified fencing and shooting on sight those approaching the fences—and later implemented similar rules and regulations, with local variations and modifications, throughout the system itself.

It was at Dachau also that the first medical experiments on prisoners were implemented. Among the most well-known of those experiments were high altitude and deep seawater experiments designed for the German *Luftwaffe,* and inoculation with malaria and experimental vaccines. It is estimated that close to 400 prisoners unwillingly took part in these experiments and close to 25 percent of them died as a result.

As the war progressed, prisoners representing the various countries occupied by Germany found themselves at Dachau, including Soviet soldiers who were murdered there without ever having been listed in the prison rolls. Though all prisoners were brutally victimized, there was no planned extermination of the inmates of Dachau; ironically, the gas chamber built at Dachau was never used.

On April 29, 1945, Dachau was liberated by the United States Seventh Army. More than 650 of those responsible for the administration of Dachau and the implementation of its programs were put on trial; 260 were tried and sentenced to death and the remainder imprisoned. At war's end, the camp itself was temporarily used as a transit camp for those awaiting repatriation to their countries of origin.

—Steven L. Jacobs

TREBLINKA

Treblinka, located approximately sixty-two miles northeast of Warsaw in a heavily-wooded area, was not one but two camps: Treblinka I, which was in operation from December 1941 until July 1944, was a penal camp primarily for Jews waiting ultimately to be exterminated, as well as for Polish economic and political dissidents from the General Government under Nazi administration.

Treblinka II (referred to cryptically as "T.II" in official communications), the more notorious of the two, was an extermination center that ultimately saw the murder of approximately 870,000 prisoners according to official Polish estimates compiled after the Second World War by the Main State Commission for the Investigation of Nazi Crimes. It began its existence in July 1942 and continued its grisly task until October 1943. Both camps together were staffed by approximately thirty men of the SS, 200–300 Ukrainian support personnel primarily for security purposes, and 1,000 to 1,500 rotating Jewish prisoners who themselves were charged with the most onerous tasks relating to the extermination process: the removal of fecal- blood- and urine-covered bodies, and the collection of gold teeth and other possible hidden valuables after examination of both rectal and vaginal orifices. In addition to Polish Jews, Jews from Germany, Austria, Bohemia-Moravia, Slovakia, Holland, Belgium, Luxemburg, Greece, and Bulgaria were also murdered there as were the Sinti-Romani.

Treblinka II was a model of efficiency. With the addition of ten gas chambers to the original two, its size became large enough to accommodate twenty full railroad cars of prisoners who were herded directly from the cars themselves, after having been stripped naked and separated from their clothing and other obvious valuables, directly into the "showers" and then to the gas chambers. Prior to the construction of these additional ten gas chambers, bodies were taken to huge pits and buried.

The Treblinka camps were headed by SS Commandant Franz Stangl who was sentenced to life imprisonment in 1971; his assistant Kurt Franz received a similar sentence in 1965, as did one Joseph (Sepp) Hirtreiter in 1951. Nine other defendants received sentences ranging from two to twelve years. All of the trials of those associated with Treblinka were held in Germany.

Concentration camps in the Holocaust. (With the kind permission of Sir Martin Gilbert, Map 8, p. 16, in Gilbert, Martin [1978]. The Holocaust: Maps and Photographs. A Record of the Destruction of Jewish Life in Europe during the Dark Years of Nazi Rule. *London: Board of Deputies of British Jews. Published in Jerusalem by the* Jerusalem Post.)

Resistance efforts took place from the beginning of the operation of the camps in 1941, with the most famous in August 1943 when inmates revolted and many escaped. Ultimately, however, given the location of the camps themselves and the hostility of the surrounding Polish peasant population, almost all were unsuccessful, with the majority of those who escaped caught and those who planned and organized such resistance efforts hanged or shot.

—*Steven L. Jacobs*

References and Recommended Reading

Donat, Alexander (1980). *The Death Camp Treblinka: A Documentary.* New York: Holocaust Library.

Steiner, Jean-François (1967). *Treblinka.* New York: Simon and Schuster.

THE HOLOCAUST

The Holocaust was the Nazi plan for the total annihilation of the Jewish people, and the actual murder of close to six million of them during World War II by Nazi Germany and its collaborators from among other nations. While the Nazis also murdered many millions of Poles, Russians, Roma ("Gypsies"), Serbs, Czechs, and political opponents, only the Jews were slated for total annihilation. *[Some scholars believe that all Gypsies were also earmarked for total annihilation.—Ed.]*

Antisemitism was a central component of Nazi ideology. Based on a long, Christian antisemitic tradition, it became secularized in the eighteenth century, and in its extreme form turned against Christianity, which it accused of stemming from Judaism. A particularly virulent form arose in the late nineteenth century: a racist, violently nationalist form of Jew-hatred. Such groups, though small, sprouted all over Europe, and much of the antisemitic and racist ideology penetrated conservative mainstream parties. As a result of the defeat of Germany and Austria in World War I, racist groups found eager listeners among the disappointed and uprooted there. One of these groups was the National Socialist German Workers' Party, or the Nazis, who were joined in 1919 by Adolf Hitler, an Austrian who had served as a German soldier, and who became their leader and spokesman. In 1923, Hitler attempted to gain power in Bavaria, his base, by means of a military uprising, but failed, was caught and sentenced to a short term of imprisonment. There he wrote his main book, called *Mein Kampf (My Struggle).*

Between 1918, the end of World War I, and 1923, a severe economic crisis shook Germany, and the Nazi party seemed to gain influence. But a period of prosperity between 1924 and 1929 made the Nazi message irrelevant and the party became marginal (2.6 percent of the vote in the 1928 elections). However, with the Great Depression spreading into Germany from 1929 on, the Nazi Party grew by leaps and bounds, and in 1932 garnered 37 percent of the votes. A reverse in late 1932 (33 percent of the votes—a loss of two million) appeared to guarantee to the right-wing camarilla around a senile German president (Paul von Hindenburg) that the Hitler party was no longer dangerous and would support their program. Hitler became Chancellor (Prime Minister), soon abolished all other parties and established his dictatorship.

What Hitler himself may have thought or planned we do not know, beyond the Nazis' violent hatred of Jews and their desire to deprive them of their citizenship and their economic and social positions. This they did between attaining power (January 30, 1933) and October 1933: Jews were fired from governmental and public employment as lawyers,

HOLOCAUST CONTROVERSIES: A POINT OF VIEW

This entry aims to describe several areas of conflict and controversy in the field of Holocaust studies. The following controversies are examined: the intentionalist vs. functionalist theses; the uniqueness vs. comparability theses; the mystification thesis; the antisemitism vs. racism theses; Holocaust-centered vs. genocide-centered scholars; the definitional abuse thesis; Holocaust denial vs. genocide denial; the resistance controversy; and the Goldhagen controversy. In conclusion, the question is posed whether there are really two fields of study—Holocaust studies and genocide studies—or one; some controversies have widened the gap and could divide the discipline. Nonetheless, with hopeful caution, I conclude that these controversies can and will be mediated, for they are quite bridgeable; and that in teaching the Holocaust at the college or high school level, one can blend the two fields into one course.

The Controversies

A. Intentionalist vs. Functionalist Theses. Was there an intent from the very beginning to destroy the Jews, or was the process of destruction of the Jews more complex and evolutionary? Did the lethal process of the Final Solution emerge from the beginning of Nazi thinking, or did the Final Solution really begin only after the invasion of Russia in June 1941? The intentionalist thesis is that there was a clear-cut intent to destroy the Jews from the beginning of Hitler's thinking and the rise of the Nazi party. The functionalist thesis is that although vicious antisemitism and persecution of the Jews were the hallmarks of nazism, and images of getting rid of the Jews were evoked from early on, the plan and actuality of the Final Solution emerged only as an unfolding sequence, with each earlier stage as it was unopposed by the world leading to the next. The term "intentionalist" is also used in section B below in respect of arguments for the uniqueness of the Holocaust, especially by Steven Katz [*The Holocaust in Historical Context, Vol. 1.* New York: Oxford University Press, 1994] when he states that "the Holocaust is phenomenologically unique by virtue of the fact that never before has a state set out, as a matter of intentional principle and actualized policy, to annihilate physically every man, woman, and child belonging to a specific people" (p. 28).

B. Uniqueness vs. Comparability Theses. Is the Holocaust so unique that there is no other case of full-blown genocide? This is the controversial Katz hypothesis. Many scholars hope to develop a common agreement on what was genocide, to the effect that the homosexuals, the Gypsies, the Armenians, the Cambodians, the Indians and many others were all victims of genocide, but Katz attempts to demolish any such consensus. He is implacable in his demands that the Holocaust was unique. Many other scholars, like Michael Berenbaum, adopt a more benign position that the Holocaust was the most prominent and in a sense the most evil genocide in the twentieth century, but that there were many other victims of the Holocaust besides the Jews, some victims of genocide (Jews and Gypsies), some victims of non-genocidal persecution (homosexuals, the disabled, political opponents, Jehovah's Witnesses); and that, following more or less the UN definition, there were many other genocides in the twentieth century such as

continues

continued

the Armenian Genocide; and that other persecuted groups should be (and are to an extent) represented in the US Holocaust Memorial Museum. For Berenbaum, there is no problem doing full honor to the Jewish memory and the singularity of the Jewish experience and paying full respect to the totality of the Nazis' victims.

Indeed, this issue comes up as a "very practical issue" in decisions about what to include and what to exclude in a museum on the Holocaust. Edward Linenthal's book on the creation of the US Holocaust Memorial Museum [*Preserving Memory: The Struggle to Create America's Holocaust Museum.* New York: Viking Press, 1996] illuminates this controversy well. Ironically, while the Wiesenthal Museum of Tolerance in Los Angeles begins with a very universalistic, inclusivistic message that group hatred and intolerance led to the Holocaust, it rejects that message at the end of the tour by focusing on a particularistic "Never Again" theme. Conversely, while the US Holocaust Memorial Museum in Washington, DC focuses on the particularism of the Jews, it has a greater universalistic impact than the ostensibly universal Los Angeles Museum of Tolerance. The US Holocaust Memorial Museum works on many levels because it honors and commemorates the Jews who died as well as recognizing the other victims—political prisoners, homosexuals, lesbians, Jehovah's Witnesses, and the disabled. Although the museum is, in fact, devoted to the Holocaust, it contains a universal message and educates on many levels. It is a profound experience that succeeds in applying the meaning of the Holocaust to other acts of genocide and oppression. The Los Angeles Museum of Tolerance seems less successful and Yad Vashem in Jerusalem does not really attempt a universal message. As Michael Lerner, editor of *Tikkun,* so eloquently puts it: "'Never Again' does not mean never again to Jews; it means 'Never Again' to any group, any race, any culture." Elie Wiesel echoes this same sentiment when he says that the particularist message of the Holocaust is the most universalistic.

C. The Mystification Thesis. Tied closely with the "uniqueness controversy" is the idea that the Holocaust is so ineffable, so evil, that it is beyond comprehension. It is an evil that it is beyond evil. This is the thesis of Emil Fackenheim, that there is no language to describe the Holocaust. It is beyond words. This is the Elie Wiesel thesis. However, most scholars have taken the position that ordinary men and women committed these cruel acts, and ordinary men and women can study them. Perhaps the Holocaust is beyond our moral understanding. One may be upset, angered, shocked, or deeply moved by the answers we find, but human beings committed these acts and not aliens from another planet. Hitler and his comrades were not insane or irrational. They were—sociologically speaking—perverted deviants, spiteful, hateful little men, but they were not insane. They knew exactly what they were doing, like serial killers. This is itself a chilling thought, more chilling than insanity, this bifurcation of the mind to killer and saint.

D. Antisemitism vs. Racism Theses. Best-selling Harvard University author,

continues

continued

Daniel Jonah Goldhagen [see *The Goldhagen Controversy,* below] has argued that antisemitism was the sole cause of the Holocaust. Years ago, Helen Fein argued in her award-winning book [*Accounting for Genocide: National Responses and Jewish Victimization during the Holocaust.* New York: Free Press, 1979] that extermination of the Jews in different European countries correlated with the long-standing tradition and prevailing political levels of antisemitism of the different countries. Antisemitism was part of racism—and also forms of white supremacy, patriarchal, sexist and even homophobic attitudes all together gave an ideological basis for the Holocaust. The Jew was the epitome of evil but there were many other targets—Bolsheviks, modernists, radicals, socialists, Communists, free thinkers, the effete, the weak, the meek, and the lame. Aryanism was the religion of the Nazi Supermen (though Nietzsche might not have sided with them and could have gone into the ovens along with the Jews because he was a radical and innovative thinker). If one concentrates only on antisemitism, then the Holocaust becomes a Jewish interest and a uniquely Jewish event. However, if one sees antisemitism as part of racism, one sees a broader, more universalistic and more accurate picture. At the same time, antisemitism is of course crucial to understanding the Holocaust.

E. Holocaust-Centered vs. Genocide-Centered Scholars. This is a subset of section B. We need to find the golden mean between people who are not sensitive to the special persecution of Jews during the Holocaust and who make statements like, "The Ukrainians or the Poles suffered just as much as the Jews"; and the "special pleading" of the Jews that says that Jews suffered more than any other persecuted and murdered people ever in history. Many Jews tend to be Holocaust-centered particularists and to use the Holocaust as a special badge.

Holocaust-centered scholars too often ignore the genocides of other peoples. Genocide-centered scholars, on the other hand, are at times insensitive to the uniqueness of the Holocaust. Helen Fein (1990) has pointed out that sociologists especially have the greatest difficulty handling unique events such as Hiroshima, the Vietnam War, or the Holocaust because sociology is best with stable, recurring, non-provocative, normative events.

F. The Definitional Abuse Thesis. Do we exclude the mass murders of certain groups from being defined as genocide if they do not pass our definitional test? Or do we label every case of mass murder genocide just in case? Does the label help save lives, meaning does labeling something a genocide help the United Nations and other agencies move into action and intervene?

Not all killings or mass murders need be considered genocides. What makes genocide unique? There are scholars who argue that there must be intention, whether carried out or not, whether successful or not: an intention to kill every man, woman and child of that particular group. According to this point of view, if that intention is not there, it is not genocide. The extreme of this point of view leads to a position such as that of Katz who said that the Holocaust is the only

continues

continued

real genocide because it was the only state-sponsored genocide that had as its intent the destruction of an entire group. In all other genocidal killings of witches, women, Gypsies, homosexuals, even Armenians and Cambodians, or Rwandans and Bosnians, there was never any intent to kill every single man, woman and child of the targeted population.

I do not accept Katz's tortured arguments. His definition of genocide is idiosyncratic and is not accepted by most scholars in genocide studies. Most scholars accept some variation of the UN definition. But what is and what is not genocide? Is intent important? Is completion crucial? Who is excluded and why? What's in a name, in the ideological semantics of Armageddon—decimation, democide, extermination, genocide, Holocaust with a small "h" or a "capital H," mass murder, auto-genocide, politicide, nuclear omnicide?

G. Holocaust Denial vs. Genocide Denial. Holocaust denial is a serious problem, but genocide denial is even more complicated. To deny the Holocaust or to say that a major aspect of it, such as crematoria, is a fabrication is clearly to lie. But to claim that a case of mass murder is not genocide is not to deny the event, or even its seriousness, but to assign the event a lesser significance. Such "genocide denial," can be as offensive to Armenians, Gypsies, and gays as outright Holocaust denial is to Jews.

H. The Resistance Controversy. Genocide scholarship was a field in turmoil from the outset, long before a discipline of genocide studies began to emerge. For immediately after the Holocaust, there developed the controversies of the "sheep to slaughter" thesis—did Jews resist enough?; and the Judenrat controversy—did Jews collaborate in their own deaths?; and the Arendt-Eichmann controversy about the banality of evil thesis—were the Nazis lunatics or bureaucrats or both? Now, years later, there seems to have emerged a quieting consensus that the Jews were not so much "sheep" as trapped in circumstances none of us can judge; that they did not so much collaborate with the Nazis as they were drawn under desperate conditions to mistaken efforts to save Jews by undue cooperation with their mad oppressors; and that much of the killing was indeed by ordinary people serving the bureaucratic machinery. But the passions and partial truths of the contrary theses are not, and perhaps cannot ever be, extinguished.

I. The Goldhagen Controversy. Daniel Goldhagen's *Hitler's Willing Executioners* [see "ORDINARY PEOPLE" AS PERPETRATORS OF GENOCIDE] is arguably the most controversial book since Hannah Arendt's *Eichmann in Jerusalem.* It was an extraordinary phenomenon. His argument was threefold: one, that the Holocaust was monocausal, that is, only antisemitism caused the Holocaust, not following orders, not peer pressure, not careerism, but ordinary Germans harboring "eliminationalist antisemitism" who carried out the Holocaust. Second, these ordinary Germans willingly participated in the killing, not banal bureaucrats simply following orders as Arendt wrote. Third, antisemitism is deeply rooted in the German culture. Germany itself has a racist character going back to Martin Luther. The Holocaust could only have taken place

continues

continued

in Germany. No other country had the technological power, ideological will and bureaucratic style to carry out such an awesome undertaking.

A "two-step solution" seems much more accurate. Goldhagen is half right. Antisemitism, deeply rooted in German culture since the Middle Ages, was the animus that began the Holocaust; and then peer pressure, obedience to orders, careerism, fear, police state threats and punishments, and other social and psychological mechanisms came into play. One needs both elements, antisemitism and the social psychological, to understand so complex a phenomenon as the Shoah.

J. The Future of Holocaust and Genocide Studies: Two Fields or One? What is the future of these two fields? Can they be bridged? I believe they can, for we are one field and we need to heal these divisions

Conclusion

All historical events are unique to some degree. All are comparative. Instead of fighting over what is and what is not genocide, we should do much more research into the Holocaust and other genocides through diligent work in archives and personal interviews and solid analyses of issues.

—Jack Nusan Porter

References and Recommended Reading

Fein, Helen (1993). *Genocide: A Sociological Perspective.* London: Sage Publications (originally published in *Current Sociology,* 1990, 38(1), 1–126 [whole issue]).

Porter, Jack Nusan (Ed.) (1982). *Genocide and Human Rights: A Global Anthology.* Lanham, MD: University Press of America.

Porter, Jack Nusan (1998). *The Sociology of Genocide.* Washington, DC: American Sociological Association.

judges, doctors, officials, journalists, and subsequently from positions for which membership in trade unions or associations was required (entertainment industry, factory workers, and so on). Already on April 1, 1933, a one-day boycott was organized against Jewish shops and offices of Jewish professionals, accompanied by violent propaganda.

The Nazi regime instituted a regime of terror against its German opponents. In March 1933, the elite SS ("Protection Squad") led by Heinrich Himmler, established the Dachau concentration camp—to be followed by many others—where torture and humiliation were developed into a fine art. Until 1938, Jews were generally incarcerated only if they were opponents of the regime.

Nazi policies toward the Jews seemed to vaccilate; in 1934, an internal party struggle postponed any further anti-Jewish actions. In September 1935, in order to whip up renewed enthusiasm from the masses, the Nazis decreed the so-called Nuremberg Laws, which deprived the Jews of their citizenship and made marriages and sexual liasions between Jews and non-Jews illegal. In 1936 there was another pause, as Germany hosted the Olympic Games, and desisted from escalating anti-Jewish measures. Many German Jews thought that the worst had passed.

German Jews had no central organization. Most were liberals who thought of themselves as Germans of the Jewish religion; some were Zionists, who saw themselves as an ethnic minority in Germany and looked toward a future time when they would move to Palestine (now Israel); some were Orthodox, who also saw themselves as Germans, but who would in some future be called by the Messiah to leave for the Holy Land.

After the Nazi accession to power, in September 1933, a Reich Representation of German Jews (acronym RV) under the leadership of Rabbi Leo Baeck was set up to represent German Jews toward the regime. The RV supported emigration of youth and of those who could not maintain themselves in Germany, but proposed that all the others should stay in the Fatherland. The Zionists were in favor of a carefully prepared emigration to Palestine. An agreement with Nazi Germany engineered by the Jewish Agency for Palestine, the main Zionist political body, which enabled wealthy German Jews to transfer much of their property to Palestine increased the emigration possibility, but ran afoul of many Jews who did not favor any contacts with the Nazis.

Nazi policy crystallized into a desire to see the Jews leave Germany, and increasing pressure was applied to that end. Out of the roughly 525,000 German Jews, 129,000 emigrated between 1933 and the end of 1937. The Nazis considered this to be too little. In 1936, Hitler ordered his top henchman, Hermann Goering, to prepare Germany for war within four years, in order to prevent, as he put it, the replacement of the ruling elites of the world by "International Jewry." The ideological imperative dictated the removal of the Jews, to assure the "purity" of the Germanic peoples of the Aryan race in their struggle for world dominance. From March 1938, when Austria was annexed, anti-Jewish policies intensified—Viennese Jews were humiliated and dispossessed. Large-scale arrests culminated in the so-called "Night of Crystal" *(Krystallnacht)* (November 9–10, 1938), when all over Germany synagogues were set on fire, and 26,000 Jewish men arrested and put into concentration camps, with the purpose of causing a mass flight of Jews. However, the world was closed to Jewish immigration, and an attempt by President Roosevelt, who initiated a Conference at Evian (France) to arrange for an orderly emigration by international agreement (July 1938) had failed. The US, too, filled its small quota for Germany and Austria (27,000 possible immigrants) only in 1938–39. Nevertheless, a total of 317,000 Jews left the German Reich between 1938 and 1941, when all Jewish emigration was stopped.

In January 1939, Hitler made a public speech in which he threatened the Jews of Europe with annihilation if another world war broke out. However, it appears that this was intended to move the Western Powers to take in Central European Jews, and though Hitler himself may well have thought of more radical measures, there is no evidence that mass murder was planned at that stage. When Germany started World War II by attacking Poland in September 1939, there was no plan of what to do with the 1.7 million Polish Jews in the conquered territories (1.6 million lived in, or fled to, the Polish areas occupied by the Soviets). Subsequently, Hitler foresaw the expulsion of all the Jews under German rule into an area in southeastern Poland, with the aim of pushing them into Soviet-occupied territory (September 21, 1939). This plan failed because of objections raised by German bureaucrats in charge of occupied Poland, as did another plan, in June 1940, to deport all European Jews to Madagascar. In the meantime, Jewish communities in Poland were forced to establish Jewish Councils (*Judenrat,* plural *Judenraete*) who were charged by the Nazis to fulfill all their orders. In most cases the Judenraete tried to look after the interests of their communities, established soup kitchens, hospitals, took care of orphans, organized the forced labor that the Nazis demanded, and had to satisfy the greed of the Germans who confiscated, usually for private gain,

HITLER AND THE NAZI DECISION-MAKING PROCESS TO COMMIT THE HOLOCAUST: A NEW PROPOSAL

Despite more than 50 years of research, Adolf Hitler's role in the decision-making process which led to the Holocaust still belongs to the heavily disputed questions in contemporary history. Written evidence is generally weak and key documents are so vague that they have led to contradictory interpretations. No direct or indirect evidence—like the one on euthanasia from October 1939, backdated to the outbreak of the war—has been delivered which could prove the existence of a formal written order by Hitler to start the mass extermination of the Jews. The research tradition has split into two major schools of interpretation on this topic due to different models of historical explanations.

The Intentionalist View

The intentionalists (e.g., Karl Dietrich Bracher, Philippe Burrin, Lucy S. Dawidowicz, Eberhard Jäckel, Gerald Fleming) stress the role of Hitler's exterminationalist view found in his political speeches and writing—beginning with his first political comments on Jews in 1919, and continuing throughout the rest of his life until his final political testament in 1945. A key argument from this point of view is Hitler's public prophecy in the Reichstag on January 30, 1939, when he prophecied that a new world war would invariably lead to "the annihiliation of the Jewish race in Europe." Later he referred several times to this prophecy, using it as his legitimation of the foreseen destiny of the Jews. The intentionalists argue that Hitler consequently initiated the Holocaust through an oral order, although they suggest different dates for such an order, pointing to specific events in the spring, summer or fall of 1941.

The Functionalist View

The functionalists (e.g., Götz Aly, Christopher R. Browning, Daniel J. Goldhagen, Hans Mommsen, Karl A. Schleunes) emphasize the fact that even if Hitler himself was the key factor in Nazi ideology, the decisions to kill the Jews emerged progressively, stage after stage in the Holocaust, until a decision to commit mass murder was made; also that much actual decision-making was made at lower levels in the system and thus for some time Hitler did not formally initiate the killings but rather approved local initiatives once they were made, as there does exist evidence to show that Hitler followed the extermination process closely. The functionalists generally tend to see events either in the late fall–early winter of 1940 or late winter–early spring of 1941 as the decisive phase in the process which led to the Holocaust. The Nazis started killing the Jews at the beginning of the invasion of the Soviet Union in June 1941, and the Holocaust was formally confirmed and administratively organized at the Wannsee Conference on January 20, 1942.

Most modern explanations use elements from both schools, stressing the development of the Holocaust as a complex process which created for the first time in civilization's history a machinery of industralized killing.

The Semiotic View

Based on the notion that non-written sources also should be included in an integrated analysis of the decision-making

continues

continued

process, this writer, a Danish historian, has recently suggested a new, more precise chronology, using semiotics (i.e., the theory of the interrelation between verbal and nonverbal signs, messages and representations) and the sociological notion of the social construction of reality in the person of Adolf Hitler as well as modern knowledge of the character of war trauma (Post-Traumatic Stress Disorder or PTSD). According to this interpretation, Hitler's symbolic behavior during the Campaign of France in May-June 1940 is of importance. Hitler at this time considered visiting his own battlefields from World War I to be more important than the ongoing war; and it was here, on June 1, 1940, while visiting the battlefield of Werwicq in Belgium where he had temporarily lost his eyewight during WW I due to poison gas, that Hitler himself took the final decision. This visit acted as a concrete, visual confirmation for him of his accomplishing what he had set out to do, when, on November 10, 1918, during another temporary "blindness," he had decided to become a politician. After the armistice ceremony in Compiègne on June 21, 1940, he paid a visit to the place, where he had been awarded the Iron Cross First Class by his Jewish superior officer, Hugo Gutmann, and ordered the establishing of a Fuehrer Headquarters ("Wolfsschlucht 2") on this site. According to Himmler's personal doctor, Felix Kersten, Hitler gave an oral order to Himmler immediately after the captulation of France (i.e., on June 22, 1940). Himmler was ordered in the utmost secrecy to make the necessary preparations for the extermination of European Jewry to begin with the attack on Soviet Russia. Heinrich Himmler was reluctant to take this responsibility upon himself and was often rebuked by the Fuehrer—who carefully checked Himmler's speeches and initiatives—for not being efficient enough. Himmler was to build up the core of the killing force with the new Waffen-SS, but as he delegated the responsibility to Reinhard Heydrich—who himself used it as a strategic means in his own struggle to become Hitler's successor—it was not the Waffen-SS as such, but primarily the so-called "Einsatzgruppen" (consisting of a mix of the SS, SD, Ordnungs and Schutzpolizei and foreign volunteers), which were responsible for the killing. Adolf Hitler did not need to be present at the Wannsee Conference on January 20, 1942. It sufficed that Heydrich referred to the authority of a Fuehrer wish.

Both perpetrators and bystanders were mentally prepared through the two propaganda films *Jud Süss* and *Der Ewige Jude,* which were produced by the Minister of Propaganda, Joseph Goebbels, and personally approved by Hitler. The latter used allegedly documentary footage and climaxed in the juxtapositioning of ritual Jewish slaughtering and Hitler's notorious prophecy of January 30, 1939 that a future war would lead to the annihilation of European Jewry. This author contends that it was Hitler's viewing of this—his own prophecy in *Der Ewige Jude,* which convinced him of the 'necessity' of launching the "Final Solution."

—Stig Hornshøj-Møller

References and Recommended Reading

Breitman, Richard (1991). *The Architect of Genocide: Himmler and the Final Solution.* New York: Alfred A. Knopf.

continues

continued

Browning, Christopher R. (1992). *The Path to Genocide: Essays on Launching the Final Solution.* Cambridge: Cambridge University Press.

Fleming, Gerald (1996). *Hitler and the Final Solution.* Berkeley, CA: University of California Press.

Herbert, Ulrich (1998). *Nationalsozialistische Vernichtungspolitik 1939–1945: Neue Forschungen und Kontroversen.* Frankfurt am Main: Fischer Taschenbuch. (German)

Hornshøj-Møller, Stig (1996). *Føremyten. Adolf Hitler, Joseph Goebbels og historien bag et folkemord.* Copenhagen: Tiderne Skifter. (Danish)

everything that was of any worth. There were infinite variations in the behavior of the Judenraete, from supine yielding to every German demand to undercover or open opposition. At German behest, unarmed Jewish Order Police units were established, who in most cases betrayed their fellow-Jews and collaborated fully with the German authorities—but in some cases were the core of armed opposition.

The Nazis established ghettoes in Poland—closed-in areas, usually in the most decrepit neighborhoods—from October 1939, to the summer of 1943. In many cases, especially in some larger cities, the establishment of the ghettoes led to mass starvation, diseases, mainly typhoid epidemics, and mass death. Illegal schooling, illegal prayer meetings, social aid, and illegal political activity were the means by which Jews tried to keep up morale.

After it became clear, in late 1940, that it would be impossible to deport all the Jews to Madagascar, the idea began to take root that the solution would be to kill them. It seems that at first it was decided to murder the Jews in the Soviet territories. Preparations to that end were made in April and May 1941 with the training of four *Einsatzgruppen* (Action Groups). These followed hard on the heels of the German Army, which invaded the Soviet Union on June 22, 1941, killing at first Jewish males, and after a few weeks Jewish women and children as well. A large number of other units, police, SS, and others, also participated. Over one million, and some claim close to two million Jews were murdered within about eighteen months, by shooting, and in small part by exhaust gas pumped into trucks into which the victims were squeezed. By September/October 1941, preparations were started for the mass murder of Jews by gas vans at Chelmno, in western Poland. *By December 1941, the decision was taken for the "Final Solution," that is, the total mass murder of all Jews under German rule or influence, wherever they might be found.* Hitler conveyed his decision orally on December 12, 1941. A meeting of a number of government agencies with the SS leadership on January 20, 1942 (the so-called "Wannsee Conference") coordinated intents of implementation.

Death camps, whose purpose was to murder Jews—some thousands of Roma, Poles and Soviet POWs were included as well—were set up in Chelmno, in western Poland, in December 1941, and at Belzec, Sobibor and Treblinka, all in eastern Poland, between March and July 1942. Other camps, such as Majdanek and Auschwitz, were both concentration camps, where not only Jews were incarcerated and where inmates were also used as slaves in German enterprises, and death camps. The Nazis rounded up Jews in all the countries they occupied, and from March 1942, began to deport them to the death camps in Poland. Of the roughly 9 million European Jews, probably about 1.1 million were killed in Auschwitz, largely in the gas chambers, using a derivative of prussic acid called

THE HOLOCAUST—A WARNING TO THE MURDERERS OF TOMORROW

My activities have focused on the administration of justice and explanation of the greatest crime in human history. Linked with this aim there has always been the hope that future generations might be spared similar horrors.

My contemporaries and I had been brought up to believe in the civilized greatness of the twentieth century. We believed in progress, in cultural development toward true human nobility, in friendship, and in tolerance. We could not even imagine the possibility of a cultured nation such as Germany relapsing into medieval behavior patterns. We were convinced that a character like Hitler had no chance. An entire wall of the living room in my parents' house was filled with bookshelves containing the German classics—how then could a man like Adolf Hitler be anything more than just a minor episode in German history? Surely the nightmare would soon be over. Not only we Jews were convinced of this; all of Germany's neighbors and the entire world believed that Hitler could be rendered inert if one simply ignored him. With the worsening of the economic crisis, however, the democratic parties failed to find ways of giving people hope. The only ones who had ready answers for the millions of unemployed and discontented were the Nazis, so Hitler had little trouble taking over Germany.

During the Nuremberg Trials after the war, I once spoke with a Sturmbannfuhrer who had been a member of the SS secret service in Budapest and who now served as a witness for the prosecution. He told me of the following incident: "It was in October of 1944. We—5 SS men and Eichmann—were sitting in the SS-Casino in Budapest. One of the younger officers, referring to the number of Jews to be annihilated, asked, 'How many are there?' Eichmann replied, 'About five.' We all knew that he meant five million people. Then someone else said, somewhat incautiously, 'What about after the war? Will people ask what happened to these millions?' Eichmann just flicked his hand and said: 'One hundred dead are a catastrophe; one million dead are a statistic.'"

Eichmann was right. One million dead exceeds our power of imagination. *The Diary of Anne Frank* had a much greater impact than the entire Nuremberg Trials, because it gave people something they could identify with. They were able to say, "That could have been my sister, my granddaughter, or a friend of my daughter." In the course of my work, I have often recalled Eichmann's words. Again and again I have tried to take the ill-fated victims out of the anonymity of the statistics to let them become persons, each with his or her own personal history, someone with whom people could identify.

The first and most serious obstacle, in my opinion, was the Cold War, which began in 1947–1948. Because of it, a thorough investigation of National Socialism in all of its phases, with all of its implications and consequences, could not take place. This also meant that there was no immunization against this kind of misanthropic ideology; no system of defense was established—and the developments in the past years show what far-reaching consequences this has had. In the final analysis, the winners of the Cold War were Nazis.

continues

continued

The Cold War, which began less than three years after the end of National Socialism, brought a new danger to Europe and the entire world—and that was Stalinism. First, Stalin swallowed up the Eastern European countries; then he got an appetite for the rest of Europe. This very real danger in the East saved the Nazis from having to answer for themselves; it changed the attitude of the Western Allies toward defeated Germany. The period of the Cold War continued for many years, even outlasting Stalin. During these years of the Cold War, the voice of justice remained silent where the crimes of the Nazis were concerned. During this period, many Nazi criminals managed to leave their various hiding places in Germany and Austria and flee to South America as well as to the Arabic countries in the Near East.

I have dedicated myself to the struggle against forgetting. I feel it is our generation's most important responsibility to do everything in our power to help our descendants prevent a repetition of what happened to us.

If we want to do something for the future, we must not allow the crimes of the Nazi period to be forgotten. I am frequently reproached for searching for old and often ill men who committed crimes as Nazis or who were Nazi collaborators in the occupied European countries and who voluntarily helped the Nazis put their inhuman programs into practice. These helpers from the Baltic countries—the Ukraine and White Russia, to name the most important—were in a sense more guilty than the Nazis themselves.

The history of mankind is a history of crimes. If enough time has elapsed after the committing of a crime, the criminal is safe. If we want to contribute to a better future, it is important that in the future every criminal should be aware that our planet has become so small that there is not even a tiny corner left for him to hide in.

I have always described my work as a warning to the murderers of tomorrow who may already be born today. When we look around us today and see young people enjoying their freedom and all the advantages of our modern times—even taking all this for granted—it becomes clear that we must try to make them aware that freedom is like health: you don't appreciate its value until you've lost it. My generation was made to feel the full force of this bitter lesson. Freedom is not a gift from the heavens, you have to fight for it every day of your life.

Hitler did not even have to give written orders. His immediate staff members knew what he wanted and how to translate his plans into reality, without having to be told to do so explicitly. Since there is no document containing Hitler's explicit orders to exterminate the Jews, some contemporary historians—like a certain David Irving *[Irving is a leading revisionist-denier of the Holocaust in England—Ed.]*—maintain that Hitler knew nothing about the murder of the Jews and that this happened against his will. The people who try to whitewash Nazi crimes go even further: they say that since Hitler did not give an order to exterminate the Jews, he knew nothing about it.

With the help of underground organizations such as "Odessa," "Spider" and "Six-Star," which were shooting up like mushrooms during the Cold War

continues

continued

period, many wanted Nazis were able to leave Germany and Austria and thus avoid being called to responsibility. Equipped with assumed names and false papers, these Nazis often took advantage of the relief organizations of the Catholic Church which were giving aid to refugees from Communist countries such as Poland, Slovakia, Croatia, etc. These church organizations supplied them with visas and many times even with funds to emigrate via Rome to South America and other far-away places.

A big obstacle to my work was the use of the term "war crimes" to describe the monstrous deeds of the Nazis. Describing the Nazi crimes as war crimes amounts to a whitewashing of the Nazi horrors and does not capture the nature of what really happened. The crimes of the Nazis have very little to do with the war. During the war years 1942 and 1943, the crimes reached their peak in the concentration and extermination camps which were located about 1,000 kilometers from the front. The mass murders that took place in these camps had absolutely no bearing on the progress of the war.

After the war and after the Nuremberg Trials, other military and other special courts were appointed to try Nazi criminals. Only in two countries, Holland and Italy, were Nazi criminals sentenced to true life imprisonment. In the other countries, life prison sentences were limited to between 15 and 20 years. The ratio of the number of victims and the number of years in prison could amount to months, days or even minutes for each individual victim.

Our century has been a time of atrocity and brutality, marked by aggression and a desire to kill. All of the achievements and innovations of our technological and industrial society, such as radio, television and film, but also the latest developments in the computer field with its computer games, are being used to poison consumers with racial hatred and antisemitism. Extreme right-wing activity has increased from year to year. Not in all cases can the underlying ideology be termed as a Nazi one, but the views and actions of some groups such as the "Republikaner," the "Deutsche Volksunion" certainly do have neo-Nazi characteristics. Evidently, the democratic parties lack programs that are sufficiently attractive to many of the young people, while dictatorships, both on the right and on the left, do succeed in attracting too many young people.

—Simon Wiesenthal

"zyklon-B," and about 2.25 million were killed in the other camps by carbon monoxide gas. Some 300,000 Jews were killed by Nazi Einsatzgruppen and Romanian troops in areas now constituting the republic of Moldova in 1941–1942. Close to a million Jews were killed locally in Poland and elsewhere, in concentration camps other than Auschwitz and Majdanek, or died of starvation and disease in the Nazi-imposed ghettoes.

The Nazis set up Judenraete in all the countries occupied by them. These, like those in Poland, behaved differently in different places, ranging from full compliance with Nazi instructions, for example, in the Netherlands, to vigorous attempts to rescue people as in Slovakia.

Armed Jewish resistance was almost impossible because the local populations, especially in Eastern Europe, evinced a mostly hostile or indifferent attitude to

Photograph taken during the liberation of the camp of bodies of victims of the Bergen-Belsen Concentration Camp, April 1945. (Yad Vashem, Jerusalem)

their Jewish neighbors; there was no access to arms and there was no coordinated Jewish leadership. Only when it became clear that the Nazis were out to murder all Jews was physical resistance organized. After the deportation to their deaths of most of the Jews of the largest Polish ghetto in Warsaw, Zionist, Communist and Jewish Socialist (Bundist) youth groups managed to set up fighting units that attacked the Germans in January 1943, and then in the main Ghetto Rebellion, in April 1943. With very few arms, the rebels held out for over a month, and sporadic resistance in the ruins of the ghetto lasted for at least three months more. Fighting or attempts at armed escape into the forests took place in sixteen other ghettoes in Central Poland and Lithuania. In what had formerly been Eastern Poland and Soviet Belorussia (Belarus), armed resistance groups operated in 63 more ghettoes. From Minsk, about 7,500 Jews escaped to the forests in order to fight, helped by a Judenrat that engaged in resistance. In the forests of Belorussia and Poland, some 30,000 Jews attempted to resist, some of them in Jewish units, most of them in Soviet units, but not many survived. Apart from German murderers, they were faced with hostility among the civilian population and some of the Soviet partisans.

In Western Europe, where no ghettoes were established, the Nazis tried to recruit the local populations in their drive to kill the Jews. In France they were abetted by the collaborationist Vichy regime led by Marshal Petain. Less than one third of the roughly 350,000 Jews then (1940) in France were caught, deported and murdered, because the rest were helped and hidden by many French, including some Catholic prelates and the whole Protestant community, the underground communists and socialists. Others managed to flee France. There

Photograph taken during the liberation of the camp of human bones near the ovens at the Majdanek Concentration Camp in Poland, April 1945. (Yad Vashem, Jerusalem)

were Jewish armed resistance groups, and considerable Jewish participation in the anti-Nazi underground. In Belgium, about half of the roughly 60,000 Jews were deported, the others having been rescued as a result of collaboration between an active Jewish underground and friendly Belgian groups. In Holland, the Germans were helped by Dutch Nazis—about 9 percent of the populace—and by Dutch bureaucrats who were running the civilian administration. However, some 24,000 of the 110,000 Jews in Holland hid with courageous Dutch people. Of these, one-third was found out, betrayed and deported. In Italy, 8,000 of the 45,000 Italian Jews were deported, the others being supported and hidden by Italians, the vast majority of whom, from Catholic priests to communist guerillas, sympathized with the Jews. Italian Army units, though allied to Nazi Germany, rescued Jews in areas occupied by them in Southeastern France, Greece, and along the Yugoslav coast. In the last stages of the war, about 2,000 Jews were members of the anti-German Italian guerilla forces. In Greece, the large community of Saloniki (56,000) was deported and almost all were murdered; in the south, Greek Orthodox prelates, resistance groups, and ordinary Greek people rescued most of the small Jewish communities. Jews on Greek islands were trapped, caught and murdered. In Bulgaria, the Nazi demand to deliver the 50,000 Jews there to them resulted first in the deportation of some 13,000 Jews of Bulgarian-occupied Yugoslav and Greek territory to their deaths, but then (March 1943), in refusal by the Orthodox Church, the democratic and communist underground, and even the monarch and some of the fascist rulers, to deliver the other Jews to them. In both Greece and Bulgaria, there was Jewish participation in anti-Nazi guerrilla fighting. In Romania, while most of the Jews in the northern parts of the country were killed, by Romanians as well as by Einsatzgruppen, the roughly 360,000 Jews of Central Romania (the *Regat*) were saved in August 1942, by a decision of the fascist regime that was motivated by diplomatic considerations and the military situation. There were interventions by some of the religious dignitaries and by an underground Jewish leadership group. In Hungary, 18,000 of the roughly 800,000 Jews were deported and, mostly, murdered in 1941; Jewish labor battallions attached to the Hungarian Army fighting alongside the Germans in Russia were largely killed, starved to death or driven over mines by their Hungarian commanders. However, the bulk of the Jewish population remained relatively unscathed until the occupation of the country by the Germans in March 1944. Adolf Eichmann, who had all this time been the responsible SS officer for the mass deportations of Jews throughout Europe, organized the deportations to Auschwitz of 437,000 Jews

The Holocaust Challenges Human Civilization

The key question is whether the Holocaust is a unique or a universal event. It was rooted to a specific time, a specific place and a specific people. At the same time, it fundamentally challenges the foundations on which human civilization rests, and has generated a credibility crisis of major proportions in our most basic assumptions about the nature of humankind, society, the modern state and our responsibilities as citizens of the world.

—From a Report in the Jerusalem Post *of an International Conference on the Holocaust and Education, October 1996, at Yad Vashem in Jerusalem*

from the Hungarian provinces between May and July, 1944 by the Hungarian gendarmerie. The deportation of the roughly 250,000 Jews from the capital, Budapest, was narrowly avoided, largely through international protests and threats. When Hungary attempted to switch sides in October 1944—as Romania had done in August—the Germans occupied the capital and established an outright Nazi Hungarian regime, which murdered large numbers of Jews, despite heroic attempts of Jewish rescuers and neutral diplomats to prevent it.

In Yugoslavia, the Jews in Serbia were murdered during the first year—1941—of the German occupation. In Croatia, a collaborationist regime (the Ustashe) murdered very large numbers of Serbs and Gypsies, and the small Jewish community. About 10 percent of the 75,000 Yugoslav Jews participated in the anti-Nazi guerilla army of Tito. In Slovakia, another collaborationist regime under a Catholic priest (Jozef Tiso) initiated the deportation of its Jews to Poland in March 1942, starting with single girls from the age of 16. Despite protests from the Vatican, 58,000 of the 90,000 Slovak Jews were deported in 1942, but some 7,000–8,000 fled to Hungary, and the rest were temporarily saved, largely through bribes by a Jewish underground leadership group. In late 1944, many Jews were caught and deported. Some 1,600 Jews participated in the anti-Nazi guerilla fighting in the Slovak mountains. In Denmark, the small Jewish population of close to 8,000 was rescued, in October 1943, by being transported to neutral Sweden by a concerted effort of the Danish people.

The attitudes of churchmen differed. The Vatican intervened diplomatically, in Slovakia (1942), Romania (1942) and Hungary (1944) in favor of the Jews. On the other hand, it approved of antisemitic actions in France, and Pope Pius XII refused to condemn the Nazi murder of the Jews in public. Individual Catholic prelates acted differently, from a thundering silence (Adam Sapieha in Kracow, Augustus Hlond of Poland in his French exile), to open opposition to the Nazis (Jean-Marie Saliege in Toulouse, Ernest van Roey in Antwerp). Similarly, Protestant reactions varied from full collaboration with the Nazis by the German Lutherans, to determined opposition by Danish Lutherans. There were thousands of individuals who helped Jews, from the Ukraine and Lithuania, where the vast majority of the population was anti-Jewish, to Western Europe, where it was relatively easier to help Jews. Neutral diplomats such as the Swiss, Charles Lutz, the Swede, Raoul Wallenberg in Hungary, the Japanese, Chiune Sugihara in Lithuania, and the Portuguese, Aristides de Sousa Mendes in France, among others, endangered themselves in helping Jews. But all these helpers and rescuers were a small minority among Europeans who observed the mass murder and remained passive.

The Soviets had no interest in the fate of the Jews, but neither did they prevent the massive Jewish flight into the Soviet interior when the Germans attacked the USSR, and some 250,000 Polish and Lithuanian Jews saved themselves. Britain tried to prevent Jewish escape to Palestine, which in 1939 it had decided to hand over to an Arab majority opposed to further Jewish immigration. However, in 1938–1939 it was the only country that took in large numbers (45,000) Jewish refugees from Central Europe, including 10,000 Jewish children whose parents had to remain under the Nazis. The United States strictly adhered to its quota laws, prevented the landing on its territory of desperate refugees on boats, and after 1939 refused to admit any significant number of Jews.

Stirred by the first reports of the mass murder, the Allies publicized, on December 17, 1942 the fact of the murders and warned the Nazis that the criminals would be punished. However, in April 1943, American and British diplomats met at Bermuda and decided not to do anything to rescue Jews, beyond opening a camp in North Africa that in the end accommodated a few hundred people. In early 1944, Roosevelt appointed a special War Refugee Board charged with implementing rescue of Jews and others whose lives were threatened, and some action was taken, but most Jewish victims of the Holocaust were no longer alive. By June 1944, the Western Allies had received detailed information about the killing center at Auschwitz from the report of four Jewish escapees, but refused, for various reasons, to bomb it. Jewish leadership groups, in Palestine, Britain and the US, tried to persuade the Allies to negotiate with the Nazis to keep the Jews alive or enable some of them to escape, but the Allied policy of non-negotation with the Germans, and the powerlessness of the Jews thwarted these attempts.

As the war neared its end, the Nazis began evacuating the camps nearest to the advancing fronts. In January 1945, they evacuated 58,000 inmates of Auschwitz; these were followed by many hundreds of thousands more, Jews and non-Jews. The inmates were marched, without food or water, for weeks on end, or transported in open carriages in European winter conditions. About 60 percent of them died. For the survivors, this was the ultimate horror. When the war ended, 200,000 surviving Jews emerged from the Nazi camps. About 5.8 million had been killed, the victims of a racist illusion seeking to dominate the earth.

Last Days of the Holocaust

In January 1945, the Soviets began an all-out onslaught on the German Armies in Poland and Southeastern Europe. Some 58,000 prisoners (out of 65,000) in the huge concentration-camp complex of Auschwitz (Oswiecim) were marched out on January 18, leaving the rest behind, to be liberated by the Soviets on January 27. From then on, in line with what was probably an oral directive from Hitler, prisoners from camps about to be liberated, Jews and non-Jews, were marched into the contracting area of the Nazi Reich. The purpose was not to let enemies of the Reich fall alive into the hands of the Allies. Officially, there were some 714,000 men and women prisoners in all Nazi camps (January 1945), but the real number was probably higher, possibly up to one million. It is estimated that about 40 percent of these were Jews, but there is no reliable documentation. The prisoners were either marched or transported in open cattle wagons. Little and often no food was supplied, nor was water. The harsh winter took many lives as well. Marchers lagging behind were in all cases shot. Jews were treated worse than the others. March routes were artificially prolonged so as to kill off as many prisoners as possible. Estimates of Jewish casualties vary between 40 to 60 percent. Increasingly chaotic conditions, and either absence of clear orders from above, or contradictory orders, made local commanders the arbiters of life and death.

In the remaining camps, arriving prisoners from the marches were herded into overcrowded barracks, and as food ran out and the water supply broke down, mass starvation and epidemics took their toll. The worst case was Bergen-Belsen (liberated by the British Army on April 14, 1945). A planned continuation of the "Final Solution" is not in evidence, but a general German consensus that as few Jews as possible should survive made these final months part of the genocide of the Jews.

—*Yehuda Bauer*

References and Recommended Reading

Arad, Yitzhak; Gutman, Yisrael; and Margaliot, Abraham (Eds.) (1981). *Documents on the Holocaust: Selected Sources on the Destruction of the*

Photograph taken during the liberation of the Bergen-Belsen Concentration Camp, April 1945. (Yad Vashem, Jerusalem)

Jews of Germany and Austria, Poland and the Soviet Union. Jerusalem: Yad Vashem.

Bauer, Yehuda (1982). *A History of the Holocaust.* New York: Franklin Watts.

Bauer, Yehuda (1989). The death marches. In Marrus, Michael R. (Ed.). *The Nazi Holocaust, Vol. 9: The End of the Holocaust.* London: Meckler, pp. 491–511.

Cesarani, David (Ed.) (1994). *The Final Solution: Origins and Implementation.* London and New York: Routledge.

Cesarani, David (1997). *Genocide and Rescue: The Holocaust in Hungary 1944.* Oxford (England): Berg.

Friedlander, Saul (1997). *Nazi Germany and the Jews. Volume 1: The Years of Persecution, 1933–1939.* New York: HarperCollins.

Gilbert, Martin (1986). *The Holocaust.* London: Collins.

Goldhagen, Daniel J. (1996). *Hitler's Willing Executioners: Ordinary Germans and the Holocaust.* New York: Knopf, pp. 327–371.

Gutman, Yisrael (1982). *The Jews of Warsaw, 1939–1943: Ghetto Underground, Revolt.* Bloomington, IN: Indiana University Press.

Hilberg, Raul (1985). *The Destruction of the European Jews.* Three volumes. Revised and Definitive Edition. New York: Holmes and Meier.

Katsh, Abraham I. (1973). *The Warsaw Diary of Chaim A. Kaplan.* New York: Collins.

Krakowski, Shmuel (1989). The death marches in the period of the evacuation of the camps. In Marrus, Michael R. (Ed.), *ibid,* London: Meckler, pp. 476–489.

Marrus, Michael R., and Paxton Robert O. (1981). *Vichy France and the Jews.* New York: Basic Books.

Porat, Dina (1990). *The Blue and the Yellow Stars of David: The Zionist Leadership in Palestine and the Holocaust, 1939–1945.* Cambridge, MA: Harvard University Press.

Wyman, David S. (1984). *The Abandonment of the Jews: America and the Holocaust, 1941–1945.* New York: Pantheon Books.

THE HOLOCAUST, NON-JEWISH VICTIMS IN

Throughout Nazi rule, Jews were a central target of Nazi policy and ideology, but they were not the only one. Some groups were victimized for what they did, others for what they refused to do, still others, for what they were.

Political dissidents—communists, socialists and liberals alike—and trade unionists were persecuted because of their politics, and their resistance to Nazi domination of Germany. Dissenting clergy were arrested. In the concentration camps, communists, social democrats and trade unionists were marked by the red triangles they wore. Bound by political ties, they were the most organized of all prisoner groups. Some were active in the underground and resistance.

German and, after 1938, Austrian male homosexuals were arrested and their institutions destroyed because of their sexual practices. Their sexual orientation was seen as a threat to breeding the Aryan "master race." Since their status as Aryans was never in question, they were not targeted for systematic murder. Incarceration was both a form of punishment and an effort at sexual reorientation. In the camps, homosexuals were identified by pink triangles. There is no evidence of the systematic persecution of lesbians.

Jehovah's Witnesses, who would not swear allegiance to the state nor register for the draft or serve in the army of the Third Reich, were targeted, as were pacifists. The Nazis believed the Witnesses to have American connections and internationalist aspirations. They read religious descriptions of Witnesses literature as a political message. Prophecies about the return of Jews to the Holy Land prior to Armageddon classified the Witnesses in Nazi eyes as Zionists. Persecution began immediately in 1933 and continued until 1945. After 1937, Witnesses were sent to concentration camps. Outside the camps, Witnesses lost children, jobs, pensions, and all civil rights. Some five thousand Jehovah's Witnesses were sent to concentration camps where they alone were "voluntary prisoners," since the moment they recanted their views, they could be freed

Freemasons were regarded as an ideo logical foe of the Third Reich as well as part of the Jewish problem. The Nazis believed that Jews exploited the Freemasons' international connections to achieve world domination. Initially, the pattern of persecution was virtually identical to that of Jews, but as the campaign against Jews intensified after 1938, the persecution of Freemasons slackened and persecution of Freemasons inside Germany was limited.

Mentally retarded, physically handicapped or emotionally disturbed Germans were not considered suitable raw material for breeding the "master race." In the fall of 1939, Hitler signed an order empowering his personal physician and the chief of the Fuehrer Chancellery to put to death those considered unsuited to live. He backdated it to September 1, 1939, the day World War II began, to give it the appearance of a wartime measure. In the directive:

> Reich leader Philip Bouhler and Dr. Brandt are charged with responsibility for expanding the authority of physicians, to be designated by name, to the end that patients considered incurable according to the best human judgment of their state of health, can be granted a mercy killing.

Within a few months, the T-4 program (named for Tiergarten 4, the street on which the Berlin Chancellery which directed it was located) involved a considerable sector of the German psychiatric community. A new bureaucracy, headed by physicians, was established with a mandate to "take executive measures against those defined as 'life unworthy of living.'"

Six killing centers were established: Hartheim, Sonnenstein, Grafeneck, Bernburg, Hadamar and Brandenburg. The members of the SS in charge of the transports donned white coats to keep up the charade of a medical procedure. Killing itself "progressed" from starvation to lethal injections and then gassing. Pseudoscientific and economic rationalizations were offered.

Some of the physicians who became specialists in the technology of cold-blooded murder in the late 1930s later staffed the death camps. All their moral, professional and ethical inhibitions had long been lost. Historians consider the "euthanasia program" an antecedent to the Holocaust. It was the training ground for death camp personnel.

Local initiatives against the Roma and Sinti [Gypsies] preceded policy decision from Berlin. Long-festering prejudices were fueled by Nazi racism. Thus, in 1935 the city of Frankfurt established a fenced and guarded Gypsy camp. By 1936, the city banned immigration of new Gypsies and authorized "biological heredity examinations." Social marginality, which characterized the Gypsy plight, became embedded into racial theory. In 1936, the Reich Interior Ministry issued guidelines "For Fighting the Gypsy Plague," which required the photographing and fingerprinting of the Gypsies. This information proved lethal when persecution and incarceration later gave way to murder. In 1937, Himmler ordered the Reich Center for Fighting the Gypsy Menace to draft racial definitions. Later that year, "preventative custody" (in Nazi parlance—concentration camp imprisonment) was authorized for Gypsies.

With the onset of war, Gypsies were interned, and then deported to slave labor and death camps. The fate of the Roma and Sinti closely paralleled that of the Jews. Gypsies were singled out according to their purported racial identity as defined by Nazi ideology and so-called racial science. They were despised because of their social status. The existence of Gypsies was also seen as a threat to Aryan blood purity. What the Germans most feared was the mixing of Gypsy and German blood. While Germans Jews of mixed blood might escape deportation, Gypsies of mixed blood were hunted down relentlessly. Tens of thousand were killed by the *Einsatzgruppen* in the East, and tens of thousands more were deported and killed in camps.

Thousands more were incarcerated in Bergen-Belsen, Buchenwald, Dachau, Mauthausen and Ravensbruck. Five thousand Gypsies were transported from Lodz to the killing center of Chelmno, where they were gassed in mobile killing vans. In concentration camps, only Jews and Gypsies were without any legal protection. There was no need to account for the dead, to give a reason or a cause.

Twenty thousand Gypsies were registered as inmates of Auschwitz-Birkenau where a special camp was built to house Gypsy inmates, who continued to live in family units. Gypsy children were subjected to brutal and inhumane "medical experiments" by Dr. Mengele and his staff. On July 31, 1944, the Gypsy camp at Birkenau was "liquidated." All its men, women and children were sent to the gas chambers.

The magnitude of Gypsy dead cannot be currently known. Somewhere between 20 and 50 percent of the entire population of European Gypsies was killed by the Nazis.

From the time of the German invasions of the Soviet Union in June 1941 to the end of World War II in May 1945, more than 3.3 million Soviet prisoners of war died at the hands of the Germans. Most were killed during the first year. The German army, which had custody of some prisoners of war, was responsible for virtually all of these deaths. Fifty-seven percent of all Soviet POWs died in incarceration as compared to 3.6 percent of Anglo-American POWs in German custody. After 1942, when the POWs became essential to the German war economy, the death rate decreased. By 1943, half-a-million Soviet POWs were working as slaves. Many were sent to concentration camps.

The fate of Soviet POWs was doubly tragic. They were disgraced at home. Stalin believed that no Soviet soldier should have ever allowed himself to be taken prisoner.

The Germans considered Poles *Untermenchen* (subhumans) standing in the way of German expansion. German policy in Poland represented a departure from traditional warfare. Terror was intensified *after* a state was subdued and its people had surrendered. In Western Poland, the Nazis instituted a program of colonization. In the General-Government, members of the Polish intelligentsia and political leadership were systematically and brutally killed. The aim was to harness a leaderless, subservient population of laborers who would be used to serve their German masters as migrant workers. Terror was central to this policy. The German General-Governor Hans Frank said: "Poles will become slaves to the German Empire." Polish priests were a particular target. Those Polish children who were considered to be sufficiently Germanic were kidnapped and sent to Germany as part of a forced Aryanization program.

—*Michael Berenbaum*

References and Recommended Reading

Berenbaum, Michael (1990). *A Mosaic of Victims: Non-Jews Persecuted and Murdered by the Nazis.* New York: New York University Press.

Friedlander, Henry (1995). *The Origins of Nazi Genocide: From Euthanasia to the Final Solution.* Chapel Hill, NC: University of North Carolina.

Grau, Gunther (1995). *Hidden Holocaust?: Gay and Lesbian Persecution in Germany 1933–45.* London and New York: Cassell.

Kendrick, Donald, and Paxon, Grattan (1973). *The Destiny of Europe's Gypsies.* New York: Basic Books.

THE HOLOCAUST: RESPONSES OF THE JEWISH COMMUNITY IN PALESTINE

The Jewish community in Palestine ("Yishuv") on the eve of World War II counted 470,000 persons. The strained relations with the British Mandatory power were aggravated by the publication of the 1939 White Paper, which restricted Jewish immigration into Palestine to a total of 75,000 for the following five years. As a result, "Aliya Bet" (illegal immigration) became one of the principal means that the Yishuv used in its struggle with the British.

Despite the conflict with the British over immigration, the Jews of Palestine regarded themselves as a natural ally of the countries that were fighting Hitler, and as soon as the war broke out, the Yishuv's institutions declared that they were rallying to the Allies' side. Some thirty thousand Jewish Palestinians volunteered for service in the British army, even though the British systematically sought to put a brake on such enlistment and to keep the Jewish volunteers from getting proper military training and battle experience. Only in September 1944 was approval given for the formation of the Jewish Brigade Group which was eventually to see action in Italy under its own flag.

A cardinal problem was to understand the real truth behind the reports coming from Europe concerning the situation of the Jews. In the second half of 1940 and in 1941, the prevailing view in Palestine was that the situation of the Jews in the occupied areas was very serious but that it had stabilized, and that most of the Jews, including those in the ghettos in Poland, would survive, albeit at the price of terrible suffering of life and loss of property. Even after the invasion by Germany of the Soviet Union and the systematic mass murder of the Jews in the newly occupied territories, the assumption in the Yishuv was that the fate of Soviet Jews would be similar to that of the Jews of Poland. Then, during 1942, several significant factual reports came into the Yishuv which began to detail the extent of the extermination of the Jews by the Nazis. Toward the end of 1942, the Yishuv itself faced the danger of German conquest of Palestine which would mean the end of the Yishuv. Even so, it was only at the end of 1942 that the Yishuv was shocked by increasingly dread infor-

The Armenian Genocide Alarmed Jews in Palestine

Many documentary evidences have remained from the Armenian Genocide. One of the famous testimonies was given by Sarah Aharonson of Zichron Yaakov, a Jewish settlement in then-Palestine, which was transmitted by her brother, Aharon Aharonson to the British authorities in 1916. "From the time of that trip, she has a fit of hysteria whenever anyone mentions the Armenians," Aharon wrote of his sister. She had seen hundreds of bodies of men, women and children strewn on both sides of the railroad and dogs eating their carcasses. Thousands of others starving and sick Armenians lay near the railroad. When the train came and the engineer saw the Armenians on the tracks he went straight on and wounded 15 people, then leaped triumphantly from his train and called out, "I got those pigs."

Aharon and Sarah Aharonson drew their conclusion from the shocking experience: "We must see the holocaust that has come on the Armenians as an example of what can happen to all the races and peoples who are under the control of the Turks," Aharon wrote in his memorandum.

—*Excerpted from an article in* Hatzofe, *a newspaper of the Center Israeli Religious Movement*

From the same article: The Chief Rabbi of Haifa has concluded: "Every person and every people, and especially the people of Israel who have suffered the Holocaust, must raise their voices to prevent murder and killing. No consideration of personal self-interest or national or public self-interest can override this holy obligation."

mation about the fate of the Jews in Europe, and even then there was still no full realization of the true situation.

Two centers of the Jewish Agency dealt with organizing rescue efforts and the immigration of refugees, one in Geneva since the beginning of the war and the second in Istanbul since the end of 1942. In January 1942 the Joint Rescue Committee of the Jewish Agency was set up, but in practice, the committee had neither the authority nor the means that were required. There were discussions over the finances to be allocated for the rescue operation, but the executive leaders of the Yishuv held that the Yishuv's meager resources had to be handled carefully and with restraint.

The Yishuv institutions were involved in several rescue programs, but the Yishuv leadership was in a trap during the Holocaust. It is clear that the Yishuv could not save millions of Jews, and so the Yishuv concentrated on the saving of thousands (the "small rescue"). On the other hand, there are accusations that the Yishuv could have done more in spite of the difficult circumstances in which it operated.

—*Yair Auron*

References and Recommended Reading

Porat, Dina (1990). Yishuv. In Gutman, Israel (Ed.), *Encyclopedia of the Holocaust.* Volume 4. New York: Macmillan, pp. 1686–1694.

Segev, Tom (1993). *The Seventh Million: The Israelis and the Holocaust.* New York: Hill and Wang.

THE HOLOCAUST: RESPONSES OF THE UNITED STATES AND ALLIES

Prior to World War II, US and British willingness to absorb Jewish refugees from the expanding German Reich was limited by American quotas and British unwillingness to accept immigrants generally, and Jews in particular. There was no way the Western governments could have foreseen the Holocaust; they were refusing entry to a persecuted minority, not to certain candidates for death. However, in 1938–39, the small US quota for Germany and Austria (27,000) was overfulfilled, and Britain accepted some 45,000 Central European Jews, including close to 10,000 children, between the 9–10 November 1938 pogrom in Germany and the outbreak of war in September 1939.

Knowledge about what was happening in German-occupied Europe was fairly accurate in 1939–40, before the German decision to murder the Jews. Britain was fighting for her life, the neutral US was afraid of Nazi or communist infiltration and reduced Jewish immigration to a minimum. Antisemitic government officials also had some influence, as did unfriendly consuls in Europe, who could accept or refuse pleas for visas.

The mass murder of European Jews began with the German invasion of the USSR in June 1941. For the first year after that, information was uncertain and scattered. Although British code-breakers read occasional German police messages about murder of Jews in various places in occupied Soviet areas between June and September 1941, knowledge of a systematic murder campaign could not be deduced from that. A Soviet announcement (January 5, 1942) about mass murder of Jews was seen as propaganda. A first detailed report reached Britain from underground Polish sources, and was published in the British press in late June and early July 1942. A cable message by Gerhard Riegner of the World Jewish Congress in Geneva on mass murder to be committed in the near future was received in London and Washington in August. By early November 1942, this had been confirmed by a number of sources. As a result of the pressure of the Polish Government-in-Exile, a public announcement by all the Allied Powers that the Germans were annihilating the Jews was read out in the British House of Commons on December 17, 1942. In Britain, public opinion demanded that something be done to come to the rescue of Jews. In the US, Jewish organizations demanded the same. However, an Anglo-American conference at Bermuda, in April 1943, in effect refused to do anything substantial, such as guaranteeing to the neutrals (Switzerland, Spain, Portugal, Turkey, Sweden) that any Jewish refugees from Nazi-occupied Europe would be kept at Allied expense, and given a home elsewhere after the war; or agreeing to spread propaganda among Germans and others threatening retribution for the crimes committed; or accompanying bombing missions with leaflets in the same spirit. Funds were permitted to be transferred to Switzerland for rescue purposes only after considerable delays in the Fall of 1943. Generally, both the US and Britain played down Nazi anti-Jewish actions for fear they would be accused of conducting the war on behalf of the Jews. Antisemitism was clearly on the rise in the US during the war—though not in Britain, it seems, despite anxieties of British ministers to the contrary—and the Roosevelt Administration was fearful of its possible effects.

The British government refused permits to enter Palestine during the war to all but a small number of refugees (some 55,000) in six years. These came at first from Central Europe, and then mainly from Balkan countries. The reason was British fear of alienating Arab countries such as Egypt and Iraq, and Palestinian Arabs. Arab political leaderships were tending toward the Nazis, such as in the case of the acknowledged leader of the Palestinian Arabs, the Mufti of Jerusalem, Hajj Amin el-Husseini, who joined and helped the Nazis.

Bombing the death camps was an impossibility up to the end of 1943, when the airfields of Foggia in Italy became usable for the US Air Force. By that time however, all the death camps except for Auschwitz had stopped operations. Information about Auschwitz as the main site of mass murder of Jews was only obtained after the escape of two Jewish prisoners in

April 1944. Demands to bomb the camp were made in and after June 1944, but were refused by the Western Allies, the reason apparently being that a prior decision of January 1944 had rejected all use of military forces for nonmilitary purposes. Murder of civilians in gas chambers fell within the nonmilitary category. The official reason given was technical difficulties, but most historians reject that as being an excuse. Whether the bombing of the murder camp (the nearby complex of the camp where industrial production was taking place was bombed) would have stopped the murder may be doubtful. Yet had it been done, it would certainly have made a clear statement that the outside world knew and cared; that is what the inmates felt and wanted.

Increased public awareness in the US, in part caused by a group of rightist Palestinian Jewish activists around "Peter Bergson" (pseudonym for Hillel Kook) on the one hand, and the personal involvement of a number of (non-Jewish) officials in the Treasury Department on the other hand, in the end made President Roosevelt take the step of establishing the War Refugee Board (WRB—January 1944). The WRB, through its emissaries in a number of US diplomatic missions in Europe, tried its best to rescue especially endangered persons, which in fact mostly meant Jews. Its successes were limited, but it did aid rescue attempts by Jewish groups and organizations, and tried to provide sustenance to those entrapped in Nazi Europe.

Allied air forces made no effort to come to the aid of marching columns of prisoners from concentration camps in the final weeks of the war. The numbers of victims in these "death marches" has not yet been clarified, but it was in the hundreds of thousands.

The USSR evinced no interest in the fate of the Jews. This was partly due to rising antisemitism within the Soviet leadership, but also to the general Soviet view that saw the Nazi murder machine directed chiefly against the Slavs and the Communist regime. When Germany invaded the USSR in June 1941, some Soviet authorities tried to stop Jews (and others) from the territories recently acquired in Eastern Poland, the Baltic States and Northern Romania from fleeing into the pre-1939 Soviet areas. However, after a few days the attitude changed and at least 300,000 Jews from these areas, as well as large but as yet undetermined numbers of Jews from the pre-1939 Soviet territories, fled into the Soviet interior, largely to Central Asia. They were treated just as all other refugees were—the situation was chaotic, there was lack of food, and diseases were rampant. Many thousands died, but detailed numbers are still unavailable. The fact that the rest survived was due to the Soviet Army's victories and the friendly indifference of the Soviet politicians. The survivors left the USSR after the war.

—Yehuda Bauer

References and Recommended Reading

Gilbert, Martin (1981). *Auschwitz and the Allies.* New York: Holt, Rinehart and Winston.

Levin, Dov (1977). The attitude of the Soviet Union to the rescue of Jews. In Gutman, Yisrael, and Zuroff, Efraim (Ed.), *Rescue Attempts during the Holocaust.* Jerusalem: Yad Vashem, pp. 225–236.

Wasserstein, Bernard (1988). *Britain and the Jews of Europe, 1939–1945.* Oxford: Oxford University Press (originally published in Oxford: Clarendon, 1970).

Wyman, David S. (1984). *The Abandonment of the Jews: America and the Holocaust, 1941–1945.* New York: Pantheon.

THE HOLOCAUST AND THE RISE OF THE STATE OF ISRAEL

The basic facts of the Nazi murder of the Jews had become clear to the outside world from November 1942 on. Nevertheless, the Jewish authorities in Palestine were hard hit by the realization of the full extent of the disaster. The Zionist—Jewish national—enterprise had been built on the notion that especially the Jews of Eastern Europe needed to leave their homes because of economic and political pressures as well as their growing group consciousness, and that the only place they could build a politically autonomous home for themselves would be Palestine. But of the close to seven million Jews in that region, up to five million had been killed, and most of the others were Soviet Jews whose government would prevent them from leaving the USSR.

Some 55,000 survivors of camps and hiding places remained in postwar Germany, and were joined in 1945–47 by another 250,000 Jewish returnees to Poland from Central Asia (whence they had fled when Germany invaded the USSR) and survivors from other East European countries. Most of these people concentrated in the Western occupation zones of Germany and Austria, and in Italy. The lesson they had drawn from their experiences was that they needed a new home. The West was closed to them until 1948 and 1950, at which times the US passed laws that enabled less than a third of them to emigrate there. Some also emigrated to other Western countries. The urge of most of the rest—about two-thirds—to emigrate to Palestine was very strong, and convinced the Truman Administration to exert pressure on the British government to permit 100,000 so-called "displaced" Jewish persons (DPs) to go there. The British refused, because they believed that Arab resistance to such a move would spell trouble for the British position in the Middle East. An Anglo-American Commission of Inquiry (November 1945–April 1946) agreed with Truman's demand, but again the British government refused. Had it agreed, the pressure to open the gates of Palestine might have been removed.

The Jewish Agency, the Zionist leadership of Palestine Jewry, which had formerly demanded that all of Palestine become a Jewish State, now (August 1946) agreed to be content with a partition of the country between Jews and Arabs. This seeming readiness to compromise made it easier for the US to press for a solution that would include the immigration of the DPs to Palestine.

The US Army demanded of its government to remove the Jewish survivors for financial reasons and because of the beginning Cold War. As the US was not interested in absorbing them, and as American Jews massively supported the demand of their DP brethren and sisters to go to Palestine, President Harry S. Truman's problems mounted. Large-scale attempts at illegal immigration to Palestine faced determined and occasionally brutal British opposition, and created a favorable climate for Zionist aspirations, for example, in France and Italy. This and American pressure on the British finally caused the British to turn the Jewish DP and Palestine problems over to the UN (February 1947). They hoped that there the Jewish influence would be neutralized. However, the formerly anti-Zionist USSR, wishing to evict the British from Palestine, surprisingly began to support Jewish aspirations (April 1947), as did most of the Latin American countries. A further United Nations Special Committee of Inquiry on Palestine, in a majority report, recommended (August 1947) partition, and hence the immigration of Holocaust survivors. The UN adopted the recommendation on November 29, 1947, thus enabling the Jews of Palestine to fight for the establishment of Israel.

There is no evidence to support the idea that remorse for the non-action of the Powers during the Holocaust was involved in the tortuous path that led to the establishment of Israel on May 14, 1948, at least not on the conscious level as reflected in diplomatic and political documentation. In fact, arguably, had the Holocaust not occurred, pressure by an increasingly desperate Jewish population in Eastern Europe might have caused a much stronger pressure on the British than exercised by the Holocaust survivors. As it was, the impact of the Holocaust lay in the fact that the inconvenient presence of the survivors in Germany and Austria moved the US to put pressure on the British, which led to the British retreat from Palestine. There is no doubt, however, that the Holocaust crucially influenced Jewish policies, as well as significant parts of European public opinion. Most Jews were convinced that with the murder of European Jewry, the national Jewish project would fail unless a desperate struggle brought about the immediate establishment of an independent state with what remained of Europe's Jews and, following May 1948, with Asian-African Jews now expelled or edged out or responding to the Zionist call. This sense of crisis was repeatedly emphasized in speeches by Zionist leaders such as Chaim Weizmann and David Ben-Gurion in Palestine, Rabbi Abba Hillel Silver in the US, and survivors' leaders such as Abba Kovner. The Israeli poet Nathan Alterman and other literary figures gave expression to the same sentiments.

—Yehuda Bauer

References and Recommended Reading

Bauer, Yehuda (1996). The impact of the Holocaust on the establishment of the State of Israel. In Gutman, Yisrael, and Saf, Avital (Eds.), *Major Changes within the Jewish People in the Wake of the Holocaust: Proceedings of the Ninth Yad Vashem International Historical Conference.* Jerusalem: Yad Vashem, pp. 545–552.

Cohen, Michael J. (Spring 1982). Truman, the Holocaust and the establishment of the State of Israel. *The Jerusalem Quarterly,* 23, 79–96.

Dinnerstein, Leonard (1982). *America and the Survivors of the Holocaust.* New York: Columbia University Press.

Friesel, Evyatar (1996). The Holocaust: Factor in the birth of Israel? In Gutman, Yisrael, and Saf, Avital (Eds.), *ibid,* pp. 519–544.

THE HOLOCAUST: UNDERSTANDING THE HOLOCAUST AND ITS IMPLICATIONS

LESSONS FROM THE HOLOCAUST

The sad words written in 1948 by Lagi Countess Ballestrem-Solf, a person who opposed the Nazis with great courage, remain for today's world: "I do not want to think of the past because it has lost its meaning. The world has learned nothing from it—neither slaughterers nor victims nor onlookers. Our time is like a dance of death whose uncanny rhythm is understood by few. Everyone whirls confusedly without seeing the abyss."

By their nature, humans are extraordinarily capable of being either killers or victims. It would be comforting to believe that only perverse sadistic devils could be killers. To be sure, Nazi policies led to a natural selection of persons of minimum or non-existent moral restraints and maximum pathological behavior. But genocide did not just happen. It was deliberately organized by the government. The appointed executioners marshalled the instruments of violence of the state, and plotted in great detail the logistics of death. Obedience, considered to be a supreme virtue in a society with an authoritarian orientation, or in a given situation such as war, can greatly exacerbate the hazard of genocide. For instance, Rudolf Höess, the head of the Auschwitz death camp, perceived himself as a law-abiding citizen who did his duty. When obedience is coupled with an expediential ethic, in which all means are justified by an end, we reach a point of maximum risk for the potential victim. In any deliberation on the role of values we must also ask ourselves to what degree the secularization of our world and abandonment of moral precepts taught by organized religions can facilitate the rationalizations involved in genocidal behavior. Yet we must recognize that although religious faith has served to restrain brutal behavior, organized religions have often served as vehicles for fanaticism leading to genocidal behavior.

Two experiments of recent years have shed some frightening light on dangerous patterns in human behavior. The experiments of Professor Stanley Milgram of Yale University, conducted in 1960, were generated by questions posed concerning psychosocial characteristics of Germans: Were they different, especially in their willingness to obey authority? Did Germans possess a basic character flaw that brutalized them? To answer his questions, Milgram designed an experiment to test the readiness to obey instructions and orders from a particular authority. A volunteer "teacher" was instructed to administer to a "learner" what the "teacher" was led to believe were electric shocks. The pain from the shocks was simulated by the learner, who had been instructed by Professor Milgram in advance. The teacher had no way of determining if these shocks, which allegedly went up to 450 volts (for wrong answers) might not in fact electrocute the learner. The experiment was designed so that there was genuine reason to believe that when the learner no longer gave evidence of pain as the voltage was escalated, he may in fact be comatose or dead. Some teachers resisted somewhat, but often not to the extent that they actually refused to continue following the orders of the perpetrator of the "experiment" (or crime?). Altogether, two-thirds of the subjects followed orders. These are Milgram's conclusions: "The results, as seen and felt in the laboratory are disturbing. They raise the possibility that human nature, or more specifically the kind of character produced in American democratic society, cannot be counted on to insulate its citizens from brutality and inhumane treatment at the direction of malevolent authority. A substantial portion of people do what they are told to do, irrespective of the content of the act and without limitations of conscience, so long as they perceive that the command comes from a legitimate authority. If, in this study, an anonymous experimenter can successfully command adults to subdue a fifty-year-old man and force on him painful electric shocks against his protests, one can only wonder what government, with its vastly greater authority and prestige, can command of its subjects."

The second experiment, by Professor Philip G. Zimbardo, Stanford University, involved hiring students to simulate a prison situation. He concluded: "At the end of only six days we had to close down our mock prison because what we saw was frightening. It was no longer apparent to most of the subjects (or to us) where reality ended and their roles began. The majority had indeed become prisoners or guards, no longer able to clearly differentiate between role playing and self. There were dramatic changes in virtually every aspect of their behavior, thinking and feeling."

The extraordinary vulnerability of human beings, illustrated by these two experiments, does not suggest a totally undifferentiated conclusion that all human beings are capable of committing mass slaughter under any circumstance. Such a jump in logic is not only wrong, but dangerous. Instead we need to examine the factors which heighten or minimize the hazard. In what context does a particular historical circumstance reach the critical point that leads to genocidal behavior? By contrast, what are the conditions of safety?

Clearly we must recognize that the nature of the particular government is critical. A highly authoritarian and totalitarian state, without restraints on its leaders, creates a much more dangerous context. If, in addition, some leaders at the top of the hierarchy possess deeply flawed personalities they may be able to co-opt similar types into the government. These persons may then force their pathological fantasies to be acted out by their more paranoid followers thereby creating an explosive situation of the type experienced with Hitler in Nazi Germany.

Other critical factors are derived from the study of psychohistory. A generation that has been severely traumatized and brutalized as were the Germans in World War I, and later with the near destruction of the fabric of their society, is at risk when then further affected by successive traumas.

There appears to be a direct correlation between an individual's or a society's pathology and the readiness to escape self-blame through the search for a scapegoat. Many societies have readily identified scapegoats. The Jews were the convenient scapegoats in Europe, and Nazi ideology, with its concept of "belonging" (to the Aryan race), was well served by antisemitism.

In the modern era, governments enjoy the technological capability to render mass killing both easier and more remote. Modern warfare engenders horrible genocidal potential, and remoteness from killer to victim makes rationalization easier. A society that legitimizes brutality and codifies the search for scapegoats also creates victims.

When is the scapegoat in danger of being sacrificed—of becoming the victim? An individual becomes defenseless when stripped of constitutional and legal safeguards. A society that denies humans these safeguards can quickly make them into victims. In the twentieth century we have had numerous demonstrations of the relative inefficacy of individuals or groups of people resisting against the state, with its ability to marshal all instruments of power.

What is the paradigm of a nation that has maximum potential for engaging in genocidal behavior? Its government is authoritarian in nature or in a state of crisis, such as war. Its people, through circumstances arising from consensus or nurtured by propaganda, have been persuaded that its particular ideology justifies an expediential ethic in which the end justifies the means. The sense of connection that humans have with the vital and nourishing symbols of their cultural traditions are broken down by the expediential ethic. Psychologically, the culture is likely to be inclined towards overly severe child-rearing habits, physical punishment, or instruction in absolute obedience. Its people have been severely traumatized by recent historical events, and brutalized by war. Timing itself is critical: a war or violent event in itself enhances the expediental ethic and leads to callousness. The emerging pathologies can be of such severity that a scapegoat is ultimately identified and stamped as subhuman. Then sadism gone rampant results in slaughter—the elimination of the sacrificial scapegoat.

By contrast, what is the paradigm of a nation that is safe for those who could be identified as potential victims? It is a society engaged in the rule of law, a culture in which childrearing habits are supportive of loving and caring relationships. It is a society with high moral principles, a society that teaches the importance of human dignity and worth, a society that is not troubled by deep traumas or subject to brutalization by wars. It is a nation with a positive attitude toward a diversity of views, in which a large number of minorities display well-developed and positive self-identities. Under conditions of hazard, strong minority organizations will prevail if civil disobedience or resistance to arbitrary authority is needed to safeguard that society's health. Such a society offers the hope of protection against genocide.

The study of the Holocaust is not an esoteric or antiquarian subject, but a matter of vital concern to us all. It is a matter that demands constant awareness and alertness.

—Eric H. Boehm

References and Recommended Reading

Boehm, Eric H. (1985). *We Survived: Fourteen Histories of the Hidden and Hunted in Germany.* 1985 Reprint Edition with Epilogue by Author. Santa Barbara, CA: ABC-CLIO Information Services (originally published in 1949 by Yale University Press).

Meyer, Philip (1987). If Hitler asked you to electrocute a stranger, would you? Probably. In Charon, Joel M. (Ed.), *The Meaning of Sociology: A Reader.* 2nd edition. Englewood Cliffs, NJ: Prentice Hall, pp. 155–168.

MEANINGS OF THE HOLOCAUST

The meaning of some events may be measured by their consequences. The storming of the Bastille in August of 1789 began a process that would transform European society: government by monarchs believing themselves to be accountable only to God gave way to institutions that would permit "the people" to govern themselves.

Holocaust Survivor Warns of Dangers of Omnicide

Writing in *The Voice of Auschwitz Survivors in Israel,* Dr. Erich Kulka, historian and Holocaust survivor, warned: "We, the survivors, also see another meaning of Auschwitz. A repetition of Auschwitz seems to us very probable. A future cataclysm would hit not only the Jews, but also much larger groups and nations. Technological progress creates and harbors unimaginable possibilities of annihilation. Persecutions, deportations, selections, gas chambers, crematoria and firepits no longer will be necessary. Atomic and nuclear means of destruction are present, stowed conveniently in silos, and capable of multiple 'overkill.' Air-borne crematoria and 'gas chambers on wings' could cause absolute havoc over the territories of nations—killing, burning, annihilating every organism and turning the very soil sterile and polluted.

"We, the survivors of the hell of Auschwitz, who went through the [illegible] daily, and survived, see a real, actual, physical danger hovering over our world today. We can sense it because we have been sensitized by the past. We raise our voice; we call for respecting the rights of man; we warn of the insensible craze of armaments. We wish to prevent the coming of doomsday."

In one sense, the Holocaust has not caused any general transformation of society. Except for its role in the establishment of the State of Israel, it has had no significant political effect. Yet the meaning of an event is not only determined by its material impacts. Beyond any material changes, the Holocaust has *radically altered what it means to be in the world.*

The eighteenth-century Enlightenment set forth the idea of progress as the governing principle of history. What made progress possible was the cumulative nature of knowledge, where each generation could build upon the accomplishment of others. By drastically increasing human productivity, the marriage of science and technology provided a new material basis for life that need not constantly be dedicated to struggling for sustenance. Joined to this was the belief that somehow the new scientific achievement would not only provide a new mastery of the natural world, but also lead to moral progress. Rational knowledge could destroy intolerant religious obscurantism, and more generally undermine the legitimacy of irrational institutions. Faith in progress did not rest only upon improvements in the material conditions of life, but was supported by the spread of democracy, the absence of major wars, the increasing sensitivity toward humane values—the nineteenth century for example witnessed the founding of numerous societies for the prevention of cruelty to animals and children—and the elimination of judicial torture.

The new political realities generated an alternate view of human nature that affirmed the Enlightenment view of a fundamental goodness of human nature. It placed its faith in education as a means of striving toward human perfectibility and posited that human beings possessed a fundamental sense of morality.

The Holocaust with its unprecedented destructiveness of human life was carried out by one of Europe's most advanced countries. It utilized the very instruments that had made progress possible—science, technology, industry and bureaucracy. Recognizing that injustices, exploitation and violence still existed, Europeans had believed that they were being steadily reduced. That millions could be killed at the very center of European civilization because they were deemed unacceptable to those in power was unthinkable. *The Holocaust destroyed the idea of history as the embodiment of an upward movement toward a higher form of civilization.*

In the wake of the discovery of the death camps with their horrifying visual imagery, the question of how people could do these things, and do them with apparently good conscience kept being asked. To answer this, social psychologist, Stanley Milgram, set up a brilliant experiment to test blind obedience to authority in which he had individuals administer (what they believed to be) electric shocks to subjects to determine how far people would go in carrying out "orders." He found that most people continued to increase the amount of shock even though the victims screamed that they were in pain. He concluded that: "Ordinary people, simply doing their jobs . . . can become agents in a terrible destructive process" (p. 6). These experiments, repeated with variations by others, made it clear that most individuals will carry out destructive actions when ordered to do so with few qualms. This conclusion received a new validation by Christopher Browning's investigation of a German police battalion in Poland. He showed how "ordinary men"—not members of the SS, not fanatical Nazis—could readily accommodate to participating in mass killing, even when they were told that if any felt that they could not do this, they could withdraw from participation without fear of punishment.

The Holocaust was a political act on the part of a government utilizing all its resources. Holocaust research has rightly emphasized the bureaucratic nature of the process. (Raul Hilberg has written the classic work that delineates how the German bureaucratic apparatus functioned in implementing the Holocaust.) Yet during the Holocaust the perpetrators did more than just carry out orders. As accounts are examined, one sees time and time again how individuals, freed from external restraints, engaged in spontaneous acts of cruelty of hitherto unimaginable proportions, seemingly because they enjoyed them. Clearly our previous definition of human nature stands in need of revision.

Two recent works have sought to locate the causes of the Holocaust primarily in German history and culture [Goldhagen, Daniel Jonah (1996). *Hitler's Willing Executioners: Ordinary Germans and the Holocaust.* New York: Alfred A. Knopf; and Weiss, John (1996). *Ideology of Death: Why the Holocaust Happened in Germany.* Chicago: Ivan R. Dee]. Yet nearly everywhere the Germans went in Europe they found individuals who enthusiastically participated in Germany's program of deportations and mass killings of Jews, Gypsies, Serbs and others, suggesting that willingness to engage in mass destructive behavior is widespread if not universal.

History, from the Athenian destruction of Melos to the Armenian Genocide and beyond, abounds with examples of human cruelty and destructiveness. The Holocaust has revealed a new dimension of destructiveness, just when the Western world believed it had achieved a new and higher level of civilization characterized by respect for the individual. It has demonstrated that the modern state may, when it chooses to do so, seek out groups for destruction and then use all its power for that purpose. It may also count upon the positive support of many who, either out of a sense of duty, or because they endow the victims with demonic qualities, or for other reasons, are willing, frequently enthusiastically, to participate in mass killing. The meaning of the Holocaust is, therefore based on realization of the Janus face of modernity, for good or evil, to which all of us are vulnerable.

—George M. Kren and Leon Rappoport

References and Recommended Reading

Browning, Christopher (1992). *Ordinary Men: Reserve Police Battalion 101 and The Final Solution in Poland.* New York: HarperCollins.

Hilberg, Raul (1985). *The Destruction of the European Jews.* Three volumes. Revised and Definitive Edition. New York: Holmes and Meier.

Kren, George, and Rappoport, Leon (1994). *The Holocaust and the Crisis of Human Behavior.* Revised Edition. New York: Holmes and Meier (originally published in 1980).

Milgram, Stanley (1974). *Obedience to Authority: An Experimental View.* New York: Harper and Row.

SIGNIFICANCE OF THE HOLOCAUST IN THE TWENTY-FIRST CENTURY

It is already apparent that, as the Holocaust recedes further into history, its presence in the consciousness of Western Civilization has been growing steadily larger. Witness the expanding accumulation of literature, scholarship, films, museums, and memorials. Moreover, insofar as any current event even remotely suggests the reality or the threat of genocide, the Holocaust is invoked as a reflexive image or metaphor. Our view is that this general expansive trend is bound to continue well into, if not throughout, the next century because *the Holocaust has become an indispensable standard against which all of the moral issues defining the modern human condition must be tested.*

Less obvious but no less significant as a force projecting concern with the Holocaust into the future is its uniquely problematic metaphysical status. Ever since the massive genocide occurred, its religious significance has remained as a major source of contention both within and between organized Christianity and Judaism. Christian theologians are divided over the question of whether it requires formal church renunciation of all forms of antisemitism; Jewish theologians divide over the question of how to relate the Holocaust to the Jewish covenant with God. Furthermore, despite efforts toward ecumenical reconciliations, including new papal initiatives to finally condemn aspects of church complicity in the Holocaust, the behavior of the Catholic hierarchy remains as a still not fully resolved point of conflict between Catholic and Jewish theologians.

It is also appropriate to consider the Holocaust in the context of how the twentieth century as a whole will be viewed in the larger perspective of history. Will it be possible to arrive at any overarching interpretation or understanding of the modern era, the century of modernity, without acknowledging the Holocaust as one of the handful of definitive events, alongside the world wars, the landings on the moon, and nuclear power? In our view, the answer is clearly "no." That is, apart from the formidable technological innovations characterizing the twentieth century, the period is chiefly defined by the massive sociopolitical disasters that made it an era of unparalleled destruction. If this "long view" is approximately correct, then it follows that for future scholars and thinkers nothing will serve so well as the Holocaust to epitomize this destructiveness.

Finally, it may be suggested that in the next century the conceptual status of the Holocaust will inevitably change. As survivors and other witnesses alive at the time pass away, the Holocaust of lived experience is likely to become more and more the Holocaust of myth and the imagination. This raises the possibility that despite the vast accumulation of documentary evidence and scholarly analyses, a process of reification at the level of popular culture may yield an oversimplified, mythic image of the Holocaust detached from its concrete realities.

—*Leon Rappoport and George M. Kren*

References and Recommended Reading

Kren, George, and Rappoport, Leon (1994). *The Holocaust and the Crisis of Human Behavior.* Revised Edition. New York: Holmes and Meier (originally published in 1980).

Totten, Samuel; Parsons, William S.; and Charny, Israel W. (1997). *Century of Genocide: Eyewitness Accounts and Critical Views.* New York: Garland Publishing. Paperback, expanded, with title change of original hardcover, *Genocide in the Twentieth Century: Critical Essays and Eyewitness Accounts,* 1995.

HOMOSEXUALS: GENOCIDE OF HOMOSEXUALS IN THE HOLOCAUST

There were many kinds of victims in the Nazi camps. Different groups wore different triangles, and different triangles denoted different "crimes." Jews wore yellow stars but also red triangles—political triangles. One of the biggest groups consisted of Germans who were made to wear black triangles, meaning saboteurs. Green triangles were worn by murderers. There were other triangles or strips for Jehovah's Witnesses, vagrants, emigrants, Gypsies, "race defiler (male)," "race defiler (female)," escape suspects, special inmates, repeaters (those who were incarcerated more than once), and members of armed forces. A bewildering array of stigmatization.

Holocaust research in general is difficult, but for research on homosexuals the problems multiply. First, the data that exist are often unreliable, and primary data are scant and inadequate. Many records were lost or destroyed. Complete reports are hard to find. Even after the war, "homosexual" was still a dirty word; paragraphs 175 and 175a of the 1935 Nazi revision of the long-existing German law proscribing homosexual acts remained in force until June 1969 when much of paragraph 175 and all of 175a were abolished. Gay men (and women) were thus stigmatized for many years after the war. Unlike Jews and other victims, they could not receive *wiedergutmachung* (restitution) payments, since West German courts decreed that gays had been criminals under the Nazis and thus not eligible for such payments. Furthermore, under the laws in which genocide was defined after the war, the killing of homosexuals was not considered a crime against humanity or a war crime. In addition, gay men and women who wished to emigrate from Europe after World War II had to keep their sexual identity secret because many nations, including the United States, enforced laws that forbade homosexuals from immigrating or even visiting those countries. For all these reasons, it was very difficult to find and interview gay survivors of the Holocaust. Some scholars have also been homophobic on the subject, either overlooking homosexuals or simply dismissing them.

In the 1930s, there began in Germany a persecution of male homosexuals that was, like that of Jews, the worst in their respective histories. Lesbians, since they could continue to breed children, presented no practical reproductive problems to the Nazi state.

The Nazis' murder of some homosexuals started earlier than that of the Jews with the murders of Ernst Roehm and other brownshirts in his paramilitary group known as the SA, although the major reason for these murders was to eliminate a potentially rival force to the SS. Roehm was a major Nazi leader, second only to Hitler as they rose to power in the 1920s and early 1930s. He and his cadre of "brownshirts" were homosexuals, which was not a problem at the beginning for Hitler, but later did prove an embarrassment and a threat. Roehm and other SA leaders were murdered without warning in a famous blood purge which was led by Himmler and other SS offi-

Homosexuals and the Holocaust: Victimization Is Not Genocide

[The following is an example of the position of many scholars of genocide who do not consider the Nazi murders of homosexuals genocide—while many others use qualifying terms such as genocidal massacre, or genocidal killing.—Ed.]

Between 1933 and 1945 no more than 50,000 men were charged with the crime of homosexuality. (It would be enlightening to know how many faced that charge between 1871 and 1933—Nazi mistreatment of male homosexuals was based on a pre-1933 law dating back to 1871 [Law #175], not to mention how many were found guilty and what the punishment was.) According to Germany's leading historian of homosexuals, Joachim Müller, around ten to fifteen thousand were found "guilty" of whom a majority was sentenced to incarceration in a concentration camp. In other words, 35,000 to 40,000 of the accused homosexuals were not sent into the German Gulag, hardly a sign of genocidal intent!

Of those 10,000 to 15,000, most survived their sentences, though several hundreds (again according to Müller) died from the brutal treatment meted out to them. But again, this is not a percentage suggesting a determination to exterminate all those imprisoned. Thus the victimization of male homosexuals under the Nazi regime in no way approaches the category of genocide and should not be classified as such.

—Henry R. Huttenbach

cers at the instigation of Hitler and began on June 30, 1934, which has been called "The Night of Long Knives."

In writing about the Holocaust, the "gay genocide" has often been either a taboo subject too delicate to touch upon, a topic obscured by other issues, or simply omitted. However, there are well-researched books—for example, John Lauritsen and David Thorstad, *The Early Homosexual Rights Movement: 1864–1935* [New York: Times Change Press, 1974]; Heinz Heger, *The Men with the Pink Triangle* [Boston: Alyson Publications, 1980]. Richard Plant's *The Pink Triangle: The Nazi War against Homosexuals* is one of the most outstanding, clearly and eloquently written.

Controversy surrounds every aspect of this genocide, even the label "genocide." Since gays could "pass" (unlike Jews or Gypsies), most survived the war. If they remained celibate or "in the closet," they could elude the Nazis and survive. Because they were difficult to detect, a considerable number were never rounded up. Thus, there are strong arguments not to call this a genocide.

On the other hand, there are strong arguments for this to be seen as a genocide: first, the stigmatization of homosexuals as "vermin," "plague," "cancerous ulcer," and "a tumor" is racist and the kind of dehumanization that enables genocide to occur. Under Himmler's direction, the ferocity of attack gained impetus to seek out and destroy or sterilize every homosexual the Nazis could find. By the United Nations definition, these acts of sterilization fall under the category of limiting births, thus genocide. It is not an easy decision, but overall I personally adopt a non-genocide label, though it could fall under the rubric of what I would call *genocidal acts*. As for a planned, systematic genocide, I have reluctantly come to the conclusion that there was none. Gays were victims of the Third Reich and therefore belong in any Holocaust museum, but I would conclude that gays were victims of a genocidal mentality, and not of outright genocide.

[See DEFINITIONS OF GENOCIDE for more on controversies in defining genocide, including the differing opinion of the editor of this Encyclopedia.—Ed.]

Overall, we can estimate the number of males convicted of homosexuality from 1933–1944 at between 50,000 to 63,000. The number of homosexuals incarcerated in the Nazi concentation camps is not known, much less the number who died there. Rudiger Lautmann in his *Gesellschaft und Homosexualität: Seminar* [Frankfurt: Suhrkamp, 1977], whose figures are used by Plant and other writers, estimates that somewhere between 5,000 to 15,000 homosexuals perished behind the barbed-wire fences. These were victims who were labeled and processed as homosexuals. A figure of about 10,000 homosexuals is the one accepted by most scholars (although figures are thrown about wildly and estimates run as high as Jean Boisson's one million dead). Gay leaders and writers insist on higher figures in order to legitimate their claim of special pleading. Yet, why indeed are 10,000 killed less tragic than one million? In the aftermath of the Holocaust, numbers themselves seem to lose their significance. In any case, the major Holocaust institution in the US, the US Holocaust Memorial Museum, recognizes the "gay genocide."

Did Hitler despise homosexuals? Was he ashamed of his own homosexual or asexual identity? These are areas of psychohistory that are beyond known knowledge. My own feelings are that Hitler was asexual in the traditional sense and had bizarre sexual fetishes. All these things were of course kept highly secret from the German people. But there were other political considerations. Perhaps Hans Peter Bleuel [*Sex and Society in Nazi Germany,* New York: Lippincott, 1973] summarizes the issue best: "Hitler's misgivings about homosexuality stemmed primarily from self-interest. His objection to it as a vice or symptom of effeminacy was only secondary. The main danger, as he saw it, was that it would infiltrate the political leadership and constitute itself a secret Order of the Third Sex. He was also concerned at the thought that population growth might be curbed by the heterosexual abstinence of those affected."

The Nazi purge of homosexuals from their own ranks was only the beginning. On June 23, 1935, the first anniversary of the Roehm killings, the Nazis began a legal campaign against homosexuals by adding to paragraph 175 another law, 175a, which created ten new criminal offenses including kisses between men, embraces, even homosexual fantasies. The Gestapo and the SS, under the notoriously anti-homosexual leadership of Heinrich Himmler, became involved in a stepped-up campaign to work gays to death in the camps. Himmler is quoted as follows: "Just as we today have gone back to the ancient Germanic view of the question of marriage mixing different races, so too in our judgment of homosexuality—a symptom of degeneracy that could destroy our race—we must return to the guiding Nordic principle: extermination." Reich Legal Director, Hans Frank, commented on the new penal code: "Particular attention should be addressed to homosexuality, which is clearly expressive of a disposition opposed to the normal national community . . . Homosexual behavior, in particular, merits no mercy."

—Jack Nusan Porter

References and Recommended Reading

Lautmann, Ruediger (1990). Gay prisoners in concentration camps as compared with Jehovah's Witnesses and political prisoners. In Berenbaum, Michael (Ed.), *A Mosaic of Victims: Non-Jews Persecuted and Murdered by the Nazis.* New York: New York University Press, pp. 200–206.

Plant, Richard (1986). *The Pink Triangle: The Nazi War Against Homosexuals.* New York: Henry Holt.

Porter, Jack Nusan (1998). *Sexual Politics in Nazi Germany: The Persecution of the Homosexuals during the Holocaust.* Newton, MA: The Spencer Press.

HUMANITARIAN INTERVENTION IN GENOCIDE

The debate over whether or not humanitarian intervention is a moral command, a legal doctrine or should be part of the strategic arsenal of states as a response to humanitarian crises parallels and continues the philosophical debate on whether or not it is possible to fight a "just" war.

Humanitarian intervention has been defined as "reliance upon force for the justifiable purpose of protecting the inhabitants of another state from treatment which is so arbitrary and persistently abusive as to exceed the limits of that authority within which the sovereign is presumed to act within reason and justice" [Stowell, Ellery C. (1921). *Intervention in International Law.* Washington, DC: John Bryne].

The current trend in international law is moving toward codification of principles and identification of appropiate conditions under which humanitarian imperatives will override national sovereignty. Humanitarian intervention is slowly approaching the status equivalent of "intervention by right" (see below). In moral discourse, scholars have accepted by and large that in cases of massive human rights violations, drastic action (including the use of force) may be necessary, if not desirable. Thorny issues remain; states and international organizations that intend to intervene lack clear parameters for identifying situations that warrant humanitarian intervention, and lack specific laws that attach sanctions (punishment), such as humanitarian intervention, to crimes against humanity. Despite the rise in ethnic conflicts and humanitarian disasters since the end of the Cold War, with a few notable exceptions such as Tanzania in Uganda (1979), and more recently in the Former Yugoslavia, policy makers remain reluctant to intervene in the internal affairs of a sovereign state, perhaps because until recently legal standards and precedents were few. More typically, crisis management takes the form of a flurry of ad hoc reactive responses.

However, humanitarian intervention has been resurrected from legal, moral and strategic pariah to legally acceptable and morally desirable sanction in cases of massive human rights violations. This change can be attributed to several factors. One is informed citizen pressure on policy makers, especially in Western societies, to halt massive human rights disasters. A second is policy makers' recognition that after the Cold War, ethnic warfare and political mass murders can be equally destructive to interests of the advanced industrial world. It is becoming fashionable to think of NATO as potential troubleshooter and thus intervention per se may lose its imperialist connotation. Under the leadership of the previous Secretary General of the UN, Boutros Boutros-Ghali, diplomats pressured member states for greater commitment in terms of resources and political will to respond, including the use of force, to ethnopolitical crises and flagrant human rights abuses.

The Legal Evolution of Humanitarian Intervention

International law is common law and thus relies on precedent, juristic decisions, legal opinions, and habitual behavior by states to alter the legal status of a particular type of behavior. Humanitarian intervention, meaning the use of force by one sovereign state into the internal affairs of another state for purported humanitarian reasons, had been considered unlawful because it threatened the territorial integrity and political independence of a state, guaranteed under international law. Nonintervention was to be the general rule in international law as exemplified in Article 2, paragraph 7 of the UN Charter. However, Chapter VIII and Article 51 allow for self-defense and collective action. Article 35 empowers the Security Council to investigate disputes that endanger peace, and Article 46 should assist member states to take action when needed. In addition, there are numerous exceptions to the rule of nonintervention known as intervention by right. For example, intervention is allowed when the lawful government of a state asks for outside help, or when the rights of neutrals are violated during a conflict.

Intervention was an ambiguous concept from its inception in international law. Definitional problems abound. Typically, humanitarian intervention is understood as interference using force analogous to fighting aggressively, albeit for a "just" cause. With the emergence of human rights provisions as part of international law after World War II, humanitarian intervention was once again under consideration as last resort punishment/sanction of state violators of human rights norms. The doctrine's historical antecedents can be discovered in the philosophical debates centering around the principle of *bellum justum* (just war). Two scholarly camps emerged; the one dismissed humanitarian intervention on grounds that any kind of intervention was unlawful in a legal system that for centuries claimed as its cornerstone the protection of the sovereign personality and political independence of states. Protection of the rights of individuals in another state was thus relegated to a lesser status, typically states were urged to abide by international norms. In contrast, a growing minority of scholars urged that humanitarian intervention be elevated to the status of intervention by right on the grounds that human rights violations not accompanied by some form of punishment were open invitations to would-be violators. Essentially the debate centered on the status of laws that granted individuals rights vis-à-vis their states versus the right of states. In recent years, judgments emanating from the European Court of Human Rights have helped to bolster individuals' claims against abusing states; now citizens can claim restitution from their own government.

We can safely assume now that international law in the twentieth century has evolved from a system that was primarily concerned with the relations of states with one another to one that embraces both the rights of states and the rights of individuals and groups. But contentious issues remain. Protection and enforcement of rights, especially of group rights remain difficult. The Genocide Convention (1948) and the United Nations Commission on Human Rights draft declaration on the *Rights of Persons Belonging to National or Ethnic, Religious and Linguistic Minorities* (February 21, 1992) dealing with the rights of indigenous peoples forbid governments to destroy ethnic, racial or religious groups. In theory, would-be violations of legal rights thus could be assessed and dealt with commensurate to the crime committed, yet it is the state as a legal person who is responsible for upholding principles and protecting the rights of groups and individuals. It is here that humanitarian intervention could play its most significant role. When groups or states commit atrocities against members of ethnic and religious minorities, they seldom face serious punishment. If sanctions were attached to violations of rights or were at least among the discretionary measures available for those willing to protect threatened minorities, obligations under the Charter would be fulfilled.

The moral debate on whether the international community should use force to save lives, or better said whether or not to risk some peoples' lives to save others has almost ceased. Those who once argued that using force could and should not be justified (even for a good cause) often rationalized that position by arguing that humanitarian intervention was typically a prelude to even greater forms of oppression. Recent tragedies may have changed their minds. Europeans mired in pacifistic traditions, especially since World War II, had to come to the realization that, despite great advances made in the protection of basic human rights, genocides were not a thing of the past and again could happen in countries perceived as relatively stable. Not only do we witness tribunals meting out punishment against perpetrators of genocide (albeit more symbolic than real), but the language of intervention has changed to include its peaceful intentions. Peacemaking and peacebuilding have become an integral part of strategic and legal language. However, we have yet to persuade policy makers to intervene routinely in escalating crises, despite legal obligation and moral desirability. Why is this so?

Humanitarian intervention is costly, both in terms of lives and material. But as Cambodia has shown, such costs can be minimal in contrast to the possibility of rebuilding a shattered society. Unfortunately Rwanda and Burundi, countries that have yet to recover from recent bloodbaths, have been of little interest to Western policy makers or the general public at large. Zaire (now known again as the Congo), however, may generate more interest due to the country's potential wealth and influence.

In the wake of recent humanitarian crises, regional stability also has become a greater issue. Neighboring countries typically absorb huge refugee flows, and international agencies are burdened with enormous costs and organizational nightmares to take care of thousands of displaced peoples. Environmental and economic crises that disrupt global exchanges are additional problems. From a reality perspective, early action is more cost efficient, morally desirable, and strategically sound. More so than ever, humanitarian intervention should become an accepted means in the arsenal of strategic planning and preventative diplomacy in cases of massive human rights violations. However, the political will to mobilize timely action still depends on an acceptable degree of certainty that action will enhance long-term stability in the targeted country.

—*Barbara Harff*

References and Recommended Reading

Franck, Thomas M., and Rodley, Nigel S. (1973). After Bangladesh: The law of humanitarian intervention by military force. *American Journal of International Law*, 67(2), 235–305.

Harff, Barbara (1984). *Genocide and Human Rights: International Legal and Political Issues.* Denver, CO: University of Denver, Graduate School of International Studies, Monograph Series in World Affairs.

Harff, Barbara (1995). Rescuing endangered peoples: Missed opportunities. *Social Research*, 62(1), 2–40.

HUMAN RIGHTS AND GENOCIDE

On December 9, 1948, one day before the Universal Declaration of Human Rights was adopted and proclaimed by UN General Assembly Resolution 217, the United Nations approved and proposed for signature and ratification the *Convention on the Prevention and Punishment of the Crime of Genocide* (Resolution 260). The closeness in time is indicative of the substantive proximity between adherence to human rights and the prohibition of genocide.

The Genocide Convention is one of 72 human rights conventions (Marie, 1996). Paradoxically and tragically, while dealing with the worst kind of human rights violations, the Genocide Convention has been invoked only once by a government (Bosnia in 1993) despite the fact that 48 instances of genocides and politicides (incidents where the victims were defined as political rather than communal groups) have been recorded since the end of the Second World War (Harff and Gurr, 1995) The reasons for governmental reluctance to invoke the power of the Genocide Convention have to do mainly with state sovereignty, the limits of international law, narrow national interest consideration and Cold War exigencies. However, to some extent the reluctance is also the result of a certain vagueness of the definition of genocide in the Convention.

The relationship between human rights violations and genocide is one that also requires clarification. A genocide does not come "out of the blue," but is generally preceded by a variety of other human rights violations such as political and economic discrimination, restrictions to freedom of movement for members of certain groups or the violation of the right to cohabit with one's family. The genocide itself consists of multiple human rights violations which culminate in extrajudicial executions of members of certain groups. Where killing of members of a national, ethnic, racial or religious group occurs purposefully on a large scale and/or repeatedly, mass killings can reach genocidal proportions. Since there is no accepted numerical threshold as to when certain gross human rights violation amount to genocide, the term genocide has been used (and abused) for a wide variety of less than large-scale human rights violations. The intent behind a loose use of the loaded label of genocide has generally been to criminalize the behavior of a political opponent. However, both national and international law have already outlawed a wide variety of attacks on the life and integrity of persons so there is no need to use the charge of genocide for—relatively speaking—more minor human rights violations.

The *International Bill of Rights* contains no fewer than 76 specific rights. While some people consider all human rights of equal importance, the violations of certain rights is considered more serious than the violation of others by many human rights lawyers and scholars. The category gross human rights violations, for instance, encompasses a set of life integrity violations which includes violations of (1) the right to life, (2) the right to be free from torture, (3) the right not to be arbitrarily arrested, and (4) the right to be free from fear of prolonged detention without trial (Fein, 1994).

Contrary to the concept of "crime against humanity" which was used at the Nuremberg Trials against Nazi war criminals, the crime of genocide is not linked to wartime conditions only, nor is it confined to interstate situations. In one sense, the concept of *genocide* serves as a bridge between humanitarian law which deals mainly with wartime and interstate situations affecting soldiers and civilians, and human rights law referring mainly to domestic "peace-time" situations of human beings, whether they are citizens or aliens.

Human rights are inherently egalitarian in that they are meant to apply to all human beings. Practitioners of genocide, on the other hand, deny this by singling out certain groups of people defined in racial, ethnic, national, or religious terms and marking them for destruction. The annihilation of such groups of people usually occurs in a domestic state context where the sovereignty of the perpetrator overrules the prohibition contained in the Genocide Convention. While human rights law and humanitarian law recognize and announce rights that groups of human beings have, the effective protection of these rights is still predominantly a matter of the constitutional state under the rule of law. Where the state fails to abide by a Bill of Rights and the terms of the Genocide Convention, the international community, generally only reluctantly and belatedly, if at all, musters enough political determination and manpower to intervene to stop genocides against the citizens of another state.

Human rights are "claim rights." In the case of genocide, the claim for prevention or suppression of genocide has to come from states who have signed the Genocide Convention (Art. VIII). The punishment of genocide is, on the other hand, not directed against a genocidal state but against persons charged with genocide (Art. VI). While there is some hope of increasing prosecution of perpetrators by the international community following approval of a permanent international penal tribunal, the current situation is one where only ad hoc tribunals (such as the one on Former Yugoslavia and Rwanda) or a "competent tribunal of the State in the territory of which the act was committed" (Art. VI) are envisaged by the Convention. The latter possibility is only likely to materialize after the genocidal regime has been overthrown from inside or defeated by an outside power.

As long as there is no effective suprastate authority which acts on signals received both from states and non-governmental actors, the destruction of intrastate national, ethical, racial or religious groups remains a recurring possibility, despite the fact that it is condemned by the civilized world as a crime under international law.

—*Alex P. Schmid*

References and Recommended Reading

Fein, Helen (1994). Genocide, terror, life integrity, and war crimes: The case for discrimination. In Andreopoulos, George J. (Ed.), *Genocide: Conceptual and Historical Dimensions.* Philadelphia, PA: University of Pennsylvania Press, pp. 95–107.

Harff, Barbara, and Gurr, Ted Robert (1996). Victims of the state: Genocides, politicides and group repression from 1945 to 1995. In Jongman, Albert J. (Ed.), *Contemporary Genocides: Causes, Cases, Consequences.* Leiden, The Netherlands: Leiden University, PIOOM (Interdisciplinary Research Program on Root Causes of Human Rights Violations), pp. 49–51.

Marie, Jean-Bernard (1996). International instruments relating to human rights: Classification and status of ratifications as of 1 January 1996. *Human Rights Law Journal,* 17(1–2), 61–78.